CHAMBERS

SPORTS FACTFINDER

CHAMBERS

CHAMBERS
An imprint of Chambers Harrap Publishers Ltd
7 Hopetoun Crescent
Edinburgh, EH7 4AY

www.chambers.co.uk

First published by Chambers Harrap Publishers Ltd 2005

We have made every effort to mark as such all words which we believe to be trademarks. We should also like to make it clear that the presence of a word in this book, whether marked or unmarked, in no way affects its legal status as a trademark.

A CIP catalogue record for this book is available from the British Library.

ISBN 0550 10161 6

Designed and typeset by Chambers Harrap Publishers Ltd, Edinburgh
Printed in Great Britain by Bath Press Ltd

Contributors

Editor and Publishing Manager

Patrick White

Project Manager

Camilla Rockwood

Compilers

Ian Brookes *(American football, baseball, basketball)*
Nadia Cornuau *(handball)*
Andrew Holmes *(Australian rules football, boxing, Canadian football, equestrian sports, football, Gaelic football, greyhound racing, horse racing, polo, snooker, wrestling)*
Simon Hill *(cycling)*
Mark MacKarel *(mountain biking)*
Alison Pickering *(all other sports)*
Tom Pinder *(athletics, tennis)*
Stewart Roberts *(ice hockey)*
Camilla Rockwood *(sailing)*
Patrick White *(bowls, cricket, darts, golf, motorcycle racing, motor racing, pool, rally driving, rugby league, rugby union)*

Editorial Assistance

Vicky Aldus
Katie Brooks

Prepress Manager

Sharon McTeir

Prepress

Kirsteen Wright

Acknowledgements

Thanks are due to the following individuals who offered valuable comments on the text: Paul Cook (Wasdale Mountain Rescue), Steph and Wilf Divens, Martin C Harris, Barny Hill, Peter Lennon, Janice McNeillie, Elaine O'Donoghue, David Rhys Jones, Duthie Thomson (Royal Caledonian Curling Club), Alan Williamson, Mike Williamson.

Introduction

Chambers Sports Factfinder is the ideal reference book for all those who love sport, both sedentary enthusiasts and active participants. It gives reliable and entertaining information for over 100 sports, running the whole gamut of sporting endeavour.

All of the sports included begin with a discussion of their origins, whether definitive (such as rugby league, where a precise date and place can be given) or speculative (such as darts, where different stories exist), and a description of the main features and rules of the sport. A selection of results is then given for the most important competitions. For reasons of space, these cannot be comprehensive, but complete results are given for very well-known events such as the Grand National, the FA Cup or the Ashes. All statistics are accurate as of 1 January 2005.

Most sports also feature an A-Z section that explains the key terms used in the sport, as well as some of the often obscure slang. Biographies of famous players are included for the higher-profile sports. Liberally sprinkled throughout this wealth of information are boxes which reveal interesting, and often amusing, little-known facts about the sports and the people who play them.

Lastly, an index has been provided of all the terms in the A-Z section, as well as those sportspeople mentioned in the biographies.

Whether you want to check a result, find out the meaning of a term or just learn more about a new sport, *Chambers Sports Factfinder* will have the answer.

Contents

CONTENTS

AEROBATICS

Origins

As soon as man learned how to fly a heavier-than-air craft, the desire to perform tricks and mimic the flight of birds was born. The loop was first demonstrated around 1913 by the French aviator Adolphe Pégoud in a Blériot monoplane. Air combat in World War I sharpened pilots' skills and after the conflict many planes and pilots formed the basis of 'barnstorming shows' for delighted spectators. A pilot who had flown in the Spanish Civil War (1936–9), Colonel José Luis de Aresti Aguirre, was responsible for a standardized catalogue of manoeuvres.

Rules and description

Aerobatics, from 'aerial' and 'acrobatics', is the name given to coordinated manoeuvres or stunts made in aircraft. It is also known as 'acrobatic flying' or 'akro'. Competition takes place within an aerial box (generally a 100m cube) and flyers perform a sequence of moves, potentially including manoeuvres from the Aresti notation, such as lines, angles, rolls (revolutions around the longitudinal axis), loops (forwards and backwards) and figures of eight, spins, tail-slides and stall-turns. Judges score each performance.

Display teams also put on aerobatic demonstrations, reminiscent of the early barnstorming shows. Famous teams include the RAF aerobatic team, the Red Arrows; the Tricolour Arrows from Italy; and the Blue Angels from the USA.

Ruling body: Fédération Aéronautique Internationale (FAI)

FAI World Aerobatic Championships

Since 1964, male competitors have competed for the Aresti Cup; since 1986, women have competed for the Royal Aero Club Trophy. There is also a team trophy.

	Men	**Women**
1968	Erwin Bläske (West Germany)	Madeline Delcroix (France)
1970	Igor Egorov (USSR)	Svetlana Savitskaya (USSR)
1972	Charlie Hillard (USA)	Mary Gaffaney (USA)
1974	*Not held*	
1976	Victor Letsko (USSR)	Lydia Leonova (USSR)
1978	Ivan Tucek (Czechoslovakia)	Valentina Yaikova (USSR)
1980	Leo Loudenslager (USA)	Betty Stewart (USA)
1982	Viktor Smolin (USSR)	Betty Stewart (USA)
1984	Petr Jirmus (Czechoslovakia)	Khalide Makagonova (USSR)
1986	Petr Jirmus (Czechoslovakia)	Lyubov Nemkova (USSR)
1988	Henry Haigh (USA)	Catherine Maunoury (France)
1990	Claude Bessière (France)	Natalia Sergeeva (USSR)
1992	*Abandoned because of bad weather*	

	Men	Women
1994	Xavier de Lapparent (France)	Christine Genin (France)
1996	Viktor Chmal (Russia)	Svetlana Kapanina (Russia)
1998	Patrick Paris (France)	Svetlana Kapanina (Russia)
2000	Eric Vazeille (France)	Catherine Maunoury (France)
2001	Mikhail Mamistov (Russia)	Svetlana Kapanina (Russia)
2003	Sergei Rakhmanin (Russia)	Svetlana Kapanina (Russia)

AIKIDO

Origins

The Japanese martial art and philosophy of aikido was created by Morihei Ueshiba (1883–1969), known as 'O-sensei' or the Great Teacher, during the early 20th century. In its earliest incarnations it was known as 'aikijutsu', and then 'aiki-budo' and was primarily a martial art (Morihei had studied ju-jitsu as a youngster). Later, he developed the spiritual element as a reflection of his way of life as a pacifist.

Rules and description

Aikido comes from the Japanese words ai, 'union, harmony'; ki, 'vital breath, energy'; do, 'way' or 'path', so literally means 'The Way to Harmonize with the Energy of the Universe'. The skills and techniques of the sport are taught in 'dojo' (schools) by 'sensei' (teachers). Practitioners or students (known as 'aikidoka') learn to work together in partnership rather than as competitors. The sport is regarded as non-aggressive – where there are throws and blows they are designed purely for self-defence.

There are many different schools or offshoots of aikido. Aikido depends particularly on two categories of movement: those of control ('katame-waza') and those of throwing an opponent ('nage-waza'). There are more than 700 movements associated with them but the basic forms ('kata') are throwing an opponent to the ground by applying pressure to the limbs ('rofiwe'), immobilizing an opponent by applying pressure to the joints ('kansetsu-gaeshi') and releasing an opponent's grip ('te-hodoki'). Some schools concentrate on the ki philosophy – the ki-aikido school – and others concentrate more on the sporting aspect – the Tomiki-ryō. Sporting contests take place on a mat approximately 9m^2. Participants wear jackets and trousers as in judo; one aikidoka wears a white belt, the other a red.

Ruling body: International Aikido Federation (IAF)

A-Z

aikidoka a practitioner of aikido
ikkyo an arm immobilization
kaiten-nage a rotation throw

kata-tori	a one-handed grip on a shoulder
katate-tori	a one-handed grip on one wrist
koshi-nage	a hip throw
morote-tori	a two-handed grip on one wrist
nage	the defender
nikyo	an **ikkyo** with hand turning
ryokata-tori	a two-handed grip, one on each shoulder
ryote-tori	a two-handed grip, one on each wrist
sankyo	an **ikkyo** with hand twisting
shomen-uchi	a vertical strike to the middle of the head with one hand
sode-tori	a one-handed grip on one sleeve
tsuki	a straight punch
udekime-nage	an arm-lock throw
uke	the assailant
yokomen-uchi	a diagonal strike to the side of the head with one hand
yonkyo	an **ikkyo** with pressure on the wrist

AMERICAN FOOTBALL

Origins

In 1869 the first intercollegiate game was played (between teams from Rutgers and Princeton) following a modified form of the rules of soccer. Over the next decade, rugby became more influential than soccer: an oval ball was introduced in 1874, and the first set of rules for American football was drawn up at the Massasoit convention of 1876. At Yale University between 1888 and 1892, Walter Camp ('the father of American football') helped to shape the current rules, introducing the eleven-man side, the line of scrimmage, the concept of 'downs' and 'yards gained', and a new points-scoring system (which was later to be adjusted several times). The distinction from rugby was further accentuated in 1906 by the legalization of the forward pass.

Rules and description

Players wear heavy padding and helmets, and passing of the ball by hand, including one forward pass per play, is permitted. The game is played on a rectangular field, divided gridiron-like into segments; the object is to score 'touchdowns' by moving the ball into the opposing team's 'end zone', but progress has to be made upfield by a series of 'plays': a team must make 9.14m/10yd of ground within four plays, otherwise it loses possession of the ball. Six points are awarded for a touchdown. An extra point can then be gained by kicking the ball between the posts and over the crossbar, or two points can be gained by advancing the ball (through play rather than kicking) from the two-yard line into the end zone in a 'two-point conversion'. A goal kicked from anywhere on the field (a 'field goal') is worth three points. Teams consist of more than 40 members, but only eleven are allowed on the field at any one time; separate units of players are used for attacking play, defensive play, kicking off, etc.

American Football

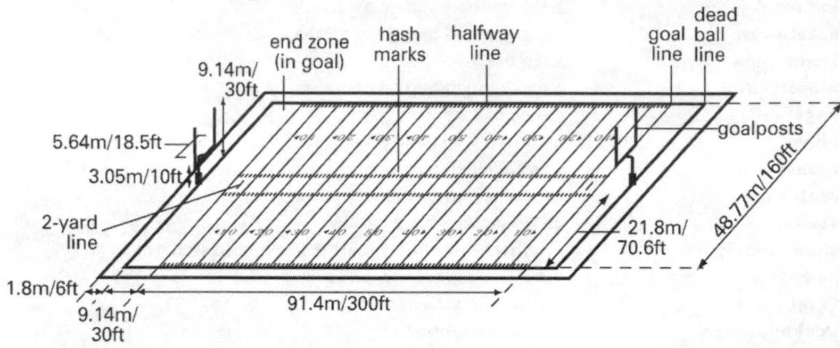

Ruling bodies (USA): National Football League (NFL); National Collegiate Athletic Association (NCAA)

Super Bowl

First held in January 1967 between the champions of the National Football League (NFL) and the American Football League (AFL); after the 1970 game, the two leagues amalgamated into an expanded NFL, with the Super Bowl played between the champions of the National Football Conference (NFC) and the American Football Conference (AFC).

	Champion	Defeated finalist	Score	Venue
1967	Green Bay Packers (NFL)	Kansas City Chiefs (AFL)	35–10	Los Angeles
1968	Green Bay Packers (NFL)	Oakland Raiders (AFL)	33–14	Miami
1969	New York Jets (AFL)	Baltimore Colts (NFL)	16–7	Miami
1970	Kansas City Chiefs (AFL)	Minnesota Vikings (NFL)	23–7	New Orleans
1971	Baltimore Colts (AFC)	Dallas Cowboys (NFC)	16–13	Miami
1972	Dallas Cowboys (NFC)	Miami Dolphins (AFC)	24–3	New Orleans
1973	Miami Dolphins (AFC)	Washington Redskins (NFC)	14–7	Los Angeles
1974	Miami Dolphins (AFC)	Minnesota Vikings (NFC)	24–7	Houston
1975	Pittsburgh Steelers (AFC)	Minnesota Vikings (NFC)	16–6	New Orleans
1976	Pittsburgh Steelers (AFC)	Dallas Cowboys (NFC)	21–17	Miami
1977	Oakland Raiders (AFC)	Minnesota Vikings (NFC)	32–14	Pasadena
1978	Dallas Cowboys (NFC)	Denver Broncos (AFC)	27–10	New Orleans
1979	Pittsburgh Steelers (AFC)	Dallas Cowboys (NFC)	35–31	Miami
1980	Pittsburgh Steelers (AFC)	Los Angeles Rams (NFC)	31–19	Pasadena
1981	Oakland Raiders (AFC)	Philadelphia Eagles (NFC)	27–10	New Orleans
1982	San Francisco 49ers (NFC)	Cincinnati Bengals (AFC)	26–21	Pontiac
1983	Washington Redskins (NFC)	Miami Dolphins (AFC)	27–17	Pasadena
1984	Los Angeles Raiders (AFC)	Washington Redskins (NFC)	38–9	Tampa
1985	San Francisco 49ers (NFC)	Miami Dolphins (AFC)	38–16	Stanford
1986	Chicago Bears (NFC)	New England Patriots (AFC)	46–10	New Orleans
1987	New York Giants (NFC)	Denver Broncos (AFC)	39–20	Pasadena
1988	Washington Redskins (NFC)	Denver Broncos (AFC)	42–10	San Diego
1989	San Francisco 49ers (NFC)	Cincinnati Bengals (AFC)	20–16	Miami
1990	San Francisco 49ers (NFC)	Denver Broncos (AFC)	55–10	New Orleans

	Champion	Defeated finalist	Score	Venue
1991	New York Giants (NFC)	Buffalo Bills (AFC)	20–19	Tampa
1992	Washington Redskins (NFC)	Buffalo Bills (AFC)	37–24	Minneapolis
1993	Dallas Cowboys (NFC)	Buffalo Bills (AFC)	52–17	Pasadena
1994	Dallas Cowboys (NFC)	Buffalo Bills (AFC)	30–13	Atlanta
1995	San Francisco 49ers (NFC)	San Diego Chargers (AFC)	49–26	Miami
1996	Dallas Cowboys (NFC)	Pittsburgh Steelers (AFC)	27–17	Tempe
1997	Green Bay Packers (NFC)	New England Patriots (AFC)	35–21	New Orleans
1998	Denver Broncos (AFC)	Green Bay Packers (NFC)	31–24	San Diego
1999	Denver Broncos (AFC)	Atlanta Falcons (NFC)	34–19	Miami
2000	St Louis Rams (NFC)	Tennessee Titans (AFC)	23–16	Atlanta
2001	Baltimore Ravens (AFC)	New York Giants (NFC)	34–7	Tampa
2002	New England Patriots (AFC)	St Louis Rams (NFC)	20–17	New Orleans
2003	Tampa Bay Buccaneers (NFC)	Oakland Raiders (AFC)	48–21	San Diego
2004	New England Patriots (AFC)	Carolina Panthers (NFC)	32–29	Houston
2005				Jacksonville
2006				Detroit

Star-spangled Super Bowl

The singing of the US National Anthem at the Super Bowl is a time-honoured tradition. While in the early years of the Super Bowl the anthem was often sung with great ceremony by bands or choirs, in later years it has usually been the luminaries of US pop music who belt out the Banner. Thus, Super Bowl audiences have been treated to the patriotic warblings of Diana Ross (1982), Whitney Houston (1991) and Mariah Carey (2002), the country croonings of Garth Brooks (1993), the Dixie Chicks (2003) and Faith Hill (2000), plus the star-spangled likes of Barry Manilow (1984), Cher (1999) and the Backstreet Boys (2001).

National Football League (NFL) Champions

The NFL was inaugurated in 1920; at that time teams played schedules of varying size and strength, the championship being determined by the teams' win–loss percentage. From 1933 the league was divided into an Eastern and Western conference with the two winners meeting in a championship game; home-field advantage for the championship game alternated between the two conferences. From 1966 to 1969, the NFL champions played against the American Football League champions in the following year's Super Bowl.

OT = after overtime

	Champion	Defeated finalist	Score
1920	Akron Pros		
1921	Chicago Staleys		
1922	Canton Bulldogs		
1923	Canton Bulldogs		
1924	Cleveland Bulldogs		
1925	Chicago Cardinals		
1926	Frankford Yellow Jackets		
1927	New York Giants		
1928	Providence Steam Roller		

Where have you gone, Crimson Giants?

Many short-lived teams graced the NFL in its early years. Among the teams consigned to NFL oblivion are the charmingly named Dayton Triangles, the Pottsville Maroons and the Evansville Crimson Giants.

	Champion	Defeated finalist	Score
1929	Green Bay Packers		
1930	Green Bay Packers		
1931	Green Bay Packers		
1932	Chicago Bears		
1933	Chicago Bears	New York Giants	23–21
1934	New York Giants	Chicago Bears	30–13
1935	Detroit Lions	New York Giants	26–7
1936	Green Bay Packers	Boston Redskins	21–6, at Polo Grounds, NY
1937	Washington Redskins	Chicago Bears	28–21
1938	New York Giants	Green Bay Packers	23–17
1939	Green Bay Packers	New York Giants	27–0
1940	Chicago Bears	Washington Redskins	73–0
1941	Chicago Bears	New York Giants	37–9
1942	Washington Redskins	Chicago Bears	14–6
1943	Chicago Bears	Washington Redskins	41–21
1944	Green Bay Packers	New York Giants	14–7
1945	Cleveland Rams	Washington Redskins	15–14
1946	Chicago Bears	New York Giants	24–14
1947	Chicago Cardinals	Philadelphia Eagles	28–21
1948	Philadelphia Eagles	Chicago Cardinals	7–0
1949	Philadelphia Eagles	Los Angeles Rams	14–0
1950	Cleveland Browns	Los Angeles Rams	30–28
1951	Los Angeles Rams	Cleveland Browns	24–17
1952	Detroit Lions	Cleveland Browns	17–7
1953	Detroit Lions	Cleveland Browns	17–16
1954	Cleveland Browns	Detroit Lions	56–10
1955	Cleveland Browns	Los Angeles Rams	38–14
1956	New York Giants	Chicago Bears	47–7
1957	Detroit Lions	Cleveland Browns	59–14
1958	Baltimore Colts	New York Giants	23–17 (OT)
1959	Baltimore Colts	New York Giants	31–16
1960	Philadelphia Eagles	Green Bay Packers	17–13
1961	Green Bay Packers	New York Giants	37–0
1962	Green Bay Packers	New York Giants	16–7
1963	Chicago Bears	New York Giants	14–10
1964	Cleveland Browns	Baltimore Colts	27–0
1965	Green Bay Packers	Cleveland Browns	23–12
1966	Green Bay Packers	Dallas Cowboys	34–27
1967	Green Bay Packers	Dallas Cowboys	21–17
1968	Baltimore Colts	Cleveland Browns	34–0
1969	Minnesota Vikings	Cleveland Browns	27–7

American Football League (AFL) Champions

Inaugurated in 1960 as a rival to the National Football League. From 1966 to 1969, the AFL champions played against the NFL champions in the following year's Super Bowl. Amalgamated with the NFL in 1970, with the AFL franchises forming the bulk of the American Football Conference.

OT = after overtime

	Champion	Defeated finalist	Score
1960	Houston Oilers	Los Angeles Chargers	24–16
1961	Houston Oilers	San Diego Chargers	10–3
1962	Dallas Texans	Houston Oilers	20–17 (OT)
1963	San Diego Chargers	Boston Patriots	51–10
1964	Buffalo Bills	San Diego Chargers	20–7
1965	Buffalo Bills	San Diego Chargers	23–0
1966	Kansas City Chiefs	Buffalo Bills	31–7
1967	Oakland Raiders	Houston Oilers	40–7
1968	New York Jets	Oakland Raiders	27–23
1969	Kansas City Chiefs	Oakland Raiders	17–7

The Rose Bowl

The most prestigious of the end-of-season college bowl games; held in the Rose Bowl, Pasadena, traditionally on New Year's Day between teams invited on the basis of their performance in the regular season; first played in 1902 as part of the Pasadena Tournament of Roses; it has been played annually since 1916.

USC = University of Southern California; UCLA = University of California at Los Angeles

	Winner	Defeated team	Score
1902	Michigan	Stanford	49–0
1916	Washington State	Brown	14–0
1917	Oregon	Pennsylvania	14–0
1918	Mare Island	Camp Lewis	19–7
1919	Great Lakes	Mare Island	17–0
1920	Harvard	Oregon	7–6
1921	California	Ohio State	28–0
1922	California *tied with* Washington & Jefferson		0–0
1923	USC	Penn State	14–3
1924	Navy *tied with* Washington		14–14
1925	Notre Dame	Stanford	27–10
1926	Alabama	Washington	20–19
1927	Alabama *tied with* Stanford		7–7
1928	Stanford	Pittsburgh	7–6
1929	Georgia Tech	California	8–7
1930	USC	Pittsburgh	47–14
1931	Alabama	Washington State	24–0
1932	USC	Tulane	21–12
1933	USC	Pittsburgh	35–0
1934	Columbia	Stanford	7–0
1935	Alabama	Stanford	29–13

American Football

	Winner	Defeated team	Score
1936	Stanford	Southern Methodist	7–0
1937	Pittsburgh	Washington	21–0
1938	California	Alabama	13–0
1939	USC	Duke	7–3
1940	USC	Tennessee	14–0
1941	Stanford	Nebraska	21–13
1942	Oregon State	Duke	20–16 (at Durham, North Carolina)
1943	Georgia	UCLA	9–0
1944	USC	Washington	29–0
1945	USC	Tennessee	25–0
1946	Alabama	USC	34–14
1947	Illinois	UCLA	45–14
1948	Michigan	USC	49–0
1949	Northwestern	California	20–14
1950	Ohio State	California	17–14
1951	Michigan	California	14–6
1952	Illinois	Stanford	40–7
1953	USC	Wisconsin	7–0
1954	Michigan State	UCLA	28–20
1955	Ohio State	USC	20–7
1956	Michigan State	UCLA	17–14
1957	Iowa	Oregon State	35–19
1958	Ohio State	Oregon	10–7
1959	Iowa	California	38–12
1960	Washington	Wisconsin	44–8
1961	Washington	Minnesota	17–7
1962	Minnesota	UCLA	21–3
1963	USC	Wisconsin	42–37
1964	Illinois	Washington	17–7
1965	Michigan	Oregon State	34–7
1966	UCLA	Michigan State	14–12
1967	Purdue	USC	14–13
1968	USC	Indiana	14–3
1969	Ohio State	USC	27–16
1970	USC	Michigan	10–3
1971	Stanford	Ohio State	27–17
1972	Stanford	Michigan	13–12
1973	USC	Ohio State	42–17
1974	Ohio State	USC	42–21
1975	USC	Ohio State	18–17
1976	UCLA	Ohio State	23–10
1977	USC	Michigan	14–6
1978	Washington	Michigan	27–20
1979	USC	Michigan	17–10
1980	USC	Ohio State	17–16
1981	Michigan	Washington	23–6
1982	Washington	Iowa	28–0
1983	UCLA	Michigan	24–14

	Winner	Defeated team	Score
1984	UCLA	Illinois	45–9
1985	USC	Ohio State	20–17
1986	UCLA	Iowa	45–28
1987	Arizona State	Michigan	22–15
1988	Michigan State	USC	20–17
1989	Michigan	USC	22–14
1990	USC	Michigan	17–10
1991	Washington	Iowa	46–34
1992	Washington	Michigan	34–14
1993	Michigan	Washington	38–31
1994	Wisconsin	UCLA	21–16
1995	Penn State	Oregon	38–20
1996	USC	Northwestern	41–32
1997	Ohio State	Arizona State	20–17
1998	Michigan	Washington State	21–16
1999	Wisconsin	UCLA	38–31
2000	Wisconsin	Stanford	17–9
2001	Washington	Purdue	34–24
2002	Miami (Florida)	Nebraska	37–14
2003	Oklahoma	Washington State	34–14
2004	USC	Michigan	28–14
2005	Texas	Michigan	38-37

No bowl of roses

The first Rose Bowl game was played in 1902 as part of the Pasadena Tournament of Roses. However, the game proved to be a mismatch as a powerful University of Michigan team racked up 49 unanswered points and opponents Stanford gave up in the third quarter. The lopsided scoreline prompted the tournament organizers to drop football from the programme until 1916 – replacing it with Roman chariot races.

World Bowl

First held in 1991 as the championship game of the World League of American Football; revived in 1995 as the championship game of NFL Europe.

	Champion	Defeated finalist	Score	Venue
1991	London Monarchs	Barcelona Dragons	21–0	London
1992	Sacramento Surge	Orlando Thunder	21–17	Montreal
1995	Frankfurt Galaxy	Amsterdam Admirals	26–22	Amsterdam
1996	Scottish Claymores	Frankfurt Galaxy	32–27	Edinburgh
1997	Barcelona Dragons	Rhein Fire	38–24	Barcelona
1998	Rhein Fire	Frankfurt Galaxy	34–10	Frankfurt
1999	Frankfurt Galaxy	Barcelona Dragons	38–24	Düsseldorf
2000	Rhein Fire	Scottish Claymores	13–10	Frankfurt
2001	Berlin Thunder	Barcelona Dragons	24–17	Amsterdam
2002	Berlin Thunder	Rhein Fire	26–20	Düsseldorf
2003	Frankfurt Galaxy	Rhein Fire	35–16	Glasgow
2004	Berlin Thunder	Frankfurt Galaxy	30–24	Schalke

Associated Press Most Valuable Player Award

A trophy awarded by Associated Press to the most valuable player (MVP) in the NFL for the regular season; similar awards are made by other bodies.

1957 Jim Brown (Cleveland Browns)
1958 Gino Marchetti (Baltimore Colts)
1959 Charley Conerly (New York Giants)
1960 Joe Schmidt (Detroit Lions) and Norm Van Brocklin (Philadelphia Eagles)
1961 Paul Hornung (Green Bay Packers)
1962 Jim Taylor (Green Bay Packers)
1963 Y A Tittle (New York Giants)
1964 Johnny Unitas (Baltimore Colts)
1965 Jim Brown (Cleveland Browns)
1966 Bart Starr (Green Bay Packers)
1967 Johnny Unitas (Baltimore Colts)
1968 Earl Morrall (Baltimore Colts)
1969 Roman Gabriel (Los Angeles Rams)
1970 John Brodie (San Francisco 49ers)
1971 Alan Page (Minnesota Vikings)
1972 Larry Brown (Washington Redskins)
1973 O J Simpson (Buffalo Bills)
1974 Ken Stabler (Oakland Raiders)
1975 Fran Tarkenton (Minnesota Vikings)
1976 Bert Jones (Baltimore Colts)
1977 Walter Payton (Chicago Bears)
1978 Terry Bradshaw (Pittsburgh Steelers)
1979 Earl Campbell (Houston Oilers)
1980 Brian Sipe (Cleveland Browns)
1981 Ken Anderson (Cincinnati Bengals)
1982 Mark Moseley (Washington Redskins)
1983 Joe Theismann (Washington Redskins)
1984 Dan Marino (Miami Dolphins)
1985 Marcus Allen (Los Angeles Raiders)
1986 Lawrence Taylor (New York Giants)
1987 John Elway (Denver Broncos)
1988 Boomer Esiason (Cincinnati Bengals)
1989 Joe Montana (San Francisco 49ers)
1990 Joe Montana (San Francisco 49ers)
1991 Thurman Thomas (Buffalo Bills)
1992 Steve Young (San Francisco 49ers)
1993 Emmitt Smith (Dallas Cowboys)
1994 Steve Young (San Francisco 49ers)
1995 Brett Favre (Green Bay Packers)
1996 Brett Favre (Green Bay Packers)
1997 Brett Favre (Green Bay Packers) and Barry Sanders (Detroit Lions)
1998 Terrell Davis (Denver Broncos)
1999 Kurt Warner (St Louis Rams)
2000 Marshall Faulk (St Louis Rams)
2001 Kurt Warner (St Louis Rams)

A natural-born Thrower

The first African-American to play quarterback in the NFL was aptly named Willie Thrower, who played for the Chicago Bears in 1953.

One for the Gipper

George Gipp (1895–1920) helped Notre Dame to unbeaten seasons in 1919 and 1920, but his career was cut tragically short by his death from pneumonia. His last words to coach Knute Rockne were, ‘Some time, Rock, when the team’s up against it, when things are wrong and the breaks are beating the boys – tell them to go in there with all they’ve got and win just one for the Gipper.’ Rockne told the team about Gipp’s request before a game in 1928, and inspired an injury-depleted Notre Dame squad to a famous victory. ‘Win one for the Gipper’ subsequently became a catchphrase throughout American sport.

2002 Rich Gannon (Oakland Raiders)
2003 Peyton Manning (Indianapolis Colts) and Steve McNair (Tennessee Titans)
2004 Peyton Manning (Indianapolis Colts)

Super Bowl Most Valuable Player

1967 Bart Starr (Green Bay Packers)
1968 Bart Starr (Green Bay Packers)
1969 Joe Namath (New York Jets)
1970 Len Dawson (Kansas City Chiefs)
1971 Chuck Howley (Dallas Cowboys)
1972 Roger Staubach (Dallas Cowboys)
1973 Jake Scott (Miami Dolphins)
1974 Larry Csonka (Miami Dolphins)
1975 Franco Harris (Pittsburgh Steelers)
1976 Lynn Swann (Pittsburgh Steelers)
1977 Fred Biletnikoff (Oakland Raiders)
1978 Randy White and Harvey Martin (Dallas Cowboys)
1979 Terry Bradshaw (Pittsburgh Steelers)
1980 Terry Bradshaw (Pittsburgh Steelers)
1981 Jim Plunkett (Oakland Raiders)
1982 Joe Montana (San Francisco 49ers)
1983 John Riggins (Washington Redskins)
1984 Marcus Allen (Los Angeles Raiders)
1985 Joe Montana (San Francisco 49ers)
1986 Richard Dent (Chicago Bears)
1987 Phil Simms (New York Giants)
1988 Doug Williams (Washington Redskins)
1989 Jerry Rice (San Francisco 49ers)
1990 Joe Montana (San Francisco 49ers)
1991 Ottis Anderson (New York Giants)
1992 Mark Rypien (Washington Redskins)
1993 Troy Aikman (Dallas Cowboys)
1994 Emmitt Smith (Dallas Cowboys)
1995 Steve Young (San Francisco 49ers)
1996 Larry Brown (Dallas Cowboys)
1997 Desmond Howard (Green Bay Packers)
1998 Terrell Davis (Denver Broncos)
1999 John Elway (Denver Broncos)
2000 Kurt Warner (St Louis Rams)
2001 Ray Lewis (Baltimore Ravens)
2002 Tom Brady (New England Patriots)
2003 Dexter Jackson (Tampa Bay Buccaneers)
2004 Tom Brady (New England Patriots)

The comeback kids

The greatest ever comeback in NFL history occurred on 3 January 1993. Houston had amassed a 35–3 lead over Buffalo in the third quarter of a first-round play-off game, but stand-in quarterback Frank Reich threw four touchdown passes to rally Buffalo to a 41–38 win.

Let's all celebrate

Most players like to draw attention to a touchdown or a big play. Notorious celebrations include the 'sack dance' performed by New York Jets' Mark Gastineau; the 'Icky shuffle' patented by Cincinnati's Icky Woods; the 'Lambeau leap' into the crowd following a Packer touchdown in Green Bay's Lambeau Field; and the more restrained 'Mile High salute' by the Denver Broncos. But the league is not always amused, and efforts to stamp out excessive celebrating have led to suggestions that NFL stands for 'No Fun League'.

Un-American activities

The all-time leading points scorer in the NFL is not even an American. Gary Anderson, who has amassed 2,434 points over a 23-year career, was born in Cape Town, South Africa. Other famous players born outside the USA include Mark Rypien (Canada), who was the Super Bowl MVP in 1992, and kickers Morten Andersen (Denmark) and Jan Stenerud (Norway).

Player records

(in the following sections, figures are up to date at the start of the 2004 season)

Leading career points scorers

Gary Anderson	2,434
Morten Andersen	2,358
George Blanda	2,002

Quarterbacks with 45,000 career passing yards

Dan Marino	61,361
John Elway	51,475
Brett Favre	49,734
Warren Moon	49,325
Fran Tarkenton	47,003

Quarterbacks with 300 career touchdown passes

Dan Marino	420
Brett Favre	376
Fran Tarkenton	342
John Elway	300

Quarterbacks with 4,000 career pass completions

Dan Marino	4,967
Brett Favre	4,306
John Elway	4,123

Most passing yards in a season

5,084	Dan Marino (Miami Dolphins, 1984)

Most touchdown passes in a season

49	Peyton Manning (Indianapolis Colts, 2004)

Most passing yards in a game

554	Norm Van Brocklin (Los Angeles Rams v New York Yankees, 1951)

Quarterbacks who have thrown seven touchdown passes in a game

Sid Luckman (Chicago Bears v New York Giants, 1943)
Adrian Burk (Philadelphia Eagles v Washington Redskins, 1954)
George Blanda (Houston Oilers v New York Titans, 1961)
Y A Tittle (New York Giants v Washington Redskins, 1962)
Joe Kapp (Minnesota Vikings v Baltimore Colts, 1969)

Players with 15,000 career rushing yards

Emmitt Smith	18,355
Walter Payton	16,726
Barry Sanders	15,269

Before they were famous

What links actor Burt Reynolds, author Jack Kerouac, civil-rights activist Jesse Jackson, and former president Gerald Ford? They all went to college on football scholarships.

Most rushing yards in a season

2,105	Eric Dickerson (Los Angeles Rams, 1984)

Most rushing yards in a game

295	Jamal Lewis (Baltimore Ravens v Cleveland Browns, 2003)

Players with 1000 career pass receptions

	Receptions	Receiving Yards
Jerry Rice	1,519	22,466
Cris Carter	1,101	13,899
Tim Brown	1,070	14,734

Most receiving yards in a season

1,848	Jerry Rice (San Francisco 49ers, 1995)

Most pass receptions in a season

143	Marvin Harrison (Indianapolis Colts, 2002)

Most receiving yards in a game

336	Willie Anderson (Los Angeles Rams v New Orleans Saints, 1989)

Most pass receptions in a game

20	Terrell Owens (San Francisco 49ers v Chicago Bears, 2000)

Players who have caught five touchdown passes in a game

Bob Shaw (Chicago Cardinals v Baltimore Colts, 1950)
Kellen Winslow (San Diego Chargers v Oakland Raiders, 1981)
Jerry Rice (San Francisco 49ers v Atlanta Falcons, 1990)

Nicknames

Some players have earned nicknames due to their talent and personality; others have acquired them more as result of quirks of rhyme or euphony. Here is a selection of famous nicknames of NFL players:

Jerome Bettis	'The Bus'
Red Grange	'The Galloping Ghost'
Joe Greene	'Mean Joe Greene'
George Halas	'Pappa Bear'
Elroy Hirsch	'Crazy Legs' (because of his running style)
Jim Kelly	'Machine Gun'
Dick Lane	'Night Train'
Joe Namath	'Broadway Joe'
Walter Payton	'Sweetness'
William Perry	'The Refrigerator' (because of his remarkable size)
Jake Plummer	'Jake the Snake'
Andre Rison	'Bad Moon Rison' (a pun on the title of the song *Bad Moon Rising*)
Deion Sanders	'Primetime'
O J Simpson	'Juice' (OJ being a common American short form of orange juice)
Ken Stabler	'The Snake' (because of his elusive running style)

Norm Van Brocklin 'The Flying Dutchman'
Reggie White 'The Minister of Defense' (an allusion to his being an ordained minister, as well as a dominant defensive player)

A-Z

all-American a college player who is selected to a team made up of the best college players at each position
all-pro a professional player who is chosen to play in the **Pro Bowl** as one of the best in his position
audible a play called out in coded form by the **quarterback** at the **line of scrimmage** to replace the previously arranged play
backfield the collective name for the players in a team who line up behind the **line of scrimmage**
back judge a member of the officiating team, positioned downfield of the **line of scrimmage** at the side of the field, who rules on whether passes are caught fairly
blitz a defensive tactic in which a **linebacker** or **defensive back** abandons his usual role and tries to **sack** the **quarterback**
block to hinder the progress of an opposing player who does not have possession
bootleg a deceptive play in which the **quarterback** simulates a **handoff** to a runner and runs in the opposite direction concealing the ball behind his hip before running or passing
center the player in the centre of the offensive line who begins the play by **snapping** the ball to a player in the **backfield**
chains a device used by the officiating team to measure the yardage required to achieve a new set of **downs**. A team that advances the required ten yards is said to 'move the chains'
chop block an illegal block below the knees
clip an illegal block below the waist made from behind
complete pass, completion a pass that is successfully caught by a **receiver**
conversion an additional score after a **touchdown**, worth one or two points
cornerback a **defensive back** who lines up at the side of the field, usually covering an opposing **wide receiver**
counter play an offensive play in which the ball carrier moves in the opposite direction to the other players
curl pattern a route taken by a **receiver** involving running up the field and then turning back towards the **line of scrimmage**
defense the team that does not have possession of the ball at the start of a play
defensive back a defensive player who begins the play away from the **line of scrimmage**, primarily concerned with defending against passes
defensive end a defensive player who lines up at the end of the **line of scrimmage**
dime defense a defensive formation involving six **defensive backs** (so called because it involves more players than a **nickel defense**, a dime being worth two nickels)
down one of four attempts allowed for the offense to advance the football a minimum of ten yards. If successful, the offense is awarded a new set of four downs
draw a deceptive play in which the offense simulates a passing play but executes a running play

drive a sequence of plays executed by one team without losing possession

eligible receiver an offensive player, usually a back or a player on the end of the **line of scrimmage**, who is legally allowed to catch a pass

end around an offensive play in which a **wide receiver** runs behind the **line of scrimmage**, is handed the ball, and continues running to the opposite side of the field

end zone the area behind the goal line, into which the offense attempts to take the ball to score a **touchdown**

extra point a point scored after a **touchdown** by **snapping** the ball from the two-yard line and kicking it through the goalposts

face mask the protective grille attached to a player's helmet

fair catch an unopposed catch of a **punt** or kickoff, after which the receiver cannot advance the ball

field goal a score achieved by kicking the ball through the opposition's goalposts, worth three points

field judge a member of the officiating team, positioned downfield of the **line of scrimmage** in the middle of the field

flag a marker thrown by a member of the officiating team to show that an infringement of the rules has occurred

flea flicker a deceptive play in which a runner or receiver pitches the ball backwards to a team-mate who attempts to advance it

franchise any of the organizations who operate a team in the National Football League

franchise player a player paid at a premium rate and not eligible to be signed by other teams

fullback an offensive player who lines up behind the **quarterback** and **halfback**, primarily concerned with blocking for other runners

fumble if a player fumbles the ball, he loses hold of it while in possession

gridiron the field on which American football is played, with lines marked across it every five yards

guard one of the players positioned on either side of the **center** on the offensive line

halfback an offensive player who lines up between the **quarterback** and **fullback**, primarily used to carry the ball

Hall of Fame an institution based in Canton, Ohio, that honours outstanding figures in the game's history

handoff the transfer of the ball from the **quarterback** to a **running back**

hang time the time that a kick remains in the air. A kick with a long hang time gives a greater opportunity for the kicking team to move upfield and tackle the player returning the kick

hash mark one of a series of short marks at intervals of one yard, running the length of the field. There are two sets of hash marks on the **gridiron**, marking the furthest distance from the centre of the field at which the ball can be placed to restart play

Heisman trophy a trophy awarded each year to the outstanding player in college football

holding the offence of illegally grasping an opponent with the hands

huddle a gathering together of players on the field between plays to call instructions for the forthcoming play

hurry-up offense an offensive strategy involving taking the minimum time to **huddle** and line up between plays; see **no-huddle offense**

incomplete pass a pass that is not caught by a **receiver**

intentional grounding the offence of deliberately throwing the ball to a place where it cannot be caught in order to avoid being **sacked**

interception a pass thrown by the **quarterback** that is caught by a member of the defense

lateral any pass thrown behind or parallel to the passer

linebacker a defensive player whose position is just behind the **line of scrimmage**

line judge a member of the officiating team, positioned opposite the **linesman**, with special responsibility for the timing of the game

lineman any player who lines up on the **line of scrimmage**

line of scrimmage an imaginary line across the field, behind which the **linemen** of a team position themselves at the start of a play

linesman a member of the officiating team, positioned on one side of the field, responsible for monitoring the **line of scrimmage**

man coverage a defensive strategy based on assigning a defender to each **eligible receiver**; see **zone coverage**

muff a failure to field a **punt** or kickoff securely

naked bootleg a **bootleg** in which no players attempt to block in front of the **quarterback**

neutral zone the area between the two **lines of scrimmage**

nickelback an additional defensive back brought into the game when the offensive team is likely to pass the football

nickel defense a defensive formation involving five **defensive backs** rather than the standard four (so called because a nickel is worth five cents); see **dime defense**

no-huddle offense an offensive strategy based on lining up for each play without a **huddle**, used either to prevent time elapsing unnecessarily or to disrupt the defense

nose tackle a defensive **lineman** who lines up facing the offensive **center**

offense the team that has possession of the ball at the start of a play

offside a player is offside if he is in front of the **line of scrimmage** at the time of the **snap**

onside kick a kickoff that travels only a short distance forward so that the kicking team has an opportunity to recover possession of the football

option play a play in which an offensive player runs with the ball and may decide either to continue running or to pass, depending on the defensive formation

outlet receiver a receiver near the **line of scrimmage** who is available to catch a pass if players further downfield are covered

overtime an additional period of up to 15 minutes played at the end of a tied game, ending as soon as one team scores

pass interference illegal contact with an opponent in order to prevent a catch being made

pass rush an attempt to tackle the **quarterback** before he is able to pass the ball

play a single period of activity, starting with the **snap**, in which players follow prearranged actions

play action an attempt to disguise a passing play by simulating a running play

pocket the area behind the offensive **line of scrimmage**, usually offering protection to the **quarterback** when attempting to pass

point after same as **extra point**

pooch kick a short high kick made with the intention of forcing the receiving team to restart behind its own 20-yard line

post pattern a route taken by a **receiver** involving running straight up the field and then turning infield towards the goalposts

prevent defense a defensive strategy based on allowing the offense to advance the ball in small increments, but denying the opportunity to advance and score quickly

primary receiver the offensive player who is intended to catch the ball if the play proceeds as planned

Pro Bowl an end-of-season game played in Hawaii between teams selected from the best players in the American Football Conference and the National Football Conference

punt to kick the football upfield (by dropping it from the hands and kicking it in mid-air), usually on fourth **down**, so that the opponents will have a greater distance to move the ball when they gain possession

punter a player who specializes in **punting** the football

quarter one of four 15-minute periods into which a game is divided

quarterback the player between the **linemen** and the **running backs**, who directs the attacking play of the team

receiver a player on the offense who catches passes from the **quarterback**

reception an instance of catching a pass from the **quarterback**

red zone the area between the goal line and the 20-yard line

referee the person in overall charge of the officiating team

running back an offensive player whose role is to advance the ball beyond the **line of scrimmage** by running with it

rushing attempting to advance the football by running with it

sack to tackle the opposing **quarterback** behind the **line of scrimmage**

safety 1. either of two defensive backs, the **strong safety** and **free safety**, positioned behind the other defenders 2. a play in which the offense carries the ball over its own goal line and does not take it back into the field of play, scoring two points for the defense

scramble if a **quarterback** scrambles, he tries to evade tacklers while running with the football

screen pass a passing play in which offensive **linemen** move across to form a barrier in front of a receiver with the aim of blocking opponents after the pass is caught

scrimmage the play between the two teams, beginning with the **snap** and ending when the ball is dead

secondary the area of the field behind the **linebackers**, defended by the **defensive backs**

shift the movement of two or more players into different starting positions before the **snap**

shotgun an offensive alignment with the **quarterback** lined up some distance behind the **center**, used mainly when passing the football

shovel pass a short pass made by flicking the ball out of the hand without extending the arm backwards

side judge a member of the officiating team with similar duties to the **back judge**

slant pattern a route taken by a **receiver** involving running diagonally from the outside of the field towards the middle of the field

slot receiver a **receiver** who lines up further infield than a **wide receiver**

snap — the action of starting a **play**, involving the **center** propelling the ball through his legs to the **quarterback** or **punter**

sneak — an attempt to advance the ball a short distance by diving forward immediately after receiving the **snap**

special teams — the groups of players who play in situations involving kicking the ball, as opposed to the regular offense and defense

spike — if a player spikes the ball, he throws the ball forcefully into the ground, either to celebrate a **touchdown** or to stop the official game clock

spiral — the characteristic pattern of movement of a well thrown pass

split end — an offensive player lined up slightly apart from the end of the **line of scrimmage**

strong side — the side of a standard offensive formation on which the **tight end** lines up; compare **weak side**

tackle — 1. an offensive player positioned outside a **guard** on the **line of scrimmage** 2. a defensive player positioned on the inside of the **line of scrimmage** 3. the act of forcing the ball carrier to the ground

tailback — a **running back** who lines up behind a **fullback**

take a knee — if a **quarterback** takes a knee, he makes no effort to pass or run with the ball after receiving the **snap**, usually to prevent the possibility of losing possession when defending a lead late in the game

tight end — an **eligible receiver** lined up next to a **tackle** at the end of the **line of scrimmage**

time out — a period when the official game clock is stopped and the teams can discuss strategy. Each team is allowed to take three time outs per half

touchback — a play in which the ball is made dead by a player on or behind his own goal line after it has been sent across the line by the opposing team

touchdown — the possession of the ball by a player behind the opponents' goal line, worth six points

turnover — an instance of the offensive team losing possession before fourth **down**

two-minute warning — a mandatory **time out** occurring with two minutes remaining in the second and fourth quarters of a game

umpire — a member of the officiating team, positioned behind the defensive line, with special responsibility for equipment and keeping score

Vince Lombardi Trophy — the trophy awarded to the winners of the Super Bowl

weak side — the side of a standard offensive formation on which there is no **tight end**; compare **strong side**

wide receiver — a member of the offense who lines up at the side of the field, primarily used to catch passes and run with the ball

zone coverage — a defensive strategy based on assigning defenders to specific areas of the field rather than to specific players; see **man coverage**.

The executioner's song

In 1976 the newly formed Tampa Bay Buccaneers went through the entire season without winning a single game. Asked by a reporter after one game how he felt about the execution of his offense, coach John McKay replied, 'I'm in favour of it.'

Some American football slang

bomb	a pass thrown deep downfield
bullet	a fast, accurate pass
chain gang	the members of the officiating team concerned with measuring the ten yards required to gain a new set of **downs**
climb the ladder	to jump extremely high in order to catch the ball
hail Mary	a high pass thrown into the **end zone** at the end of a half
Monday-morning quarterbacking	expressing opinions about strategic decisions after the outcome of a game is known
on the numbers	if a pass is thrown on the numbers, it is thrown accurately, reaching the receiver at chest height and allowing an easy catch to be made
pigskin	the football
prayer	a desperate pass thrown in spite of the fact that no receiver is obviously in a position to catch it
thread the needle	to pass the ball into a small gap between two defenders
traffic	if a **quarterback** passes into traffic, there are a lot of players in the area where the ball is thrown
trenches	the offensive and defensive lines, regarded as the site of strenuous and unappreciated effort
wobbly duck	a badly thrown pass that travels with an eccentric motion
X's and O's	the tactical manoeuvres formulated by coaches and traditionally explained to players through diagrams on which offensive players are marked with an X and defensive players with an O
zebra	a member of the officiating team (from the black-and-white striped shirts worn by officials)

Some famous American football players and coaches

Jim Brown, 1936–

Born in St Simon Island, Georgia, he won attention as an All-American halfback at Syracuse University (1956) and went on to become an NFL star with the Cleveland Browns (1957–66). Fast and powerful, he scored a total of 126 touchdowns and led the league eight times in rushing. After retiring as a player he established a film career in Hollywood.

Paul Brown, 1908–91

Born in Norwalk, Ohio, he was a highly successful and innovative coach. Using pioneering methods, he built up the Cleveland Browns (who are named in his honour) from a minor-league team into three-time NFL champions (1950, 1954, 1955), and had only one losing season in 17 years. He later coached the Cincinnati Bengals.

John Elway, 1960–

Born in Port Angeles, Washington, he played as a quarterback for the Denver Broncos from 1983 to 1998. He became famous for his ability to engineer comebacks, leading the Broncos on 47 game-winning or game-tying drives in the final quarter. He also led the Broncos to Super Bowl victories in both of his last two seasons as a player.

Brett Favre, 1969–

Born in Gulfport, Mississippi, he played college football for Southern Mississippi University. He was initially drafted by the Atlanta Falcons, but was traded to the Green

Bay Packers, whom he then led to Super Bowl appearances in 1997 and 1998. Noted for his durability and leadership, he has been voted the league's Most Valuable Player on three occasions (1995, 1996, 1997).

Otto Graham, 1921–2003

Born in Waukegan, Illinois, he was a tailback at college, but became a quarterback as a professional and guided the Cleveland Browns to ten division or league titles in ten years. He threw four touchdown passes in the 1950 NFL title game, and in the 1954 title game had three running touchdowns and passed for three more. In the course of his career he passed for 23,584 yards and 174 touchdowns, as well as running for 46 touchdowns.

Red Grange, 1903–91

Born Harold Edward Grange in Forksville, Pennsylvania, he was a star runner at the University of Illinois, selected to the All-American team three times (1923–5). His elusive running style earned him the nickname of 'The Galloping Ghost'. Joining the Chicago Bears in 1925, he did much to popularize the professional game, attracting huge crowds on a 17-game barnstorming tour. The following year he left the Bears to found a rival league.

George Halas, 1895–1983

Born in Chicago, he founded the Decatur Staleys football team, and was present at the NFL's league organizational meeting in 1920. He was associated with the NFL throughout its first 50 years, coaching the Chicago Bears for 40 seasons and winning six NFL titles. His record of 324 career wins was only surpassed in 1993 (by **Don Shula**).

Don Hutson, 1913–97

Born in Pine Bluff, Arkansas, he was an All-American at the University of Alabama (1934). An outstanding receiver, he also played as a safety and place kicker. As a professional with the Green Bay Packers, he led the NFL in receiving eight times and was leading points scorer five times. He was voted the league's Most Valuable Player in 1941 and 1942. At the time of his retirement he held 18 major NFL records.

Curly Lambeau, 1898–1965

Born Earl Louis Lambeau in Green Bay, Wisconsin, he founded the Green Bay Packers in 1919, playing for eleven seasons as a halfback, and continuing as coach and general manager until 1949, in which time he established the small town of Green Bay as a national force. He was the first coach to use the forward pass as an integral part of his team's offense. He won six NFL championships with the Packers, whose stadium, Lambeau Field, is named after him.

Tom Landry, 1924–2000

Born in Mission, Texas, he was a player with the New York Yankees and New York Giants before becoming coach of the Dallas Cowboys. He coached the Cowboys for 29 years, including 20 consecutive winning seasons, five NFL championships and two Super Bowl wins. As a coach, he was noted as both an offensive and defensive strategist, as well as for his impassive demeanour and trademark fedora hat.

Vince Lombardi, 1913–70

Born in Brooklyn, New York, he was a noted defensive guard in his playing days with Fordham University, although he was better known as an inspirational coach. His best work was done with the Green Bay Packers (1959–69), lifting five NFL titles and leading them to victory in the first two Super Bowls (1967 and 1968). The Super Bowl trophy is named in his honour.

Dan Marino, 1961–

Born in Pittsburgh, he played as quarterback with the Miami Dolphins, and in the 1984 season he gained 5,084 yards passing to create an NFL record. In 1986 he established another record by completing 378 passes in a single season. By the time he retired in 2000, he was the NFL's all-time leader in career passing yards (61,361), completed passes (4,967) and touchdown passes (420).

Joe Montana, 1956–

Born in New Eagle, Pennsylvania, he joined the San Francisco 49ers in 1979, and played in their winning Super Bowl teams in 1982, 1985, 1989 and 1990. He has been voted the Super Bowl's Most Valuable Player on an unprecedented three occasions (1982, 1985, 1990). He joined the Kansas City Chiefs in 1993, retiring in 1995.

Joe Namath, 1943–

Born in Beaver Halls, Pennsylvania, he was noted for his high living off the field. An outstanding quarterback in Alabama University's unbeaten team of 1964, he joined the New York Jets in 1965. In a phenomenally successful career, he played for a total of 23 seasons, passing for a total of 27,663 yards and 173 touchdowns. In 1969 he inspired the Jets to an upset victory over the Baltimore Colts in the Super Bowl.

Walter Payton, 1954–99

Born in Columbia, Mississippi, he joined the Chicago Bears as a running back in 1975. Between then and 1987 he rushed for 16,726 yards, including 275 yards in a single game (then a record) and scored 125 touchdowns. At the time of his retirement he was the NFL's all-time rushing leader. He was also part of the Bears' Super Bowl winning team in 1986.

Jerry Rice, 1962–

Born in Starkville, Mississippi, he turned professional in 1985 with the San Francisco 49ers, and by 1986 led the League in receiving with 86 catches. In 1987 he broke an NFL record when he caught 22 touchdown passes in just 12 games. By the end of the 2003 season he held almost every meaningful NFL receiving record, including 1,519 career pass receptions for 22,466 yards. He helped the 49ers to three victories in the Super Bowl (1989, 1990, 1995) before joining the Oakland Raiders in 2001 and the Seattle Seahawks in 2004. By the end of the 2004 season he held almost every meaningful NFL receiving record, including 1,549 career pass receptions for 22,895 yards.

Knute Rockne, 1888–1931

Born in Voss, Norway, he was taken to the USA as a child. He graduated from Notre Dame in 1914 and became head football coach there shortly after the end of World War I. He dominated US college football, shifting the emphasis from sheer physical brawn to pace, elusiveness and ball handling, and built Notre Dame into a national collegiate football power with a record of 105 wins, 12 losses and 5 draws. He died in an air crash.

Don Shula, 1930–

Born in Grand River, Ohio, he played as a defensive back for Cleveland, Baltimore and Washington before turning to coaching in 1958. He is noted for his success as a coach with the Miami Dolphins, who won an unprecedented 100 games in 10 seasons and in 1972 became the only team to complete a perfect season in the NFL, winning every game. He retired in 1995 with a record 328 career victories as a coach.

O J Simpson, 1947–

Born Orenthal James Simpson in San Francisco, he played college football for the University of Southern California, before playing professionally with the Buffalo Bills (1969–77) and San Francisco 49ers (1978–9). He combined blistering pace with an astute strategic sense, and in 1973 he became the first running back to gain over 2,000 yards in a season. After retiring from football, he became a popular commentator and film actor (he appeared in *The Towering Inferno*, *Roots* and the *Naked Gun* films). In 1994 he was charged with the murder of his former wife. Huge interest centred on the subsequent televised trial, at which he was eventually acquitted.

Emmitt Smith, 1969–

Born in Pensacola, Florida, he played for Florida State University before signing for the Dallas Cowboys in 1990. Considered one of the greatest running backs in NFL history, he was a member of three Super Bowl champion teams (1993, 1994, 1996) and was the NFL rushing leader four times (1991–3, 1995). In 2003 he joined the Arizona Cardinals with whom he eventually broke **Walter Payton**'s record for most career rushing yards.

Lawrence Taylor, 1959–

Born in Williamsburg, Virginia, he played as a linebacker for the New York Giants from 1981 to 1993. He is known as one of the greatest defensive players of all time, combining great aggression, speed and strength. He was named an All-Pro in each of his first nine seasons and is one of the few defensive players to have been named the NFL's Most Valuable Player (1986).

Jim Thorpe, 1888–1953

Born in Prague, Oklahoma, of Native American descent, he was a superb all-round athlete. Besides being an All-American halfback at Carlisle Indian Industrial School, he was also the Olympic pentathlon and decathlon champion in 1912. He became the first prominent collegiate athlete to play professional football, signing with the Canton Bulldogs in 1915. He later became the first president of the NFL.

Johnny Unitas, 1933–2002

Born in Pittsburgh, he joined the home-town Steelers, but was released in 1955. He then signed with the Baltimore Colts, and soon achieved a heroic status as an exceptional leader who thrived on the pressure of important games. He led the Colts to NFL titles in 1958 and 1959, helping to establish American football as a popular television sport. He performed the remarkable feat of throwing at least one touchdown pass in 47 consecutive games.

ANGLING

Origins

Angling, or fishing, is one of the most ancient of occupations; early man used a flint 'gorge' instead of hook to secure fish on the end of line made from vines. Fishing with hooks is mentioned in the Bible but one of the most important and celebrated books on angling is Izaak Walton's *The Compleat Angler* (1653). Angling's development as a sport is much more modern, with organized participation angling dating from 1829 and the establishment of the Ellem Fishing Club in Scotland. The British National Championships were first held in 1906.

Rules and description

Angling is the practice of catching fish by means of a baited hook (or 'angle'). There are two main categories of fishing – in fresh water and in the sea. In rivers, fish are caught at the surface, in mid-water and near the bottom of rivers and the skills for each differ. Fly-fishing takes place at the surface level with a lure (an imitation insect) resting on the surface encouraging the fish to bite ('dry-fly fishing'). If the fly is set to sink in the water it is known as 'wet-fly fishing'. Mid-water fishing utilizes a bait that mimics a small fish or a dead bait. Bottom fishers use worms, paste, or other items to attract the fish. Winners of competition or 'match' fishing events are usually decided by the greatest weight of fish caught within a set period of time, although there are also competitions for the heaviest single fish caught.

Ruling body: Fédération Internationale de la Pêche Sportive

World Fly-Fishing Champions

	Individual	**Team**
1981	C Wittkamp (The Netherlands)	The Netherlands
1982	Viktor Diez (Spain)	Italy
1983	Segismondo Fernandez (Spain)	Italy
1984	Tony Pawson (England)	Italy
1985	Leslaw Frasik (Poland)	Poland
1986	Slivoj Svoboda (Czechoslovakia)	Italy
1987	Brian Leadbetter (England)	England
1988	John Pawson (England)	England
1989	Wladislaw Trzebuinia (Poland)	Poland
1990	Franciszek Szajnik (Poland)	Czechoslovakia
1991	Brian Leadbetter (England)	New Zealand
1992	Pierluigi Coccito (Italy)	Italy
1993	Russell Owen (Wales)	England
1994	Pascal Cognard (France)	Czech Republic
1995	Jeremy Herrmann (England)	England
1996	Pierluigi Coccito (Italy)	Czech Republic
1997	Pascal Cognard (France)	France

Angling

	Individual	Team
1998	Tomas Starychfojtu (Czech Republic)	Czech Republic
1999	Ross Stewart (Australia)	Australia
2000	Pascal Cognard (France)	France
2001	Vladimir Sedivy (Czech Republic)	France
2002	Jérôme Brossutti (France)	France
2003	Stefano Cotugno (Italy)	France
2004	Miroslav Antal (Slovakia)	Slovakia

World Freshwater Angling Champions

The competition was first held in 1957 and takes place annually.

	Individual	Team
1981	Dave Thomas (England)	France
1982	Kevin Ashurst (England)	The Netherlands
1983	Wolf-Rüdiger Kremkus (West Germany)	Belgium
1984	Bobby Smithers (Ireland)	Luxembourg
1985	Dave Roper (England)	England
1986	Lud Wever (The Netherlands)	Italy
1987	Clive Branson (Wales)	England
1988	Jean-Pierre Fougeat (France)	England
1989	Tom Pickering (England)	Wales
1990	Bob Nudd (England)	France
1991	Bob Nudd (England)	England
1992	David Wesson (Australia)	Italy
1993	Mario Barros (Portugal)	Italy
1994	Bob Nudd (England)	England
1995	Paul Jean (France)	France
1996	Alan Scotthorne (England)	Italy
1997	Alan Scotthorne (England)	Italy
1998	Alan Scotthorne (England)	England
1999	Bob Nudd (England)	Spain
2000	Jacopo Falsini (Italy)	Italy
2001	Umberto Ballabeni (Italy)	England
2002	Juan Blasco (Spain)	Spain
2003	Alan Scotthorne (England)	Hungary
2004	Walter Tamas (Hungary)	France

A Treatyse of Fysshynge wyth an Angle

This famous treatise on fishing was published in 1496 at Westminster by Wynkyn de Worde. It gave specific details about how to use a fishing rod and hooks. It also gave advice on making flies. Most surprisingly, it has been attributed to Dame Juliana Berners, who was a prioress at an abbey near St Albans.

A-Z of match fishing terms

catch and release	the practice of releasing fish after they have been caught and weighed
coarse fish	freshwater fish other than those of the salmon family
dry-fly	a method of angling where the fly does not sink in the water
game fish	any freshwater fish of the salmon family except the grayling
keep net	a mesh bag, closed at one end, for storing fish in the water until an official weighing can be made
landing net	a mesh net used for scooping fish out of the water
peg	a section of the river or lake designated for a single angler in match fishing
weigh sling	a bag attached to a gauge, used for weighing caught fish
wet-fly	a method of angling where the fly sinks in the water

First literary mention of fly-fishing

In the 3rd century, Aelian, a Greek writer, made perhaps the first mention of fly-fishing in *De Natura Animalium* (*Natural History*). He described how he witnessed Macedonians capturing a spotted fish in the water: 'They fasten red wool round a hook, and fix on to the wool two feathers which grow under a cock's wattles, and which in colour are like wax...'.

ARCHERY

Origins

Bows and arrows were used as hunting tools at least 10,000 years ago. Archery was played as a sport in the Middle Ages as well as being a vital instrument in war. English archers won decisive battles against the French at Crécy (1346) and Agincourt (1415). The Royal Toxopholite (Greek for 'bow lover') Society was formed in 1787 and developed into the Grand National Archery Association in 1844.

Shoot the birdie!

The Ancient Society of Kilwinning Archers is the oldest archery society in Britain, if not the world. In 1688 the first Kilwinning Papingo was held. The aim was to dislodge a wooden parrot from the top of the abbey tower in Kilwinning in Ayrshire, by shooting at it from directly below. The first to knock the papingo off the perch was awarded the 'Benn of Crimson Taffety' and a silver arrow.

Rules and description

Archery is the art of using a bow to shoot arrows at a target. Archers participate in singles and team competitions. Bows, once made of wood (preferably yew), are now mainly composed of plastic, fibreglass or graphite and carbon composites.

Archery

Competitive bows made from wood are termed 'primitive'. Arrows are made of carbon graphite or aluminium with feathers at one end. There are three different types of bow: 'recurve' or 'classic'; 'compound' (a bow augmented with pulleys and cables); and 'barebow' (a recurve bow with no sights or stabilizer).

There are two main types of competition: target archery and field archery. In target archery competitors shoot at circular paper targets attached to an upright coiled-straw boss. Points are scored according to how close to the centre an archer hits. From the centre outwards there is a gold inner bull (10 points); gold outer (9); red inner (8); red outer (7); blue inner (6); blue outer (5); black inner (4); black outer (3); white inner (2); white outer (1). Archers shoot a specified number of arrows over a predetermined variety of distances up to 90m (70m for women).

In field archery competitors move along a course or path aiming at targets, or targets fashioned to look like animals. The World Field Archery Championships is held in three bow divisions (barebow since 1959, recurve or classic since 1969 and compound since 1990).

Other forms of archery include:

archery darts archers shoot at a target that has the same arrangement as the numbers on a dartboard. The target is set at 18m

clout archery this is a form of long-distance shooting where the target, called a clout, is a flat surface on the ground divided in concentric circles. The distances vary between 125m/136.7yd and 185m/202.3yd. Archers fire arrows high into the air to land on the target

flight archery the object is to fire an arrow as far as possible. World records are set for different bow types

indoor target archery as target archery but staged indoors with a target set at 18m

popinjay archery the wooden targets are disguised with feathers and called 'birds', 'chicks' or 'hens'. They are arranged in a 'roost' atop a 26m pole. Archers aim to dislodge them by firing from below

ski archery a combination of archery and Nordic cross-country skiing

Ruling body: Fédération Internationale de Tir à l'Arc (FITA)

Olympic Champions

Archery was in the 1900, 1904, 1908 and 1920 Olympics when there were numerous different events, with medals awarded for each, including a 'perche' event where archers fired at birds fastened to the top of a pole. Reintroduced in 1972, with team events from 1988.

	Men	Women	Men's team	Women's team
1972	John Williams (USA)	Doreen Wilber (USA)		
1976	Darrell Pace (USA)	Luann Ryon (USA)		
1980	Tomi Poikolainen (Finland)	Keto Losaberidze (USSR)		
1984	Darrell Pace (USA)	Seo Hyang-soon (South Korea)		
1988	Jay Barrs (USA)	Kim Soo-nyung (South Korea)		
1992	Sebastien Flute (France)	Cho Youn-jeong (South Korea)	Spain	South Korea

	Men	Women	Men's team	Women's team
1996	Justin Huish (USA)	Kim Kyung-wook (South Korea)	USA	South Korea
2000	Simon Fairweather (Australia)	Yun Mi-jin (South Korea)	South Korea	South Korea
2004	Marco Galiazzo (Italy)	Park Sung-hyun (South Korea)	South Korea	South Korea

A-Z

back the part of the bow handle that faces the target when the archer is shooting

belly the part of the bow handle that faces the archer when shooting

bowsight a sighting device attached to the bow to help the archer aim

bull('s eye) the central spot of the target

butt a mound of earth behind a target

classic bow same as **recurve bow**

compound bow a bow with pulleys and cables that enable an archer to impart less force to pull back the bowstring

draw to pull back the bowstring and arrow ready to shoot

draw weight the force required to pull back the bowstring to its maximum – in men's competition it is about 22kg; in women's competition about 15kg

end a group of arrows, usually three, shot in one sequence

finger tab a piece of leather worn to prevent injury when the finger releases an arrow

fletchings the feathers of an arrow; they are designed to make the arrow fly straight

limb the upper or lower portion of a bow from the handle to the tip

nock the groove or notch at the rear of an arrow that holds it in place on the bowstring

petticoat the part of an archery target outside the scoring area

pin hole the exact centre of the **bullseye**

quiver a long narrow case for holding arrows, worn by an archer

recurve bow a bow where the limbs curve away from the archer

Robin Hood the act of splitting the shaft of an arrow already in the target with another arrow

round a specified number of arrows shot over certain different distances

rover a field archer

spotter an appointed person who identifies each archer's score

stabilizer a device attached to the bow to increase stability during a shot

tip the pointed end of an arrow

upshot the last shot in an archery contest

Target Archery World Championships

First held in 1931. Held annually except 1940–5, 1951, 1954, 1956; since 1959 it has been a biennial competition. A compound bow event for men and women was introduced in 1995.

	Venue	Individual men's	Men's team	Individual women's	Women's team
1931	Lvov, Poland	Michal Sawicki (Poland)	France	Janina Kurkowska (Poland)	
1932	Warsaw, Poland	Laurent Reth (Belgium)	Poland	Janina Kurkowska (Poland)	
1933	London, UK	Donald Mackenzie (USA)	Belgium	Janina Kurkowska (Poland)	Poland
1934	Båstad, Sweden	Henry Kjellson (Sweden)	Sweden	Janina Kurkowska (Poland)	Poland
1935	Brussels, Belgium	Adrien van Kolen (Belgium)	Belgium	Ina Catani (Sweden)	Great Britain
1936	Prague, Czechoslovakia	Emil Heilborn (Sweden)	Czechoslovakia	Janina Kurkowska (Poland)	Poland
1937	Paris, France	Georges De Rons (Belgium)	Poland	Erna Simon (GB)	Great Britain
1938	London, UK	Frantisek Hadas (Czechoslovakia)	Czechoslovakia	Nora Weston-Martyr (GB)	Poland
1939	Oslo, Norway	Roger Beday (France)	France	Janina Kurkowska (Poland)	Poland
1946	Stockholm, Sweden	Einar Tang-Holbek (Denmark)	Denmark	Nilla de Wharton Burr (GB)	Great Britain
1947	Prague, Czechoslovakia	Hans Deutgen (Sweden)	Czechoslovakia	Janina Kurkowska (Poland)	Denmark
1948	London, UK	Hans Deutgen (Sweden)	Sweden	Nilla de Wharton Burr (GB)	Czechoslovakia
1949	Paris, France	Hans Deutgen (Sweden)	Czechoslovakia	Barbara Waterhouse (GB)	Great Britain
1950	Copenhagen, Denmark	Hans Deutgen (Sweden)	Denmark	Jean Lee (USA)	Finland
1952	Brussels, Belgium	Stellan Andersson (Sweden)	Sweden	Jean Lee (USA)	USA
1953	Oslo, Norway	Bror Lundgren (Sweden)	Sweden	Jean Richards (USA)	Finland
1955	Helsinki, Finland	Nils Andersson (Sweden)	Sweden	Katarzyna Wisniowska (Poland)	Great Britain
1957	Prague, Czechoslovakia	Oziek Smathers (USA)	USA	Carole Meinhart (USA)	USA
1958	Brussels, Belgium	Stig Thysell (Sweden)	Finland	Sigrid Johansson (Sweden)	USA
1959	Stockholm, Sweden	James Caspers (USA)	USA	Ann Corby (USA)	USA
1961	Oslo, Norway	Joe Thornton (USA)	USA	Nancy Vonderheide (USA)	USA
1963	Helsinki, Finland	Charles Sandlin (USA)	USA	Victoria Cook (USA)	USA
1965	Västerås, Sweden	Matti Haikonen (Finland)	USA	Maire Lindholm (Finland)	USA
1967	Amersfoort, The Netherlands	Ray Rogers (USA)	USA	Maria Maczyńska (Poland)	Poland
1969	Valleyforge Park, USA	Hardy Ward (USA)	USA	Dorothy Lidstone (Canada)	USSR
1971	York, UK	John Williams (USA)	USA	Emma Gaptchenko (USSR)	Poland

	Venue	Individual men's	Men's team	Individual women's	Women's team
1973	Grenoble, France	Viktor Sidoruk (USSR)	USA	Linda Myers (USA)	USSR
1975	Interlaken, Switzerland	Darrell Pace (USA)	USA	Zebiniso Rustamova (USSR)	USSR
1977	Canberra, Australia	Richard McKinney (USA)	USA	Luann Ryon (USA)	USA
1979	Berlin, Germany	Darrell Pace (USA)	USA	Kim Jin-ho (South Korea)	South Korea
1981	Punta Ala, Italy	Kyosti Laasonen (Finland)	USA	Natalia Butuzova (USSR)	USSR
1983	Los Angeles, USA	Richard McKinney (USA)	USA	Kim Jin-ho (South Korea)	South Korea
1985	Seoul, South Korea	Richard McKinney (USA)	South Korea	Irina Soldatova (USSR)	USSR
1987	Adelaide, Australia	Vladimir Yesheyev (USSR)	West Germany	Ma Xiangjun (China)	USSR
1989	Lausanne, Switzerland	Stanislav Zabrodsky (USSR)	South Korea	Kim Soo-nyung (South Korea)	South Korea
1991	Kraków, Poland	Simon Fairweather (Australia)	South Korea	Kim Soo-nyung (South Korea)	South Korea
1993	Antalya, Turkey	Park Kyung-mo (South Korea)	France	Kim Hyo-jung (South Korea)	South Korea
1995	Jakarta, Indonesia	*Recurve:* Lee Kyung-chul (South Korea)	South Korea	*Recurve:* Natalia Valeyeva (Moldova)	South Korea
		Compound: Gary Broadhead (USA)	France	*Compound:* Angela Moscarelli (USA)	USA
1997	Victoria, Canada	*Recurve:* Kim Kyung-ho (South Korea)	South Korea	*Recurve:* Kim Du-ri (South Korea)	South Korea
		Compound: Dee Wilde (USA)	Hungary	*Compound:* Fabiola Palazzini (Italy)	Italy
1999	Riom, France	*Recurve:* Hong Sung-chil (South Korea)	Italy	*Recurve:* Lee Eun-kyung (South Korea)	Italy
		Compound: David Cousins (USA)	USA	*Compound:* Cathérine Pellen (France)	Taiwan
2001	Beijing, China	*Recurve:* Jung Ki-yeon (South Korea)	South Korea	*Recurve:* Park Sung-hyun (South Korea)	China
		Compound: Dejan Sitar (Slovakia)	Norway	*Compound:* Ulrika Sjoewall (Sweden)	France
2003	New York, USA	*Recurve:* Michele Frangilli (Italy)	South Korea	*Recurve:* Yun Mi-jin (South Korea)	South Korea
		Compound: Clint Freeman (Australia)	USA	*Compound:* MaryZorn (USA)	USA

Fans of the sport

In 1545 English scholar and author Sir Roger Ascham (1515–68) published a popular treatise on archery called *Toxophilus*. It was a defence of the physical benefits for scholars of archery, and it was dedicated to King Henry VIII. The essay pleased the king, who granted the author an annual pension of 10 pounds a year. An ascham is a term for a tall narrow cupboard for the storage of bows and arrows.

ATHLETICS

Origins

The most natural of sports, testing the limits of the human body, athletics can be traced back to organized running competitions held around 3800 BC in Egypt. Competitive athletics truly took off in Ancient Greece, where games were held to celebrate victories on the battlefield and to honour the dead. A number of the events competed in today originated at the Ancient Greek games. The first modern Olympiad of 1896 sparked the rise of athletics as a global competitive sport.

Rules and description

Athletic events can be split into two categories: track events and field events, with field events divided into jumps and throws (see A-Z section for description of events). The aim is to go faster, further or higher than the other competitors. Competitions take place both indoors and outdoors, with the track encircling the area for the field events.

Ruling body: International Association of Athletics Federations (IAAF)

Olympic Games

1896

Men	
100m	Thomas Burke (USA)
400m	Thomas Burke (USA)
800m	Edwin Flack (Australia)
1,500m	Edwin Flack (Australia)
110m Hurdles	Thomas Curtis (USA)
High Jump	Ellery Clark (USA)
Pole Vault	William Welles Hoyt (USA)
Long Jump	Ellery Clark (USA)
Triple Jump	James Connolly (USA)
Shot Put	Robert Garrett (USA)
Discus	Robert Garrett (USA)

1900

Men	
60m	Alvin Kraenzlein (USA)
100m	Frank Jarvis (USA)
200m	Walter Tewksbury (USA)
400m	Maxwell Long (USA)

See separate sections on **Cross-country running**, **Decathlon**, **Heptathlon**, **Marathon** and **Walking**

800m	Alfred Tysoe (Great Britain)
1,500m	Charles Bennett (Great Britain)
110m Hurdles	Alvin Kraenzlein (USA)
400m Hurdles	Walter Tewksbury (USA)
200m Hurdles	Alvin Kraenzlein (USA)
3,000m Steeplechase	George Orton (Canada)
4,000m Steeplechase	John Rimmer (Great Britain)
High Jump	Irving Baxter (USA)
Pole Vault	Irving Baxter (USA)
Long Jump	Alvin Kraenzlein (USA)
Triple Jump	Meyer Prinstein (USA)
Shot Put	Richard Sheldon (USA)
Discus	Rudolf Bauer (Hungary)
Hammer	John Flanagan (USA)
Standing High Jump	Ray Ewry (USA)
Standing Long Jump	Ray Ewry (USA)
Standing Triple Jump	Ray Ewry (USA)

1904

Men

60m	Archie Hahn (USA)
100m	Archie Hahn (USA)
200m	Archie Hahn (USA)
400m	Harry Hillman (USA)
800m	James Lightbody (USA)
1,500m	James Lightbody (USA)
110m Hurdles	Frederick Schule (USA)
200m Hurdles	Harry Hillman (USA)
400m Hurdles	Harry Hillman (USA)
3,000m Steeplechase	James Lightbody (USA)
High Jump	Samuel Jones (USA)
Pole Vault	Charles Dvorak (USA)
Long Jump	Meyer Prinstein (USA)
Triple Jump	Meyer Prinstein (USA)
Shot Put	Ralph Rose (USA)
Discus	Martin Sheridan (USA)
Hammer	John Flanagan (USA)
56lb Weight	Etienne Desmarteau (Canada)
Standing High Jump	Ray Ewry (USA)
Standing Long Jump	Ray Ewry (USA)
Standing Triple Jump	Ray Ewry (USA)

See separate sections on **Cross-country running, Decathlon, Heptathlon, Marathon** and **Walking**

1908

Men

100m	Reginald Walker (South Africa)
200m	Robert Kerr (Canada)
400m	Wyndham Halswelle (Great Britain)
800m	Melvin Sheppard (USA)
1,500m	Melvin Sheppard (USA)
5 Miles	Emil Voigt (Great Britain)
110m Hurdles	Forrest Smithson (USA)
400m Hurdles	Charles Bacon (USA)
3,200m Steeplechase	Arthur Russell (Great Britain)
4x400m Relay	USA
High Jump	Harry Porter (USA)
Pole Vault	Edward Cooke (USA) and Alfred Gilbert (USA)
Long Jump	Frank Irons (USA)
Triple Jump	Timothy Ahearne (Ireland)
Shot Put	Ralph Rose (USA)
Discus	Martin Sheridan (USA)
Greek Style Discus	Martin Sheridan (USA)
Hammer	John Flanagan (USA)
Javelin	Eric Lemming (Sweden)
Freestyle Javelin	Eric Lemming (Sweden)
Standing High Jump	Ray Ewry (USA)
Standing Long Jump	Ray Ewry (USA)
Standing Triple Jump	Ray Ewry (USA)

1912

Men

100m	Ralph Craig (USA)
200m	Ralph Craig (USA)
400m	Charles Reidpath (USA)
800m	James Meredith (USA)
1,500m	Arnold Jackson (Great Britain)
5,000m	Hannes Kolehmainen (Finland)
10,000m	Hannes Kolehmainen (Finland)
110m Hurdles	Frederick Kelly (USA)
4x100m Relay	Great Britain
4x400m Relay	USA
High Jump	Alma Richards (USA)
Pole Vault	Harry Babcock (USA)
Long Jump	Albert Gutterson (USA)
Triple Jump	Gustav Lindblom (Sweden)
Shot Put	Patrick Mcdonald (USA)
Discus	Armas Taipale (Finland)
Hammer	Matthew McGrath (USA)

See separate sections on **Cross-country running, Decathlon, Heptathlon, Marathon** and **Walking**

Javelin	Eric Lemming (Sweden)
Standing High Jump	Platt Adams (USA)
Standing Long Jump	Konstantinos Tsiclitiras (Greece)
Discus Both Hands	Armas Taipale (Finland)
Javelin Both Hands	Juho Saaristo (Finland)
Shot Put Both Hands	Ralph Rose (USA)

1920

Men

100m	Charles Paddock (USA)
200m	Allen Woodring (USA)
400m	Bevil Rudd (South Africa)
800m	Albert Hill (Great Britain)
1,500m	Albert Hill (Great Britain)
5,000m	Joseph Guillemot (France)
10,000m	Paavo Nurmi (Finland)
110m Hurdles	Earl Thomson (Canada)
400m Hurdles	Frank Loomis (USA)
3,000m Steeplechase	Percy Hodge (Great Britain)
4x100m Relay	USA
4x400m Relay	Great Britain
High Jump	Richmond Landon (USA)
Pole Vault	Frank Foss (USA)
Long Jump	William Petersson (Sweden)
Triple Jump	Vilho Tuulos (Finland)
Shot Put	Frans Pörhölä (Finland)
Hammer	Patrick Ryan (USA)
Discus	Elmer Niklander (Finland)
Javelin	Jonni Myrrä (Finland)
56lb Weight	Patrick Mcdonald (USA)

1924

Men

100m	Harold Abrahams (Great Britain)
200m	Jackson Scholz (USA)
400m	Eric Liddell (Great Britain)
800m	Douglas Lowe (Great Britain)
1,000m	Paavo Nurmi (Finland)
5,000m	Paavo Nurmi (Finland)
10,000m	Ville Ritola (Finland)
110m Hurdles	Daniel Kinsey (USA)
400m Hurdles	F Morgan Taylor (USA)
3,000m Steeplechase	Ville Ritola (Finland)
4x100m Relay	USA

See separate sections on **Cross-country running, Decathlon, Heptathlon, Marathon** and **Walking**

4x400m Relay	USA
High Jump	Harold Osborn (USA)
Pole Vault	Lee Barnes (USA)
Long Jump	William Hubbard (USA)
Triple Jump	Anthony Winter (Australia)
Shot Put	Clarence Houser (USA)
Discus	Clarence Houser (USA)
Hammer	Frederick Tootell (USA)
Javelin	Jonni Myyrä (Finland)

1928

Men		Women	
100m	Percy Williams (Canada)	100m	Elizabeth Robinson (USA)
200m	Percy Williams (Canada)	800m	Lina Radke (Germany)
400m	Raymond Barbuti (USA)	4x100m Relay	Canada
800m	Douglas Lowe (Great Britain)	High Jump	Ethel Catherwood (Canada)
1,500m	Harri Larva (Finland)	Discus	Halina Konopacka (Poland)
5,000m	Ville Ritola (Finland)		
10,000m	Paavo Nurmi (Finland)		
110m Hurdles	Sydney Atkinson (South Africa)		
400m Hurdles	David Burghley (Great Britain)		
3,000m Steeplechase	Toivo Loukola (Finland)		
4x100m Relay	USA		
4x400m Relay	USA		
High Jump	Robert King (USA)		
Long Jump	Edward Hamm (USA)		
Triple Jump	Mikio Oda (Japan)		
Pole Vault	Sabin Carr (USA)		
Shot Put	John Kuck (USA)		
Discus	Clarence Houser (USA)		
Hammer	Patrick O'Callaghan (Ireland)		
Javelin	Erik Lundqvist (Sweden)		

1932

Men		Women	
100m	Eddie Tolan (USA)	100m	Stanislawa Walasiewicz (Poland)
200m	Eddie Tolan (USA)		
400m	William Carr (USA)	80m Hurdles	Mildred Didrikson (USA)
800m	Thomas Hampson (Great Britain)	4x100m Relay	USA
1,500m	Luigi Beccali (Italy)	High Jump	Jean Shiley (USA)
5,000m	Lauri Lehtinen (Finland)	Discus	Lillian Copeland (USA)
10,000m	Januscz Kusocinski (Poland)	Javelin	Mildred Didrikson (USA)
110m Hurdles	George Saling, Jr (USA)		
400m Hurdles	Robert Tisdall (Ireland)		

See separate sections on **Cross-country running, Decathlon, Heptathlon, Marathon** and **Walking**

3,000m Steeplechase	Volmari Iso-Hollo (Finland)
4x100m Relay	USA
4x400m Relay	USA
High Jump	Duncan McNaughton (Canada)
Long Jump	Edward Gordon (USA)
Triple Jump	Chuhei Nambu (Japan)
Pole Vault	William Miller (USA)
Shot Put	Leo Sexton (USA)
Discus	John Anderson (USA)
Hammer	Patrick O'Callaghan (Ireland)
Javelin	Matti Jarvinen (Finland)

1936

Men

100m	Jesse Owens (USA)
200m	Jesse Owens (USA)
400m	Archibald Williams (USA)
800m	John Woodruff (USA)
1,500m	John Lovelock (New Zealand)
5,000m	Gunnar Höckert (Finland)
10,000m	Ilmari Salminen (Finland)
110m Hurdles	Forrest Towns (USA)
400m Hurdles	Glenn Hardin (USA)
3,000m Steeplechase	Volmari Iso-Hollo (Finland)
4x100m Relay	USA
4x400m Relay	Great Britain
High Jump	Cornelius Johnson (USA)
Long Jump	Jesse Owens (USA)
Triple Jump	Naoto Tajima (Japan)
Pole Vault	Earle Meadows (USA)
Shot Put	Hans Wollcke (Germany)
Discus	William Carpenter (USA)
Hammer	Karl Hein (Germany)
Javelin	Gerhard Stöck (Germany)

Women

100m	Helen Stephens (USA)
80m Hurdles	Trebisonda Valla (Italy)
4x100m Relay	USA
High Jump	Ibolya Csak (Hungary)
Discus	Gisela Mauermayer (Germany)
Javelin	Mathilde Fleischer (Germany)

1948

Men

100m	Harrison Dillard (USA)
200m	Melvin Patton (USA)
400m	Arthur Wint (Jamaica)
800m	Malvin Whitfield (USA)
1,500m	Henry Eriksson (Sweden)
5,000m	Gaston Reiff (Belgium)
10,000m	Emil Zatopek (Czechoslovakia)

Women

100m	Fanny Blankers-Koen (The Netherlands)
200m	Fanny Blankers-Koen (The Netherlands)
80m Hurdles	Fanny Blankers-Koen (The Netherlands)
4x100m Relay	The Netherlands

See separate sections on **Cross-country running, Decathlon, Heptathlon, Marathon** and **Walking**

110m Hurdles	William Porter (USA)	High Jump	Alice Coachman (USA)
400m Hurdles	Roy Cochran (USA)	Long Jump	Olga Gyarmati (Hungary)
3,000m Steeplechase	Tore Sjöstrand (Sweden)	Shot Put	Micheline Ostermeyer (France)
4x100m Relay	USA	Discus	Micheline Ostermeyer (France)
4x400m Relay	USA	Javelin	Herma Bauma (Austria)
High Jump	John Winter (Australia)		
Long Jump	Willie Steele (USA)		
Triple Jump	Arne Ahman (Sweden)		
Pole Vault	Guinn Smith (USA)		
Shot Put	Wilbur Thompson (USA)		
Discus	Adolfo Consolini (Italy)		
Hammer	Imre Nemeth (Hungary)		
Javelin	Kaj Rautavaara (Finland)		

1952

Men		Women	
100m	Lindy Remigino (USA)	100m	Marjorie Jackson-Nelson (Australia)
200m	Andrew Stanfield (USA)	200m	Marjorie Jackson-Nelson (Australia)
400m	George Rhoden (Jamaica)	80m Hurdles	Shirley Strickland de la Hunty (Australia)
800m	Malvin Whitfield (USA)	4x100m Relay	USA
1,500m	Josy Barthel (Luxembourg)	High Jump	Esther Brand (South Africa)
5,000m	Emil Zatopek (Czechoslovakia)	Long Jump	Yvette Williams (New Zealand)
10,000m	Emil Zatopek (Czechoslovakia)	Shot Put	Galina Zybina (USSR)
110m Hurdles	Harrison Dillard (USA)	Discus	Nina Romaschkova-Ponomareva (USSR)
400m Hurdles	Charles Moore (USA)	Javelin	Dana Ingrova-Zatopkova (Czechoslovakia)
3,000m Steeplechase	Horace Ashenfelter (USA)		
4x100m Relay	USA		
4x400m Relay	Jamaica		
High Jump	Buddy Davis (USA)		
Long Jump	Jerome Biffle (USA)		
Triple Jump	Adhemar Ferreira da Silva (Brazil)		
Pole Vault	Robert Richards (USA)		
Shot Put	Parry O'Brien (USA)		
Discus	Sim Iness (USA)		
Hammer	Jozsef Csermak (Hungary)		
Javelin	Cyrus Young (USA)		

1956

Men		Women	
100m	Bobby Morrow (USA)	100m	Betty Cuthbert (Australia)
200m	Bobby Morrow (USA)	200m	Betty Cuthbert (Australia)
400m	Charles Jenkins (USA)	80m Hurdles	Shirley Strickland de la Hunty (Australia)
800m	Tom Courtney (USA)	4x100m Relay	Australia
1,500m	Ron Delany (Ireland)		

See separate sections on **Cross-country running, Decathlon, Heptathlon, Marathon** and **Walking**

5,000m	Vladimir Kuts (USSR)	High Jump	Mildred McDaniel (USA)
10,000m	Vladimir Kuts (USSR)	Long Jump	Elzbieta Dunska-Krzesinska (Poland)
110m Hurdles	Lee Calhoun (USA)	Shot Put	Tamara Tyshkevich (USSR)
400m Hurdles	Glenn Davis (USA)	Discus	Olga Fikotova-Connolly (Czechoslovakia)
3,000m Steeplechase	Chris Brasher (Great Britain)	Javelin	Inese Jaunzeme (USSR)
4x100m Relay	USA		
4x400m Relay	USA		
High Jump	Charles Dumas (USA)		
Long Jump	Gregory Bell (USA)		
Triple Jump	Adhemar Ferreira da Silva (Brazil)		
Pole Vault	Robert Richards (USA)		
Shot Put	Parry O'Brien (USA)		
Discus	Al Oerter (USA)		
Hammer	Harold Connolly (USA)		
Javelin	Egil Danielsen (Norway)		

1960

Men		Women	
100m	Armin Hary (Germany)	100m	Wilma Rudolph (USA)
200m	Livio Berruti (Italy)	200m	Wilma Rudolph (USA)
400m	Otis Davis (USA)	800m	Lyudmila Lisenko-Shevtsova (USSR)
800m	Peter Snell (New Zealand)	80m Hurdles	Iryna Press (USSR)
1,500m	Herb Elliott (Australia)	4x100m Relay	USA
5,000m	Murray Halberg (New Zealand)	High Jump	Iolanda Balas (Romania)
10,000m	Pyotr Bolotnikov (USSR)	Long Jump	Vera Kolashnikova-Krepkina (USSR)
110m Hurdles	Lee Calhoun (USA)	Shot Put	Tamara Press (USSR)
400m Hurdles	Glenn Davis (USA)	Discus	Nina Romaschkova-Ponomareva (USSR)
3,000m Steeplechase	Zdzislaw Krzyszkowiak (Poland)	Javelin	Elvira Ozolina (USSR)
4x100m Relay	Germany		
4x400m Relay	USA		
High Jump	Robert Shavlakadze (USSR)		
Long Jump	Ralph Boston (USA)		
Triple Jump	Józef Schmidt (Poland)		
Pole Vault	Donald Bragg (USA)		
Shot Put	William Nieder (USA)		
Discus	Al Oerter (USA)		
Hammer	Vasili Rudenkov (USSR)		
Javelin	Viktor Tsybulenko (USSR)		

1964

Men		Women	
100m	Robert Hayes (USA)	100m	Wyomia Tyus (USA)
200m	Henry Carr (USA)	200m	Edith McGuire (USA)
400m	Michael Larrabee (USA)	400m	Betty Cuthbert (Australia)

See separate sections on **Cross-country running, Decathlon, Heptathlon, Marathon** and **Walking**

800m	Peter Snell (New Zealand)	800m	Ann Packer (Great Britain)
1,500m	Peter Snell (New Zealand)	80m Hurdles	Karin Richert-Balzer (Germany)
5,000m	Robert Schul (USA)	4x100m Relay	Poland
10,000m	William Mills (USA)	High Jump	Iolanda Balas (Romania)
110m Hurdles	Hayes Jones (USA)	Long Jump	Mary Bignal-Rand (Great Britain)
400m Hurdles	Rex Cawley (USA)	Shot Put	Tamara Press (USSR)
3,000m Steeplechase	Gaston Roelants (Belgium)	Discus	Tamara Press (USSR)
4x100m Relay	USA	Javelin	Mihaela Penes (Romania)
4x400m Relay	USA		
High Jump	Valeri Brumel (USSR)		
Long Jump	Lynn Davies (Great Britain)		
Triple Jump	Józef Schmidt (Poland)		
Pole Vault	Frederick Hansen (USA)		
Shot Put	Dallas Long (USA)		
Discus	Al Oerter (USA)		
Hammer	Romuald Klim (USSR)		
Javelin	Pauli Nevala (Finland)		

1968

Men		Women	
100m	James Hines (USA)	100m	Wyomia Tyus (USA)
200m	Tommie Smith (USA)	200m	Irena Szewinska (Poland)
400m	Lee Evans (USA)	400m	Colette Besson (France)
800m	Ralph Doubell (Australia)	800m	Madeline Manning-Jackson (USA)
1,500m	Kip Keino (Kenya)	80m Hurdles	Maureen Caird (Australia)
5,000m	Mohamed Gammoudi (Tunisia)	4x100m Relay	USA
10,000m	Naftali Temu (Kenya)	High Jump	Miloslava Rezkova-Hubner (Czechoslovakia)
110m Hurdles	Willie Davenport (USA)	Long Jump	Viorica Viscopoleanu (Romania)
400m Hurdles	David Hemery (Great Britain)	Shot Put	Margitta Helmbold-Gummel (East Germany)
3,000m Steeplechase	Amos Biwott (Kenya)	Discus	Lia Manoliu (Romania)
4x100m Relay	USA	Javelin	Angela Nemeth-Ranky (Hungary)
4x400m Relay	USA		
High Jump	Dick Fosbury (USA)		
Long Jump	Bob Beamon (USA)		
Triple Jump	Viktor Saneyev (USSR)		
Pole Vault	Bob Seagren (USA)		
Shot Put	James Matson (USA)		
Discus	Al Oerter (USA)		
Hammer	Gyula Zsivotzky (Hungary)		
Javelin	Yanis Lusis (USSR)		

1972

Men		Women	
100m	Valeri Borzov (USSR)	100m	Renate Stecher (East Germany)
200m	Valeri Borzov (USSR)		

See separate sections on **Cross-country running, Decathlon, Heptathlon, Marathon** and **Walking**

400m	Vincent Matthews (USA)	200m	Renate Stecher (East Germany)
800m	Dave Wottle (USA)	400m	Monika Zehrt (East Germany)
1,500m	Pekka Vasala (Finland)	800m	Hildegard Falck-Janze (West Germany)
5,000m	Lasse Viren (Finland)	1,500m	Lyudmila Bragina (USSR)
10,000m	Lasse Viren (Finland)	100m Hurdles	Annelie Ehrhardt (East Germany)
110m Hurdles	Rodney Milburn (USA)	4x100m Relay	West Germany
400m Hurdles	John Akii-Bua (Uganda)	4x400m Relay	East Germany
3,000m Steeplechase	Kip Keino (Kenya)	High Jump	Ulrike Meyfarth (West Germany)
4x100m Relay	USA	Long Jump	Heidemarie Rosendahl (West Germany)
4x400m Relay	Kenya	Shot Put	Nadezhda Chizhova (USSR)
High Jump	Yuri Tarmak (USSR)	Discus	Faina Melnik (USSR)
Long Jump	Randy Williams (USA)	Javelin	Ruth Fuchs (East Germany)
Triple Jump	Viktor Saneyev (USSR)		
Pole Vault	Wolfgang Nordwig (East Germany)		
Shot Put	Wladyslaw Komar (Poland)		
Discus	Ludvik Danek (Czechoslovakia)		
Hammer	Anatoli Bondarchuk (USSR)		
Javelin	Klaus Wolfermann (West Germany)		

1976

Men		Women	
100m	Hasely Crawford (Trinidad and Tobago)	100m	Annegret Richter-Irrgang (West Germany)
200m	Don Quarrie (Jamaica)	200m	Bärbel Eckert-Wöckel (East Germany)
400m	Alberto Juantorena (Cuba)	400m	Irena Szewinska (Poland)
800m	Alberto Juantorena (Cuba)	800m	Tatiana Kazankina (USSR)
1,500m	John Walker (New Zealand)	1,500m	Tatiana Kazankina (USSR)
5,000m	Lasse Viren (Finland)	100m Hurdles	Johanna Schaller-Klier (East Germany)
10,000m	Lasse Viren (Finland)	4x100m Relay	East Germany
110m Hurdles	Guy Drut (France)	4x400m Relay	East Germany
400m Hurdles	Edwin Moses (USA)	High Jump	Rosemarie Witschas-Ackermann (East Germany)
3,000m Steeplechase	Anders Garderud (Sweden)	Long Jump	Angela Voigt (East Germany)
4x100m Relay	USA	Shot Put	Ivanka Christova-Todorova (Bulgaria)
4x400m Relay	USA	Discus	Evelin Schlaak-Jahl (East Germany)
High Jump	Jacek Wszola (Poland)	Javelin	Ruth Fuchs (East Germany)
Long Jump	Arnie Robinson (USA)		
Triple Jump	Viktor Saneyev (USSR)		
Pole Vault	Tadeusz Slusarski (Poland)		
Shot Put	Udo Beyer (East Germany)		
Discus	Mac Wilkins (USA)		
Hammer	Yuri Sedykh (USSR)		
Javelin	Miklos Nemeth (Hungary)		

See separate sections on **Cross-country running, Decathlon, Heptathlon, Marathon** and **Walking**

1980

Men		Women	
100m	Allan Wells (Great Britain)	100m	Lyudmila Kondratieva (USSR)
200m	Pietro Mennea (Italy)	200m	Bärbel Eckert-Wöckel (East Germany)
400m	Viktor Markin (USSR)	400m	Marita Koch (East Germany)
800m	Steve Ovett (Great Britain)	800m	Nadiya Olizarenko (USSR)
1,500m	Sebastian Coe (Great Britain)	1,500m	Tatiana Kazankina (USSR)
5,000m	Miruts Yifter (Ethiopia)	100m Hurdles	Vera Komisova (USSR)
10,000m	Miruts Yifter (Ethiopia)	4x100m Relay	East Germany
110m Hurdles	Thomas Munkelt (East Germany)	4x400m Relay	USSR
400m Hurdles	Volker Beck (East Germany)	High Jump	Sara Simeoni (Italy)
3,000m Steeplechase	Bronislaw Malinowski (Poland)	Long Jump	Tatiana Kolpakova (USSR)
4x100m Relay	USSR	Shot Put	Ilona Schoknecht-Slupianek (East Germany)
4x400m Relay	USSR	Discus	Evelin Schlaak-Jahl (East Germany)
High Jump	Gerd Wessig (East Germany)	Javelin	Maria Colon-Ruenes (Cuba)
Long Jump	Lutz Dombrowski (East Germany)		
Triple Jump	Yaak Uudmae (USSR)		
Pole Vault	Wladyslaw Kozakiewicz (Poland)		
Shot Put	Vladimir Kiselev (USSR)		
Discus	Viktor Rashchupkin (USSR)		
Hammer	Yuri Sedykh (USSR)		
Javelin	Dainis Kula (USSR)		

1984

Men		Women	
100m	Carl Lewis (USA)	100m	Evelyn Ashford (USA)
200m	Carl Lewis (USA)	200m	Valerie Brisco-Hooks (USA)
400m	Alonzo Babers (USA)	400m	Valerie Brisco-Hooks (USA)
800m	Joaquim Cruz (Brazil)	800m	Doina Besliu-Melinte (Romania)
1,500m	Sebastian Coe (Great Britain)	1,500m	Gabriella Dorio (Italy)
5,000m	Said Aouita (Morocco)	3,000m	Maricica Puica (Romania)
10,000m	Alberto Cova (Italy)	100m Hurdles	Benita Fitzgerald-Brown (USA)
110m Hurdles	Roger Kingdom (USA)	400m Hurdles	Nawal El Moutawakel (Morocco)
400m Hurdles	Edwin Moses (USA)	4x100m Relay	USA
3,000m Steeplechase	Julius Korir (Kenya)	4x400m Relay	USA
4x100m Relay	USA	High Jump	Ulrike Meyfarth (West Germany)
4x400m Relay	USA	Long Jump	Anisoara Cusmir-Stanciu (Romania)
High Jump	Dietmar Mögenburg (West Germany)	Shot Put	Claudia Losch (West Germany)
Long Jump	Carl Lewis (USA)	Discus	Ria Stalman (The Netherlands)
Triple Jump	Al Joyner (USA)		
Pole Vault	Pierre Quinon (France)		
Shot Put	Alessandro Andrei (Italy)		
Discus	Rolf Danneberg (West Germany)		

See separate sections on **Cross-country running**, **Decathlon**, **Heptathlon**, **Marathon** and **Walking**

Hammer	Juha Tiainen (Finland)	Javelin	Tessa Sanderson (Great Britain)
Javelin	Arto Harkonen (Finland)		

1988

Men		Women	
100m	Carl Lewis (USA)	100m	Florence Griffith-Joyner (USA)
200m	Joe DeLoach (USA)	200m	Florence Griffith-Joyner (USA)
400m	Steve Lewis (USA)	400m	Olga Bryzgina (USSR)
800m	Paul Ereng (Kenya)	800m	Sigrun Wodars (East Germany)
1,500m	Peter Rono (Kenya)	1,500m	Paula Ivan (Romania)
5,000m	John Ngugi (Kenya)	3,000m	Tatiana Samolenko-Dorovskikh (USSR)
10,000m	Brahim Boutayeb (Morocco)	10,000m	Olga Bondarenko (USSR)
110m Hurdles	Roger Kingdom (USA)	100m Hurdles	Yordanka Donkova (Bulgaria)
400m Hurdles	Andre Phillips (USA)	400m Hurdles	Debbie Flintoff-King (Australia)
3,000m Steeplechase	Julius Kariuki (Kenya)	4x100m Relay	USA
4x100m Relay	USSR	4x400m Relay	USSR
4x400m Relay	USA	High Jump	Louise Ritter (USA)
High Jump	Gennadi Avdeyenko (USSR)	Long Jump	Jackie Joyner-Kersee (USA)
Long Jump	Carl Lewis (USA)	Shot Put	Natalya Lisovskaia (USSR)
Triple Jump	Kristo Markov (Bulgaria)	Discus	Martina Hellmann (East Germany)
Pole Vault	Sergei Bubka (USSR)	Javelin	Petra Felke-Meier (East Germany)
Shot Put	Ulf Timmermann (East Germany)		
Discus	Jürgen Schult (East Germany)		
Hammer	Sergei Litvinov (USSR)		
Javelin	Tapio Korjus (Finland)		

1992

Men		Women	
100m	Linford Christie (Great Britain)	100m	Gail Devers (USA)
200m	Mike Marsh (USA)	200m	Gwen Torrence (USA)
400m	Quincy Watts (USA)	400m	Marie-José Pérec (France)
800m	William Tanui (Kenya)	800m	Ellen van Langen (The Netherlands)
1,500m	Fermin Cacho (Spain)	1,500m	Hassiba Boulmerka (Algeria)
5,000m	Dieter Baumann (Germany)	3,000m	Elena Romanova (Unified Team)
10,000m	Khalid Skah (Morocco)	10,000m	Derartu Tulu (Ethiopia)
110m Hurdles	Mark McKoy (Canada)	100m Hurdles	Paraskevi Patoulidou (Greece)
400m Hurdles	Kevin Young (USA)	400m Hurdles	Sally Gunnell (Great Britain)
3,000m Steeplechase	Mathew Birir (Kenya)	4x100m Relay	USA
4x100m Relay	USA		
4x400m Relay	USA		

See separate sections on **Cross-country running, Decathlon, Heptathlon, Marathon** and **Walking**

High Jump	Javier Sotomayor (Cuba)	4x400m Relay	Unified Team
Long Jump	Carl Lewis (USA)	High Jump	Heike Henkel (Germany)
Triple Jump	Mike Conley (USA)	Long Jump	Heike Drechsler (Germany)
Pole Vault	Maksim Tarasov (Unified Team)	Shot Put	Svetlana Kriveleva (Unified Team)
Shot Put	Mike Stulce (USA)		
Discus	Romas Ubartas (Lithuania)	Discus	Maritza Marten (Cuba)
Hammer	Andrei Abduvaliyev (Unified Team)	Javelin	Silke Renk (Germany)
Javelin	Jan Zelezný (Czechoslovakia)		

From shot put to line-out

Young shot putter Victor Costello, who represented Ireland to no great acclaim at the 1992 Barcelona Olympics, went on to a successful rugby union career, gaining 39 caps as number eight for the Irish international side.

1996

Men		Women	
100m	Donovan Bailey (Canada)	100m	Gail Devers (USA)
200m	Michael Johnson (USA)	200m	Marie-José Pérec (France)
400m	Michael Johnson (USA)	400m	Marie-José Pérec (France)
800m	Vebjørn Rodal (Norway)	800m	Svetlana Masterkova (Russia)
1,500m	Noureddine Morceli (Algeria)	1,500m	Svetlana Masterkova (Russia)
5,000m	Venuste Niyongabo (Burundi)	5,000m	Wang Junxia (China)
10,000m	Haile Gebrselassie (Ethiopia)	10,000m	Fernanda Ribeiro (Portugal)
110m Hurdles	Allen Johnson (USA)	100m Hurdles	Ludmila Engquist (Sweden)
400m Hurdles	Derrick Adkins (USA)	400m Hurdles	Deon Hemmings (Jamaica)
3,000m Steeplechase	Joseph Keter (Kenya)	4x100m Relay	USA
4x100m Relay	Canada	4x400m Relay	USA
4x400m Relay	USA	High Jump	Stefka Kostadinova (Bulgaria)
High Jump	Charles Austin (USA)	Long Jump	Chioma Ajunwa (Nigeria)
Long Jump	Carl Lewis (USA)	Triple Jump	Inessa Kravets (Ukraine)
Triple Jump	Kenny Harrison (USA)	Shot Put	Astrid Kumbernuss (Germany)
Pole Vault	Jean Galfione (France)		
Shot Put	Randy Barnes (USA)	Discus	Ilke Wyludda (Germany)
Discus	Lars Riedel (Germany)	Javelin	Heli Rantanen (Finland)
Hammer	Balazs Kiss (Hungary)		
Javelin	Jan Zelezný (Czech Republic)		

2000

Men		Women	
100m	Maurice Greene (USA)	100m	Marion Jones (USA)
200m	Konstantinos Kenteris (Greece)	200m	Marion Jones (USA)

See separate sections on **Cross-country running, Decathlon, Heptathlon, Marathon** and **Walking**

400m	Michael Johnson (USA)	400m	Cathy Freeman (Australia)
800m	Nils Schumann (Germany)	800m	Maria Mutola (Mozambique)
1,500m	Noah Ngenyi (Kenya)	1,500m	Nouria Merah-Benida (Algeria)
5,000m	Millon Wolde (Ethiopia)	5,000m	Gabriela Szabo (Romania)
10,000m	Haile Gebrselassie (Ethiopia)	10,000m	Derartu Tulu (Ethiopia)
110m Hurdles	Anier Garcia (Cuba)	100m Hurdles	Olga Shishigina (Kazakhstan)
400m Hurdles	Angelo Taylor (USA)	400m Hurdles	Irina Privalova (Russia)
3,000m Steeplechase	Reuben Kosgei (Kenya)	4x100m Relay	Bahamas
4x100m Relay	USA	4x400m Relay	USA
4x400m Relay	USA	High Jump	Yelena Yelesina (Russia)
High Jump	Sergei Kliugin (Russia)	Long Jump	Heike Drechsler (Germany)
Long Jump	Iván Pedroso (Cuba)	Triple Jump	Tereza Marinova (Bulgaria)
Triple Jump	Jonathan Edwards (Great Britain)	Pole Vault	Stacy Dragila (USA)
Pole Vault	Nick Hysong (USA)	Shot Put	Yanina Karolchik (Belarus)
Shot Put	Arsi Harju (Finland)	Discus	Ellina Zvereva (Belarus)
Discus	Virgilijus Alekna (Lithuania)	Hammer	Kamila Skolimowska (Poland)
Hammer	Szymon Ziolkowski (Poland)	Javelin	Trine Hattestad (Norway)
Javelin	Jan Zelezný (Czech Republic)		

2004

Men		Women	
100m	Justin Gatlin (USA)	100m	Yuliya Nesterenko (Belarus)
200m	Shawn Crawford (USA)	200m	Veronica Campbell (Jamaica)
400m	Jeremy Wariner (USA)	400m	Tonique Williams-Darling (Bahamas)
800m	Yuri Borzakovskiy (Russia)	800m	Kelly Holmes (Great Britain)
1,500m	Hicham El Guerrouj (Morocco)	1,500m	Kelly Holmes (Great Britain)
5,000m	Hicham El Guerrouj (Morocco)	5,000m	Meseret Defar (Ethiopia)
10,000m	Kenenisa Bekele (Ethiopia)	10,000m	Xing Huina (China)
110m Hurdles	Xiang Liu (China)	100m Hurdles	Joanna Hayes (USA)
400m Hurdles	Felix Sánchez (Dominican Republic)	400m Hurdles	Fani Halkia (Greece)
3,000m Steeplechase	Ezekiel Kemboi (Kenya)	4x100m Relay	Jamaica
4x100m Relay	Great Britain	4x400m Relay	USA
4x400m Relay	USA	High Jump	Yelena Slesarenko (Russia)
High Jump	Stefan Holm (Sweden)	Long Jump	Tatiana Lebedeva (Russia)
Long Jump	Dwight Phillips (USA)	Triple Jump	Françoise Mbango Etone (Cameroon)
Triple Jump	Christian Olsson (Sweden)		
Pole Vault	Timothy Mack (USA)	Pole Vault	Yelena Isinbayeva (Russia)
Shot Put	Yuri Bilonog (Ukraine)	Shot Put	Yumileidi Cumba (Cuba)
Discus	Virgilijus Alekna (Lithuania)	Discus	Natalia Sadova (Russia)
Hammer	Koji Murofushi (Japan)	Hammer	Olga Kuzenkova (Russia)
Javelin	Andreas Thorkildsen (Norway)	Javelin	Osleidys Menéndez (Cuba)

See separate sections on **Cross-country running, Decathlon, Heptathlon, Marathon** and **Walking**

Trevor the Tortoise

Twenty-one-stone Trevor Misapeka of American Samoa came to the 1991 World Championships to compete in the shot put, but after rules changes left him ineligible, decided to enter the 100m. His time of 14.28s meant he came in over four seconds behind heat winner Kim Collins. The lumbering Misapeka, affectionately nicknamed Trevor the Tortoise, went on to a more appropriate career as defensive lineman for San Diego Riptide in the National West division of the Arena Football League.

World Athletics Championships

The first World Athletics Championships were held in Helsinki in 1983. The Championships took place every four years until 1991, when they became biennial.

1983 Helsinki, Finland

Men		Women	
100m	Carl Lewis (USA)	100m	Marlies Oelsner-Gohr (East Germany)
200m	Calvin Smith (USA)	200m	Marita Koch (East Germany)
400m	Bert Cameron (Jamaica)	400m	Jarmila Kratochvílová (Czechoslovakia)
800m	Willi Wülbeck (West Germany)	800m	Jarmila Kratochvílová (Czechoslovakia)
1,500m	Steve Cram (Great Britain)	1,500m	Mary Decker (USA)
5,000m	Eamonn Coghlan (Ireland)	3,000m	Mary Decker (USA)
10,000m	Alberto Cova (Italy)	100m Hurdles	Bettine Jahn (East Germany)
3,000m Steeplechase	Patriz Ilg (West Germany)	400m Hurdles	Yekaterina Fesenko-Grun (USSR)
110m Hurdles	Greg Foster (USA)	4x100m Relay	East Germany
400m Hurdles	Edwin Moses (USA)	4x400m Relay	East Germany
4x100m Relay	USA	High Jump	Tamara Bykova (USSR)
4x400m Relay	USSR	Long Jump	Heike Daute (East Germany)
High Jump	Gennadi Avdeyenko (USSR)	Discus	Martina Opitz-Hellmann (East Germany)
Pole Vault	Sergei Bubka (USSR)	Javelin	Tiina Lillak (Finland)
Long Jump	Carl Lewis (USA)		
Triple Jump	Zdzislaw Hoffmann (Poland)		
Shot Put	Edward Sarul (Poland)		
Discus	Imrich Bugár (Czechoslovakia)		
Hammer	Sergei Litvinov (USSR)		
Javelin	Detlef Michel (East Germany)		

1987 Rome, Italy

Men		Women	
100m	Carl Lewis (USA)	100m	Silke Gladisch (East Germany)
200m	Calvin Smith (USA)	200m	Silke Gladisch (East Germany)
400m	Thomas Schonlebe (East Germany)	400m	Olga Bryzgina (USSR)
800m	Billy Konchellah (Kenya)		

See separate sections on **Cross-country running, Decathlon, Heptathlon, Marathon** and **Walking**

1,500m	Abdi Bile (Somalia)	800m	Sigrun Wodars (East Germany)
5,000m	Said Aouita (Morocco)	1,500m	Tatiana Samolenko (USSR)
10,000m	Paul Kipkoech (Kenya)	3,000m	Tatiana Samolenko (USSR)
3,000m Steeplechase	Francesco Panetta (Italy)	10,000m	Ingrid Kristiansen (Norway)
110m Hurdles	Greg Foster (USA)	100m Hurdles	Ginka Zagorcheva (Bulgaria)
400m Hurdles	Edwin Moses (USA)	400m Hurdles	Sabine Busch (East Germany)
4x100m Relay	USA	4x100m Relay	USA
4x400m Relay	USA	4x400m Relay	East Germany
High Jump	Patrik Sjoberg (Sweden)	High Jump	Stefka Kostadinova (Bulgaria)
Pole Vault	Sergei Bubka (USSR)	Long Jump	Jackie Joyner-Kersee (USA)
Long Jump	Carl Lewis (USA)	Shot Put	Natalia Lisovskaya (USSR)
Triple Jump	Kristo Markov (Bulgaria)	Discus	Martina Opitz-Hellman (East Germany)
Shot Put	Werner Günthör (Switzerland)	Javelin	Fatima Whitbread (Great Britain)
Discus	Jürgen Schult (East Germany)		
Hammer	Sergei Litvinov (USSR)		
Javelin	Seppo Roty (Finland)		

1991 Tokyo, Japan

Men		Women	
100m	Carl Lewis (USA)	100m	Katrin Krabbe (Germany)
200m	Michael Johnson (USA)	200m	Katrin Krabbe (Germany)
400m	Antonio Pettigrew (USA)	400m	Marie-José Pérec (France)
800m	Billy Konchellah (Kenya)	800m	Liliya Nurutdinova (USSR)
1,500m	Noureddine Morceli (Algeria)	1,500m	Hassiba Boulmerka (Algeria)
5,000m	Yobes Ondieki (Kenya)	3,000m	Tatiana Samolenko-Dorovskikh (USSR)
10,000m	Moses Tanui (Kenya)	10,000m	Liz McColgan (Great Britain)
3,000m Steeplechase	Moses Kiptanui (Kenya)	100m Hurdles	Ludmila Engquist (USSR)
110m Hurdles	Greg Foster (USA)	400m Hurdles	Tatiana Ledovskaya (USSR)
400m Hurdles	Samuel Matete (Zambia)	4x100m Relay	Jamaica
4x100m Relay	USA	4x400m Relay	USSR
4x400m Relay	Great Britain	High Jump	Heike Redetzky-Henkel (Germany)
High Jump	Charles Austin (USA)	Long Jump	Jackie Joyner-Kersee (USA)
Pole Vault	Sergei Bubka (Ukraine)	Shot Put	Huang Zhihong (China)
Long Jump	Mike Powell (USA)	Discus	Tsvetanka Khristova (Bulgaria)
Triple Jump	Kenny Harrison (USA)	Javelin	Xu Demei (China)
Shot Put	Werner Günthör (Switzerland)		
Discus	Lars Riedel (Germany)		
Hammer	Yuri Sedykh (USSR)		
Javelin	Kimmo Kinnunen (Finland)		

1993 Stuttgart, Germany

Men		Women	
100m	Linford Christie (Great Britain)	100m	Gail Devers (USA)
200m	Frankie Fredericks (Namibia)	200m	Merlene Ottey (Jamaica)

See separate sections on **Cross-country running, Decathlon, Heptathlon, Marathon** and **Walking**

400m	Michael Johnson (USA)	400m	Jearl Miles-Clark (USA)
800m	Paul Ruto (Kenya)	800m	Maria Mutola (Mozambique)
1,500m	Noureddine Morceli (Algeria)	1,500m	Liu Dong (China)
5,000m	Ismael Kirui (Kenya)	3,000m	Qu Yunxia (China)
10,000m	Haile Gebrselassie (Ethiopia)	10,000m	Wang Junxia (China)
3,000m Steeplechase	Moses Kiptanui (Kenya)	100m Hurdles	Gail Devers (USA)
110m Hurdles	Colin Jackson (Great Britain)	400m Hurdles	Sally Gunnell (Great Britain)
400m Hurdles	Kevin Young (USA)	4x100m Relay	Russia
4x100m Relay	USA	4x400m Relay	USA
4x400m Relay	USA	High Jump	Ioamnet Quintero (Cuba)
High Jump	Javier Sotomayor (Cuba)	Long Jump	Heike Drechsler (Germany)
Pole Vault	Sergei Bubka (Ukraine)	Triple Jump	Anna Biryukova (Russia)
Long Jump	Mike Powell (USA)	Shot Put	Huang Zhihong (China)
Triple Jump	Mike Conley (USA)	Discus	Olga Burova-Chernyavskaya (Russia)
Shot Put	Werner Günthör (Switzerland)		
Discus	Lars Riedel (Germany)	Javelin	Trine Hattestad (Norway)
Hammer	Andrei Abduvaliyev (Tajikistan)		
Javelin	Jan Zelezný (Czech Republic)		

1995 Gothenburg, Sweden

Men		Women	
100m	Donovan Bailey (Canada)	100m	Gwen Torrence (USA)
200m	Michael Johnson (USA)	200m	Merlene Ottey (Jamaica)
400m	Michael Johnson (USA)	400m	Marie-José Pérec (France)
800m	Wilson Kipketer (Denmark)	800m	Ana Quirot (Cuba)
1,500m	Noureddine Morceli (Algeria)	1,500m	Hassiba Boulmerka (Algeria)
5,000m	Ismael Kirui (Kenya)	5,000m	Sonia O'Sullivan (Ireland)
10,000m	Haile Gebrselassie (Ethiopia)	10,000m	Fernanda Ribeiro (Portugal)
3,000m Steeplechase	Moses Kiptanui (Kenya)	100m Hurdles	Gail Devers (USA)
110m Hurdles	Allen Johnson (USA)	400m Hurdles	Kim Batten (USA)
400m Hurdles	Derrick Adkins (USA)	4x100m Relay	USA
4x100m Relay	Canada	4x400m Relay	USA
4x400m Relay	USA	High Jump	Stefka Kostadinova (Bulgaria)
High Jump	Troy Kemp (Bahamas)	Long Jump	Fiona May (Italy)
Pole Vault	Sergei Bubka (Ukraine)	Triple Jump	Inessa Kravets (Ukraine)
Long Jump	Iván Pedroso (Cuba)	Shot Put	Astrid Kumbernuss (Germany)
Triple Jump	Jonathan Edwards (Great Britain)		
Shot Put	John Godina (USA)	Discus	Ellina Zvereva (Belarus)
Discus	Lars Riedel (Germany)	Javelin	Natalia Shikolenko (Belarus)
Hammer	Andrei Abduvaliyev (Tajikistan)		
Javelin	Jan Zelezný (Czech Republic)		

1997 Athens, Greece

Men		Women	
100m	Maurice Greene (USA)	100m	Marion Jones (USA)
200m	Ato Boldon (Trinidad)	200m	Zhanna Pintusevich (Ukraine)

See separate sections on **Cross-country running**, **Decathlon**, **Heptathlon**, **Marathon** and **Walking**

400m	Michael Johnson (USA)
800m	Wilson Kipketer (Denmark)
1,500m	Hicham El Guerrouj (Morocco)
5,000m	Daniel Komen (Kenya)
10,000m	Haile Gebrselassie (Ethiopia)
3,000m Steeplechase	Wilson Kipketer (Denmark)
110m Hurdles	Allen Johnson (USA)
400m Hurdles	Stéphane Diagana (France)
4x100m Relay	Canada
4x400m Relay	USA
High Jump	Javier Sotomayor (Cuba)
Pole Vault	Sergei Bubka (Ukraine)
Long Jump	Iván Pedroso (Cuba)
Triple Jump	Yoelbi Quesada (Cuba)
Shot Put	John Godina (USA)
Discus	Lars Riedel (Germany)
Hammer	Heinz Weis (Germany)
Javelin	Marius Corbett (South Africa)

400m	Cathy Freeman (Australia)
800m	Ana Quirot (Cuba)
1,500m	Carla Sacramento (Portugal)
5,000m	Gabriela Szabo (Romania)
10,000m	Sally Barsosio (Kenya)
100m Hurdles	Ludmila Engquist (Sweden)
400m Hurdles	Nezha Bidouane (Morocco)
4x100m Relay	USA
4x400m Relay	Germany
High Jump	Hanne Haugland (Norway)
Long Jump	Lyudmila Galkina (Russia)
Triple Jump	Sarka Kasparkova (Czech Republic)
Shot Put	Astrid Kumbernuss (Germany)
Discus	Beatrice Faumuina (New Zealand)
Javelin	Trine Hattestad (Norway)

1999 Seville, Spain

Men

100m	Maurice Greene (USA)
200m	Maurice Greene (USA)
400m	Michael Johnson (USA)
800m	Wilson Kipketer (Denmark)
1,500m	Hicham El Guerrouj (Morocco)
5,000m	Salah Hissou (Morocco)
10,000m	Haile Gebrselassie (Ethiopia)
3,000m Steeplechase	Christopher Koskei (Kenya)
110m Hurdles	Colin Jackson (Great Britain)
400m Hurdles	Fabrizio Mori (Italy)
4x100m Relay	USA
4x400m Relay	USA
High Jump	Vyacheslav Voronin (Russia)
Pole Vault	Maksim Tarasov (Russia)
Long Jump	Iván Pedroso (Cuba)
Triple Jump	Charles Friedek (Germany)
Shot Put	CJ Hunter (USA)
Discus	Anthony Washington (USA)
Hammer	Karsten Kobs (Germany)
Javelin	Aki Parviainen (Finland)

Women

100m	Marion Jones (USA)
200m	Inger Miller (USA)
400m	Cathy Freeman (Australia)
800m	Ludmila Formanová (Czech Republic)
1,500m	Svetlana Masterkova (Russia)
5,000m	Gabriela Szabo (Romania)
10,000m	Gete Wami (Ethiopia)
100m Hurdles	Gail Devers (USA)
400m Hurdles	Daimí Pernia (Cuba)
4x100m Relay	Bahamas
4x400m Relay	Russia
High Jump	Inga Babakova (Ukraine)
Pole Vault	Stacy Dragila (USA)
Long Jump	Niurka Montalvo (Spain)
Triple Jump	Paraskevi Tsiamita (Greece)
Shot Put	Astrid Kumbernuss (Germany)
Discus	Franka Dietzsch (Germany)
Hammer	Mihaela Melinte (Romania)
Javelin	Mirela Manjani-Tzelili (Greece)

See separate sections on **Cross-country running, Decathlon, Heptathlon, Marathon** and **Walking**

Athletics

2001 Edmonton, Canada

Men

100m	Maurice Greene (USA)
200m	Konstantinos Kenteris (Greece)
400m	Avard Moncur (Bahamas)
800m	André Bucher (Switzerland)
1,500m	Hicham El Guerrouj (Morocco)
5,000m	Richard Limo (Kenya)
10,000m	Charles Kamathi (Kenya)
3,000m Steeplechase	Reuben Kosgei (Kenya)
110m Hurdles	Allen Johnson (USA)
400m Hurdles	Felix Sánchez (Dominican Republic)
4x100m Relay	USA
4x400m Relay	USA
High Jump	Martin Buss (Germany)
Pole Vault	Dmitri Markov (Austria)
Long Jump	Iván Pedroso (Cuba)
Triple Jump	Jonathan Edwards (Great Britain)
Shot Put	John Godina (USA)
Discus	Lars Riedel (Germany)
Hammer	Szymon Ziolkowski (Poland)
Javelin	Jan Zelezný (Czech Republic)

Women

100m	Zhanna Pintusevich-Block (Ukraine)
200m	Marion Jones (USA)
400m	Amy Mbacke Thiam (Senegal)
800m	Maria Mutola (Mozambique)
1,500m	Gabriela Szabo (Romania)
5,000m	Olga Yegorova (Russia)
10,000m	Derartu Tulu (Ethiopia)
100m Hurdles	Anjanette Kirkland (USA)
400m Hurdles	Nezha Bidouane (Morocco)
4x100m Relay	Germany
4x400m Relay	Jamaica
High Jump	Hestrie Cloete (South Africa)
Pole Vault	Stacy Dragila (USA)
Long Jump	Fiona May (Italy)
Triple Jump	Tatiana Lebedeva (Russia)
Shot Put	Yanina Korolchik (Belarus)
Discus	Natalia Sadova (Russia)
Hammer	Yipsi Moreno (Cuba)
Javelin	Osleidys Menéndez (Cuba)

2003 Paris, France

Men

100m	Kim Collins (St Kitts and Nevis)
200m	John Capel (USA)
400m	Jerome Young (USA)
800m	Djabir Saïd-Guerni (Algeria)
1,500m	Hicham El Guerrouj (Morocco)
5,000m	Eliud Kipchoge (Kenya)
10,000m	Kenenisa Bekele (Ethiopia)
3,000m Steeplechase	Saif Shaheen (Qatar)
110m Hurdles	Allen Johnson (USA)
400m Hurdles	Felix Sánchez (Dominican Republic)
4x100m Relay	USA
4x400m Relay	USA
High Jump	Jacques Freitag (South Africa)
Pole Vault	Giuseppe Gibilisco (Italy)
Long Jump	Dwight Phillips (USA)
Triple Jump	Christian Olsson (Sweden)
Shot Put	Andrei Mikhnevich (Belarus)

Women

100m	Torri Edwards (USA)
200m	Anastasia Kapachinskaya (Russia)
400m	Ana Guevara (Mexico)
800m	Maria Mutola (Mozambique)
1,500m	Tatiana Tomashova (Russia)
5,000m	Tirunesh Dibaba (Ethiopia)
10,000m	Berhane Adere (Ethiopia)
100m Hurdles	Perdita Felicien (Canada)
400m Hurdles	Jana Pittman (Australia)
4x100m Relay	France
4x400m Relay	USA
High Jump	Hestrie Cloete (South Africa)
Pole Vault	Svetlana Feofanova (Russia)
Long Jump	Eunice Barber (France)
Triple Jump	Tatiana Lebedeva (Russia)
Shot Put	Svetlana Krivelyova (Russia)
Discus	Irina Yatchenko (Belarus)

See separate sections on **Cross-country running**, **Decathlon**, **Heptathlon**, **Marathon** and **Walking**

Discus	Virgilijus Alekna (Lithuania)	Hammer	Yipsi Moreno (Cuba)
Hammer	Ivan Tikhon (Belarus)	Javelin	Mirela Manjani-Tzelili (Greece)
Javelin	Sergei Makarov (Russia)		

Progression of Men's 100m World Record

		Date set	**Location**
10.6	Donald Lippincott (USA)	6 July 1912	Stockholm, Sweden
10.4	Charles Paddock (USA)	23 April 1921	Redlands, USA
10.3	Percy Williams (Canada)	9 August 1930	Toronto, Canada
10.2	Jesse Owens (USA)	20 June 1936	Chicago, USA
10.1	Willie Williams (USA)	3 August 1956	West Berlin, Germany
10.0	Armin Hary (West Germany)	21 June 1960	Zurich, Switzerland
9.9*	Jim Hines (USA)	20 June 1968	Sacramento, USA
9.95	Jim Hines (USA)	14 October 1968	Mexico City, Mexico
9.93	Calvin Smith (USA)	3 July 1983	Colorado Springs, USA
9.92	Carl Lewis (USA)	24 September 1988	Seoul, South Korea
9.90	Leroy Burrell (USA)	14 June 1991	New York, USA
9.86	Carl Lewis (USA)	25 August 1991	Tokyo, Japan
9.85	Leroy Burrell (USA)	6 July 1994	Lausanne, Switzerland
9.84	Donovan Bailey (Canada)	27 July 1996	Atlanta, USA
9.79	Maurice Greene (USA)	16 June 1999	Athens, Greece
9.78	Tim Montgomery (USA)	14 September 2002	Paris, France

*hand-timed

A-Z

back straight — the straight part of a running track on the other side from the **home straight**

bar — the 4m-long crossbar which an athlete must clear in the high jump (4.5m in the pole vault)

baton — the 30.48cm-long metal cylinder that must be passed between athletes in a **relay**

bend — 1. a curved section of a running track 2. the part of a race run around these sections, eg *she's run a good bend*

blocks — used by an athlete to brace his or her feet and get a fast start to the race, eg, *he's quick out of the blocks*

board — the point at the end of the **runway** from where an athlete takes off in the long jump and triple jump

box — the support in which an athlete plants the base of his or her pole when vaulting

box in — if an athlete is boxed in, he or she is trapped by other competitors against the inside of the track and is unable to move out to overtake

break — when an athlete breaks, he or she moves from their **lane** towards the inside of the track – permitted after the first **bend** of the **800m** and after the first **bend** of the second **leg** of the **4x400m relay**

See separate sections on **Cross-country running, Decathlon, Heptathlon, Marathon** and **Walking**

World Records

Men

		Date set	Location	Time/distance (m)/points
100m	Tim Montgomery (USA)	14 September 2002	Paris, France	9.78
200m	Michael Johnson (USA)	1 August 1996	Atlanta, USA	19.32
400m	Michael Johnson (USA)	26 August 1999	Seville, Spain	43.18
800m	Wilson Kipketer (Denmark)	24 August 1997	Cologne, Germany	1:41.11
1,500m	Hicham El Guerrouj (Morocco)	14 July 1998	Rome, Italy	3:26.00
5,000m	Kenenisa Bekele (Ethiopia)	31 May 2004	Hengelo, The Netherlands	12:37.35
10,000m	Kenenisa Bekele (Ethiopia)	8 June 2004	Ostrava, Czech Republic	26:20.31
Marathon	Paul Tergat (Kenya)	28 September 2003	Berlin, Germany	2:04:55
110m Hurdles	Colin Jackson (Great Britain)	20 August 1993	Stuttgart, Germany	12.91
400m Hurdles	Kevin Young (USA)	6 August 1992	Barcelona, Spain	46.78
3,000m Steeplechase	Saif Saeed Shaheen (Qatar)	3 September 2004	Brussels, Belgium	7:53.63
4x100m Relay	USA	8 August 1992	Barcelona, Spain	37.40
4x400m Relay	USA	22 July 1998	Uniondale, USA	2:54.20
20km Walk	Jefferson Pérez (Ecuador)	23 August 2003	Paris, France	1:17:21
50km Walk	Robert Korzeniowski (Poland)	27 August 2003	Paris, France	3:36:03
High Jump	Javier Sotomayor (Cuba)	27 July 1993	Salamanca, Spain	2.45
Long Jump	Mike Powell (USA)	30 August 1991	Tokyo, Japan	8.95
Pole Vault	Sergei Bubka (Ukraine)	31 July 1994	Sestrière, Italy	6.14
Triple Jump	Jonathan Edwards (Great Britain)	7 August 1995	Gothenburg, Sweden	18.29
Shot Put	Randy Barnes (USA)	20 May 1990	Los Angeles, USA	23.12
Discus	Jürgen Schult (East Germany)	6 June 1986	Neubrandenburg, East Germany	74.08
Hammer	Yuri Sedykh (USSR)	30 August 1986	Stuttgart, West Germany	86.74
Javelin	Jan Zelezný (Czech Republic)	25 May 1996	Jena, Germany	98.48
Decathlon	Roman Šebrle (Czech Republic)	27 May 2001	Götzis, Austria	9026

See separate sections on **Cross-country running, Decathlon, Heptathlon, Marathon** and **Walking**

Women

		Date set	Location	Time/distance (m)/points
100m	Florence Griffith-Joyner (USA)	16 July 1988	Indianapolis, USA	10.49
200m	Florence Griffith-Joyner (USA)	29 September 1988	Seoul, South Korea	21.34
400m	Marita Koch (East Germany)	6 October 1985	Canberra, Australia	47.60
800m	Jarmila Kratochvílová (Czechoslovakia)	26 July 1983	Munich, West Germany	1:53.28
1,500m	Qu Yunxia (China)	11 September 1993	Beijing, China	3:50.46
5,000m	Elvan Abeylegesse (Turkey)	11 June 2004	Bergen, Norway	14:24.68
10,000m	Wang Junxia (China)	8 September 1993	Beijing, China	29:31.78
Marathon	Paula Radcliffe (Great Britain)	13 April 2003	London, UK	2:15:25
100m Hurdles	Yordanka Donkova (Bulgaria)	20 August 1988	Stara Zagora, Bulgaria	12.21
400m Hurdles	Yuliya Pechonkina (Russia)	8 August 2003	Tula, Russia	52.34
4x100m Relay	East Germany	6 October 1985	Canberra, Australia	41.37
4x400m Relay	USSR	1 October 1988	Seoul, South Korea	3:15.17
20km Walk	Yan Wang (China)	19 November 2001	Guangzhon, China	1:26:22
High Jump	Stefka Kostadinova (Bulgaria)	30 August 1987	Rome, Italy	2.09
Long Jump	Galina Chistyakova (USSR)	11 June 1988	Leningrad, USSR	7.52
Pole Vault	Yelena Isinbayeva (Russia)	3 September 2004	Brussels, Belgium	4.92
Triple Jump	Inessa Kravets (Ukraine)	10 August 1995	Gothenburg, Sweden	15.50
Shot Put	Natalia Lisovskaya (USSR)	7 June 1987	Moscow, USSR	22.63
Discus	Gabriele Reinsch (East Germany)	9 July 1988	Neubrandenburg, East Germany	76.80
Hammer	Mihaela Melinte (Romania)	29 August 1999	Rüdlingen, Switzerland	76.07
Javelin	Osleidys Menéndez (Cuba)	1 July 2001	Rethimnon, Greece	71.54
Heptathlon	Jackie Joyner-Kersee (USA)	24 September 1988	Seoul, South Korea	7291

The double life of Stella Walsh

Born Stanislawa Walaziewcz in 1911 in Poland, Stella Walsh was one of the greatest sprinters of the 1930s. She emigrated to the United States as a child but competed for Poland, winning 100m gold at the 1932 Los Angeles Olympics and silver at the 1936 Berlin Games. She became a US citizen in 1947, winning 41 US track and field titles, but never competing for the US Olympic team. Walsh was shot dead in a parking lot in Cleveland, Ohio, during a robbery in 1980. An autopsy revealed the secret of her speed: she was not technically a woman. Walsh had a rare condition known as mosaicism, characterized by both male and female chromosomes and genitals.

See separate sections on **Cross-country running, Decathlon, Heptathlon, Marathon** and **Walking**

circle	the area within which an athlete must stay when throwing the hammer, discus or shot
crouching start	a starting position for a race with the knees bent; first used in 1888 by US athlete Charles Sherrill
dash	the former name for a **sprint**
dip	when an athlete dips, he or she lunges for the finish line, eg *he lost out on the line because he dipped too early*
discus	a throwing event in which the athlete spins to gain speed before throwing a metal disc (weighing 2kg/4.4lb for men and 1kg/2.2lb for women) as far as possible
800m	a **middle-distance** race over two laps of the track; athletes must stay in lane for the first bend, but may then **break** to the inside
fail	if an athlete fails at a height in the high jump or pole vault, he or she fails to clear the **bar**
false start	if an athlete false starts, he or she shifts from the **blocks** before the starting pistol is fired; the rules now state that once a false start has occurred, any subsequent athlete who false starts is disqualified
field events	the jumping and throwing competitions, as distinct from **track events**
1,500m	a **middle-distance** event run over three and three-quarter laps of the track, also known as the 'metric mile'
50km walk	a walking event over a street course, ending at the **finish line** of the stadium
finish line	the line marking the end of the race
5,000m	a **long-distance** race over twelve and a half laps of the track
following wind	a tailwind that assists an athlete to run faster or jump further; times or distances are not considered for official records if the following wind is over the legal limit
Fosbury flop	a method of high-jumping in which an athlete goes over the **bar** horizontally on his or her back; now used universally, it is named after US athlete Dick Fosbury, who pioneered the technique in the 1960s
foul	an athlete fouls in the long jump and triple jump when his or her **spikes** imprint in or beyond the red section of the **plasticine** on the **board**; in the discus, hammer or shot put when he or she steps outside the circle or the throw lands outside the designated area; and in the javelin when he or she steps over the end of the **runway**, even after the javelin is released, or the throw lands outside the designated area. Fouls in all cases are designated by a **red flag**
4x100m relay	a team event with four runners completing in total a single lap of the track
4x400m relay	a team event with four runners completing a lap of the track each; athletes must stay in lane until the end of the first bend of the second **leg**, but may then **break** to the inside
400m	a **sprint** from **blocks** over one **lap** of the track
400m hurdles	a single-lap **sprint** from **blocks** over ten hurdles 3ft/0.914m high (2.5ft/0.762m high for women), with 114.83ft/35m between hurdles
half mile	the predecessor and imperial equivalent of the **800m** (half a mile = 804.67m)

See separate sections on **Cross-country running**, **Decathlon**, **Heptathlon**, **Marathon** and **Walking**

hammer a throwing event in which an athlete throws a metal ball (weighing 7.26kg/16lb for men and 4kg/8.8lb for women) attached to a steel wire as far as possible by rotating it around the head and then releasing it

heptathlon a multi-event for women, consisting of seven events held on two consecutive days and contested in the following order – first day: 100m hurdles, high jump, shot put, 200m; second day: long jump, javelin, 800m

high hurdles the men's 110m and women's 100m hurdles

high jump a jumping event in which an athlete must clear a 4m-long crossbar, taking off on one foot

hitch kick a long-jumping technique in which an athlete moves his or her legs in the air as if he or she is running

home straight the final **straight** on a **lap**, the approach to the **finish line**

hop the first stage of the **triple jump**

hop, step, jump same as **triple jump**

javelin a throwing event in which an athlete throws a pointed metal pole (weighing 800g for men and 600g for women) as far as possible from over the shoulder while running at speed

jump the final phase of the **triple jump**

kick if an athlete kicks, he or she puts on an extra spurt of speed, usually on the final lap of a long-distance race, eg *he's kicked for the line and the rest of the field can't stay with him*

lane one of eight marked divisions of the track, within which an athlete must stay when running sprint races

lap a single circuit of a running track (400m)

leg a single athlete's section of a **relay**

long distance the long-distance events are the 3,000m, 5,000m and 10,000m

long jump a jumping event in which an athlete sprints down a **runway** before leaping off a board into a sandpit; distance is measured from the **board** to the nearest mark caused by the athlete's body in the sand

marathon a street race, run over a 26mi, 385yd long course (42.19km), ending at the **finish line** of the stadium

middle distance the middle-distance events are the 800m and 1,500m

mile the predecessor and imperial equivalent of the **1,500m** (1 mile = 1,609.344m)

no jump a **foul** in the long jump or triple jump

100m a **sprint** from **blocks** along the length of the **home straight**

100m hurdles the women's equivalent of the **110m hurdles**, with hurdles 2.75ft/0.84m high, and 27.88ft/8.5m between hurdles

110m hurdles a **sprint** from **blocks** along the length of the **home straight** with ten hurdles 3.5ft/1.067m high to be cleared and a distance of 30ft/9.14m between hurdles

pacemaker an athlete who aids a record attempt by ensuring the race starts off at the required speed

personal best (PB) if an athlete achieves a personal best, it is his or her career best time or distance

pit the sanded landing area in the long jump and triple jump

plasticine the soft rubber section of the **board** in the long jump or triple jump, upon which an athlete's **spikes** imprint on takeoff, determining whether the jump is a **foul** or not

See separate sections on **Cross-country running, Decathlon, Heptathlon, Marathon** and **Walking**

pole vault	a jumping event in which an athlete attempts to clear a crossbar with the aid of a pole, planting the end in a **box** and bending it to lever themselves up and over the bar
reaction time	the split-second taken by an athlete to propel themselves out of the **blocks**
red flag	if an athlete receives a red flag, the jump or throw is a **foul**, eg *that's a huge jump, but she's got the red flag*
relay	a team event in which each of the four athletes that make up the team run the same distance, each runner passing a **baton** to the next team member
runway	the corridor of track along which an athlete approaches a jump or throw
season's best (SB)	if an athlete achieves a season's best, it is his or her best time or distance of the current year
shot put	a throwing event in which an athlete throws a heavy metal ball (weighing 7.26kg/16lb for men and 4kg/8.8lb for women) as far as possible, holding it in one hand against the neck and driving it upwards and outwards
60m	a sprint in indoor competitions
60m hurdles	a hurdles race in indoor competitions
skip	same as **step**
spikes	running shoes with spiked soles
sprint	sprint races are the 100m, 200m and 400m
sprint hurdles	the 100m hurdles (for women) or 110m hurdles (for men)
staggered start	when athletes are spaced at intervals along the track to compensate for the curve of the **bend**
starter	the official who fires the starting pistol
step	the second phase of the **triple jump**
straight	a straight section of a running track
take-over zone	the 20m/66ft-long area of the track within which the baton must be passed in a **relay**
10,000m	a **long-distance** race over 25 laps of the track
300m	a little-run event, combining the speed of the **200m** and the strength of the **400m**
3,000m	a **long-distance** event run over seven and a half laps of the track, competed in by women until replaced by the **5,000m** in 1995 – it is also run indoors in place of the longer events
3,000m steeplechase	a **long-distance** event run over seven and a half laps of the track, consisting of a total of 28 3ft/0.91m-high hurdles and seven **water jumps**, 12ft/3.66m long
track events	the running and hurdling competitions, as distinct from **field events**
triple jump	a jumping event in which an athlete sprints down a **runway** before performing a **hop**, **step** and **jump** into a sandpit; distance is measured from the **board**, the starting point of the hop, to the nearest mark caused by the athlete's body in the sand
20km walk	a walking event over a street course, ending at the **finish line** of the stadium
200m	a **sprint** from **blocks** around the **bend** then along the **home straight**
water jump	one of the hurdles of the 3,000m steeplechase, where athletes land in a shallow pool of water

See separate sections on **Cross-country running, Decathlon, Heptathlon, Marathon** and **Walking**

white flag — if an athlete receives a white flag, his or her jump or throw is fair

wind-assisted — a wind-assisted distance or time is achieved with a **following wind** and is therefore ineligible for any official records

Some famous athletes

Iolanda Balas, 1936–

Born in Timosoaru, Romania, she first broke the high jump world record in July 1956 and improved upon it 13 times over the next eight years. She finished fifth at the 1956 Olympics, then did not lose again until 1967, winning 140 consecutive competitions, including the European Championships in 1958 and 1962, and the 1960 and 1964 Olympics. Her final world record, set in 1961, lasted for ten years and was a full 7cm higher than the second-best woman jumper.

Sir Roger Bannister, 1929–

Born in Harrow, England, he was the first man to break the 'four-minute mile'. He won the mile event in the Oxford v Cambridge match four times (1947–50), and was a finalist in the 1,500m in the 1952 Olympic Games in Helsinki. At an athletics meeting at Iffley Road, Oxford, in 1954, he ran the mile in under four minutes (3 minutes 59.4 seconds). His record did not stand for long; Australian John Landy eclipsed his time just six weeks later. He was knighted in 1975.

Bob Beamon, 1946–

Born in New York City, USA, he smashed the world long jump record at the 1968 Olympic Games in Mexico City, with a jump of 8.90m (29ft 2ins) – 55cm (21ins) further than the previous record. The record stood until 1991, when it was broken by Mike Powell in Tokyo. He almost failed to make the final, fouling on his first two qualifying jumps and being forced to take off for his final qualifying attempt from well behind the board.

Fanny Blankers-Koen, 1918–2004

Born in Amsterdam, the Netherlands, she achieved success at the comparatively late age of 30 when she dominated women's track events in the London Olympics of 1948. The mother-of-two won four gold medals: the 100m, 200m, 80m hurdles and the 4×100m relay, and earned the nickname 'the flying Dutch housewife'. She at various times also held world records for both high and long jumps.

Hassiba Boulmerka, 1968–

Born in Constantine, Algeria, she upset the odds to win 1,500m gold at the 1991 World Championships. Hailed as a national heroine on her return home, she became a role model for Arab women's liberation. However, she was also condemned by fundamentalists for 'running with naked legs' and was forced to move to Europe. She also won gold in the 1,500m at the Barcelona Olympics in 1992 and the 1995 world championships.

See separate sections on **Cross-country running, Decathlon, Heptathlon, Marathon** and **Walking**

Sergei Bubka, 1963–

Born in Donetsk, Ukraine, he made his international debut as a pole-vaulter at the 1983 world championship in Helsinki, where he won the gold medal. He retained this title in 1987, 1991, 1993, 1995 and 1997, and also won gold at the 1988 Olympics. In his career he broke no fewer than 35 world records and, in 1994, took the world pole vault record to 6.14m.

Sebastian Coe, 1956–

Born in Chiswick, London, England, he won the 1,500m gold medal and the silver medal in the 800m at the 1980 Moscow Olympics and at Los Angeles four years later. In 1981 he broke the world record for the 800m, 1,000m and the mile. Between September 1976 and June 1983 he did not lose the final of any race over 1,500m or a mile. Following the 1990 Commonwealth Games, he retired from athletics to pursue a career in politics. He was Conservative MP for Falmouth and Cambourne from 1992 to 1997, and was made a life peer in 2000.

Heike Drechsler, 1964–

Born in Gera, East Germany, she won the world long jump championship in 1983 under her maiden name of Daute, becoming the youngest-ever world champion, and in 1985 added wins in the European and World Cup events. She consistently jumped over seven metres, winning 27 successive competitions before 1987, when she was injured, and setting three world records before 1988. She was also a strong sprinter, picking up a variety of Olympic and world medals at 100m and 200m and equalling Marita Koch's 200m world record. She won the Olympic gold medal for long jump in 1992 and again in 2000, and won the world championship in 1993.

Jonathan Edwards, 1966–

Born in London, England, he gave up work as a genetics research officer to specialize in the triple jump. He was the first man to pass 18m and in 1995 became world champion, twice breaking his own world record to jump 18.29m. He won silver medals in the Olympic Games (1996), the world championships (1997 and 1999) and world indoor championships (2001) and further golds in the European championships (1998), the European indoor championships (1998), the Olympic Games (2000), the world championships (2001), and the Commonwealth Games (2002). He retired in 2003 to become a television presenter and media regulator.

Cathy Freeman, 1973–

Born in Mackay, Queensland, Australia, she won a gold medal in the 4×100m relay at the 1990 Commonwealth Games and in 1992 became the first Australian Aboriginal to compete in the Olympic Games. She won gold medals in the 400m and 200m events at the 1994 Commonwealth Games and Olympic 400m silver in 1996. A controversial defender of Aboriginal rights, she was chosen to light the Olympic flame at the 2000 Sydney Olympics and went on to win the 400m gold medal, to the delight of the home audience. She retired in 2003.

Haile Gebrselassie, 1973–

Born in Arsi, Ethiopia, he had to run 10km each day to and from school. He attracted international attention in 1992 when he won the 5,000m and 10,000m events at the world

See separate sections on **Cross-country running**, **Decathlon**, **Heptathlon**, **Marathon** and **Walking**

junior championships. Subsequently he established himself as the greatest long-distance runner ever, including among his triumphs 15 track world records, four world titles in the 10,000m and gold medals in the same event at the Olympic Games of 1996 and 2000, on both occasions passing Kenyan rival Paul Tergat on the last lap.

Florence Griffith-Joyner, 1959–98

Born in Los Angeles, California, USA, she won three gold medals at the 1988 Olympics (100m, 200m and 4×100m relay), and also won silver in the 4×400m relay. Known as Flo-Jo and famous for her long painted fingernails, she broke the 200m world record to go with the 100m record she had set two months earlier, but retired immediately after the Games for a career in fashion. She died following a heart seizure, aged 38.

Dame Kelly Holmes, 1970–

Born in Pembury, Kent, England, she joined the army as a fitness instructor at 18. After leaving in 1992, she devoted herself to athletics, her first medals coming at the Commonwealth Games in 1994 when she won the 1500m, taking silver in the same event in 1998 and reclaiming the gold medal at the Games in 2002. She also came third in the 800m and second in the 1500m at the world championships in 1995 and 2003, and at the Olympics in Sydney in 2000 she won the bronze medal in the 800m. All of this was, however, a preamble to her glory year of 2004 when, following training with **Maria Mutola**, she became the first British female athlete to take two Olympic golds (in the 800m and 1500m) and was voted BBC Sports Personality of the Year and European Female Athlete of the Year. She was made a Dame in the New Year's honours list of 2005.

Michael Johnson, 1967–

Born in Dallas, Texas, USA, he won world championship races in the 200m in 1991 and 1995 and in the 400m in 1993 and 1995. At the 1996 Olympics in Atlanta, he tempted fate by wearing gold running shoes but nevertheless won gold medals in both the 200m and 400m, the first man ever to do so. At the same time he set a new world record in the 200m, breaking the world record he himself set at the Olympic trials. He became the Olympic champion in the 400m again in Sydney in 2000 before retiring.

Kip Keino, 1940–

Born in Kipsano, Kenya, he beat American Jim Ryun to 1,500m gold at the 1968 Olympics, despite suffering from gallstones and arriving at the track only minutes before the start, after jogging to the stadium when his bus became stuck in traffic. Four years later he won gold in the 3,000m steeplechase, despite only having run the distance four times before. As well as paving the way for a long line of Kenyan distance stars, he is renowned for his charity work, having adopted over 60 orphans. He is currently president of the Kenyan Olympic Committee.

Wilson Kipketer, 1970–

Born in Kapchemoiywo, Kenya, he became a specialist in the 800m, representing Kenya and then Denmark, where he settled in 1990. Having won gold medals in the 800m at the world championships in 1995 and 1997 and in the world indoor championships in 1997, he set a new world record of 1min 41.11s in the event in 1997, but was beaten into second place at the 2000 Sydney Olympics. He took bronze in his farewell Olympics in Athens in 2004.

See separate sections on **Cross-country running, Decathlon, Heptathlon, Marathon** and **Walking**

Carl Lewis, 1961–

Born in Birmingham, Alabama, USA, he was a brilliant all-round athlete at Houston University (1979–82). He won four gold medals at the 1984 Los Angeles Olympics (100m, 200m, 4×100m relay and long jump). At the 1988 Seoul Olympics he won a gold medal in the long jump and was awarded the 100m gold medal after Ben Johnson was stripped of the title. In 1992 at the Barcelona Olympics he acquired two more golds in the long jump and the 4×100m relay, and in the 1996 Atlanta Olympics he earned the ninth and final gold medal of his career in the long jump, only the fourth Olympian to win as many.

Maria Mutola, 1972–

Born in a shanty town in Maputo, Mozambique, she was spotted playing football, the only girl in a boys' team, by poet José Craveirinha, who saw her potential and introduced her to the world of athletics. She competed at the 1988 Seoul Olympics at the age of 15, but came to prominence in 1993, winning the 800m at the world championships. She won gold again in 2001 and 2003 and won Commonwealth gold in 1998 and 2002. At the Sydney Olympics in 2000, she became Mozambique's first Olympic gold medallist.

Paavo Nurmi, 1897–1973

Born in Turku, Finland, he dominated long-distance running in the 1920s, winning nine gold medals at three Olympic Games (1920, 1924, 1928). From 1922 to 1926 he set four world records at 3,000m, bringing the time down to 8min 20.4s. Known as 'the Flying Finn', he also established world records at six miles (1921), one mile (1923) and two miles (1931). Disqualified in 1932 for alleged professionalism, he nevertheless remained a Finnish national hero.

Merlene Ottey, 1960–

Born in Pondside, Jamaica, she has won a record 14 world championship outdoor medals – the most by any female athlete – although she has never won an Olympic gold. Beaten on the line in Atlanta in 1996, she had earlier lost the 1993 world 100m title by 0.001 seconds. Fired up, she went on to take the 1993 world 200m title, setting a then world-record time of 21.98s. At the 2000 Olympics, she became the oldest athlete to win a track medal, picking up bronze in the 4×100m at the age of 40. She took Slovenian citizenship in 2002 and appeared at her seventh consecutive Olympics in 2004.

Jesse Owens, 1913–80

He was born in Danville, Alabama, USA. While competing for the Ohio State University team in 1935, he set three world records and equalled another, all within the space of an hour. At the 1936 Olympics in Berlin he won four gold medals (100m, 200m, long jump, and 4×100m relay), which caused the German Nazi leader, Adolf Hitler, to leave the stadium. Back in the USA, Owens gained no recognition for his feat and was reduced to running 'freak' races against horses and dogs. Later he held an executive position with the Illinois Athletic Commission, and attended the 1956 Olympics as President Dwight Eisenhower's personal representative. He is considered the greatest sprinter of his generation.

Don Quarrie, 1951–

Born in Kingston, Jamaica, he won a gold, silver and two bronze medals at the Olympic Games. However, he first came to notice at the 1970 Commonwealth Games in

See separate sections on **Cross-country running, Decathlon, Heptathlon, Marathon** and **Walking**

Edinburgh, capturing three gold medals (100m, 200m and 4×100m relay). He won further Commonwealth gold medals in 1974 (100m and 200m) and 1978 (100m). Quarrie also set four sprint world records.

Paula Radcliffe, 1973-

Born in Northwich, Cheshire, England, she won the 2002 London Marathon, her first, in a record debut time of 2hrs, 18min, 55s, then broke the word record in Chicago, in her second marathon, clocking 2hrs, 17min, 18s. After taking Commonwealth 5,000m gold in Manchester, she won the 10,000m at the European championships, slashing 24s from her personal best and 13s from the European record. At the 2003 London Marathon she took a further 1min, 53s off her world record and later set a new world record in the half-marathon. Despite being favourite for the marathon at the Athens Olympics, she was dramatically forced to pull up, in tears and suffering from the heat.

Daley Thompson, 1958-

Born in London, England, he competed in the decathlon at the 1976 Olympic Games at just 18 years old, returning to win back-to-back golds in 1980 and 1984. He was victorious in the 1983 world championships, but at Seoul in 1988 was affected by injury and came fourth. A fierce competitor with ready charm, he courted controversy, notably in the 1984 Olympics when he questioned the sexuality of Carl Lewis. He broke the world record four times between 1980 and 1984, and retired in 1992.

Lasse Viren, 1949-

Born in Helsinki, Finland, he arrived at the 1972 Munich Olympics as an unknown policeman. After recovering from a fall halfway through the 10,000m, he went on to win gold and break the world record. He also triumphed in the 5,000m ten days later. At the 1976 Games in Montreal he repeated this long-distance double, becoming the only man to successfully defend the 5,000m title. In 1994 he put his four gold medals up for sale at $200,000 apiece.

Emil Zatopek, 1922-2000

He was born in Moravia, Czechoslovakia. After many successes in Czechoslovak track events, he won the gold medal for the 10,000m at the 1948 Olympics in London. For the next six years, despite an astonishingly laboured style, he proved himself to be the greatest long-distance runner of his time, breaking 13 world records. In the 1952 Olympics in Helsinki, he won a historic triple gold, retaining his 10,000m title and also winning the 5,000m and the marathon, the first he had competed in, setting Olympic records in all three. His wife and fellow athlete Dana Zatopekova also won Olympic gold (for the javelin) in 1952.

Jan Zelezný, 1966-

Born in Mlada Boleslav, Czechoslovakia, he is the only javelin thrower in Olympic history to win three gold medals in the event (1992, 1996, 2000). His record would be even more impressive were it not for Tapio Korjus of Finland, the final thrower at the 1988 Games, whose last-ditch effort pushed Zelezný into second place. Zelezný cemented his dominance of the event in 1995, recording 21 throws over 89m, while the rest of the world could manage only one. He has set four javelin world records and was the first man to throw over 87, 95 and 98m.

See separate sections on **Cross-country running, Decathlon, Heptathlon, Marathon** and **Walking**

AUSTRALIAN RULES FOOTBALL

Origins

Australian Rules Football, or Aussie rules, was invented in the mid-1800s by Tom Wills, W J Hammersley and J B Thompson. English-educated Wills was a keen cricketer and also football captain at Rugby public school. On his return down under, Wills suggested that cricketers could maintain fitness during the winter months by playing a version of rugby football. In 1858 Wills and his associates drew up some rules (which have since been modified), the Melbourne Football Club was formed, and the code's first recorded game was played between Melbourne Grammar School and Scotch College. In 1877 the game's first league, the Victorian Football Association, was formed. The game soon spread to other Australian colonies, although Queensland and New South Wales chose rugby union and rugby league as their winter games.

Rules and description

A field game played between two teams of 18 players, generally on cricket ovals during the winter months. The object of the game is to score 'goals' by kicking an inflated oval ball between the four posts erected at either end of the oval. A goal scored between the two inner posts is worth six points; a goal scored between an inner post and an outer post is worth one point. The ball may be kicked, caught, or passed to another player by punching, but may not be thrown. Players may run with the ball but must bounce it to the ground every ten metres. A player who

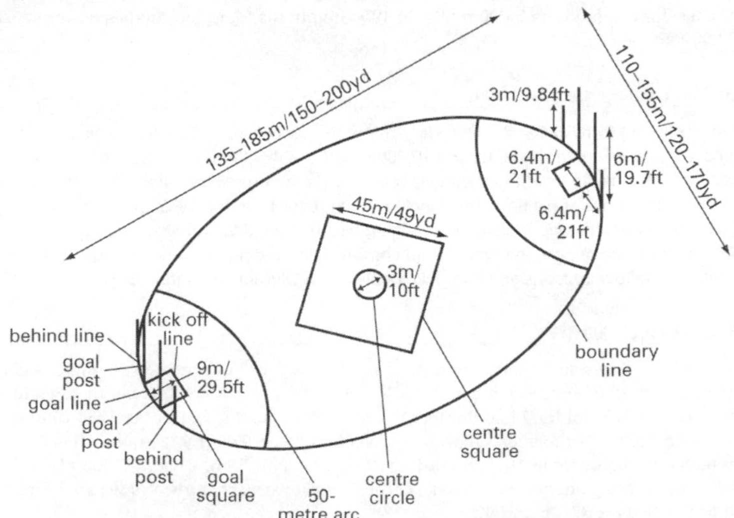

catches the ball cleanly may call for a 'mark', which entitles them to an unimpeded kick. The game is regulated by field umpires, goal umpires, and boundary umpires. Each game consists of four quarters of 20 minutes. Each team has four 'interchange' players (substitutes), who can come on and off the pitch at any time during the match.

Ruling body: Australian Football League (AFL)

Premiership Trophy

Australian Rules Football's major trophy. First held in 1897 as the Victorian Football League (1897–1989). In 1990 the Australian Football League replaced the Victorian Football League as the main governing body for the sport. The majority of finals have been played at the MCG (Melbourne Cricket Ground).

	Winner
1897	Essendon
1898	Fitzroy
1899	Fitzroy
1900	Melbourne
1901	Essendon
1902	Collingwood
1903	Collingwood
1904	Fitzroy
1905	Fitzroy
1906	Carlton
1907	Carlton
1908	Carlton
1909	South Melbourne
1910	Collingwood
1911	Essendon
1912	Essendon
1913	Fitzroy
1914	Carlton
1915	Carlton
1916	Fitzroy
1917	Collingwood
1918	South Melbourne
1919	Collingwood
1920	Richmond
1921	Richmond
1922	Fitzroy
1923	Essendon
1924	Essendon
1925	Geelong
1926	Melbourne
1927	Collingwood
1928	Collingwood
1929	Collingwood

	Winner
1930	Collingwood
1931	Geelong
1932	Richmond
1933	South Melbourne
1934	Richmond
1935	Collingwood
1936	Collingwood
1937	Geelong
1938	Carlton
1939	Melbourne
1940	Melbourne
1941	Melbourne
1942	Essendon
1943	Richmond
1944	Fitzroy
1945	Carlton
1946	Essendon
1947	Carlton
1948	Melbourne
1949	Essendon
1950	Essendon
1951	Geelong
1952	Geelong
1953	Collingwood
1954	Footscray
1955	Melbourne
1956	Melbourne
1957	Melbourne
1958	Collingwood
1959	Melbourne
1960	Melbourne
1961	Hawthorn
1962	Essendon

	Winner		Winner
1963	Geelong	**1984**	Essendon
1964	Melbourne	**1985**	Essendon
1965	Essendon	**1986**	Hawthorn
1966	St Kilda	**1987**	Carlton
1967	Richmond	**1988**	Hawthorn
1968	Carlton	**1989**	Hawthorn
1969	Richmond	**1990**	Collingwood
1970	Carlton	**1991**	Hawthorn
1971	Hawthorn	**1992**	West Coast
1972	Carlton	**1993**	Essendon
1973	Richmond	**1994**	West Coast
1974	Richmond	**1995**	Carlton
1975	North Melbourne	**1996**	North Melbourne
1976	Hawthorn	**1997**	Adelaide
1977	North Melbourne	**1998**	Adelaide
1978	Hawthorn	**1999**	North Melbourne
1979	Carlton	**2000**	Essendon
1980	Richmond	**2001**	Brisbane
1981	Carlton	**2002**	Brisbane
1982	Carlton	**2003**	Brisbane
1983	Hawthorn	**2004**	Adelaide

A-Z

back pocket a defensive player who runs the ball out of defence

ball up commencement of play in which the umpire bounces the ball in the centre of the field and **ruckmen** compete for possession

behind a goal scored between an inner post and an outer post, worth one point

boundary line the line surrounding the playing surface of the pitch beyond which the ball is out of play

centre a creative player operating in midfield

centre bounce same as **ball up**

centre halfback defensive player who operates near the middle of the **50-metre arc**, in the front of the **fullback**

centre half-forward an attacking player who operates behind the **full forward** and **forward pockets**

centre square 45m/49yd-square area marked in the centre of the oval

dispose if a player disposes of the ball after he is tackled, he passes or kicks the ball immediately and does not hold on to it. Holding on to the ball after a tackle is an infringement

50-metre arc semi-circular line surrounding the goals at either end of the pitch

forward pocket an opportunistic player operating in the **50-metre arc** near the goal

free kick an unimpeded kick awarded to a team for an infringement. The following infringements result in a free kick: a neck tackle; pushing an opponent in the back; throwing the ball; dropping the ball while being tackled; tackling an opponent who doesn't have the ball; kicking the ball out of bounds on the full; running with ball for more than 10m without bouncing it

fullback a defensive player who counters a **full forward**

full forward attacking player playing near the opponents' goal

goal a successful kick of the ball between the two inner posts, worth six points

goal square a square marked in the front of the goals. After a **behind** the game recommences with a **free kick** to the defending side from the goal square

halfback flank a running defender who plays on the flank

half-forward flank an attacking player who plays on the flank near the **50-metre arc**

handpass if a player handpasses the ball to a team-mate, he punches the ball to him

mark if a player marks the ball, he catches it. If the ball has travelled more than 15m and the ball is caught cleanly, the catcher is entitled to an unimpeded **free kick** or **handpass**

playfield the area of the pitch marked by the boundary lines within which the game is played

quarter one of four 20-minute periods into which a match is divided

rover a small, mobile player who feeds off a **ruck**

ruck the three players, a **rover** and two **ruckmen**, who follow the ball closely and who do not have fixed positions

ruckman one of the three ruck players who follow the ball closely

tackle a legal attempt to stop an opponent. Illegal attempts result in a **free kick**

time on time added on for injuries and when the ball goes out of play

umpire one of the officials who referee the match. There are field, goal, and boundary umpires

wing attacking player who operates on the flanks

BADMINTON

Origins

The Chinese are reputed to have played the game more than 2,000 years ago. However, the game it most closely resembles is 'battledore and shuttlecock' (the former a taut leather paddle; the latter a small feathered cork), a children's pastime from the Middle Ages. The modern game takes its name from Badminton Hall, in South Gloucestershire, a seat of the Dukes of Beaufort, where games were played in the 1870s. Badminton was also being played in India by British army officers that same decade and the first rules were drawn up in 1873.

Rules and description

Badminton is a game for two or four people, played mainly on indoor courts. The court measures 13.4 x 6.1m/44 x 20ft and is divided in two by a net, which is suspended 1.55m/5ft above the floor. The court size varies for singles and doubles play. The game is played with lightweight rackets and a 'shuttlecock', a cone fashioned from a cork base stuck with 16 goose feather flights (cheaper alternatives are made of plastic). The object of the game is to win more points than the opposition by preventing the shuttlecock from hitting the ground. The server serves into the diagonally opposite service court and a rally continues until the shuttlecock falls outside the court or the opposition cannot retrieve it or a fault is committed. Only the server can score points; if the opposition player wins the point the service advantage moves to him/her.

In the men's and doubles game the first to 15 points wins. If the score reaches 14-14 the player that reaches 14 first decides either to play on to 15 or to 'set' the game to 17 points. In the women's game players need to reach 11 points – there is the option to 'set' the play at 10-10 to play the best of a further 3 points. Matches are the best of three games. In doubles play both players on a side get the opportunity to serve before it passes to the opposition.

Ruling body: The International Badminton Federation (IBF)

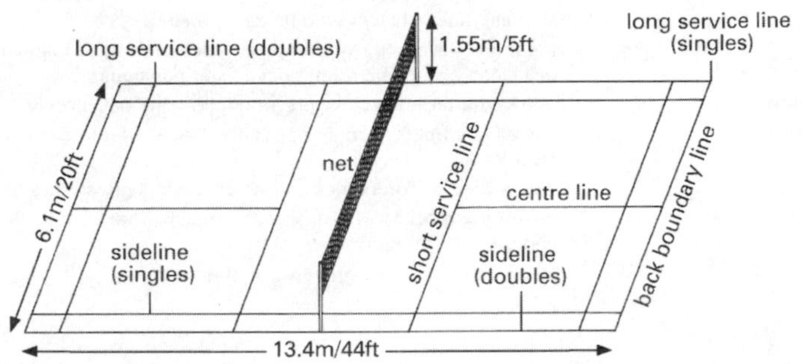

Olympic Champions

Introduced as an Olympic sport in 1992

	Men's singles	**Women's singles**
1992	Allan Budi Kusuma (Indonesia)	Susi Susanti (Indonesia)
1996	Poul-Erik Høyer-Larsen (Denmark)	Bang Soo-hyun (Indonesia)
2000	Ji Xinpeng (China)	Gong Zhichao (China)
2004	Taufik Hidayat (Indonesia)	Ning Zhang (China)

Letting the officers in

When the game was popularized in India at the end of the 19th century, the court differed from a modern badminton court in that there were segments taken out of its centre, giving it an hourglass appearance. Reputedly this was because the game was played in the officers' mess in Madras and the doors to the room opened inwards, explaining why the court was 'cut away' to accommodate pedestrian traffic. The hourglass court was phased out after 1901.

Thomas Cup

An international team competition for men comprising six players per team. It was contested every three years from 1949 to 1984 and thereafter ever two years. The cup is named after Sir George Thomas (1881–1972), winner of 21 All-England titles from 1903–28.

	Winner	Runner-up	Score	Venue
1949	Malaya	Denmark	8-1	Preston, UK
1952	Malaya	USA	7-2	Singapore
1955	Malaya	Denmark	8-1	Singapore
1958	Indonesia	Malaya	6-3	Singapore
1961	Indonesia	Thailand	6-3	Jakarta, Indonesia
1964	Indonesia	Denmark	5-4	Tokyo, Japan
1967	Malaysia	Indonesia	6-3	Jakarta, Indonesia
1970	Indonesia	Malaysia	7-2	Kuala Lumpur, Malaysia
1973	Indonesia	Denmark	8-1	Jakarta, Indonesia
1976	Indonesia	Malaysia	9-0	Bangkok, Thailand
1979	Indonesia	Denmark	9-0	Kuala Lumpur, Malaysia
1982	China	Indonesia	5-4	London, UK
1984	Indonesia	China	3-2	Kuala Lumpur, Malaysia
1986	China	Indonesia	3-2	Jakarta, Indonesia
1988	China	Malaysia	4-1	Kuala Lumpur, Malaysia
1990	China	Malaysia	4-1	Tokyo, Japan
1992	Malaysia	Indonesia	3-2	Kuala Lumpur, Malaysia
1994	Indonesia	Malaysia	3-0	Jakarta, Indonesia
1996	Indonesia	Denmark	5-0	Hong Kong
1998	Indonesia	Malaysia	3-2	Hong Kong
2000	Indonesia	China	3-0	Kuala Lumpur, Malaysia
2002	Indonesia	Malaysia	3-2	Guangzhou, China
2004	China	Denmark	3-1	Jakarta, Indonesia

Uber Cup

An international team competition for women comprising six players per team. It was contested every three years from 1957 to 1984 and thereafter every two years. The cup is named after English player Betty Uber (c 1905–83).

	Winner	Runner-up	Score	Venue
1957	USA	Denmark	6-1	Lytham St Annes, UK
1960	USA	Denmark	5-2	Philadelphia, USA
1963	USA	England	4-3	Wilmington, USA
1966	Japan	USA	5-2	Wellington, New Zealand
1969	Japan	Indonesia	6-1	Tokyo, Japan
1972	Japan	Indonesia	6-1	Tokyo, Japan
1975	Indonesia	Japan	5-2	Jakarta, Indonesia
1978	Japan	Indonesia	5-2	Auckland, New Zealand
1981	Japan	Indonesia	6-3	Tokyo, Japan
1984	China	England	5-0	Kuala Lumpur, Malaysia
1986	China	Indonesia	3-2	Jakarta, Indonesia

Badminton

	Winner	Runner-up	Score	Venue
1988	China	South Korea	5-0	Kuala Lumpur, Malaysia
1990	China	South Korea	3-2	Tokyo, Japan
1992	China	South Korea	3-2	Kuala Lumpur, Malaysia
1994	Indonesia	China	3-2	Jakarta, Indonesia
1996	Indonesia	China	4-1	Hong Kong
1998	China	Indonesia	4-1	Hong Kong
2000	China	Denmark	3-0	Kuala Lumpur, Malaysia
2002	China	Korea	3-1	Guangzhou, China
2004	China	Korea	3-1	Jakarta, Indonesia

World Championships

First held in 1977.

	Men's singles	Women's singles	Venue
1977	Flemming Delfs (Denmark)	Lene Køppen (Denmark)	Malmö, Sweden
1980	Rudy Hartono (Indonesia)	Wiharjo Verawaty (Indonesia)	Jakarta, Indonesia
1983	Icuk Sugiarto (Indonesia)	Li Lingwei (China)	Copenhagen, Denmark
1985	Han Jian (China)	Han Aiping (China)	Calgary, Canada
1987	Yang Yang (China)	Han Aiping (China)	Beijing, China
1989	Yang Yang (China)	Li Lingwei (China)	Jakarta, Indonesia
1991	Zhao Jianhua (China)	Tang Jiuhong (China)	Copenhagen, Denmark
1993	Joko Suprianto (Indonesia)	Susi Susanti (Indonesia)	Birmingham, UK
1995	Heryanto Arbi (Indonesia)	Ye Zhaoying (China)	Lausanne, Switzerland
1997	Peter Rasmussen (Denmark)	Ye Zhaoying (China)	Glasgow, UK
1999	Sun Jun (China)	Camilla Martin (Denmark)	Copenhagen, Denmark
2001	Hendrawan (Indonesia)	Gong Ruina (China)	Seville, Spain
2003	Xia Xuanze (China)	Zhang Ning (China)	Birmingham, UK

All-England Championship

Badminton's premier event prior to the inauguration of the World Championships; first held in 1900.

	Men	Women
1979	Liem Swie King (Indonesia)	Lene Køppen (Denmark)
1980	Prakash Padukone (India)	Lene Køppen (Denmark)
1981	Liem Swie King (Indonesia)	Hwang Sun-ai (South Korea)
1982	Morten Frost (Denmark)	Zhang Ailing (China)
1983	Luan Jin (China)	Zhang Ailing (China)
1984	Morten Frost (Denmark)	Li Lingwei (China)
1985	Zhao Jianhua (China)	Han Aiping (China)
1986	Morten Frost (Denmark)	Kim Yun-ja (South Korea)
1987	Morten Frost (Denmark)	Kirsten Larsen (Denmark)
1988	Ib Frederikson (Denmark)	Gu Jiaming (China)
1989	Yang Yang (China)	Li Lingwei (China)
1990	Zhao Jianhua (China)	Susi Susanti (Indonesia)
1991	Ardi Wiranata (Indonesia)	Susi Susanti (Indonesia)

	Men	Women
1992	Liu Jun (China)	Tang Jiuhong (China)
1993	Heryanto Arbi (Indonesia)	Susi Susanti (Indonesia)
1994	Heryanto Arbi (Indonesia)	Susi Susanti (Indonesia)
1995	Poul-Erik Høyer-Larsen (Denmark)	Lim Xiao Qing (Sweden)
1996	Poul-Erik Høyer-Larsen (Denmark)	Bang Soo-hyun (South Korea)
1997	Dong Jiong (China)	Ye Zhaoying (China)
1998	Sun Jun (China)	Ye Zhaoying (China)
1999	Peter Gade Christensen (Denmark)	Ye Zhaoying (China)
2000	Xia Xuanze (China)	Gong Zichao (China)
2001	Pulella Gopichand (India)	Gong Zichao (China)
2002	Chen Hong (China)	Camilla Martin (Denmark)
2003	Muhammad Hafiz Hashim (Malaysia)	Mi Zhou (China)
2004	Lin Dan (China)	Gong Ruina (China)

Left is best

It is generally accepted that the best shuttlecocks are made from goose feathers rather than nylon or other plastics. However, did you realize that professional players are even fussier than that? The best feathers reputedly come from the left wing of the goose, as they are meant to be stronger than those plucked from the right!

A-Z

bird a nickname used for the shuttlecock

clear an overhead shot where the shuttlecock travels from baseline to baseline. In general there are two types of clear shot: a high defensive clear and an attacking clear

drive a hard low shot that is hit with the racquet horizontal and travels horizontally over the net

drop shot a gentle shot hit from the baseline at the back of the court that drops just over the net

flick an apparently gentle shot that moves out of the reach of an opponent because of the wristy power imparted to it

kill a **smash** from near the net that cannot be returned

rally an exchange of shots, starting with the service

service court one of the two boxes into which the rear part of the court is divided and from which a player must serve diagonally across the net into the opponent's service court

set if you set a game, you decide to extend it by a specified number of points

shuttlecock the cone–shaped object hit; in professional play it is made of 16 goose feathers

smash a powerful overhead stroke hit downwards

underarm clear an underarm shot that is hit both high and deep

wood shot a shot where the shuttlecock comes off the rim (once wooden) of the racquet

Some famous badminton players

Tonny Ahm, 1914–1993

Born in Gentofte, Denmark, as Tonny Olsen, she represented her country of birth for 23 years. With Ruth Dalsgard she won the women's doubles title at the All-England Championships in 1939 but World War II brought her career to a standstill. She returned in 1947 and between then and her retirement she won a further five All-England titles with Dalsgard, Kirsten Thorndahl and Aase Jacobsen, as well as four mixed doubles with Poul Holm and two singles (1950 and 1952).

Morten Frost, 1958–

Born in Nykøbing, Denmark, he was the best European player of the 1980s. He won four All-England singles titles (1982, 1984, 1986–7) and the European men's singles title in 1984 and 1986. Frost reached two World singles finals but lost to Chinese players on both occasions.

Rudy Hartono Kurniawan, 1948–

Born in Surabaya, Indonesia, he won the World men's singles title in 1980. He holds the record for All-England singles titles with eight (1968–74, 1976). He represented Indonesia in the Thomas Cup, and helped the side to win the trophy in 1970, 1973 and 1976.

Judy Hashman (née Devlin), 1936–

Born in Winnipeg, Canada, she was coached from the age of seven by her father. In her career she won 31 US Open titles including singles, doubles and mixed doubles. She holds the record for All-England singles titles with ten and also claimed seven doubles titles. Her Irish-born father Frank (1900–88) went one better with 18 All-England titles.

BALLOONING

Origins

Wealthy French papermakers Jacques Étienne and Joseph Michel Montgolfier invented the first practical hot-air balloon in the 1780s. In tests in September 1783 they sent aloft the first living creatures: a duck, a cock and a sheep. The first human pilots were Jean-François Pilâtre de Rozier and the Marquis d'Arlandes, who flew for 25 minutes above Paris in November of the same year. The first flight of a manned gas balloon took place days later.

Rules and description

Hot-air balloons were eventually replaced by gas-filled (hydrogen or helium) balloons, which are lighter than air. The balloon was originally made from silk or rubber but is now more likely to be made from polyester or nylon. Pilots and co-pilots fly the balloon from a basket or gondola carried beneath it and attached by cables.

Modern hot-air balloons heat the air in the balloon using propane carried aboard the craft. The fuel system and burner are attached to a frame above the pilot's head. The pilots can make the balloon ascend or descend by heating or cooling the gas. Rozier balloons are hybrids of gas and hot-air balloons. There are different categories of competition for all three types of balloon.

Balloon races often include competition for altitude, distance, and the amount of time spent in the air. There are also various tests of a pilot's skill, including maintaining a specific altitude, making a controlled descent or following a predetermined flight plan.

Ruling body: Fédération Aéronautique Internationale (FAI)

World Hot-Air Balloon Championships

	Winner	Venue
1973	Dennis Floden (USA)	Albuquerque, USA
1975	David Schaffer (USA)	Albuquerque, USA
1977	Paul Woessner (USA)	York, UK
1979	Paul Woessner (USA)	Uppsala, Sweden
1981	Bruce Comstock (USA)	Battle Creek, USA
1983	Peter Vizzard (Australia)	Nantes, France
1985	David Levin (USA)	Battle Creek, USA
1987	Albert Nels (USA)	Schielleiten, Austria
1989	Benedikt Haggeney (East Germany)	Saga, Japan
1991	Albert Nels (USA)	St Jean-sur-Richelieu, Canada
1993	Alan Blount (USA)	Larochette, Luxembourg
1995	Joe Heartsill (USA)	Battle Creek, USA
1997	David Bareford (Great Britain)	Saga, Japan
1999	Bill Arras (USA)	Bad Waltersdorf, Austria
2002	David Bareford (Great Britain)	Châtellerault, France
2004	Markus Pieper (Germany)	Mildura, Australia

Gordon Bennett!

The most celebrated trophy in hot-air ballooning is the Coupe Aéronautique Gordon Bennett, first awarded in 1906 and named after the American newspaper tycoon. The aim of the event is to fly the furthest distance. The first competition saw 16 balloons set off from the Tuileries Gardens in Paris, France. The winner, American Frank P Lahm, landed his balloon 22 hours later in Fylingdales, North Yorkshire, UK.

BANDY

Origins

The modern game originated in the Fenland counties of England in the 1790s when stick-and-ball games were played on frozen low-lying land in Lincolnshire and Cambridgeshire. The first club was the Bury Fen club and from here enthusiasts took the game first to the Netherlands and then to Sweden, the rest of Scandinavia, the Baltic countries and Russia. Bandy is rarely played in England nowadays.

Rules and description

Bandy is an eleven-a-side, stick-and-rink game with similarities to both ice hockey and field hockey. The object of the game is to score goals. Players wear skates and use a curved stick, similar to a hockey stick, to score goals. The goalkeeper does not use a stick but uses his or her hands and legpads to defend the goal. Players can also use their skates to initially kick or place the orange-coloured ball ready for a stick shot. Free strokes, penalty strokes and penalty shots are awarded for differing levels of foul play. Matches comprise two halves of 45 minutes each. When rinks are unavailable the game is played on ice-covered football pitches. An indoor version of the game, called rink bandy, is played by teams of six.

Ruling bodies: National Bandy Association; Federation of International Bandy

World Bandy Championships

The championship was first held in 1957, with the next competition following in 1961 and thence every two years until 2003 when it became an annual event. An inaugural women's bandy world championship was held in 2004 and was won by Sweden.

	Winner
1957–79	USSR
1981–3	Sweden
1985	USSR
1987	Sweden
1989–91	USSR
1993–7	Sweden
1999–2001	Russia
2003	Sweden
2004	Finland

Winter football

Some English football clubs such as Sheffield United and Nottingham Forest had bandy in their original names. In the winter months, when the pitches froze over, players amused themselves by taking part in bandy matches.

An attempt to give bandy to the world

Bandy was a demonstration sport at the 1952 Olympic Games in Oslo, Norway. However, it failed to catch on, with the similar, some say usurper, sport of ice hockey continuing to dominate, especially in North America.

BASEBALL

Origins

The sport developed from the British bat-and-ball game of rounders, which was played by colonists in North America at town meeting days. References to baseball have been found in American newspapers and civic documents from as early as 1791, and there is a tradition (now discredited) that the rules of the game were laid down by Abner Doubleday (1819–93) at Cooperstown, New York, in 1839. The first recorded organized game was played between the Knickerbockers and the New York Nine at Hoboken, New Jersey, on 19 June 1846 under rules drawn up by Alexander Cartwright (1820–92). Rules concerning equipment, numbers of 'balls' and 'strikes' allowed, and dimensions of the field of play developed over the next 50 years. The distance from the pitcher's mound to home plate was finally fixed at 18.4m/60ft 6in in 1893, since when there have been only minor changes to the game.

Rules and description

Team game played between two sides on a field containing a diamond-shaped 'infield' which has 'bases' at the corners, 27.4m/90ft apart, and an 'outfield' lying beyond this. Each side consists of nine players who 'bat' and 'field', but players may be replaced during the game by substitutes from a total squad of up to 25. Essential pieces of equipment are long solid bats, the hard ball 'pitched' from the

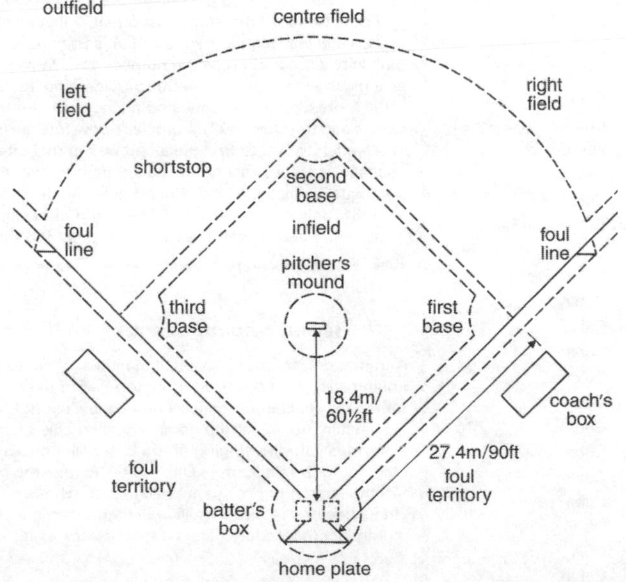

'mound', and the glove worn by each fielder; the team 'at bat' tries to score runs during each 'inning' by having its players hit the ball, circle the bases and return to home plate before being put out by the team 'in the field'; players are out if their hit is caught, if they are tagged with the ball when 'off-base', if the base is touched by a fielder with the ball before they arrive at it, or if they 'strike out', ie fail to hit the ball after three pitches have been judged 'strikes' by the umpire; the team at bat is retired after three players are put out, ending the inning; a game consists of nine innings for each team, plus unlimited extra innings in the event of a tie.

Under National League rules, all nine players who field also bat; under American League rules, the pitcher is not required to bat, and there is a 'designated hitter', who bats but does not field.

Ruling bodies: International Baseball Federation (IBAF); Major League Baseball (MLB) governs the professional game in North America

World Cup

Instituted in 1938, it was initially held at irregular intervals, with two competitions (editions XXI and XXII) held in 1973; currently held every two years.

(* Puerto Rico won the 1950 tournament, but was later disqualified for fielding professional players.)

	Winner
1938	Great Britain
1939	Cuba
1940	Cuba
1941	Venezuela
1942	Cuba
1943	Cuba
1944	Venezuela
1945	Venezuela
1947	Colombia
1948	Dominican Republic
1950	Cuba*
1951	Puerto Rico
1952	Cuba
1953	Cuba
1961	Cuba
1965	Colombia
1969	Cuba
1970	Cuba
1971	Cuba
1972	Cuba
1973	Cuba
1973	USA
1974	USA
1976	Cuba

Short story

The smallest player to play major-league baseball was Eddie Gaedel, who stood just 3 feet, 7 inches tall. Gaedel was signed by the St Louis Browns as a publicity stunt and given the number 1/8. He was used as a pinch hitter against the Detroit Tigers on 19 August 1951, presenting the opposing pitcher with a minute strike zone to throw at. The pitcher threw four balls, and Gaedel walked to first base and was immediately substituted. As a result, the league banned the use of unusually small players. When Eddie Gaedel died in 1961, only one person from the world of baseball attended his funeral: the Detroit pitcher, Bob Cain.

The seventh-inning stretch

A traditional feature of baseball matches is the 'seventh-inning stretch', a break after the top half of the seventh inning for spectators to stand up and walk about before settling to watch the game's climax. This often coincides with the singing of the baseball anthem 'Take Me out to the Ballgame'. One story ascribes the origin of the stretch to President William Taft, who is said to have become restless while watching a game in 1910, but in fact the tradition can be traced back as far as the 1860s.

	Winner
1978	Cuba
1980	Cuba
1982	South Korea
1984	Cuba
1986	Cuba
1988	Cuba
1990	Cuba
1994	Cuba
1998	Cuba
2001	Cuba
2003	Cuba

The shot heard round the world

In 1951, the Brooklyn Dodgers and New York Giants finished level at the top of the National League and played a three-game play-off to decide the pennant. In the deciding game, the Giants trailed 4-2 with two men on base and a man out in the bottom half of the ninth inning, but Bobby Thomson hit a home run, allowing himself and the two baserunners to score, meaning that the Giants won the game and the league pennant. Thomson's dramatic home run has passed into baseball history as 'the shot heard round the world', and the scene was later recreated in Don DeLillo's novel *Underworld* (1997).

Women's World Cup

First held in Edmonton, Canada, in 2004.

	Winner
2004	USA

Olympic Champions

Played as a demonstration sport in 1912, 1936, 1984 and 1988; became an official Olympic sport in 1992.

1992	Cuba
1996	Cuba
2000	USA
2004	Cuba

World Series

First held in 1903, it takes place in October as a best-of-seven-match series. Professional baseball's leading event, it is an end-of-season meeting between the winners of the two major baseball leagues in North America, the National League (NL) and American League (AL).

	Winner	Defeated team	Score
1903	Boston Red Sox (AL)	Pittsburgh Pirates (NL)	5-3
1904	*Not held*		

Baseball

	Winner	Defeated team	Score
1905	New York Giants (NL)	Philadelphia Athletics (AL)	4-1
1906	Chicago White Sox (AL)	Chicago Cubs (NL)	4-2
1907	Chicago Cubs (NL)	Detroit Tigers (AL)	4-0 (one tie)
1908	Chicago Cubs (NL)	Detroit Tigers (AL)	4-1
1909	Pittsburgh Pirates (NL)	Detroit Tigers (AL)	4-3
1910	Philadelphia Athletics (AL)	Chicago Cubs (NL)	4-1
1911	Philadelphia Athletics (AL)	New York Giants (NL)	4-2
1912	Boston Red Sox (AL)	New York Giants (NL)	4-3 (one tie)
1913	Philadelphia Athletics (AL)	New York Giants (NL)	4-1
1914	Boston Braves (NL)	Philadelphia Athletics (AL)	4-0
1915	Boston Red Sox (AL)	Philadelphia Phillies (NL)	4-1
1916	Boston Red Sox (AL)	Brooklyn Dodgers (NL)	4-1
1917	Chicago White Sox (AL)	New York Giants (NL)	4-2
1918	Boston Red Sox (AL)	Chicago Cubs (NL)	4-2
1919	Cincinnati Reds (NL)	Chicago White Sox (AL)	5-3
1920	Cleveland Indians (AL)	Brooklyn Dodgers (NL)	5-2
1921	New York Giants (NL)	New York Yankees (AL)	5-3
1922	New York Giants (NL)	New York Yankees (AL)	4-0 (one tie)
1923	New York Yankees (AL)	New York Giants (NL)	4-2
1924	Washington Senators (AL)	New York Giants (NL)	4-3
1925	Pittsburgh Pirates (NL)	Washington Senators (AL)	4-3
1926	St Louis Cardinals (NL)	New York Yankees (AL)	4-3
1927	New York Yankees (AL)	Pittsburgh Pirates (NL)	4-0
1928	New York Yankees (AL)	St Louis Cardinals (NL)	4-0
1929	Philadelphia Athletics (AL)	Chicago Cubs (NL)	4-1
1930	Philadelphia Athletics (AL)	St Louis Cardinals (NL)	4-2
1931	St Louis Cardinals (NL)	Philadelphia Athletics (AL)	4-3
1932	New York Yankees (AL)	Chicago Cubs (NL)	4-0
1933	New York Giants (NL)	Washington Senators (AL)	4-1
1934	St Louis Cardinals (NL)	Detroit Tigers (AL)	4-3
1935	Detroit Tigers (AL)	Chicago Cubs (NL)	4-2
1936	New York Yankees (AL)	New York Giants (NL)	4-2
1937	New York Yankees (AL)	New York Giants (NL)	4-1
1938	New York Yankees (AL)	Chicago Cubs (NL)	4-0
1939	New York Yankees (AL)	Cincinnati Reds (NL)	4-0
1940	Cincinnati Reds (NL)	Detroit Tigers (AL)	4-3
1941	New York Yankees (AL)	Brooklyn Dodgers (NL)	4-1
1942	St Louis Cardinals (NL)	New York Yankees (AL)	4-1
1943	New York Yankees (AL)	St Louis Cardinals (NL)	4-1
1944	St Louis Cardinals (NL)	St Louis Browns (AL)	4-2
1945	Detroit Tigers (AL)	Chicago Cubs (NL)	4-3
1946	St Louis Cardinals (NL)	Boston Red Sox (AL)	4-3
1947	New York Yankees (AL)	Brooklyn Dodgers (NL)	4-3
1948	Cleveland Indians (AL)	Boston Braves (NL)	4-2
1949	New York Yankees (AL)	Brooklyn Dodgers (NL)	4-1
1950	New York Yankees (AL)	Philadelphia Phillies (NL)	4-0
1951	New York Yankees (AL)	New York Giants (NL)	4-2
1952	New York Yankees (AL)	Brooklyn Dodgers (NL)	4-3
1953	New York Yankees (AL)	Brooklyn Dodgers (NL)	4-2

	Winner	Defeated team	Score
1954	New York Giants (NL)	Cleveland Indians (AL)	4-0
1955	Brooklyn Dodgers (NL)	New York Yankees (AL)	4-3
1956	New York Yankees (AL)	Brooklyn Dodgers (NL)	4-3
1957	Milwaukee Braves (NL)	New York Yankees (AL)	4-3
1958	New York Yankees (AL)	Milwaukee Braves (NL)	4-3
1959	Los Angeles Dodgers (NL)	Chicago White Sox (AL)	4-2
1960	Pittsburgh Pirates (NL)	New York Yankees (AL)	4-3
1961	New York Yankees (AL)	Cincinnati Reds (NL)	4-1
1962	New York Yankees (AL)	San Francisco Giants (NL)	4-3
1963	Los Angeles Dodgers (NL)	New York Yankees (AL)	4-0
1964	St Louis Cardinals (NL)	New York Yankees (AL)	4-3
1965	Los Angeles Dodgers (NL)	Minnesota Twins (AL)	4-3
1966	Baltimore Orioles (AL)	Los Angeles Dodgers (NL)	4-0
1967	St Louis Cardinals (NL)	Boston Red Sox (AL)	4-3
1968	Detroit Tigers (AL)	St Louis Cardinals (NL)	4-3
1969	New York Mets (NL)	Baltimore Orioles (AL)	4-1
1970	Baltimore Orioles (AL)	Cincinnati Reds (NL)	4-1
1971	Pittsburgh Pirates (NL)	Baltimore Orioles (AL)	4-3
1972	Oakland Athletics (AL)	Cincinnati Reds (NL)	4-3
1973	Oakland Athletics (AL)	New York Mets (NL)	4-3
1974	Oakland Athletics (AL)	Los Angeles Dodgers (NL)	4-1
1975	Cincinnati Reds (NL)	Boston Red Sox (AL)	4-3
1976	Cincinnati Reds (NL)	New York Yankees (AL)	4-0
1977	New York Yankees (AL)	Los Angeles Dodgers (NL)	4-2
1978	New York Yankees (AL)	Los Angeles Dodgers (NL)	4-2
1979	Pittsburgh Pirates (NL)	Baltimore Orioles (AL)	4-3
1980	Philadelphia Phillies (NL)	Kansas City Royals (AL)	4-2
1981	Los Angeles Dodgers (NL)	New York Yankees (AL)	4-2
1982	St Louis Cardinals (NL)	Milwaukee Brewers (AL)	4-3
1983	Baltimore Orioles (AL)	Philadelphia Phillies (NL)	4-1
1984	Detroit Tigers (AL)	San Diego Padres (NL)	4-1
1985	Kansas City Royals (AL)	St Louis Cardinals (NL)	4-3
1986	New York Mets (NL)	Boston Red Sox (AL)	4-3
1987	Minnesota Twins (AL)	St Louis Cardinals (NL)	4-3
1988	Los Angeles Dodgers (NL)	Oakland Athletics (AL)	4-1
1989	Oakland Athletics (AL)	San Francisco Giants (NL)	4-0
1990	Cincinnati Reds (NL)	Oakland Athletics (AL)	4-0
1991	Minnesota Twins (AL)	Atlanta Braves (NL)	4-3
1992	Toronto Blue Jays (AL)	Atlanta Braves (NL)	4-2
1993	Toronto Blue Jays (AL)	Philadelphia Phillies (NL)	4-2
1994	*Not held*		
1995	Atlanta Braves (NL)	Cleveland Indians (AL)	4-2
1996	New York Yankees (AL)	Atlanta Braves (NL)	4-2
1997	Florida Marlins (NL)	Cleveland Indians (AL)	4-3
1998	New York Yankees (AL)	San Diego Padres (NL)	4-0
1999	New York Yankees (AL)	Atlanta Braves (NL)	4-0
2000	New York Yankees (AL)	New York Mets (NL)	4-1
2001	Arizona Diamondbacks (NL)	New York Yankees (AL)	4-3
2002	Anaheim Angels (AL)	San Francisco Giants (NL)	4-3

	Winner	Defeated team	Score
2003	Florida Marlins (NL)	New York Yankees (AL)	4-2
2004	Boston Red Sox (AL)	St Louis Cardinals (NL)	4-0

Pre-World-Series League Pennant Winners

The National League was organized in 1876, and the American League became a major league in 1901. The winners of each league are shown up to the point when the World Series became an annual event in 1905, subsequent winners being deducible from the World Series results above.

	National League	American League
1876	Chicago Cubs	
1877	Boston Braves	
1878	Boston Braves	
1879	Providence Grays	
1880	Chicago Cubs	
1881	Chicago Cubs	
1882	Chicago Cubs	
1883	Boston Braves	
1884	Providence Grays	
1885	Chicago Cubs	
1886	Chicago Cubs	
1887	Detroit Wolverines	
1888	New York Giants	
1889	New York Giants	
1890	Brooklyn Dodgers	
1891	Boston Braves	
1892	Boston Braves	
1893	Boston Braves	
1894	Baltimore Orioles	
1895	Baltimore Orioles	
1896	Baltimore Orioles	
1897	Boston Braves	
1898	Boston Braves	
1899	Brooklyn Dodgers	
1900	Brooklyn Dodgers	
1901	Pittsburgh Pirates	Chicago White Sox
1902	Pittsburgh Pirates	Philadelphia Athletics
1903	Pittsburgh Pirates	Boston Red Sox
1904	New York Giants	Boston Red Sox

On the cards

Cards featuring baseball players were first distributed with tobacco in 1887 as a marketing exercise. Since then, the pastime of collecting baseball cards has become part of American life. A rare card from 1909 featuring Honus Wagner has been sold at auction for over a million dollars.

Most Valuable Player

An annual award to the player judged most valuable to his team in each of the major leagues.

	American League	National League
1931	Lefty Grove (Philadelphia Athletics)	Frankie Frisch (St Louis Cardinals)

	American League	National League
1932	Jimmie Foxx (Philadelphia Athletics)	Chuck Klein (Philadelphia Phillies)
1933	Jimmie Foxx (Philadelphia Athletics)	Carl Hubbell (New York Giants)
1934	Mickey Cochrane (Detroit Tigers)	Dizzy Dean (St Louis Cardinals)
1935	Hank Greenberg (Detroit Tigers)	Gabby Hartnett (Chicago Cubs)
1936	Lou Gehrig (New York Yankees)	Carl Hubbell (New York Giants)
1937	Charlie Gehringer (Detroit Tigers)	Joe Medwick (St Louis Cardinals)
1938	Jimmie Foxx (Boston Red Sox)	Ernie Lombardi (Cincinnati Reds)
1939	Joe DiMaggio (New York Yankees)	Bucky Walters (Cincinnati Reds)
1940	Hank Greenberg (Detroit Tigers)	Frank McCormick (Cincinnati Reds)
1941	Joe DiMaggio (New York Yankees)	Dolph Camilli (Brooklyn Dodgers)
1942	Joe Gordon (New York Yankees)	Mort Cooper (St Louis Cardinals)
1943	Spud Chandler (New York Yankees)	Stan Musial (St Louis Cardinals)
1944	Hal Newhouser (Detroit Tigers)	Marty Marion (St Louis Cardinals)
1945	Hal Newhouser (Detroit Tigers)	Phil Cavarretta (Chicago Cubs)
1946	Ted Williams (Boston Red Sox)	Stan Musial (St Louis Cardinals)
1947	Joe DiMaggio (New York Yankees)	Bob Elliott (Boston Braves)
1948	Lou Boudreau (Cleveland Indians)	Stan Musial (St Louis Cardinals)
1949	Ted Williams (Boston Red Sox)	Jackie Robinson (Brooklyn Dodgers)
1950	Phil Rizzuto (New York Yankees)	Jim Konstanty (Philadelphia Phillies)
1951	Yogi Berra (New York Yankees)	Roy Campanella (Brooklyn Dodgers)
1952	Bobby Shantz (Philadelphia Athletics)	Hank Sauer (Chicago Cubs)
1953	Al Rosen (Cleveland Indians)	Roy Campanella (Brooklyn Dodgers)
1954	Yogi Berra (New York Yankees)	Willie Mays (New York Giants)
1955	Yogi Berra (New York Yankees)	Roy Campanella (Brooklyn Dodgers)
1956	Mickey Mantle (New York Yankees)	Don Newcombe (Brooklyn Dodgers)
1957	Mickey Mantle (New York Yankees)	Hank Aaron (Milwaukee Braves)
1958	Jackie Jensen (Boston Red Sox)	Ernie Banks (Chicago Cubs)
1959	Nellie Fox (Chicago White Sox)	Ernie Banks (Chicago Cubs)
1960	Roger Maris (New York Yankees)	Dick Groat (Pittsburgh Pirates)
1961	Roger Maris (New York Yankees)	Frank Robinson (Cincinnati Reds)
1962	Mickey Mantle (New York Yankees)	Maury Wills (Los Angeles Dodgers)
1963	Elston Howard (New York Yankees)	Sandy Koufax (Los Angeles Dodgers)
1964	Brooks Robinson (Baltimore Orioles)	Ken Boyer (St Louis Cardinals)
1965	Zoilo Versalles (Minnesota Twins)	Willie Mays (San Francisco Giants)
1966	Frank Robinson (Baltimore Orioles)	Roberto Clemente (Pittsburgh Pirates)
1967	Carl Yastrzemski (Boston Red Sox)	Orlando Cepeda (St Louis Cardinals)
1968	Denny McLain (Detroit Tigers)	Bob Gibson (St Louis Cardinals)
1969	Harmon Killebrew (Minnesota Twins)	Willie McCovey (San Francisco Giants)
1970	Boog Powell (Baltimore Orioles)	Johnny Bench (Cincinnati Reds)
1971	Vida Blue (Oakland Athletics)	Joe Torre (St Louis Cardinals)
1972	Richie Allen (Chicago White Sox)	Johnny Bench (Cincinnati Reds)
1973	Reggie Jackson (Oakland Athletics)	Pete Rose (Cincinnati Reds)
1974	Jeff Burroughs (Texas Rangers)	Steve Garvey (Los Angeles Dodgers)
1975	Fred Lynn (Boston Red Sox)	Joe Morgan (Cincinnati Reds)
1976	Thurman Munson (New York Yankees)	Joe Morgan (Cincinnati Reds)
1977	Rod Carew (Minnesota Twins)	George Foster (Cincinnati Reds)
1978	Jim Rice (Boston Red Sox)	Dave Parker (Pittsburgh Pirates)
1979	Don Baylor (California Angels)	Keith Hernandez (St Louis Cardinals) and Willie Stargell (Pittsburgh Pirates)

	American League	National League
1980	George Brett (Kansas City Royals)	Mike Schmidt (Philadelphia Phillies)
1981	Rollie Fingers (Milwaukee Brewers)	Mike Schmidt (Philadelphia Phillies)
1982	Robin Yount (Milwaukee Brewers)	Dale Murphy (Atlanta Braves)
1983	Cal Ripken, Jr (Baltimore Orioles)	Dale Murphy (Atlanta Braves)
1984	Willie Hernandez (Detroit Tigers)	Ryne Sandberg (Chicago Cubs)
1985	Don Mattingly (New York Yankees)	Willie McGee (St Louis Cardinals)
1986	Roger Clemens (Boston Red Sox)	Mike Schmidt (Philadelphia Phillies)
1987	George Bell (Toronto Blue Jays)	Andre Dawson (Chicago Cubs)
1988	Jose Canseco (Oakland Athletics)	Kirk Gibson (Los Angeles Dodgers)
1989	Robin Yount (Milwaukee Brewers)	Kevin Mitchell (San Francisco Giants)
1990	Rickey Henderson (Oakland Athletics)	Barry Bonds (Pittsburgh Pirates)
1991	Cal Ripken, Jr (Baltimore Orioles)	Terry Pendleton (Atlanta Braves)
1992	Dennis Eckersley (Oakland Athletics)	Barry Bonds (Pittsburgh Pirates)
1993	Frank Thomas (Chicago White Sox)	Barry Bonds (San Francisco Giants)
1994	Frank Thomas (Chicago White Sox)	Jeff Bagwell (Houston Astros)
1995	Mo Vaughn (Boston Red Sox)	Barry Larkin (Cincinnati Reds)
1996	Juan Gonzalez (Texas Rangers)	Ken Caminiti (San Diego Padres)
1997	Ken Griffey, Jr (Seattle Mariners)	Larry Walker (Colorado Rockies)
1998	Juan Gonzalez (Texas Rangers)	Sammy Sosa (Chicago Cubs)
1999	Ivan Rodriguez (Texas Rangers)	Chipper Jones (Atlanta Braves)
2000	Jason Giambi (Oakland Athletics)	Jeff Kent (San Francisco Giants)
2001	Ichiro Suzuki (Seattle Mariners)	Barry Bonds (San Francisco Giants)
2002	Miguel Tejada (Oakland Athletics)	Barry Bonds (San Francisco Giants)
2003	Alex Rodriguez (Texas Rangers)	Barry Bonds (San Francisco Giants)
2004	Vladimir Guerrero (Anaheim Angels)	Barry Bonds (San Francisco Giants)

World Series Most Valuable Player

Awarded since 1955 to the Most Valuable Player in the World Series.

1955	Johnny Podres (Brooklyn Dodgers)
1956	Don Larsen (New York Yankees)
1957	Lew Burdette (Milwaukee Braves)
1958	Bob Turley (New York Yankees)
1959	Larry Sherry (Los Angeles Dodgers)
1960	Bobby Richardson (New York Yankees)
1961	Whitey Ford (New York Yankees)
1962	Ralph Terry (New York Yankees)
1963	Sandy Koufax (Los Angeles Dodgers)
1964	Bob Gibson (St Louis Cardinals)
1965	Sandy Koufax (Los Angeles Dodgers)
1966	Frank Robinson (Baltimore Orioles)
1967	Bob Gibson (St Louis Cardinals)
1968	Mickey Lolich (Detroit Tigers)
1969	Donn Clendenon (New York Mets)
1970	Brooks Robinson (Baltimore Orioles)
1971	Roberto Clemente (Pittsburgh Pirates)
1972	Gene Tenace (Oakland Athletics)

The curse of the Bambino

In January 1920, Harry Frazee, owner of the Boston Red Sox, sold his star player, Babe Ruth, to the New York Yankees to raise money for his production of the musical *No, No, Nanette*. Over the next 84 years, the Yankees won 26 World Series titles while the Red Sox won none, often losing to the Yankees in heart-breaking circumstances. Boston's continuing failure was widely ascribed to 'the curse of the Bambino' ('The Bambino' being Ruth's nickname). The curse was finally lifted in 2004, when the Red Sox won the World Series after making an unprecedented comeback to defeat the Yankees in the American League Championship.

1973 Reggie Jackson (Oakland Athletics)
1974 Rollie Fingers (Oakland Athletics)
1975 Pete Rose (Cincinnati Reds)
1976 Johnny Bench (Cincinnati Reds)
1977 Reggie Jackson (New York Yankees)
1978 Bucky Dent (New York Yankees)
1979 Willie Stargell (Pittsburgh Pirates)
1980 Mike Schmidt (Philadelphia Phillies)
1981 Ron Cey, Pedro Guerrero and Steve Yeager (Los Angeles Dodgers)
1982 Darrell Porter (St Louis Cardinals)
1983 Rick Dempsey (Baltimore Orioles)
1984 Alan Trammell (Detroit Tigers)
1985 Bret Saberhagen (Kansas City Royals)
1986 Ray Knight (New York Mets)
1987 Frank Viola (Minnesota Twins)
1988 Orel Hershiser (Los Angeles Dodgers)
1989 Dave Stewart (Oakland Athletics)
1990 Jose Rijo (Cincinnati Reds)
1991 Jack Morris (Minnesota Twins)
1992 Pat Borders (Toronto Blue Jays)
1993 Paul Molitor (Toronto Blue Jays)
1994 *Not awarded*
1995 Tom Glavine (Atlanta Braves)
1996 John Wetteland (New York Yankees)
1997 Livan Hernandez (Florida Marlins)
1998 Scott Brosius (New York Yankees)
1999 Mariano Rivera (New York Yankees)
2000 Derek Jeter (New York Yankees)
2001 Randy Johnson and Curt Schilling (Arizona Diamondbacks)
2002 Troy Glaus (Anaheim Angels)
2003 Josh Beckett (Florida Marlins)
2004 Manny Ramirez (Boston Red Sox)

No handicap

Jim Abbott became a successful pitcher despite being born without a right hand. He pitched for the US team in the final of the World Championship in 1988, and went on to have an eleven-year career in the major leagues, throwing a no-hitter for the New York Yankees in 1993.

Working overtime

On 4 August 1982, Joel Youngblood was traded from the New York Mets to the Montreal Expos. Youngblood heard about the trade while playing for the Mets in an afternoon game in Chicago, and promptly took a plane to Philadelphia where his new team-mates were playing that evening. He arrived in time to be used as a substitute, and not only achieved the unique feat of playing for two different teams in two different cities on the same day, but also scored a hit in both games.

Cy Young Award

Instituted in 1956, it is awarded to the outstanding pitcher in the major leagues. From 1967 a separate award was made for each league.

Winner

1956 Don Newcombe (Brooklyn Dodgers)
1957 Warren Spahn (Milwaukee Braves)
1958 Bob Turley (New York Yankees)
1959 Early Wynn (Chicago White Sox)
1960 Vernon Law (Pittsburgh Pirates)
1961 Whitey Ford (New York Yankees)
1962 Don Drysdale (Los Angeles Dodgers)
1963 Sandy Koufax (Los Angeles Dodgers)
1964 Dean Chance (Los Angeles Angels)

In a league of their own

With many of America's baseball fields lying empty as the country's young men fought overseas, the All-American Girls' Professional Baseball League was set up in 1943 to provide the American public with the opportunity to watch baseball. The league continued to run until 1954, when it folded because of low attendances.

	Winner
1965	Sandy Koufax (Los Angeles Dodgers)
1966	Sandy Koufax (Los Angeles Dodgers)

	American League	National League
1967	Jim Lonborg (Boston Red Sox)	Mike McCormick (San Francisco Giants)
1968	Denny McLain (Detroit Tigers)	Bob Gibson (St Louis Cardinals)
1969	Mike Cuellar (Baltimore Orioles) and Denny McLain (Detroit Tigers)	Tom Seaver (New York Mets)
1970	Jim Perry (Minnesota Twins)	Bob Gibson (St Louis Cardinals)
1971	Vida Blue (Oakland Athletics)	Ferguson Jenkins (Chicago Cubs)
1972	Gaylord Perry (Cleveland Indians)	Steve Carlton (Philadelphia Phillies)
1973	Jim Palmer (Baltimore Orioles)	Tom Seaver (New York Mets)
1974	Jim 'Catfish' Hunter (Oakland Athletics)	Mike Marshall (Los Angeles Dodgers)
1975	Jim Palmer (Baltimore Orioles)	Tom Seaver (New York Mets)
1976	Jim Palmer (Baltimore Orioles)	Randy Jones (San Diego Padres)
1977	Sparky Lyle (New York Yankees)	Steve Carlton (Philadelphia Phillies)
1978	Ron Guidry (New York Yankees)	Gaylord Perry (San Diego Padres)
1979	Mike Flanagan (Baltimore Orioles)	Bruce Sutter (Chicago Cubs)
1980	Steve Stone (Baltimore Orioles)	Steve Carlton (Philadelphia Phillies)
1981	Rollie Fingers (Milwaukee Brewers)	Fernando Valenzuela (Los Angeles Dodgers)
1982	Pete Vuckovich (Milwaukee Brewers)	Steve Carlton (Philadelphia Phillies)
1983	LaMarr Hoyt (Chicago White Sox)	John Denny (Philadelphia Phillies)
1984	Willie Hernandez (Detroit Tigers)	Rick Sutcliffe (Chicago Cubs)
1985	Bret Saberhagen (Kansas City Royals)	Dwight Gooden (New York Mets)
1986	Roger Clemens (Boston Red Sox)	Mike Scott (Houston Astros)
1987	Roger Clemens (Boston Red Sox)	Steve Bedrosian (Philadelphia Phillies)
1988	Frank Viola (Minnesota Twins)	Orel Hershiser (Los Angeles Dodgers)
1989	Bret Saberhagen (Kansas City Royals)	Mark Davis (San Diego Padres)
1990	Bob Welch (Oakland Athletics)	Doug Drabek (Pittsburgh Pirates)
1991	Roger Clemens (Boston Red Sox)	Tom Glavine (Atlanta Braves)
1992	Dennis Eckersley (Oakland Athletics)	Greg Maddux (Chicago Cubs)
1993	Jack McDowell (Chicago White Sox)	Greg Maddux (Atlanta Braves)
1994	David Cone (Kansas City Royals)	Greg Maddux (Atlanta Braves)
1995	Randy Johnson (Seattle Mariners)	Greg Maddux (Atlanta Braves)
1996	Pat Hentgen (Toronto Blue Jays)	John Smoltz (Atlanta Braves)
1997	Roger Clemens (Toronto Blue Jays)	Pedro Martinez (Montreal Expos)
1998	Roger Clemens (Toronto Blue Jays)	Tom Glavine (Atlanta Braves)
1999	Pedro Martinez (Boston Red Sox)	Randy Johnson (Arizona Diamondbacks)
2000	Pedro Martinez (Boston Red Sox)	Randy Johnson (Arizona Diamondbacks)
2001	Roger Clemens (New York Yankees)	Randy Johnson (Arizona Diamondbacks)
2002	Barry Zito (Oakland Athletics)	Randy Johnson (Arizona Diamondbacks)
2003	Roy Halladay (Toronto Blue Jays)	Eric Gagne (Los Angeles Dodgers)
2004	Johan Santana (Minnesota Twins)	Roger Clemens (Houston Astros)

Some Major-league Baseball Records

(In the following sections, figures are up to date at the start of the 2005 season; single-season records before 1903 not included due to differences in rules and scoring)

Players with over 600 career home runs

Hank Aaron	755
Babe Ruth	714
Barry Bonds	703
Willie Mays	660

Most home runs in a season

73 Barry Bonds (San Francisco Giants, 2001)

Players with over 2,000 runs batted in

Hank Aaron	2,297
Babe Ruth	2,213
Cap Anson	2,076

Most runs batted in in a season

191 Hack Wilson (Chicago Cubs, 1930)

Players with over 4,000 career hits

Pete Rose	4,256
Ty Cobb	4,191

Most hits in a season

262 Ichiro Suzuki (Seattle Mariners, 2004)

Most consecutive games with a hit

56 Joe DiMaggio (New York Yankees, 1941)

Highest career batting average

.367 Ty Cobb

Highest season batting average

.424 Rogers Hornsby (St Louis Cardinals, 1924)

(Several players before 1903 have been credited with a higher average, the highest being .440 by Hugh Duffy of the Boston Braves in 1894)

Pitchers with over 400 career wins

Cy Young	511
Walter Johnson	417

Most wins in a season

41 Jack Chesbro (New York Yankees, 1904)

(Many players before 1903 have been credited with more wins, the most being 59 by Charles 'Old Hoss' Radbourn of the Providence Grays in 1884)

Most career strikeouts

5,714 Nolan Ryan

Out in left field

In the 1920s, fans of the New York Yankees had a couple of good reasons for taking seats behind the right-field fence: that was the place where the left-handed Babe Ruth tended to hit home runs, and right field was also Ruth's fielding position. It seemed perverse to choose seats on the other side of the outfield. Hence the term 'left-field' came to be used to refer to any sort of unconventional behaviour or thinking.

Baseball goes to the movies

Baseball's status as 'America's pastime' has made it a popular subject for Hollywood film-makers. Baseball films range from comedies such as *Major League* (1989) to dramas such as *The Natural* (1984) and *Bull Durham* (1988) and biopics, which have cast John Goodman as Babe Ruth in *The Babe* (1992), Tommy Lee Jones as Ty Cobb in *Cobb* (1994), and Gary Cooper as Lou Gehrig in *The Pride of the Yankees* (1942).

Most strikeouts in a season

383 Nolan Ryan (California Angels, 1973)

(Charlie Buffinton of the Boston Braves is credited with 417 strikeouts in 1884)

Most career saves

478 Lee Smith

Most saves in a season

57 Bobby Thigpen (Chicago White Sox, 1990)

Lowest career earned run average

1.82 Ed Walsh

Lowest season earned run average

0.96 Dutch Leonard (Boston Red Sox, 1914)

(The lowest ERA for a pitcher throwing more than 300 innings is 1.12 by Bob Gibson of the St Louis Cardinals in 1968)

Perfect games

The ultimate achievement for a pitcher is to complete a game by retiring the minimum number of batters (27), without allowing any to reach first base. This feat has been achieved 17 times in major-league history:

Lee Richmond (Worcester Ruby Legs v Cleveland Blues, 1880)
John 'Monte' Ward (Providence Grays v Buffalo Bison, 1880)
Cy Young (Boston Red Sox v Philadelphia Athletics, 1904)
Addie Joss (Cleveland Indians v Chicago White Sox, 1908)
Charlie Robertson (Chicago White Sox v Detroit Tigers, 1922)
Don Larsen (New York Yankees v Brooklyn Dodgers, 1956)
Jim Bunning (Philadelphia Phillies v New York Mets, 1964)
Sandy Koufax (Los Angeles Dodgers v Chicago Cubs, 1965)
Jim 'Catfish' Hunter (Oakland Athletics v Minnesota Twins, 1968)
Len Barker (Cleveland Indians v Toronto Blue Jays, 1981)
Mike Witt (California Angels v Texas Rangers, 1984)
Tom Browning (Cincinnati Reds v Los Angeles Dodgers, 1988)
Dennis Martinez (Montreal Expos v Los Angeles Dodgers, 1991)
Kenny Rogers (Texas Rangers v California Angels, 1994)
David Wells (New York Yankees v Minnesota Twins, 1998)
David Cone (New York Yankees v Montreal Expos, 1999)
Randy Johnson (Arizona Diamondbacks v Atlanta Braves, 2004)

Most no-hitters thrown by a pitcher in a career

7 Nolan Ryan

Most stolen bases in a career

1,406 Rickey Henderson

Most stolen bases in a season

130 Rickey Henderson (Oakland Athletics, 1982)

(Hugh Nicol of the Cincinnati Reds is credited with 138 stolen bases in 1887)

Most consecutive games played

2,632 Cal Ripken, Jr (Baltimore Orioles, 1982–98)

Think I'll buy me a baseball team

Among the better-known people who have owned major-league baseball teams are the chewing-gum manufacturer William Wrigley (Chicago Cubs), singing cowboy Gene Autry (Los Angeles/California/Anaheim Angels), media mogul Ted Turner (Atlanta Braves), tennis champion Pam Shriver (a part-owner of the Baltimore Orioles), and future president George W Bush (Texas Rangers).

Nicknames

A selection of famous nicknames of baseball players:

Hank Aaron	Hammerin' Hank
James Bell	'Cool Papa' Bell
Mordecai Brown	'Three Fingers' Brown
Roger Clemens	The Rocket
Ty Cobb	The Georgia Peach
Joe DiMaggio	Joltin' Joe; The Yankee Clipper
Lou Gehrig	The Iron Horse
Rogers Hornsby	The Rajah
Jim Hunter	Catfish
Joe Jackson	'Shoeless' Joe
Reggie Jackson	Mr October (because of his feats in the World Series, held in October)
Randy Johnson	The Big Unit
Walter Johnson	The Big Train
Mark McGwire	Big Mac
Willie Mays	The Say Hey Kid
Stan Musial	Stan the Man
Pete Rose	Charlie Hustle (because of his aggressive style of play)
Babe Ruth	The Sultan of Swat; the Bambino
Nolan Ryan	The Ryan Express
Ozzie Smith	The Wizard (because of his skill as a fielder)
Sammy Sosa	Slammin' Sammy
Honus Wagner	The Flying Dutchman
Ted Williams	The Splendid Splinter

A-Z

ace a team's best **starting pitcher**.

alley a section of the **outfield** between two outfielders, eg *he hit the ball into the alley in left-centre;* also called **gap**

all-star a player chosen to represent his league in the **All-Star game**

All-Star game an annual challenge match between teams chosen form the best players in the **National League** and the **American League**

American League one of the two most prestigious North American professional baseball leagues

assist a play by a fielder that makes it possible for a colleague to put out a **baserunner**

Baseball

at bat a player's turn to bat, eg *three hits in four at bats*

backdoor slider a pitch that appears to be beyond the outside part of the **strike zone**, but then breaks back over the **plate**

backstop a screen, wall, etc acting as a barrier behind the **catcher**

balk an illegal action made by the pitcher to deceive a **baserunner**

ball a pitch that is outside the **strike zone**. A batter who receives four balls is automatically awarded first base

ballpark a baseball stadium

base one of the fixed points around the corners of the **infield**, which a player must cross to score a run

base hit same as **hit**

baseline a line joining two bases

base on balls same as **walk**

baserunner a player who has reached first base safely and is attempting to perform a circuit of the bases

basket catch a catch made by a fielder at waist height as the ball drops over his shoulder

batter the player attempting to hit the ball delivered by the pitcher; also called **hitter**

batter's box the place where the batter stands to receive the pitch

battery the **pitcher** and **catcher** collectively

batting average a figure calculated by dividing a batter's total number of **hits** by the number of **at bats**, used as an indication of a batter's success

bench 1. a seat for coaches and reserve players at a match 2. the reserve players collectively

bloop a stroke that sends the ball softly just beyond the **infield**

bottom the second part of an **inning**, during which the home team bats, eg *Boston scored three runs in the bottom of the eighth*

breaking ball any pitch that swerves or changes direction in flight, such as a **curveball** or **slider**

bull pen 1. the part of a baseball ground where pitchers warm up 2. a team's **relief pitchers** collectively

bunt to block the ball with the bat so that it travels only a short distance, usually done as a tactical move to allow a **baserunner** to advance

cage an enclosed area used for batting practice

catcher a fielder positioned behind the batter

centre field the part of the **outfield** immediately behind second base when viewed from **home plate**

centre fielder the fielder positioned in **centre field**

change-up a slower pitch, thrown to deceive the batter

chopper a ball that bounces high after being hit into the ground

clean-up hitter the hitter who bats fourth for the batting side, regarded as having the best opportunity to **drive in** runs

closer a pitcher who specializes in defending a lead late in the game

complete game if a pitcher throws a complete game, he records all 27 outs without being replaced by a **relief pitcher**; compare **no-hitter**, **perfect game**

count a tally of the number of **balls** and **strikes** that have been thrown during an **at bat**, eg if the count is *three and one*, the pitcher has thrown three balls and one strike to the batter

curveball a slower pitch with an arcing trajectory

cut fastball	same as **cutter**
cut-off man	a fielder who goes to meet a long throw from the **outfield** before it reaches the **infield**
cutter	a **fastball** with a late sideways movement
cycle	if a batter hits for the cycle, he hits a **single**, **double**, **triple** and **home run** in the same game
designated hitter	a player who takes a regular turn at batting, but does not field
diamond	the diamond-shaped part of a baseball field marked off by the **baselines**
double	a **hit** that allows the batter to reach second base
double-header	a set of two games played on the same day
double play	a defensive play that results in two players being put out
drive in	if a batter drives in a run, he makes a **hit** that allows a **baserunner** to score; see also **run batted in**
earned run	a run conceded by a pitcher without the intervention of an **error**
earned run average (ERA)	the number of **earned runs** conceded by a pitcher per nine innings pitched, used as an indication of a pitcher's success
error	an instance of a fielder failing to record an **out** when one could have been made using routine effort
extra innings	additional innings played to decide the winner if a game is tied after nine innings
fair ball	a ball hit between the **baselines** into the field of play; compare **foul ball**
fastball	a delivery from the pitcher thrown at maximum speed
fielder's choice	a play where the batter is allowed to reach first base, but a **baserunner** ahead is put out, eg *Gwynn hit a single but was then retired on a fielder's choice*
first base	the first of the bases to which a batter must run, situated on the right-hand side of the **infield** when viewed from **home plate**
first baseman	the fielder positioned near first base
first pitch	a ceremonial opening pitch made at the start of a season, series or game, often thrown by an honoured guest
fly ball	a ball hit in the air; compare **ground ball**
fly out	if a batter flies out, he is put out by a fielder catching a **fly ball**
foul ball	a ball hit behind the **baselines**, counting as a **strike** unless there are already two strikes against the batter; compare **fair ball**
foul pole	either of two solid structures marking the division between the edge of the **outfield** and **foul territory**. A ball that strikes the foul pole on the full is counted as a **home run**
foul territory	the part of baseball ground outside the field of play
full count	a situation where the pitcher has thrown three **balls** and two **strikes** to the batter; see also **count**
gap	same as **alley**
gold glove	an annual award made to the outstanding fielder in the league at each position
grand slam	a **home run** hit when there is a **baserunner** at each base, scoring four runs
ground ball	a ball hit along the ground; compare **fly ball**
ground out	if a batter grounds out, he hits a **ground ball** and is put out by not reaching first base before the throw from a fielder
Hall of Fame	an institution based in Cooperstown, New York, that honours outstanding figures in the game's history

hit a stroke that sends the ball into the field of play and allows the batter to reach at least first base safely

hit-and-run a tactical manoeuvre where a **baserunner** at first base begins to run as soon as the pitcher begins to throw the ball, expecting the hitter to put the ball in play. The aim is to allow the baserunner more time to advance safely and to force **infielders** to move out of position

hitter same as **batter**

home plate the **plate** over which the pitcher aims the ball, and to which the batter must return in order to score a run

home run a **hit** that goes far enough to allow the batter to make a complete circuit of all four bases, especially any hit that lands beyond the **outfield** fence between the **foul poles**

infield the part of the playing area enclosed within the **baselines**

infielder any fielder positioned around the infield, ie the **first baseman**, **second baseman**, **third baseman** or **shortstop**

inning a turn at batting for each team, lasting until three batters from each are out

inside-the-park home run a **home run** scored without the ball travelling beyond the field of play

in the hole if a batter is in the hole, he is scheduled to bat two places after the current batter; compare **on deck**

knuckleball a type of slow pitch with an unpredictable trajectory, caused by gripping the ball with the fingertips

lead-off hitter the player who bats first for the batting side

left field the part of the **outfield** to the left of second base when viewed from **home plate**

left fielder the fielder positioned in **left field**

line drive a hard-hit ball with a flat trajectory

load the bases if a pitcher loads the bases, or if the bases are loaded, there are **baserunners** at first, second and third base

long reliever a **relief pitcher** who is used to pitch several innings if the **starting pitcher** has to be removed from the game prematurely

major league either of the two most prestigious North American professional baseball leagues, the **National League** and the **American League**; also called **majors**

middle reliever any **relief pitcher** other than the **closer**

minor league any of the less prestigious North American professional baseball leagues, often used to groom younger players for the **major leagues**; also called **minors**

mitt a padded leather glove used to catch the ball

mound a raised area, 18.4m/60ft 6in from **home plate**, from which the pitcher throws the ball to the batter

National League one of the two most prestigious North American professional baseball leagues

nightcap the second of the two games in a **double-header**

no-hitter a game in which a pitcher does not allow an opponent to score a **hit**; compare **perfect game**

on deck if a batter is on deck, he is scheduled to bat after the current batter

on-deck circle a circular area in **foul territory** where the next player to bat waits

out an instance of a batter being retired by being caught, tagged out, struck out, etc. An inning ends when three outs are recorded

outfield the part of the playing area beyond the **baselines**, usually extending to a wall or fence

outfielder any fielder positioned in the outfield, ie the **left fielder**, **centre fielder** or **right fielder**

passed ball an accurately thrown pitch that the **catcher** fails to gather in time to prevent a **baserunner** from advancing; compare **wild pitch**

pennant a flag awarded to the winners of a league championship

perfect game a game in which a pitcher does not allow an opponent to reach base by any means; compare **no-hitter**

pick off if a pitcher or **catcher** picks off a **baserunner** who has strayed off base, he throws the ball to a fielder who tags the runner before he is able to return to the base

pinch hitter a substitute batter who bats in place of another because of injury or for tactical reasons

pinch runner a substitute **baserunner** who runs in place of a batter who has reached base, usually a fast runner used towards the end of a close game

pitch 1. to throw the ball to the batter 2. a ball thrown to the batter

pitcher the player who initiates play by throwing the ball to the batter

pitch-out a tactic, used when the fielding team anticipates that a **baserunner** will attempt to **steal** a base, whereby the pitcher deliberately throws the ball wide of the **plate** in order to give the **catcher** a better chance of throwing out the runner

plate a five-sided white slab over which the pitcher must throw the ball

pop up to hit the ball in the air a short distance from **home plate**

position player any player other than a pitcher

RBI see **run batted in**

relay a throw to the **infield** made by a **cut-off man** after intercepting a throw

relief pitcher, reliever a pitcher who enters the game as a substitute

right field the part of the **outfield** to the right of second base when viewed from **home plate**

right fielder the fielder positioned in **right field**

run a score awarded to a player who completes a circuit of the bases and returns to home plate without being put out

run batted in (RBI) a batter is credited with a run batted in for each run that is scored as a result of the batter's action, eg by scoring a **hit**, making a **sacrifice**, or receiving a **walk**

rundown a situation in which a **baserunner** is trapped between two bases and must attempt to reach one before being tagged out

sacrifice a play where a batter deliberately makes an **out** in order to enable a **baserunner** to score or advance to another base

safe if a player is safe, he has reached base before being thrown out by the fielding side

safety squeeze a tactical manoeuvre where a **baserunner** at third base begins to run towards **home plate** as soon as the batter makes contact with the ball; compare **suicide squeeze**

save an instance of a **relief pitcher** successfully preserving a narrow lead to the end of a game

screwball a pitch that breaks in the opposite direction to a conventional **curveball** or **slider**

second base — the second of the bases to which a player must run, situated on the far side of the pitcher's **mound** from **home plate**

second baseman — the fielder positioned near second base, on the side nearer first base

set-up man — a **relief pitcher** who usually enters the game in the seventh or eighth inning, attempting to preserve a lead for the **closer**

shortstop — the fielder positioned between second and third base

shutout — a game in which the opposition fails to score a run

single — a **hit** that allows the batter to reach first base; compare **double**, **triple**, **home run**

silver slugger — an annual award made to the outstanding hitter in the league at each position

sinker — a **fastball** with a downward movement; also called **sinking fastball**

slider — a pitch that breaks in a horizontal plane

slugger — a batter who specializes in hitting home runs

splitter — a **fastball** thrown with fingers apart, imparting late downward movement; also called **split-finger pitch**

starting pitcher — a player who pitches at the beginning of a game, usually expected to continue in the game for at least five innings; compare **relief pitcher**

steal — if a **baserunner** steals a base, he runs to it safely without the help of a **hit** or an **error**

stretch — a pitching stance that is more upright than the **wind-up**, used in order to prevent a **baserunner** from **stealing** a base

strike — a ball thrown by the pitcher into the **strike zone**, or any ball at which the batter swings and misses

strike out — to dismiss or be dismissed by means of three **strikes**

strike zone — the area above **home plate** extending from the batter's knees to the middle of the torso, providing a target for the pitcher to throw at

suicide squeeze — a tactical manoeuvre where a **baserunner** at third base begins to run towards **home plate** as soon as the pitcher begins to throw the ball; compare **safety squeeze**

switch hitter — a player who is able to bat either right-handed or left-handed

tag — the act of putting out a **baserunner** by touching him with the ball or the hand holding the ball

third base — the third of the bases to which a player must run, situated on the left-hand side of the **infield** when viewed from **home plate**

third baseman — the fielder positioned near third base

throw out — to retire an opponent by throwing the ball to a fielder at the base to which the opponent is running

top — the first part of an **inning**, during which the visiting team bats, eg *the top of the ninth*

triple — a **hit** that allows the batter to reach third base

triple crown — the feat of leading the league in **home runs**, **batting average** and **runs batted in** in the same season

triple play — a defensive play that results in three players being put out

unearned run — a run conceded as a result of an **error** by the fielding side

walk — the automatic award of first base to the batter after the pitcher has thrown four **balls**; also called **base on balls**

warning track — a grass-free area in front of the **outfield** fence

wild pitch — a pitch thrown so inaccurately that the **catcher** is unable to gather the ball to stop a **baserunner** from advancing; compare **passed ball**

wind-up — a coiled position taken up by a pitcher before throwing the ball; compare **stretch**

Some baseball slang

aboard	if a batter is aboard, he has reached first base successfully
around the horn	if a **double play** is made around the horn, the ball is thrown from third base to second to first, putting out runners at second and first base
bag	a base
bandbox	a small ballpark that makes it easy to hit **home runs**
blast	a **home run**
can of corn	an easy catch for a fielder
chin music	a pitch that passes close to the batter's head
crooked number	any number other than 0 or 1 recorded on a baseball scoreboard
dinger	a **home run**
dish	the **plate**
Fall Classic	the World Series
fan	if a pitcher fans a batter, he **strikes** him **out**
filthy	if a pitch is described as filthy, it breaks so sharply that it is almost impossible to hit
flash the leather	to make a skilful defensive play
frozen rope	a ball that travels on a fast, level trajectory
gapper	a ball hit into the gap between two **outfielders**
glove	defensive ability, eg *he is not usually known for his glove, but that was a good play*
golden sombrero	a notional award given to a batter who **strikes out** four times in a game
go yard	to hit a **home run**
grand salami	a **grand slam**
heat	if a pitcher 'throws heat' or 'brings the heat', he has a powerful **fastball**
high cheese	a pitcher's **fastball** thrown at the top of or above the **strike zone**; also called **high heat**
homer	a **home run**
hot corner	the position of third baseman (where the fielder has least time to react to balls hit in his direction)
interstate	if a batter is 'on the interstate', he has a **batting average** below .100 (the saying comes from the fact that American interstate highways all have two-digit numbers)
junior circuit	the American League
K	a **strikeout**
Mendoza line	a batting average of .200, considered the lower limit of respectability for a professional hitter (named after a notoriously weak-hitting player)
Midsummer Classic	the All-Star game
moon shot	same as **tape-measure shot**
paint the black	if a pitcher paints the black, he throws the ball right over the edge of the plate
Punch-and-Judy hitter	a batter who only hits the ball softly
punch out	to **strike out** a batter
rope	same as **frozen rope**
senior circuit	the National League
stuff	the ability to throw the ball with speed and movement, eg *he has excellent stuff, but his control lets him down*

table setter	a batter, usually batting first or second, whose job is to get on base so that the team's more powerful hitters can **drive** him **in**
tape-measure shot	a **home run** that travels a very long distance beyond the field of play
tater	a **home run**
Texas Leaguer	a **bloop** that drops between an **infielder** and an **outfielder**
tools of ignorance	the protective equipment worn by the **catcher**
twin killing	a **double play**
Uncle Charlie	a **curveball**
wheelhouse	if a pitch is thrown in a hitter's wheelhouse, the hitter is able to make a powerful swing at the ball
whiff	if a batter whiffs, he **strikes out**
yakker	a **curveball**

Some famous baseball players and managers

Hank Aaron, 1934–

Born in Mobile, Alabama, he is regarded as one of the greatest hitters ever. A right-handed batting outfielder, he set almost every batting record in his 23-season career with the Milwaukee Braves (later Atlanta Braves) and the Milwaukee Brewers: 2,297 runs batted in, 1,477 extra-base hits, and 755 home runs (he broke **Babe Ruth**'s long-standing record of 714 in 1974). He is commemorated by the annual Hank Aaron award to the outstanding hitter in each major league.

Grover Cleveland Alexander, 1887–1950

Born in Elba, Nebraska, he was one of the greatest right-handed pitchers in the history of the game. In a long and brilliant career, he played for the Philadelphia Phillies (1911–17), Chicago Cubs (1918–26) and St Louis Cardinals (1926–9). His career total of 373 wins ranks equal third in major-league history. The story of his life was told in the film *The Winning Team* (1952).

Johnny Bench, 1947–

Born in Oklahoma City, he played with the Cincinnati Reds and was the outstanding catcher of the 1970s. Besides being an outstanding defensive player, he had great ability with the bat, hitting 389 home runs, and leading the league in runs batted in three times. He was twice voted the National League's Most Valuable Player (1970 and 1972) and won ten consecutive Gold Glove awards for his position.

Yogi Berra, 1925–

Born Lawrence Peter Berra, in St Louis, Missouri, he played as a catcher and outfielder with the New York Yankees from 1946 to 1963, appearing in a record 14 World Series. He was voted the American League's Most Valuable Player three times and appeared in 15 All-Star games. He went on to manage and coach the Yankees, the New York Mets and the Houston Astros. The cartoon character Yogi Bear is named after him.

Yogi Berra's baseball wisdom

Although he was a Hall-of-Fame catcher, Yogi Berra is probably as well known for his unique relationship with the English language as for his baseball skills. Among the quotations ascribed to him are, 'Baseball is 90 per cent mental; the other half is physical', 'It's déjà vu all over again' and 'It ain't over till it's over'. However, some of these statements may be falsely attributed. As Berra himself tells it: 'I didn't really say everything I said.'

Barry Bonds, 1964–

Born in Riverside, California, the son of a leading professional player, he became an outfielder for the Pittsburgh Pirates and San Francisco Giants. He was voted the National League's Most Valuable Player on an unprecedented seven occasions and is the only player to have hit over 500 home runs and stolen over 500 bases in his career. In 2001 he hit a record 73 home runs in a season.

Roger Clemens, 1962–

Born in Dayton, Ohio, he began his career with the Boston Red Sox, later playing for the Toronto Blue Jays, New York Yankees and Houston Astros. Known as 'The Rocket' because of his intimidating fastball, he won an unprecedented seven Cy Young awards as the best pitcher in the American League. He also shares the record for the most strikeouts in a single game (20), and is one of only four pitchers to have struck out 4,000 batters in a career.

Roberto Clemente, 1932–72

Born in Carolina, Puerto Rico, he was an outstanding outfielder with the Pittsburgh Pirates (1955–72), leading the National League in batting average five times and being voted Most Valuable Player in 1966. He was killed in an air crash while on a relief mission to the victims of an earthquake in Nicaragua.

Ty Cobb, 1886–1961

Born in Narrows, Georgia, he was one of the outstanding offensive players of all time. He played for the Detroit Tigers (1905–26) and the Philadelphia Athletics (1926–8), and until **Pete Rose** was the only player with more than 4,000 hits in major-league baseball. He still holds the record for the highest career batting average (.367), and was one of the first group of players inducted into the Baseball Hall of Fame.

Joe DiMaggio, 1914–99

Born in Martinez, California, he was a powerful and elegant centre fielder and hitter, and played his entire career (1936–51) with the New York Yankees. His greatest achievement was recording a hit at least once in 56 consecutive games in the 1941 season. He led the American League in batting average twice (1939, 1940), and was voted the Most Valuable Player three times. During his career he hit 361 home runs and compiled a lifetime average of .325. In 1954 he married (briefly) the film actress Marilyn Monroe.

Lou Gehrig, 1903–41

Born in New York City, he earned his nickname of 'The Iron Horse' through his endurance. His record number of 2,130 consecutive major league games for the New

York Yankees (1925–39) stood for 56 years before being beaten by **Cal Ripken, Jr**, and he was voted Most Valuable Player four times. His career was cut short by a form of motor neurone disease which is now named after him (Lou Gehrig's disease). The story of his life was told in the film *The Pride of the Yankees* (1942).

The luckiest man on the face of this earth

In 1939, after not missing a single game for 14 years, Lou Gehrig's form began to slump as he felt increasingly tired. Doctors at the Mayo Clinic diagnosed him as having amyotrophic lateral sclerosis, a form of motor neurone disease. On 4 July that year, Gehrig was honoured by the Yankees, but at the ceremony he made light of his misfortune, focusing instead on the pleasure he had gained from baseball and pronouncing himself 'the luckiest man on the face on this earth'.

Bob Gibson, 1935–

Born in Omaha, Nebraska, he was a noted pitcher with the St Louis Cardinals from 1959 to 1975. He twice won the Cy Young award as the best pitcher in the National League and in 1968 became Most Valuable Player in the league on the strength of his exceptionally low earned-run average of 1.12. In 1968 he set a record for the most strikeouts in a World Series game.

Josh Gibson, 1911–47

He was born in Buena Vista, Georgia. He played in era before integration in sport, and as an African-American was confined to the Negro Leagues. Playing as a catcher for the Pittsburgh Homestead Grays and the Pittsburgh Crawfords, he became a legendary hitter, credited with more than 950 home runs in his career, including 84 in a single season. In 1972 he was elected to the Baseball Hall of Fame.

Rickey Henderson, 1958–

Born in Chicago, he played for numerous clubs, principally the Oakland Athletics (1979–84, 1989–93, 1994, 1995, 1998) and New York Yankees (1985–9). Probably the best lead-off hitter and baserunner of all time, he set numerous records over a long career, and is baseball's all-time leader in stolen bases (1,406) and runs scored (2,295).

Rogers Hornsby, 1896–1963

Born in Winters, Texas, he played as a second baseman with the St Louis Cardinals, later joining the New York Giants, Boston Braves and Chicago Cubs. His lifetime batting average of .358 is second only to **Ty Cobb**, and his season average of .424 in 1924 is the highest in the modern era. He also won the triple crown in 1921 and 1925, leading the league in home runs, batting average and runs batted in.

'Shoeless' Joe Jackson, 1888–1951

Born in Pickens County, South Carolina, he is said to have earned his nickname after discarding his boots during a minor-league game because of blisters. He played as an outfielder for the Philadelphia Athletics, Cleveland Indians and Chicago White Sox, compiling a lifetime batting average of .356, bettered only by **Ty Cobb** and **Rogers Hornsby**. He was banned from baseball after White Sox players were found to have accepted money to lose the World Series in 1919, although it is doubtful whether he was personally involved.

Say it ain't so, Joe!

One of the most infamous episodes in baseball history is the 'Black Sox' scandal of 1919. That year the Chicago White Sox were favourites to win the World Series, but surprisingly lost to the Cincinnati Reds. It was afterwards revealed that several Chicago players had received payments from gamblers. As a result, eight players were given life bans from organized baseball. Among them was the legendary 'Shoeless' Joe Jackson – despite the fact that Jackson had the highest batting average of any player in the series. Legend has it that when Jackson left the courthouse after the hearing, a young boy ran up to him and cried, 'Say it ain't so, Joe!'

Walter Johnson, 1887–1946

Born in Allen County, Kansas, he pitched for the Washington Senators (1907–27), winning a total of 417 games, including a record 110 shutouts, despite playing for a perennially poor team. He was the first pitcher to record 3,000 strikeouts, and was one of the original inductees into the Baseball Hall of Fame.

Sandy Koufax, 1935–

Born in Brooklyn, New York City, he played as a pitcher for the Dodgers there, then in Los Angeles. His short career (1955–66) reached its peak in the 1960s, and in 1963 he was named Most Valuable Player as the Dodgers beat the New York Yankees in the World Series. In 1965 he again helped the Dodgers to a World Series victory over Minnesota. During his career he threw four no-hitters, including a perfect game, and won the Cy Young award three times (1963, 1965, 1966). In 1966, aged only 31, he had to retire from baseball with arthritis of the left elbow.

Mark McGwire, 1963–

Born in Pomona, California, he played as a pitcher in college, but in the major leagues was converted to a first baseman for the Oakland Athletics and St Louis Cardinals. In his first season (1987), he hit 49 home runs, a record for a rookie, and with Jose Canseco formed the 'Bash Brothers', leading Oakland to three consecutive World Series appearances (1988–90). In 1998 he became the first player to hit 70 home runs in a season.

Connie Mack, 1862–1956

Born in East Brookfield, Massachusetts, he was closely involved in the early days of US baseball. He was catcher with various teams from 1886 to 1916, and began his managerial career as player/manager at Pittsburgh (1894–96). He moved on to the Philadelphia Athletics in 1901 and stayed for 50 years. He holds the record for most years managing (53), most games won (3,776), and most games lost (4,025), and won World Series titles in 1910–11, 1913 and 1929–30.

Micky Mantle, 1931–95

Born in Spavinaw, Oklahoma, he achieved legendary status as a star outfielder with the New York Yankees. Highlights of his career included seven World Series titles and, in

1956, his winning of the triple crown for leading the league in batting average, home runs and runs batted in. Possessing exceptional ability as a hitter, baserunner and centre fielder, he won three Most Valuable Player awards and was elected to the Baseball Hall of Fame in 1974.

Christie Mathewson, 1880–1925

Born in Factoryville, Pennsylvania, he had, for his time, an unlikely baseball background, being college educated and known for his interest in music and literature. He pitched for the New York Giants, winning 373 games in his career, leading the National League in wins four times and strikeouts five times. He was one of the original inductees into the Baseball Hall of Fame.

Willie Mays, 1931–

Born in Fairfield, Alabama, he played for the Giants in New York (1951–7) and San Francisco (1958–72), and later for the New York Mets (1972–3). A magnificent outfielder, batter and baserunner, only he and **Hank Aaron** have achieved the double of more than 3000 hits and 600 home runs. He was voted the Most Valuable Player in 1954 and 1965, and was voted the Baseball Player of the Decade (1960–9).

Stan Musial, 1920–

Born in Donora, Pennsylvania, he played as an outfielder with the St Louis Cardinals (1941–63). He led the National League in batting average seven times, was voted the league's Most Valuable Player three times, and played in 24 All-Star games.

Sadaharo Oh, 1940–

Born in Tokyo, Japan, he played as first baseman for the Yomiuri Giants in the Japanese League (1959–1980). He attributed his success at hitting to his study of samurai swordsmanship, and over the course of his career hit 868 home runs, an international record for professional baseball. He became manager of the Giants after retiring as a player.

Satchel Paige, 1906–1982

Born Leroy Robert Paige in Mobile, Alabama, he was a highly successful pitcher in the Negro Leagues in the period before integrated baseball. After integration, he signed to play for the Cleveland Indians at the age of 42, and helped them to win the World Series. He finally retired in 1953, but made a return with the Kansas City Athletics in 1965 at the astonishing age of 59, giving up no runs in three innings.

Branch Rickey, 1881–1965

Born in Stockdale, Ohio, he had a profound influence on top-class baseball. In 1919, as manager of the St Louis Cardinals, he introduced the 'farm system' whereby major league clubs linked themselves to lower-grade clubs to develop their own young players. This brought his team four world championships and made them the most profitable in baseball.

Cal Ripken, Jr, 1960–

Born in Havre de Grace, Maryland, the son of a professional coach, he played as a shortstop for the Baltimore Orioles, becoming one of the first players in that position to be known for hitting home runs, and twice being named the American League's Most Valuable Player. He is noted especially for his record of playing 2,632 consecutive games between 1982 and 1998, breaking the mark set by **Lou Gehrig**.

Frank Robinson, 1935–

Born in Beaumont, Texas, he played as an outfielder principally with the Cincinnati Reds and Baltimore Orioles, hitting 586 home runs and becoming the first player to be named Most Valuable Player in both the National League and American League. In 1975 he became the first African-American to manage a team in the major leagues.

Jackie Robinson, 1919–72

Born in Cairo, Georgia, he was the first African-American to play in the major leagues. After World War II he became a star infielder and outfielder for the Brooklyn Dodgers (1947–56), helping the team to six National League pennants and one World Series victory (1955). He retired in 1956 with a lifetime batting average of .311. He was largely responsible for the acceptance of African-American athletes in American professional sport, and wrote of the pressures on him in his autobiography *I Never Had It Made* (1972). Major League Baseball now celebrates 15 April, the anniversary of his breaking the colour bar, as Jackie Robinson Day.

Pete Rose, 1941–

Born in Cincinnati, Ohio, he played with the Cincinnati Reds from 1963 to 1978, then went on to Philadelphia and Montreal before returning to the Reds as player-manager in 1984. In September 1985 he broke **Ty Cobb**'s 57-year-old record of career base hits (4,191). By the time he retired from playing in 1986 he had amassed 4,256 base hits, an all-time record. He was manager of the Reds from 1987 to 1989, when an investigation into an alleged gambling offence led to his being banned from baseball for life.

Babe Ruth, 1895–1948

Born George Herman Ruth in Baltimore, Maryland, he started his career as a left-handed pitcher with the Boston Red Sox (1914–19), but converted to an outfielder and became famous for his powerful hitting after being traded to the New York Yankees (1920–34). His 1927 season record of 60 home runs stood until 1961. In all he played in ten World Series and hit 714 home runs, a record that stood for 30 years until it was surpassed by **Hank Aaron**. In 1935 he moved to the Boston Braves, and ended his career as a coach for the Brooklyn Dodgers (1938). He is considered by many to be the greatest player in the history of the game.

Nolan Ryan, 1947–

Born in Refugio, Texas, he was a pitcher for the New York Mets, California Angels, Houston Astros and Texas Rangers. Noted for his searing fastball, he holds numerous major-league pitching records, including most seasons pitched (27), most strikeouts (5,714) and most no-hitters (7).

Sammy Sosa, 1968–

Born in San Pedro de Marcoris, Dominican Republic, he entered the major leagues as an outfielder with the Texas Rangers before joining the Chicago White Sox and Chicago

Cubs. In 1998, he hit 65 home runs, four more than the previous record, only for **Mark McGwire** to hit 70. He went on to become the only player to hit more than 60 home runs in three separate seasons.

Honus Wagner, 1874–1951

Born John Peter Wagner in Carnegie, Pennsylvania, he worked in the coalmines from the age of 12 to 16 before becoming a baseball player. He played for the Louisville Colonels (1897–9) and Pittsburgh Pirates (1900–17), leading the league in batting average eight times on the way to a lifetime average of .329 over 21 seasons. He played in the first World Series and was one of the five original members of the Baseball Hall of Fame.

Ted Williams, 1918–2002

Born in San Diego, California, he won acclaim as one of the greatest hitters in baseball history as an outfielder with the Boston Red Sox in the 1940s and 1950s. Despite missing nearly five full seasons through injury and military service in World War II and Korea, he notched up 521 home runs, two triple crowns (1942, 1947) and two Most Valuable Player awards (1946, 1949) and led the American League in batting average six times. He was the last major-league player to record a season batting average of .400.

Cy Young, 1867–1955

Born Denton True Young in Gilmore, Ohio, he was a pitcher with several teams, principally the Cleveland Spiders and Boston Red Sox, and recorded a total of 511 wins between 1890 and 1911, a mark that is unlikely ever to be surpassed. In 1904, he pitched the first perfect game under modern rules. He is commemorated by the annual Cy Young award to the most successful pitcher in the major leagues.

BASKETBALL

Origins

A Canadian, James Naismith (1861–1939), is regarded as being the originator of basketball, although a similar game is believed to have been played in Mexico in the 10th century. Naismith invented the game in 1891 at the YMCA college in Springfield, Massachusetts, USA, using peach baskets on a gym wall. The game was originally designed merely to bridge the gap between the baseball and American football seasons, but it soon became popular in its own right.

Rules and description

Five-a-side team ball game played on a hard-surface court with a bottomless basket at each end. The object is to move the ball by a series of passing and bouncing moves and throw it through the opponent's basket. If a shot is not attempted within a prescribed time (24 seconds in the NBA), possession is awarded to the other team. Throwing the ball through the basket from open play scores a 'field goal', worth two or three points depending on the distance of the shot. Fouls may be penalized by a series of 'free throws' at the basket for one point each.

Ruling bodies: International Basketball Federation (FIBA; Fédération Internationale de Basketball); the National Basketball Association (NBA) governs the professional game in North America; the National Collegiate Athletic Association (NCAA) governs the sport at collegiate level in the USA

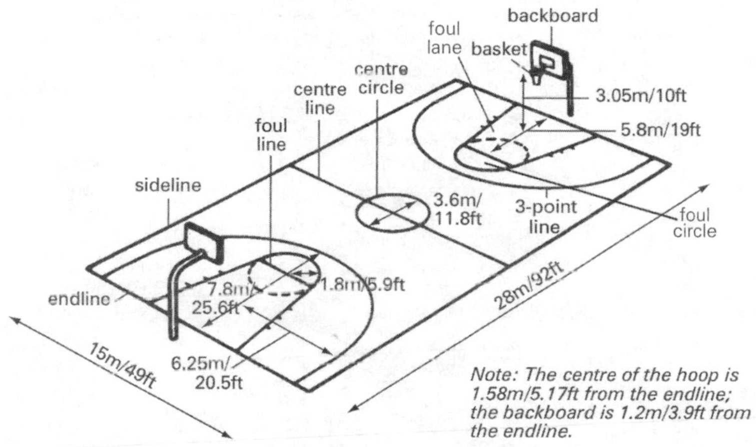

Note: The centre of the hoop is 1.58m/5.17ft from the endline; the backboard is 1.2m/3.9ft from the endline.

Hoops in the rain

When basketball was first included in the Olympic Games in 1936, the games were played outdoors on courts of sand and clay. The final took place in pouring rain which turned the playing area into a swamp.

World Championship

First held in 1950 for men, 1953 for women; takes place approximately every four years.

Men

	Winner	Runner-up	Venue
1950	Argentina	USA	Buenos Aires, Argentina
1954	USA	Brazil	Rio de Janeiro, Brazil
1959	Brazil	USA	Santiago, Chile
1963	Brazil	Yugoslavia	Rio de Janeiro, Brazil
1967	USSR	Yugoslavia	Montevideo, Uruguay
1970	Yugoslavia	Brazil	Ljubljana, Yugoslavia
1974	USSR	Yugoslavia	San Juan, Puerto Rico
1978	Yugoslavia	USSR	Manila, Phillipines
1982	USSR	USA	Cali, Colombia

	Winner	Runner-up	Venue
1986	USA	USSR	Madrid, Spain
1990	Yugoslavia	USSR	Buenos Aires, Argentina
1994	USA	Russia	Toronto, Canada
1998	Yugoslavia	Russia	Athens, Greece
2002	Yugoslavia	Argentina	Indianapolis, USA
2006			Saitama, Japan

Women

	Winner	Runner-up	Venue
1953	USA	Chile	Santiago, Chile
1957	USA	USSR	Rio de Janeiro, Brazil
1959	USSR	Bulgaria	Moscow, USSR
1964	USSR	Czechoslovakia	Lima, Peru
1967	USSR	South Korea	Prague, Czechoslavakia
1971	USSR	Czechoslovakia	Sao Paulo, Brazil
1975	USSR	Japan	Cali, Colombia
1979	USA	South Korea	Seoul, South Korea
1983	USSR	USA	Sao Paulo, Brazil
1986	USA	USSR	Moscow, USSR
1990	USA	Yugoslavia	Kuala Lumpur, Malaysia
1994	Brazil	China	Sydney, Australia
1998	USA	Russia	Germany
2002	USA	Russia	China
2006			Brazil

Foul trouble

In a game between Argentina and Uruguay in the 1952 Olympic Games, so many players fouled out that there were only four players from Uruguay and three from Argentina eligible to be on court at the end of the game. At one point, 25 players were involved in an on-court brawl. In their previous match, against France, Uruguay had finished with only three eligible players.

Olympic Champions

First held in 1936 for men, 1976 for women.

	Men	Women
1936	USA	
1948	USA	
1952	USA	
1956	USA	
1960	USA	
1964	USA	
1968	USA	
1972	USSR	
1976	USA	USSR
1980	Yugoslavia	USSR
1984	USA	USA

	Men	Women
1988	USSR	USA
1992	USA	Unified Team
1996	USA	USA
2000	USA	USA
2004	Argentina	USA

NBA Championship

First held in 1947 as the Basketball Association of America (BAA) Championship; renamed the National Basketball Association (NBA) Championship in 1949. This is the major competition in professional basketball in North America; an end-of-season best-of-seven-game play-off involving the champion teams from the Eastern Conference (EC) and Western Conference (WC). (In the 1949–50 season, following expansion of the league, the NBA was divided into Eastern, Central and Western Divisions, reverting to East and West the following year.)

	Champion	Defeated finalist	Score
1947	Philadelphia Warriors (EC)	Chicago Stags (WC)	4-1
1948	Baltimore Bullets (WC)	Philadelphia Warriors (EC)	4-2
1949	Minneapolis Lakers (WC)	Washington Capitols (EC)	4-2
1950	Minneapolis Lakers (Central Division)	Syracuse Nationals (Eastern Division)	4-2
1951	Rochester Royals (WC)	New York Knicks (EC)	4-3
1952	Minneapolis Lakers (WC)	New York Knicks (EC)	4-3
1953	Minneapolis Lakers (WC)	New York Knicks (EC)	4-1
1954	Minneapolis Lakers (WC)	Syracuse Nationals (EC)	4-3
1955	Syracuse Nationals (EC)	Fort Wayne Pistons (WC)	4-3
1956	Philadelphia Warriors (EC)	Fort Wayne Pistons (WC)	4-1
1957	Boston Celtics (EC)	St Louis Hawks (WC)	4-3
1958	St Louis Hawks (WC)	Boston Celtics (EC)	4-2
1959	Boston Celtics (EC)	Minneapolis Lakers (WC)	4-0
1960	Boston Celtics (EC)	St Louis Hawks (WC)	4-3
1961	Boston Celtics (EC)	St Louis Hawks (WC)	4-1
1962	Boston Celtics (EC)	Los Angeles Lakers (WC)	4-3
1963	Boston Celtics (EC)	Los Angeles Lakers (WC)	4-2
1964	Boston Celtics (EC)	San Francisco Warriors (WC)	4-1
1965	Boston Celtics (EC)	Los Angeles Lakers (WC)	4-1
1966	Boston Celtics (EC)	Los Angeles Lakers (WC)	4-3
1967	Philadelphia 76ers (EC)	San Francisco Warriors (WC)	4-2
1968	Boston Celtics (EC)	Los Angeles Lakers (WC)	4-2
1969	Boston Celtics (EC)	Los Angeles Lakers (WC)	4-3
1970	New York Knicks (EC)	Los Angeles Lakers (WC)	4-3
1971	Milwaukee Bucks (WC)	Baltimore Bullets (EC)	4-0
1972	Los Angeles Lakers (WC)	New York Knicks (EC)	4-1
1973	New York Knicks (EC)	Los Angeles Lakers (WC)	4-1
1974	Boston Celtics (EC)	Milwaukee Bucks (WC)	4-3
1975	Golden State Warriors (WC)	Washington Bullets (EC)	4-0
1976	Boston Celtics (EC)	Phoenix Suns (WC)	4-2
1977	Portland Trail Blazers (WC)	Philadelphia 76ers (EC)	4-2

	Champion	Defeated finalist	Score
1978	Washington Bullets (EC)	Seattle SuperSonics (WC)	4-3
1979	Seattle SuperSonics (WC)	Washington Bullets (EC)	4-1
1980	Los Angeles Lakers (WC)	Philadelphia 76ers (EC)	4-2
1981	Boston Celtics (EC)	Houston Rockets (WC)	4-2
1982	Los Angeles Lakers (WC)	Philadelphia 76ers (EC)	4-2
1983	Philadelphia 76ers (EC)	Los Angeles Lakers (WC)	4-0
1984	Boston Celtics (EC)	Los Angeles Lakers (WC)	4-3
1985	Los Angeles Lakers (WC)	Boston Celtics (EC)	4-2
1986	Boston Celtics (EC)	Houston Rockets (WC)	4-2
1987	Los Angeles Lakers (WC)	Boston Celtics (EC)	4-2
1988	Los Angeles Lakers (WC)	Detroit Pistons (EC)	4-3
1989	Detroit Pistons (EC)	Los Angeles Lakers (WC)	4-0
1990	Detroit Pistons (EC)	Portland Trail Blazers (WC)	4-1
1991	Chicago Bulls (EC)	Los Angeles Lakers (WC)	4-1
1992	Chicago Bulls (EC)	Portland Trail Blazers (WC)	4-2
1993	Chicago Bulls (EC)	Phoenix Suns (WC)	4-2
1994	Houston Rockets (WC)	New York Knicks (EC)	4-3
1995	Houston Rockets (WC)	Orlando Magic (EC)	4-0
1996	Chicago Bulls (EC)	Seattle SuperSonics (WC)	4-2
1997	Chicago Bulls (EC)	Utah Jazz (WC)	4-2
1998	Chicago Bulls (EC)	Utah Jazz (WC)	4-2
1999	San Antonio Spurs (WC)	New York Knicks (EC)	4-1
2000	Los Angeles Lakers (WC)	Indiana Pacers (EC)	4-2
2001	Los Angeles Lakers (WC)	Philadelphia 76ers (EC)	4-1
2002	Los Angeles Lakers (WC)	New Jersey Nets (EC)	4-0
2003	San Antonio Spurs (WC)	New Jersey Nets (EC)	4-2
2004	Detroit Pistons (EC)	Los Angeles Lakers (WC)	4-1

Why the Lakers don't have a lake

Many of the NBA's franchises have relocated several times, and some now play on the other side of the continent from their original home. This accounts for the rather inappropriate current names of some teams: the Minneapolis Lakers ended up in the arid surroundings of Los Angeles, and the New Orleans Jazz moved to Utah, better known for religious austerity than its love of good-time music.

Most Valuable Player

An annual award made to the outstanding player in the NBA.

1956	Bob Pettit (St Louis Hawks)
1957	Bob Cousy (Boston Celtics)
1958	Bill Russell (Boston Celtics)
1959	Bob Pettit (St Louis Hawks)
1960	Wilt Chamberlain (Philadelphia Warriors)
1961	Bill Russell (Boston Celtics)
1962	Bill Russell (Boston Celtics)

1963 Bill Russell (Boston Celtics)
1964 Oscar Robertson (Cincinnati Royals)
1965 Bill Russell (Boston Celtics)
1966 Wilt Chamberlain (Philadelphia 76ers)
1967 Wilt Chamberlain (Philadelphia 76ers)
1968 Wilt Chamberlain (Philadelphia 76ers)
1969 Wes Unseld (Baltimore Bullets)
1970 Willis Reed (New York Knicks)
1971 Kareem Abdul-Jabbar (Milwaukee Bucks)
1972 Kareem Abdul-Jabbar (Milwaukee Bucks)
1973 Dave Cowens (Boston Celtics)
1974 Kareem Abdul-Jabbar (Milwaukee Bucks)
1975 Bob McAdoo (Buffalo Braves)
1976 Kareem Abdul-Jabbar (Los Angeles Lakers)
1977 Kareem Abdul-Jabbar (Los Angeles Lakers)
1978 Bill Walton (Portland Trail Blazers)
1979 Moses Malone (Houston Rockets)
1980 Kareem Abdul-Jabbar (Los Angeles Lakers)
1981 Julius Erving (Philadelphia 76ers)
1982 Moses Malone (Houston Rockets)
1983 Moses Malone (Philadelphia 76ers)
1984 Larry Bird (Boston Celtics)
1985 Larry Bird (Boston Celtics)
1986 Larry Bird (Boston Celtics)
1987 Magic Johnson (Los Angeles Lakers)
1988 Michael Jordan (Chicago Bulls)
1989 Magic Johnson (Los Angeles Lakers)
1990 Magic Johnson (Los Angeles Lakers)
1991 Michael Jordan (Chicago Bulls)
1992 Michael Jordan (Chicago Bulls)
1993 Charles Barkley (Phoenix Suns)
1994 Hakeem Olajuwon (Houston Rockets)
1995 David Robinson (San Antonio Spurs)
1996 Michael Jordan (Chicago Bulls)
1997 Karl Malone (Utah Jazz)
1998 Michael Jordan (Chicago Bulls)
1999 Karl Malone (Utah Jazz)
2000 Shaquille O'Neal (Los Angeles Lakers)
2001 Allen Iverson (Philadelphia 76ers)
2002 Tim Duncan (San Antonio Spurs)
2003 Tim Duncan (San Antonio Spurs)
2004 Kevin Garnett (Minnesota Timberwolves)

Don't shoot!

In 1956, a four-day ceasefire was declared in a civil war raging in Peru to allow the Harlem Globetrotters to play a series of exhibition games.

Mine's a triple

The idea of rewarding players for shooting from long range originated in the American Basketball Association, a rival league to the NBA that ran for nine years from 1967. In an attempt to make the game more exciting, the ABA introduced a new line, 6.7m/22ft from the basket, and awarded three points, rather than two, for field goals scored from beyond that point. The experiment was a success, and the NBA adopted the three-point line in 1979.

The long and short of it

The average height for a professional basketball player is around 6 feet, 7 inches. Romanian-born Gheorghe Muresan and Sudanese-born Manute Bol are the tallest players to have played in the NBA at 7 feet, 7 inches. However, shortness of stature is not necessarily a barrier to success: Muggsy Bogues made a career in the NBA despite standing just 5 feet, 3 inches tall.

Major NBA Career Records

(figures are up to date at the end of the 2003–4 season; not including play-off games)

Points

Kareem Abdul-Jabbar	38,387
Karl Malone	36,928
Michael Jordan	32,292
Wilt Chamberlain	31,419

Steals

John Stockton	3,265
Michael Jordan	2,514
Maurice Cheeks	2,310
Scottie Pippen	2,307
Gary Payton	2,243

Blocked shots

Hakeem Olajuwon	3,830
Kareem Abdul-Jabbar	3,189
Mark Eaton	3,064
Dikembe Mutombo	2,996
David Robinson	2,954
Patrick Ewing	2,894

Rebounds

Wilt Chamberlain	23,924
Bill Russell	21,620
Kareem Abdul-Jabbar	17,440
Elvin Hayes	16,279
Moses Malone	16,212

Assists

John Stockton	15,806
Mark Jackson	10,334
Magic Johnson	10,141
Oscar Robertson	9,887
Isiah Thomas	9,061

Sore losers

Perhaps the most memorable basketball match of all time was the final of the men's Olympic tournament at Munich in 1972 between the USA and USSR. The USSR scored in controversial circumstances in the final seconds of the game to turn a one-point deficit into a surprise 51-50 victory. The defeated American players were so incensed at the manner of their defeat that they declined to accept their silver medals, which remain in a Munich bank vault to this day.

Hats off to Harlem

Perhaps the most famous basketball team of all, the Harlem Globetrotters were founded in 1927 by Abe Saperstein, and have kept busy ever since, playing their 20,000th game in 1998. In that time they won 19,668 and lost just 332 games. Curiously, the team did not actually play a game in Harlem until 1968, the name being coined solely to reflect the fact that all the players were black.

WNBA Championship

First held in 1997 under the auspices of the Women's National Basketball Association (WNBA), it is the major competition in women's professional basketball in North America. In 1997 the final was played as a single game; subsequently, the winner has been decided by a best-of-three-game series.

	Champion	Defeated finalist	Score
1997	Houston Comets	New York Liberty	65-51
1998	Houston Comets	Phoenix Mercury	2-1
1999	Houston Comets	New York Liberty	2-1

	Champion	Defeated finalist	Score
2000	Houston Comets	New York Liberty	2-0
2001	Los Angeles Sparks	Charlotte Sting	2 0
2002	Los Angeles Sparks	New York Liberty	2-0
2003	Detroit Shock	Los Angeles Sparks	2-1
2004	Seattle Storm	Connecticut Sun	2-1

WNBA Most Valuable Player

1997 Cynthia Cooper (Houston Comets)
1998 Cynthia Cooper (Houston Comets)
1999 Yolanda Griffith (Sacramento Monarchs)
2000 Sheryl Swoopes (Houston Comets)
2001 Lisa Leslie (Los Angeles Sparks)
2002 Sheryl Swoopes (Houston Comets)
2003 Lauren Jackson (Seattle Storm)
2004 Lisa Leslie (Los Angeles Sparks)

Every second counts

Before 1954 there was no limit to the time that a team could hold on to the ball. Games were often blighted because once a team held a lead it simply chose to retain possession without attempting to score. So the NBA introduced a 24-second clock to limit the time that a team could retain possession before shooting.

NCAA Championship

First held in 1939, it is an end-of-season tournament between the leading US college teams under the auspices of the National Collegiate Athletic Association to decide the national champion. Teams progress through regional rounds to the 'Final Four', culminating in a championship game.

OT = after overtime; 3OT = after triple overtime; UCLA = University of California at Los Angeles; UNLV = University of Nevada at Las Vegas; USC = University of Southern California

Men

	Champion	Defeated finalist	Score
1939	Oregon	Ohio State	46-33
1940	Indiana	Kansas	60-42
1941	Wisconsin	Washington State	39-34
1942	Stanford	Dartmouth	53-38
1943	Wyoming	Georgetown	46-34
1944	Utah	Dartmouth	42-40 (OT)
1945	Oklahoma A&M	New York University	49-45
1946	Oklahoma A&M	North Carolina	43-40
1947	Holy Cross	Oklahoma	58-47
1948	Kentucky	Baylor	58-42
1949	Kentucky	Oklahoma A&M	46-36
1950	City College of New York	Bradley	71-68
1951	Kentucky	Kansas State	68-58
1952	Kansas	St John's (New York)	80-63
1953	Indiana	Kansas	69-68
1954	La Salle	Bradley	92-76
1955	San Francisco	La Salle	77-63
1956	San Francisco	Iowa	83-71
1957	North Carolina	Kansas	54-53 (3OT)

Basketball

	Champion	Defeated finalist	Score
1958	Kentucky	Seattle	84-72
1959	California	West Virginia	71-70
1960	Ohio State	California	75-55
1961	Cincinnati	Ohio State	70-65 (OT)
1962	Cincinnati	Ohio State	71-59
1963	Loyola (Illinois)	Cincinnati	60-58 (OT)
1964	UCLA	Duke	98-83
1965	UCLA	Michigan	91-80
1966	Texas Western	Kentucky	72-65
1967	UCLA	Dayton	79-64
1968	UCLA	North Carolina	78-55
1969	UCLA	Purdue	92-72
1970	UCLA	Jacksonville	80-69
1971	UCLA	Villanova	68-62
1972	UCLA	Florida State	81-76
1973	UCLA	Memphis State	87-66
1974	North Carolina State	Marquette	76-64
1975	UCLA	Kentucky	92-85
1976	Indiana	Michigan	86-68
1977	Marquette	North Carolina	67-59
1978	Kentucky	Duke	94-88
1979	Michigan State	Indiana State	75-64
1980	Louisville	UCLA	59-54
1981	Indiana	North Carolina	63-50
1982	North Carolina	Georgetown	63-62
1983	North Carolina State	Houston	54-52
1984	Georgetown	Houston	84-75
1985	Villanova	Georgetown	66-64
1986	Louisville	Duke	72-69
1987	Indiana	Syracuse	74-73
1988	Kansas	Oklahoma	83-79
1989	Michigan	Seton Hall	80-79 (OT)
1990	UNLV	Duke	103-73
1991	Duke	Kansas	72-65
1992	Duke	Michigan	71-51
1993	North Carolina	Michigan	77-71
1994	Arkansas	Duke	77-72
1995	UCLA	Arkansas	89-78
1996	Kentucky	Syracuse	76-67
1997	Arizona	Kentucky	84-79 (OT)
1998	Kentucky	Utah	78-69
1999	Connecticut	Duke	77-74
2000	Michigan State	Florida	89-76
2001	Duke	Arizona	82-72
2002	Maryland	Indiana	64-52
2003	Syracuse	Kansas	81-78
2004	Connecticut	Georgia Tech	82-73

Women

	Champion	Defeated finalist	Score
1982	Louisiana Tech	Cheyney State	76-62
1983	USC	Louisiana Tech	69-67
1984	USC	Tennessee	72-61
1985	Old Dominion	Georgia	70-65
1986	Texas	USC	97-81
1987	Tennessee	Louisiana Tech	67-44
1988	Louisiana Tech	Auburn	56-54
1989	Tennessee	Auburn	76-60
1990	Stanford	Auburn	88-81
1991	Tennessee	Virginia	70-67 (OT)
1992	Stanford	Western Kentucky	78-62
1993	Texas Tech	Ohio State	84-82
1994	North Carolina	Louisiana Tech	60-59
1995	Connecticut	Tennessee	70-64
1996	Tennessee	Georgia	83-65
1997	Tennessee	Old Dominion	68-59
1998	Tennessee	Louisiana Tech	93-75
1999	Purdue	Duke	62-45
2000	Connecticut	Tennessee	71-52
2001	Notre Dame	Purdue	68-66
2002	Connecticut	Oklahoma	80-72
2003	Connecticut	Tennessee	73-68
2004	Connecticut	Tennessee	70-61

FIBA European Champions

First held in 1958 as the European Champions Cup; originally a knockout competition between the national champion clubs but from 1992 reorganized on a league basis as the European League, with an end-of-season play-off series to decide the champion; later renamed Euroleague (1996–2000), Suproleague (2001, after the rival ULEB set up its own Euroleague competition), Champions Cup (2003) and Europe League (2004).

	Champion	Defeated finalist	Score
1958	ASK Riga (USSR)	Akademic Sofia (Bulgaria)	86-81, 84-71
1959	ASK Riga (USSR)	Akademic Sofia (Bulgaria)	79-58, 69-67
1960	ASK Riga (USSR)	Dinamo Tbilisi (USSR)	61-51, 69-62
1961	CSKA Moscow (USSR)	ASK Riga (USSR)	61-66, 87-62
1962	Dinamo Tbilisi (USSR)	Real Madrid (Spain)	90-83
1963	CSKA Moscow (USSR)	Real Madrid (Spain)	69-86, 91-74, 99-80
1964	Real Madrid (Spain)	Spartak Brno (Czechoslovakia)	99-110, 84-64
1965	Real Madrid (Spain)	CSKA Moscow (USSR)	81-88, 76 62
1966	Milan (Italy)	Slavia Prague (Czechoslovakia)	77-72
1967	Real Madrid (Spain)	Milan (Italy)	91-83
1968	Real Madrid (Spain)	Spartak Brno (Czechoslovakia)	98-95
1969	CSKA Moscow (USSR)	Real Madrid (Spain)	103-99
1970	Varese (Italy)	CSKA Moscow (USSR)	79-74
1971	CSKA Moscow (USSR)	Varese (Italy)	67-53

Basketball

	Champion	Defeated finalist	Score
1972	Varese (Italy)	Split (Yugoslavia)	70-69
1973	Varese (Italy)	CSKA Moscow (USSR)	71-66
1974	Real Madrid (Spain)	Varese (Italy)	84-82
1975	Varese (Italy)	Real Madrid (Spain)	79-66
1976	Varese (Italy)	Real Madrid (Spain)	81-74
1977	Maccabi Tel Aviv (Israel)	Varese (Italy)	78-77
1978	Real Madrid (Spain)	Varese (Italy)	75-67
1979	Bosna Sarajevo (Yugoslavia)	Varese (Italy)	96-93
1980	Real Madrid (Spain)	Maccabi Tel Aviv (Israel)	89-85
1981	Maccabi Tel Aviv (Israel)	Bologna (Italy)	80-79
1982	Cantu (Italy)	Maccabi Tel Aviv (Israel)	86-80
1983	Cantu (Italy)	Milan (Italy)	69-68
1984	Roma (Italy)	Barcelona (Spain)	79-73
1985	Cibona Zagreb (Yugoslavia)	Real Madrid (Spain)	87-78
1986	Cibona Zagreb (Yugoslavia)	Zalgiris Kaunas (USSR)	94-82
1987	Milan (Italy)	Maccabi Tel Aviv (Israel)	71-69
1988	Milan (Italy)	Maccabi Tel Aviv (Israel)	90-84
1989	Split (Yugoslavia)	Maccabi Tel Aviv (Israel)	75-69
1990	Split (Yugoslavia)	Barcelona (Spain)	72-67
1991	Split (Yugoslavia)	Barcelona (Spain)	70-65
1992	Partizan Belgrade (Yugoslavia)	Badalona (Spain)	71-70
1993	Limoges (France)	Treviso (Italy)	59-55
1994	Badalona (Spain)	Olympiakos Piraeus (Greece)	59-57
1995	Real Madrid (Spain)	Olympiakos Piraeus (Greece)	73-61
1996	Panathinaikos (Greece)	Barcelona (Spain)	67-66
1997	Olympiakos Piraeus (Greece)	Barcelona (Spain)	73-58
1998	Bologna (Italy)	AEK Athens (Greece)	58-44
1999	Zalgiris Kaunas (Lithuania)	Bologna (Italy)	82-74
2000	Panathinaikos (Greece)	Maccabi Tel Aviv (Israel)	73-67
2001	Maccabi Tel Aviv (Israel)	Panathinaikos Athens (Greece)	81-67
2002	*Not held*		
2003	Aris Thessaloniki (Greece)	Trefl (Poland)	84-83
2004	Unics Kazan (Russia)	Maroussi (Greece)	87-63

ULEB Euroleague Winners

First contested in 2001 under the auspices of the Union of European Basketball Leagues (ULEB) as a rival to the FIBA-run competition.

	Winner	Defeated finalist	Score
2001	Bologna (Italy)	Tau Ceramica Vitoria (Spain)	3-2 (best of 5 matches)
2002	Panathinaikos (Greece)	Bologna (Italy)	89-83
2003	Barcelona (Spain)	Treviso (Italy)	76-65
2004	Maccabi Tel Aviv (Israel)	Bologna (Italy)	118-74

British Basketball League Champions

First administered by the British Basketball League in 1987–8; formerly contested as the National Basketball League. From 2000 to 2002 the league was divided into two conferences.

1988 Portsmouth
1989 Glasgow Rangers
1990 Kingston Wildcats
1991 Kingston Wildcats
1992 Kingston Wildcats
1993 Worthing Bears
1994 Thames Valley Tigers
1995 Sheffield Sharks
1996 London Towers
1997 Greater London Leopards
1998 Greater London Leopards
1999 Sheffield Sharks
2000 Manchester Giants (Northern Conference); London Towers (Southern Conference)
2001 Sheffield Sharks (Northern Conference); London Towers (Southern Conference)
2002 Chester Jets (Northern Conference); London Towers (Southern Conference)
2003 Sheffield Sharks
2004 Brighton Bears

No contest

The former Ugandan dictator Idi Amin was a basketball enthusiast and arranged games in which he took part himself. However, the outcome of these matches was rarely in doubt, as nobody else on the court was allowed to score.

British Basketball League Play-Off Winners

An annual end-of-season play-off tournament between the leading teams in the British Basketball League.

	Winner	Defeated finalist	Score
1988	Livingston	Portsmouth	81-72
1989	Glasgow Rangers	Livingston	89-86
1990	Kingston Wildcats	Sunderland	87-82
1991	Kingston Wildcats	Sunderland	94-72
1992	Kingston Wildcats	Thames Valley Tigers	84-67
1993	Worthing Bears	Thames Valley Tigers	75-74
1994	Worthing Bears	Guildford Kings	71-65
1995	Worthing Bears	Manchester Giants	77-73
1996	Birmingham Bullets	London Towers	78-72
1997	London Towers	Greater London Leopards	89-88
1998	Birmingham Bullets	Thames Valley Tigers	78-75
1999	London Towers	Thames Valley Tigers	82-71
2000	Manchester Giants	Birmingham Bullets	74-65
2001	Leicester Riders	Sheffield Sharks	84-75
2002	Chester Jets	Sheffield Sharks	93-82
2003	Scottish Rocks	Brighton Bears	83-76
2004	Sheffield Sharks	Chester Jets	86-74

Hair today...

In the 1970s, American basketball players such as Julius Erving and Darnell Hillman led the way in popularizing the Afro hairstyle. In later years, Dennis Rodman amazed and astonished fans by sporting a variety of hair colours that often changed on a daily basis, while Allen Iverson has done much to make braided hair or 'cornrows' fashionable in urban culture.

A-Z

alley-oop	a manoeuvre in which the ball is thrown high in the air so that a player running towards the basket may catch it and score
assist	a pass to a colleague that allows a basket to be scored
backboard	a rigid vertical panel placed above and behind the basket to deflect the ball
backcourt violation	the offence of passing the ball back across the centre line to a team-mate; punishable by loss of possession
bank shot	a shot that sends the ball off the **backboard** and into the basket
baseball pass	a long fast pass made by throwing the ball overarm
basket	1. a hoop with an open net attached, used as a goal 2. an instance of scoring
block	to deflect the ball on its upward trajectory towards the basket; compare **goal-tending**
bounce pass	a pass where a player bounces the ball to the recipient
box out	to position oneself between an opponent and the basket in order to establish a good position to catch a **rebound**
centre	a player, usually the tallest player on a team, who takes up a position immediately under the basket, often specializing in blocking shots and catching **rebounds**
charging	the offence of running into a stationary defender while in possession of the ball
chest pass	a pass where the player holds the ball with both hands at chest height and passes it without bouncing to a team-mate
crossover dribble	a **dribble** made using first one hand, then the other
double dribble	the illegal act of **dribbling** with two hands or, more commonly, resuming a **dribble** after stopping
double pump	a play in which a shooter attempts to deceive a defender by feinting to shoot in mid-air before taking a shot
double team	the defensive strategy of assigning two defenders to one attacking player
dribble	to move around the court while bouncing the ball with one hand
drive	to advance forcefully towards the basket with the ball
dunk	if a player dunks the ball, he jumps up and pushes it down through the basket from close range; see also **slam dunk**
fadeaway	a shot taken while leaning or falling away from the basket
fast break	an attempt to score by moving the ball forwards quickly after gaining possession
field goal	a goal scored from normal play, rather than from a **free throw**
forward	a tall player who plays mainly in the area around the basket and whose primary roles are to catch **rebounds** and shoot from close range; compare **guard**
foul circle	the circular painted area behind the **foul line**, inside which a player taking a **free throw** stands

foul lane — the area (often painted) between the basket and the **foul line**, outside which the other players must stand when a **free throw** is being attempted

foul line — a line 4.6m/15ft from the **backboard**, from which **free throws** are taken

foul out — to be ejected from the game for committing more than the allowed number of **personal fouls**

free throw — an unhindered throw to the basket, awarded as a penalty after an infringement by the opposing side

full-court press — a tactic in which the defensive team challenges opponents in all areas of the court rather than retreating to its own defensive area

goal-tending — the illegal touching of the ball on its downward trajectory towards the basket

guard — a usually shorter player who plays mainly away from the basket, whose primary roles are to pass, dribble and shoot the ball; compare **forward**

hang time — the time a player is able to remain in the air while shooting or jumping for the ball

hesitation dribble — a **dribble** in which a player feints to stop before continuing to advance the ball

high post — the area of the court near the **foul circle** during an attack

hook shot — a shot made by a player from side-on to the basket by making a curving motion with the farther-away arm

hoop — the hard, circular part of the basket, from which a net is suspended

inbounds — the area within the end lines and sidelines of the court

jump ball — a ball thrown up between opposing players by an official to restart the game

jump hook — a **hook shot** made while the shooter's feet are off the ground

jump shot — a shot made when the shooter's feet are off the ground

key — the (often painted) area on a basketball court including the **foul lane** and the **foul circle**; so-called because it resembles a keyhole

kick out — to pass the ball from inside the **foul lane** to a player outside it, especially after **driving** to the basket

lay-up — a shot taken from near the basket, releasing the ball gently with one hand at the top of one's jump so that it bounces off the **backboard** and into the basket

low post — the area of the court just outside the **foul lane** and under the basket

NBA — the National Basketball Association, a professional basketball association in North America

perimeter — the area of the court beyond the **key**

personal foul — a foul recorded against an individual player for physical contact that results in an unfair advantage; see **foul out**

pick and roll — a tactic in which an attacking player establishes a **screen** before rolling away from the defender and accepting a pass

pivot — same as **centre**

point guard — a **guard** whose primary responsibility is to direct the side's attacking play; compare **shooting guard**

post up — to establish possession outside the **key** with one's back to the basket

power forward — the taller of a team's two forwards, usually specializing in catching **rebounds**; compare **small forward**

rebound	an instance of catching the ball in the air after a missed shot has bounced off the **backboard** or the rim of the basket
rim out	if the ball rims out, it hits the rim of the basket and bounces away
screen	a manoeuvre involving positioning an attacking player between a defender and the ball carrier
shooting guard	a **guard** who specializes in taking long-range shots; compare **point guard**
shot clock	a clock that records the amount of time a team retains possession before attempting a shot
shot-clock violation	the offence of maintaining possession for more than the prescribed time (24 seconds in the NBA) without attempting a shot
sixth man	the best substitute player on a basketball team
sky hook	a variation of the **jump hook** in which the ball is released from a point high above the shooter's head
slam dunk	a forceful and dramatic instance of **dunking** the ball to score
small forward	the smaller of a team's two forwards; compare **power forward**
steal	if a player steals the ball, he takes possession of it away from an opponent
tap-in	an act of striking the ball in the air with the hand so that it goes into the basket
team foul	any **personal foul**, counting towards a team's permitted number of a fouls in a period of play. After the permitted number has been reached, further fouls are penalized by **free throws**
technical foul	a foul awarded for a non-contact offence, especially for dissent or unsporting conduct
three-point line	an arc painted on the court 6.25m/20ft 6in from the basket under FIBA rules (6.7m/22ft in the NBA). A **field goal** made from beyond this line scores three points rather than two
time out	an occasion when a team calls for play to be suspended, eg to discuss strategy
tip-off	the opening **jump ball** in a game
transition	the period of play immediately following a change of possession
trap	to guard the ball handler with two defenders in order to deprive the player of the opportunity to pass
travelling	the offence of carrying the ball for too many steps without dribbling
triple double	the feat of recording double figures in three categories (usually points, **rebounds** and **assists**, but sometimes including **steals** or blocked shots) in a game
turnaround jump shot	a **jump shot** executed by jumping with one's back to the basket and twisting in mid-air
turnover	loss of possession of the ball by a team, following an error or a breach of a rule
zone defence	a defensive strategy based on assigning defenders to specific areas of the court rather than to specific players

Some basketball slang

air	the distance between the ground and a player's feet when shooting or jumping for the ball
board	a **rebound**, eg *he came up with two steals and grabbed some tough boards*
brick	an inaccurate and poorly thrown shot
bucket	the basket, or a basket
charity stripe	the **foul line**
dish	to pass the ball, eg *Stockton dished to Marshall for a three-pointer*
downtown	the area beyond the **three-point line**
drain	to shoot the ball cleanly through the basket, eg *she drained a three-pointer*
glass	the **backboard**, eg *he caught ten rebounds including seven off the offensive glass*
hoops	the game of basketball
hops	the ability to jump high in the air
jumper	a **jump shot**
paint	the **key**
reject	to **block** a shot
rock	the ball, especially in the phrase *shoot the rock*
shake'n'bake	showy play, involving fast changes of direction and dextrous handling of the ball
stroke	to shoot the ball smoothly, eg *Jackson's not stroking it well tonight*
T	a **technical foul**
trey	a three-point field goal

Some famous basketball players

Kareem Abdul-Jabbar, 1947–

Born in New York City, he played with the Milwaukee Bucks and Los Angeles Lakers, earning six Most Valuable Player awards. Born Lewis Ferdinand Alcindor, Jr, he took the name Kareem Abdul-Jabbar when he converted to Islam in 1971. By the time of his retirement in 1989 he was recognized as one of the greatest players in the history of the game, holding several all-time records including most points scored (38,387).

Charles Barkley, 1963–

Born in Leeds, Alabama, he established a reputation as one of the most talented and volatile players of the 1980s and 1990s, playing for the Philadelphia 76ers, the Phoenix Suns and the Houston Rockets. Although not exceptionally tall for the position, he was one of the great power forwards in the game, earning the nicknames 'The Round Mound of Rebound' and 'Sir Charles'. He is one of only four players to have collected over 20,000 points, 10,000 rebounds and 4,000 assists in an NBA career.

Larry Bird, 1956–

Brought up in French Lick, Indiana, in 1979 he became a professional with the Boston Celtics, leading the team to an NBA championship in 1981. He was the Most Valuable Player in the 1984 and 1986 NBA championship finals and the league MVP three times (1984–6). He retired from the game in 1992, after playing in the gold-medal-winning US Olympic team. He later coached the Indiana Pacers.

Wilt Chamberlain, 1936–99

Born in Philadelphia, he was 7ft, 1in tall, earning him the nickname 'Wilt the Stilt'. He began his professional career with the Harlem Globetrotters, and in 1959 signed for the Philadelphia (later San Francisco) Warriors. At various times he also played with the New York Knicks, the Philadelphia 76ers and the Los Angeles Lakers. He was the NBA's Most Valuable Player on four occasions. He was an irresistible offensive force, and in 1962 achieved the unique feat of scoring 100 points in a single game.

Wilt the Stilt's century of points

In 1962, Wilt Chamberlain scored an astonishing 100 points for the Philadelphia Warriors against the New York Knicks. With the opposition's tallest player absent through illness, Chamberlain's team-mates took advantage by giving him the ball at every opportunity. He responded by shooting 36 field goals and adding 28 free throws when the Knicks attempted to stop him by repeated fouling.

Bob Cousy, 1928–

Born in New York City, he played professionally with the Boston Celtics (1950–63), becoming recognized as one of the greatest passers and playmakers in the game's history and earning the nickname 'The Houdini of the Hardwood'. After retiring, he went on to coach with the Cincinnati Royals (later the Kansas City–Omaha Kings) before becoming a commentator.

Julius Erving, 1950–

Born in Roosevelt, New York, he played in the American Basketball Association for the Virginia Squires (1971–3) and New York Nets (1973–6) before joining the Philadelphia 76ers in the NBA (1976–87). Known as 'Dr J', he was noted for his athletic and flamboyant style of play. He was named Most Valuable Player four times (ABA, 1974–6; NBA, 1981) and scored a career total of 30,026 points (in the ABA and NBA combined).

Earvin 'Magic' Johnson, 1959–

Born in Lansing, Michigan, he played college basketball for Michigan State University, then played with the Los Angeles Lakers (1979–91, 1996) and was a member of the USA's 'dream team' that won the Olympic basketball gold medal in 1992. He was named NBA Most Valuable Player in 1987, 1989 and 1990. He retired in 1992 after revealing that he had been diagnosed HIV-positive, but made a brief comeback in 1996.

Michael Jordan, 1963–

Born in Brooklyn, New York, he played college basketball at the University of North Carolina, then joined the Chicago Bulls (1984–93, 1995–8). Perhaps the finest all-round player in the history of the game, he possessed a remarkable combination of grace, speed, power and competitive flair. He was a member of the US Olympic gold-medal-winning teams in 1984 and 1992, and was named the NBA's Most Valuable Player five times (1988, 1991, 1992, 1996, 1998). After leading Chicago to three consecutive NBA championships, he retired in 1993 to play baseball, but rejoined the Bulls in the 1994–5 season and led them to another three championships (1996–8). Having retired again in 1999, he came out of retirement for a second time in 2001 and played for two seasons with the Washington Wizards.

Karl Malone, 1963–

Born in Summerfield, Louisiana, he played as power forward for the Utah Jazz from 1985 to 2003, when he joined the Los Angeles Lakers. Known as 'The Mailman' (because he always delivers), he was voted the NBA's Most Valuable Player in 1997 and 1999, and played on the USA's Olympic gold-medal-winning teams of 1992 and 1996.

Shaquille O'Neal, 1972–

Born in Newark, New Jersey, he played for the Orlando Magic from 1992 to 1996, when he joined the Los Angeles Lakers. He won three consecutive NBA championships with the Lakers (2000–2), being the Most Valuable Player in the championship finals on each occasion. In 2004 he joined the Miami Heat. He was a member of the US team that won the Olympic basketball gold medal in 1996, and has appeared in films and released rap records.

Oscar Robertson, 1938–

Born in Charlotte, Tennessee, he played college basketball for the University of Cincinnati and was a member of the US team that won the Olympic basketball gold medal in 1960. He then played professionally with the Cincinnati Royals and Milwaukee Bucks. Known as 'the Big O', he was one of the great all-round players, regularly posting double figures in points, rebounds and assists.

Bill Russell, 1934–

Born in Monroe, Louisiana, he played for the dominant Boston Celtics team that won eleven NBA championships between 1957 and 1969. He was voted the NBA's Most Valuable Player five times. A commanding defensive player, he amassed 21,620 career rebounds, an average of 22.5 per game, and led the league in rebounding four times.

John Stockton, 1962–

Born in Spokane, Washington, he played as point guard for the Utah Jazz, leading his team to the play-offs in every season of his 19-year NBA career. He was also part of the USA's Olympic gold-medal-winning teams of 1992 and 1996. He holds the records for the most assists (15,806) and steals (3,265) in a career.

BIATHLON

Origins

Generally regarded as a winter sport, the biathlon combines cross-country skiing and rifle shooting. It started in Norway as a training exercise for soldiers. The first competition took place in 1767 between soldiers guarding the border with Sweden. A precursor to the biathlon, the military patrol, was first demonstrated at the 1924 Winter Olympics in Chamonix, France.

Rules and description

Biathletes ski, at 30-second intervals, on a cross-country course, stopping at intervals to shoot at targets with a 22-calibre small-bore rifle. There are four shooting intervals in the individual event – in two the competitors shoot from a standing position, in the other two from a prone position. Competitors must hit five targets with five bullets at each stop and the targets are 50m from the firing line. Biathletes carry their rifle throughout the competition. Winners are the fastest to cover the course; missed target shots incur penalties, such as having time added to the total or the skier is required to ski an extra loop on the course. In the sprint events competitors stop twice at the firing range. Relay races begin with mass starts, with handovers to team members within a designated zone.

Ruling body: International Biathlon Union (IBU)

Olympic Champions

	Men's 20km	Men's 10km (sprint)
1960	Klas Lestander (Sweden)	
1964	Vladimir Melanin (USSR)	
1968	Magnar Solberg (Norway)	
1972	Magnar Solberg (Norway)	
1976	Nikolai Kruglov (USSR)	
1980	Anatoly Alyabyev (USSR)	Frank Ullrich (East Germany)
1984	Peter Angerer (West Germany)	Eirik Kvalfoss (Norway)
1988	Frank-Peter Rötsch (East Germany)	Frank-Peter Rötsch (East Germany)
1992	Yevgeny Redkin (Unified Team)	Mark Kirchner (Germany)
1994	Sergei Tarasov (USSR)	Sergei Chepikov (USSR)
1998	Halvard Hanevold (Norway)	Ole Einar Bjørndalen (Norway)
2002	Ole Einar Bjørndalen (Norway)	Ole Einar Bjørndalen (Norway)

	Women's 15km	Women's 7.5km (sprint)
1992	Antje Miserky (Germany)	Anfisa Reztsova (Unified Team)
1994	Myriam Bédard (Canada)	Myriam Bédard (Canada)
1998	Ekaterina Dafovska (Bulgaria)	Galina Kukleva (Canada)
2002	Andrea Henkel (Germany)	Kati Wilhelm (Germany)

...And when the snow fails to arrive

Keen to export the thrills of biathlon to non-snowy countries, a summer version of the sport was born. The skiing element is replaced by cross-country running. The first World championships were held in 1996 at Hochfilzen in Austria.

A-Z

double poling using both ski poles at the same time; used to generate speed at starts

mass start 1. when all competitors start at the same time, in a relay 2. an event for individual competitors with four shooting stages and in which they all start at the same time

pursuit	an event in which competitors start at times based upon where they finished in a previously held sprint race
V1	technique used for climbing, where the ski pole is used on one side only
V2	technique used for sprinting, where both ski poles are used, the skier pushing back on a pole at the same time as he or she pushes back with his/her leg on that side

BILLIARDS

Origins

The earliest mention of billiards comes from early 15th-century France and the game of *billard*. Louis XI of France is believed to have taken a game that was previously played outdoors on grass to an inside table. Mary Queen of Scots was also reputed to enjoy the game.

Rules and description

The term billiards describes a number of games played with a cue and balls on a baize-covered table, and is sometimes used as a catch-all term to include snooker and pool. There are two major forms of the game billiards itself: English billiards and carom billiards (also known as three-cushion billiards). English billiards is played on a table measuring 12 x 6ft/3.65 x 1.8m. The baize is marked with a 'baulk line', a 'D', and three 'spots'; the table has six pockets, one in each corner and one midway along each long side of the table. Three balls are used: white, spot white (which has two small black spots on it) and red. The white balls are cue balls; the red is never hit with the cue. The object of the game is to score points. Three points are scored if a red is potted or if the cue ball goes into a pocket after striking a red. If a red is missed the opponent scores two points. Two points are scored for potted whites. 'Cannons', also known as 'caroms' (hitting both other balls in a single shot) also score two points and up to 75 consecutive cannons can be made in a single break.

Carom billiards dates from 1878. It is played on a billiards table (measuring 10 x 9ft/3 x 1.5m) with no pockets and the same three balls as in English billiards. A carom scores one point and is similar to the cannon in English billiards. There are four varieties: straight rail, baulk line, cushion and three-cushion. Three-cushion is the most popular form – in this game the cue ball must contact three or more cushions, as well as both object balls, in order to score.

Ruling bodies: The World Confederation of Billiard Sports (WCBS) is the overarching ruling body for three further major ruling bodies that cover billiard sport. They are the World Pool-Billiard Association (WPA); the World Snooker Federation (WSF); and the Union Mondiale de Billard (UMB)

World Professional Championship

The championship was held as a challenger tournament from 1825 to 1912 and from 1951 (when the competition was reintroduced) to 1979. It has been held on a knockout basis since 1980.

* = declared champion

	Winner
1825*	Edwin Kentfield
1849*	John Roberts, Sr (England)
1870	William Cook (England)
1870	John Roberts, Jr (England)
1870	Joseph Bennett (England)
1871	John Roberts, Jr (England)
1871	William Cook (England)
1875	John Roberts, Jr (England)
1876*	William Cook (England)
1877	John Roberts, Jr (England)
1878*	William Cook (England)
1880	Joseph Bennett (England)
1881*	William Cook (England)
1885	John Roberts, Jr (England)
1887	Billy Mitchell (England)
1888	William Peall (England)
1889	Billy Mitchell (England)
1890–1	William Peall (England)
1892	Billy Mitchell (England)
1892	William Peall (England)
1893–4	Billy Mitchell (England)
1899	Charles Dawson (England)
1901	H(enry) W(illiam) Stevenson (England)
1901	Charles Dawson (England)
1901*	H(enry) W(illiam) Stevenson (England)
1903	Charles Dawson (England)
1908*	Melbourne Inman (England)
1909*	H(enry) W(illiam) Stevenson (England)
1909	Melbourne Inman (England)
1910–11	H(enry) W(illiam) Stevenson (England)
1912–19	Melbourne Inman (England)
1920	Willie Smith (England)
1921–2	Tom Newman (England)
1923	Willie Smith (England)
1924-7	Tom Newman (England)
1928–32	Joe Davis (England)
1933–4	Walter Lindrum (Australia)
1951	Clark McConachy (New Zealand)
1968	Rex Williams (England)
1971	Leslie Driffield (England)
1971	Rex Williams (England)
1980–1	Fred Davis (England)

Sacrebleu!

A French infantry captain named Mingaud is credited with inventing the leather tip for a cue. In 1807, while serving time as a political prisoner in Revolutionary France, he is said to have punched out small leather discs from a horse's harness and attached them to the end of his cue. This improved his control of the ball. His enjoyment of the game was so extreme that when his release from prison was due he asked to be incarcerated for longer so he could perfect his game!

1982–3	Rex Williams (England)
1984	Mark Wildman (England)
1985	Ray Edmonds (England)
1986	Robbie Foldvari (Australia)
1987–8	Norman Dagley (England)
1989	Mike Russell (England)
1990	*Not held*
1991	Mike Russell (England)
1992–3	Geet Sethi (India)
1994	Peter Gilchrist (England)
1995	Geet Sethi (India)
1996	Mike Russell (England)
1997	*Not held*
1998	Geet Sethi (India)
1999	Mike Russell (England)
2000	*Not held*
2001	Peter Gilchrist (England)
2002–4	Mike Russell (England)

Jumbo balls

In the late 19th century, before the advent of billiard balls made from synthetic materials, it was elephants that provided the ivory for making the balls. It was not even the case that you could reckon on getting dozens of balls from the tusks. One dead elephant would yield fewer than ten billiard balls—elephants' tusks are solid towards the end but become hollower towards the mouth.

BOBSLEIGH

Origins

Bobsleighing (known as bobsledding in North America) reputedly originated in St Moritz in Switzerland in 1888 when an Englishman named Wilson Smith, a member of a holidaying party, lashed together two sleighs with a wooden board. The first competition was held on the Cresta Run in 1898, although the course was meant for toboggans; the first purpose-built bob run was constructed alongside it in 1902.

Rules and description

At the start of the race the crew push the bobsleigh to get it moving. The driver is the person who sits at the front of the bob and steers it. He/she is usually the first to get into the bobsleigh. The 'brakeman' is the last to enter the bob, sits at the back and applies the brakes only after the race is over. The bobsleigh plus crew should not weigh more than 390kg/860lb (or 630kg/1389lb for a four-man bob). The runs are artificially built and the winners are decided by which team makes four descents in the shortest time. Bobsleighs are made of fibreglass with steel runners.

Ruling body: FIBT (Fédération Internationale de Bobsleigh et de Tobogganing)

Cool Runnings

The story of the Jamaican bobsleigh performance in the 1988 Calgary Winter Olympics inspired a Hollywood film and caught the imagination of fans all around the world. For a team who had no home ice to train on, they surprised everyone by performing credibly (they had one of the fastest starting times) but a spectacular crash saw them finish down the field. Their fame led to a world tour and even a guest appearance with the Los Angeles Lakers. Their success was largely due to the team's sprinting prowess that gave them an explosive start; former or current athletes have often made Olympic bobsledders (such as American Willie Gault and Briton Marcus Adam).

World Championships and Olympic Champions

Held every year except in Olympic years (indicated by an asterisk), when the gold-medal winners become automatic world champions. (NB: there was no bobsleigh event in the 1960 Winter Olympics). Women's bobsleigh was introduced at the 2003 world championships, with a German team winning on both occasions it has been held. A team from the USA won the inaugural event at the 2002 Olympic Games.

	Two-man	Four-man	Venue
1924*	Switzerland		Chamonix, France
1925–7	*Not held*		
1928*	USA		St Moritz, Switzerland[1]
1929	*Not held*		
1930	Italy		Caux-Montreux, Switzerland
1931	Germany	Germany	Oberhof, Germany/St Moritz, Switzerland
1932*	USA	USA	Lake Placid, USA
1933	Romania	*Not held*	Schreiberhau, Germany
1934	Romania	Germany	Engelberg, Switzerland/Garmisch-Partenkirchen, Germany
1935	Switzerland	Germany	Igls, Austria/St Moritz, Switzerland
1936*	USA	Switzerland	Garmisch-Partenkirchen, Germany
1937	Great Britain	Great Britain	Cortina d'Ampezzo, Italy/St Moritz, Switzerland
1938	Germany	Great Britain	St Moritz, Switzerland/Garmisch-Partenkirchen, Germany
1939	Belgium	Switzerland	St Moritz, Switzerland/Cortina d'Ampezzo, Italy
1940–6	*Not held*		
1947	Switzerland	Switzerland	St Moritz, Switzerland
1948*	Switzerland	USA	St Moritz, Switzerland
1949	Switzerland	USA	Lake Placid, USA
1950	Switzerland	USA	Cortina d'Ampezzo, Italy
1951	Germany	Germany	Alpe d'Huez, France
1952*	Germany	Germany	Oslo, Norway
1953	Switzerland	USA	Garmisch-Partenkirchen, West Germany
1954	Italy	Switzerland	Cortina d'Ampezzo, Italy
1955	Switzerland	Switzerland	St Moritz, Switzerland

	Two-man	Four-man	Venue
1956*	Italy	Switzerland	Cortina d'Ampezzo, Italy
1957	Italy	Switzerland	St Moritz, Switzerland
1958	Italy	West Germany	Garmisch-Partenkirchen, West Germany
1959	Italy	USA	St Moritz, Switzerland
1960	Italy	Italy	Cortina d'Ampezzo, Italy
1961	Italy	Italy	Lake Placid, USA
1962	Italy	West Germany	Garmisch-Partenkirchen, West Germany
1963	Italy	Italy	Igls, Austria
1964*	Great Britain	Canada	Igls, Austria
1965	Great Britain	Canada	St Moritz, Switzerland
1966	Italy	*Not held*	St Moritz, Switzerland
1967	Austria	*Not held*	Alpe d'Huez, France
1968*	Italy	Italy	Alpe d'Huez, Grenoble, France[2]
1969	Italy	West Germany	Lake Placid, USA
1970	West Germany	Italy	St Moritz, Switzerland
1971	Italy	Switzerland	Cervinia, Italy
1972*	West Germany	Switzerland	Sapporo, Japan
1973	West Germany	Switzerland	Lake Placid, USA
1974	West Germany	West Germany	St Moritz, Switzerland
1975	Italy	Switzerland	Cervinia, Italy
1976*	East Germany	East Germany	Igls, Austria
1977	Switzerland	East Germany	St Moritz, Switzerland
1978	Switzerland	East Germany	Lake Placid, USA
1979	Switzerland	West Germany	Königssee, West Germany
1980*	Switzerland	East Germany	Lake Placid, USA
1981	East Germany	East Germany	Cortina d'Ampezzo, Italy
1982	Switzerland	Switzerland	St Moritz, Switzerland
1983	Switzerland	Switzerland	Lake Placid, USA
1984*	East Germany	East Germany	Sarajevo, Yugoslavia
1985	East Germany	East Germany	Cervinia, Italy
1986	East Germany	Switzerland	Königssee, West Germany
1987	Switzerland	Switzerland	St Moritz, Switzerland
1988*	USSR	Switzerland	Calgary, Canada
1989	East Germany	Switzerland	Cortina d'Ampezzo, Italy
1990	Switzerland	Switzerland	St Moritz, Switzerland
1991	Germany	Germany	Altenberg, Germany
1992*	Switzerland	Austria	Albertville, France
1993	Germany	Switzerland	Igls, Austria
1994*	Switzerland	Germany	Lillehammer, Norway
1995	Germany	Germany	Winterberg, Germany
1996	Germany	Germany	Calgary, Canada
1997	Switzerland	Germany	St Moritz, Switzerland
1998*	Canada	Germany	Nagano, Japan
1999	Italy	France	Cortina d'Ampezzo, Italy
2000	Germany	Germany	Altenberg, Germany
2001	Germany	Germany	St Moritz, Switzerland
2002*	Germany	Germany	Salt Lake City, USA

	Two-man	Four-man	Venue
2003	Germany	Germany	Winterberg, Germany
2004	Canada	Germany	Königssee, Germany

[1] A five-man bob competition
[2] Games awarded to the town of Grenoble

BOULES

Origins

The game of boules or pétanque, commonly seen played in French town squares, originated in southeastern France in the Provence region (hence the closely related game 'jeu Provençal'). Indeed, it is believed that boules evolved from jeu Provençal in about 1910 when the citizens playing jeu Provençal tired of the game with its run-up before releasing the ball, and invented a game that could be played from a stationary position.

Rules and description

Boules is an umbrella term used to describe games played with metal balls (and the balls themselves) that are thrown at a smaller target ball (the 'jack' or 'cochonnet'; French for piglet). The two most popular forms of the game are pétanque and jeu Provençal. In pétanque a pitch usually measures around 15 x 4m/16.4 x 4.37yd and is of a hard surface, gravel or sand. The jack measures 25 to 35mm/0.98 to 1.37in in diameter. The player (or side) who wins the toss traces a circle on the ground large enough for any player to stand within. The first player throws the jack from within the circle and then the first ball to attempt to get as close as possible to the jack. Players can toss the ball high in the air or roll it along the ground. Most games go to 13 points, but they may be to 11, 15, 18, or 21. As a rule, a match consists of three games. Pétanque is played as singles, pairs or triples.

Ruling body: The Fédération Internationale de Pétanque et Jeu Provençal (FIPJP) looks after the two most prominent boules games: pétanque and jeu Provençal. An overarching organization – the Confédération Mondiale Sports Boules (CMSB) – is also concerned with the similar games of boules Lyonnaise (played with larger balls) and rafle.

Pétanque World Championships

The World Championships were inaugurated in 1959 and in 2000 a new event was added – precision shooting. This competition involves shooting at various targets from different distances. The women's world championships are held separately.

Men's Triples

	Winner	Venue
1959	France	Spa, Belgium
1961	France	Cannes, France
1963	France	Casablanca, Morocco
1964	Algeria	Geneva, Switzerland
1965	Switzerland	Madrid, Spain
1966	Switzerland	Palma, Spain
1971	Spain	Nice, France
1972	France	Geneva, Switzerland
1973	Switzerland	Casablanca, Morocco
1974	France	Alicante, Spain
1975	Italy	Quebec, Canada
1976	France	Monaco
1977	France	Luxembourg
1978	Italy	Mons, Belgium
1979	Italy	Southampton, UK
1980	Switzerland	Nevers, France
1981	Belgium	Ghent, Belgium
1982	Monaco	Geneva, Switzerland
1983	Tunisia	Tunis, Tunisia
1984	Morocco	Rotterdam, The Netherlands
1985	France	Casablanca, Morocco
1986	Tunisia	Épinal, France
1987	Morocco	Boumerdes, Algeria
1988	France	Genoa, Italy
1989	France	Pineda de Mar, Spain
1990	Morocco	Monaco
1991	France	Les Escaldes, Andorra
1992	France	Aosta, Italy
1993	France	Chiang Mai, Thailand
1994	France	Clermont-Ferrand, France
1995	France	Brussels, Belgium
1996	France	Essen, Germany
1997	Tunisia	Montpellier, France
1998	France	Maspalomas, Spain
1999	Madagascar	St-Denis, Réunion
2000	Belgium	Faro, Portugal
2001	France	Monaco
2002	France	Grenoble, France
2003	France	Geneva, Switzerland
2004	France	Grenoble, France

Men's Precision Shooting

	Winner	Venue
2000	Philippe Quintais (France)	Faro, Portugal
2001	Philippe Quintais (France)	Monaco
2002	Philippe Quintais (France)	Grenoble, France

	Winner	Venue
2003	Philippe Quintais (France)	Geneva, Switzerland
2004	Samy Attalah (Tunisia)	Grenoble, France

Women's Triples

	Winner	Venue
1988	Thailand	Palma, Spain
1990	Thailand	Bangkok, Thailand
1992	France	Lausanne, Switzerland
1994	France	Luxembourg
1996	Spain	Pori, Finland
1998	Spain	Stockholm, Sweden
2000	Belgium	Hyères, France
2002	Spain	La Tuque, Canada
2004	Thailand	San Fernando, Spain

Women's Precision Shooting

	Winner	Venue
2002	Yolanda Mattaranz (Spain)	La Tuque, Canada
2004	Thongsri Thamakord (Thailand)	San Fernando, Spain

A-Z

carreau similar to **tirer** but with the advantage of leaving the attacking ball in the position vacated by the ball knocked away

cochonnet the target ball

mène the basic unit of the game, similar to an end in bowls

petit bois same as **cochonnet**

plomber the technique that sees the player toss the ball high in the air so that it lands near the **cochonnet** and stops dead

pointer the first ball played after the **cochonnet**

rouler the technique of rolling the ball along the ground

tirer the technique of throwing the ball onto the winning ball and knocking it away

BOWLS

Origins

It is believed that bowls developed from a game played by Egyptians with skittles with round stones. Variants of the game are now played around the world, eg in Italy (bocce), Denmark (bolle), France (boules; see above) and Polynesia (ula miaka). The oldest bowls green still in use is in Southampton, England, records showing that bowls have been played there since AD 1299. Henry VIII was a keen bowler but thought it should only be played by the nobility, banning 'Bowyers, Fletchers, Stringers and Arrowhead makers' from taking part as they were being distracted from their trades, and imposing a fee of 100 pounds for anyone who wanted to keep a private green. Bowls was introduced into North America in the early 17th century (George Washington is believed to have been a keen player). The game spread throughout the British Empire, with reports of it first being played in Canada (Nova Scotia) in 1730, Australia (Tasmania) in 1844, and New Zealand in 1860.

Rules and description

Outdoor or 'lawn' bowls is played in 44 countries worldwide on a flat lawn or 'green' surrounded by a shallow ditch, enclosed by a low bank and divided into strips known as 'rinks' on which each game takes place. Games are contested between individuals, or teams of two, three or four. Bowls (which are flattened on one side to give them a bias) are delivered alternately and rolled towards a small white target ball (the 'jack'), the aim being to place as many of your bowls as possible closer to the jack than your opponent's nearest bowl, one point counting for each. Each set of deliveries is called an 'end'. Singles is normally played to 21 shots, or to a sets format, with pairs and fours games being the best of 21 ends, and triples the best of 18. After each end, players play in the reverse direction, back up the rink. Bowlers must have one foot on or over a small mat when delivering the bowl. Similar rules apply for indoor bowls, although competitions are usually played on a piece of carpet with a single rink.

Crown green bowls is played predominantly in northern England on a square green, larger than that used for lawn bowls and with a raised 'crown' at the centre. Each player (the usual game is singles) bowls two bowls towards a 'jack' and, as in lawn bowls, counts a point for each bowl closer to the jack than his opponent's nearest bowl. Players start each new end from the position of the jack of the previous end. Games are usually played to 21 points.

Ruling bodies: World Bowls Ltd; World Indoor Bowls Council (WIBC); British Crown Green Bowling Association. The World Bowls Tour (WBT) stages professional events for members of the Professional Bowls Association (PBA)

Doctor Bowls

Dr W G Grace was not only a cricketing legend but also turned his hand to bowls, being the first President of the English Bowling Association when it was founded in 1903. It was at his suggestion that the first indoor bowls club was founded in 1906 at the Crystal Palace, London, where bowlers played on carpets placed in one of the long galleries.

Outdoor World Championships

The men's championships started in 1966 as a development of the Commonwealth Games, when the host country that year (Jamaica) was unable to include lawn bowls as it had no greens.

Bowls

Men

Leonard Trophy

Donated by William Leonard, the then managing director of the first sponsors of the event, Ampol. It is a team trophy, awarded to the country which has accumulated the most points in the championship.

	Winner	Venue
1966	Australia	Kyeemagh, New South Wales, Australia
1972	Scotland	Worthing, England
1976	South Africa	Johannesburg, South Africa
1980	England	Frankston, Victoria, Australia
1984	Scotland	Aberdeen, Scotland
1988	England	Auckland, New Zealand
1992	Scotland	Worthing, England
1996	Scotland	Adelaide, Australia
2000	Australia	Johannesburg, South Africa
2004	Scotland	Ayr, Scotland

	Men's singles	Men's pairs
1966	David Bryant (England)	Bert Palm & Geoff Kelly (Australia)
1972	Maldwyn Evans (Wales)	Clementi Cecil Delgado & Eric Liddell (Hong Kong)
1976	Doug Watson (South Africa)	Bill Moseley & Doug Watson (South Africa)
1980	David Bryant (England)	Alf Sandercock & Peter Rheuben (Australia)
1984	Peter Belliss (New Zealand)	George Adrain & Skippy Arculli (USA)
1988	David Bryant (England)	Rowan Brassey & Peter Belliss (New Zealand)
1992	Tony Allcock (England)	Richard Corsie & Alex Marshall (Scotland)
1996	Tony Allcock (England)	Jeremy Henry & Sammy Allen (Ireland)
2000	Jeremy Henry (Ireland)	George Sneddon & Alex Marshall (Scotland)
2004	Steve Glasson (Australia)	Keith Roney & Ryan Bester (Canada)

Women

The women's outdoor world championship was introduced in 1969 and held separately from the men's competition, although the two are due to be merged in Christchurch, New Zealand, in 2008.

	Team prize	Venue
1969	South Africa	Sydney, Australia
1973	New Zealand	Wellington, New Zealand
1977	Australia	Worthing, England
1981	England	Willowdale, Toronto, Canada
1985	Australia	Melbourne, Australia
1988	England	Henderson, Auckland, New Zealand
1992	Scotland	Ayr, Scotland
1996	South Africa	Royal Leamington Spa, England
2000	England	Moama, New South Wales, Australia
2004	England	Royal Leamington Spa, England

	Women's singles	Women's pairs
1969	Gladys Doyle (Papua New Guinea)	E Mcdonald & M Cridlan (South Africa)
1973	Elsie Wilkie (New Zealand)	Lorna Lucas & Dot Jenkinson (Australia)
1977	Elsie Wilkie (New Zealand)	Helen Wong & Elvie Chok (Hong Kong)
1981	Norma Shaw (England)	Eileen Bell & Nan Allely (Ireland)
1985	Merle Richardson (Australia)	Fay Craig & Merle Richardson (Australia)
1988	Janet Ackland (Wales)	Phillis Nolan & Margaret Johnston (Ireland)
1992	Margaret Johnston (Ireland)	Phillis Nolan & Margaret Johnston (Ireland)
1996	Carmen Anderson (Norfolk Island)	Phillis Nolan & Margaret Johnston (Ireland)
2000	Margaret Johnston (Ireland)	Margaret Letham & Joyce Lindores (Scotland)
2004	Margaret Johnston (Ireland)	Sharon Sims & Jo Edwards (New Zealand)

Commonwealth Games Champions

	Men's singles	Men's pairs
1930	Robert Colquhoun (England)	George Wright & Tommy Hills (England)
1934	Robert Sprot (Scotland)	George Wright & Tommy Hills (England)
1938	Horace Harvey (South Africa)	Lance Masey & Walter Denison (New Zealand)
1950	James Pirret (New Zealand)	Phil Exelby & Bob Henry (New Zealand)
1954	Ralph Hodges (S Rhodesia)	Percy Watson & William Rosbotham (Northern Ireland)
1958	Pinkie Danilowitz (South Africa)	John Morris & Richard Pilkington (New Zealand)
1962	David Bryant (England)	Hugh Robson & Bob McDonald (New Zealand)
1966	*Not held*	
1970	David Bryant (England)	Norman King & Peter Line (England)
1974	David Bryant (England)	John Christie & Alex McIntosh (Scotland)
1978	David Bryant (England)	Clementi Cecil Delgado & Eric Liddell (Hong Kong)
1982	Willie Wood (Scotland)	John Watson & David Gourlay, Sr (Scotland)
1986	Ian Dickison (New Zealand)	Grant Knox & George Adrain (Scotland)
1990	Rob Parrella (Australia)	Ian Schuback & Trevor Morris (Australia)
1994	Richard Corsie (Scotland)	Cameron Curtis & Rex Johnston (Australia)
1998	Roy Garden (Zimbabwe)	Brett Duprez & Mark Jacobsen (Australia)
2002	Bobby Donnelly (South Africa)	George Sneddon & Alex Marshall (Scotland)

	Women's singles	Women's pairs
1986	Wendy Line (England)	Freda Elliott & Margaret Johnston (Northern Ireland)
1990	Geua Vada Tau (Papua New Guinea)	Marie Watson & Judy Howat (New Zealand)
1994	Margaret Johnston (Northern Ireland)	Sarah Gourlay & Frances Whyte (Scotland)
1998	Lesly Hartwell (South Africa)	Margaret Letham & Joyce Lindores (Scotland)
2002	Siti Zalina Ahmad (Malaysia)	Sharon Sims & Jo Edwards (New Zealand)

World Indoor Championships

Men's singles

	Champion	Defeated finalist
1979	David Bryant (England)	Jimmy Donnelly (Ireland)
1980	David Bryant (England)	Philip Chok (Hong Kong)
1981	David Bryant (England)	John Thomas (Wales)

Bowls

	Champion	Defeated finalist
1982	John Watson (Scotland)	Jim Baker (Ireland)
1983	Bob Sutherland (Scotland)	Burnie Gill (Canada)
1984	Jim Baker (Ireland)	Nigel Smith (England)
1985	Terry Sullivan (Wales)	Cecil Bransky (Israel)
1986	Tony Allcock (England)	Phil Skoglund (New Zealand)
1987	Tony Allcock (England)	David Bryant (England)
1988	Hugh Duff (Scotland)	Wynne Richards (England)
1989	Richard Corsie (Scotland)	Willie Wood (Scotland)
1990	John Price (Wales)	Ian Schuback (Australia)
1991	Richard Corsie (Scotland)	Ian Schuback (Australia)
1992	Ian Schuback (Australia)	John Price (Wales)
1993	Richard Corsie (Scotland)	Jim McCann (Scotland)
1994	Andy Thomson (England)	Richard Corsie (Scotland)
1995	Andy Thomson (England)	Richard Corsie (Scotland)
1996	David Gourlay, Jr (Scotland)	Hugh Duff (Scotland)
1997	Hugh Duff (Scotland)	Andy Thomson (England)
1998	Paul Foster (Scotland)	Mervyn King (England)
1999	Alex Marshall (Scotland)	David Gourlay, Jr (Scotland)
2000	Robert Wheale (Wales)	John Price (Wales)
2001	Paul Foster (Scotland)	Richard Corsie (Scotland)
2002	Tony Allcock (England)	Richard Corsie (Scotland)
2003	Alex Marshall (Scotland)	John Price (Wales)
2004	Alex Marshall (Scotland)	Mark McMahon (Australia)

Men's pairs champions

1986	David Bryant & Tony Allcock (England)
1987	David Bryant & Tony Allcock (England)
1988	Jim Yates & Ian Schuback (Australia)
1989	David Bryant & Tony Allcock (England)
1990	David Bryant & Tony Allcock (England)
1991	David Bryant & Tony Allcock (England)
1992	David Bryant & Tony Allcock (England)
1993	Gary Smith & Andy Thomson (England)
1994	Cameron Curtis & Ian Schuback (Australia)
1995	Alex Marshall & Richard Corsie (Scotland)
1996	Kelvin Kerkow & Ian Schuback (Australia)
1997	Mervyn King & Tony Allcock (England)
1998	Graham Robertson & Richard Corsie (Scotland)
1999	Stephen Rees & John Price (Wales)
2000	David Gourlay, Jr & Alex Marshall (Scotland)
2001	Les Gillett & Mark McMahon (England)
2002	Hugh Duff & Paul Foster (Scotland)
2003	David Holt & Tony Allcock (England)
2004	Ian McClure & Jeremy Henry (Ireland)

Women's singles

	Champion	Defeated finalist
1988	Margaret Johnston (Ireland)	Edna Bessell (England)
1989	Margaret Johnston (Ireland)	Mavis Steele (England)
1990	Fleur Bougourd (Guernsey)	Liz Wren (Scotland)
1991	Mary Price (England)	Margaret Johnston (Ireland)
1992	Sarah Gourlay (Scotland)	Mary Price (England)
1993	Kate Adams (Scotland)	Jayne Roylance (England)
1994	Jan Woodley (Scotland)	Mary Price (England)
1995	Joyce Lindores (Scotland)	Margaret Johnston (Ireland)
1996	Sandy Hazell (England)	Jean Baker (England)
1997	Norma Shaw (England)	Caroline McAllister (Scotland)
1998	Caroline McAllister (Scotland)	Carol Ashby (England)
1999	Caroline McAllister (Scotland)	Kate Adams (Scotland)
2000	Marlene Castle (New Zealand)	Margaret Johnston (Ireland)
2001	Betty Brown (Scotland)	Marilyn Peddell (Australia)
2002	Carol Ashby (England)	Betty Morgan (Wales)
2003	Carol Ashby (England)	Wendy Jensen (New Zealand)
2004	Julie Forrest (Scotland)	Carol Ashby (England)

Better at warring than drawing

Bowls is associated with one of the best-loved stories of British history: of how, on 18 July 1588, Sir Francis Drake is said to have been playing a game at Plymouth Hoe when he was told that the Spanish Armada was approaching. His famous (probably apocryphal) reply was that 'We still have time to finish the game and to thrash the Spaniards, too'. He then proceeded to finish the match (which he lost) before setting off to take on the battle with the Armada (which he won).

A-Z

backhand — the left-hand side of the **rink** (for a right-handed bowler), where the bowl is delivered to the left and swings back to the right

blocker — a bowl played so that it finishes deliberately short of the **head**, making it harder for an opponent to attack the **jack**

carpet — the surface on which indoor bowls is played

dead — a bowl is dead if it rolls into the **ditch** without first touching the **jack** during its original course on the **green**, or if it goes out of play (off the **rink**)

dead draw — a **draw** played with **dead weight**

dead end — an end is termed dead, and has to be replayed, when the **jack** is hit off the **rink**, ie onto the next rink or beyond the bank

dead weight — if a bowler bowls a wood dead weight, it comes to rest right next to the **jack** or to a target bowl

ditch — the shallow trough around a **green** or at either end of an indoor **carpet**

draw — a gently delivered shot where the bowl curves in from the edge of the **rink** or **carpet**, towards the **head**

drive to bowl a straight fast bowl, eliminating the bias, with the intention of breaking up the **head** and/or sending the **jack** into the **ditch** or off the rink

end a complete sequence of play in one direction, at the end of which shots are counted and the score updated; so called because play alternates from one end of the **rink** to the other

fire same as **drive**

footer a round **mat** (sense 1) used in crown green bowls

forehand the right-hand side of the **rink** (for a right-handed bowler), where the bowl is delivered to the right and swings back to the left

green a 34–40m square area of closely cut grass on which outdoor bowls is played

head the collection of bowls around the **jack**

jack the small, usually white (although sometimes yellow) object ball; in crown green bowls it has a bias

jack high a bowl that is jack high is level with the **jack**; this term is now officially obsolete

lead the first bowler in a team, who also bowls the **jack**

lollipops small coloured lollipop-shaped pieces of plastic held up by the **marker** to indicate the number of shots gained in an **end**

marker the official who assists the players in a singles game, placing the **jack** in the centre of the **rink**, answering questions, keeping the score etc

mat 1. the small, rectangular piece of rubber on which a bowler has his or her back foot when delivering a bowl 2. same as **carpet**

measure a situation when the naked eye cannot determine which bowl is closer to the **jack**; measuring devices are then used, at the completion of the end, to decide

rink 1. one of the playing areas into which a **green** is divided 2. a team of four bowlers

shortmat bowls a variety of the game played on a mat measuring 40–45 x 6ft with full-size bowls, with a block placed in the centre of the mat which prevents bowlers from driving, all bowls having to curl around the block

shot 1. the point gained for having a bowl closer to the **jack** than your opponent's nearest bowl, eg *she picked up two shots in the third end* 2. the position closest to the **jack**, eg *Corke has shot*

shot bowl the bowl that is closest to the **jack**

skip the captain of a team, who dictates tactics and bowls last

three the third bowler in a **rink**, who assists the **skip** and normally measures disputed shots

toucher a bowl that touches the **jack** during its original course on the green; all such bowls are marked with chalk, sometimes sprayed on, and are live even if knocked into the **ditch**

trail the jack a bowler trails the **jack** when a bowl in motion hits it flush and moves it away in the same direction as the path of the bowl

two the second bowler in a **rink**, who is normally expected to keep the scorecard up to date

umpire the official who is responsible for ensuring that the laws are adhered to

wood a bowl; formerly made of heavy-density wood (lignum vitae) and then rubber; modern bowls are made from a composite material

Some famous bowlers

Tony Allcock, 1955–

Born in Leicester, England, he formed with **David Bryant** an all-conquering pairs team, taking six world indoor titles, and he added to that tally with two more wins in 1997 and 2003 with different partners. He has also won the world indoor singles three times (1986, 1987 and 2002) and the outdoor twice (1992, 1996). An MBE, he is chief executive of the English Bowling Association; outside bowls he is also well known in the dog-breeding world as a breeder of Japanese chins.

David Bryant, 1931–

Born in Clevedon, Somerset, England, he is unquestionably the most famous and successful bowler of all time. In the course of a long career, he won the world outdoor singles gold three times (1966, 1980 and 1988), and the world indoor singles three times (1979–81), as well as five Commonwealth Games medals. With **Tony Allcock**, he won the world indoor pairs no fewer than six times. Known for his trademark pipe, he was awarded the MBE in 1960 and the CBE in 1980.

Margaret Johnston, 1943–

Born in Upperlands, County Londonderry, Northen Ireland, she is universally regarded as the best woman bowler ever. After winning the Commonwealth Games pairs title in 1986, she has lifted the world outdoor singles three times, the indoor singles twice, and, with Dublin's Phillis Nolan, the outdoor pairs three times. She was awarded the MBE for services to bowls.

Alex Marshall, 1967–

Born in Edinburgh, Scotland, and nicknamed 'Tattie', he is one of the leading bowlers in the world, having won the world indoor singles championship three times (1999, 2003 and 2004), the world indoor pairs title twice (1995 and 2000) and the world outdoor pairs championship twice (1992 and 2000). He works as a sales representative for a leading firm of bowls distributors.

Willie Wood, 1938–

Born in Haddington, Scotland, this most appropriately-named bowler played in a record-breaking seven Commonwealth Games (taking gold in the 1982 men's singles) and is the most capped Scottish Commonwealth Games athlete ever. He twice took silver in the outdoor world championships (in 1984 and 1988) and was awarded the MBE in 1992.

BOXING

Origins

Fighting with fists can be traced back over 6000 years to the part of Africa now known as Ethiopia. It reached Egypt and then eventually spread throughout the

Mediterranean region. Homer mentions boxing in the *Iliad* and it became an Olympic sport in 688 BC. The Greeks wore leather gloves and protective headguards; they also used punchbags for training. The ancient Roman version of boxing was a far more brutal affair; iron-studded gauntlets were used and bouts were often fought to the death. The sport died out after the fall of the western Roman empire in AD 476 and did not reappear in Europe until the 17th century. It was revived in England and James Figg became Britain's first heavyweight champion in 1719. His successor, Jack Broughton, drew up a set of rules (1743) to make bouts less like street fighting and more like the sport we know today. A ring of spectators was replaced by a square bounded by ropes, and hitting below the belt was outlawed. The era of bareknuckle boxing lasted until 1866 when the Marquess of Queensberry drew up the rules that are still used to govern boxing today. The use of gloves became mandatory, gouging and wrestling were outlawed, and three-minute rounds were introduced. Gloveless bouts became far less common and the modern era of boxing was ushered in when James J Corbett defeated the last of the great bareknuckle boxers, John L Sullivan, in 1892 under the new rules for the heavyweight championship of the world.

Rules and description

A combat sport in which two boxers (usually men; official matches between women were only introduced in 1993) trade punches with fists enclosed in leather gloves weighing 6 to 8oz. Matches ('bouts') take place in a square ring (3.7 to 6.1m/4.04 to 6.67yd on each side) enclosed by ropes. Amateur fights consist of three three-minute rounds, professional fights last up to twelve rounds. Bouts are won if a boxer is sent to the floor by a punch and cannot get up within a count of ten by the referee (a 'knockout') or by one boxer landing more scoring hits (clean punches landed with force on the front or side of the opponent's head or on his body above an imaginary belt around his waist). A doctor or the referee can also intervene and stop the fight if one boxer is considered too injured or defenceless to carry on.

Ruling bodies: The professional sport is governed by the following organizations: International Boxing Federation (IBF); World Boxing Association (WBA); World Boxing Council (WBC); World Boxing Foundation (WBF); World Boxing Organization (WBO). Amateur boxing is governed by the Association Internationale de Boxe Amateur (AIBA)

Professional Boxing Weight Categories

mini flyweight/strawweight	under 48kg/105lb
light flyweight/junior flyweight	maximum 49kg/108lb
flyweight	maximum 51kg/112lb
superflyweight/junior bantamweight	maximum 52kg/115lb
bantamweight	maximum 54kg/118lb
superbantamweight/junior featherweight	maximum 55kg/122lb
featherweight	maximum 57kg/126lb
superfeatherweight/junior lightweight	maximum 59kg/130lb
lightweight	maximum 61kg/135lb

superlightweight/junior welterweight	maximum 63.5kg/140lb
welterweight	maximum 67kg/147lb
superwelterweight/junior middleweight	maximum 70kg/154lb
middleweight	maximum 73kg/160lb
supermiddleweight	maximum 76kg/168lb
light heavyweight	maximum 79kg/175lb
cruiserweight	maximum 86kg/190lb
heavyweight	above 86kg/190lb
superheavyweight (amateur only)	above 91kg/201lb

Professional World Heavyweight Title Fights

Boxers are US unless specified.

	Champion	Title	Opponent
1892	James J Corbett	undisputed	John L Sullivan
1894	James J Corbett	undisputed	Charlie Mitchell (Great Britain)
1897	Bob Fitzsimmons (Great Britain)	undisputed	James J Corbett
1899	James J Jeffries	undisputed	Bob Fitzsimmons (Great Britain)
1899	James J Jeffries	undisputed	Tom Sharkey (Ireland)
1900	James J Jeffries	undisputed	James J Corbett
1901	James J Jeffries	undisputed	Gus Ruhlin
1902	James J Jeffries	undisputed	Bob Fitzsimmons (Great Britain)
1903	James J Jeffries	undisputed	James J Corbett
1904	James J Jeffries	undisputed	Jack Monroe
1905	Marvin Hart	undisputed	Jack Root
1906	Tommy Burns (Canada)	undisputed	Marvin Hart
1906	Tommy Burns (Canada)	undisputed	Jim Flynn
1906	Tommy Burns (Canada)	undisputed	Jack O'Brien
1907	Tommy Burns (Canada)	undisputed	Jack O'Brien
1907	Tommy Burns (Canada)	undisputed	Bill Squires (Australia)
1907	Tommy Burns (Canada)	undisputed	Gunner Moir (Great Britain)
1908	Tommy Burns (Canada)	undisputed	Jack Palmer (Great Britain)
1908	Tommy Burns (Canada)	undisputed	Jem Roche (Ireland)
1908	Tommy Burns (Canada)	undisputed	Jewey Smith (Great Britain)
1908	Tommy Burns (Canada)	undisputed	Bill Squires (Australia)
1908	Tommy Burns (Canada)	undisputed	Bill Squires (Australia)
1908	Tommy Burns (Canada)	undisputed	Bill Laing (Australia)
1908	Jack Johnson	undisputed	Tommy Burns (Canada)
1915	Jess Willard	undisputed	Jack Johnson
1916	Jess Willard	undisputed	Frank Moran
1919	Jack Dempsey	undisputed	Jess Willard
1920	Jack Dempsey	undisputed	Billy Miske
1920	Jack Dempsey	undisputed	Bill Brennan
1921	Jack Dempsey	undisputed	Georges Carpentier (France)
1923	Jack Dempsey	undisputed	Tom Gibbons
1923	Jack Dempsey	undisputed	Luis Firpo (Argentina)
1926	Gene Tunney	undisputed	Jack Dempsey
1927	Gene Tunney	undisputed	Jack Dempsey

	Champion	Title	Opponent
1928	Gene Tunney	undisputed	Tom Heeney (New Zealand)
1930	Max Schmeling (Germany)	undisputed	Jack Sharkey
1931	Max Schmeling (Germany)	undisputed	William 'Young' Stribling
1932	Jack Sharkey	undisputed	Max Schmeling (Germany)
1933	Primo Carnera (Italy)	undisputed	Jack Sharkey
1933	Primo Carnera (Italy)	undisputed	Paolino Uzcudun (Spain)
1934	Primo Carnera (Italy)	undisputed	Tommy Loughran
1934	Max Baer	undisputed	Primo Carnera (Italy)
1935	James J Braddock	undisputed	Max Baer
1937	Joe Louis	undisputed	James J Braddock
1937	Joe Louis	undisputed	Tommy Farr (Great Britain)
1938	Joe Louis	undisputed	Nathan Mann
1938	Joe Louis	undisputed	Harry Thomas
1938	Joe Louis	undisputed	Max Schmeling (Germany)
1939	Joe Louis	undisputed	John Henry Lewis
1939	Joe Louis	undisputed	Jack Roper
1939	Joe Louis	undisputed	Tony Galento
1939	Joe Louis	undisputed	Bob Pastor
1940	Joe Louis	undisputed	Arturo Godoy (Chile)
1940	Joe Louis	undisputed	Johnny Paycheck
1940	Joe Louis	undisputed	Arturo Godoy
1940	Joe Louis	undisputed	Al McCoy
1941	Joe Louis	undisputed	Red Burman
1941	Joe Louis	undisputed	Gus Dorazio
1941	Joe Louis	undisputed	Abe Simon
1941	Joe Louis	undisputed	Tony Musto
1941	Joe Louis	undisputed	Buddy Baer
1941	Joe Louis	undisputed	Billy Conn
1941	Joe Louis	undisputed	Lou Nova
1942	Joe Louis	undisputed	Buddy Baer
1942	Joe Louis	undisputed	Abe Simon
1946	Joe Louis	undisputed	Billy Conn
1946	Joe Louis	undisputed	Tami Mauriello
1947	Joe Louis	undisputed	Jersey Joe Walcott
1948	Joe Louis	undisputed	Jersey Joe Walcott
1949	Ezzard Charles	undisputed	Jersey Joe Walcott
1949	Ezzard Charles	undisputed	Gus Lesnevich
1949	Ezzard Charles	undisputed	Pat Valentino
1950	Ezzard Charles	undisputed	Freddie Beshore
1950	Ezzard Chalres	undisputed	Joe Louis
1950	Ezzard Charles	undisputed	Nick Barone
1951	Ezzard Charles	undisputed	Lee Oma
1951	Ezzard Charles	undisputed	Jersey Joe Walcott
1951	Ezzard Charles	undisputed	Joey Maxim
1951	Jersey Joe Walcott	undisputed	Ezzard Charles
1952	Jersey Joe Walcott	undisputed	Ezzard Charles
1952	Rocky Marciano	undisputed	Jersey Joe Walcott
1953	Rocky Marciano	undisputed	Jersey Joe Walcott
1954	Rocky Marciano	undisputed	Ezzard Charles

	Champion	Title	Opponent
1954	Rocky Marciano	undisputed	Ezzard Charles
1955	Rocky Marciano	undisputed	Don Cockell
1955	Rocky Marciano	undisputed	Archie Moore
1956	Floyd Patterson	undisputed	Archie Moore
1957	Floyd Patterson	undisputed	Tommy Jackson
1958	Floyd Patterson	undisputed	Roy Harris
1959	Floyd Patterson	undisputed	Brian London (Great Britain)
1959	Ingemar Johansson (Sweden)	undisputed	Floyd Patterson
1960	Floyd Patterson	undisputed	Ingemar Johansson (Sweden)
1961	Floyd Patterson	undisputed	Ingemar Johansson (Sweden)
1961	Floyd Patterson	undisputed	Tom McNeeley
1962	Sonny Liston	undisputed	Floyd Patterson
1963	Sonny Liston	undisputed	Floyd Patterson
1964	Cassius Clay	undisputed	Sonny Liston
1965	Ernie Terrell	WBA	Eddie Machen
1965	Muhammad Ali	WBC	Sonny Liston
1965	Ernie Terrell	WBA	George Chuvalo (Canada)
1965	Muhammad Ali	WBC	Floyd Patterson
1966	Muhammad Ali	WBC	George Chuvalo (Canada)
1966	Muhammad Ali	WBC	Henry Cooper (Great Britain)
1967	Muhammad Ali	undisputed	Ernie Terrell
1967	Muhammad Ali	undisputed	Zora Folley
1968	Joe Frazier	WBC	Buster Mathis
1968	Jimmy Ellis	WBA	Floyd Patterson
1968	Joe Frazier	WBC	Oscar Bonavena (Argentina)
1969	Joe Frazier	WBC	Jerry Quarry
1970	Joe Frazier	undisputed	Jimmy Ellis
1970	Joe Frazier	undisputed	Bob Foster
1971	Joe Frazier	undisputed	Muhammad Ali
1972	Joe Frazier	undisputed	Ron Stander
1973	George Foreman	undisputed	Joe Frazier
1973	George Foreman	undisputed	Jose Roman (Puerto Rico)
1974	George Foreman	undisputed	Ken Norton
1974	Muhammad Ali	undisputed	George Foreman
1975	Muhammad Ali	undisputed	Chuck Wepner
1975	Muhammad Ali	undisputed	Ron Lyle
1975	Muhammad Ali	undisputed	Joe Bugner (Great Britain)
1975	Muhammad Ali	undisputed	Joe Frazier
1976	Muhammad Ali	undisputed	Jean-Pierre Coopman (Belgium)
1976	Muhammad Ali	undisputed	Jimmy Young
1976	Muhammad Ali	undisputed	Richard Dunn (Great Britain)
1976	Muhammad Ali	undisputed	Ken Norton
1977	Muhammad Ali	undisputed	Alfredo Evangelista (Italy)
1977	Muhammad Ali	undisputed	Earnie Shavers
1978	Leon Spinks	undisputed	Muhammad Ali
1978	Larry Holmes	WBC	Ken Norton
1978	Muhammad Ali	WBA	Leon Spinks
1978	Larry Holmes	WBC	Alfredo Evangelista (Italy)
1979	Larry Holmes	WBC	Ossie Ocasio (Puerto Rico)

	Champion	Title	Opponent
1979	Larry Holmes	WBC	Mike Weaver
1979	Larry Holmes	WBC	Earnie Shavers
1979	John Tate	WBA	Gerrie Coetzee (South Africa)
1980	Larry Holmes	WBC	Lorenzo Zanon (Italy)
1980	Mike Weaver	WBA	John Tate
1981	Larry Holmes	WBC	Trevor Berbick (Jamaica)
1981	Larry Holmes	WBC	Leon Spinks
1981	Mike Weaver	WBA	James Tillis
1981	Larry Holmes	WBC	Renaldo Snipes
1982	Larry Holmes	WBC	Gerry Cooney
1982	Larry Holmes	WBC	Randall 'Tex' Cobb
1982	Michael Dokes	WBA	Mike Weaver
1983	Larry Holmes	WBC	Lucien Rodriguez (France)
1983	Michael Dokes	WBA	Mike Weaver
1983	Larry Holmes	WBC	Tim Witherspoon
1983	Larry Holmes	WBC	Scott Frank
1983	Gerrie Coetzee (South Africa)	WBA	Michael Dokes
1984	Larry Holmes	WBC	Marvis Frazier
1984	Tim Witherspoon	WBC	Greg Page
1984	Pinklon Thomas	WBC	Tim Witherspoon
1984	Larry Holmes	IBF	James 'Bonecrusher' Smith
1984	Greg Page	WBA	Gerrie Coetzee (South Africa)
1985	Larry Holmes	IBF	David Bey
1985	Tony Tubbs	WBA	Greg Page
1985	Larry Holmes	IBF	Carl Williams
1985	Pinklon Thomas	WBC	Mike Weaver
1985	Michael Spinks	IBF	Larry Holmes
1986	Tim Witherspoon	WBA	Tony Tubbs
1986	Trevor Berbick (Canada)	WBC	Pinklon Thomas
1986	Michael Spinks	IBF	Larry Holmes
1986	Tim Witherspoon	WBC	Frank Bruno (Great Britain)
1986	Michael Spinks	IBF	Steffen Tangstad (Norway)
1986	Mike Tyson	WBC	Trevor Berbick (Canada)
1986	James 'Bonecrusher' Smith	WBA	Tim Witherspoon
1987	Mike Tyson	WBC	James 'Bonecrusher' Smith
1987	Mike Tyson	WBC	Pinklon Thomas
1987	Tony Tucker	IBF	James 'Buster' Douglas
1987	Mike Tyson	undisputed	Tony Tucker
1987	Mike Tyson	undisputed	Tyrell Biggs
1988	Mike Tyson	undisputed	Larry Holmes
1988	Mike Tyson	undisputed	Tony Tubbs
1988	Mike Tyson	undisputed	Michael Spinks
1989	Mike Tyson	undisputed	Frank Bruno
1989	Mike Tyson	undisputed	Carl Williams
1989	Francesco Damiani (Italy)	WBO	Johnny du Plooy (South Africa)
1989	Francesco Damiani (Italy)	WBO	Daniel Netto (Argentina)
1990	James 'Buster' Douglas	undisputed	Mike Tyson
1990	Evander Holyfield	undisputed	James 'Buster' Douglas
1990	Evander Holyfield	undisputed	George Foreman

	Champion	Title	Opponent
1991	Evander Holyfield	undisputed	Bert Cooper
1991	Ray Mercer	WBO	Francesco Damiani (Italy)
1991	Ray Mercer	WBO	Tommy Morrison
1992	Evander Holyfield	undisputed	Larry Holmes
1992	Riddick Bowe	undisputed	Evander Holyfield
1992	Michael Moorer	WBO	Bert Cooper
1993	Riddick Bowe	WBA	Michael Dokes
1993	Lennox Lewis	WBC	Tony Tucker
1993	Riddick Bowe	WBA	Jesse Ferguson
1993	Tommy Morrison	WBO	George Foreman
1993	Lennox Lewis	WBC	Frank Bruno (Great Britain)
1993	Evander Holyfield	WBA	Riddick Bowe
1993	Michael Bentt	WBO	Tommy Morrison
1994	Michael Moorer	WBA	Evander Holyfield
1994	Lennox Lewis	WBC	Phil Jackson
1994	Oliver McCall	WBC	Lennox Lewis
1994	George Foreman	WBA	Michael Moorer
1994	Herbie Hide (Great Britain)	WBO	Michael Bentt
1995	Oliver McCall	WBC	Larry Holmes
1995	Riddick Bowe	WBO	Herbie Hide (Great Britain)
1995	Bruce Seldon	WBA	Tony Tucker
1995	George Foreman	IBF	Axel Schultz (Germany)
1995	Tony LaRosa	IBO	Frank Hinton
1995	Bruce Seldon	WBA	Joe Hipp
1995	Riddick Bowe	WBO	Jorge Luis Gonzalez (Cuba)
1995	Frank Bruno (Great Britain)	WBC	Oliver McCall
1995	Frans Botha (South Africa)	IBF	Axel Schultz (Germany)
1996	Brian Nielson	IBO	Tony LaRosa
1996	Mike Tyson	WBC	Frank Bruno (Great Britain)
1996	Henry Akinwande (Great Britain)	WBO	Jeremy Williams
1996	Brian Nielson	IBO	Phil Jackson
1996	Brian Nielson	IBO	Mike Hunter
1996	Michael Moorer	IBF	Axel Schultz (Germany)
1996	Henry Akinwande (Great Britain)	WBO	Aleksandr Zolkin (Russia)
1996	Mike Tyson	WBA	Bruce Seldon
1996	Evander Holyfield	WBA	Mike Tyson
1996	Michael Moorer	IBF	Frans Botha (South Africa)
1997	Brian Nielson	IBO	Larry Holmes
1997	Henry Akinwande (Great Britain)	WBO	Scott Welch (Great Britain)
1997	Lennox Lewis (Great Britain)	WBC	Oliver McCall
1997	Herbie Hide (Great Britain)	WBO	Tony Tucker
1997	Michael Moorer	IBF	Vaughn Bean
1997	Evander Holyfield	WBA	Mike Tyson
1997	Lennox Lewis (Great Britain)	WBC	Henry Akinwande (Great Britain)
1997	Lennox Lewis (Great Britain)	WBC	Andrew Golota (Poland)
1997	Herbie Hide (Great Britain)	WBO	Tony Tucker
1997	Evander Holyfield	WBA	Michael Moorer
1997	Brian Nielson	IBO	Don Steele
1998	Herbie Hide (Great Britain)	WBO	Damon Reed

	Champion	Title	Opponent
1998	Lennox Lewis (Great Britain)	WBC	Shannon Briggs
1998	Brian Nielsen	IBO	Lionel Butler
1998	Evander Holyfield	IBF	Vaughn Bean
1998	Herbie Hide (Great Britain)	WBO	Willi Fischer (Germany)
1998	Lennox Lewis (Great Britain)	WBC	Zeljko Mavrovic (Croatia)
1999	Vitali Klitschko (Ukraine)	WBO	Herbie Hide (Great Britain)
1999	Vitali Klitschko (Ukraine)	WBO	Ed Mahone
1999	Lennox Lewis (Great Britain)	undisputed	Evander Holyfield
1999	Vitali Klitschko (Ukraine)	WBO	Obed Sullivan
1999	Lennox Lewis (Great Britain)	undisputed	Evander Holyfield
2000	Lennox Lewis (Great Britain)	WBC	Michael Grant
2000	Chris Byrd (USA)	WBO	Vitali Klitschko (Ukraine)
2000	Lennox Lewis (Great Britain)	WBC	Frans Botha (South Africa)
2000	Evander Holyfield	WBA	John Ruiz
2000	Vladimir Klitschko (Ukraine)	WBO	Chris Byrd
2000	Lennox Lewis (Great Britain)	IBF	David Tua (Samoa)
2001	John Ruiz	WBA	Evander Holyfield
2001	Vladimir Klitschko (Ukraine)	WBO	Derrick Jefferson
2001	Hasim Rahman	WBC	Lennox Lewis (Great Britain)
2001	Lennox Lewis (Great Britain)	WBC	Hasim Rahman
2001	John Ruiz	WBA	Evander Holyfield
2001	Vladimir Klitschko (Ukraine)	WBO	Charles Shufford
2002	Lennox Lewis (Great Britain)	WBC	Mike Tyson
2002	John Ruiz	WBA	Kirk Johnson
2002	Vladimir Klitschko (Ukraine)	WBO	Frans Botha (South Africa)
2002	Vladimir Klitschko (Ukraine)	WBO	Ray Mercer
2002	Chris Byrd	IBF	Evander Holyfield
2002	Vladimir Klitschko (Ukraine)	WBO	Jameel McCline
2003	Corrie Sanders (South Africa)	WBO	Vladimir Klitschko (Ukraine)
2003	Roy Jones, Jr	WBA	John Ruiz
2003	Lennox Lewis (Great Britain)	WBC	Vitali Klitschko (Ukraine)
2003	Chris Byrd	IBF	Fres Oquendo (Puerto Rico)
2004	Lamon Brewster	WBO	Vladimir Klitschko (Ukraine)
2004	John Ruiz	WBA	Fres Oquendo (Puerto Rico)
2004	Chris Byrd	IBF	Andrew Golota (Poland)
2004	Lamon Brewster	WBO	Kali Meehan (Australia)
2004	Vitali Klitschko (Ukraine)	WBC	Corrie Sanders (South Africa)
2004	Chris Byrd	IBF	Jameel McCline
2004	John Ruiz	WBA	Andrew Golota (Poland)
2004	Vitali Klitschko (Ukraine)	WBC	Danny Williams (Great Britain)

Pop that packed a punch

Irish featherweight champion Barry McGuigan has two connections with the world of popular music. In 1968 his father Pat represented Ireland in the European Song Contest, performing third-placed 'A Chance of a Lifetime'. In 1986, after Barry had won the world title, comedian Dermot Morgan (later of Father Ted fame) released 'Thank you very much, Mr Eastwood'. The song, which got to number one in Ireland, gently satirizes McGuigan's modesty and his devotion to his manager, Barney Eastwood, whom he was in the habit of praising at every opportunity.

British Heavyweight Title Fights

	Winner	Opponent
1895	Jem Smith	Ted Pritchard
1901	Jack Scales	Cloggy Saunders
1901	Jack Scales	Jack Palmer
1902	Jack Scales	Ben Taylor
1902	Jack Scales	Harry Dixon
1902	Charlie Wilson	Jack Scales
1903	Jack Palmer	Ben Taylor
1905	Jack Palmer	Geoffrey Thorne
1906	Gunner Moir	Jack Palmer
1907	Gunner Moir	James Smith
1909	William Hague	Gunner Moir
1910	William Hague	Jewey Smith
1910	William Hague	Jewey Smith
1911	Billy Wells	William Hague
1913	Billy Wells	Packey Mahoney
1913	Billy Wells	Pat O'Keefe
1913	Billy Wells	Gunner Moir
1914	Billy Wells	Gus Rawles
1914	Billy Wells	Jack Blake
1914	Billy Wells	Bandsman Rice
1915	Billy Wells	Bandsman Rice
1915	Billy Wells	Dick Smith
1915	Billy Wells	Bandsman Rice
1916	Billy Wells	Dick Smith
1916	Billy Wells	P O Curran
1916	Billy Wells	Dick Smith
1916	Billy Wells	Dan Voyles
1919	Joe Beckett	Billy Wells
1919	Frank Goddard	Jack Curphy
1920	Joe Beckett	Dick Smith
1920	Joe Beckett	Billy Wells
1921	Joe Beckett	Boy McCormick
1923	Joe Beckett	Dick Smith
1923	Frank Goddard	Jack Bloomfield
1924	Frank Goddard	Jack Stanley
1926	Phil Scott	Frank Goddard
1926	Phil Scott	Boy McCormick
1931	Reggie Meen	Charlie Smith
1932	Jack Petersen	Reggie Meen
1933	Jack Petersen	Jack Pettifer
1933	Len Harvey	Jack Petersen
1934	Jack Petersen	Len Harvey
1934	Jack Petersen	George Cook
1936	Jack Petersen	Len Harvey
1936	Jack Petersen	Jock McAvoy
1936	Ben Foord	Jack Petersen
1937	Tommy Farr	Ben Foord

What's in a name?

Jersey Joe Walcott was a powerful presence in the boxing ring. In the early 50s he won the world heavyweight title, and so became the most feared man in sport. Perhaps he would have seemed a less terrifying figure to his opponents had they known his real name, the less than rugged Arnold Cream.

I coulda been a virtuoso

Heavyweight legend Joe Louis, the world champion who made a record 25 defences of his title during the 30s and 40s, could have had a rather different career had he followed his parents' instructions. When 12 years old he was given money and told to learn the violin. However, instead of practising his scales he skipped class and spent the cash on boxing lessons.

Boxing

	Winner	Opponent
1938	Len Harvey	Eddie Phillips
1944	Jack London	Freddie Mills
1945	Bruce Woodcock	Jack London
1946	Bruce Woodcock	Freddie Mills
1949	Bruce Woodcock	Freddie Mills
1950	Jack Gardner	Bruce Woodcock
1952	Johnny Williams	Jack Gardner
1953	Don Cockell	Johnny Williams
1956	Joe Erskine	Johnny Williams
1957	Joe Erskine	Henry Cooper
1958	Brian London	Joe Erskine
1959	Henry Cooper	Brian London
1961	Henry Cooper	Joe Erskine
1962	Henry Cooper	Joe Erskine
1963	Henry Cooper	Dick Richardson
1964	Henry Cooper	Brian London
1965	Henry Cooper	Johnny Prescott
1967	Henry Cooper	Jack Bodell
1967	Henry Cooper	Billy Walker
1969	Jack Bodell	Carl Gizzi
1970	Henry Cooper	Jack Bodell
1971	Joe Bugner	Henry Cooper
1971	Jack Bodell	Joe Bugner
1972	Danny McAlinden	Jack Bodell
1975	Bunny Johnson	Danny McAlinden
1975	Richard Dunn	Bunny Johnson
1975	Richard Dunn	Danny McAlinden
1976	Joe Bugner	Richard Dunn
1978	John Gardner	Billy Aird
1979	John Gardner	Paul Sykes
1981	Gordon Ferris	Billy Aird
1981	Neville Meade	Gordon Ferris
1983	David Pearce	Neville Meade
1985	Hughroy Currie	Funso Banjo
1986	Horace Notice	Hughroy Currie
1987	Horace Notice	Dave Garside
1987	Horace Notice	Paul Lister
1988	Horace Notice	Hughroy Currie
1989	Gary Mason	Hughroy Currie
1989	Gary Mason	Jess Harding
1991	Lennox Lewis	Gary Mason
1991	Lennox Lewis	Glenn McCrory
1992	Lennox Lewis	Derek Williams
1993	Herbie Hide	Michael Murray
1994	James Oyebola	Clifton Mitchell
1995	Scott Welch	James Oyebola
1997	Julius Francis	Garry Delaney
1999	Julius Francis	Pele Reid
1999	Julius Francis	Danny Williams

Boxer dwarfed by devotees

Sugar Ray Robinson was a boxer of almost superhuman strength and endurance. However, outside the ring he liked to pamper himself, particularly when he was on tour. In one visit to Europe in 1951, the world middleweight champion brought with him an entourage that included a hairdresser, a masseur, a shoeshine man, and, most strange of all, a dwarf.

	Winner	Opponent
1999	Julius Francis	Scott Welch
2000	Michael Holden	Julius Francis
2000	Danny Williams	Mark Potter
2001	Danny Williams	Julius Francis
2002	Danny Williams	Michael Sprott
2002	Danny Williams	Keith Long
2003	Danny Williams	Michael Sprott
2004	Michael Sprott	Danny Williams
2004	Matt Skelton	Michael Sprott
2004	Matt Skelton	Keith Long

Olympic Light Heavyweight Boxing Champions

Introduced in 1920.

1920 Eddie Eagen (USA)
1924 Harry Mitchell (Great Britain)
1928 Victor Avendaño (Argentina)
1932 David Carstens (South Africa)
1936 Roger Michelot (France)
1948 George Hunter (South Africa)
1952 Norvel Lee (USA)
1956 James Boyd (USA)
1960 Cassius Clay (USA)
1964 Cosimo Pinto (Italy)
1968 Danas Pozniakas (USSR)
1972 Mate Parlov (Yugoslavia)
1976 Leon Spinks (USA)
1980 Slobodan Kacar (Yugoslavia)
1984 Anton Josipovic (Yugoslavia)
1988 Andrew Maynard (USA)
1992 Torsten May (Germany)
1996 Vasiliy Zhirov (Kazakhstan)
2000 Aleksandr Lebziak (Russia)
2004 Andre Ward (USA)

Olympic Heavyweight Boxing Champions

Introduced in 1904.

1904 Samuel Berger (USA)
1908 Albert Oldham (Great Britain)
1912 *Not held*
1920 Ronald Rawson (Great Britain)
1924 Otto von Porat (Norway)
1928 Arturo Rodriguez Jurado (Argentina)
1932 Santiago Lovell (Argentina)
1936 Herbert Runge (Germany)
1948 Rafael Iglesias (Argentina)
1952 H Edward Sanders (USA)
1956 Peter Rademacher (USA)
1960 Franco De Piccolo (Italy)
1964 Joe Frazier (USA)
1968 George Foreman (USA)
1972 Teofilo Stevenson (Cuba)
1976 Teofilo Stevenson (Cuba)
1980 Teofilo Stevenson (Cuba)
1984 Henry Tillman (USA)
1988 Ray Mercer (USA)
1992 Felix Savon (Cuba)
1996 Felix Savon (Cuba)
2000 Felix Savon (Cuba)
2004 Odlanier Solis Fonte (Cuba)

Olympic Superheavyweight Boxing Champions

Introduced in 1984.

1984	Tyrell Biggs (USA)	**1996**	Vladimir Klitschko (Ukraine)
1988	Lennox Lewis (Canada)	**2000**	Audley Harrison (Great Britain)
1992	Roberto Balado (Cuba)	**2004**	Aleksandr Povetkin (Russia)

Nicknames

Some boxers' nicknames have become so fixed that they are routinely used when referring to them, eg Sugar Ray Robinson and Buster Douglas. Here is a selection of some of the better known:

Muhammad Ali	'The Louisville Lip', 'The Greatest'
Rocky Balboa	'The Italian Stallion'
Jim Corbett	'Gentleman Jim'
Jack Dempsey	'The Manassa Mauler'
James Douglas	'Buster'
Roberto Duran	'Hands of Stone' (because of the strength of his punch)
Joe Frazier	'Smokin' Joe'
Tony Galento	'Two Ton Tony'
Marvin Hagler	'Marvellous'
Tommy Hearns	'The Hitman'
Evander Holyfield	'The Real Deal'
Oscar de la Hoya	'The Golden Boy' (because he won an Olympic gold in 1992 and because of his good looks)
Joe Louis	'The Brown Bomber'
Rocky Marciano	'The Brockton Blockbuster' (because he was born in Brockton, Massachusetts)
Jake La Motta	'Raging Bull'
Archie Moore	'The Mongoose' (because of his defensive skills)
Hasim Rahman	'The Rock'
Ray Robinson	'Sugar'
Donovan Ruddock	'Razor'
James Smith	'Bonecrusher'
Mike Tyson	'Iron Mike'
Pernell Whitaker	'Sweet Pea'

A-Z

apron	that part of a boxing **ring** that extends beyond the ropes
belt	an imaginary line from the top of the hips to the navel, below which boxers are not allowed to punch their opponent
blocking	the use of the shoulders, arms or hands in order to prevent an opponent's punch from landing cleanly
bout	a boxing contest
canvas	the floor of a boxing **ring**

caution an instruction by the referee to a boxer following an infringement of the rules. Usually, three cautions will lead to a **warning**

clinch the act of a boxer holding his opponent such that the opponent cannot throw punches

combination a series of punches thrown in quick succession

corner one of the four corners of the boxing ring. One is assigned to each boxer, and it is that corner where he sits, assisted by his **seconds**, in the intervals between rounds. The other two corners are called the neutral corners

corner man same as **second**

count the counting up to ten seconds by the referee when a boxer is down on the canvas, after which a win to his opponent by a **knockout** is declared

counter an attack launched immediately after an opponent throws a punch, in order to exploit an opening in his defences

cross a straight punch delivered from the side

disqualification the elimination of a boxer from a contest because he has received three **warnings** from the referee for infringements of the rules

distance if a bout goes the distance, it lasts the full number of **rounds**

down when a boxer is down, a part of his body other than his feet is touching the **canvas** or he is in a helpless condition on the ropes or is judged by the referee to be unable to continue boxing

eight-count a count of eight seconds made by the referee that a downed boxer must take while the referee decides whether or not to continue the bout. If a boxer takes three eight-counts in one round or four in a bout, the fight is stopped and the opponent is declared the winner

feint the faking of a punch in order to put the opponent into a vulnerable position

foul an illegal move, such as holding onto one's opponent or hitting him below the **belt** or behind the head

guard a posture of defence, with the gloves raised, protecting the face

headguard a protective head covering that must be worn by amateur boxers

hold when a boxer holds his opponent, he clutches him so that punches cannot be thrown

hook a short punch in which the boxer swings from the shoulder with the elbow bent, bringing the fist to the centre from the side

infighting boxing at very close quarters so that punches using the full reach of the arm cannot be thrown

jab a straight punch thrown with the **lead** hand

judge one of the three ring-side officials who keep a tally of the number of **scoring hits** during a bout

knockout a decision made by the referee whereby a boxer is declared the winner of the bout if his opponent has been **down** for the count of ten

lead if a boxer leads with a particular fist, he habitually opens attacks with it

mouthpiece a piece of plastic placed in a boxer's mouth in order to protect his teeth and to stop him biting his tongue

neutral corner see **corner**

one-two a combination of punches in which a **jab** with the leading hand is followed by a **cross** with the other hand

outclassed when a boxer is outclassed, he is considered by the referee to be taking excessive punishment from his opponent and the bout is stopped

out for the count when a boxer is out for the count, he has failed to beat the referee's **count** of ten

passbook a record of a boxer's matches, including injuries, time between bouts, medical examinations, etc

pugilism the art or practice of boxing. The word is from Latin *pugil*, a boxer

pull if a boxer pulls a punch, he holds back the full force of the blow

punch drunk suffering from a form of cerebral concussion from past blows in boxing, resulting in movement that resembles drunkenness

Queensberry Rules a set of rules adhered to in modern boxing, drawn up by the 8th Marquess of Queensberry, a British nobleman, in 1867

rabbit punch an illegal blow to the back of the neck

reach a boxer's reach is the distance between the fingertips of one arm to those of his other arm, when standing with arms outstretched to either side

ring the rectangular space, bounded by ropes on all four sides, on which a boxing match takes place

ringside physician the doctor who checks the physical condition of each boxer before the start of a bout, and who determines whether a dazed boxer is fit enough to continue

round a period of action over a certain number of minutes, separated by rests, which makes up a boxing match

scoring hit a clean blow with force, using the knuckle area of a closed glove, on the opponent's body above the belt or on the side or front of his head. If the three **judges** agree within a one-second period that the blow was landed successfully, the boxer scores one point

second an assistant who helps a boxer before a bout and during the rests between **rounds**

shadow boxing sparring practice with an imaginary opponent

shortarm a shortarm punch is delivered with a bent, rather than an extended, arm

southpaw a boxer who **leads** with his right hand

spar when two boxers spar, they practise by trading light blows

speed bag a relatively small suspended padded bag used when practising

split decision a decision by the **judges** that is not unanimous but is arrived at by a majority

throw in the towel if a boxer's trainer or second throws in the towel, he indicates to the referee that the fight should be stopped to save the boxer from unnecessary punishment. Originally, this was done by the throwing of a towel into the ring

TKO an abbreviation of technical **knockout**, a decision of a knockout given by the referee when one boxer is too badly beaten to continue the fight without risk of serious injury

uppercut an upward punch that comes from underneath an opponent's **guard**

warning when a boxer infringes the rules he is given a warning by the referee. Three warnings leads to **disqualification** from the bout

weave if a boxer weaves, he eludes punches by making twisting and turning movements

Some boxing slang

haymaker	a wild swinging punch
the noble art, the noble science	other names for boxing
palooka	a clumsy or stupid boxer. This word dates from the 1920s but is of uncertain origin
rope-a-dope	the strategy of feigning to be trapped on the ropes in order to encourage one's opponent, the 'dope', into tiring himself out with punches. This phrase was coined by Muhammad Ali in the 1970s, who employed the tactic with George Foreman to great effect in the 'Rumble in the Jungle' title fight in 1974
roundhouse	a wild swinging punch or style of punching
sweet science	another name for boxing

Some famous boxing personalities

Muhammad Ali, 1942–

Born Cassius Clay in Louisville, Kentucky, USA, he was a controversial figure in the sixties, became a legend in the seventies, and is still one of the most popular and recognizable men in the world. He came to prominence at the 1960 Olympics in Rome, winning the light heavyweight gold as a teenager. After returning to the US in triumph he was refused entry to a diner because of his colour. In disgust, he threw his medal into a river and began a lifetime of involvement in the civil rights movement. After he turned professional it was not long before he had a shot at Sonny Liston's world title. Odds of 7/1 suggested the cocky young challenger had no chance, but it took only six rounds before he won his first world title. After becoming involved with the radical Islamic section of the civil rights movement, he abandoned his 'slave name' of Cassius Clay and became known as Muhammad Ali. After refusing to serve in the US Army in Vietnam, Ali was banned from boxing for three years. On his return, his showboating evolved into a more attritional style. This served him well in the memorable contests he had in the seventies with Joe Frazier and **George Foreman**, beating the latter to regain the world title in the 'Rumble in the Jungle' in Zaire in 1974 and the former to retain it in the 'Thriller in Manila' a year later. He lost then regained the title against Leon Spinks in 1978 and should have retired. However, he unwisely came out of retirement to fight Larry Holmes and Trevor Berbick before finally calling it a day in 1981. His boxing prowess, charisma, bravery in confronting prejudice, and the dignity with which he is dealing with Parkinson's syndrome, have made him a legend and an inspiration to many. It was fitting that in 2000, in front of a TV audience of billions, the greatest sportsman of the 20th century should have lit the flame at the first Olympics of the 21st.

Jim Corbett, 1866–1933

Born in San Francisco, California, USA, he was boxing's first world champion of the gloved era. A skilled boxer, he used 'science' to defeat his opponents rather than brute force. His technique helped him to defeat the much heavier John L Sullivan, the last of the great bareknuckle fighters, for the first world heavyweight title fight in 1892. Corbett's disciplined approach had a huge effect on the sport, helping it to evolve from bareknuckle brawling to the 'noble art of self-defence'. His articulacy outside the ring also made him a popular figure, and he appeared on a number of occasions on stage and screen.

George Foreman, 1948–

Born in Marshall, Texas, USA, he is one of boxing's most remarkable characters. He won heavyweight gold at the 1968 Olympics after only 18 amateur fights. A year later he turned professional and knocked out 34 of his first 37 opponents. In 1973 he took on Joe Frazier for the world title, knocking the champion to the canvas six times before the fight was stopped in round two. He was considered unbeatable and many feared for **Muhammad Ali**'s life when he took on Foreman in Zaire in 1974. Foreman's assault on Ali was fearsome but by round eight he had punched himself out and Ali put the big man on the floor to win the most famous fight in history. After retiring in 1977, Foreman became a minister. Ten years later, in order to raise funds for his church, he became the Punching Preacher and entered the ring again. He shocked the sporting world in 1994 when, as a 46-year-old grandfather, he knocked out Michael Moorer to win the WBA title. He has now retired and makes money from TV commentary work and, bizarrely but lucratively, endorsing a cooking device called the Lean Mean Grillin' Machine.

Jack Johnson, 1878–1946

Born John Arthur Johnson in Galveston, Texas, USA, he was the first black heavyweight champion of the world. This was a considerable achievement at a time when white champion boxers either refused to, or were prevented from, fighting black challengers. Johnson had to travel half way around the world to take part in his first title fight, squaring up to Canadian Tommy Burns in Sydney, Australia, in 1908. He won the fight in the fourteenth round and was crowned champion. Many in the white establishment were shocked by this victory, and further enraged by Johnson's fast living and penchant for white women. His wins sometimes provoked race riots; in 1910, when he demolished former champion James J Jeffries, twelve black people were killed in violence following the fight. Johnson continued boxing until he was 60 years old before finally hanging up his gloves in 1938. He died in a car crash in 1946.

Don King, 1932–

Born in Cleveland, Ohio, USA, he is one of the most powerful men in boxing. Known for his unorthodox methods, outlandish fashions, and 'Van de Graaff generator' hairstyle, he has promoted fights involving most of the world's top boxers since the 1970s. Perhaps his greatest coup was the 'Rumble in the Jungle', the world heavyweight title fight between **Muhammad Ali** and **George Foreman** in 1974, which he organized in the unlikely setting of Kinshasa, the capital of Mobutu's dictatorship in Zaire. His success has come despite a notorious past which included a prison sentence for murder.

Joe Louis, 1914–81

Born Joseph Louis Barrow in Alabama, USA, he was easily the best heavyweight boxer of his generation. He held the world title for a record twelve years between 1937 and 1949, the year in which he retired undefeated. Weighed down by debts, he was forced to resume his career but lost title fights against Ezzard Charles and **Rocky Marciano**, after which latter fight, in 1951, he finally retired. Troubled once again by debt and unpaid taxes, he was rescued by President John F Kennedy who wrote off Joe's back taxes in recognition for fundraising and morale-boosting work for the US Army during World War II. He later worked as a greeter at a Las Vegas casino.

Rocky Marciano, 1923-69

Born Rocco Francis Marchegiano in Massachusetts, USA, he is the only world heavyweight champion to retire with a perfect record. He started boxing in Britain while enlisted in the US Army during World War II, and turned professional in 1947. Although relatively small for a heavyweight (under 6ft tall and just over 13 stone) he more than made up for his stature with aggression, persistence and brute force. Despite being floored in a number of title fights, he always beat the referee's count and went on to beat his opponent, invariably within the distance. His record of 49 fights, 49 wins and 43 knockouts may never be matched. He sensibly retired undefeated in 1956 and was never lured back into the ring. He did not get the long retirement he deserved though, dying in a plane crash aged 45.

Sugar Ray Robinson, 1920-89

Born Walker Smith in Detroit, Michigan, USA, he is pound-for-pound arguably the greatest boxer of all time. He had 202 fights, including 110 knockouts, and just 19 defeats, most at the tail end of his 25-year career. He was five-time world middleweight champion and undisputed world welterweight champion for four years. He won his first 40 professional fights and, after a points defeat by Jake 'Raging Bull' La Motta in 1943, went unbeaten for eight years, during which time he did not lose an astonishing 91 fights. He retired in 1953 but had to put on his gloves again after problems with the taxman. During this second period he won another three world middleweight titles, eventually retiring in 1965 at the age of 44. During his long career he was never once knocked out.

Teofilo Stevenson, 1952-

Born in Delicias-Puerto Madre, Cuba, he became the first man to win three consecutive Olympic boxing gold medals. The tall and elegant Stevenson began his reign in Munich in 1972. His semi-final opponent, Peter Hussing, said, 'I have never been hit so hard in all my 212 bouts'. Four years later, he dispatched his first three opponents in a record 7 minutes and 22 seconds. In Moscow in 1980, his semi-final opponent, Istvan Levai, became the first man to go the distance with Stevenson – but only because he ran round the ring to avoid the giant Cuban. The Communist boycott of the Los Angeles Olympics denied him a fourth gold, but he was still good enough to win a third title at the world championships in 1986. During the seventies, he was offered a number of lucrative contracts to turn professional in the US. He declined them all, saying, 'What is a million dollars compared to the love of my people?'

CANADIAN FOOTBALL

Origins

Canadian football traces its lineage to the game of rugby football played in Britain in the early Victorian era. The game was introduced to North America by the British Army, whose Montreal Garrison played a series of games with McGill University. McGill headed south of the border into the United States and played a number of games with Harvard University, thus helping to establish the oval-ball game as the dominant form of football in Ivy League sport at the expense of the round-ball version. The Canadian and American forms of the game evolved in tandem from that point and remain very similar, although there are a number of differences. In 1884 the Canadian Rugby Football Union was formed and within a few years the game had spread to every Canadian province.

Rules and description

A field game, similar to American football, played on a rectangular pitch. Two teams of twelve players compete to gain possession of an oval ball and score 'touchdowns' over the opponents' goal line and kick 'field goals' and 'converts' over the crossbar of the opponents' goal. Teams advance down the field through a series of short plays in which the ball can be carried and passed to team-mates. Only one forward pass is permitted in each play. Three 'downs' (attempts) are permitted to move the ball forward ten yards, or the team with the ball must surrender possession. Body tackling is permitted and when a successful tackle is made the play is stopped for a 'scrimmage' (a clash of opposing players lined up against each other). Play lasts one hour and is divided into four 15-minute quarters.

Ruling body: Canadian Football League (CFL)

Grey Cup

The Grey Cup is Canadian football's premier trophy. In 1909 Lord Grey, the Governor-General of Canada, donated a trophy for the Rugby Football Championship of Canada. Originally the trophy was open to teams from the Canadian Rugby Union but, since 1954, the Grey Cup has been presented to the champion team of the Canadian Football League (CFL).

1909	University of Toronto	**1933**	Toronto Argonauts
1910	University of Toronto	**1934**	Sarnia Imperials
1911	University of Toronto	**1935**	Winnipeg 'Pegs
1912	Hamilton Alerts	**1936**	Sarnia Imperials
1913	Hamilton Tigers	**1937**	Toronto Argonauts
1914	Toronto Argonauts	**1938**	Toronto Argonauts
1915	Hamilton Tigers	**1939**	Winnipeg Blue Bombers
1920	University of Toronto	**1940**	Ottawa Rough Riders
1921	Toronto Argonauts	**1941**	Winnipeg Blue Bombers
1922	Queen's University	**1942**	Toronto RACF
1924	Queen's University	**1943**	Hamilton Wildcats
1925	Ottawa Senators	**1944**	Montreal HMCS
1926	Ottawa Senators	**1945**	Toronto Argonauts
1927	Toronto Balmy Beach	**1946**	Toronto Argonauts
1928	Hamilton Tigers	**1947**	Toronto Argonauts
1929	Hamilton Tigers	**1948**	Calgary Stampeders
1930	Toronto Balmy Beach	**1949**	Montreal Alouettes
1931	Montreal AAA	**1950**	Toronto Argonauts
1932	Hamilton Tigers	**1951**	Ottawa Rough Riders

1952	Toronto Argonauts	**1979**	Edmonton Eskimos
1953	Hamilton Tiger-Cats	**1980**	Edmonton Eskimos
1954	Edmonton Eskimos	**1981**	Edmonton Eskimos
1955	Edmonton Eskimos	**1982**	Edmonton Eskimos
1956	Edmonton Eskimos	**1983**	Toronto Argonauts
1957	Hamilton Tiger-Cats	**1984**	Winnipeg Blue Bombers
1958	Winnipeg Blue Bombers	**1985**	British Columbia Lions
1959	Winnipeg Blue Bombers	**1986**	Hamilton Tiger-Cats
1960	Ottawa Rough Riders	**1987**	Edmonton Eskimos
1961	Winnipeg Blue Bombers	**1988**	Winnipeg Blue Bombers
1962	Winnipeg Blue Bombers	**1989**	Saskatchewan Roughriders
1963	Hamilton Tiger-Cats	**1990**	Winnipeg Blue Bombers
1964	British Columbia Lions	**1991**	Toronto Argonauts
1965	Hamilton Tiger-Cats	**1992**	Calgary Stampeders
1966	Saskatchewan Roughriders	**1993**	Edmonton Eskimos
1967	Hamilton Tiger-Cats	**1994**	British Columbia Lions
1968	Ottawa Rough Riders	**1995**	Baltimore Stallions
1969	Ottawa Rough Riders	**1996**	Toronto Argonauts
1970	Montreal Alouettes	**1997**	Toronto Argonauts
1971	Calgary Stampeders	**1998**	Calgary Stampeders
1972	Hamilton Tiger-Cats	**1999**	Hamilton Tiger-Cats
1973	Ottawa Rough Riders	**2000**	British Columbia Lions
1974	Montreal Alouettes	**2001**	Calgary Stampeders
1975	Edmonton Eskimos	**2002**	Montreal Alouettes
1976	Ottawa Rough Riders	**2003**	Edmonton Eskimos
1977	Montreal Alouettes	**2004**	Toronto Argonauts
1978	Edmonton Eskimos		

Border rivalry

In 1995 the Baltimore Stallions became the only team from outside Canada to win the Grey Cup. Their success came during a short-lived experiment to expand the sport into the United States.

A-Z

See **American football** as most terminology is shared by both sports; but see also table below for key differences.

Key differences between Canadian football and American football

Canadian football	American football
➤ 12 players on each team	➤ 11 players on each team
➤ Field of play is 110 yards long	➤ Field of play is 100 yards long
➤ End zone is 20 yards deep	➤ End zone is 10 yards deep
➤ Team in possession has three downs to move 10 yards	➤ Team in possession has four downs to move 10 yards
➤ All backfield players except the quarterback may be in motion before the snap	➤ Only one backfield player may be in motion before the snap

- Play must restart within 20 seconds after the ball is dead
- An extra score after a touchdown is called a 'convert', and is attempted from two-the five-yard line
- A 'rouge' (worth one point) is awarded played when the ball is played into the opponents' goal area and becomes dead

- Play must restart within 45 seconds after the ball is dead
- An extra score after a touchdown is called a 'conversion' and is attempted from the yard line
- No score is awarded when the ball is into the opponents' goal area and becomes dead; the defending team is awarded a 'touchback'

CANOEING

Origins

Native North and South American Indians are believed to have been the originators of the canoes we recognize today. They were built from hollowed-out tree trunks or were constructed from birchbark. The Inuit people of North America and Greenland created their own form of canoe: the sealskin vessels they called kayaks. As a competitive sport canoeing was invented by the Scotsman John MacGregor, who in 1866 founded the Canoe Club at Richmond, Surrey.

Rules and description

Competitive canoeing is divided into two types, depending largely upon the paddle and craft used. 'Kayaking' has a paddle with a blade on each end and the kayaker sits in the boat, paddling on alternate sides of the craft. The kayak is a closed-decked craft. In 'Canadian canoeing' the paddler has just one blade and adopts a half-kneeling position in the canoe, switching the paddle from side to side. The Canadian canoe is an open-decked craft.

In flatwater contests canoeists and kayakers race in lanes over a set distance – generally 500m or 1,000m. In the past distances of 10,000m were competed over. Flatwater contests are also known as 'sprints', irrespective of the distance. Whitewater or slalom events are held over rivers (natural or man-made) with a series of rapids, currents and eddies. Competitors have to negotiate a series of 18 to 25 gates on a 250–400m course, heading downstream and reversing direction to go upstream. They are timed over the length of the course and can incur penalty points for missing gates or touching gate poles.

Ruling bodies: International Canoe Federation (ICF)

Olympic Champions

Men

Kayak slalom K-1

1972	Siegbert Horn (East Germany)
1976-88	*Not held*
1992	Pierpaolo Ferrazzi (Italy)
1996	Oliver Fix (Germany)
2000	Thomas Schmidt (Germany)
2004	Benoit Peschier (France)

	Canadian slalom C-1	**Canadian slalom C-2**
1972	Reinhard Eiben (East Germany)	Walter Hofmann & Rolf-Dieter Amend (East Germany)
1976-88	*Not held*	*Not held*
1992	Lukáš Pollert (Czechoslovakia)	Scott Strausbaugh & Joe Jacobi (USA)
1996	Michal Martikan (Slovakia)	Franck Adisson & Wilfrid Forgues (France)
2000	Tony Estanguet (France)	Pavol Hochschorner & Peter Hochschorner (Slovakia)
2004	Tony Estanguet (France)	Pavol Hochschorner & Peter Hochschorner (Slovakia)

	Kayak sprint K-1 (500m)	**Kayak sprint pairs K-2 (500m)**
1976	Vasile Diba (Romania)	Joachim Mattern & Bernd Olbricht (East Germany)
1980	Vladimir Parfenovich (USSR)	Vladimir Parfenovich & Sergei Chukhrai (USSR)
1984	Ian Ferguson (New Zealand)	Ian Ferguson & Paul MacDonald (New Zealand)
1988	Zsolt Gyulay (Hungary)	Ian Ferguson & Paul MacDonald (New Zealand)
1992	Mikko Kolehmainen (Finland)	Kay Bluhm & Torsten Gutsche (Germany)
1996	Antonio Rossi (Italy)	Kay Bluhm & Torsten Gutsche (Germany)
2000	Knut Holmann (Norway)	Zoltan Kammerer & Botond Storcz (Hungary)
2004	Adam van Koeverden (Canada)	Ronald Rauhe & Tim Wieskoetter (Germany)

	Kayak sprint K-1 (1,000m)	**Kayak sprint pairs K-2 (1,000m)**
1936	Gregor Hradetsky (Austria)	Adolf Kainz & Alfons Dorfner (Austria)
1948	Gert Fredriksson (Sweden)	Hans Berglund & Lennart Klingström (Sweden)
1952	Gert Fredriksson (Sweden)	Kurt Wires & Yrjö Hietanen (Finland)
1956	Gert Fredriksson (Sweden)	Michael Scheuer & Meinrad Miltenberger (Germany)
1960	Erik Hansen (Denmark)	Gert Fredriksson & Sven-Olov Sjödelius (Sweden)
1964	Rolf Peterson (Sweden)	Sven-Olov Sjödelius & Nils Gunnar Utterberg (Sweden)
1968	Mihály Hesz (Hungary)	Aleksandr Shaparenko & Vladimir Morozov (USSR)
1972	Aleksandr Shaparenko (USSR)	Nikolai Gorbachev & Viktor Kratasyuk (USSR)
1976	Rüdiger Helm (East Germany)	Sergei Nagorny & Vladimir Romanovsky (USSR)
1980	Rüdiger Helm (East Germany)	Vladimir Parfenovich & Sergei Chukhrai (USSR)
1984	Alan Thompson (New Zealand)	Hugh Fisher & Alwyn Morris (Canada)
1988	Gregory Barton (USA)	Gregory Barton & Norman Bellingham (USA)
1992	Clint Robinson (Australia)	Kay Bluhm & Torsten Gutsche (Germany)
1996	Knut Holmann (Norway)	Antonio Rossi & Daniele Scarpa (Italy)
2000	Knut Holmann (Norway)	Antonio Rossi & Beniamino Bonomi (Italy)
2004	Eirik Larsen (Norway)	Markus Oscarsson & Henrik Nilsson (Sweden)

Kayak sprint K-4 (1,000m)

1964	USSR
1968	Norway
1972	USSR
1976	USSR
1980	East Germany
1984	New Zealand
1988	Hungary
1992	Germany
1996	Germany
2000	Hungary
2004	Hungary

	Canadian sprint C-1 (500m)	Canadian sprint C-2 (500m)
1976	Aleksandr Rogov (USSR)	Sergei Petrenko & Aleksandr Vinogradov (USSR)
1980	Sergei Postryekhin (USSR)	László Foltán & István Vaskuti (Hungary)
1984	Larry Cain (Canada)	Matija Ljubek & Mirko Nišović (Yugoslavia)
1988	Olaf Heukrodt (East Germany)	Viktor Reneisky & Nikolai Zhuravsky (USSR)
1992	Nikolai Bukhalov (Bulgaria)	Aleksandr Masseikov & Dmitri Dovgalyonok (Belarus)
1996	Martin Doktor (Czech Republic)	Csaba Horvath & György Kolonics (Hungary)
2000	György Kolonics (Hungary)	Ferenc Novák & Imre Pulai (Hungary)
2004	Andreas Dittmer (Germany)	Meng Guanliang & Yang Wenjun (China)

	Canadian sprint C-1 (1,000m)	Canadian sprint C-2 (1,000m)
1936	Francis Amyot (Canada)	Vladimir Syrovátka & Jan Brzák-Felix (Czechoslovakia)
1948	Josef Holeček (Czechoslovakia)	Jan Brzák-Felix & Bohumil Kudrna (Czechoslovakia)
1952	Josef Holeček (Czechoslovakia)	Bent Peder Rasch & Finn Haunstoft (Denmark)
1956	Leon Rotman (Romania)	Alexe Dumitru & Simion Ismailciuc (Romania)
1960	János Parti (Hungary)	Leonid Geishtor & Sergei Makarenko (USSR)
1964	Jürgen Eschert (East Germany)	Andriy Khymych & Stepan Oschepkov (USSR)
1968	Tibor Tatai (Hungary)	Ivan Patzaichin & Serghei Covaliov (Romania)
1972	Ivan Patzaichan (Romania)	Vladislavas Chessyunas & Yuri Lobanov (USSR)
1976	Matija Ljubek (Yugoslavia)	Sergei Petrenko & Aleksandr Vinoradov (USSR)
1980	Lyubomir Lyubenov (Bulgaria)	Ivan Patzaichin & Toma Simionov (Romania)
1984	Ulrich Eicke (West Germany)	Ivan Patzaichin & Toma Simionov (Romania)
1988	Ivans Klemenjevs (USSR)	Viktor Reneisky & Nikolai Zhuravsky (USSR)
1992	Nikolai Bukhalov (Bulgaria)	Ulrich Papke & Ingo Spelly (Germany)
1996	Martin Doktor (Czech Republic)	Andreas Dittmer & Gunar Kirchbach (Germany)
2000	Andreas Dittmer (Germany)	Florin Popescu & Mitica Pricop (Romania)
2004	David Cal (Spain)	Christian Gille & Tomasz Wylenzek (Germany)

Women

Kayak slalom K-1

1972	Angelika Bahmann (East Germany)
1976-88	*Not held*
1992	Elisabeth Micheler (Germany)
1996	Stepanka Hilgertová (Czech Republic)
2000	Stepanka Hilgertová (Czech Republic)
2004	Elena Kaliska (Slovakia)

	Kayak sprint K-1 (500m)
1948	Karen Hoff (Denmark)
1952	Sylvi Saimo (Finland)
1956	Yelizaveta Dementyeva (USSR)
1960	Antonina Seredina (USSR)
1964	Lyudmila Khvedosyuk (USSR)
1968	Lyudmila Pinayeva (née Khvedosyuk) (USSR)
1972	Yulia Ryabchynska (USSR)
1976	Carola Zirzow (East Germany)
1980	Birgit Fischer (East Germany)
1984	Agneta Andersson (Sweden)
1988	Vania Gesheva (Bulgaria)
1992	Birgit Schmidt (née Fischer) (Germany)
1996	Rita Köbán (Hungary)
2000	Josefa Idem Guerrini (Italy)
2004	Natasa Janics (Hungary)

	Kayak sprint K-2	Kayak sprint K-4
1960	Maria Chubina & Antonina Seredina (USSR)	
1964	Roswitha Esser & Annemarie Zimmermann (Germany)	
1968	Roswitha Esser & Annemarie Zimmermann (Germany)	
1972	Lyudmila Pinayeva (née Khvedosyuk) & Katerina Nahima-Kuryshko (USSR)	
1976	Nina Gopova & Galina Kreft (USSR)	
1980	Carsta Genäuss & Martina Bischof (East Germany)	
1984	Agneta Andersson & Anna Olsson (Sweden)	Romania
1988	Birgit Schmidt (née Fischer) & Anke Nothnagel (East Germany)	East Germany
1992	Ramona Portwich & Anke von Seck (née Nothnagel) (Germany)	Hungary
1996	Agneta Andersson & Susanne Gunnarsson (Sweden)	Germany
2000	Birgit Fischer & Katrin Wagner (Germany)	Germany
2004	Katalin Kovacs & Natasa Janics (Hungary)	Germany

A-Z

back paddling pushing the paddle forwards to reverse the direction of the canoe or kayak

brace a recovery stroke used to prevent the canoe from capsizing

C-1, C-2, C-4 one-, two- or four-person **Canadian canoe**

Canadian canoe an open canoe in which the canoeist uses a single-bladed paddle

chute an area of river that narrows causing an increase in speed

coaming raised rim of a **cockpit**, to which a **spray skirt** is attached

cockpit the space in the deck of a **kayak** in which the kayaker sits

downstream gate on a **slalom** course, a **gate** (marked by green and white stripes) that has to be negotiated following the direction of the river

draw a stroke, taken at right-angles to the direction of travel, which turns the canoe

Eskimo roll a method of using the paddle against the water to right a boat that has tipped or rolled over

feathered paddle a kayaking paddle in which the blades are at right-angles to each other

flatwater	calm water; describes sprint as opposed to **slalom** races
free gate	a **gate** indicated by black and white stripes that can be entered from either direction
gate	on a **slalom** course, an obstacle marked by two free-hanging poles; paddlers have to go between the poles without touching them
K-1, K-2	one- or two-person **kayak**
kayak	a fully decked canoe. The paddler sits in the kayak and uses a double-bladed paddle
petit final	a race that is used to determine the placing of paddlers who fail to reach the final
repechage	a competitive round in which paddlers who lost in the first heat are given a chance to advance further; from the French for 'fishing again'
slalom	a type of **whitewater** race in which paddlers have to pass through gates
spray skirt, spray deck	waterproof (usually Neoprene®) cockpit cover worn around the waist by a kayaker and which attaches tightly to the **coaming** in order to prevent water entering the kayak
Telemark turn	a fast turn that uses the paddle to pivot
upstream gate	on a **slalom** course, a **gate** (marked by red and white stripes) that has to be negotiated against the direction of the stream
whitewater	the type of water created by rapids. It describes **slalom** rather than **flatwater** racing

Some famous canoeists and kayakers

Birgit Fischer, 1962–

Born in Brandenburg in the former German Democratic Republic, she won the kayak singles aged 18 to become the youngest canoeing champion in Olympic history. She was part of the GDR boycott at the Los Angeles Games in 1984, but won three medals at the 1988 Games (two golds and a silver) under her married name Schmidt. She further added to the haul with golds and silvers in the 1992, 1996, 2000 and 2004 Games. As well as being the greatest German Olympian of all time with seven gold medals, she won 27 World championship gold medals.

Richard Fox, 1960–

Born in Winsford, Cheshire, England, he won a record five world titles for canoe slalom in the K-1 class (1981, 1983, 1985, 1989 and 1993) and five gold team medals (1981, 1983, 1985, 1987 and 1993). His sister was a British champion and his wife, Myriam Jérusalmi, a world champion canoeist.

Gert Fredriksson, 1919–

Born in Nyköping, Sweden, he started canoeing aged 17. Because of the hiatus for World War II his first major international triumph was at the 1948 London Olympics, where he won two gold medals in the 1,000m K-1 and the 10,000m K-1 events. He retained the former title in 1952, gaining a silver medal in the 10,000m and then won golds in both events four years later in Melbourne, Australia. His final Olympic gold (of six) was in the pairs event of 1960. In addition he won four world titles.

COMMONWEALTH GAMES

Origins

The idea for a multi-event sporting contest between countries of the British Empire was first proposed in 1891 by the Reverend J Astley Cooper, and the first Inter-Empire sports meeting was held at Crystal Palace, London, in 1911 as part of King George V's coronation celebrations. The first Games proper (called the British Empire Games) were held in Hamilton, Canada, in 1930. Eleven countries and 400 athletes took part.

Festival of the Empire

The coronation of King George V was celebrated at Crystal Palace, London, in 1911 with a series of games. The festival was contested by athletes from Great Britain and Ireland, Australasia, Canada and South Africa and five athletics events were held (100 yards, 220 yards, 880 yards, 1 mile and 120 yards hurdles) as well as heavyweight boxing, middleweight wrestling, and 100 yards and 1 mile swimming races.

Rules and description

The Commonwealth Games are open to competitors from all Commonwealth countries, colonies and dependent or associated territories. Mozambique is the only member of the Commonwealth not to have experienced direct or indirect British rule. Ireland and Zimbabwe have either left or been excluded from the Commonwealth. Like the Olympic Games, these Games take place every four years. In 1954 they were renamed the British Empire and Commonwealth Games; from 1966 to 1974, the British Commonwealth Games; and they adopted their present name in 1978. The home countries of the UK compete separately as England, Northern Ireland, Scotland and Wales, as do the individual Channel Islands and the Isle of Man. Known as the 'friendly games', they are notable in that all competitors share a common language – English.

Ruling body: Commonwealth Games Federation (CGF)

Commonwealth Games Venues

The host city for each Commonwealth Games is chosen by the Commonwealth Games Federation (CGF) seven years in advance of competition.

1930 Hamilton, Canada
1934 London, England
1938 Sydney, Australia
1942 *Not held*
1946 *Not held*
1950 Auckland, New Zealand
1954 Vancouver, Canada

Commonwealth Games

1958 Cardiff, Wales
1962 Perth, Australia
1966 Kingston, Jamaica
1970 Edinburgh, Scotland
1974 Christchurch, New Zealand
1978 Edmonton, Canada
1982 Brisbane, Australia
1986 Edinburgh, Scotland
1990 Auckland, New Zealand
1994 Victoria, Canada
1998 Kuala Lumpur, Malaysia
2002 Manchester, England
2006 Melbourne, Australia
2010 New Delhi, India

Athletes' Villages

At the first Commonwealth Games in Hamilton in 1930 the facilities were somewhat spartan: the 400-odd competitors slept at a school near the stadium, with up to 24 athletes sharing each classroom. In contrast, the athletes' village at the 2002 Games in Manchester included a bar, cinema, entertainment marquee, games room, gym, Internet cafe, medical centre, religious centre and restaurant. The organizers estimated beforehand that the beds would be made 120,500 times, 530km/331mi of toilet roll would be used and a stack of towels 4km/2.4mi high would be needed to cater for the thousands of athletes attending.

Leading Medal Winners

Includes medals won in 2002.

	Gold	**Silver**	**Bronze**	**Total**
Australia	646	551	488	1,685
England	542	513	528	1,583
Canada	388	413	430	1,231
New Zealand	118	156	221	495
Scotland	71	87	142	300
South Africa	80	79	83	242
India	80	79	63	222
Wales	46	64	85	195
Kenya	53	42	49	144
Nigeria	35	41	50	126

Commonwealth Games Sports

Until 1998 ten sports were competed for at each Games, though the individual sports themselves differed every four years (apart from athletics and swimming which were ever-presents). From 2010 five sports will be obligatory: athletics, lawn bowls, netball, rugby sevens and swimming. The host country selects the rest of the programme from an approved list of sports and may also select one or more additional team sports.

Athletics
Badminton
Bowls
Boxing
Cricket
Cycling
Diving
Gymnastics
Hockey
Judo
Netball
Rugby
Shooting
Squash
Swimming
Synchronized swimming
Table tennis
Tenpin bowling
Triathlon
Weightlifting
Wrestling

Shooting prowess on the islands

In the Commonwealth Games, Jersey, Guernsey and the Isle of Man each compete in their own right as separate teams rather than as part of Great Britain. Both Guernsey and Jersey have one gold medal each to their name—in the men's rapid-fire pistol (1990) and the full-bore rifle shooting (1990) respectively. Not to be left out of the action, the Isle of Man has won two gold medals, again in the shooting with a men's skeet gold in 1986, but also expanding its horizons somewhat to win a 1966 gold medal in the 120-mile cycle road race.

Commonwealth Games Countries

Africa	Americas/ Caribbean	Asia	Europe	Oceania
Botswana	Anguilla	Bangladesh	England	Australia
Cameroon	Antigua & Barbuda	Brunei	Cyprus	Cook Islands
Gambia	Bahamas	India	Gibraltar	Fiji
Ghana	Barbados	Malaysia	Guernsey	Kiribati
Kenya	Belize	Maldives	Isle of Man	Nauru
Lesotho	Bermuda	Pakistan	Jersey	New Zealand
Malawi	British Virgin Islands	Singapore	Malta	Niue
Mauritius	Canada	Sri Lanka	Northern Ireland	Norfolk Islands
Mozambique	Cayman Islands		Scotland	Papua New Guinea
Namibia	Dominica		Wales	Samoa
Nigeria	Falkland Islands			Solomon Islands
Seychelles	Grenada			Tonga
Sierra Leone	Guyana			Tuvalu
South Africa	Jamaica			Vanuatu
Swaziland	Montserrat			
Tanzania	St Helena			
Uganda	St Kitts and Nevis			
Zambia	St Lucia			
	St Vincent and the Grenadines			
	Trinidad and Tobago			
	Turks and Caicos			

CRICKET

Origins

Although there is a reference in the household accounts of Edward I to a game like cricket being played in Kent in 1300, the precise origins of the game are obscure. It is believed that it began as a game played by shepherds in the pastures of south-east England where the cropped grass meant that the ball (made of wool or rags) could be literally bowled along the ground. The target was the wicket-gate of the sheepfold, which was defended with a shepherd's crook (which explains why early bats had a curved blade). The first recorded match was played at Coxheath in Kent in 1646. At this time the game was mostly a rural pastime but by the 18th century cricket was being played at all levels of society throughout England. The first set of rules was written in 1744, although the MCC produced a revised official set in 1835, which still largely apply today.

Rules and description

An eleven-a-side team game. A 'wicket' consisting of three 'stumps' (wooden sticks) surmounted by a pair of 'bails' (smaller sticks) is placed at each end of a grassy pitch 20.1m/22yd in length. Each team takes it in turn to bat (with long flat-sided wooden bats) and bowl (with a solid ball), the object being to defend the wicket while trying to score as many runs as possible. A bowler delivers an 'over' of six balls to a batsman standing in front of one of the wickets before a different bowler attacks the other wicket. If the batsman hits the ball (and in certain other circumstances) he can attempt to run to the other end of the pitch and thus score a run. A ball reaching the boundary of the field scores four runs automatically, and six if it has not bounced on the way. A batsman can be got out by being 'caught' (a fielder catches the ball before it reaches the ground), 'bowled' (the ball from the bowler knocks the bails off the stumps), 'stumped' (the wicketkeeper knocks the bails off the stumps with the ball while the defending batsman is standing outside his 'safe ground' or 'crease'), 'run out' (the bails on the wicket towards which one of the batsmen is running are knocked off before the safe ground is reached), 'leg before wicket' or 'lbw' (see below) and 'hit wicket' (the batsman accidentally knocks the bails off the stumps). Once ten batsmen have been dismissed, the innings comes to a close, but a team can stop its innings or 'declare' if it thinks it has made enough runs. In limited-overs games, each team has one innings and the team with the greater number of runs at the end of the match wins. In most other games, however, each team has two innings and a team has to bowl the opposition out twice for a lower total score in order to win; if two innings have not been completed at the end of the time allotted for the match, the result is a draw, regardless of which team has scored more runs.

Ruling bodies: International Cricket Council (ICC), Marylebone Cricket Club (MCC), England and Wales Cricket Board (ECB)

Ludicrous Baffling Waffle

So might seem the lbw rule to non-cricket fans. However, it can be explained relatively simply: a batsman is given out lbw when the lower part of the his leg prevents the ball bowled by the bowler from hitting the wicket, as long as: (i) the batsman has not first hit the ball with his bat; (ii) the ball strikes the leg directly in line with stumps when the batsman is trying to hit the ball (this requirement does not apply if he makes no attempt to hit it); (iii) the ball has not pitched outside the leg stump. Given that the umpire has to asses all these variables instantly, it is not surprising that this is one of the most controversial aspects of cricket.

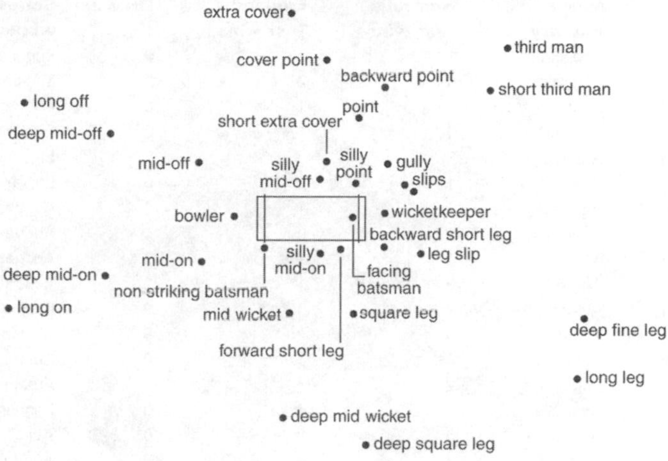

On and on and on and on

Test matches are now played over five days, but 'timeless tests', where there was no restriction on the length of the game, were played before World War II. Only one timeless test was not completed. England scored 654 for five in their second innings against South Africa at Durban in 1938, chasing 696 to win. Despite being so close to victory, the tourists realized that they might miss their boat home, and so the game was declared a draw on the tenth day of play.

Ashes Series Winners

The Ashes

The Ashes is the name given to the trophy that England and Australia have played for in Test series since 1882, and to such series themselves. The trophy itself is a small urn, which contains the ashes of a burnt bail. The trophy was devised following a mock obituary of English cricket that appeared in *The Sporting Times* after Australia defeated England at the Oval in 1882. The full text read: 'In Affectionate Remembrance Of ENGLISH CRICKET WHICH DIED AT THE OVAL On 29th August, 1882, Deeply lamented by a large circle of sorrowing friends and acquaintances R. I. P. N.B. - The body will be cremated and the ashes taken to Australia.'

	Host country	**Australia Test wins**	**England Test wins**	**Drawn**	**Series winner**
1882–3	Australia	1	2	0	England
1884	England	0	1	2	England
1884–5	Australia	2	3	0	England
1886	England	0	3	0	England
1886–7	Australia	0	2	0	England
1887–8	Australia	0	1	0	England

	Host country	Australia Test wins	England Test wins	Drawn	Series winner
1888	England	1	2	0	England
1890	England	0	2	0	England
1891–2	Australia	2	1	0	Australia
1893	England	0	1	2	England
1894–5	Australia	2	3	0	England
1896	England	1	2	0	England
1897–8	Australia	4	1	0	Australia
1899	England	1	0	4	Australia
1901–2	Australia	4	1	0	Australia
1902	England	2	1	2	Australia
1903–4	Australia	2	3	0	England
1905	England	0	2	3	England
1907–8	Australia	4	1	0	Australia
1909	England	2	1	2	Australia
1911–2	Australia	1	4	0	England
1920–1	Australia	5	0	0	Australia
1921	England	3	0	2	Australia
1924–5	Australia	4	1	0	Australia
1926	England	0	1	4	England
1928–9	Australia	1	4	0	England
1930	England	2	1	2	Australia
1932–3	Australia	1	4	0	England
1934	England	2	1	2	Australia
1936–7	Australia	3	2	0	Australia
1938	England	1	1	2	Drawn
1946–7	Australia	3	0	2	Australia
1948	England	4	0	1	Australia
1950–1	Australia	4	1	0	Australia
1953	England	0	1	4	England
1954–5	Australia	1	3	1	England
1956	England	1	2	2	England
1958–9	Australia	4	0	1	Australia
1961	England	2	1	2	Australia
1962–3	Australia	1	1	3	Drawn
1964	England	1	0	4	Australia
1965–6	Australia	1	1	3	Drawn
1968	England	1	1	3	Drawn
1970–1	Australia	0	2	4	England
1972	England	2	2	1	Drawn
1974–5	Australia	4	1	1	Australia
1975	England	1	0	3	Australia
1977	England	0	3	2	England
1978–9	Australia	1	5	0	England
1979–80	Australia	3	0	0	Australia
1981	England	1	3	2	England
1982–3	Australia	2	1	2	Australia
1985	England	1	3	2	England
1986–7	Australia	1	2	2	England

	Host country	Australia Test wins	England Test wins	Drawn	Series winner
1989	England	4	0	2	Australia
1990–1	Australia	3	0	2	Australia
1993	England	4	1	1	Australia
1994–5	Australia	3	1	1	Australia
1997	England	3	2	1	Australia
1998–9	Australia	3	1	1	Australia
2001	England	4	1	0	Australia
2002–3	Australia	4	1	0	Australia

World Cup

Played approximately every four years; limited-over games with teams grouped into pools, followed by a knockout phase.

	Winner	Beaten finalist	Host country
1975	West Indies	Australia	England
1979	West Indies	England	England
1983	India	West Indies	England
1987	Australia	England	India and Pakistan
1992	Pakistan	England	Australia and New Zealand
1996	Sri Lanka	Australia	India, Pakistan and Sri Lanka
1999	Australia	Pakistan	England
2003	Australia	India	South Africa
2007			West Indies

English County Championship

The oldest cricket competition in the world; although games between counties are recorded as early as the 18th century, 1873 is generally regarded as the year in which the championship began (it being officially recognized in 1890, when a proper points system was introduced). Before that, unofficial champions were decided by newspapers. Games were played over three days (except for 1919 when they were shortened to two days); four-day games were introduced for some matches in 1988 and then for all in 1993. In 2000 the Championship was split into two divisions of nine teams, each team playing 16 matches. Three teams are relegated from Division 1 and three promoted from Division 2 each year.

1890	Surrey
1891	Surrey
1892	Surrey
1893	Yorkshire
1894	Surrey
1895	Surrey
1896	Yorkshire
1897	Lancashire
1898	Yorkshire
1899	Surrey
1900	Yorkshire
1901	Yorkshire
1902	Yorkshire
1903	Middlesex
1904	Lancashire
1905	Yorkshire
1906	Kent
1907	Nottinghamshire
1908	Yorkshire
1909	Kent
1910	Kent
1911	Warwickshire
1912	Yorkshire
1913	Kent

1914	Surrey
1915-18	*Not held*
1919	Yorkshire
1920	Middlesex
1921	Middlesex
1922	Yorkshire
1923	Yorkshire
1924	Yorkshire
1925	Yorkshire
1926	Lancashire
1927	Lancashire
1928	Lancashire
1929	Nottinghamshire
1930	Lancashire
1931	Yorkshire
1932	Yorkshire
1933	Yorkshire
1934	Lancashire
1935	Yorkshire
1936	Derbyshire
1937	Yorkshire
1938	Yorkshire
1939	Yorkshire
1940-5	*Not held*
1946	Yorkshire
1947	Middlesex
1948	Glamorgan
1949	Middlesex and Yorkshire
1950	Lancashire and Surrey
1951	Warwickshire
1952	Surrey
1953	Surrey
1954	Surrey
1955	Surrey
1956	Surrey
1957	Surrey
1958	Surrey
1959	Yorkshire
1960	Yorkshire
1961	Hampshire
1962	Yorkshire
1963	Yorkshire
1964	Worcestershire
1965	Worcestershire
1966	Yorkshire
1967	Yorkshire
1968	Yorkshire
1969	Glamorgan
1970	Kent
1971	Surrey
1972	Warwickshire
1973	Hampshire
1974	Worcestershire
1975	Leicestershire
1976	Middlesex
1977	Middlesex and Kent
1978	Kent
1979	Essex
1980	Middlesex
1981	Nottinghamshire
1982	Middlesex
1983	Essex
1984	Essex
1985	Middlesex
1986	Essex
1987	Nottinghamshire
1988	Worcestershire
1989	Worcestershire
1990	Middlesex
1991	Essex
1992	Essex
1993	Middlesex
1994	Warwickshire
1995	Warwickshire
1996	Leicestershire
1997	Glamorgan
1998	Leicestershire
1999	Surrey
2000	Surrey (Division 2 Northamptonshire)
2001	Yorkshire (Division 2 Sussex)
2002	Surrey (Division 2 Essex)
2003	Sussex (Division 2 Worcestershire)
2004	Warwickshire (Division 2 Nottinghamshire)

Ball of the century

It is universally agreed that this was bowled by Shane Warne to Mike Gatting in the first Test of the Ashes series at Old Trafford in 1993. It was Warne's very first ball in an Ashes test and spun a huge amount, beating Gatting's defensive prod, removing the off bail and leaving the former England captain nonplussed – a typically eyecatching way for Shane Warne to announce his arrival in international cricket.

English County Teams

	Year formed	First-class status	Home ground	Other grounds	Crest	One-day name
Derbyshire	1870	1871	Racecourse Ground (Derby)		Rose and crown	Phantoms
Durham	1882	1992	Riverside (Chester-le-Street)		Four lions rampant	Dynamos
Essex	1876	1895	County Ground (Chelmsford)	Southend-on-Sea, Colchester	Three scimitars	Eagles
Glamorgan	1888	1921	Sophia Gardens (Cardiff)	Swansea, Colwyn Bay	Daffodil	Dragons
Gloucestershire	1870	1870	County Ground (Bristol)	College Ground (Cheltenham), Archdeacon Meadow (Gloucester)	Bristol coat of arms	Gladiators
Hampshire	1863	1864	The Rose Bowl (Southampton)		Tudor rose and crown	Hawks
Kent	1859	1864	St Lawrence Ground (Canterbury)	Nevill Ground (Tunbridge Wells), The Mote (Maidstone)	White horse	Spitfires
Lancashire	1864	1865	Old Trafford (Manchester)	Liverpool	Red rose	Lightning
Leicestershire	1879	1895	Grace Road (Leicester)	Oakham	Running fox	Foxes
Middlesex	1864	1864	Lord's (London)	Southgate, Richmond, Shenley	Three seaxes	Crusaders
Northamptonshire	1878	1905	County Ground (Northampton)	Wardown Park (Luton)	Tudor rose	Steelbacks
Nottinghamshire	1841	1864	Trent Bridge (Nottingham)	Cleethorpes	Stag	Outlaws
Somerset	1875	1882	County Ground (Taunton)	Bath	Wessex wyvern	Sabres
Surrey	1845	1864	The Oval (London)	Whitgift School (Croydon), Guildford	Prince of Wales's feathers	Lions
Sussex	1839	1864	County Ground (Hove)	Horsham, Arundel	Six martlets	Sharks
Warwickshire	1882	1895	Edgbaston (Birmingham)	Stratford-on-Avon	Bear and ragged staff	Bears
Worcestershire	1865	1899	New Road (Worcester)		Shield with three pears	Royals
Yorkshire	1863	1864	Headingley (Leeds)	Scarborough	White rose	Phoenix

Mind games

Mike Brearley was England captain for two spells between 1977 and 1981. After retiring, he became a psychotherapist and there is no doubt that he put his insights into the human character and mind to good use when on the cricket field in order to get the best from his players (Australian fast bowler Rodney Hogg said of him that 'He has a degree in people'). He himself likened man management to gardening: 'some plants need fertilizer to thrive, others need pruning'. In the astounding 1981 Headingley Ashes Test where England came back from a seemingly impossible position to win, Brearley fired up his leading fast bowler Bob Willis by making him bowl up the hill at the start of the crucial Australian second innings. When he was switched to the other end, Willis tore in and destroyed the Australian batting, taking a match-winning 8 for 43.

Totesport National Cricket League

Known as the John Player League from 1969 to 1987, the Refuge Assurance League until 1991, the Axa Equity and Law League until 1999, the CGU League until 2000, and the Norwich Union National Cricket League until 2003. The format was 40 overs per side (with 50 overs in 1993) until a two-division structure was introduced in 1999. Division 1 now has nine teams and Division 2 ten (Scotland took part for the first time in 2003), each team playing each other twice in 45-over one-day matches. Three teams are relegated from Division 1 and three promoted from Division 2 each year.

1969	Lancashire
1970	Lancashire
1971	Worcestershire
1972	Kent
1973	Kent
1974	Leicestershire
1975	Hampshire
1976	Kent
1977	Leicestershire
1978	Hampshire
1979	Somerset
1980	Warwickshire
1981	Essex
1982	Sussex
1983	Yorkshire
1984	Essex
1985	Essex
1986	Hampshire
1987	Worcestershire
1988	Worcestershire
1989	Lancashire
1990	Derbyshire
1991	Nottinghamshire
1992	Middlesex
1993	Glamorgan
1994	Warwickshire
1995	Kent
1996	Surrey
1997	Warwickshire
1998	Lancashire
1999	Lancashire (Division 2 Sussex)
2000	Gloucestershire (Division 2 Surrey)
2001	Kent (Division 2 Glamorgan)
2002	Glamorgan (Division 2 Gloucestershire)
2003	Surrey (Division 2 Lancashire)
2004	Glamorgan (Division 2 Middlesex)

The bowler's Holding, the batsman's Willey

These words were uttered by Brian Johnston on Radio 4's *Test Match Special* when commentating on an England v West Indies Test match. Famous for his gaffes and love of cakes as much as his descriptive skills, Johnners also memorably said of the then England captain, 'Ray Illingworth has just relieved himself at the pavilion end'. His most notorious moment, however, was probably when fellow commentator Jonathan Agnew, talking about Ian Botham's dismissal when he hit his own wicket, remarked, 'he couldn't get his leg over'. Brian Johnston tried to restrain the surging tide of giggles as he persevered with his live commentary but eventually became speechless with laughter.

He's had a good innings

For nearly 42 years the record for the longest first-class innings belonged to Pakistan batsman, Hanif Mohammed, who batted for 970 minutes (999 according to him) in scoring 337 against West Indies at Bridgetown in January 1958. It is said that a young boy fell out of a tree overlooking the ground soon after Hanif started his innings. He was taken to hospital with suspected fractures, and released three days later. Returning to the ground he was amazed to find that Hanif was still batting. Hanif's record was overtaken in November 1999 by Indian Rajiv Nayyar who took 1,015 minutes (16 hours 55 minutes) to score 271 for Himachal Pradesh against Jammu & Kashmir.

Cheltenham & Gloucester Trophy

Known as the Gillette Cup until 1981 and the NatWest Bank Trophy until 2000. Now 50 overs per side (65 overs in 1963 and 60 until 1998), with the final played at Lord's.

	Winner	**Beaten finalist**
1963	Sussex	Worcestershire
1964	Sussex	Warwickshire
1965	Yorkshire	Surrey
1966	Warwickshire	Worcestershire
1967	Kent	Somerset
1968	Warwickshire	Sussex
1969	Yorkshire	Derbyshire
1970	Lancashire	Sussex
1971	Lancashire	Kent
1972	Lancashire	Warwickshire
1973	Gloucestershire	Sussex
1974	Kent	Lancashire
1975	Lancashire	Middlesex
1976	Northamptonshire	Lancashire
1977	Middlesex	Glamorgan
1978	Sussex	Somerset
1979	Somerset	Northamptonshire
1980	Middlesex	Surrey
1981	Derbyshire	Northamptonshire
1982	Surrey	Warwickshire
1983	Somerset	Kent
1984	Middlesex	Kent
1985	Essex	Nottinghamshire
1986	Sussex	Lancashire
1987	Nottinghamshire	Northamptonshire
1988	Middlesex	Worcestershire
1989	Warwickshire	Middlesex
1990	Lancashire	Northamptonshire
1991	Hampshire	Surrey
1992	Northamptonshire	Lancashire
1993	Warwickshire	Sussex
1994	Worcestershire	Warwickshire
1995	Warwickshire	Northamptonshire
1996	Lancashire	Essex
1997	Essex	Warwickshire
1998	Lancashire	Derbyshire
1999	Gloucestershire	Somerset
2000	Gloucestershire	Warwickshire
2001	Somerset	Leicestershire
2002	Yorkshire	Somerset
2003	Gloucestershire	Worcestershire
2004	Gloucestershire	Worcestershire

Twenty20 Cup

Each team has 20 overs for its innings. The four best teams from three regional groups go through to semi-finals and finals that are played on the same day.

	Winner	Beaten finalist	Venue
2003	Surrey	Warwickshire	Trent Bridge
2004	Leicestershire	Surrey	Edgbaston
2005			The Oval

In, out, shake it all about

It can be hard to explain cricket to newcomers to the sport. The following famous description doesn't help:

'You have two sides, one out in the field and one in. Each man that's in the side that's in goes out, and when he's out he comes in and the next man goes in until he's out. When they are all out, the side that's out comes in and the side that's been in goes out and tries to get those coming in, out. Sometimes you get men still in and not out. When a man goes out to go in, the men who are out try to get him out, and when he is out he goes in and the next man in goes out and goes in. There are two men called umpires who stay out all the time and they decide when the men who are in are out. When both sides have been in and all the men have been given out, and both sides have been out twice after all the men have been in, including those who are not out, that is the end of the game!'

Benson and Hedges Cup

Competition ran from 1972 to 2002. The 17 first-class counties (18 since 1992) plus various Minor Counties, University sides and Scotland competed, with the addition of Ireland in 1995. Each team had 55 overs until 1995 when the number was reduced to 50. Up until 1992 the format was round-robin matches in four groups, and then knockout games. In 1993 and 1994 the tournament was played just on a knockout basis. In 1999, for one year only, the competition was renamed the Super Cup and played between the top eight teams in the previous year's county championship.

	Winner	Beaten finalist
1972	Leicestershire	Yorkshire
1973	Kent	Worcestershire
1974	Surrey	Leicestershire
1975	Leicestershire	Middlesex
1976	Kent	Worcestershire
1977	Gloucestershire	Kent
1978	Kent	Derbyshire
1979	Essex	Surrey
1980	Northamptonshire	Essex
1981	Somerset	Surrey
1982	Somerset	Nottinghamshire
1983	Middlesex	Essex
1984	Lancashire	Warwickshire
1985	Leicestershire	Essex
1986	Middlesex	Kent
1987	Yorkshire	Northamptonshire

	Winner	Beaten finalist
1988	Hampshire	Derbyshire
1989	Nottinghamshire	Essex
1990	Lancashire	Worcestershire
1991	Worcestershire	Lancashire
1992	Hampshire	Kent
1993	Derbyshire	Lancashire
1994	Warwickshire	Worcestershire
1995	Lancashire	Kent
1996	Lancashire	Northamptonshire
1997	Surrey	Kent
1998	Essex	Leicestershire
1999	Gloucestershire	Yorkshire
2000	Gloucestershire	Glamorgan
2001	Surrey	Gloucestershire
2002	Warwickshire	Essex

Pura Cup

Australia's leading domestic competition; contested inter-state since 1892–3; known as the Sheffield Shield (after Lord Sheffield who brought an England team to Australia in 1891–2 and donated 150 pounds towards a trophy) until 1999.

1893	Victoria
1894	South Australia
1895	Victoria
1896	New South Wales
1897	New South Wales
1898	Victoria
1899	Victoria
1900	New South Wales
1901	Victoria
1902	New South Wales
1903	New South Wales
1904	New South Wales
1905	New South Wales
1906	New South Wales
1907	New South Wales
1908	Victoria
1909	New South Wales
1910	South Australia
1911	New South Wales
1912	New South Wales
1913	South Australia
1914	New South Wales
1915	Victoria
1920	New South Wales
1921	New South Wales
1922	Victoria
1923	New South Wales
1924	Victoria
1925	Victoria
1926	New South Wales
1927	South Australia
1928	Victoria
1929	New South Wales
1930	Victoria
1931	Victoria
1932	New South Wales
1933	New South Wales
1934	Victoria
1935	Victoria
1936	South Australia
1937	Victoria
1938	New South Wales
1939	South Australia
1940	New South Wales
1940–6	*Not held*
1947	Victoria
1948	Western Australia
1949	New South Wales
1950	New South Wales
1951	Victoria
1952	New South Wales
1953	South Australia
1954	New South Wales
1955	New South Wales

1956	New South Wales	**1981**	Western Australia
1957	New South Wales	**1982**	South Australia
1958	New South Wales	**1983**	New South Wales
1959	New South Wales	**1984**	Western Australia
1960	New South Wales	**1985**	New South Wales
1961	New South Wales	**1986**	New South Wales
1962	New South Wales	**1987**	Western Australia
1963	Victoria	**1988**	Western Australia
1964	South Australia	**1989**	Western Australia
1965	New South Wales	**1990**	New South Wales
1966	New South Wales	**1991**	Victoria
1967	Victoria	**1992**	Western Australia
1968	Western Australia	**1993**	New South Wales
1969	South Australia	**1994**	New South Wales
1970	Victoria	**1995**	Queensland
1971	South Australia	**1996**	South Australia
1972	Western Australia	**1997**	Queensland
1973	Western Australia	**1998**	Western Australia
1974	Victoria	**1999**	Western Australia
1975	Western Australia	**2000**	Queensland
1976	South Australia	**2001**	Queensland
1977	Western Australia	**2002**	Queensland
1978	Western Australia	**2003**	New South Wales
1979	Victoria	**2004**	Victoria
1980	Victoria		

Unlucky numbers

Cricketers appear to be particularly superstitious sportsmen. The score of 111 is meant to be unlucky for English cricketers and is known as 'nelson' (see A-Z section). Whenever this score (or a multiple of it) is reached in a game in which he is officiating, English umpire David Shepherd hops about, believing it is unlucky to keep both feet on the ground for long. The Australian unlucky number is 87, as it is 13 below 100.

ING Cup

Australian domestic one-day competition that also included New Zealand until 1975. Started in 1970 when known as the Vehicle & General Australasian Knock-out Competition; Coca-Cola Australasian Knock-out Competition (1972–3); Gilette Cup (1974–9); McDonald's Cup (1980–88); FAI Cup (1989–92); Mercantile Mutual Cup (1993–2001). Current format is 50 overs per side.

	Winner	**Beaten finalist**
1970	New Zealand	Victoria
1971	Western Australia	Queensland
1972	Victoria	South Australia
1973	New Zealand	Queensland
1974	Western Australia	New Zealand
1975	New Zealand	Western Australia
1976	Queensland	Western Australia

	Winner	Beaten finalist
1977	Western Australia	Victoria
1978	Western Australia	Tasmania
1979	Tasmania	Western Australia
1980	Victoria	New South Wales
1981	Queensland	Western Australia
1982	Queensland	New South Wales
1983	Western Australia	New South Wales
1984	South Australia	Western Australia
1985	New South Wales	South Australia
1986	Western Australia	Victoria
1987	South Australia	Tasmania
1988	New South Wales	South Australia
1989	Queensland	Victoria
1990	Western Australia	South Australia
1991	Western Australia	New South Wales
1992	New South Wales	Western Australia
1993	New South Wales	Victoria
1994	New South Wales	Western Australia
1995	Victoria	South Australia
1995	Queensland	Western Australia
1997	Western Australia	Queensland
1998	Queensland	New South Wales
1999	Victoria	New South Wales
2000	Western Australia	Queensland
2001	New South Wales	Western Australia
2002	New South Wales	Queensland
2003	New South Wales	Western Australia
2004	Western Australia	Queensland

Player Records

Most appearances in Test cricket

Steve Waugh (Australia)	168
Allan Border (Australia)	156
Alec Stewart (England)	133
Courtney Walsh (West Indies)	132
Kapil Dev (India)	131
Mark Waugh (Australia)	128
Sunil Gavaskar (India)	125
Javed Miandad (Pakistan)	124
Viv Richards (West Indies)	121

Most runs in Test career

Allan Border (Australia)	11,174
Steve Waugh (Australia)	10,927
Sunil Gavaskar (India)	10,122
Brian Lara (West Indies)	10,094

Bad luck, old chap

John MacBryan of Somerset is the least successful Test cricketer. He was selected by England for the Old Trafford Test against South Africa in 1925 but torrential rain ended play at 4.00pm on the first day (of three) after 165 minutes of play. Play never resumed and MacBryan was not selected again, making him the only Test cricketer who never batted, bowled or dismissed anyone in the field.

Cricket

Most runs in Test career

Sachin Tendulkar (India)	9,879
Graham Gooch (England)	8,900
Javed Miandad (Pakistan)	8,832
Viv Richards (West Indies)	8,540
Alec Stewart (England)	8,463
David Gower (England)	8,231
Geoffrey Boycott (England)	8,114
Garry Sobers (West Indies)	8,032
Mark Waugh (Australia)	8,029

Highest individual score in a Test innings

	Batsman	Opponent	Venue	Year
400*	Brian Lara (West Indies)	England	St John's, Antigua	2004
380	Matthew Hayden (Australia)	Zimbabwe	Perth, Australia	2003
375	Brian Lara (West Indies)	England	St John's, Antigua	1994
365*	Garry Sobers (West Indies)	Pakistan	Kingston, Jamacia	1958
364	Len Hutton (England)	Australia	The Oval, London, England	1938
340	Sanath Jayasuriya (Sri Lanka)	India	Colombo, Sri Lanka	1997
337	Hanif Mohammad (Pakistan)	West Indies	Bridgetown, Barbados	1958
336*	Wally Hammond (England)	New Zealand	Auckland, New Zealand	1933
334*	Mark Taylor (Australia)	Pakistan	Peshawar, Pakistan	1998
334	Don Bradman (Australia)	England	Leeds, England	1930
333	Graham Gooch (England)	India	Lord's, London, England	1990
329	Inzamam-ul-Haq (Pakistan)	New Zealand	Lahore, Pakistan	2002
325	Andrew Sandham (England)	West Indies	Kingston, Jamaica	1930
311	Bobby Simpson (Australia)	England	Manchester, England	1964
310*	John Edrich (England)	New Zealand	Leeds, England	1965
309	Virender Sehwag (India)	Pakistan	Multan, Pakistan	2004
307	Bob Cowper (Australia)	England	Melbourne, Australia	1966
304	Don Bradman (Australia)	England	Leeds, England	1934
302	Lawrence Rowe (West Indies)	England	Bridgetown, Barbados	1974

* = not out

Most wickets in Test career

Shane Warne (Australia)	561
Muttiah Muralitharan (Sri Lanka)	532
Courtney Walsh (West Indies)	519
Glenn McGrath (Australia)	477
Anil Kumble (India)	444
Kapil Dev (India)	434
Richard Hadlee (New Zealand)	431
Wasim Akram (Pakistan)	414
Curtly Ambrose (West Indies)	405

Best bowling in a Test innings

	Bowler	Opponent	Venue	Year
10/53	Jim Laker (England)	Australia	Manchester, England	1956
10/74	Anil Kumble (India)	Pakistan	Delhi, India	1999
9/28	George Lohmann (England)	South Africa	Johannesburg, South Africa	1896

	Bowler	Opponent	Venue	Year
9/37	Jim Laker (England)	Australia	Manchester, England	1956
9/51	Muttiah Muralitharan (Sri Lanka)	Zimbabwe	Kandy, Sri Lanka	2002
9/52	Richard Hadlee (New Zealand)	Australia	Brisbane, Australia	1985
9/56	Abdul Qadir (Pakistan)	England	Lahore, Pakistan	1987
9/57	Devon Malcolm (England)	South Africa	The Oval, London, England	1994
9/65	Muttiah Muralitharan (Sri Lanka)	England	The Oval, London, England	1998
9/69	Jasubhai Patel (India)	Australia	Kanpur, India	1959
9/83	Kapil Dev (India)	West Indies	Ahmedabad, India	1983
9/86	Sarfraz Nawaz (Pakistan)	Australia	Melbourne, Australia	1979
9/95	Jack Noreiga (West Indies)	India	Port-of-Spain, Trinidad	1971
9/102	Subash Gupte (India)	West Indies	Kanpur, India	1958
9/103	Sydney Barnes (England)	South Africa	Johannesburg, South Africa	1913
9/113	Hugh Tayfield (South Africa)	England	Johannesburg, South Africa	1957
9/121	Arthur Mailey (Australia)	England	Melbourne, Australia	1921

Leading Test all-rounders (2,000 runs and 200 wickets)

	Runs	Wickets
Wasim Akram (Pakistan)	2,898	414
Richie Benaud (Australia)	2,201	248
Ian Botham (England)	5,200	383
Kapil Dev (India)	5,248	434
Richard Hadlee (New Zealand)	3,124	431
Imran Khan (Pakistan)	3,807	362
Sean Pollock (South Africa)	3,109	361
Garry Sobers (West Indies)	8,032	235
Shane Warne (Australia)	2,449	561

Most runs in first-class career

	Runs	Matches	Innings
Jack Hobbs	61,760	834	1,325
Frank Woolley	58,959	978	1,530
Patsy Hendren	57,611	833	1,300
Phil Mead	55,061	814	1,340
W G Grace	54,211	870	1,478
Herbert Sutcliffe	50,670	754	1,098
Wally Hammond	50,551	634	1,005

Most wickets in first-class career

	Wickets	Matches
Wilfred Rhodes	4,204	1,110
Tich Freeman	3,776	592
Charlie Parker	3,278	635
Jack Hearne	3,061	639
Tom Goddard	2,979	593
Alex Kennedy	2,874	677
Derek Shackleton	2,857	647
Tony Lock	2,844	654
Fred Titmus	2,830	792
W G Grace	2,809	870

Nicknames

Although often all too predictable ('Inzy' for Inzamam-ul-Haq, 'Athers' for Michael Atherton, 'Mushy' for Mushtaq Mohammed), some more colourful nicknames have been given to cricketers:

Shoaib Akhtar	'The Rawalpindi Express' (because of the speed of his bowling)
Ian Botham	'Beefy'/'Guy the Gorilla'
Don Bradman	'The Don'
Phil DeFreitas	'Daffy'
Allan Donald	'White Lightning' (because he was a white South African fast bowler)
Andrew Flintoff	'Freddie' (because his large frame and muscular style of play gave him the nickname Fred Flintstone)
Joel Garner	'Big Bird'
Sunil Gavaskar	'The Little Master'
W G Grace	'The Doctor'
Richard Hadlee	'Paddles' (because of his large feet)
Michael Holding	'Whispering Death'
Lance Klusener	'Zulu'
Glenn McGrath	'Pigeon' (because of his skinny legs)
Ken Mackay	'Slasher' (an ironic name as he was a very defensive batsman)
Ricky Ponting	'Punter' (because of his fondness for gambling)
Derek Randall	'Arkle' (because he was fast like the racehorse)
Viv Richards	'Master Blaster'
Harbhajan Singh	'The Turbanator' (because he is a Sikh and wears a turban)
Alec Stewart	'The Gaffer'
Marcus Trescothick	'Banger' (because of his love of sausages)
Fred Trueman	'Fiery'
Phil Tufnell	'The Cat' (because of his languid character and less than agile fielding)
Frank Tyson	'Typhoon'
Derek Underwood	'Deadly'
Shane Warne	'Hollywood' (because of his celebrity status)
Steve Waugh	'Tug'

A-Z

all-rounder	a player who is skilled at both batting and bowling
arm ball	a delivery by a spin bowler that continues in the direction of the bowler's arm, not deviating as is normal
armguard	protection worn by a batsman on the forearm facing the bowler
away swing	movement of the ball in the air from the **leg** to the **off** side
bails	the two small pieces of wood that rest on top of the **stumps**; one of them must be dislodged if a batsman is to be given out **bowled** or **run out**
ball	1. the hard, leather-covered spherical object bowled by bowlers 2. an instance of a bowler bowling the ball to a batsman, eg *that was a good ball*
Barmy Army	the name given to the group of England fans who travel around the world to support their team

bat-pad catch a catch (usually from a slow delivery) taken after the ball has struck the bat and then rebounded off the batsman's **pad**

batsman a player who attempts to hit the ball with his bat and so score runs

beamer a **full toss** at head height

bite the amount of turn a spinner is able to extract from a particular wicket

bouncer a fast delivery that bounces up high off the pitch to around shoulder height

boundary 1. the outer limit of the playing area, usually marked by a rope or painted white line 2. a hit by a batsman that reaches (a four) or clears (a six) the boundary

bowled when a ball bowled by the bowler strikes the stumps and dislodges the **bails**, and the batsman is thus out

bowler a player who projects the ball overarm from the **stumps** at one end towards the stumps at the other in an attempt to get the batsman **out**

bowling crease a horizontal line marked at each end of the pitch, indicating from where the bowler should bowl and on which the **stumps** are placed (compare **popping crease**)

box a hard plastic form of protection for the genitals, worn inside the trousers by batsmen and wicketkeepers (and sometimes close fielders)

bumper same as **bouncer**

bye an **extra** awarded when the batsmen complete a run after the ball has not made contact with the bat or body

central contract when a player is contracted to his national team as well as to a county or state team

centurion a batsman who scores a **century**

century a score of 100 runs or more by a batsman

Chinaman the standard delivery of a left-arm wrist-spin bowler, ie one that moves from **off** to **leg** (for a right-handed batsman) after pitching

Chinese cut an inadvertent stroke by a batsman where the ball is deflected off the inside edge of the bat, behind the wicket

cover a fielding position on the **off** side between **point** and **mid-off**

cover drive a **drive** by a batsman that goes through the **cover** area

cover point same as **cover**

crease 1. any of the lines marked at either end of the pitch; see **bowling crease**, **popping crease** and **return crease** 2. a batsman is said to be 'in his crease' if he is behind the **popping crease**

cross-batted a cross-batted shot is one played with the bat horizontal

cut a shot on the **off** side, between **cover** and **third man**, played with the bat close to the horizontal

dab if a batsman dabs the ball, he deflects it with minimal bat movement on the **off** side

dead the ball is dead if it is not in play (in accordance with various laws)

dead bat if a batsman plays the ball with a dead bat, he defensively allows the ball to hit the bat so that it falls in front of him

declare when the captain of the batting side declares, he ends his side's **innings** before all ten wickets have been taken

doosra a top-spinning delivery by an **off-break** bowler that moves from **off** to **leg**, rather than the usual **leg** to **off**

dot ball a delivery from which no runs are scored and no wicket taken, so called because in such circumstances the scorer places a dot in the score book

drive a shot played with a vertical bat so that the ball runs along the ground in front of the batsman

drop-in wicket a portable batting surface that is laid into the playing surface

duck a score of no runs by a batsman

Duckworth-Lewis method see below

The Duckworth-Lewis method

Frustrated by rain delays having an unfair influence on the result of one-day games, statisticians Frank Duckworth and Tony Lewis invented a method for calculating the total required for a team batting second in a rain-affected one-day game. The actual formula used is complicated to the layman (and most cricketers) but essentially looks at the 'resources' available to a team, these being how many wickets they still have and how many balls are still to be bowled. Each time rain stops play, the required total will be adjusted downwards, taking into account how many fewer balls will be bowled. In games where the method is employed, the abbreviation D/L will appear next to the score.

edge if a batsman edges the ball, he gets a slight touch to it from the edge of his bat

extra a run scored by the batting side from a **bye**, **leg-bye**, **wide** or **no-ball**

extra cover a fielding position on the **off** side between **cover** and **mid-off**

feather if a batsman feathers the ball, he gets a very faint edge to it

field the arrangement of the **fielders**, eg *the captain set a very defensive field*

fielder a player who catches and stops the ball

fine leg a fielding position, on the **leg** side boundary at a more acute angle to the batsman than **long leg**

flipper a delivery by a leg-spin bowler which comes at the batsman faster than a standard ball, with backspin, skids on low and does not deviate on pitching

fly slip a fielding position behind the **slips**, between them and the boundary

follow-on when a team has to start its second innings immediately after the first, as the result of scoring a total that is lower than that of the opposing team by more than a predetermined amount

full toss a ball bowled by the bowler that does not pitch before it reaches the batsman

Gabba Test cricket ground in Brisbane, Australia; from the suburb of Woolloongabba where it is situated

gate the gap between the batsman's pad and bat when playing a shot, eg *he was bowled through the gate*

glance if a batsman glances the ball, he hits it so that it deviates only slightly from its line of flight

golden duck when a batsman is given out to the first ball he faces

googly an **off-break** bowled with an apparent **leg-break** action by a right-arm bowler to a right-handed batsman, or conversely for a left-arm bowler

ground — a batsman's ground is the space behind the **popping crease** with which the batsman must be in touch by bat or person if he is not to be **stumped** or **run out**

grubber — a delivery that keeps low after leaving the bowler's hand

guard — the position of a batsman's bat relative to the stumps when standing ready to receive a ball, eg *he takes a leg stump guard*

gully — a fielding position on the **off** side, between **point** and **slips**

half-century — a score of 50 runs or more by a batsman

handled the ball — when a batsman deliberately touches the ball with his hand, especially in order to prevent if from hitting the **stumps**, and is thus out

Harrow drive — same as **Chinese cut**

hat trick — the taking of three wickets with consecutive balls; so called because the feat was considered as deserving a new hat

hit wicket — when a batsman strikes the stumps with his bat or part of his body and dislodges the **bails**, and is thus out

hole out — if a batsman holes out, he is out caught

hook — an attacking stroke played with a horizontal bat sending the ball from shoulder height or above onto the **leg** side behind the wicket

how's that, howzat — the appeal of the fielding side to the umpire to give the batsman out

ICC — International Cricket Council

innings — a team's or individual batsman's turn at batting

inswinger — a ball bowled so as to swerve from **off** to **leg**

king pair — two **golden ducks** in the same match

late cut — a **cut** shot played so that the ball deflects more finely than usual

lbw — short for leg before wicket (see box on p156)

leg — that half of the field on the side on which the batsman stands when waiting to receive the ball, separated from the **off** side by an imaginary line drawn from wicket to wicket

leg-break — a ball bowled by a slow bowler that breaks from the **leg** side towards the **off** side on pitching

leg-bye — a run made after the ball has touched any part of the batsman's person except his hands or bat, credited to the batsman's team but not to his individual score

leg-cutter — a fast bowler's delivery that moves from **leg** to **off** after pitching

leg glance — a shot played with a vertical bat in which the ball is deflected finely on the **leg** side towards **fine leg**

leg slip — a fielding position slightly behind the batsman on the **leg** side

leg spin — spin imparted to a ball to cause a **leg-break**

leg spinner — someone who bowls **leg-breaks**

length — the distance from the bowler at which the ball pitches; if a bowler bowls 'a good length' or 'on a length', the ball pitches at a distance such that the batsman cannot easily play an attacking stroke

line — the trajectory of a ball bowled by a bowler; for example an 'off stump line' would mean that the ball was directed at **off stump**

long hop — a short-pitched, high-bouncing ball that is easy to hit

long leg — a fielding position, on the boundary behind the batsman on the **leg** side

long off — a fielding position, on the boundary behind the bowler on the **off** side

long on — a fielding position, on the boundary behind the bowler on the **leg** side

Lord's — Test cricket ground in St John's Wood, London, founded by Thomas Lord in 1814; considered the spiritual home of English cricket, it is also the county ground of Middlesex and headquarters of the ECB and **MCC**

maiden — an **over** in which no runs are scored by the batsmen and no **wide** or **no-ball** is bowled

MCC — the Marylebone Cricket Club; founded in 1787, it is responsible for lawmaking and promotes cricket worldwide

MCG — Melbourne Cricket Ground

meat — the meat of the bat is the centre of the blade, eg *the shot came out of the meat of the bat*

middle — if a batsman middles the ball, he hits it in the centre of the bat so that it travels a long way

mid-off — a fielding position, behind the bowler on the **off** side

mid-on — a fielding position, behind the bowler on the **leg** side

midwicket — a fielding position, on the **leg** side, about midway between **mid-on** and **square leg**

net — 1. a practice pitch surrounded by nets to stop the ball from travelling far 2. a practice session in a net

nick — if a batsman nicks the ball, he gets a slight touch to it from the edge of his bat

night watchman — a relatively unskilled batsman who is sent in to bat towards the end of the day's play in order to prevent a more skilled batsman from having to go in

no-ball — a ball bowled in a way that it is disallowed by the rules (most commonly because the bowler's front foot is over the **popping crease** when he releases the ball), and which counts as one run to the batting side

ODI — (short for one-day international); a limited-overs game between national teams

off — that half of the field on the opposite side to that on which the batsman stands when waiting to receive the ball, separated from the **leg** side by an imaginary line drawn from wicket to wicket

off-break — a ball bowled by a slow bowler that breaks from the **off** side towards the **leg** side on pitching

off-cutter — a fast bowler's delivery that moves from **off** to **leg** after pitching

off-drive — a **drive** to the **off** side

off spin — spin imparted to a ball to cause an **off-break**

off spinner — a bowler who bowls **off-breaks**

on — same as **leg**

on-drive — a **drive** to the **leg** side

opener — one of the two batsmen who start the batting side's **innings**

order — the list of the batsmen in the order in which they take turns at batting; hence top order (broadly numbers 1 to 4), middle order (broadly numbers 5 to 8) and bottom order (broadly numbers 9 to 11)

outfield — the outer part of the field, near the **boundary**

outswinger — a ball bowled so as to swerve from **leg** to **off**

Oval — Test cricket ground in south London, county ground of Surrey

over — a series of six balls after which play changes from one end to the other; previously eight-ball overs were also used

overthrow — a return of the ball to the wicket that is missed by the fielders there, and a run scored as a consequence

pad — a protective covering worn by batsmen and wicketkeepers on the front of the lower leg

paddle sweep — a **sweep** played gently, with a short stroke

pair — two **ducks** in the same match; compare **king pair**

partnership — 1. the time for which two batsmen bat together, eg *a long partnership of over two hours* 2. the number of runs scored during that time, eg *a partnership of 153 for the third wicket*

pinch hitter — a term borrowed from baseball to describe a player in a limited-overs game who bats higher up the order than normally

point — a fielding position, on the **off** side on a line with the **popping crease**

popping crease — a horizontal line marked at each end of the pitch, beyond which the batsman is in his **ground** and behind which the bowler must have his front foot when releasing the ball

pull — if a batsman pulls the ball, he hits it with a horizontal bat from waist height round onto the **leg** side

referee — an official at Test matches who deals with disciplinary matters

retire hurt — if a batsman retires hurt, he leaves the pitch after being injured; he can return at a later point in the innings if desired

reverse sweep — a **sweep** shot played on the **off** side by reversing the grip on the bat

reverse swing — a phenomenon that causes a ball that has become roughened on one side to swing in the opposite direction to a new ball

run — the basic unit of scoring; when a batsman runs from one **popping crease** to the other

runner — a player who runs on behalf of an injured batsman

run out — when a fielder throws the ball and dislodges the **bails** before the batsman has reached his **ground**, the batsman thus being out

SCG — Sydney Cricket Ground

seam — a ball seams if it deviates after pitching on the raised stitching that joins together the two pieces of leather which encase the ball

seamer — a medium-pace or fast bowler who bowls balls that **seam**

short — a fielding position that is described as short is closer than normal to the batsman, eg *short midwicket*

short leg — the fielding position of **short square leg**

shoulder — the shoulder of the bat is the slightly curved upper edge of the blade, near to where it joins the handle

sight screen — a large, usually white screen placed on the **boundary** behind the bowler, providing a backdrop against which the batsman can more easily see the approaching ball

silly — a fielding position that is described as silly is very close to the batsman, eg *silly mid-on*

slip — any of several fielders (eg first slip, second slip, etc) positioned in a row next to the wicketkeeper on the **off** side

slog — a shot played with the intention of hitting the ball hard but without great control and not using the correct technique

slog overs — in limited-overs games, the overs at the end of an innings when the batting team attempt to score a lot of runs quickly

slog sweep — a **sweep** shot in which the ball is hit hard and in the air, in front of **square**

snick — a slight deflection off the edge of the bat

spell	a number of overs bowled consecutively by a bowler, eg *he bowled two five-over spells*
spinner	a slow bowler who twists the ball with his wrist or fingers, in order to make it deviate after striking the ground
splice	the part of the handle of the bat that fits into the blade
square	1. the rectangular area in the centre of the ground, on which the wickets are prepared 2. at right angles to the wicket, eg *this batsman is strong square of the wicket*
square cut	a shot **square** on the **off** side, played with the bat close to the horizontal
square leg	a fielding position, on the **leg** side in a line with the **popping crease**
stand	same as **partnership**
strike	if a batsman has the strike, he will receive the next ball
stump	one of the three sticks forming (with the **bails**) a **wicket**
stumped	when the wicketkeeper dislodges the **bails** with the ball before the batsman on **strike** has regained his **ground**, the batsman thus being out
stumps	1. same as **wicket** (sense 1) 2. the end of the day's play
sweep	a stroke in which the batsman goes down on one knee to play the ball to the **leg** side with a horizontal bat
sweeper	a fielder positioned on the **boundary** in front of **square** to stop balls hit through the infield
swing	a ball swings when it swerves in the air
tail	the weaker batsmen at the end of a team's batting **order**
Test match	a five-day match between international teams that have been awarded Test-match status by the **ICC**
thigh pad	a plastic or fabric protective covering for the thigh worn inside the trousers by batsmen
third man	a fielding position, near the **boundary** on the **off** side behind the **slips**
third umpire	an official who does not appear on the field of play but adjudicates on **run out** decisions and disputed catches with the use of TV replays
throw-down	a throw of a ball from a short distance to a batsman for practice
tickle	same as **feather**
twelfth man	a player selected beyond the necessary eleven to play if required as a substitute fielder
two	the **guard** of middle and leg, in full 'two leg'
umpire	one of the two onfield officials who ensure that the rules are upheld and give decisions; in some matches there is also a **third umpire**
V	the V is the area between **mid-on** and **mid-off**, used in descriptions of where a batsman hits the ball
WACA	(pronounced *wacker*) Test cricket ground in Perth of the Western Australian Cricket Association
walk	if a player walks, he leaves the pitch without waiting for the umpire to adjudicate on an appeal
wicket	1. the arrangement of the three stumps with two **bails** on top which the batsman defends against the bowling 2. a **stump** 3. the pitch, eg *the wicket was a fast one* 4. a batsman's stay at the wicket, or his joint stay there with another, eg *they put on 211 for the third wicket*

wicketkeeper the fielder who stands immediately behind the batsman's wicket and whose main object is to stop balls missed by the batsman

wide a delivery that is judged by the umpire to be beyond the batsman's reach and which counts as one run to the batting side

wrong 'un same as **googly**

yorker a ball bowled so as to pitch on the **popping crease** and pass under the bat

zooter a delivery by a leg spinner that does not spin and dips late in flight

Some cricket slang

blob a score of nought, so called because it is round

bunny same as **rabbit**

bunsen rhyming slang (Bunsen burner = turner) for a wicket on which the ball spins a long way after pitching

chin music bowling **bouncers** that rear up close to the batsman's head; a term invented and a practice mastered by West Indian fast bowlers

coffin a case used to carry a player's equipment and clothing

corridor of uncertainty the area outside a batsman's **off stump**, where he is unsure whether to play a stroke or not; a phrase popularized by England batsman-turned-commentator Geoffrey Boycott

cow corner a fielding position on the boundary on the **leg** side between deep **midwicket** and **long on** to which **cow shots** are hit

cow shot a slog to the leg side

dig an **innings**, eg *they only scored 156 in their first dig*

dolly an easy catch

four ball a poorly bowled ball that can be easily hit to the **boundary**

gardening when a batsman prods down loose areas of the pitch with the end of his bat

good areas if a bowler is said to be putting the ball in good areas, he is bowling in such away that the batsman is not able to score easily

hutch the pavilion, eg *by lunch they had made 100 with five men back in the hutch*

jaffa an exceptionally good ball that **seams** or spins a lot and so is difficult to play

knock a batsman's innings, eg *a match-winning knock from Lara*

leggy a leg spinner

Michelle five wickets by a bowler; rhyming slang (Michelle Pfeiffer = five for)

nelson the score of 111, believed by English players to be unlucky; said to originate from the widely but erroneously held belief that Lord Nelson had one eye, one arm and one leg

nine, ten, jack the last three batsmen (numbers nine, ten and eleven)

nurdle if you nurdle the ball in a certain direction, you hit it there but not hard and usually into a gap between fielders

pair of spectacles same as **pair**

peg a **stump**, eg *the ball hit the off peg*

pie chucker a pejorative term for an inexpert bowler

plumb unquestionably **leg before wicket**

pyjama cricket a pejorative term for one-day cricket, from the brightly coloured clothes that are often worn

rabbit 1. an inferior batsman 2. a batsman who is often dismissed by a certain bowler, eg *he's Warne's rabbit*

sandshoe crusher an Australian term for a ball that pitches on the batsman's boots

shooter a delivery that keeps abnormally low after pitching

show the bowler the maker's name to play a forward defensive stroke with exaggerated correctness

sit on the splice	to bat defensively, with no attempt to score runs
skier	a ball hit high into the air
skittle out	if a team is skittled out, they are dismissed for a low score
sledging	offensive, sometimes humorous, remarks made to a batsman in order to disturb his concentration
stick	same as **peg**
sticky dog	a pitch affected by rain (no longer a feature of Test matches where pitches are always covered)
stonewall	to bat extremely defensively
timbers	the **stumps**, eg *Knott was sharp behind the timbers*
ton	same as **century**
track	the pitch, eg *the track at Kingston is always a quick one*
turn one's arm over	to bowl, especially said of someone who is not a recognized bowler, eg *even Taylor turned his arm over in the course of the long Indian innings*
twirler	a spin bowler
Windies	the West Indies team
yahoo	an exuberant attempt to hit the ball hard, often with disappointing results

Some famous cricketers

Wasim Akram, 1966–

Born in Lahore, he played 104 tests for Pakistan (second only to **Javed Miandad**), taking 414 wickets with his left-arm swing and seam bowling. He captained the side 25 times but it is in the one-day international game that he stands supreme: 356 appearances and 502 wickets are both world records. In Britain he played for Lancashire for many years, and latterly Hampshire.

Michael Atherton, 1968–

Born in Failsworth, Manchester, England, he played for Lancashire throughout his career and captained England a record 54 times between 1993 and 2001 with only moderate success (13 wins) but held an average team together from his opening batsman position. He played 115 tests and scored 7,728 runs with 16 centuries. His highest score of 185 not out against South Africa at Johannesburg summed up his gutsy attitude to cricket: a doughty match-saving rearguard action that spanned 643 minutes. He was awarded the OBE in 1997.

Mohammad Azharuddin, 1963–

Born in Hyderabad, India, he emerged as a formidable batsman, making his Test debut for India in 1985 and scoring three centuries in each of his first three matches. Named captain of India in 1989, he went on to become his country's most successful captain, with 14 Test victories. In 2000, with a total of 99 Test appearances, he was banned for life by the Indian Board of Control for involvement in match-fixing.

Richie Benaud, 1930–

Born in Penrith, New South Wales, Australia, he first played for New South Wales in 1948 and went on to appear in 63 Test matches for Australia, captaining the team 28 times and participating in three successful tours of England (1953, 1956 and 1961). In all he took

248 Test wickets and scored 2,201 Test runs, becoming the first man to achieve 2,000 runs and 200 wickets in Test cricket. For many he has become the voice of cricket in his job as a commentator. He was awarded the OBE in 1961.

Dickie Bird, 1933–

Born in Barnsley, Yorkshire, England, he played for Yorkshire (1956–9) and Leicestershire (1960–4) and by the end of his playing career had scored 3,314 runs in first-class cricket. He became better known, however, as an umpire (1970–98), celebrated as much for his sense of humour and eccentricities as for his authority on the pitch. He umpired a record 67 Test matches in the years 1973–96, 93 limited-overs internationals and the first three finals of the World Cup. He was awarded the MBE in 1986 ('It means more to me than my life', he said).

Allan Border, 1955–

Born in Cremorne, Sydney, Australia, he made his Test debut for Australia in 1978, and captained the team from 1984 to 1994. He established world records for most Test match and ODI appearances (now superseded), and holds the record for the most runs scored in Test matches. He has played county cricket in England for Gloucestershire and Essex. He retired from Test cricket in 1995 and from Sheffield Shield cricket in 1996. A medal named after him is now awarded to the outstanding Australian cricketer of the preceding twelve months.

Ian Botham, 1955–

Born in Heswall, Merseyside, England, he is regarded as one of the greatest all-rounders of all time. He played for England in 102 Test matches, took 383 wickets, and scored 5,200 runs. His performances for England in 1981 (149 not out at Headingley to set up the most unlikely of victories, a 5 wickets for 1 run spell at Edgbaston) led to the Test series win over Australia becoming known as 'Botham's Ashes'. He played for Somerset (1974–86), Worcestershire (1987–91) and Durham (1992–3), before his retirement in 1993. Off-the-field brushes with authority alternated with successful charity fund-raising campaigns. He was awarded the OBE in 1992 and is now a commentator.

Geoffrey Boycott, 1940–

Born in Fitzwilliam, Yorkshire, England, he is the most celebrated batsman in postwar English cricket. An opening batsman with a technically perfect defence, he regularly frustrated bowling attacks and is the only England player to bat on all days of a five-day Test (at Trent Bridge in 1977 against Australia). He played 108 times for England between 1964 and 1982, and scored 151 first-class centuries, but there was controversy over his value as a team player. He was awarded the OBE in 1980.

Sir Don(ald) Bradman, 1908–2001

Born in Cootamundra, New South Wales, Australia, he is regarded as the greatest batsman in the history of the game. He played for Australia from 1928 to 1948 (captain 1936–48). A prodigious scorer, he made the highest aggregate and largest number of centuries in Tests against England, and holds the record for the highest Australian Test score against England (334 at Leeds in 1930). His batting average in Test matches was an astonishing 99.94 runs per innings. He was the first Australian cricketer to be knighted, in 1949, and was named as one of the five Wisden cricketers of the century in 2000.

No average cricketer

Batsmen's averages are calculated by dividing the total number of runs they have scored by the number of times they have been out. A Test average of over 50 is exceptional. When Don Bradman came to play his final innings, he needed to score only 4 runs in order to ensure himself a career Test average of 100. The story has it that he was still misty-eyed from the emotional reception he received as he walked onto the pitch; he was promptly bowled by Eric Hollies for nought, leaving him with an average of 99.94. This remains a remarkable 39 runs above the second-best Test batting average.

Denis Compton, 1918–97

Born in Hendon, England, he first played for Middlesex in 1936, and was first capped for England the following year. He played in 78 Test matches, scoring 17 Test centuries. In his first-class career he scored over 38,000 runs, including 123 centuries; in 1947 he scored a record 18 centuries. He was also a talented footballer, a member of the Cup-winning Arsenal team in 1950, and was capped for England in 1943. He was awarded the CBE in 1958.

Sir Learie Constantine, 1901–71

Born in Petit Valley, Trinidad, he was an accomplished all-rounder and respected fast bowler. In 1928 he became the first West Indian cricketer to achieve 1,000 runs and 100 wickets in a single season. He was knighted in 1962 and given a life peerage in 1969.

Sir Colin Cowdrey, 1932–2000

Born in Bangalore, India, he was educated at Brasenose College, Oxford. He played in a record 114 Tests for England (23 as captain), despite being dogged by injuries and illness, and made six tours of Australia, also a record. In his long first-class career (1951–75) he was captain of Kent from 1957 to 1971. He became International Cricket Council chairman between 1989 and 1993, overseeing the return of South Africa to international cricket and the agreement of the international code of conduct in 1991. He was knighted in 1992.

Basil D'Oliveira, 1931–

Born in Cape Town, South Africa, he was prohibited from playing cricket as a Cape Coloured and so moved to England, where he played league cricket in Lancashire before joining Worcestershire. He made his debut for England in 1966 and went on to win 44 caps and score five Test centuries. The South African government's refusal to admit him to the country with the England team in 1968–9 resulted in the tour being cancelled and South Africa being banned from international cricket.

Godfrey Evans, 1920–99

Born in Finchley, London, he joined the Kent county cricket staff at the age of 16. First capped for England in 1946, he played in 91 Test matches, and set many new records, including 218 Test dismissals (75 against Australia). He was the first wicketkeeper to have dismissed more than 200 batsmen and scored 2,000 runs in Test cricket. He was awarded the CBE in 1960.

Sunil Gavaskar, 1949–

Born in Bombay, India, and educated at St Xavier's College and Bombay University, the perfection of his style as well as his short stature earned him his nickname 'the Little Master'. He played in 125 Test matches for India from 1971 to 1987, and scored 10,122 runs, including a record 34 Test centuries. He was the first player to score more than 10,000 Test runs.

Graham Gooch, 1953–

Born in Leytonstone, London, England, he made his debut for Essex in 1973, and was captain of the club (apart from 1988) from 1986 to 1994. First capped for England in 1975 (he made an inauspicious debut, scoring a pair), he went on to play in over 100 Test matches, with a memorable top score of 333 in 1990 against India at Lord's. An enigmatic character with a strong work ethic, he was initially a flamboyant big-hitter but modified his game in later years. He received the OBE in 1991.

David Gower, 1957–

Born in Tunbridge Wells, Kent, England, he came to the fore quickly, scoring a 50 in his first Test innings and demonstrating elegant left-handed stroke play. He was captain of England in the mid-1980s, though without particular success. He was recalled as captain in 1989, only to lose the captaincy and his place in the team after a heavy defeat in that year's Ashes series. He received the OBE in 1992. He is now a TV commentator and is a member of the St Moritz Tobogganing Club.

W G Grace, 1848–1915

Born in Downend, near Bristol, England, Dr William Gilbert Grace is considered the first genuinely great cricketer of modern times. He started playing cricket for Gloucestershire in 1864, and was immediately picked for the Gentlemen v Players match. He scored 2,739 runs in a season in 1871, and in 1876 he scored 344 runs in an innings for MCC. He took his medical degree in 1879 and had a practice in Bristol, but devoted most of his time to cricket. He toured Canada and the USA, and twice captained the Test team against Australia, in 1880 and 1882. By 1895 he had scored 100 first-class centuries, and by the end of his career in 1908 he was a national hero. Once, when given out, he is alleged to have refused to leave, saying to the umpire, 'They haven't come to see you umpiring, they have come to see me bat.'

Sir Richard Hadlee, 1948–

He was born in Christchurch, New Zealand. He and his father Walter and brother Dayle all represented New Zealand at Test level. He made his Test debut in 1973 and in 1988 he became the first bowler to take more than 400 Test wickets, several times taking 10 or more wickets in a match. He set a new world record of 431 wickets in 1990, the year he retired, and still holds the New Zealand record for most wickets in a series.

Sir Jack Hobbs, 1882–1963

Born in Cambridge, England, he became one of England's greatest batsmen. He first played first-class cricket for Cambridgeshire in 1904, but joined Surrey the following year and played for them for 30 years (1905–35). He played in 61 Test matches between 1907 and 1930, when he and Herbert Sutcliffe established themselves as an unrivalled pair of opening batsmen, and he captained England in 1926. In his first-class career he made 197 centuries, and scored 61,237 runs. He also made the highest ever score in the

Gentlemen v Players match, 266 not out. He was knighted in 1953 and named as one of the five Wisden cricketers of the century in 2000.

Sir Leonard Hutton, 1916–90

Born in Fulneck, Yorkshire, England, he was a Yorkshire player throughout his career. He first played for England in 1937, and in the Oval Test against Australia in 1938 scored a world record of 364 runs, which stood for 20 years. Renowned for the perfection of his batting technique, he made 129 centuries in his first-class career. After World War II he captained England in 23 Test matches. Under his captaincy England regained the Ashes from Australia in the Test series of 1953, and retained them during the Australian tour of 1954–5, thus ending 20 years of Australian supremacy. He retired in 1956 and was knighted that year.

Kapil Dev, 1959–

Born in Chandigarh, Punjab, India, an all-rounder, he made his first-class debut for Haryana at the age of 16, and played county cricket in England for Northamptonshire and Worcestershire. He led India to victory in the 1983 World Cup. In 1994 he retired from the game, having set a then world record of 434 Test wickets.

Imran Khan, 1952–

He was born in Lahore, Pakistan, and educated at Oxford University. He played county cricket for Worcestershire and Sussex, and made his Test debut in 1971. He captained Pakistan on several occasions (1982–3, 1985–7 and 1988–92), and led them to victory in the World Cup in 1992. He scored over 3,000 Test runs, and took over 325 wickets in Test matches, before announcing his retirement from cricket in 1992. He made an unsuccessful bid to enter Pakistani politics, his party failing to win a single seat in the 1997 elections.

Jim Laker, 1922–86

He was born in Frizinghall, West Yorkshire, England. His outstanding achievement was to take 19 Australian wickets in the Fourth Test at Old Trafford in 1956. His figures for the match were 9 for 37 and 10 for 53. This is the only time a bowler has taken more than 17 wickets in first-class cricket and, until Anil Kumble repeated the feat in 1999, was the only time a bowler had taken all 10 wickets in a Test innings. As a spin bowler he played 46 Tests for England, and at county level represented Surrey and Essex. He retired in 1964 to become a television commentator.

Brian Lara, 1969–

Born in Santa Cruz, Trinidad, he is a supremely talented batsman who likes to break records: he made 375 runs for the West Indies against England in the fifth Test in Antigua in 1994, the then highest individual Test innings, before Australia's Matthew Hayden surpassed it with 380 in 2003, but regained the record with 400 not out in 2004 on the same ground and against the same opposition. He also holds the record for the highest individual score in first-class cricket with a score of 501 for Warwickshire against Durham at Edgbaston in 1994, which overtook the record of **Hanif Mohammed**.

Harold Larwood, 1904–95

He was born in Nuncargate, Nottinghamshire, England. His career was comparatively brief and he played in only 21 Test matches. He was employed by captain Douglas Jardine to bowl 'bodyline' (short and fast towards the body of the batter) in the controversial 1932–3 tour of Australia when several of the home batsmen were seriously hurt, and diplomatic relations between the two countries suffered. On his return, feeling that he had not been supported in official quarters, he retired from Test cricket and in later life settled happily in Australia. He was belatedly awarded the MBE in 1993.

Dennis Lillee, 1949–

Born in Perth, Western Australia, he epitomized the move towards a more combative approach to international cricket in both his fast bowling and his attitude. An automatic choice for his country when fit, he took 355 wickets in 70 Tests. His attempts to introduce a metal bat (which is illegal) into Test matches prompted just one of many well-publicized clashes with the Australian cricketing authorities. He retired in 1984 and now runs a fast bowling academy in Australia.

Ray Lindwall, 1921–96

He was born in Sydney, Australia. A classic fast bowler, with **Keith Miller** he formed an invincible Australian opening attack in the five years after World War II. He took 228 wickets in 61 Tests, and also scored more than 1,500 runs, including two Test centuries.

Clive Lloyd, 1944–

Born in Georgetown, Guyana, his first West Indies Test cap was in 1966. He then went to England to play for Haslingden in the Lancashire League before joining Lancashire (1968–86). A magnificent batsman and fielder, he played in 110 Test matches (captain 1974–85), scoring 7,515 runs and making 19 centuries. He captained the West Indies in 18 Test matches, losing only two, which made him the most successful Test captain. He also captained the West Indies sides which won the World Cup in 1975 and 1979. He later became a British citizen.

Rodney Marsh, 1947–

Born in Armadale, Perth, Western Australia, he established his reputation as a wicketkeeper playing for Western Australia, often in close collaboration with legendary fast bowler **Dennis Lillee**. He made his debut as wicketkeeper for Australia in 1970 and continued in the role for 14 years, making a record total of 355 dismissals. He was also highly effective as a batsman. After retirement he ran the Australian cricket academy, before switching sides in 2002 to take up the roles of director of the England academy and an England selector.

Javed Miandad, 1957–

Born in Karachi, Pakistan, he is considered the finest batsman ever produced by Pakistan. As well as playing for Karachi, Sindh, Sussex and Glamorgan, he excelled as a Test player, making his debut for Pakistan in 1975 and going on to amass 8,832 runs in 124 Tests (both national records) and 7,381 runs in one-day internationals (often as captain). He took part in the first six Cricket World Cups, winning the title with Pakistan in 1992 and becoming the first man to score 1,000 runs in World Cup matches. His often abrasive manner almost led to an on-pitch fight with **Dennis Lillee** in 1983.

Keith Miller, 1919–2004

He was born in Melbourne, Australia. He established himself as the world's leading all-rounder of the time, playing in the great Australian Test side of 1948 and forming a formidable new-ball partnership with **Ray Lindwall**. Miller scored 2,598 runs in 55 Test matches including seven centuries, and took 170 wickets.

Hanif Mohammed, 1934–

Born in Junagadh, Pakistan, and a member of the great cricketing family which produced two other Test players (his brothers Mushtaq and Sadiq), he made the first of his 55 appearances when only 17. In his Test career he scored twelve centuries, including two in the match against England at Dacca in 1961–2. A natural stroke-maker, he holds the world's second-highest score, with 499 runs for Karachi against Bahawalpur in 1958–9 (**Brian Lara** broke his record in 1994 with 501).

Muttiah Muralitharan, 1972–

Born in Kandy, Sri Lanka, Murali, as he is commonly known, rivals **Shane Warne** for the title of the most successful Test bowler of all time. He can make the ball spin prodigiously and has taken his wickets extremely quickly since his Test debut in 1992 (532 in 91 matches with 5 wickets in an innings 44 times, as of December 2004) but his career has been dogged with controversy as to the legitimacy of his bowling action. He has played for Lancashire and Kent in the County Championship.

Graeme Pollock, 1944–

He was born in Durban, South Africa. One of the great batsmen of the 1960s, he was the last South African cricketer to make an impact at international level before that country's exclusion from Test cricket. A stylish left-hander with perfect timing, he has a Test average of 60.97 from 23 Tests that is second only to **Don Bradman**'s.

Wilfred Rhodes, 1877–1973

Born in Kirkheaton, Yorkshire, England, he played for Yorkshire and England, and during his long career (1898–1930) took a world-record 4,187 wickets and scored 39,722 runs. He took 100 wickets in a season 23 times with his slow left-arm deliveries, and performed the double feat of 1,000 runs and 100 wickets 16 times. The oldest man to play Test cricket, he was 52 years and 165 days old when he played for England against the West Indies at Kingston in April 1930.

Sir Viv Richards, 1952–

Born in St John's, Antigua, he played in the UK for Somerset (1974–86) and Glamorgan (1990–3), and set the record for most Test runs in a calendar year with 1,710 in 1976. He usually wore a cap and not a helmet, and his timing, power and range enabled him to score Test cricket's fastest century (off 56 balls) against England in 1986. He was captain of the West Indies from 1985 to 1991 and holds the West Indies record for the most caps. He was knighted in 1999 and named as one of the five Wisden cricketers of the century in 2000.

Sir Garfield (Garry) Sobers, 1936–

He was born in Bridgetown, Barbados. In 93 Test matches for the West Indies (captain 1965–74), he scored more than 8,000 runs (including 26 centuries) and took 235 wickets and 110 catches. A cricketing phenomenon, he could deliver three kinds of bowling (fast, medium and spin) and bat with tireless brilliance and power. He held the world record for the highest Test innings (365 not out, made at Kingston, Jamaica, in 1958) until **Brian Lara** made 375 against England in 1994. He famously scored six sixes in one over off Malcolm Nash at Swansea in 1968 when playing for Nottinghamshire, a feat that has only been repeated once in first-class cricket (by Ravi Shastri). He was knighted on his retirement from cricket in 1975 and named as one of the five Wisden cricketers of the century in 2000.

Sachin Tendulkar, 1973–

Born in Bombay, India, he was recognized as a prodigious batting talent while still at school, and at the age of 15 made a century for Bombay in his debut first-class match. He made seven Test centuries before he was 21, making him the only batsman ever to have done this. He is noted for his flamboyant style and for the last decade has been recognized as one of the world's leading batsmen as well as being a national megastar in India. In December 2004 he equalled **Sunil Gavaskar**'s record of 34 Test-match centuries.

Fred Trueman, 1931–

Born in Stainton, South Yorkshire, England, he became an apprentice bricklayer before developing into the first genuine fast bowler in postwar English cricket. A Yorkshire player for 19 years (1949–68), he played in 67 Tests between 1952 and 1965 and took a then record 307 wickets, forming a formidable partnership with Brian Statham. Bluff and not afraid to speak his mind, he became a forthright radio commentator on the game after retirement. He was awarded the OBE in 1989.

Courtney Walsh, 1962–

Born in Kingston, Jamaica, he established an international reputation as a fast bowler playing for Jamaica, Gloucestershire and the West Indies. He made his debut for the West Indies in Perth in 1984, going on to form a legendary partnership with fellow fast bowler Curtly Ambrose and becoming the side's regular captain in 1996. By the time of his retirement from international competition in 2001, he had overtaken **Kapil Dev** as the all-time leading wicket-taker in Test cricket with 519.

Shane Warne, 1969–

Born in Ferntree Gully, Victoria, Australia, he is now recognized as one of the greatest spinners the world has ever known, having the complete armoury of leg-spin deliveries, all bowled with considerable accuracy. Despite being banned from cricket for a year in 2003 after testing positive for a banned substance, as of December 2004 he has taken 561 Test wickets, making him the highest Test wicket-taker of all time. He was selected as one of five Wisden cricketers of the century in 2000 and played for Hampshire in 2000-4.

Steve Waugh, 1965–

Born in Canterbury, Sydney, Australia, he became one of the most respected players in international cricket. The twin of the almost equally talented Mark Waugh, he played for New South Wales (from 1984), Somerset (1987–8) and Kent (2002) and made his debut for Australia in 1985, subsequently playing many times alongside his brother, together becoming the most capped set of brothers in Test history. Steve captained Australia from 1999, in which year the team won the World Cup. He retired from Test cricket Jan 2004 after 168 matches (a record). A fiercely driven player, he superstitiously always batted with a red rag sticking out of his trouser pocket.

CROQUET

Origins

The origins of croquet are uncertain. Its name may be derived from the French word *croche*, meaning shepherd's crook; the game itself seems to have developed from a French game called *jeu de mail* (mallet game) that was popular in the 12th century. Certainly by the 17th century this game was being popularized in England by the court of Charles II, who played it in St James's Park. The name of the game – paille-maille ('ball-mallet') – was anglicized to pall mall, which then became attributed to the nearby street. More recently, a game resembling croquet (called 'crokey') was played in Ireland in the 1830s and by the early 1850s had been introduced into England.

Rules and description

Croquet is an outdoor mallet-and-ball game for two or four players. It is played on a grass pitch 31.9m/105ft long by 25.6m/84ft wide. Six hoops are arranged in a pattern around the field. The object is to use the long-handled mallet to hit the wooden balls through all six hoops twice (on an outward and inward course) and finish by hitting the centre peg. In singles each player has two balls: blue and black always play against red and yellow. In doubles each player has one coloured ball. Each hoop has a coloured clip corresponding to the colours of the balls and indicates the next hoop to play in the sequence.

Each turn generally consists of one stroke. If a hoop is scored the striker is allowed a free turn (a 'continuation stroke'). A player can also hit his or her ball so that it hits any of the other three balls (a 'roquet'). In this case the player gets two free turns. The first involves picking up the ball and placing it against the hit ball, then hitting the strike ball so that the other ball moves (called a 'croquet shot'); the second is another free shot, attempting another roquet or a hoop shot. The turn ends if another roquet or a hoop point is not scored. In this way a player can build up a break of points similar to snooker.

There are several variations on the game, including a shorter, faster version called golf croquet. In the USA a smaller-scale game called 'roque' with 9 hoops was first popularized in the early 1900s.

Ruling bodies: The Wimbledon All-England Croquet Club was founded in 1868 and established the first standardized rules. The Croquet Association was founded in 1896 to revive a sport that was becoming overshadowed by tennis; it regulates the sport in the UK, except in Scotland. The world governing body is the World Croquet Federation

MacRobertson International Shield

Tournament played between Great Britain, Australia, New Zealand (since 1930) and the United States (since 1993). The Shield is named after Sir Macpherson Robertson, an Australian philanthropist who made his money as a confectionery manufacturer.

	Winner	Host country
1925	England	England
1927-8	Australia	Australia
1930	Australia	Australia
1935	Australia	Australia
1937	England	England
1950-1	New Zealand	New Zealand
1956	England	England
1963	England	New Zealand
1969	England	Australia
1974	Great Britain	Great Britain
1979	New Zealand	New Zealand
1982	Great Britain	Australia
1986	New Zealand	Great Britain
1990	Great Britain and Ireland	New Zealand
1993	Great Britain and Ireland	Australia
1996	Great Britain	Great Britain
2000	Great Britain	New Zealand
2003	Great Britain	USA

World Singles Championship

British winner unless indicated otherwise.

	Winner	Venue
1989	Joe Hagan (New Zealand)	Hurlingham, UK
1990	Robert Fulford	Hurlingham, UK
1991	John Walters	Hurlingham, UK
1992	Robert Fulford	Newport, USA
1994	Robert Fulford	Carden Park, UK
1995	Chris Clarke	Fontenay le Comte, France
1997	Robert Fulford	Bunbury, Australia
2001	Reg Bamford (South Africa)	Hurlingham, UK
2002	Robert Fulford	Wellington, New Zealand

UK Open Championship

First held in 1867. British winner unless indicated otherwise.

	Singles	Doubles
1980	William de R Prichard	William de R Prichard & Stephen Mulliner
1981	David Openshaw	Stephen Mulliner & Mark Ormerod
1982	Nigel Aspinall	Martin Murray & Andrew Hope
1983	Nigel Aspinall	John McCullough & Phil Cordingley

	Singles	Doubles
1984	Nigel Aspinall	Nigel Aspinall & Stephen Mulliner
1985	David Openshaw	David Openshaw & Mark Avery
1986	Joe Hogan (New Zealand)	Nigel Aspinall & Stephen Mulliner
1987	Mark Avery	David Openshaw & Mark Avery
1988	Stephen Mulliner	Nigel Aspinall & Stephen Mulliner
1989	Joe Hogan (New Zealand)	Joe Hogan & Bob Jackson (both New Zealand)
1990	Stephen Mulliner	Robert Fulford & Chris Clarke
1991	Robert Fulford	Robert Fulford & Chris Clarke
1992	Robert Fulford	Robert Fulford & Chris Clarke
1993	Reg Bamford (South Africa)	Robert Fulford & Chris Clarke
1994	Reg Bamford (South Africa)	Reg Bamford (South Africa) & Stephen Mulliner
1995	Reg Bamford (South Africa)	Steve Comish & David Maugham
1996	Robert Fulford	Robert Fulford & Chris Clarke
1997	Chris Clarke	Reg Bamford (South Africa) & Stephen Mulliner
1998	Robert Fulford	Robert Fulford & Chris Clarke
1999	Reg Bamford (South Africa)	Chris Farthing & Chris Patmore
2000	Stephen Mulliner	Reg Bamford (South Africa) & Stephen Mulliner
2001	Reg Bamford (South Africa)	Robert Fulford & Chris Clarke
2002	Reg Bamford (South Africa)	Chris Clarke & David Maugham
2003	Robert Fulford	Robert Fulford & Chris Clarke; Mark Avery & David Maugham
2004	Robert Fulford	Robert Fulford & Chris Clarke

Croquet at the Olympics

In 1900 in Paris, the only time the game was played at the Olympics, all the winners were French, Aumoitte winning the singles one-ball, Waydelich the singles two-ball, and Aumoitte and Johin the doubles. Two other French players, Madame Brohy and Mademoiselle Ohnier, were the first women to compete in the modern Olympics. The variant roque also made one appearance, in the St Louis Games of 1904.

Golf Croquet World Champions

	Winner	Venue
1996	Khaled Younis (Egypt)	Milan, Italy
1997	Salah Hassan (Egypt)	Cairo, Egypt
1998	Khaled Younis (Egypt)	Royal Leamington Spa, UK
2000	Salah Hassan (Egypt)	Cairo, Egypt
2002	Khaled Younis (Egypt)	Palm Beach, USA
2004	Ahmed Nasr (Egypt)	Southwick, UK

A-Z

angle of split	the angle at which the balls diverge in a split **croquet shot**
baulk line	a line drawn at each end of a croquet court from which players start
bisque	a free turn that is awarded to the weaker player in a handicap game

break	a turn in which more than one point is scored in consecutive scoring shots
cannon	a stroke in which three or four balls are in contact and the player takes a **croquet shot** and makes a **roquet** in one stroke
carrot	the part of the hoop sunk below the ground
continuation stroke	the bonus stroke taken after **running a hoop** or the second bonus stroke after making a **roquet**
croquet shot	played after a **roquet**, a shot made when the striker's ball is in contact with an opposing ball
entice	same as **tice**
peel	to send a ball other than the **striker's ball** through its hoop in order
peg out	if a **rover ball** is pegged out it strikes the peg and thus completes its circuit
pioneer ball	the ball sent to the 'next hoop plus one' to be ready for when that next hoop is attempted
pivot ball	a ball that is placed in the centre of play to allow the **striker's ball** to change direction or pivot
roquet	a stroke by which the **striker's ball** is played against another ball
rover ball	a ball that has run all twelve hoops and can be **pegged out**
rover hoop	the last hoop in the sequence; it has a red crown
run a hoop	to hit the ball through the hoop
striker's ball	the ball played at the start of a turn
Test	an international match
tice	a ball played as a decoy to tempt one's opponent in the hope that he or she will miss it
wire	1. the part of the hoop above the ground 2. a strategy used to ensure the hoop is placed between a **striker's ball** and the next shot to impede progress. Similar to the use of a snooker in that game

CROSS-COUNTRY RUNNING

Origins

Running is as old as time but cross-country running developed in England in the 17th century. The great diarist Samuel Pepys's entry for 27 May, 1663, states: 'This day there was great thronging to Banstead Downs, upon a great horse-race and foot-race.' The horse race was probably a forerunner of the Derby. Later on, races were organized by wealthy landowners who wagered on the chances of their footmen and other servants winning races across the countryside.

'Hare and hounds races' (also known as 'paper chases') were popular at English public schools in the 19th century and saw the 'hare' set off, throwing pieces of paper behind him and leaving a trail (or 'scent') for the 'hounds' to follow. Some of the earliest athletics clubs that concentrated on cross-country running included the Thames Hare and Hounds (1868) and the Cheshire Tally-Ho Hare and Hounds (1871). Other clubs incorporated 'harrier' in their title. However, the honour of being the first cross-country running club in England is generally attributed to the Thames Rowing Club, whose members ran during the winter in order to keep fit. The first English championship race was held in 1876.

Rules and description

Cross-country races are foot races where runners negotiate sections of countryside with natural obstacles, such as hedges, ditches, stiles and so on. Races tend to be held in the autumn, winter and spring when poor weather conditions add to the challenge. At championship level many of the obstacles are excluded and runners are left tackling an undulating but often unforgiving terrain. The first men's international race was run in 1903 and the corresponding women's race in 1931 in Douai, France.

Men run distances of 12km/7.5mi and women 5km/3mi; juniors run 8km/5mi and 4km/2.5mi respectively. In team events the aggregate scores (based on finishing positions of one point for first place, two points for second, and so on) of the runners are added together and the team with the lowest total wins.

Ruling body: International Association of Athletics Federations (IAAF)

World Cross-Country Championships

The International Cross-Country Championships were first held in 1903 at Hamilton Park racecourse in Glasgow over a distance of 8mi (13km). The winner was Alfred Shrubb of England but the race only included runners from England, Ireland, Scotland and Wales. The IAAF gave the championships world status from 1973; the first women's race was held in 1967.

The current race distances are 12km for men's long-course races; 8km for women's long course; and 4km for both short-course races. Team scores are calculated by aggregating the positions of the first four finishers from a maximum of six competitors (or six finishers from nine competitors for men prior to 1997). The team with the lowest points total wins.

Individual Winners — Long Course

	Men	Women	Venue
1973	Pekka Päivärinta (Finland)	Paola Pigni-Cacchi (Italy)	Waregem, Belgium
1974	Eric De Beck (Belgium)	Paola Pigni-Cacchi (Italy)	Monza, Italy
1975	Ian Stewart (Scotland)	Julie Brown (USA)	Rabat, Morocco
1976	Carlos Lopes (Portugal)	Carmen Valero (Spain)	Chepstow, UK
1977	Léon Schots (Belgium)	Carmen Valero (Spain	Düsseldorf, West Germany
1978	John Treacy (Ireland)	Grete Waitz (Norway)	Glasgow, UK
1979	John Treacy (Ireland)	Grete Waitz (Norway)	Limerick, Ireland
1980	Craig Virgin (USA)	Grete Waitz (Norway)	Paris, France
1981	Craig Virgin (USA)	Grete Waitz (Norway)	Madrid, Spain
1982	Mohammed Kedir (Ethiopia)	Maricica Puica (Romania)	Rome, Italy

	Men	Women	Venue
1983	Bekele Debele (Ethiopia)	Grete Waitz (Norway)	Gateshead, UK
1984	Carlos Lopes (Portugal)	Maricica Puica (Romania)	New York, USA
1985	Carlos Lopes (Portugal)	Zola Budd (England)	Lisbon, Portugal
1986	John Ngugi (Kenya)	Zola Budd (England)	Neuchâtel, Switzerland
1987	John Ngugi (Kenya)	Annette Sergent (France)	Warsaw, Poland
1988	John Ngugi (Kenya)	Ingrid Kristiansen (Norway)	Auckland, New Zealand
1989	John Ngugi (Kenya)	Annette Sergent (France)	Stavanger, Norway
1990	Khalid Skah (Morocco)	Lynn Jennings (USA)	Aix-les-Bains, France
1991	Khalid Skah (Morocco)	Lynn Jennings (USA)	Antwerp, Belgium
1992	John Ngugi (Kenya)	Lynn Jennings (USA)	Boston, USA
1993	William Sigei (Kenya)	Albertina Dias (Portugal)	Amorebieta, Spain
1994	William Sigei (Kenya)	Hellen Chepngeno (Kenya)	Budapest, Hungary
1995	Paul Tergat (Kenya)	Derartu Tulu (Ethiopia)	Durham, UK
1996	Paul Tergat (Kenya)	Gete Wami (Ethiopia)	Stellenbosch, South Africa
1997	Paul Tergat (Kenya)	Derartu Tulu (Ethiopia)	Turin, Italy
1998	Paul Tergat (Kenya)	Sonia O'Sullivan (Ireland)	Marrakech, Morocco
1999	Paul Tergat (Kenya)	Gete Wami (Ethiopia)	Belfast, UK
2000	Mohammed Mourhit (Belgium)	Derartu Tulu (Ethiopia)	Vilamoura, Portugal
2001	Mohammed Mourhit (Belgium)	Paula Radcliffe (Great Britain)	Ostend, Belgium
2002	Kenenisa Bekele (Ethiopia)	Paula Radcliffe (Great Britain)	Dublin, Ireland
2003	Kenenisa Bekele (Ethiopia)	Werknesh Kidane (Ethiopia)	Lausanne-La Broye, Switzerland
2004	Kenenisa Bekele (Ethiopia)	Benita Johnson (Australia)	Brussels, Belgium

Individual Winners — Short Course

	Men	Women	Venue
1998	John Kibowen (Kenya)	Sonia O'Sullivan (Ireland)	Marrakech, Morocco
1999	Benjamin Limo (Kenya)	Jackline Maranga (Kenya)	Belfast, UK
2000	John Kibowen (Kenya)	Kutre Dulecha (Ethiopia)	Vilamoura, Portugal
2001	Enock Koech (Kenya)	Gete Wami (Ethiopia)	Ostend, Belgium
2002	Kenenisa Bekele (Ethiopia)	Edith Masai (Kenya)	Dublin, Ireland
2003	Kenenisa Bekele (Ethiopia)	Edith Masai (Kenya)	Lausanne-La Broye, Switzerland
2004	Kenenisa Bekele (Ethiopia)	Edith Masai (Kenya)	Brussels, Belgium

Team Winners — Men's Long Course

1973-4	Belgium
1975	New Zealand
1976	England
1977	Belgium
1978	France
1979-80	England
1981-5	Ethiopia

1986-2003	Kenya
2004	Ethiopia

Running from steeple to steeple

The 3,000m steeplechase event takes place on an athletics track but it is an attempt to mimic cross-country running with hurdles representing hedges and even a water jump to simulate a ditch. The word steeplechasing comes from the fact that early cross-country runners used to run towards a church whose steeple was visible throughout the course of the race.

Team Winners — Women's Long Course

1973-4	England
1975	USA
1976-7	USSR
1978	Romania
1979	USA
1980-2	USSR
1983-5	USA
1986	England
1987	USA
1988-90	USSR
1991	Ethiopia and Kenya
1992-3	Kenya
1994	Portugal
1995-6	Kenya
1997	Ethiopia
1998	Kenya
1999-2000	Ethiopia
2001	Kenya
2002-4	Ethiopia

The Crick and Barby runs

The hare and hounds at Rugby School gained great popularity thanks to being written about by Thomas Hughes in *Tom Brown's Schooldays* (1857). Rugby School has a Crick Run that was first staged at Rugby School in 1838. It is a ten-mile race across the countryside. There has been a girls' race since 1986. The Barby Run, for junior boys and girls, is mentioned in *Tom Brown's Schooldays*: '...nine miles at least, and hard ground; no chance of getting in at the finish, unless you're a first-rate scud.'

Team — Short Course

	Men	**Women**
1998	Kenya	Morocco
1999	Kenya	France
2000	Kenya	Portugal
2001-2	Kenya	Ethiopia
2003	Kenya	Kenya
2004	Ethiopia	Ethiopia

Olympic Games

A cross-country event formed part of the Olympic Games in 1904 at St Louis, and then from 1912 to 1924 before it was discontinued. In 1904 only two teams entered, both from the USA, with the New York Athletic Club beating the Chicago Athletic Association into second. The event was probably discontinued as a result of the 1924 event, run in the full heat of a Parisian summer when less than half the field finished.

	Individual gold medal	**Team gold medal**
1912	Hannes Kolehmainen (Finland)	Sweden
1920	Paavo Nurmi (Finland)	Finland
1924	Paavo Nurmi (Finland)	Finland

Some famous cross-country runners

John Ngugi, 1962-

Born in Nyahururu, Kenya, he took the world cross-country title four years in succession from 1986–9 and again in 1992. At the 1988 Olympic Games he won gold at 5,000m, and ran a record 10,000m of 27min 19.15s at the 1990 Commonwealth Games.

Paul Tergat, 1969-

Born in Kabarnet, Barango, Kenya, he was a former basketball player and airforce sergeant. He won the Kenyan cross-country title in 1992, and in 1995–6, and went on to win five consecutive world cross-country titles (1995–9). He also won two world half-marathon championships and four silver medals at the Olympics and World Championships 10,000m.

Grete Waitz, 1953-

Born in Oslo, Norway, she was, for a time in the 1970s and 1980s, the world's best women's long-distance runner. She won five world cross-country world titles (1978–81, 1983) and led the marathon craze, winning the London Marathon in 1983 and 1986, the New York Marathon (1978–80, 1982–6, 1988) and the World Championships marathon in 1983.

CURLING

Origins

Curling has been played in Scotland since the 16th century, at first on frozen lakes. The oldest curling stone is the Stirling Stone which is inscribed with the date 1511 and was discovered in Dunblane, Scotland. Scottish soldiers introduced the game to Canada in the 1760s. The name 'curling' comes from the natural movement of the granite stones on the ice.

Rules and description

Curling resembles the game of lawn bowls but is played on an ice rink. Curling stones are heavy (44lb/20kg maximum), made of granite, and with a handle at the top. Competitive events generally comprise two teams of four curlers. Playing in turn, each player sends down two stones, propelling them down the ice towards a circular target (the 'house') and aiming to get them as close to the centre spot (the 'tee') as possible. A team scores a point for each stone that is closer to the tee than their opponents' nearest stone, as long as the stone is within the house. The final two stones for each side are played by the 'skip', who either protects a winning lead or aims to hit the opposition's stone away. The novel aspect of the game is the brooms, which are swept across the ice in front of the curling stone to help dictate its speed and direction. Once a stone has passed the tee, opposing team members can sweep the ice to try to coax the stone out of the rink. Games consist of ten 'ends'.

Ruling bodies: The Royal Caledonian Curling Club; World Curling Federation (previously known as the International Curling Federation)

The Roaring Game

The sounds the stones make on the ice mean that curling is commonly known as the 'Roaring Game'.

World Curling Championships

The World Championships were first contested in 1959 as the Scotch Whisky Cup. Since then the tournament has been held annually and has had various sponsors, including Air Canada Silver Broom trophy (1968–79). The women's tournament was introduced in 1979.

Men

	Champion	Skip	Beaten finalist	Score	Venue
1990	Canada	Ed Werenich	Scotland	3-1	Västerås, Sweden
1991	Scotland	David Smith	Canada	7-2	Winnipeg, Canada
1992	Switzerland	Markus Eggler	Scotland	6-3	Garmisch, Germany
1993	Canada	Russ Howard	Scotland	8-4	Geneva, Switzerland
1994	Canada	Rick Folk	Sweden	3-2	Oberstdorf, Germany
1995	Canada	Kerry Burtnyk	Scotland	4-2	Brandon, Canada
1996	Canada	Jeff Stoughton	Scotland	6-2	Hamilton, Canada
1997	Sweden	Peter Lindholm	Germany	6-3	Bern, Switzerland
1998	Canada	Wayne Middaugh	Sweden	7-4	Kamloops, Canada
1999	Scotland	Hammy McMillan	Canada	6-5	Saint John, Canada
2000	Canada	Greg McAulay	Sweden	9-4	Glasgow, UK
2001	Sweden	Peter Lindholm	Switzerland	6-3	Lausanne, Switzerland
2002	Canada	David Nedohin	Norway	10-5	Bismarck, USA
2003	Canada	David Nedohin	Switzerland	10-6	Winnipeg, Canada
2004	Sweden	Peter Lindholm	Germany	7-6	Gävle, Sweden

Women

Champion		Skip	Beaten finalist	Score	Venue
1990	Norway	Dordi Nordby	Scotland	4-2	Västerås, Sweden
1991	Norway	Dordi Nordby	Canada	4-3	Winnipeg, Canada
1992	Sweden	Elisabet Johansson	USA	8-4	Garmisch, Germany
1993	Canada	Sandra Peterson	Germany	5-3	Geneva, Switzerland
1994	Canada	Sandra Peterson	Scotland	5-3	Oberstdorf, Germany
1995	Sweden	Elisabet Gustafson	Canada	6-5	Brandon, Canada
1996	Canada	Marilyn Bodogh	USA	5-2	Hamilton, Canada
1997	Canada	Sandra Schmirler	Norway	8-4	Bern, Switzerland
1998	Sweden	Elisabet Gustafson	Denmark	7-3	Kamloops, Canada
1999	Sweden	Elisabet Gustafson	USA	8-5	Saint John, Canada
2000	Canada	Kelley Law	Switzerland	7-6	Glasgow, UK
2001	Canada	Colleen Jones	Sweden	5-2	Lausanne, Switzerland
2002	Scotland	Jackie Lockhart	Sweden	6-5	Bismarck, USA
2003	USA	Debbie McCormick	Canada	5-3	Winnipeg, Canada
2004	Canada	Colleen Jones	Norway	8-4	Gävle, Sweden

The Fairy Rock

The World Curling Federation stipulates that all new curling stones should be manufactured from Ailsa Craig granite. Ailsa Craig, from the Gaelic for 'fairy rock', is a seabird island sanctuary in the Firth of Clyde.

Olympic Champions

Curling was introduced into the Olympics in 1998.

	Men	Skip	Women	Skip
1998	Switzerland	Patrick Hürlimann	Canada	Sandra Schmirler
2002	Norway	Paal Trulsen	Great Britain	Rhona Martin

A-Z

biter a stone just touching the outer circle of the **house**

bonspiel a curling match

broom the instrument used for sweeping the ice ahead of the stone. It is made of horsehair or synthetic fibres

button same as **tee**

counter a stone in the **house** that may be worth a point at the completion of the **end**

draw 1. the amount of curve in the trajectory of a stone 2. a shot played with enough weight to reach the **house**

end the completion of 16 stones, each player having played their two stones. Scores are decided at the conclusion of each end and each match is the best of ten ends

freeze a **draw** where a stone stops adjacent to another stone

guard a stone played into a position so it can protect another stone from being hit. It is generally played just short of the **house**

hack metal or rubber footholds at each end of the **rink** from where curlers can push off

hammer if a **rink** has the hammer, they have the right to play the last stone in an **end**

hog a stone that fails to reach the **hog line**

hog line the hog line is marked 10m/33ft from the **hack** and 6.4m/21ft from the **tee**. Only when the stone passes the hog line is it considered in play. If it fails to reach the hog line it is removed from play

house the target, a set of three concentric rings on the ice with the **tee** in the centre. The house is 3.66m/12ft in diameter. Stones must sit within the house to score

lead the member of the **rink** who plays first

pebble fine water droplets sprayed onto the ice before play and which freeze instantly, creating an optimum curling surface

peel a **takeout** where both the stone played and the stone hit leave the **house**

raise a type of **draw** that knocks another stone into the **house** or into a better position within the house

rink 1. the playing area of prepared ice 2. a curling team, eg *the Scottish rink*

second the member of the rink who plays second

sheet the strip of ice upon which the game is played

skip the captain of the team, the fourth player to deliver stones at each **end**. The skip delivers the final and often crucial stone

takeout a shot that hits another stone and completely removes it from play (also double takeout when two stones are removed)

tee the small centre spot in the centre of the **house**

tee-line a line that passes through the **tee** across the width of the **sheet**

third the member of the **rink** who plays third; usually also the vice-skip

CYCLING

Origins

Bicycle racing is probably as old as the bicycle itself. The first pedal cycle was built by Scottish blacksmith Kirkpatrick Macmillan in 1839. The pedals took the form of treadles, operating levers that drove the rear wheel. However, the modern style of cycling was really born in 1861 when the French coachbuilder Pierre Michaux began to manufacture the velocipede, a bicycle driven by pedals turning cranks. Further innovations such as chain-drive, gears, pneumatic tyres and brakes followed rapidly during the latter part of the 19th century. The first officially recorded cycle race took place in the Parc de Saint-Cloud in Paris in 1868 and was won by James Moore of England. The popularity of cycle racing rapidly spread, with banked tracks (velodromes) being built in many cities so that racing could take place in front of a stadium crowd. The first World Track Championships were held in 1895 and cycling was included in the programme of the first modern Olympic Games the following year.

Rules and description

There are a wide range of cycle racing disciplines, each with their own comprehensive set of rules, covering all areas from race distances, team numbers and the use of team support through to the dimensions of the bikes used and the licensing of individual riders. Since the very earliest days of cycling competition there have been two main sub-divisions of the sport – road and track racing. The events covered here are competed in using one-person, two-wheeled cycles which comply with the Union Cycliste Internationale (UCI) regulations relating to geometry, dimensions and components. There are variations on some of the following disciplines which are raced on tricycles, tandems or recumbent bicycles although these tend still to be very much minority sports. Some competitions for disabled riders employ hand-powered bicycles or tandems shared with a guide rider.

Road Racing: Road races are ridden on the road either from place to place or around a road circuit. They can take the form of a mass-start 'road race', a 'time trial', a 'criterium' or a 'stage race'.

Track Racing: Track races take place at either indoor or outdoor velodromes (banked wooden or concrete circuits). Velodromes vary in size but Olympic class velodromes must be at least 333m/364yd in length. Events ridden individually or head-to-head generally take the form of a knockout competition. Events include the 'sprint', 'team sprint', 'time trial', the 'keirin', 'individual pursuit', 'team pursuit', 'madison', 'scratch race' and the 'hour' time trial.

Ruling body: Union Cycliste Internationale (UCI)

Tour de France

First held in 1903 starting and finishing in Paris and ridden over 2,428km in six stages between 1 and 21 July. A three-week-long stage race held every July, the Tour de France is the largest annual sporting event in the world. The overall winner is the rider that completes the whole distance in the fastest time. A separate King of the Mountains competition was added in 1933 for the best climber and a points competition was added in 1953 for the best sprinter. In some of the early years the whole event was run as a points competition.

Leaving it to the last minute

The 1989 Tour de France was won by the smallest ever margin. Unusually, the final stage into Paris was a time trial. Going into the stage Greg Lemond was in second place overall, 50 seconds behind Laurent Fignon. With a dramatic performance, Lemond made up the deficit during the time trial to win the Tour by just eight seconds. Always one of cycling's innovators, he was using aero bars for the first time in the Tour and it was suggested that these gave him the necessary aerodynamic advantage to win. Aero bars are now used universally by time trialists.

Cycling

Men

	Winner	Points winner	King of the Mountains
1903	Maurice Garin (France)		
1904	Henri Cornet (France)		
1905	Louis Trousselier (France)		
1906	René Pottier (France)		
1907	Lucien Petit-Breton (France)		
1908	Lucien Petit-Breton (France)		
1909	François Faber (Luxembourg)		
1910	Octave Lapize (France)		
1911	Gustave Garrigou (France)		
1912	Odile Defraye (Belgium)		
1913	Philippe Thys (Belgium)		
1914	Philippe Thys (Belgium)		
1919	Firmin Lambot (Belgium)		
1920	Philippe Thys (Belgium)		
1921	Léon Scieur (Belgium)		
1922	Firmin Lambot (Belgium)		
1923	Henri Pélissier (France)		
1924	Ottavio Bottechia (Italy)		
1925	Ottavio Bottechia (Italy)		
1926	Lucien Buysse (Belgium)		
1927	Nicolas Frantz (Luxembourg)		
1928	Nicolas Frantz (Luxembourg)		
1929	Maurice Dewaele (Belgium)		
1930	André Leducq (France)		
1931	Antonin Magne (France)		
1932	André Leducq (France)		
1933	Georges Speicher (France)	Vincente Trueba (Spain)	
1934	Antonin Magne (France)	René Vietto (France)	
1935	Romain Maes (Belgium)	Félicien Vervaecke (Belgium)	
1936	Sylvère Maes (Belgium)	Julian Berrendero (Spain)	
1937	Roger Lapébie (France)	Félicien Vervaecke (Belgium)	
1938	Gino Bartali (Italy)	Gino Bartali (Italy)	
1939	Sylvère Maes (Belgium)	Sylvère Maes (Belgium)	
1947	Jean Robic (France)	Pierre Brambilla (Italy)	
1948	Gino Bartali (Italy)	Gino Bartali (Italy)	
1949	Fausto Coppi (Italy)	Fausto Coppi (Italy)	
1950	Ferdi Kubler (Switzerland)	Louison Bobet (France)	
1951	Hugo Koblet (Switzerland)	Raphael Geminiani (France)	
1952	Fausto Coppi (Italy)	Fausto Coppi (Italy)	
1953	Louison Bobet (France)	Fritz Schaer (Switzerland)	Jésus Lorono (Spain)
1954	Louison Bobet (France)	Ferdi Kubler (Switzerland)	Federico Bahamontès (Spain)
1955	Louison Bobet (France)	Constant Ockers (Belgium)	Charly Gaul (Luxembourg)
1956	Roger Walkowiak (France)	Constant Ockers (Belgium)	Charly Gaul (Luxembourg)
1957	Jacques Anquetil (France)	Jean Forestier (France)	Gastone Nencini (Italy)
1958	Charly Gaul (Luxembourg)	Jean Graczyk (France)	Federico Bahamontès (Spain)
1959	Federico Bahamontès (Spain)	André Darrigade (France)	Federico Bahamontès (Spain)
1960	Gastone Nencini (Italy)	Jean Graczyk (France)	Imerio Massignan (Italy)

Human greyhounds

Keirin is a hugely popular betting sport in Japan, second only to horse racing in revenue. Following the first race in Kokura City in 1948 it grew rapidly. It has always been taken extremely seriously by the fans and the stars are amongst Japan's highest paid sportsmen. A mechanical fault with the favourite's bicycle at the Naruo Keirin in 1950 resulted in a riot.

	Winner	Points winner	King of the Mountains
1961	Jacques Anquetil (France)	André Darrigade (France)	Imerio Massignan (Italy)
1962	Jacques Anquetil (France)	Rudi Altig (West Germany)	Federico Bahamontès (Spain)
1963	Jacques Anquetil (France)	Rik Van Looy (Belgium)	Federico Bahamontès (Spain)
1964	Jacques Anquetil (France)	Jan Janssen (The Netherlands)	Federico Bahamontès (Spain)
1965	Felice Gimondi (Italy)	Jan Janssen (The Netherlands)	Julio Jiminez (Spain)
1966	Lucien Aimar (France)	Willy Planckaert (Belgium)	Julio Jiminez (Spain)
1967	Roger Pingeon (France)	Jan Janssen (The Netherlands)	Julio Jiminez (Spain)
1968	Jan Janssen (The Netherlands)	Franco Bitossi (Italy)	Aurelio Gonzales (Spain)
1969	Eddy Merckx (Belgium)	Eddy Merckx (Belgium)	Eddy Merckz (Belgium)
1970	Eddy Merckx (Belgium)	Walter Godefroot (Belgium)	Eddy Merckx (Belgium)
1971	Eddy Merckx (Belgium)	Eddy Merckx (Belgium)	Lucien Van Impe (Belgium)
1972	Eddy Merckx (Belgium)	Eddy Merckx (Belgium)	Lucien Van Impe (Belgium)
1973	Luis Ocaña (Spain)	Herman Van Springel (Belgium)	Pedro Torrès (Spain)
1974	Eddy Merckx (Belgium)	Patrick Sercu (Belgium)	Domingo Perurena (Spain)
1975	Bernard Thévenet (France)	Rik Van Linden (Belgium)	Lucien Van Impe (Belgium)
1976	Lucien Van Impe (Belgium)	Freddy Maertens (Belgium)	Giancarlo Bellini (Italy)
1977	Bernard Thévenet (France)	Jaques Esclassan (France)	Lucien Van Impe (Belgium)
1978	Bernard Hinault (France)	Freddy Maertens (Belgium)	Mariano Martinez (Spain)
1979	Bernard Hinault (France)	Bernard Hinault (France)	Giovanni Battaglin (Italy)
1980	Joop Zoetemelk (The Netherlands)	Rudy Pevenage (Belgium)	Raymond Martin (France)
1981	Bernard Hinault (France)	Freddy Maertens (Belgium)	Lucien Van Impe (Belgium)
1982	Bernard Hinault (France)	Sean Kelly (Ireland)	Bernard Vallet (France)
1983	Laurent Fignon (France)	Sean Kelly (Ireland)	Lucien Van Impe (Belgium)
1984	Laurent Fignon (France)	Frank Hoste (Belgium)	Robert Millar (Great Britain)
1985	Bernard Hinault (France)	Sean Kelly (Ireland)	Luis Herrera (Colombia)
1986	Greg LeMond (USA)	Eric Vanderaerden (Belgium)	Bernard Hinault (France)
1987	Stephen Roche (Ireland)	Jean-Paul Van Poppel (The Netherlands)	Luis Herrera (Colombia)
1988	Pedro Delgado (Spain)	Eddy Planckaert (Belgium)	Steven Rooks (The Netherlands)
1989	Greg LeMond (USA)	Sean Kelly (Ireland)	Gert Jan Theunisse (The Netherlands)
1990	Greg LeMond (USA)	Olaf Ludwig (Germany)	Thierry Claveyrolat (France)
1991	Miguel Indurain (Spain)	Djamolidine Abdoujaparov (Uzbekistan)	Claudio Chiappucci (Italy)
1992	Miguel Indurain (Spain)	Laurent Jalabert (France)	Claudio Chiappucci (Italy)
1993	Miguel Indurain (Spain)	Djamolidine Abdoujaparov (Uzbekistan)	Tony Rominger (Switzerland)
1994	Miguel Indurain (Spain)	Djamolidine Abdoujaparov (Uzbekistan)	Richard Virenque (France)
1995	Miguel Indurain (Spain)	Laurent Jalabert (France)	Richard Virenque (France)
1996	Bjarne Riis (Denmark)	Erik Zabel (Germany)	Richard Virenque (France)
1997	Jan Ullrich (Germany)	Erik Zabel (Germany)	Richard Virenque (France)
1998	Marco Pantani (Italy)	Erik Zabel (Germany)	Christophe Rinero (France)
1999	Lance Armstrong (USA)	Erik Zabel (Germany)	Richard Virenque (France)
2000	Lance Armstrong (USA)	Erik Zabel (Germany)	Santiago Botero (Colombia)
2001	Lance Armstrong (USA)	Erik Zabel (Germany)	Laurent Jalabert (France)
2002	Lance Armstrong (USA)	Robbie McEwen (Australia)	Laurent Jalabert (France)

	Winner	Points winner	King of the Mountains
2003	Lance Armstrong (USA)	Baden Cooke (Australia)	Richard Virenque (France)
2004	Lance Armstrong (USA)	Robbie McEwen (Australia)	Richard Virenque (France)

The World Hour Record

To hold the world hour record is considered one of the most prestigious achievements in cycling. Many great names have held the record over the years, including Fausto Coppi, Eddy Merckx and Miguel Indurain. During the 1980s and 1990s, cyclists such as Francesco Moser, Graeme Obree and Tony Rominger used ever more aerodynamically built bicycles and extreme riding positions to push the record forward, culminating in Chris Boardman's ride of 56.375km in 1996. However, in 2000, the UCI, concerned that technological advances were overtaking athletic performance, established two separate records. The current record was re-labelled 'Best Hour Performance' and subsequent attempts at the World Hour Record had to be made on a traditional bicycle, using a traditional riding position. Chris Boardman undertook a ride in October 2000 to set a new World Hour Record in the belief that whatever the distance he achieved it would be the new record. However, two hours before his ride, he was advised that the UCI had decided that Eddy Merckx's 1972 ride of 49.431km was the last set on a traditional bicycle and that it still stood. Boardman beat it by just 10m to set the new absolute record.

World Road Race Championships

The men's competition was first held at the Nürburgring in in Germany in 1927 and was first won by Alfredo Binda (Italy). It has been held annually ever since, with the exception of the war years. The women's competition has been held since 1958.

	Men's winner	Women's winner	Venue
1980	Bernard Hinault (France)	Beth Heiden (USA)	Sallanches, France
1981	Freddy Maertens (Belgium)	Ute Enzenauer (West Germany)	Prague, Czechoslovakia
1982	Giuseppe Saronni (Italy)	Mandy Jones (Great Britain)	Goodwood, UK
1983	Greg LeMond (USA)	Marianne Berglund (Switzerland)	Altenrhein, Switzerland
1984	Claude Criquielion (Belgium)	*Not held*	Barcelona, Spain
1985	Joop Zoetemelk (The Netherlands)	Jeannie Longo (France)	Giavera Montello, Spain
1986	Moreno Argentin (Italy)	Jeannie Longo (France)	Colorado Springs, USA
1987	Stephen Roche (Ireland)	Jeannie Longo (France)	Villach, Austria
1988	Maurizio Fondriest (Italy)	Jeannie Longo (France)	Ronse, Belgium
1989	Greg LeMond (USA)	Jeannie Longo (France)	Chambéry, France
1990	Rudy Dhaenens (Belgium)	Catherine Marsal (France)	Utsunomiya, Japan
1991	Gianni Bugno (Italy)	Leontien Van Moorsel (The Netherlands)	Stuttgart, Germany
1992	Gianni Bugno (Italy)	*Not held*	Benidorm, Spain
1993	Lance Armstrong (USA)	Leontien Van Moorsel (The Netherlands)	Oslo, Norway
1994	Luc Leblanc (France)	Monica Valvik (Norway)	Agrigiento, Italy
1995	Abraham Olano Manzano (Spain)	Jeannie Longo (France)	Bogotá, Colombia
1996	Johan Museeuw (Belgium)	Barbara Heeb (Switzerland)	Lugano, Switzerland
1997	Laurent Brochard (France)	Alessandra Cappellotto (Italy)	San Sebastian, Spain
1998	Oscar Camenzind (Switzerland)	Diana Ziliute (Lithuania)	Valkenburg, The Netherlands

	Men's winner	Women's winner	Venue
1999	Oscar Freire Gomez (Spain)	Edita Pucinskaite (Lithuania)	Verona, Italy
2000	Romans Vainsteins (Latvia)	Zinaida Stahurskaia (Belarus)	Plouay, France
2001	Oscar Freire Gomez (Spain)	Rasa Polikeviciute (Lithuania)	Lisbon, Portugal
2002	Mario Cipollini (Italy)	Susanne Ljungskog (Sweden)	Zolder, Belgium
2003	Igor Astarloa (Spain)	Susanne Ljungskog (Sweden)	Hamilton, Canada
2004	Oscar Freire Gomez (Spain)	Judith Arndt (Germany)	Verona, Italy

The big three

No rider has ever won the Tour de France, Giro d'Italia and Vuelta d'España in the same season but Jacques Anquetil (France), Felice Gimondi (Italy), Eddy Merckx (Belgium) and Bernard Hinault (France) have claimed all three in the course of their careers. The best same-season performance in all three tours was by Marino Lejarreta (Spain) who came 20th in the Vuelta d'Espana, 10th in the Giro d'Italia and 5th in the Tour de France in 1989.

Paris–Roubaix

Paris–Roubaix is the most famous of the Spring Classic road races, ridden every spring (apart from the war years) since 1896, when it was won by Josef Fischer (Germany). Known as the 'Hell of the North', the race is over 250km long and sections of the race are ridden over cobbled roads (called 'pavé').

1980	Francesco Moser (Italy)
1981	Bernard Hinault (France)
1982	Jan Raas (The Netherlands)
1983	Hennie Kuiper (The Netherlands)
1984	Sean Kelly (Ireland)
1985	Marc Madiot (France)
1986	Sean Kelly (Ireland)
1987	Eric Vanderaerden (Belgium)
1988	Dirk de Mol (Belgium)
1989	Jean-Marie Wampers (Belgium)
1990	Eddy Planckaert (Belgium)
1991	Marc Madiot (France)
1992	Gilbert Duclos-Lassalle (France)
1993	Gilbert Duclos-Lassalle (France)
1994	Andrei Tchmïl (Russia)
1995	Franco Ballerini (Italy)
1996	Johan Museeuw (Belgium)
1997	Frédéric Guesdon (France)
1998	Franco Ballerini (Italy)
1999	Andrea Tafi (Italy)
2000	Johan Museeuw (Belgium)
2001	Servais Knaven (The Netherlands)
2002	Johan Museeuw (Belgium)
2003	Peter Van Petegem (Belgium)
2004	Magnus Backstedt (Sweden)

Track World Records – Men

Event	Record holder	Year	Time	Distance
200m	Curt Harnett (Canada)	1995	9.865s	
500m	Arnaud Duble (France)	2001	25.850s	
1km	Arnaud Tournant (France)	2001	58.875s	
4km	Chris Boardman (Great Britain)	1996	4min 11.114s	
4km (team)	Australia (Luke Roberts, Brett Lancaster, Bradley McGee, Graeme Brown)	2004	3min 56.610s	
1 hour	Chris Boardman (Great Britain)*	2000		49.441km

*The record for Best Hour Performance, set before new restrictions were applied to the bicycles used for hour record attempts in 2000, is also held by Chris Boardman with a distance of 56.375km set in 1996.

Track World Records – Women

Event	Record holder	Year	Time	Distance
200m	Olga Slioussareva (Russia)	1993	10.831s	
500m (flying start)	Erika Saloumiaee (USSR)	1987	29.655s	
500m (standing start)	Anna Meares (Australia)	2004	33.952s	
3km	Sarah Ulmer (New Zealand)	2004	3min 24.537s	
1 hour	Jeannie Longo-Ciprelli (France)	2000		45.094km

A week in the saddle

The highlights of the European winter track-racing season are the famous Six-Day races, where cycling's showmen battle it out over six successive evenings of racing. The riders race in teams of two in a programme composed of a number of Madison races, interspersed with other track events. Teams win races by gaining laps on other riders and points for winning incidental sprints. However, the original Six-Day races held in the USA at the turn of the 20th century really were races lasting six days, with only brief rest stops. The record was set by C W Miller in 1897 who covered a total distance of 3,361km.

Nicknames

Many cyclists are given nicknames (sometimes more than one) by the sporting press or TV commentators. These often reflect their appearance, sporting achievements or personality. It is also common for popular cyclists to be given pet names by their fans. Here is a selection of them:

Djamolodine Abdoujaparov 'The Tashkent Terror' or 'The Terminator' (because of his sprinting style)

Federico Bahamontès 'The Eagle of Toledo' (for his mountain-climbing prowess)

Louison Bobet Although now always known as 'Louison', this is a nickname – his actual name is Louis

Claudio Chiappucci 'Il Diabolo'

Mario Cipollini 'Super Mario', 'The Fastest Man in the World', 'The Lion King' (for his hairstyle)

Fausto Coppi 'Il Campionissimo'

Roger de Vlaeminck 'The Gypsy' (his parents ran a fairground ride), 'Mr Paris–Roubaix'

Laurent Fignon 'Le Professeur' (because of his glasses – although he does also have a degree)

Bernard Hinault 'Le Blaireau' (The Badger)

Miguel Indurain 'Miguelon', 'Big Mig' (because of his size and dominance in the Tour de France)

Eddie Merckx 'Le Cannibale' (The Cannibal)

Marco Pantani 'Diabolino', 'Il Elefantino' (because of his ears), 'The Pirate'

Lucien Petit-Breton Another cyclist now always known by his nickname – his actual name is Lucien Mazan

It wasn't so easy in the good old days!

In 1913 Eugène Christophe was leading the Tour de France, having already overcome saboteurs scattering nails onto the road in the first stage (not an uncommon occurrence in the early years), when disaster struck; his forks broke on the descent of the Tourmalet. At that time any outside help was forbidden, so he carried his bicycle for two hours to reach the nearest blacksmith and spent an hour forging it back together. He was then handed a further three-minute time penalty because the blacksmith's apprentice had pumped the bellows for him.

A–Z

aero bars extensions clamped on to the handlebars of **time trial** or **track bikes** allowing a cyclist to stretch further forward to achieve a more aerodynamic position. Sometimes called triathlon bars or tri-bars as they were first used in that sport in the 1980s

attack to make a sudden acceleration to try to ride away from another rider or group

banking the inclined track surface of a **velodrome**

bidon a water bottle carried on the bike during a road race

block 1. the **freewheel** 2. a rider's deliberate attempt to slow down a group when that rider does not want the group to catch another rider who has the lead (for tactical reasons)

bonification a time bonus given to riders in the Tour de France for achieving a place at the end of a **stage** or in incidental **sprints**

break, breakaway a rider or group of riders that has ridden away from a larger group or the **peloton**

bridge if a rider bridges, he or she catches up with a **break**

broom wagon (**voiture balai** in French); the support vehicle that picks up riders who abandon, or fall too far behind in, a stage race

bunch same as **peloton**

bunch sprint a sprint for the line involving the **bunch** at the end of a road race or **stage**

cadence the rate at which a rider is pedalling – generally between 90 and 130rpm for a competitive cyclist

chainring, chainwheel the gear wheel that drives the chain, attached to the **cranks**. There are usually two on a **road bike** and one on a **track bike**

chasers riders trying to catch up with a **break**

cleat a device attached to the bottom of a cycling shoe that engages with the mechanism on a **clipless pedal**, locking the rider to the bicycle. Can usually be disengaged by twisting the foot

clipless pedals pedals with a built-in mechanism that locks the rider's foot to the pedal. Used with **cleats**

clips, toe-clips devices attached to pedals allowing the foot to be strapped to the pedal. Now generally replaced by the use of **clipless pedals**, but sometimes used by track cyclists in addition to clipless pedals for added security

climb a section of a race or **stage** ending at the top of a long hill or mountain. In stage races such as the Tour de France the climbs are categorized by height and gradient

climber a road-racing cyclist who specializes in long hill climbs or the mountain stages of races such as the Tour de France

contre-la-montre same as **time trial**. Literally 'against the watch' in French

criterium — **road races** involving several laps around a short road circuit in a town centre

dérailleur — the mechanism that changes the gear on a road bike by moving the chain between **sprockets** at the rear or **chainrings** at the front

directeur sportif — the team manager of a professional cycling team

disc wheel — a wheel composed of a solid disc (rather than spokes), used in time trials and some track events for its superior aerodynamic properties

domestique — a rider in a professional cycling team whose job is to ride for the overall benefit of the team and the team leaders rather than for their own glory

drafting — riding closely behind another rider or riders to save energy by reducing the effects of wind resistance

drops — the lower sections of the curved handlebars on a road bike and some track bikes. Riders ride with their hands 'on the drops' to achieve a lower, more aerodynamic position

echelon — a **paceline** in which the cyclists are staggered at an angle to allow them to achieve a **drafting** effect against a crosswind

feeding station — a designated point in a road race where riders can pick up food and drink

field — same as **peloton**

fixed-wheel — a rear wheel with no **freewheel** where the wheel and pedals always turn together

flamme rouge — a red flag marking the point 1km from the finish of a road race or **stage**

freewheel — 1. the mechanism to which the **sprockets** are attached, allowing the sprockets to disengage from the rear wheel so that it may continue to turn freely when the rider stops pedalling 2. if a rider freewheels, he allows the bicycle to continue to move forwards without pedalling

general classification (GC) — the positions of riders in a stage race based on overall time

green jersey — the jersey worn by the leader in the **points competition** in the Tour de France

handsling — the way in which team-mates change places in the **Madison** by gripping hands, then releasing, so that one rider can propel the other forwards

hoods — the covers of the brake levers on a road bike. Riders sometimes ride with their hands 'on the hoods' to give an alternative, more comfortable position to riding on the **drops**

Keirin — a **track race** sprinting event from Japan. In international competition it is ridden by six to eight riders over 2km. Riders are led for the first 1,400m by a moped, the pace gradually increasing from 30kmh to 50kmh before the moped peels away, leaving the riders to sprint for the line

kermesse — a **criterium** raced around a very short town centre circuit – popular in Belgium

King of the Mountains — the leader in the competition for points gained on **climbs** in the Tour de France. Wears the **polka-dot jersey**

lapped — a rider has been lapped in a track race (such as the **points race** or **scratch race**) if they fall more than one lap behind the leader

lead-out — a tactic whereby a rider allows a team-mate to **draft** behind them as they ride at high speed to give them an advantage as they prepare to **jump** into a **sprint**

Madison a group distance **track race** (often 50km in length) with incidental sprints. It is ridden in teams of two with only one of the two riders in the race at any one time. The race is scored on a combination of distance covered and points for position in **sprints**. So-called because it was first ridden at Madison Square Garden in New York City

mass start a race in which all of the competitors start together

measuring line same as **pole line**

monocoque a one-piece construction method, usually using carbon fibre, for frames or wheels. UCI regulations restrict the extent to which such aerodynamic shaping may be used

musette a bag that can be slung over the shoulder, in which food is handed to cyclists at **feeding stations**

neutralize following an accident in a **track race**, officials may neutralize the race by telling riders to ride slowly at the top of the track and maintain their current position

neutral support a mechanic who follows the riders in a race and is provided by the race organizers (rather than an individual team) and who can give mechanical assistance to any rider

neutral zone a section of a road race where the riders must ride behind a leading vehicle and cannot **attack**

paceline a group of riders each **drafting** behind the one in front. Riders take turns to ride at the front to set the pace

pavé cobbled roads found in northern France and in Belgium

peloton the main group of riders in a stage race

points competition a subsidiary competition in stage races, such as the Tour de France, won by the rider who has accumulated most points from their finishing positions in stages and from **primes**

points race a **track race** ridden by a large group of 20–30 riders over 30km (25km for women). Riders gain points during the race for their position at the end of each lap and in incidental **sprints** throughout the race

pole line the innermost line painted around the track in a **velodrome**. This is the line around which the length of the track is measured

polka-dot jersey the jersey worn by the **King of the Mountains** in the Tour de France

prime a place during a **road race** or a **stage** of a **stage race** at which points are given in the **points competition** or a separate prize is awarded

pursuit race 1. the individual pursuit is a **track race** ridden by two riders head-to-head over a distance of 4km (3km for women). Starting at opposite sides of the track the aim is to catch the other rider or, failing this, to record the fastest time for the total distance 2. the team pursuit follows the same principle but is ridden by teams of four

repechage a round in track racing competitions in which riders who lost their heat can race again to try to re-enter the competition

road bike a bike designed for **road races**, usually with dropped handlebars and several gears (18 is now normal)

road race a cycle race ridden on the road. Distance varies from event to event but professional races will generally be more than 150km in length

rouleur a rider who specializes in riding long flat or rolling **stages** or races, often good at **time trials** and long **breakaways**

scratch race a straightforward distance **track race** ridden by up to 24 riders over 15km (10km for women)

skid lid a cycle helmet

slipstreaming same as **drafting**

soigneur a member of staff in a professional cycling team responsible for riders' food, drink and kit and for massaging riders following races or **stages**

sprint 1. sprint (or match sprint) races are **track races** ridden over 1km by individuals against one or two opponents. Riders jockey for position over the first 800m with a final explosive sprint over the last 200m (the only section of the race that is timed) 2. the final race for the line or for a **prime** in a **road race** or **stage**

sprinter a cyclist who specializes in sprinting

sprinters' lane the inner area of a track in a **velodrome**, between the **pole line** and the **sprinters' line** within which certain rules apply for cyclists sprinting for the finish of a race

sprinters' line a red line on the track in a **velodrome** marking the outside of the **sprinters' lane**

sprockets the gear wheels attached to the rear wheel of a bicycle, via the **freewheel** on a road bike or directly on a **fixed-wheel**

stage individual **road races**, **criteriums**, **time trials** or **team time trials** that make up a stage race

stage race a race that takes place over periods from two days to three weeks. It involves a series of **road races** (and sometimes **time trials** and **criteriums**) ridden on successive days

stand still a tactical manoeuvre in a track **sprint** race whereby a rider stops moving forwards totally to avoid taking the leading position prior to the final sprint. The rules restrict a stand still to a maximum of three minutes

starting block a machine that holds the rear wheel of a bicycle at the start of a **track race**. It releases the wheel when the start of the race is signalled

team sprint a **track race** ridden in teams of three over three laps. Competing teams start on opposite sides of the track. Each rider on the team takes a turn at the front for one lap, then hands over to the next. The final rider finishes alone in a **sprint** for the line

team time trial a **time trial** ridden by a team of riders

time trial a race ridden individually or in small teams, with riders (or teams) riding on their own to achieve the fastest time over a set distance (standard distances are 10km, 25km and 50km but races can be of any length) or to achieve the furthest distance in a set time (for example 1hr, 12hrs or 24hrs)

time-trial bike a road bike designed specifically for a **time trial**, usually with closer ratio gears, **aero bars** and more aerodynamic wheels and frame

toe-clips see **clips**

track bike a bike with a fixed rear wheel and no brakes, designed specifically for riding **track races**

track race a race that takes place in a **velodrome**

velodrome a banked track, either indoor or outdoor, on which **track races** are held

voiture balai see **broom wagon**

yellow jersey the jersey worn by the leader in the **general classification** in the Tour de France. It originated in a publicity stunt by French newspaper L'Auto, which was printed on yellow paper

Some cycling slang

autobus	the group of poor **climbers** who stick together in the mountain **stages** of a race to help each other to finish inside the time limit. Also known as the 'gruppetto' (little group) or laughing group
bonk	sudden fatigue during a race when body carbohydrate reserves are depleted
granny gear	a very low gear
hook	if a rider hooks, he or she deliberately moves the rear wheel of the bike to the side to force the rider behind to slow down
honking	pedalling whilst standing up out of the saddle. Usually used to achieve greater power or to rest the legs while climbing
knock, hunger knock	same as **bonk**
lanterne rouge	the rider in last place in the **general classification** in a stage race. Literally 'red light' in French, an allusion to the red light at the back of a train
natural break	relieving oneself while continuing to cycle. A technique employed by racing cyclists during long **road races**
on the rivet	if a cyclist is on the rivet, he is riding at his physical limit to maintain a fast pace. Such a rider sits right on the front of the saddle, where leather saddles used to have a rivet
road rash	skin abrasion caused by sliding across the road after a crash
sag wagon	a vehicle that follows the cyclists in a road race to give mechanical assistance or to help riders in physical difficulty
sitting in	riding very closely behind the back wheel of the rider in front to **draft**
switching	cutting up another rider by suddenly moving across in front of them when **attacking** or **sprinting**
tester	a **time trial** specialist
wheelsucking	same as **sitting in**

Some famous cyclists

Jacques Anquetil, 1934–87

Born in Normandy, France, he was the foremost of the second wave of French cyclists to emerge after World War II. He was the first rider to win the Tour de France five times, including four successes in a row (1961–4). Excelling in time-trial stages, he could make ferocious attacks, or suddenly outdistance the field on a conventional stretch of road. He retired in 1969.

Lance Armstrong, 1971–

Born in Plano, Texas, USA, he won the US Amateur Cycling Championship in 1990. He turned professional in 1992 and within a year was ranked fifth in the world. He won stages in the Tour de France in 1993 and 1995 but in 1996 was diagnosed with advanced cancer. Declared clear of cancer in 1997, in 1999 he became the second American (after **Greg LeMond**) to win the Tour de France, and went on to win it a record six times in a row.

Chris Boardman, 1968–

Born in Clatterbridge on the Wirral, England, by 1991 he was reigning British champion in the 25-mile, 50-mile and pursuit events. He created a sensation at the 1992 Olympics at Barcelona riding a revolutionary streamlined cycle and took the gold medal in the 4,000m event. He captured the world championship titles in both the pursuit and time-trial events in 1994 and also won the 4,000m title at the 1996 world championships. He is the current holder of the world hour record.

Bernard Hinault, 1954–

Born in Yffiniac, France, he won the Tour de France five times (1978–9, 1981–2, 1985). He also won the Tour of Italy three times and the Tour of Spain twice. In 1985 he won his last Tour despite a fall midway through in which he broke his nose. He retired on his 32nd birthday and became technical adviser to the Tour de France.

Miguel Indurain, 1964–

Born in Villava, Navarre, Spain, he was only the fourth cyclist to win five Tours de France (1991–5). His second win of the Giro d'Italia in 1993 ranks him among only six other cyclists ever to have won both events in the same year. As the leader of the Banesto team, he became the richest man in cycle racing and a national hero in Spain. He announced his retirement in 1997.

Greg LeMond, 1961–

Born in Lakewood, California, USA, in 1986 he became the first American to win the Tour de France, winning it again in 1989 and 1990. His 1989 victory captivated the sporting world. After 23 days and 2,253km, LeMond rode what was then the race's fastest ever time trial to beat French favourite Laurent Fignon by just eight seconds. He retired after contracting a rare muscular wasting disease.

Jeannie Longo-Ciprelli, 1958–

Born in Annecy, France. Her numerous wins include the Women's Tour de France three times, the Colorado equivalent four times and the world title 13 times. Her numerous French Women's Championship wins include eleven consecutive titles between 1979 and 1989 and she has set world records indoors and out. Widely considered the best woman road cyclist of all time.

Brad McGee, 1976–

Born in Sydney, Australia, he started competitive cycling aged ten. At the 1994 Commonwealth Games he won both the individual and team pursuit gold medals. The following year he was part of the Australian world championship team. In 1996 he won two bronze medals at the Olympics and in 1998 repeated his 1994 feat of two gold medals in the individual and team pursuits. Once more he took the 4,000m individual pursuit at the 2002 Commonwealth Games but was struck down by a virus and was not included in the team competition. McGee has also won stages of the Tour de France.

Eddy Merckx, 1945–

Born in Woluwe St Pierre, near Brussels, Belgium. In the 1969 Tour de France he won the major prizes in all three sections: overall, points classification and King of the Mountains. He won the Tour de France five times (1969–72 and 1974), the Tour of Italy five times, and all the major classics, including the Milan–San Remo race seven times. He was the world professional road race champion three times. He won more races (445 out of 1,582) and more classics than any other rider, before retiring in 1978.

DARTS

Origins

It is commonly believed that darts originated in the Middle Ages among archers who threw their arrows, or shortened versions, at barrel lids and then tree stumps. The latter were particularly suitable as the growth rings made it easy to tell who was closest to the centre. It is recorded that in 1530 Anne Boleyn gave Henry VIII a set of 'dartes of Biscayan fashion, richly ornamented' and also that passengers on *The Mayflower* in 1620 played the game.

Rules and description

An indoor game that consists of throwing three 13cm/5in darts from a distance of 2.4m/8ft at a circular board which has its 'bull' or centre 1.7m/5ft 8in from the floor. The standard board is divided into 20 segments numbered 1–20 (not in numerical order); each contains smaller segments ('beds') which either double or treble that number's score if hit. The centre ring (the 'bull') is worth 50 points, and the area around it (the 'outer') is worth 25 points. The most popular game is '501' where players start at that figure and deduct all scores from it, aiming to reduce the starting score exactly to zero; the final shot or 'game shot' must consist of a double.

Ruling bodies: World Darts Federation (WDF); British Darts Organization (BDO). The Professional Darts Corporation (PDC) was formed in 1992 (initially known as the World Darts Council) as a breakaway from the BDO and organizes a separate tour and World Championship

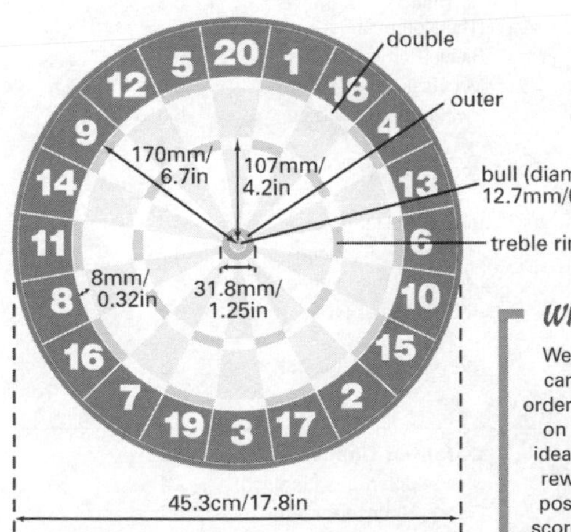

Why double top is at the top

We have Brian Gamlin (1852-1903), a carpenter from Bury, to thank for the order in which the numbers are arranged on a dartboard. He came up with the idea shortly before he died as a way of rewarding accuracy and reducing the possibility of lucky throws making big scores, low numbers being placed next to high ones. Carpenters often made dartboards as elm was the favoured material for many years.

Embassy World Professional Championship

First held at the Heart of the Midlands Club, Nottingham, in 1978; from 1979 to 1985 held at Jollees Cabaret Club, Stoke on Trent; since 1986 held at Lakeside Country Club, Frimley Green, Surrey. Women's championship introduced in 2001. The men's final is now played over eleven sets, each set consisting of five legs, the women's final over three sets of five legs each.

Men

	Champion	Defeated finalist	Score
1978	Leighton Rees (Wales)	John Lowe (England)	11-7 (legs not sets)
1979	John Lowe (England)	Leighton Rees (Wales)	5-0
1980	Eric Bristow (England)	Bobby George (England)	5-3
1981	Eric Bristow (England)	John Lowe (England)	5-3
1982	Jocky Wilson (Scotland)	John Lowe (England)	5-3
1983	Keith Deller (England)	Eric Bristow (England)	6-5
1984	Eric Bristow (England)	Dave Whitcombe (England)	7-1
1985	Eric Bristow (England)	John Lowe (England)	6-2
1986	Eric Bristow (England)	Dave Whitcombe (England)	6-0
1987	John Lowe (England)	Eric Bristow (England)	6-4
1988	Bob Anderson (England)	John Lowe (England)	6-4
1989	Jocky Wilson (Scotland)	Eric Bristow (England)	6-4
1990	Phil Taylor (England)	Eric Bristow (England)	6-1
1991	Dennis Priestley (England)	Eric Bristow (England)	6-0
1992	Phil Taylor (England)	Mike Gregory (England)	6-5
1993	John Lowe (England)	Alan Warriner (England)	6-3
1994	John Part (Canada)	Bobby George (England)	6-0
1995	Richie Burnett (Wales)	Raymond van Barneveld (The Netherlands)	6-3
1996	Steve Beaton (England)	Richie Burnett (Wales)	6-3
1997	Les Wallace (Scotland)	Marshall James (Wales)	6-3
1998	Raymond van Barneveld (The Netherlands)	Richie Burnett (Wales)	6-5
1999	Raymond van Barneveld (The Netherlands)	Ronnie Baxter (England)	6-5
2000	Ted Hankey (England)	Ronnie Baxter (England)	6-0
2001	John Walton (England)	Ted Hankey (England)	6-2
2002	Tony David (Australia)	Mervyn King (England)	6-4
2003	Raymond van Barneveld (The Netherlands)	Ritchie Davies (Wales)	6-3
2004	Andy Fordham (England)	Mervyn King (England)	6-3

Women

	Champion	Defeated finalist	Score
2001	Trina Gulliver (England)	Mandy Solomons (England)	2-1
2002	Trina Gulliver (England)	Francis Hoenselaar (The Netherlands)	2-1
2003	Trina Gulliver (England)	Anne Kirk (Scotland)	2-0
2004	Trina Gulliver (England)	Francis Hoenselaar (The Netherlands)	2-0

PDC World Championship

The PDC World Championship has been held at the Circus Tavern, Purfleet, since 1994.

	Champion	Defeated finalist	Score
1994	Dennis Priestley (England)	Phil Taylor (England)	6-1
1995	Phil Taylor (England)	Rod Harrington (England)	6-2
1996	Phil Taylor (England)	Dennis Priestley (England)	6-4
1997	Phil Taylor (England)	Dennis Priestley (England)	6-3
1998	Phil Taylor (England)	Dennis Priestley (England)	6-0
1999	Phil Taylor (England)	Peter Manley (England)	6-2
2000	Phil Taylor (England)	Dennis Priestley (England)	7-3
2001	Phil Taylor (England)	John Part (Canada)	7-0
2002	Phil Taylor (England)	Peter Manley (England)	7-0
2003	John Part (Canada)	Phil Taylor (England)	7-6
2004	Phil Taylor (England)	Kevin Painter (England)	7-0

Winmau World Masters

Competition started in 1974 and has been sponsored by dartboard manufacturers Winmau since its inception.

	Champion	Defeated finalist
1974	Cliff Inglis (England)	Harry Keenan (Scotland)
1975	Alan Evans (Wales)	David Jones (Wales)
1976	John Lowe (England)	Phil Obbard (Wales)
1977	Eric Bristow (England)	Paul Reynolds (England)
1978	Ronnie Davis (England)	Tony Brown (England)
1979	Eric Bristow (England)	Alan Hogg (Canada)
1980	John Lowe (England)	Rab Smith (Scotland)
1981	Eric Bristow (England)	John Lowe (England)
1982	Dave Whitcombe (England)	Jocky Wilson (Scotland)
1983	Eric Bristow (England)	Mike Gregory (England)
1984	Eric Bristow (England)	Keith Deller (England)
1985	Dave Whitcombe (England)	Ray Farrell (Northern Ireland)
1986	Bob Anderson (England)	Bob Sinnaeve (Canada)
1987	Bob Anderson (England)	John Lowe (England)
1988	Bob Anderson (England)	John Lowe (England)
1989	Peter Evison (England)	Eric Bristow (England)
1990	Phil Taylor (England)	Jocky Wilson (Scotland)
1991	Rod Harrington (England)	Phil Taylor (England)
1992	Dennis Priestley (England)	Mike Gregory (England)
1993	Steve Beaton (England)	Les Wallace (Scotland)
1994	Richie Burnett (Wales)	Steve Beaton (England)
1995	Erik Clarijs (Belgium)	Richie Burnett (Wales)
1996	Colin Monk (England)	Richie Burnett (Wales)
1997	Graham Hunt (Australia)	Ronnie Baxter (England)
1998	Les Wallace (Scotland)	Alan Warriner (England)
1999	Andy Fordham (England)	Wayne Jones (England)
2000	John Walton (England)	Mervyn King (England)

	Champion	Defeated finalist
2001	Raymond van Barneveld (The Netherlands)	Jarkko Komula (Finland)
2002	Mark Dudbridge (England)	Tony West (England)
2003	Tony West (England)	Raymond van Barneveld (The Netherlands)
2004	Mervyn King (England)	Tony O'Shea (England)

Are you ready? Let's play darts

This is the catchphrase of Martin Fitzmaurice, veteran compère and caller at professional darts competitions. The solidly built former Tube driver and amateur darter whips up the crowd who chant the words along with him.

Nicknames

Many, if not most, professional darts players have nicknames, which are usually written on the back of their shirts. Below are nicknames of players mentioned in this chapter.

Bob Anderson	'The Limestone Cowboy' (because of his fondness for country-and-western and his northern roots)
Raymond van Barneveld	'Barney'
Ronnie Baxter	'The Rocket'
Steve Beaton	'The Bronze Adonis' (because of his perma-tan and full head of hair)
Eric Bristow	'The Crafty Cockney'
Richie Burnett	'Prince of Wales'
Erik Clarijs	'The Sheriff'
Tony David	'Boomerang' or 'Elvis'
Ritchie Davies	'Lamb Chop'
Keith Deller	'Milky Bar Kid' (because of his clean-cut image and because he used to drink milk during games)
Mark Dudbridge	'The Flash'
Peter Evison	'The Fen Tiger'
Andy Fordham	'The Viking' (because of his size and long hair)
Bobby George	'Mr Glitter' (because of his jewellery)
Shaun Greatbatch	'Nine Dart' (because of his televised nine-dart finish in 2002)
Trina Gulliver	'The Golden Girl'
Ted Hankey	'The Count' (because of a supposed resemblance to Count Dracula)
Rod Harrington	'The Prince of Style' (because he wore a shirt and tie when playing)
Francis Hoenselaar	'The Dutch Crown'
Mervyn King	'The King'
Jarkko Komula	'Smiley' (because of his serious demeanour during a game)
Paul Lim	'The Singapore Slinger' (because he was born there)
John Lowe	'Old Stoneface' (because of his serious demeanour during a game)
Peter Manley	'One Dart'
Wayne Mardle	'Hawaii 501' (because of his Hawaiian shirts)
Colin Monk	'The Mad Monk'
Kevin Painter	'The Artist'

John Part	'Darth Maple'
Dennis Priestley	'The Menace'
Phil Taylor	'The Power'
Les Wallace	'McDanger'
John Walton	'John Boy'
Alan Warriner	'The Iceman'

Televised Nine-dart Finishes

The nine-dart finish (the fewest darts with which a game of 501 can be won) is the ultimate achievement in darts, similar to a hole-in-one at golf, a hat-trick at cricket, a 147 break in snooker or pitching a perfect game in baseball. Only four perfect dart games have been seen on television.

John Lowe (England)	1984	MFI World Matchplay Championships, Slough
Paul Lim (USA)	1990	Embassy World Championships, Frimley Green
Shaun Greatbatch (England)	2002	Dutch Open, Slagharen, The Netherlands
Phil Taylor (England)	2002	Stan James World Matchplay, Blackpool

A-Z

against the darts	if a player wins a leg against the darts, it means that his or her opponent had the advantage of throwing first; see **break the throw**
barrel	the metal front part of the dart, which is gripped by the thrower
bed	the area of a double or treble, defined by the wire of the **spider**
bounce-out	when a dart hits the wire of the board and falls to the ground
break the throw	to win a leg of darts in which your opponent threw first
bull('s eye)	the small red circle at the centre of a dartboard; worth 50 points
bust	to exceed the required score
checkout	the score successfully thrown to win a game in one turn; the highest possible checkout is 170 (two treble 20s and the bull's eye)
cover shot	a throw at another high number, usually treble 18 or 19, when the treble 20 bed is obscured by the position of a dart or darts already thrown
dartitis	unexplained syndrome (similar to the yips in golf) where a player cannot release the dart naturally or at all, resulting in a total loss of accuracy
double	the score of twice the normal amount when hitting the narrow outer ring of a dartboard
double top, tops	double 20
finish	to win a game of darts by hitting the required double
flight	usually plastic or polyester attachment with four fins that fits into the **shaft** of a dart and make it more aerodynamic. Flights were originally made from turkey feathers and paper flights were introduced around the beginning of the 20th century
game on	the traditional call of the announcer to signal the beginning of a game
game shot	the shot that wins a leg of darts

hold the throw	to win a leg in which you threw first
marker	1. a dart just outside the required double that helps the aiming of subsequent darts 2. the person who keeps the score
maximum	a score of 180 with three darts (three treble 20s)
oche	the line, groove or ridge behind which a player must stand to throw. The origin of the word is uncertain but it may come from the Old French word *ocher*, meaning to nick or cut a groove in
outer	the green circle around the **bull's eye**; worth 25 points
outshot	same as **checkout**
shaft, stem	the plastic or metal part of the dart that screws into the **barrel** and holds the **flight**
spider	the wire grid that is fixed to the face of a dartboard; the spider usually also includes the numbers so that it can be rotated and hence prolong the life of the board
treble	the score of three times the normal amount when hitting the narrow inner ring of a dartboard
with the darts	if a player wins a leg with the darts, it means that he or she had the advantage of throwing first; see **hold the throw**

Some darts slang

Annie's room	the number 1 and, sometimes, double 1. The phrase 'up in Annie's room' was used in World War I as a dismissive answer to a question about where something was, and more generally to mean any lost cause. The identity of Annie is unknown
arrows	slang for the game of darts, and for the darts themselves
bed and breakfast	the score 26, a common score of 20, 5 and 1 when aiming for treble 20. Comes from two and six, the former traditional cost of bed and breakfast
madhouse	double 1. The word expresses the frustration of the player left with this least-favoured double
middle for diddle	an expression that describes a way of deciding who throws first in an informal game of darts; both players throw one dart and the player who throws nearest to the bull starts the game
shanghai	the feat of scoring a single, double and treble of the same number with a set of three darts

Trebles for show, doubles for dough

This is an old saying in darts and reflects the fact that big scorers do not always win matches. In a sport fascinated with averages, it is normal for the best players to have a single-dart average of 30 and above. Proof of the saying came in the quarter-final of the 2004 Embassy World Championship, where Mervyn 'The King' King defeated Ritchie 'Lamb Chop' Davies by 5 sets to 4 despite the fact that Davies had a higher average of 32.04 to King's 30.76.

Some famous darts players

Raymond van Barneveld, 1967–

Born in Rijswijk, the Netherlands, he has won the Embassy World Championship three times and is the leading darts player in the BDO-organized tour. His emergence at the forefront of world darts coincided with the rise of darts in the Netherlands, where it is now one of the most popular sports. A big scorer who demoralizes opponents with single-dart averages approaching 35, he was honoured by Queen Beatrix in 1999.

Eric Bristow, 1957-

Born in London, England, he dominated darts in the 1980s, winning the Embassy World Championship five times and being runner-up five times. He was awarded the MBE in 1989, the first darts player to receive such an honour, but shortly afterwards began to suffer from dartitis, which ended his career early. Always cheeky (some would say arrogant), hence his nickname The Crafty Cockney, he is now a TV commentator.

John Lowe, 1945-

Born in New Tupton, Derbyshire, England, he won the Embassy World Championship three times and was losing finalist five times. He played over 100 times for England, and had an unbeaten record as captain, but his greatest achievement was throwing the first ever televised nine-dart finish, for which he won £100,000.

Phil Taylor, 1960-

Born in Stoke-on-Trent, England, he is simply the most successful darts player of all time. He joined the PDC tour when it was formed and had a phenomenal eight-year unbroken run of victories in the PDC World Championship. His televised nine-darter in 2002 gained him £100,000 and left him with little else to achieve in the game. In 2000 he became the second darts player to receive an MBE but had the honour withdrawn after he was convicted for indecent assault.

Gems from Sid

Excitable Geordie television commentator Sid Waddell is notorious for his flights of fancy when describing darts. Here are just a few: 'That's the greatest comeback since Lazarus'; 'When Alexander of Macedonia was 33, he cried salt tears because there were no more worlds to conquer. Bristow's only 27'; 'Steve Beaton, he's not Adonis, he's THE donis'; 'This lad has more checkouts than Tescos'; and 'If we'd had Phil Taylor at Hastings against the Normans, they'd have gone home'.

DECATHLON

Origins

Introduced into the ancient Olympic Games in 708 BC the pentathlon was a sporting event comprising five sports: sprinting, discus throwing, long jumping, throwing the javelin, and concluding with a wrestling match.

In the Much Wenlock Games, a revival of the Olympic Games held in Shropshire in the 1850s and 1860s, the pentathlon consisted of a high jump, long jump, putting a 36lb stone, a half-mile run and climbing a 55ft rope. In 1884 the American athletics authorities designed a national 'All-Around' championship. By the 1904 St Louis Olympics this had evolved into a decathlon.

Decathlon

Rules and description

The decathlon is an athletics event for men consisting of ten separate contests held on two consecutive days.

On day one is the 100m, long jump, shot put, high jump and 400m; on day two, the 110m hurdles, discus, pole vault, javelin and 1,500m. In the field events, each competitor has three throws or jumps. Points are awarded for each individual event according to a set of tables approved by the International Amateur Athletics Association. Top decathletes expect to achieve more than 8,000 points.

Ruling body: International Association of Athletics Federations

Olympic Champions

Held for the first time in 1904, the decathlon was revived in its modern form for the 1912 Games. The scoring tables are modified from time to time, most often to take into account advances in timekeeping and measuring.

1904 Thomas Kiely (Great Britain/Ireland) [1]
1912 Hugo Wieslander (Sweden) [2]
1920 Helge Lövland (Norway)
1924 Harold Osborn (USA)
1928 Paavo Yrjölä (Finland)
1932 James Bausch (USA)
1936 Glenn Morris (USA)
1948 Bob Mathias (USA)
1952 Bob Mathias (USA)
1956 Milt Campbell (USA)
1960 Rafer Johnson (USA)
1964 Willi Holdorf (West Germany)
1968 Bill Toomey (USA)
1972 Mikola Avilov (USSR)
1976 Bruce Jenner (USA)
1980 Daley Thompson (Great Britain)
1984 Daley Thompson (Great Britain)
1988 Christian Schenk (East Germany)
1992 Robert Změlík (Czechoslovakia)
1996 Dan O'Brien (USA)
2000 Erki Nool (Estonia)
2004 Roman Šebrle (Czech Republic)

A sure thing

Dan O'Brien was seen as a hot favourite for the Olympic decathlon in 1992 – so much so that Reebok pumped $25 million into an advertising campaign featuring O'Brien and fellow American Dave Johnson, proclaiming that the world's greatest athlete would be revealed in Barcelona. After dominating early events in the American trials, all O'Brien needed to do to make the team was register a height – any height – in the pole vault. He chose to open at a challenging 4.8m and failed all three attempts. Johnson went on to take Olympic bronze while the watching O'Brien commentated for NBC.

[1] The events were the 100 yards, 1 mile, 120 yards hurdles, 880 yards walk, high jump, long jump, pole vault, shot put, hammer and 56lb weight.

[2] American Jim Thorpe won the gold medal but was later disqualified for previously competing as a professional American footballer. The disqualification was overturned in 1982, nearly 30 years after his death.

Major Landmarks in the Decathlon Record

Figures have been recalculated to take into account the current scoring tables.

Landmark	Decathlete	Year	Points
Over 6,000 points	Jim Thorpe (USA)	1912	6,564
Over 7,000 points	Hans-Heinrich Sievert (Germany)	1934	7,147
Over 8,000 points	Phil Mulkey (USA)	1961	8,049
Over 8,500 points	Bruce Jenner (USA)	1976	8,634
Over 8,700 points	Daley Thompson (Great Britain)	1982	8,730
Over 8,800 points	Jürgen Hingsen (West Germany)	1983	8,825
Over 8,900 points	Tomáš Dvorák (Czech Republic)	1999	8,994
Over 9,000 points	Roman Šebrle (Czech Republic)	2001	9,026

The dizzy heights of the silver screen

If you are an American and the Olympic Games decathlon champion, chances are that you can carve yourself a career in Hollywood. A number of champions did just that. Glenn Morris and Rafer Johnson both appeared in Tarzan movies – Morris as the ape-man himself. Bob Mathias and Bruce Jenner had brief movie careers but Jim Thorpe starred in more than 50 films, though largely uncredited and often playing a token Indian.

DRAG RACING

Origins

The sport developed in the late 1930s in California, USA, from hot-rod racing, where ordinary cars were fitted with more powerful engines to give them a greater speed. Racers used the straight main streets ('drags') in towns but complaints about the danger and the noise meant the sport was transferred to salt flats. The first rules were formalized by the Southern California Timing Association (SCTA) in 1937. The first formal drag strip was opened in Goleta, California, in 1948. Drag racing continues to be more popular in the USA than anywhere else.

Rules and description

In drag racing two cars (or motorcycles) start side by side and accelerate over the distance of a quarter of a mile (402m) on a straight-line track. Most cars are rear-engined, have very large rear slick tyres to give greater contact with the track surface, and elongated bodies. They use parachutes at the end of a run to assist with the braking. Electronic devices detect the elapsed time and the terminal speed of each vehicle. 'Top fuel cars' and 'funny cars' reach speeds of over 330mph/530kph; the races are quickly over, with elapsed times of less than five seconds being the norm. In competition, the winner of each race progresses through a series of knockout rounds to a final.

Motorcycles are also ridden in drag racing, but they are often lengthened to improve their stability and have bars behind the rear wheel to prevent the front wheel from lifting off the ground and flipping the machine over. From a standing start motorcycles can reach speeds as high as 190mph/305kph over the quarter-mile.

Ruling bodies: Fédération Internationale de l'Automobile (FIA); the National Hot Rod Association (NHRA) oversees US drag racing

NHRA POWERade Series Champions

Sponsored by Winston from 1974 to 1991.

	Top fuel	Funny car	Pro-stock
1974	Gary Beck	Shirl Beck	Bob Glidden
1975	Don Garlits	Don Prudhomme	Bob Glidden
1976	Richard Tharp	Don Prudhomme	Larry Lombardo
1977	Shirley Muldowney	Don Prudhomme	Don Nicholson
1978	Kelly Brown	Don Prudhomme	Bob Glidden
1979	Rob Bruins	Raymond Beadle	Bob Glidden
1980	Shirley Muldowney	Raymond Beadle	Bob Glidden
1981	Jeb Allen	Raymond Beadle	Lee Shepherd
1982	Shirley Muldowney	Frank Hawley	Lee Shepherd
1983	Gary Beck	Frank Hawley	Lee Shepherd
1984	Joe Amato	Mark Oswald	Lee Shepherd
1985	Don Garlits	Kenny Bernstein	Bob Glidden
1986	Don Garlits	Kenny Bernstein	Bob Glidden
1987	Dick LaHaie	Kenny Bernstein	Bob Glidden
1988	Joe Amato	Kenny Bernstein	Bob Glidden
1989	Gary Ormsby	Bruce Larson	Bob Glidden
1990	Joe Amato	John Force	Darrell Alderman
1991	Joe Amato	John Force	Darrell Alderman
1992	Joe Amato	Cruz Pedregon	Warren Johnson
1993	Eddie Hill	John Force	Warren Johnson
1994	Scott Kalitta	John Force	Darrell Alderman
1995	Scott Kalitta	John Force	Warren Johnson
1996	Kenny Bernstein	John Force	Jim Yates
1997	Gary Scelzi	John Force	Jim Yates
1998	Gary Scelzi	John Force	Warren Johnson
1999	Tony Schumacher	John Force	Warren Johnson
2000	Gary Scelzi	John Force	Jeg Coughlin, Jr
2001	Kenny Bernstein	John Force	Warren Johnson
2002	Larry Dixon, Jr	John Force	Jeg Coughlin, Jr
2003	Larry Dixon, Jr	Tony Pedregon	Greg Anderson
2004	Tony Schumacher	John Force	Greg Anderson

A-Z

burnout — the process of spinning the rear tyres in water to heat and clean them prior to a run to gain better traction. Competitors perform a burnout before every run

Christmas tree — the description given to the multicoloured lighting system of yellow, green and red lights that starts a race

elapsed time — the time taken to travel the course from start line to finishing line

ET — short for **elapsed time**

funny car — front-engined car with a fibreglass body that can be folded up and resembles that of a normal car

methanol — pure methyl alcohol, it is used in **top fuel dragsters** and **funny cars** to produce more power

nitromethane — a fuel made specifically for drag racing. It is the result of a chemical reaction between nitric acid and propane

pro-stock — a type of drag racer that outwardly appears like a normal production car but with chassis and engine modifications

rail — a **top fuel dragster**

reaction time — the time it takes a driver to react to the green starting light on the **Christmas tree**; it is measured in thousandths of a second

speed trap — the final 66ft/20m to the finish line where the speed is recorded

terminal speed — the speed that is recorded as the racer crosses the finishing line

top fuel dragster — a classification of elongated, usually rear-engined car that runs on racing alcohol (**nitromethane** and **methanol**) rather than petrol. They produce around 8,000 horsepower

wheelie — the act of lifting the front wheels of the racer so that only the rear wheels are in contact with the track

EQUESTRIAN SPORTS

Origins

The history of man and horse goes back many thousands of years. Evidence for the riding of horses dates to as early as 4000BC and the use of horses as draft animals to between 3000 and 2000BC. Equestrian sports first featured in the ancient Olympic Games. In Rome professional chariot racing became immensely popular, and the huge Circus Maximus arena was built especially for the sport. Gymnastics on horseback was popular in ancient Rome and it is from this that the modern sport of 'vaulting' is derived. The disciplines of 'dressage' and 'three-day eventing' are based on the skills required of cavalry riders and their horses. Indeed, the three-day event at the Olympics was known in its infancy as the 'Militaire' and, until 1952, was open only to serving cavalry officers. In Britain during the 18th century, the increasing enclosure of hitherto common land into privately owned plots divided by fences, walls and hedges meant that foxhunters encountered more and more obstacles to be leapt. Jumping eventually became a sport in itself and the first organized events in Europe took place in the 1860s, most notably in Paris and at the 1868 Royal Dublin Society Show which featured 'high leap' and 'long leap' events. The first important 'showjumping' event in Britain took place at the Horse of the Year Show at Olympia in 1907.

Rules and description

The seven disciplines recognized by the FEI are as follows:

Dressage is the performance by the horse of set gaits and manoeuvres signalled by the rider, with each movement being marked by judges. In grand prix freestyle dressage the movements are accompanied by music.

Showjumping requires horse and rider to clear a series of high obstacles in a set order, usually within a time limit, without faults (the knocking down of walls and fences or the refusal by the horse to attempt the obstacles).

Three-day eventing is a combination of three disciplines: dressage, showjumping and cross-country (riding that tests speed, endurance, and the ability to tackle fences and natural obstacles).

Reining is a discipline of American origin, based on the skills required by ranchers, that requires horse and rider to perform a routine of figures, turns and stops at varying speeds.

Vaulting is gymnastics on horseback and requires the rider to perform a series of freestyle and compulsory moves marked by judges.

Carriage driving involves driver, carriage (two- or four-wheeled), and one, two, four or sometimes more horses in three phases of competition: dressage, marathon (a cross-country time trial) and cones (the completion of a tightly winding course marked by cones).

Endurance riding is a test of a horse's stamina over cross-country courses of between 25 and 100 miles. During competition each horse is checked regularly by vets and those animals showing signs of distress are eliminated from competition. The rider's skill, therefore, is to pace his horse so that it can complete as great a distance as possible in good condition.

Ruling body: Fédération Équestre Internationale (FEI)

Olympic Games

Equestrian sports have featured at nearly every modern Olympiad. The three disciplines competed for at the Olympics are the three-day event, showjumping, and dressage.

Olympic Three-Day Event

	Individual	Team
1912	Axel Nordlander (Sweden)	Sweden
1920	Helmer Mörner (Sweden)	Sweden
1924	Adolph van der Voort van Zijp (The Netherlands)	The Netherlands
1928	Charles Pahud de Mortanges (The Netherlands)	The Netherlands
1932	Charles Pahud de Mortanges (The Netherlands)	USA
1936	Ludwig Stubbendorff (Germany)	Germany
1948	Bernard Chevallier (France)	USA

	Individual	Team
1952	Hans von Blixen-Finecke (Sweden)	Sweden
1956	Petrus Kastenman (Sweden)	Great Britain
1960	Lawrence Morgan (Australia)	Australia
1964	Mauro Checcoli (Italy)	Italy
1968	Jean-Jacques Guyon (France)	Great Britain
1972	Richard Meade (Great Britain)	Great Britain
1976	Edmund Coffin (USA)	USA
1980	Euro Frederico Roman (Italy)	USSR
1984	Mark Todd (New Zealand)	USA
1988	Mark Todd (New Zealand)	West Germany
1992	Matthew Ryan (Australia)	Australia
1996	Blyth Tait (New Zealand)	Australia
2000	David O'Connor (USA)	Australia
2004	Leslie Law (Great Britain)	France

Olympic Showjumping

	Individual	Team
1900	Aimé Haageman (Belgium)	
1904-8	*Not held*	
1912	Jean Cariou (France)	Sweden
1920	Tommaso Lequio di Assaba (Italy)	Sweden
1924	Alphonse Gemuseus (Switzerland)	Sweden
1928	František Ventura (Czechoslovakia)	Spain
1932	Takeichi Nishi (Japan)	*No finishers*
1936	Kurt Hasse (Germany)	Germany
1948	Humberto Mariles (Mexico)	Mexico
1952	Pierre Jonquères d'Oriola (France)	Great Britain
1956	Hans Günter Winkler (West Germany)	West Germany
1960	Raimondo D'Inzeo (Italy)	West Germany
1964	Pierre Jonquères d'Oriola (France)	West Germany
1968	William Steinkraus (USA)	Canada
1972	Graziano Mancinelli (Italy)	West Germany
1976	Alwin Schockemöhle (West Germany)	France
1980	Jan Kowalczyk (Poland)	USSR
1984	Joe Fargis (USA)	USA
1988	Pierre Durand (France)	West Germany
1992	Ludger Beerbaum (Germany)	The Netherlands
1996	Ulrich Kirchhoff (Germany)	Germany
2000	Jeroen Dubbeldam (The Netherlands)	Germany
2004	Cian O'Connor (Ireland)*	USA

* Result subject to change following a positive doping test.

Olympic Dressage

	Individual	Team
1912	Carl Bonde (Sweden)	
1920	Janne Lundblad (Sweden)	
1924	Ernst Linder (Sweden)	
1928	Carl-Friedrich von Langen-Parow (Germany)	Germany
1932	Xavier Lesage (France)	France

	Individual	Team
1936	Heinz Pollay (Germany)	Germany
1948	Hans Moser (Switzerland)	France
1952	Henri Saint Cyr (France)	Sweden
1956	Henri Saint Cyr (France)	Sweden
1960	Sergei Filatov (USSR)	*Not held*
1964	Henri Chammartin (Switzerland)	West Germany
1968	Ivan Kizimov (USSR)	West Germany
1972	Liselott Linsenhoff (West Germany)	USSR
1976	Christine Stückelberger (Switzerland)	West Germany
1980	Elisabeth Theurer (Austria)	USSR
1984	Reiner Klimke (West Germany)	West Germany
1988	Nicole Uphoff (West Germany)	West Germany
1992	Nicole Uphoff (Germany)	Germany
1996	Isabell Werth (Germany)	Germany
2000	Anky van Grunsven (The Netherlands)	Germany
2004	Anky van Grunsven (The Netherlands)	Germany

World Equestrian Games (WEG)

Since 1990 the FEI-organized World Equestrian Games have brought together a number of equestrian world championships into one games, although in some cases (such as vaulting) separate championships are held between Games. The latest discipline to become a WEG event is reining, which joined the games in 2002. The World Equestrian Games have been held at the following venues:

1990	Stockholm, Sweden
1994	The Hague, The Netherlands
1998	Rome, Italy
2002	Jerez, Spain
2006	Aachen, Germany

Showjumping World Championships

	Individual	Team
1953	Francisco Goyoago (Spain)	
1954	Hans Günter Winkler (West Germany)	
1955	Hans Günter Winkler (West Germany)	
1956	Raimondo D'Inzeo (Italy)	
1960	Raimondo D'Inzeo (Italy)	
1966	Pierre Jonquères d'Oriola (France)	
1970	David Broome (Great Britain)	
1974	Hartwig Steenken (West Germany)	
1978	Gerd Wiltfang (West Germany)	Great Britain
1982	Norbert Koof (West Germany)	France
1986	Gail Greenough (Canada)	USA
1990	Eric Navet (France)	France
1994	Franke Sloothaak (Germany)	Germany
1998	Rodrigo Pessoa (Brazil)	Germany
2002	Dermott Lennon (Ireland)	France

Three-Day Eventing World Championships

	Individual	Team
1966	Carlos Moratorio (Argentina)	Ireland
1970	Mary Gordon Watson (Great Britain)	Great Britain
1974	Bruce Davidson (USA)	USA
1978	Bruce Davidson (USA)	Canada
1982	Lucinda Green (Great Britain)	Great Britain
1986	Virginia Leng (Great Britain)	Great Britain
1990	Blyth Tait (New Zealand)	New Zealand
1994	Vaughn Jefferis (New Zealand)	Great Britain
1998	Blyth Tait (New Zealand)	New Zealand
2002	Jean Teulcre (France)	USA

Dressage World Champioships

	Individual	Team
1966	Josef Neckermann (West Germany)	West Germany
1970	Yelena Petuchkova (USSR)	USSR
1974	Reiner Klimke (West Germany)	West Germany
1978	Christine Stückelberger (Switzerland)	West Germany
1982	Reiner Klimke (West Germany)	West Germany
1986	Anne Grethe Jensen (Denmark)	West Germany
1990	Nicole Uphoff (West Germany)	West Germany
1994	Anky van Grunsven (The Netherlands)	Germany
1998	Isabell Werth (Germany)	Germany
2002	Nadine Capellmann (Germany)	Germany

Endurance Riding World Championships

	Individual	Team
1986	Cassandra Schuler (USA)	Great Britain
1988	Becky Hart (USA)	USA
1990	Becky Hart (USA)	Great Britain
1992	Becky Hart (USA)	France
1994	Valerie Kanavy (USA)	France
1996	Danielle Kanavy (USA)	USA
1998	Valerie Kanavy (USA)	New Zealand
2002	Sheikh Ahmed bin Mohammad al Maktoum (UAE)	France

Vaulting World Championships

	Men	Women	Team
1986	Dietmar Otto (West Germany)	Silke Bernhard (West Germany)	West Germany
1988	Christoph Lensing (West Germany)	Silke Bernhard (West Germany)	Switzerland
1990	Michael Lehner (Germany)	Silke Bernhard (Germany)	Switzerland
1992	Christoph Lensing (Germany)	Barbara Ströbel (Germany)	Germany
1994	Thomas Fiskbaek (Denmark)	Tanja Benedetto (Germany)	Switzerland
1996	Christoph Lensing (Germany)	Tanja Benedetto (Germany)	Germany
1998	Devon Maitozo (USA)	Nadia Zülow (Germany)	Germany
2000	Matthias Lang (France)	Nadia Zülow (Germany)	Germany
2002	Matthias Lang (France)	Nadia Zülow (Germany)	Germany
2004	Kai Vorberg (Germany)	Nicola Ströh (Germany)	Germany

Equestrian Sports

Reining World Championships

	Individual	Team
2002	Shawn Flarida (USA)	USA

Carriage Driving World Championships: Four-in-hand

	Individual	Team
1972	Auguste Dubey (Switzerland)	Great Britain
1974	Sandor Fülöp (Hungary)	Great Britain
1976	Imre Abonyi (Hungary)	Hungary
1978	György Bardos (Hungary)	Hungary
1980	György Bardos (Hungary)	Great Britain
1982	Tjeerd Velstra (The Netherlands)	The Netherlands
1984	Laszlo Juhasz (Hungary)	Hungary
1986	Tjeerd Velstra (The Netherlands)	The Netherlands
1988	Ijsbrand Chardon (The Netherlands)	The Netherlands
1990	Tomas Eriksson (Sweden)	Sweden
1992	Ijsbrand Chardon (The Netherlands)	Germany
1996	Felix Brasseur (Belgium)	Belgium
1998	Werner Ulrich (Switzerland)	The Netherlands
2000	Thomas Eriksson (Sweden)	Sweden
2002	Ijsbrand Chardon (The Netherlands)	The Netherlands
2004	Michael Freund (Germany)	Hungary

Carriage Driving World Championships: Pairs

	Individual	Team
1985	Eckert Meinecke (West Germany)	Switzerland
1987	László Kecskerneti (Hungary)	West Germany
1989	Udo Hochgeschorz (Canada)	Hungary
1991	Werner Ulrich (Switzerland)	USA
1993	Georg Moser (Austria)	Austria
1995	Mieke van Tergouw (The Netherlands)	France
1997	Zoltan Lázár (Hungary)	Germany
1999	Vilmos Lázár (Hungary)	Hungary
2001	Vilmos Lázár (Hungary)	Hungary

A-Z

aid a prompt given to a horse to make it change **gaits**, turn, etc

baulk if a horse baulks, it stops short of an obstacle

canter a horse's **gait** in which three legs are off the ground at the same time. It is slower than a **gallop** and faster than a **trot**

clean round a round of jumping completed without any **faults** or penalties

cones one of the disciplines in carriage driving. The cones section involves manoeuvring the horse and carriage through a pattern of cones on top of which are balanced balls. If the balls are knocked off the cones, penalty points are incurred

cross-country type of riding event that simulates a ride through open country, including various jumps

disobedience horse misbehaviour such as **resistance** and **refusal**

fault a mistake that incurs penalty points. Faults include **disobedience**, knocking down an obstacle, the horse's hooves touching water in a **water jump**, and a fall by rider or horse

figure eight a dressage exercise in which the horse traces two connected circles, one clockwise the other anti-clockwise

gait the manner in which a horse moves, based on the rhythm and sequence of its leg movements

gallop a horse's fastest **gait**, in which all four feet are off the ground at the same time

gate a narrow, high fence

grand prix the highest stage of dressage, used to determine Olympic and world champions

grand prix freestyle the final round of a grand prix dressage competition, in which rider and horse perform a series of movements to music

groom a person who assists a driver in carriage riding. Grooms walk the course and memorize distances and turns, keep the horse and carriage well turned out, and help balance the carriage on tight turns

half pass a sideways and forward movement in dressage in which the horse crosses its legs

half pirouette a half-circle turn with the inside hind foot as pivot

jump any obstacle that a horse has to jump over or across

jump-off a tie-breaker round of jumping if two or more riders are tied for first place

lath a thin white strip, lined with plasticine, marking the boundary of a **water jump** and used to indicate if a horse failed to clear the jump

lead the leg that leads during a **canter**

lead change a dressage manoeuvre in which the horse's lead foot changes

longeur in vaulting, the person who leads round the horse while the rider performs gymnastic manoeuvres

manège the art of training riders and horses. The word derives from Italian *maneggiare*, meaning 'to manage'

marathon one of the disciplines in carriage driving. The marathon is a cross-country time trial divided into five sections, each of which must be achieved at a set **gait** (either walking or trotting). The final section involves obstacles and tight turns

movement a single manoeuvre in a dressage performance

natural aid any signal given to a horse by the rider with the legs, hands, or voice

obstacle a fence, **gate** or **water jump** that must be cleared in showjumping or a three-day event

passage a slow **trot** in which the pairs of feet diagonal to each other are raised and then lowered in alternation

piaffe a type of slow **trot** in which the horse's neck is raised and arched and the head is vertical

pirouette a full turn on the spot during which the inside hind foot is used as pivot

puissance a showjumping competition in which the horse must jump a series of large obstacles. The word is French and means 'power'

rail a wooden bar in an obstacle

refusal the failure of a horse to jump an obstacle because the horse runs around it or stops short of it. A refusal incurs penalty points

resistance	movements by a horse that indicate a refusal to jump an obstacle or continue a round
roads and tracks	a phase of the cross-country section of the three-day event, involving riding at a steady pace on the flat
routine	a series of movements in a dressage display
speed and endurance	the second day of the three-day event, consisting of the **steeplechase**, the cross-country obstacle course, and **roads and tracks**
steeplechase	a phase of the **speed and endurance** section of the three-day event, involving the hurdling of low fences over a turf track
time fault	a penalty for exceeding the time limit allowed in a round of jumps
trot	a slowish **gait** in which the horse's legs move in diagonal pairs
vertical	a high obstacle
walk	a horse's slowest **gait**, in which the legs move individually in a diagonal pattern
wall	a high jump that looks like a brick or stone wall
water jump	an obstacle consisting of a low fence or hedge followed by a stretch of water
whip	the driver in carriage driving

Some famous equestrian personalities

Raimondo D'Inzeo, 1925–

Born in Poggio Mirteto, Italy, he and his brother Piero (born 1923) became the first Olympians to compete in eight Olympic Games. They completed this remarkable achievement in the showjumping events in every Games between 1948 and 1976. Piero won two silver and four bronze medals but his younger brother was slightly more successful, winning two silvers, three bronzes, and one gold. The gold medal, appropriately and to the delight of the home crowd, came at the 1960 Olympics in Rome. Both brothers, like their father before them, were officers in the Italian cavalry.

Lucinda Green, 1953–

Born in London, England, she is one of Britain's best-known horsewomen and has achieved many notable successes in three-day eventing. At the European Championships she won individual golds in 1975 and 1977 under her maiden name Prior-Palmer and team golds with the Great Britain team in 1977, 1985 and 1987. She has also won a record six titles at the Badminton Horse Trials (1973, 1976-7, 1979, 1983-4), although her greatest achievement was in 1982 when she won the world championship individual title on Regal Realm and helped Great Britain to the team gold.

Reiner Klimke, 1936–99

Born in Münster, Germany, his achievement of eight medals in dressage stands as a record in Olympic equestrian events. He won team golds in 1964, 1968, 1976, 1984 and 1988, and the individual gold medal in the 1984 Games in Los Angeles. His record at the world championships is just as impressive, with a total of six gold medals and one bronze in four championships stretching over 20 years.

FENCING

Origins

Fencing can be traced back to ancient Egypt and originated from armed combat. It was first practised as a sport in Europe in the 14th and 15th centuries, and the names for its various movements were originally coined in 1570 by the Frenchman Henri Saint-Didier. In the 16th century the longer lighter rapier was introduced in Italy, and the art of fencing was rapidly disseminated in fencing schools around Europe. The 'épée', originally called the *colichemarde*, developed as a duelling sword; the 'foil' was a similar weapon used for practice; and the 'sabre', originally the largest of the three, was first used by 18th-century Hungarian cavalry officers.

Rules and description

In modern fencing there are three disciplines – the épée, foil and sabre – and competitions are held for men, women and teams. The object of the sport is to score 'touches', hits against the opponent with the point of the sword (or the point and edge of the blade for the sabre). Competitors wear protective clothing and a padded jacket and mask. Scoring is by means of a wire attached to the sword that connects the fencer to a scoring box. When a touch is made, a light comes on and a buzzer sounds. Bouts are generally six to nine minutes long and/or the first fencer to make 15 touches. The target area of the opponent in the épée is the full body, in the foil between the neckline and the hip, and in the sabre above the waist (including arms and the head).

Ruling body: Fédération Internationale d'Escrime (FIE)

World Championships

Held annually since 1921 (when only the men's épée was held). The men's foil competition was first held in 1922 and the sabre in 1926. World championships are not held in Olympic years. Between 1921 and 1935 the competition was known as the European Championships.

Men's World Champions

	Foil	Épée	Sabre
1985	Mauro Numa (Italy)	Philippe Boisse (France)	György Nébald (Hungary)
1986	Andrea Borella (Italy)	Philippe Riboud (France)	Sergei Mindirgassov (USSR)
1987	Mathias Gey (West Germany)	Volker Fischer (West Germany)	Jean-François Lamour (France)
1989	Alexander Koch (West Germany)	Manuel Pereira (Spain)	Grigory Kirienko (USSR)
1990	Philippe Omnès (France)	Thomas Gerull (West Germany)	György Nébald (Hungary)
1991	Ingo Weissenborn (Germany)	Andrei Shuvalov (USSR)	Grigory Kirienko (USSR)
1993	Alexander Koch (Germany)	Pavel Kolobkov (Russia)	Grigory Kirienko (USSR)
1994	Rolando Tuckers (Cuba)	Pavel Kolobkov (Russia)	Felix Becker (Germany)

	Foil	Épée	Sabre
1995	Dmitri Chevtchenko (Russia)	Eric Srecki (France)	Grigory Kirienko (USSR)
1997	Sergei Golubitsky (Ukraine)	Eric Srecki (France)	Stanislav Pozdniakov (Russia)
1998	Sergei Golubitsky (Ukraine)	Hugues Obry (France)	Luigi Tarantino (Italy)
1999	Sergei Golubitsky (Ukraine)	Arnd Schmitt (Germany)	Damien Touya (France)
2001	Salvatore Sanzo (Italy)	Paolo Milanoli (Italy)	Stanislav Pozdniakov (Russia)
2002	Simone Vanni (Italy)	Pavel Kolobkov (Russia)	Stanislav Pozdniakov (Russia)
2003	Peter Joppich (Germany)	Fabrice Jeannet (France)	Vladimir Lukashenko (Ukraine)

Women's World Champions

The foil event has been held since 1929. The épée was instituted in 1989 and the sabre in 1999. Competitions are not held in Olympic years.

	Foil	Épée	Sabre
1985	Cornelia Hanisch (West Germany)		
1986	Anja Fichtel (West Germany)		
1987	Elisabeta Tufan (Romania)		
1989	Olga Velichko (USSR)	Anja Straub (Switzerland)	
1990	Anja Fichtel (West Germany)	Taime Chappe (Cuba)	
1991	Giovanna Trillini (Italy)	Marianne Horváth (Hungary)	
1993	Francesca Bortolozzi (Italy)	Oksana Yermakova (Estonia)	
1994	Reka Szabó-Lazar (Romania)	Laura Chiesa (Italy)	
1995	Laura Badea (Romania)	Joanna Jakimiuk (Poland)	
1997	Giovanna Trillini (Italy)	Miraide Garcia (Cuba)	
1998	Sabine Bau (Germany)	Laura Fiessel (France)	
1999	Valentina Vezzali (Italy)	Laura Fiessel-Colovic (France)	Elena Jemayeva (Azerbaijan)
2001	Valentina Vezzali (Italy)	Claudia Bokel (Germany)	Anne-Lise Touya (France)
2002	Svetlana Boiko (Russia)	Hee Hyun (South Korea)	Tan Xue (China)
2003	Valentina Vezzali (Italy)	Natalia Conrad (Ukraine)	Dorina Mihai (Romania)

Olympic Champions

Men

	Foil	Épée	Sabre
1896	Eugène-Henri Gravelotte (France)		Jean Georgiadis (Greece)
1900	Emile Coste (France)	Ramón Fonst (Cuba)	Georges de la Falaise (France)
1904	Ramón Fonst (Cuba)	Ramón Fonst (Cuba)	Manuel Diaz (Cuba)
1908	*Not held*	Gaston Alibert (France)	Jeno Fuchs (Hungary)
1912	Nedo Nadi (Italy)	Paul Anspach (Belgium)	Jeno Fuchs (Hungary)
1920	Nedo Nadi (Italy)	Armand Massard (France)	Nedo Nadi (Italy)
1924	Roger Ducret (France)	Charles Delporte (Belgium)	Sandor Posta (Hungary)

	Foil	Épée	Sabre
1928	Lucien Gaudin (France)	Lucien Gaudin (France)	Odon Tersztyanszky (Hungary)
1932	Gustavo Marzi (Italy)	Giancarlo Cornaggia-Medici (Italy)	György Piller (Hungary)
1936	Giulio Gaudini (Italy)	Franco Riccardi (Italy)	Endre Kabos (Hungary)
1948	Jehan Buhan (France)	Luigi Cantone (Italy)	Aladar Gerevech (Hungary)
1952	Christian d'Oriola (France)	Edoardo Mangiarotti (Italy)	Pal Kovacs (Hungary)
1956	Christian d'Oriola (France)	Carlo Pavesi (Italy)	Rudolf Karpati (Hungary)
1960	Viktor Zhdanovich (USSR)	Giuseppe Delfino (Italy)	Rudolf Karpati (Hungary)
1964	Egon Franke (Poland)	Grigory Kriss (USSR)	Tibor Pesza (Hungary)
1968	Ion Drimba (Romania)	Gyozo Kulcsar (Hungary)	Jerzy Pawlowski (Poland)
1972	Witold Woyda (Poland)	Csaba Fenyvesi (Hungary)	Viktor Sidyak (USSR)
1976	Fabio dal Zotto (Italy)	Alexander Pusch (West Germany)	Viktor Krovopuskov (USSR)
1980	Vladimir Smirnov (USSR)	Johan Harmenberg (Sweden)	Viktor Krovopuskov (USSR)
1984	Mauro Numa (Italy)	Philippe Boisse (France)	Jean-François Lamour (France)
1988	Stefano Cerioni (Itlay)	Arnd Schmitt (West Germany)	Jean-François Lamour (France)
1992	Philippe Omnès (France)	Eric Srecki (France)	Bence Szabó (Hungary)
1996	Alessandro Puccini (Italy)	Aleksandr Beketov (Russia)	Stanislav Pozdniakov (Russia)
2000	Kim Young-ho (South Korea)	Pavel Kolobkov (Russia)	Mihai Covaliu (Romania)
2004	Brice Guyart (France)	Marcel Fischer (Switzerland)	Aldo Montano (Italy)

Women

	Foil	Épée	Sabre
1924	Ellen Osiier (Denmark)		
1928	Helene Mayer (Germany)		
1932	Ellen Preis (Austria)		
1936	Ilona Elek (Hungary)		
1948	Ilona Elek (Hungary)		
1952	Irene Camber (Italy)		
1956	Gillian Sheen (Great Britain)		
1960	Heidi Schmid (West Germany)		
1964	Ildikó Ujlaki-Rejtö (Hungary)		
1968	Yelena Novikova (USSR)		
1972	Antonella Ragno-Lonzi (Italy)		
1976	Ildikó Schwarczenberger (Hungary)		
1980	Pascale Trinquet (France)		
1984	Luan Jujie (China)		
1988	Anja Fichtel (West Germany)		
1992	Giovanna Trillini (Italy)		
1996	Laura Badea (Romania)	Laura Flessel (France)	
2000	Valentina Vezzali (Italy)	Tímea Nagy (Hungary)	
2004	Valentina Vezzali (Italy)	Tímea Nagy (Hungary)	Mariel Zagunis (USA)

A-Z

allez! the command given by the official to start a **bout**

appel a stamp of the front foot on the ground

back edge the opposite edge of a sabre from the cutting edge

balestra an attacking movement where the fencer jumps forwards with both feet, and then immediately lunges on landing

barrage a fence-off to decide ties

bib the (usually white) padded protective part of a mask that protects the throat

bout a contest between two fencers

button the soft covering over the point of a foil or épée that is used when practising

coquille the **hilt** of a sword in the shape of a shell that protects the hand on a foil or épée

corps à corps bodily contact between two fencers

cut a hit with a sabre

doigté use of the fingers to manipulate the sword; from the French meaning 'finger play'

en garde a warning to assume a defensive position in readiness for an attack. The fencer stands sideways to his or her opponent with the swordless hand crooked up behind for balance

épée a sword that weighs up to 770g, is up to 110cm/43.3in in length, and has a relatively stiff triangular blade

feint a deceptive movement or fake attack to trick the opponent into changing his or her line

flèche a short run towards the opponent or an attack in which the aggressor leaps off the leading foot, attempts to make the hit and then passes the opponent; from the French meaning 'arrow'

foible the half of the blade furthest from the **hilt**. It is more flexible than the **forte**

foil a sword that weighs up to 500g, is up to 110cm/43.3in in length, and has a flexible rectangular blade and a blunt point

forte the half of the blade nearest the **hilt**

guard the metal cup at the **hilt** end that protects the hand from being hit

hilt the handle of the sword. It includes the **guard**, and a grip and **pommel**

in quartata an attack made with a sidestep

lunge a sudden thrusting movement with the front leg extended

martingale the leather loop attached to the grip that keeps the foil in the fencer's hand

on guard same as **en garde**

parry the blocking of an opponent's thrust. There are nine standard parries, named after Old French ordinal numbers, that protect various parts of the body from attack: *prime*, *seconde*, *tierce*, *quarte*, *quinte*, *sixte*, *septime*, *octave* and *neuvième*

passata sotto an avoiding action that is executed by ducking under the opponent's blade

piste the duelling area. In competition it is a strip that measures 2 x 14m/2.18 x 15.31ft

plastron a protective undergarment worn under the fencing jacket

pommel the fastener that holds the grip to the blade

president	the controller of a bout
remise	an effective second thrust after the first one has missed
riposte	an offensive move that follows a **parry**
sabre	a sword that weighs 500g, is up to 105cm/41.3in in length, and has a flexible flattened triangular blade and a blunt point
stop hit	a thrust made at the precise moment the opponent draws breath for his or her thrust
thrust	a sudden attack with the blade, but without the footwork associated with a **lunge**
touché	the expression that acknowledges a hit (or touch) in fencing

Some famous fencers

Ilona Elek, 1907–88

Born in Hungary, she represented her country at the 1936, 1948 and 1952 Olympics, winning gold in the foil on the first two occasions and only failing by one point to take a third title at the age of 45. In addition she won six individual world championship titles in 1934, 1935 and 1951. Her achievement of winning titles both before and after World War II makes her one of the greatest fencers of all time.

Edoardo Mangiarotti, 1919–

Born in Milan, Italy, he was taught fencing by his father Giuseppe, who converted him into a left-handed swordsman. He won a team épée gold medal at the 1936 Olympic Games. In total he won 13 Olympic medals (six golds, five silvers and two bronzes). His older brother Dario also won a gold and two silvers.

Helene Mayer, 1910–53

Born in Offenbach, Germany, she was the German foil champion at 13 years old. She won an individual fencing gold medal at the 1928 Olympic Games, and was world foil champion in 1929, 1931 and 1937. She was expelled by the Nazis from Offenbach fencing club when her Jewish origins were discovered, but she went on to participate at the 1936 Berlin Games and won a silver medal. She emigrated to the USA before World War II and then won eight national foil titles (1934–5, 1937–9, 1941–2, 1946).

FIVES

Origins

The name 'fives' probably refers to the five fingers of the hand used to propel the ball in this variant of handball. In the Middle Ages peasants are known to have played hand-and-ball games against church walls; at Eton College in England, the birthplace of the modern game of Eton fives, the first court was an area outside the chapel. There are two other variants of fives, also founded at English public schools: Rugby fives and Winchester fives.

Rules and description

The Eton court was three-walled, being open at the back, with a ledge marking a horizontal line across the front wall 4ft 6in/1.37m from the ground. Courts are divided into lower and upper courts by a shallow step 10ft/3.05m from the front wall. A large buttress (called a 'pepper box') protruding from the left-hand wall provides another 'hazard'. The aim of the game is to keep the ball in play and players need to hit the ball against the side and then front wall, keeping it above the ledge. Games are won by the first to twelve points; players can only score points on serve. Eton fives is a doubles game. Rugby fives differs in that the court is enclosed by four walls and it does not have the same hazards. The winner is the first to 15 points, with only the receiver scoring. Rugby fives is a singles and doubles game. (The court for Winchester fives, a variant of Rugby fives, has a left-hand wall buttress.) Rules for both forms of the game were standardized in 1931.

Ruling bodies: Eton Fives Association; Rugby Fives Association

Eton Fives: Kinnaird Cup

The Kinnaird Cup was donated by Lord Kinnaird and first played for in 1926. It is a doubles competition. The last time it was won by an Etonian was in 1950.

	Champions	**Club**
1980	Dennis Firth & Malcolm Keeling	Berkhamstedians
1981–90	Brian Matthews & John Reynolds	Citizens
1991	John Reynolds & Manuel de Souza-Girao	Citizens/Harrovians
1992	Mark Moore & Gary Baker	Wulfrunians
1993–5	Robin Mason & Jonathan Mole	Edwardians
1996–7	Eddie Wass & Jamie Halstead	Cholmeleians
1998–9	Robin Mason & Jonathan Mole	Edwardians
2000	Matthew Wiseman & James Toop	Olavians
2001	Eddie Wass & Jamie Halstead	Cholmeleians
2002–4	Robin Mason & Tom Dunbar	Edwardians/Harrovians

Rugby Fives: National Championship

Otherwise known as the Jesters' Club Cup, it has been contested annually since 1932. By far the most successful champion has been Wayne Enstone, who won 21 titles (1973–8, 1980–94).

	Champion
1996	Neil Roberts
1997–8	Ian Fuller
1999	Hamish Buchanan
2000	Neil Roberts
2001	Hamish Buchanan
2002	Neil Roberts
2003	James Toop
2004	Matt Cavanagh

FOOTBALL

Origins

It seems that man has been kicking a ball around for at least two millennia, and a primitive kind of football is documented by writers during China's Han dynasty. The game in Britain during the Middle Ages was fairly rough and ready, with monarchs and aristocrats decrying its 'beastlike furie and extreme violence' (Sir Thomas Elyot, 1564) and occasionally trying to ban the game so that men would have more time for archery practice. Although football is often known as the 'people's game', it was the English public schools and ancient universities that were responsible for bringing structure to what were essentially disordered kickabouts where handling the ball was allowed, and codifying football into the game we know today. The FA was formed in England in 1863, and the SFA came into being north of the border in the next decade. It was players and administrators in England and Scotland who were responsible for giving the game rules (in order to distinguish it from rugby union) and exporting the game around the world. In 1904 FIFA, the world game's governing body, was formed, and in 1930 the game's first World Cup was played in Uruguay.

Rules and description

A field game using a round inflated ball, in which two teams of eleven players compete to kick or head the ball into goals formed by two posts, a crossbar, and a net at either end of the pitch. Goalkeepers are allowed to handle the ball in the box surrounding their goal (the 'penalty box'), but outfield players are not allowed to handle the ball at all except while taking 'throw-ins' when the ball is out of play over the touchline. Each match is divided into two halves of 45 minutes' duration with a break at half-time. Fouls are punishable by bookings, indicated by the referee with yellow and red cards. A red card leads to the sending-off of a player. The game's laws are upheld by a referee, two assistant referees who run the touchline, and a fourth official who patrols the technical area where the substitutes, managers, etc sit.

Ruling bodies: FIFA (the international governing body); UEFA (Europe); CONMEBOL (South America); CONCACAF (North and Central America and Caribbean); CAF (Africa); AFC (Asia); OFC (Oceania); FA (England); SFA (Scotland); FAW (Wales); IFA (Northern Ireland); FAI (Republic of Ireland)

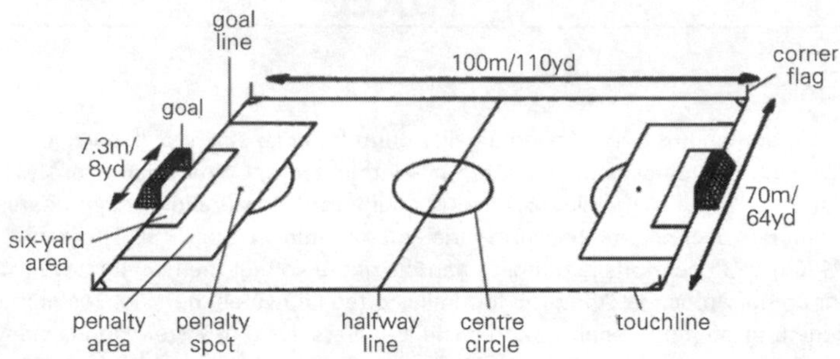

FA Cup

England's premier cup competition and the oldest in the world. For most of its history the FA Cup final has been played at Wembley, but recent ground redevelopment has seen the final moved temporarily to the Millennium Stadium in Cardiff, Wales.

aet = after extra time

	Winners	Runners-up	Score
1872	Wanderers	Royal Engineers	1-0
1873	Wanderers	Oxford University	2-0
1874	Oxford University	Royal Engineers	2-0
1875	Royal Engineers	Old Etonians	1-1; 2-0
1876	Wanderers	Old Etonians	0-0; 3-0
1877	Wanderers	Oxford University	2-1 aet
1878	Wanderers	Royal Engineers	3-1
1879	Old Etonians	Clapham Rovers	1-0
1880	Clapham Rovers	Oxford University	1-0
1881	Old Carthusians	Old Etonians	3-0
1882	Old Etonians	Blackburn Rovers	1-0
1883	Blackburn Olympic	Old Etonians	2-1 aet
1884	Blackburn Rovers	Queens Park, Glasgow	2-1
1885	Blackburn Rovers	Queens Park, Glasgow	2-0
1886	Blackburn Rovers	West Bromwich Albion	0-0; 2-0
1887	Aston Villa	West Bromwich Albion	2-0
1888	West Bromwich Albion	Preston North End	2-1
1889	Preston North End	Wolverhampton Wanderers	3-0
1890	Blackburn Rovers	Sheffield Wednesday	6-1
1891	Blackburn Rovers	Notts County	3-1
1892	West Bromwich Albion	Aston Villa	3-0
1893	Wolverhampton Wanderers	Everton	1-0
1894	Notts County	Bolton Wanderers	4-1
1895	Aston Villa	West Bromwich Albion	1-0
1896	Sheffield Wednesday	Wolverhampton Wanderers	2-1
1897	Aston Villa	Everton	3-2

	Winners	Runners-up	Score
1898	Nottingham Forest	Derby County	3-1
1899	Sheffield United	Derby County	4-1
1900	Bury	Southampton	4-0
1901	Tottenham Hotspur	Sheffield United	2-2; 3-1
1902	Sheffield United	Derby County	1-1; 2-1
1903	Bury	Derby County	6-0
1904	Manchester City	Bolton Wanderers	1-0
1905	Aston Villa	Newcastle United	2-0
1906	Everton	Newcastle United	1-0
1907	Sheffield Wednesday	Everton	2-1
1908	Wolverhampton Wanderers	Newcastle United	3-1
1909	Manchester United	Bristol City	1-0
1910	Newcastle United	Barnsley	1-1
1911	Bradford City	Newcastle United	0-0; 1-0
1912	Barnsley	West Bromwich Albion	0-0; 1-0
1913	Aston Villa	Sunderland	1-0
1914	Burnley	Liverpool	1-0
1915	Sheffield United	Chelsea	3-0
1916–19	*Not held*		
1920	Aston Villa	Huddersfield Town	1-0 aet
1921	Tottenham Hotspur	Wolverhampton Wanderers	1-0
1922	Huddersfield Town	Preston North End	1-0
1923	Bolton Wanderers	West Ham United	2-0
1924	Newcastle United	Aston Villa	2-0
1925	Sheffield United	Cardiff City	1-0
1926	Bolton Wanderers	Manchester City	1-0
1927	Cardiff City	Arsenal	1-0
1928	Blackburn Rovers	Huddersfield Town	3-1
1929	Bolton Wanderers	Portsmouth	2-0
1930	Arsenal	Huddersfield Town	2-0
1931	West Bromwich Albion	Birmingham	2-1
1932	Newcastle United	Arsenal	2-1
1933	Everton	Manchester City	3-0
1934	Manchester City	Portsmouth	2-1
1935	Sheffield Wednesday	West Bromwich Albion	4-2
1936	Arsenal	Sheffield	1-0
1937	Sunderland	Preston North End	3-1
1938	Preston North End	Huddersfield Town	1-0 aet
1939	Portsmouth	Wolverhampton Wanderers	4-1
1940–5	*Not held*		
1946	Derby County	Charlton Athletic	4-1 aet
1947	Charlton Athletic	Burnley	1-0 aet
1948	Manchester United	Blackpool	4-2
1949	Wolverhampton Wanderers	Leicester City	3-1
1950	Arsenal	Liverpool	2-0
1951	Newcastle United	Blackpool	2-0
1952	Newcastle United	Arsenal	1-0
1953	Blackpool	Bolton Wanderers	4-3
1954	West Bromwich Albion	Preston North End	3-2

	Winners	Runners-up	Score
1955	Newcastle United	Manchester City	3-1
1956	Manchester City	Birmingham City	3-1
1957	Aston Villa	Manchester United	2-1
1958	Bolton Wanderers	Manchester United	2-0
1959	Nottingham Forest	Luton Town	2-1
1960	Wolverhampton Wanderers	Blackburn Rovers	3-0
1961	Tottenham Hotspur	Leicester City	2-0
1962	Tottenham Hotspur	Burnley	3-1
1963	Manchester United	Leicester City	3-1
1964	West Ham United	Preston North End	3-2
1965	Liverpool	Leeds United	2-1 aet
1966	Everton	Sheffield Wednesday	3-2
1967	Tottenham Hotspur	Chelsea	2-1
1968	West Bromwich Albion	Everton	1-0 aet
1969	Manchester City	Leicester City	1-0
1970	Chelsea	Leeds United	2-2; 2-1
1971	Arsenal	Liverpool	2-1 aet
1972	Leeds United	Arsenal	1-0
1973	Sunderland	Leeds United	1-0
1974	Liverpool	Newcastle United	3-0
1975	West Ham United	Fulham	2-0
1976	Southampton	Manchester United	1-0
1977	Manchester United	Liverpool	2-1
1978	Ipswich Town	Arsenal	1-0
1979	Arsenal	Manchester United	3-2
1980	West Ham United	Arsenal	1-0
1981	Tottenham Hotspur	Manchester City	1-1 aet; 3-2
1982	Tottenham Hotspur	Queens Park Rangers	1-1; 1-0
1983	Manchester United	Brighton and Hove Albion	2-2; 4-0
1984	Everton	Watford	2-0
1985	Manchester United	Everton	1-0 aet
1986	Liverpool	Everton	3-1
1987	Coventry City	Tottenham Hotspur	3-2 aet
1988	Wimbledon	Liverpool	1-0
1989	Liverpool	Everton	3-2 aet
1990	Manchester United	Crystal Palace	3-3 aet; 1-0
1991	Tottenham Hotspur	Nottingham Forest	2-1 aet
1992	Liverpool	Sunderland	2-0
1993	Arsenal	Sheffield Wednesday	1-1 aet; 2-1 aet
1994	Manchester United	Chelsea	4-0
1995	Everton	Manchester United	1-0
1996	Manchester United	Liverpool	1-0
1997	Chelsea	Middlesbrough	2-0
1998	Arsenal	Newcastle United	2-0
1999	Manchester United	Newcastle United	2-0
2000	Chelsea	Aston Villa	1-0
2001	Liverpool	Arsenal	2-1
2002	Arsenal	Chelsea	2-0

2003	Arsenal	Southampton	1-0
2004	Manchester United	Millwall	3-0

Some FA Cup upsets

Hereford United 2-1 Newcastle United

FA Cup third round replay, 1972

First-Division Newcastle took the lead with a goal from Malcolm McDonald but Ronnie Radford's 30-yard equalizer and substitute Ricky George's late winner sent the non-league side into the fourth round.

Sunderland 1-0 Leeds United

FA Cup final, 1973

Bob Stokoe's team became the first Second Division club to win the cup for 40 years as Ian Porterfield's volley sank a Leeds side that had become accustomed to getting its own way both at home and in Europe.

Wrexham 2-1 Arsenal

FA Cup third round, 1992

League champions Arsenal took the lead at the Racecourse Ground but a spectacular free kick from veteran Mickey Thomas and a winner from youngster Steve Watkin put the Welsh side (then 24th in the Third Division) through to the fourth round.

Bournemouth 2-0 Manchester United

FA Cup third round, 1984

Milton Graham and Ian Thompson supplied the goals as Ron Atkinson's cup holders were humbled by Harry Redknapp's Third Division outfit.

Wimbledon 1-0 Liverpool

FA Cup final, 1988

Wimbledon's so-called Crazy Gang, managed by Don Howe and featuring future film star Vinnie Jones, beat a star-studded Liverpool side expected to add yet more silverware to its bulging trophy cabinet. Lawrie Sanchez scored the winner but captain Dave Beasant was the hero as he became the first goalkeeper to save a penalty in an FA Cup final.

FA Cup records

The biggest victory in the FA Cup was Preston North End's 26-0 thrashing of Hyde United on 15 October 1887. The honour of scoring the most FA Cup goals in a career goes to Henry Cursham of Notts County, who notched up 48; Ian Rush is second, with 43 scored for Liverpool and Chester. Ian Rush also holds the record for the most FA Cup Final goals in a career with five in the finals of 1986, 1989 and 1992.

Football League Clubs 2004–5

Club	Ground	Nickname	Chant/song
Arsenal	Highbury	Gunners	Good old Arsenal
Aston Villa	Villa Park	Villans	We'll never die
Barnsley	Oakwell	Tykes; Colliers	Oh when the league is upside down
Birmingham City	St Andrews	Blues	Come to Birmingham and you'll see
Blackburn Rovers	Ewood Park	Rovers	Forever and ever we'll follow our team
Blackpool	Bloomfield Road	Seasiders	Lancashire is wonderful
Boston United	York Street Stadium	Pilgrims	Let's all laugh at Lincoln
Bournemouth	The Fitness First Stadium	Cherries	We'll keep the red flag flying high
Bolton Wanderers	Reebok Stadium	Trotters	The Wanderers are coming up the hill, boys
Bradford City	Valley Parade	Bantams	You are my City, my only City
Brentford	Griffin Park	Bees	A goal is all we need
Brighton & Hove Albion	Withdean Stadium	Seagulls	Robbo was through but he passed it to Smith
Bristol City	Ashton Gate	Robins	Ashton Road, take me home
Bristol Rovers	Memorial Stadium	Pirates	Oh they should have built a wall not a bridge
Burnley	Turf Moor	Clarets	Ewood's now empty, it's getting knocked down
Bury	Gigg Lane	Shakers	We all follow Bury
Cambridge United	Abbey Stadium	U's	We are the famous, the famous Cambridge
Cardiff City	Ninian Park	Bluebirds	You are my Cardiff, my only Cardiff
Charlton Athletic	The Valley	Addicks	Valley, Floyd road, my only desire
Chelsea	Stamford Bridge	Blues	Blue is the colour, football is the game
Cheltenham Town	Whaddon Road	Robins	Cheltenham Town will thrash them all
Chester City	Deva Stadium	Blues	The famous CCFC
Chesterfield	Recreation Ground	Spireites	From the green, green grass of Saltergate
Colchester United	Layer Road	U's	Up the U's
Coventry City	Highfield Road	Sky Blues	Let's all sing together
Crewe Alexandria	The Alexandria Stadium	Railwaymen	I'm Alex till I die
Crystal Palace	Selhurst Park	Eagles	The famous CPFC
Darlington	Reynolds Arena	Quakers	Darlo till I die

Club	Ground	Nickname	Chant/song
Derby County	Pride Park	Rams	When the Rams go marching in
Doncaster Rovers	Belle Vue	Rovers	Donny Rovers FC
Everton	Goodison Park	Toffees	Everton, Everton, we're forever Everton
Fulham	Craven Cottage	Cottagers	You are my Fulham, my only Fulham
Gillingham	Priestfield Stadium	Gills	We all live in a Blue Rainham End
Grimsby Town	Blundell Park	Mariners	We only sing when we're fishing
Hartlepool United	Victoria Park	Pools	Two little boys
Huddersfield Town	McAlpine Stadium	Terriers	There's a team that's dear to its followers
Hull City	Kingston Communication Stadium	Tigers	We all follow a black and amber team
Ipswich Town	Portman Road	Blues	Take me home, Portman Road
Kidderminster Harriers	Aggborough Stadium	Harriers	Come on, Kiddy
Leeds United	Elland Road	United	Marching on together
Leicester City	The Walkers Stadium	Foxes; Filberts	Score, Leicester, score
Leyton Orient	Brisbane Road	O's	Come on you O's
Lincoln City	Sincil Bank	Red Imps	Don't cry for me, Boston United
Liverpool	Anfield	Reds; Pool	You'll never walk alone
Luton Town	Kenilworth Road	Hatters	I was born in the Maple Road
Macclesfield Town	Moss Rose	Silkmen	We love you Silkmen, we do
Manchester City	City of Manchester Stadium	Blues	Blue Moon
Manchester United	Old Trafford	Red Devils	Glory, glory Man United
Mansfield Town	Field Mill	Stags	To see the Mansfield aces
Middlesbrough	Riverside Stadium	Boro	We are the Boro, the cock of the north
Millwall	The New Den	Lions	No one like us, we don't care
Milton Keynes Dons (formerly Wimbledon)	National Hockey Stadium	Dons	Dons, Dons, glorious Dons
Newcastle United	St James' Park	Magpies	The Blaydon Races
Northampton Town	Sixfields Stadium	Cobblers	Cobblers, Cobblers, let's have a win today
Norwich City	Carrow Road	Canaries	Brazil of the East Country
Nottingham Forest	City Ground	Forest	We all agree Nottingham Forest are magic
Notts County	Meadow Lane	Magpies	I had a wheelbarrow, the wheel fell off

Club	Ground	Nickname	Chant/song
Oldham Athletic	Boundary Park	Latics	You are my Oldham, my only Oldham
Oxford United	The Kassam Stadium	U's	I love my Oxford, my only Oxford
Peterborough United	London Road	The Posh	Boro boys arising
Plymouth Argyle	Home Park	Pilgrims	I was born in the Devenport End
Portsmouth	Fratton Park	Pompey	The glory of the lights of Fratton Park
Port Vale	Vale Park	Valiants	The wonder of you
Preston North End	Deepdale	Lilywhites	Blackpool Tower is falling down
Queen's Park Rangers	Loftus Road	Rangers; R's	Whatever the season, we'll follow our team
Reading	Madejski Stadium	Royals	When the red, red robin...
Rochdale	Spotland	The Dale	The mighty Dale
Rushden & Diamonds	Nene Park	Diamonds	Flying high up in the sky
Rotherham United	Millmoor	Millers	Happy to be a Miller
Scunthorpe United	Glanford Park	The Iron	Scunny United FC
Sheffield United	Bramall Lane	Blades	We are Bladesmen, super Bladesmen
Sheffield Wednesday	Hillsborough	Owls	Hark now hear the Wednesday sing
Shrewsbury Town	Gay Meadow	Shrews	From the banks of the river Severn
Southampton	St Mary's Stadium	Saints	Oh when the Saints go marching in
Southend United	Roots Hall	Shrimpers	Give me blue in my heart, give me Southend
Stockport County	Edgeley Park	Hatters	Clear blue skies
Stoke City	Britannia Stadium	Potters	Tell the boys in red and white
Sunderland	Stadium of Light	Black Cats	Who put the ball in the Geordies' net?
Swansea City	Vetch Field	Swans	Swansea till I die
Swindon Town	County Ground	Robins	All things bright and beautiful
Torquay United	Plainmoor	Gulls	Have you ever seen a beach?
Tottenham Hotspur	White Hart Lane	Spurs	We are the Tottenham, the pride of the south
Tranmere Rovers	Prenton Park	Rovers	We're not Scousers, we're from Birkenhead
Walsall	Bescot Stadium	Saddlers	Hark now hear the Walsall sing
Watford	Vicarage Road	Hornets	Watford till I die
West Bromwich Albion	The Hawthorns	Baggies	Oh when the Stripes go marching in
West Ham United	Upton Park	Hammers	I'm forever blowing bubbles

Club	Ground	Nickname	Chant/song
Wigan Athletic	JJB Stadium	Latics	And it's Wigan Latics
Wolverhampton Wanderers	Molineux	Wolves	I was born under a Wanderers scarf
Wrexham	Racecourse Ground	Dragons	Oh when those Blues go steaming in
Wycombe Wanderers	Causeway Stadium	Chairboys; Blues	Wycombe Wanderers number one
Yeovil Town	Huish Park	Glovers	Drink up thy cider

Scottish League Clubs 2004–5

Club	Ground	Nickname	Chant/song
Aberdeen	Pittodrie Stadium	Dons	The northern lights of old Aberdeen
Airdrie United	New Broomfield	Diamonds	The streets of Airdrie
Albion Rovers	Cliftonhill Stadium	Wee Rovers	We're the Albion Rovers
Alloa Athletic	Recreation Park	Wasps	Alloa Ooh-Ooh
Arbroath	Gayfield Park	Red Lichties	36-nil, 36-nil, hello, hello
Ayr United	Somerset Park	Honest Men	Ayr, Ayr, Super Ayr
Berwick Rangers	Shielfield Park	Borders	Falling in love with you
Brechin City	Glebe Park	City	We can drive a tractor
Celtic	Celtic Park	Bhoys; Celts	Hail, hail the Celts are here
Clyde	Broadwood Stadium	Bully Wee	We are the famous Bully Wee
Cowdenbeath	Central Park	Blue Brazil	You are my Cowden, my only Cowden
Dumbarton	Strathclyde Homes Stadium	Sons	Come on, you Sons
Dundee	Dens Park	Dark Blues; Dees	Hello, hello, we are the Dundee boys
Dundee United	Tannadice Park	Terrors; Arabs	We won the league at Dens
Dunfermline Athletic	East End Park	Pars	Walking down the Halbeath Road
East Fife	Bayview Park	Fifers	The kingdom of Fife
East Stirlingshire	Firs Park	The Shire	Come on, you Shire
Elgin City	Borough Briggs	Black & Whites	You are my city, my Elgin City
Falkirk	Westfield	Bairns	Oh when the Bairns go marching in
Forfar Athletic	Station Park	Loons	Come on, you Loons

Club	Ground	Nickname	Chant/song
Greenock Morton	Cappielow	The Ton	A wee town that stands upon the Clyde
Gretna	Raydale Park	Black & Whites	You are my Gretna, my only Gretna
Hamilton Academical	Ballast Stadium	Accies	She wore a scarlet ribbon
Heart of Midlothian	Tynescastle Park	Hearts; Jam Tarts	Hearts, Hearts glorious Hearts
Hibernian	Easter Road	Hibs; Hibees	Glory, glory to the Hibees
Inverness Caledonian Thistle	Caledonian Stadium	Caley	ICT, ICT, ICT
Kilmarnock	Rugby Park	Killie	Paper roses
Livingston	City Stadium	Livi; Lions	Oh when the Lions go marching in
Montrose	Links Park Stadium	Gable Endies	Mo, Mo, Super Mo, Super Montrose FC
Motherwell	Fir Park	The Well	We are the Motherwell FC
Partick Thistle	Firhill	Jags; Harry Wrags	There's a well known Glasgow football team
Peterhead	Balmoor Stadium	The Blue Toon	Come on, you Toon
Queen of the South	Palmerston Park	Doonhamers	We are the Dumfries boys
Queen's Park	Hampden Park	Spiders	Allez Les Hoops
Raith Rovers	Stark's Park	Rovers	I don't want to go to Idaho
Rangers	Ibrox	Gers; Teddy Bears	Follow, Follow
Ross County	Victoria Park	County; Staggies	Who's the team that they call the County?
Stenhousemuir	Ochilview Park	Warriors	You are my Stenny, my only Stenny
Stirling Albion	Forthbank	Binos	The boys in black and gold
St Johnstone	McDiarmid Park	Saints	We love you Saintees
St Mirren	St Mirren Park	Buddies	Oh when the Saints go marching in
Stranraer	Stair Park	Blues	We are Stranraer FC

Sharp shooters

The record for the most goals in English league football is held by Arthur Rowley who put the ball in the back of the net 434 times between 1946 and 1965 for West Bromwich Albion (4 goals), Fulham (27), Leicester City (241) and Shrewsbury Town (152), while the Scottish record belongs to Jimmy McGrory who scored 410 league goals for Celtic and Clydebank from 1922 to 1938. Alan Shearer is by a long way the leading scorer in the Premiership with 243 (to the end of 2003–4 season), Henrik Larsson of Celtic topping the pile in the Scottish Premier League with 155.

Lucky thirteen

The biggest victory in English league football is 13-0, the score by which Newcastle United beat Newport County in a Division Two match on 5 October 1946, and by which Stockport County overcame Halifax Town in a Division Three (Northern) encounter on 6 January 1934. The Scottish record is Celtic's 11-0 thrashing of Dundee on 26 October 1895.

English Players' Player of the Year

An award given at the end of each season to the English league player obtaining the most votes from his peers.

	Player	Club
1974	Norman Hunter	Leeds United
1975	Colin Todd	Derby County
1976	Pat Jennings	Tottenham Hotspur
1977	Andy Gray	Aston Villa
1978	Peter Shilton	Nottingham Forest
1979	Liam Brady	Arsenal
1980	Terry McDermott	Liverpool
1981	John Wark	Ipswich
1982	Kevin Keegan	Southampton
1983	Kenny Dalglish	Liverpool
1984	Ian Rush	Liverpool
1985	Peter Reid	Everton
1986	Gary Lineker	Everton
1987	Clive Allen	Tottenham Hotspur
1988	John Barnes	Liverpool
1989	Mark Hughes	Manchester United
1990	David Platt	Aston Villa
1991	Mark Hughes	Manchester United
1992	Gary Pallister	Manchester United
1993	Paul McGrath	Aston Villa
1994	Eric Cantona	Manchester United
1995	Alan Shearer	Blackburn Rovers
1996	Les Ferdinand	Newcastle United
1997	Alan Shearer	Newcastle United
1998	Dennis Bergkamp	Arsenal
1999	David Ginola	Tottenham Hotspur
2000	Roy Keane	Manchester United
2001	Teddy Sheringham	Manchester United
2002	Ruud Van Nistelrooy	Manchester United
2003	Thierry Henry	Arsenal
2004	Thierry Henry	Arsenal

Seeing red

Two players share the distinction of the most red cards in British domestic football: Willie Johnstone (Rangers, West Bromwich Albion) and Roy McDonough (Colchester United, Southend United, Exeter City and Cambridge United) both received no fewer than 21, although only 7 and 13 of them respectively were received in Football League games. Vinnie Jones (ex-Wimbledon midfielder turned tough-guy actor) was a comparative angel with just 12.

Scottish Players' Player of the Year

An award given at the end of each season to the Scottish league player obtaining the most votes from his peers.

	Player	Club
1978	Derek Johnstone	Rangers
1979	Paul Hegarty	Dundee United
1980	Davie Provan	Celtic
1981	Mark McGhee	Aberdeen
1982	Sandy Clark	Airdrie
1983	Charlie Nicholas	Celtic

	Player	Club
1984	Willie Miller	Aberdeen
1985	Jim Duffy	Morton
1986	Richard Gough	Dundee United
1987	Brian McClair	Celtic
1988	Paul McStay	Celtic
1989	Theo Snelders	Aberdeen
1990	Jim Bett	Aberdeen
1991	Paul Elliot	Celtic
1992	Ally McCoist	Rangers
1993	Andy Goram	Rangers
1994	Mark Hateley	Rangers
1995	Brian Laudrup	Rangers
1996	Paul Gascoigne	Rangers
1997	Paolo di Canio	Celtic
1998	Jackie McNamara	Celtic
1999	Henrik Larsson	Celtic
2000	Mark Viduka	Celtic
2001	Henrik Larsson	Celtic
2002	Lorenzo Amoruso	Rangers
2003	Barry Ferguson	Rangers
2004	Chris Sutton	Celtic

Long servants

Goalkeeper Peter Shilton holds the record for the most appearances in English league football with 1,005 at the following different clubs: Leicester City (286), Stoke City (110), Nottingham Forest (202), Southampton (188), Derby County (175), Plymouth Argyle (34), Bolton Wanderers (1) and Leyton Orient (9). The record for the most appearances for the same club is held by John Trollope who turned out 770 times for Swindon Town between 1960 and 1980.

English League Division Winners

The oldest league championship in the world started as one division but has increased to four divisions over the years. In 1992 the top clubs left the Football league and formed the Premiership. In 2004, Division 1 was renamed The Championship and Divisions 2 and 3 became League 1 and League 2, respectively.

	1st Division	2nd Division	3rd Division
1889	Preston North End		
1890	Preston North End		
1891	Everton		
1892	Sunderland		
1893	Sunderland	Small Heath	
1894	Aston Villa	Liverpool	
1895	Sunderland	Bury	
1896	Aston Villa	Liverpool	
1897	Aston Villa	Notts County	
1898	Sheffield United	Burnley	
1899	Aston Villa	Manchester City	
1900	Aston Villa	The Wednesday	
1901	Liverpool	Grimsby	
1902	Sunderland	West Bromwich Albion	
1903	The Wednesday	Manchester City	
1904	The Wednesday	Preston North End	
1905	Newcastle United	Liverpool	
1906	Liverpool	Bristol City	

	1st Division	2nd Division	3rd Division
1907	Newcastle United	Nottingham Forest	
1908	Manchester United	Bradford City	
1909	Newcastle United	Bolton Wanderers	
1910	Aston Villa	Manchester City	
1911	Manchester United	West Bromwich Albion	
1912	Blackburn Rovers	Derby County	
1913	Sunderland	Preston North End	
1914	Blackburn Rovers	Notts County	
1915	Everton	Derby County	
1916–19	*Not held*		
1920	West Bromwich Albion	Tottenham Hotspur	
1921	Burnley	Birmingham City	Crystal Palace

	1st Division	2nd Division	3rd Division North	3rd Division South
1922	Liverpool	Nottingham Forest	Stockport County	Southampton
1923	Liverpool	Notts County	Nelson	Bristol City
1924	Huddersfield Town	Leeds United	Wolves	Portsmouth
1925	Huddersfield Town	Leicester City	Darlington	Swansea
1926	Huddersfield Town	Sheffield Wednesday	Grimsby Town	Reading
1927	Newcastle United	Middlesbrough	Stoke City	Bristol City
1928	Everton	Manchester City	Bradford PA	Millwall
1929	Sheffield Wednesday	Middlesbrough	Bradford City	Charlton
1930	Sheffield Wednesday	Blackpool	Port Vale	Plymouth
1931	Arsenal	Everton	Chesterfield	Notts County
1932	Everton	Wolves	Lincoln City	Fulham
1933	Arsenal	Stoke City	Hull City	Brentford
1934	Arsenal	Grimsby Town	Barnsley	Nowich City
1935	Arsenal	Brentford	Doncaster Rovers	Charlton Athletic
1936	Sunderland	Manchester United	Chesterfield	Coventry City
1937	Manchester City	Leicester City	Stockport County	Luton Town
1938	Arsenal	Aston Villa	Tranmere Rovers	Millwall
1939	Everton	Blackburn Rovers	Barnsley	Newport County
1940–6	*Not held*			
1947	Liverpool	Manchester City	Doncaster Rovers	Cardiff City
1948	Arsenal	Birmingham City	Lincoln City	Queens Park Rangers
1949	Portsmouth	Fulham	Hull City	Swansea City
1950	Portsmouth	Tottenham Hotspur	Doncaster Rovers	Notts County
1951	Tottenham Hotspur	Preston North End	Rotherham United	Nottingham Forest
1952	Manchester United	Sheffield Wednesday	Lincoln City	Plymouth Argyle
1953	Arsenal	Sheffield United	Oldham Town	Bristol Rovers
1954	Wolves	Leicester City	Port Vale	Ipswich Town
1955	Chelsea	Birmingham City	Barnsley	Bristol City
1956	Manchester United	Sheffield Wednesday	Grimsby Town	Leyton Orient
1957	Manchester United	Leicester City	Derby County	Ipswich Town
1958	Wolves	West Ham United	Scunthorpe United	Brighton & Hove Albion

Football

	1st Division	2nd Division	3rd Division	4th Division
1959	Wolves	Sheffield Wednesday	Plymouth Argyle	Port Vale
1960	Burnley	Aston Villa	Southampton	Walsall
1961	Tottenham Hotspur	Ipswich Town	Bury	Peterborough United
1962	Ipswich Town	Liverpool	Portsmouth	Millwall
1963	Everton	Stoke City	Northampton Town	Brentford
1964	Liverpool	Leeds United	Coventry City	Gillingham
1965	Manchester United	Newcastle United	Carlisle United	Brighton & Hove Albion
1966	Liverpool	Manchester City	Hull City	Doncaster Rovers
1967	Manchester United	Coventry City	Queens Park Rangers	Stockport County
1968	Manchester City	Ipswich Town	Oxford United	Luton Town
1969	Leeds United	Derby County	Watford	Doncaster Rovers
1970	Everton	Huddersfield Town	Orient	Chesterfield
1971	Arsenal	Leicester City	Preston North End	Notts County
1972	Derby County	Norwich City	Aston Villa	Grimsby Town
1973	Liverpool	Burnley	Bolton Wanderers	Southport
1974	Leeds United	Middlesbrough	Oldham Town	Peterborough United
1975	Derby County	Manchester United	Blackburn Rovers	Mansfield Town
1976	Liverpool	Sunderland	Hereford United	Lincoln City
1977	Liverpool	Wolves	Mansfield Town	Cambridge United
1978	Nottingham Forest	Bolton Wanderers	Wrexham	Watford
1979	Liverpool	Crystal Palace	Shrewsbury Town	Reading
1980	Liverpool	Leicester City	Grimsby Town	Huddersfield Town
1981	Aston Villa	West Ham United	Rotherham United	Southend United
1982	Liverpool	Luton Town	Burnley	Sheffield United
1983	Liverpool	Queens Park Rangers	Portsmouth	Wimbledon
1984	Liverpool	Chelsea	Oxford United	York City
1985	Everton	Oxford United	Bradford City	Chesterfield
1986	Liverpool	Norwich City	Reading	Swindon
1987	Everton	Derby County	Bournemouth	Northampton Town
1988	Liverpool	Millwall	Sunderland	Wolves
1989	Arsenal	Chelsea	Wolves	Rotherham United
1990	Liverpool	Leeds United	Bristol Rovers	Exeter City
1991	Arsenal	Oldham Town	Cambridge United	Darlington
1992	Leeds United	Ipswich Town	Brentford	Burnley

	Premiership	1st Division	2nd Division	3rd Division
1993	Manchester United	Newcastle United	Stoke City	Cardiff City
1994	Manchester United	Crystal Palace	Reading	Shrewsbury Town
1995	Blackburn Rovers	Middlesbrough	Birmingham City	Carlisle
1996	Manchester United	Sunderland	Swindon Town	Preston North End
1997	Manchester United	Bolton Wanderers	Bury	Wigan Athletic
1998	Arsenal	Nottingham Forest	Watford	Notts County
1999	Manchester United	Sunderland	Fulham	Brentford
2000	Manchester United	Charlton Athletic	Preston North End	Swansea City

	Premiership	1st Division	2nd Division	3rd Division
2001	Manchester United	Fulham	Millwall	Brighton & Hove Albion
2002	Arsenal	Manchester City	Brighton & Hove Albion	Plymouth Argyle
2003	Manchester United	Portsmouth	Wigan Athletic	Rushden & Diamonds
2004	Arsenal	Norwich City	Plymouth Argyle	Doncaster Rovers

Scottish Football League Division Winners

The second oldest league in the world started in 1890 with just one division. Now there are four divisions in Scottish senior football, the top teams splitting from the Scottish Football League in 1998 to form the Premier League.

	1st Division	2nd Division	3rd Division
1891	Dumbarton & Rangers		
1892	Dumbarton		
1893	Celtic		
1894	Celtic	Hibernian	
1895	Heart of Midlothian	Hibernian	
1896	Celtic	Abercorn	
1897	Heart of Midlothian	Partick Thistle	
1898	Celtic	Kilmarnock	
1899	Rangers	Kilmarnock	
1900	Rangers	Partick Thistle	
1901	Rangers	St Bernards	
1902	Rangers	Port Glasgow Athletic	
1903	Hibernian	Airdrie	
1904	Third Lanark	Hamilton Academicals	
1905	Celtic	Clyde	
1906	Celtic	Leith Athletic	
1907	Celtic	St Bernards	
1908	Celtic	Raith Rovers	
1909	Celtic	Abercorn	
1910	Celtic	Leith Athletic & Raith Rovers	
1911	Rangers	Dumbarton	
1912	Rangers	Ayr United	
1913	Rangers	Ayr United	
1914	Celtic	Cowdenbeath	
1915	Celtic	Cowdenbeath	
1916	Celtic		
1917	Celtic		
1918	Rangers		
1919	Celtic		
1920	Rangers		
1921	Rangers		
1922	Celtic	Alloa Athletic	
1923	Rangers	Queen's Park	
1924	Rangers	St Johnstone	

	1st Division	2nd Division	3rd Division
1925	Rangers	Dundee United	
1926	Celtic	Dunfermline Athletic	
1927	Rangers	Bo'ness	
1928	Rangers	Ayr United	
1929	Rangers	Dundee United	
1930	Rangers	Leith Athletic	
1931	Rangers	Third Lanark	
1932	Motherwell	East Stirlingshire	
1933	Rangers	Hibernian	
1934	Rangers	Albion Rovers	
1935	Rangers	Third Lanark	
1936	Celtic	Falkirk	
1937	Rangers	Ayr United	
1938	Celtic	Raith Rovers	
1939	Rangers	Cowdenbeath	
1940–6	*Not held*		
1947	Rangers	Dundee	
1948	Hibernian	East Fife	
1949	Rangers	Raith Rovers	
1950	Rangers	Morton	Clyde Reserves
1951	Hibernian	Queen of the South	Clyde Reserves
1952	Hibernian	Clyde	Rangers Reserves
1953	Rangers	Stirling Albion	Rangers Reserves
1954	Celtic	Motherwell	Rangers Reserves
1955	Aberdeen	Airdrie	Partick Thistle Reserves
1956	Rangers	Queen's Park	
1957	Rangers	Clyde	
1958	Heart of Midlothian	Stirling Albion	
1959	Rangers	Ayr United	
1960	Heart of Midlothian	St Johnstone	
1961	Rangers	Stirling Albion	
1962	Dundee	Clyde	
1963	Rangers	St Johnstone	
1964	Rangers	Morton	
1965	Kilmarnock	Stirling Albion	
1966	Celtic	Ayr United	
1967	Celtic	Morton	
1968	Celtic	St Mirren	
1969	Celtic	Motherwell	
1970	Celtic	Falkirk	
1971	Celtic	Partick Thistle	
1972	Celtic	Dumbarton	
1973	Celtic	Clyde	
1974	Celtic	Airdrie	
1975	Rangers	Falkirk	

I beg your pardon?

The aphorisms of English player and manager Kevin Keegan are to football what Friedrich Nietzsche's maxims and interludes are to philosophy. Well, not quite. See for yourself:

'You can't do better than go away from home and get a draw.'

'I don't think there's anyone bigger or smaller than Maradona.'

'In some ways, cramp is worse than having a broken leg.'

'Goalkeepers aren't born today until they are in their late 20s or 30s.'

Villan is no hero

In March 1976, Chris Nicholl, Aston Villa's tall central defender, scored two equalizers to earn his side an important point in a remarkable 2–2 draw away to Leicester City. And yet Chris was not fêted by the Villa fans as their hero. Earlier in the game he had managed to head both of Leicester's two goals into his own net. He must be the only player to score all four goals in a game without getting the match ball.

	Premier League	1st Division	2nd Division	3rd Division
1976	Rangers	Partick Thistle	Clydebank	
1977	Celtic	St Mirren	Stirling Albion	

	Premier League	1st Division	2nd Division	3rd Division
1978	Rangers	Morton	Clyde	
1979	Celtic	Dundee	Berwick Rangers	
1980	Aberdeen	Heart of Midlothian	Falkirk	
1981	Celtic	Hibernian	Queen's Park	
1982	Celtic	Motherwell	Clyde	
1983	Dundee United	St Johnstone	Brechin City	
1984	Aberdeen	Morton	Forfar Athletic	
1985	Aberdeen	Motherwell	Montrose	
1986	Celtic	Hamilton Academicals	Dunfermline Athletic	
1987	Rangers	Morton	Meadowbank Thistle	
1988	Celtic	Hamilton Academicals	Ayr United	
1989	Rangers	Dunfermline Athletic	Albion Rovers	
1990	Rangers	St Johnstone	Brechin City	
1991	Rangers	Falkirk	Stirling Albion	
1992	Rangers	Dundee	Dumbarton	
1993	Rangers	Raith Rovers	Clyde	
1994	Rangers	Falkirk	Stranraer	
1995	Rangers	Raith Rovers	Morton	Forfar Athletic
1996	Rangers	Dunfermline Athletic	Stirling Albion	Livingston
1997	Rangers	St Johnstone	Ayr United	Inverness Caledonian Thistle
1998	Celtic	Dundee	Stranraer	Alloa Athletic
	SPL	**SFL 1**	**SFL 2**	**SFL 3**
1999	Rangers	Hibernian	Livingston	Ross County
2000	Rangers	St Mirren	Clyde	Queen's Park
2001	Celtic	Livingston	Partick Thistle	Hamilton Academicals
2002	Celtic	Partick Thistle	Queen of the South	Brechin City
2003	Rangers	Falkirk	Raith Rovers	Morton
2004	Celtic	Inverness Caledonian Thistle	Airdrie United	Stranraer

Promotion from and Relegation to the Football Conference in England

Automatic promotion and relegation between the Football Conference and the Football League was first introduced in season 1986–7.

	Conference Champions	Relegated from Football League
1987	Scarborough	Lincoln City
1988	Lincoln City	Newport County
1989	Maidstone United	Darlington
1990	Darlington	Colchester United
1991	Barnet	Wrexham
1992	Colchester United	Carlisle United
1993	Wycombe Wanderers	Halifax Town
1994	Kidderminster Harriers*	*No relegation*

	Conference Champions	Relegated from Football League
1995	Macclesfield Town*	*No relegation*
1996	Stevenage Borough*	*No relegation*
1997	Macclesfield Town	Hereford United
1998	Halifax Town	Doncaster Rovers
1999	Cheltenham Town	Scarborough
2000	Kidderminster Harriers	Chester City
2001	Rushden & Diamonds	Barnet
2002	Boston United	Halifax Town
2003	Yeovil Town; Doncaster Rovers	Shrewsbury Town; Exeter City
2004	Chester City; Shrewsbury Town	Carlisle United; York City

*champions but not promoted

FIFA World Cup

FIFA was formed in 1904 but it took another 26 years before the first World Cup was held. Frenchman Jules Rimet was the driving force behind the World Cup's creation, but it wasn't until 1950 that the trophy first bore his name. Brazil, champions for the third time in 1970, were awarded the trophy to keep and another trophy was created in time for the 1974 World Cup. The World Cup is played every four years, with qualifying rounds played on a continental basis.

aet = after extra time
* = penalties
+ = deciding match of final group stage

Just the job for France

Just Fontaine holds the record for the number of goals scored at a single World Cup finals. The Moroccan-born striker bagged an incredible 13 goals in six games in the 1958 competition in Sweden. His tally included four against West Germany in the third-place final, which France won 6-3.

	Champions	Runners-up	Score	Host country	Top scorer
1930	Argentina	Uruguay	4-2	Uruguay	Guillermo Stábile (Argentina) 8
1934	Italy	Czechoslovakia	2-1 aet	Italy	Edmund Conen (Germany), Oldrich Nejedly (Czechoslovakia), Angelo Schiavio (Italy) 4
1938	Italy	Hungary	4-2	France	Leônidas da Silva (Brazil) 8
1950	Uruguay	Brazil	2-1+	Brazil	Ademir (Brazil) 9
1954	West Germany	Hungary	3-2	Switzerland	Sándor Kocsis (Hungary) 11
1958	Brazil	Sweden	5-2	Sweden	Just Fontaine (France) 13
1962	Brazil	Czechoslovakia	3-1	Chile	Flórián Albert (Hungary), Valentin Ivanov (USSR), Garrincha (Brazil), Leonel Sánchez (Chile), Drazen Jerkovic (Yugoslavia), Vavá (Brazil) 4
1966	England	West Germany	4-2 aet	England	Eusébio (Portugal) 9

	Champions	Runners-up	Score	Host country	Top scorer
1970	Brazil	Italy	4-1	Mexico	Gerd Müller (West Germany) 10
1974	West Germany	Holland	2-1	West Germany	Grzegorz Lato (Poland) 7
1978	Argentina	Holland	3-1 aet	Argentina	Mario Kempes (Argentina) 6
1982	Italy	West Germany	3-1	Spain	Paolo Rossi (Italy) 6
1986	Argentina	West Germany	3-2	Mexico	Gary Lineker (England) 6
1990	West Germany	Argentina	1-0	Italy	Salvatore Schillaci (Italy) 6
1994	Brazil	Italy	0-0 aet; 3-2*	USA	Oleg Salenko (Russia) 6, Hristo Stoitchkov (Bulgaria) 6
1998	France	Brazil	3-0	France	Davor Suker (Croatia) 6
2002	Brazil	Germany	2-0	Japan/South Korea	Ronaldo (Brazil) 8
2006				Germany	

One El of a beating

In six matches in World Cup finals El Salvador have scored just one goal. Was this solitary strike in Spain in 1982 a cause for celebration? Not quite. The Central American minnows' opponents, Hungary, replied with ten in what is still the largest win in the history of World Cup finals.

Packing them in

The final match in the 1950 World Cup in Brazil saw the competition's biggest ever attendance. An amazing 199,854 turned up at the Maracana stadium in Rio de Janeiro to see Uruguay lift the trophy after beating the hosts 2-1.

Where were the fans?

World Cup matches often bring whole nations to a standstill but that wasn't quite the case at the inaugural tournament in 1930 in Uruguay. Romania beat Peru 3-1 in Montevideo but only 300 spectators could be bothered to turn up for the match that holds, and is likely to keep holding, the record for the lowest attendance at the finals of the World Cup.

European Championship

The European Championship is played every four years following a round of qualifying matches played in groups. The competition is played for the Henri Delaunay Cup.

aet = after extra time
* = penalties
(R) = replay
(G) = golden goal

	Champions	Runners-up	Score	Host country
1960	USSR	Yugoslavia	2-1	France
1964	Spain	USSR	2-1	Spain
1968	Italy	Yugoslavia	1-1; 2-0 (R)	Italy
1972	West Germany	USSR	3-0	Belgium
1976	Czechoslovakia	West Germany	2-2 aet; 5-4*	Yugoslavia

	Champions	Runners-up	Score	Host country
1980	West Germany	Belgium	2-1	Italy
1984	France	Spain	2-0	France
1988	Holland	USSR	2-0	West Germany
1992	Denmark	Germany	2-0	Sweden
1996	Germany	Czech Republic	2-1 (G)	England
2000	France	Italy	2-1 (G)	Holland/Belgium
2004	Greece	Portugal	1-0	Portugal

Mischievous mascot causes panda-monium

St Mirren mascot Paisley Panda was red-carded for bad behaviour in season 2003/04 after a series of controversial performances. Bored with attempting to amuse young home fans, he turned his attention to antagonizing away supporters. First an inflatable sheep was waved provocatively at Queen of the South fans. Then a giant can of air freshener was brandished in the direction of Morton supporters at a Renfrewshire derby. Later a Falkirk jersey was placed in contact with the Panda's posterior in a manner that suggested a distinct lack of respect for the Stirlingshire club. This final incident led to a brush with the law and the resignation of the bad-mannered bear.

Copa America

The South American Championship, known since 1975 as the Copa America, is international football's oldest running competition. It is organized by South America's Confederation (CONMEBOL) but guest nations have also competed in recent years, including Mexico, the USA and Japan. Details of championship play-offs and finals have been shown where applicable. For tournaments played on a league basis, only the winners and runners-up have been listed.

* = unofficial 'extraordinarios' tournament

** = penalties

	Champions	Runners-up	Score	Host country
1910	Argentina	Uruguay		Argentina
1916	Uruguay	Argentina		Argentina
1917	Argentina	Uruguay		Uruguay
1919	Brazil	Uruguay	1-0	Brazil
1920	Uruguay	Argentina		Chile
1921	Argentina	Brazil		Argentina
1922	Brazil	Paraguay	3-1	Brazil
1923	Uruguay	Argentina		Uruguay
1924	Uruguay	Argentina		Uruguay
1925	Argentina	Brazil		Argentina
1926	Uruguay	Argentina		Chile
1927	Argentina	Uruguay		Peru
1929	Argentina	Paraguay		Argentina
1935	Uruguay	Argentina		Peru*
1937	Argentina	Brazil	2-0	Argentina
1939	Peru	Uruguay		Peru

	Champions	Runners-up	Score	Host country
1941	Argentina	Uruguay		Chile*
1942	Uruguay	Argentina		Uruguay
1945	Argentina	Brazil		Chile*
1946	Argentina	Brazil		Argentina*
1947	Argentina	Paraguay		Ecuador
1949	Brazil	Paraguay	7-0	Brazil
1953	Paraguay	Brazil	3-2	Peru
1955	Argentina	Chile		Chile
1956	Uruguay	Chile		Uruguay*
1957	Argentina	Brazil		Peru
1959	Argentina	Brazil		Argentina*
1959	Uruguay	Argentina		Ecuador
1963	Bolivia	Paraguay		Bolivia
1967	Uruguay	Argentina		Uruguay
1975	Peru	Colombia		Colombia/Peru/ Venezuela
1979	Paraguay	Chile		Paraguay/Chile/ Argentina
1983	Uruguay	Brazil	2-0	Uruguay
1987	Uruguay	Chile	1-0	Argentina
1989	Brazil	Uruguay		Brazil
1991	Argentina	Brazil		Chile
1993	Argentina	Mexico	2-1	Ecuador
1995	Uruguay	Brazil	1-1; 5-3**	Uruguay
1997	Brazil	Bolivia	3-1	Bolivia
1999	Brazil	Uruguay	3-0	Paraguay
2001	Colombia	Mexico	1-0	Colombia
2004	Brazil	Argentina	2-2; 4-2**	Peru

European Champions' Club Cup

Europe's oldest club competition is held annually and was, until 1992, played in a knock-out format and competed for by the champions of each nation's top league. Since 1993, the Champions' League format has been in place, in which the top one, two, three or four teams in each league (depending on the strength of the nation concerned) compete in league-format groups before the later knockout stages.

aet = after extra time
* = penalties

	Champions	Runners-up	Score	Venue
1956	Real Madrid	Stade de Reims	4-3	Paris
1957	Real Madrid	Fiorentina	2-0	Madrid
1958	Real Madrid	AC Milan	3-2	Brussels
1959	Real Madrid	Stade de Reims	2-0	Stuttgart
1960	Real Madrid	Eintracht Frankfurt	7-3	Glasgow
1961	Benfica	Barcelona	3-2	Berne
1962	Benfica	Real Madrid	5-3	Amsterdam
1963	AC Milan	Benfica	2-1	London

	Champions	Runners-up	Score	Venue
1964	Inter Milan	Real Madrid	3-1	Vienna
1965	Inter Milan	Benfica	1-0	Milan
1966	Real Madrid	Partizan Belgrade	2-1	Brussels
1967	Celtic	Inter Milan	2-1	Lisbon
1968	Manchester United	Benfica	4-1 aet	London
1969	AC Milan	Ajax	4-1	Madrid
1970	Feyenoord	Celtic	2-1	Milan
1971	Ajax	Panathinaikos	2-0	London
1972	Ajax	Inter Milan	2-0	Rotterdam
1973	Ajax	Juventus	1-0	Belgrade
1974	Bayern Munich	Atletico Madrid	1-1 aet; 4-0	Brussels
1975	Bayern Munich	Leeds United	2-0	Paris
1976	Bayern Munich	St Etienne	1-0	Glasgow
1977	Liverpool	Borussia Mönchen-gladbach	3-1	Rome
1978	Liverpool	Club Brugge	1-0	London
1979	Nottingham Forest	Malmö	1-0	Munich
1980	Nottingham Forest	Hamburg	1-0	Madrid
1981	Liverpool	Real Madrid	1-0	Paris
1982	Aston Villa	Bayern Munich	1-0	Rotterdam
1983	Hamburg	Juventus	1-0	Athens
1984	Liverpool	AS Roma	1-1 aet; 4-2*	Rome
1985	Juventus	Liverpool	1-0	Brussels
1986	Steaua Bucharest	Barcelona	0-0 aet; 2-0*	Seville
1987	FC Porto	Bayern Munich	2-1	Vienna
1988	PSV Eindhoven	Benfica	0-0 aet; 6-5*	Stuttgart
1989	AC Milan	Steaua Bucharest	4-0	Barcelona
1990	AC Milan	Benfica	1-0	Vienna
1991	Red Star Belgrade	Marseille	0-0 aet; 5-3*	Bari
1992	Barcelona	Sampdoria	1-0	London
1993	Marseille	AC Milan	1-0	Munich
	(Marseille stripped of their title because of match fixing)			
1994	AC Milan	Barcelona	4-0	Athens
1995	Ajax	AC Milan	1-0	Vienna
1996	Juventus	Ajax	1-1 aet; 4-2*	Rome
1997	Borussia Dortmund	Juventus	3-1	Munich
1998	Real Madrid	Juventus	1-0	Amsterdam
1999	Manchester United	Bayern Munich	2-1	Barcelona
2000	Real Madrid	Valencia	3-0	Paris
2001	Bayern Munich	Valencia	1-1 aet; 5-4*	Milan
2002	Real Madrid	Bayer Leverkusen	2-1	Glasgow
2003	AC Milan	Juventus	0-0 aet; 3-2*	Manchester
2004	Porto	Monaco	3-0	Gelsenkirchen

Record transfer fees

The world's highest transfer fee was paid when Zinedine Zidane was transferred from Juventus to Real Madrid for £45.62m in 2001. The highest fee for a transfer between British clubs is the £29.1m paid by Manchester United for Rio Ferdinand from Leeds United in 2002.

UEFA Cup

The UEFA Cup is played for by clubs finishing near the top of their domestic league. It has a knockout format, with sides competing over home and away legs in each tie, except for the final (since 1998). In recent years, the sides finishing third in their respective Champions' League groups have joined the UEFA Cup in the third round. The competition was known until 1971 as the Fairs Cup.

aet = after extra time
* = decided on away goals
** = penalties
(G) = golden goal
(S) = silver goal

	Champions	Runners-up	Score	Venue
1958	Barcelona	London Select XI	2-2, 6-0	
1960	Barcelona	Birmingham City	0-0, 4-1	
1961	AS Roma	Birmingham City	2-2, 2-0	
1962	Valencia	Barcelona	6-2, 1-1	
1963	Valencia	Dinamo Zagreb	2-1, 2-0	
1964	Real Zaragoza	Valencia `	2-1	Barcelona
1965	Ferencvaros	Juventus	1-0	Turin
1966	Barcelona	Real Zaragoza	0-1, 4-2	
1967	Dinamo Zagreb	Leeds United	2-0, 0-0	
1968	Leeds United	Ferencvaros	1-0, 0-0	
1969	Newcastle United	Ujpest Dozsa	3-0, 0-2	
1970	Arsenal	Anderlecht	1-3, 3-0	
1971	Leeds United	Juventus	2-2,-1-1*	
1972	Tottenham Hotspur	Wolverhampton Wanderers	2-1, 1-1	
1973	Liverpool	Borussia Mönchengladbach	3-0, 0-2	
1974	Feyenoord	Tottenham Hotspur	2-2, 2-0	
1975	Borussia Mönchengladbach	Twente Enschede	0-0, 5-1	
1976	Liverpool	Club Bruges	3-2, 1-1	
1977	Juventus	Athletic Bilbao	1-0, 1-2*	
1978	PSV Eindhoven	Bastia	0-0, 3-0	
1979	Borussia Mönchengladbach	Red Star Belgrade	1-1, 1-0	
1980	Eintracht Frankfurt	Borussia Mönchen-gladbach	2-3, 1-0*	
1981	Ipswich Town	AZ 67 Alkmaar	3-0, 2-4	
1982	IFK Gothenburg	Hamburg	1-0, 3-0	
1983	Anderlecht	Benfica	1-0, 1-1	
1984	Tottenham Hotspur	Anderlecht	1-1, 1-1 aet; 4-3**	
1985	Real Madrid	Videoton	3-0, 0-1	
1986	Real Madrid	Cologne	5-1, 0-2	
1987	IFK Gothenburg	Dundee United	1-0, 1-1	
1988	Bayer Leverkusen	Español	0-3, 3-0 aet; 3-2**	
1989	Napoli	Stuttgart	2-1, 3-3	
1990	Juventus	Fiorentina	3-1, 0-0	
1991	Inter Milan	AS Roma	2-0, 0-1	

	Champions	Runners-up	Score	Venue
1992	Ajax	Torino	2-2, 0-0*	
1993	Juventus	Borussia Dortmund	3-1, 3-0	
1994	Inter Milan	Salzburg	1-0, 1-0	
1995	Parma	Juventus	1-0, 1-1	
1996	Bayern Munich	Bordeaux	2-0, 3-1	
1997	Schalke	Inter Milan	1-0, 0-1 aet; 4-1**	
1998	Inter Milan	Lazio	3-0	Paris
1999	Parma	Marseille	3-0	Moscow
2000	Galatasaray	Arsenal	0-0 aet; 4-1**	Copenhagen
2001	Liverpool	Alaves	5-4 (G)	Dortmund
2002	Feyenoord	Borussia Dortmund	3-2	Rotterdam
2003	FC Porto	Celtic	3-2 (S)	Seville
2004	Valencia	Marseille	2-0	Gothenburg

Bringing the game into disrepute

In 2003 Channel 4 asked viewers to vote for the worst singles of all time. The top (or should that be bottom?) 100 included three songs by footballers. Holding off Peter Andre's 'Mysterious Girl' from the coveted number 56 position was 'Back Home' by the 1970 England World Cup squad. Sandwiched between Joe Dolce and Bob the Builder was Paul Gascoigne with his affecting interpretation of 'Fog on the Tyne'. Leading the way for the beautiful game was the mulleted midfield duo of Glenn Hoddle and Chris Waddle whose 'Diamond Lights' shone at a poptastic number 43.

European Cup Winners' Cup

The European Cup Winners' Cup, now no longer played, was the club competition intended for winners of the main domestic cup competitions. A knock-out format was played, with sides playing in home and away legs in each tie, except for the final.

aet = after extra time
(R) = replay
* = penalties

	Champions	Runners-up	Score	Venue
1961	Fiorentina	Rangers	2-0; 2-1	Glasgow; Florence
1962	Atletico Madrid	Fiorentina	1-1 aet; 3-0 (R)	Glasgow; Stuttgart
1963	Tottenham Hotspur	Atletico Madrid	5-1	Rotterdam
1964	Sporting Lisbon	MTK Budapest	3-3 aet; 1-0 (R)	Brussels; Antwerp
1965	West Ham United	TSV Munich	2-0	London (Wembley)
1966	Borussia Dortmund	Liverpool	2-1 aet	Glasgow
1967	Bayern Munich	Rangers	1-0 aet	Nuremberg
1968	AC Milan	SV Hamburg	2-0	Rotterdam
1969	Slovan Bratislava	Barcelona	3-2	Basle
1970	Manchester City	Gornik Zabrze	2-1	Vienna
1971	Chelsea	Real Madrid	1-1 (aet); 2-1 (R)	Athens
1972	Rangers	Moscow Dynamo	3-2	Barcelona
1973	AC Milan	Leeds United	1-0	Salonika

	Champions	Runners-up	Score	Venue
1974	FC Magdeburg	AC Milan	2-0	Rotterdam
1975	Dynamo Kiev	Ferencvaros	3-0	Basle
1976	Anderlecht	West Ham United	4-2	Brussels
1977	SV Hamburg	Anderlecht	2-0	Amsterdam
1978	Anderlecht	FK Austria	4-0	Paris
1979	Barcelona	Fortuna Düsseldorf	4-3 aet	Basle
1980	Valencia	Arsenal	0-0 aet; 5-4*	Brussels
1981	Dynamo Tbilisi	Carl Zeiss Jena	2-1	Düsseldorf
1982	Barcelona	Standard Liège	2-1	Barcelona
1983	Aberdeen	Real Madrid	2-1 aet	Gothenburg
1984	Juventus	FC Porto	2-1	Basle
1985	Everton	Rapid Vienna	3-1	Rotterdam
1986	Dynamo Kiev	Atletico Madrid	3-0	Lyons
1987	Ajax	Lokomotive Leipzig	1-0	Athens
1988	Mechelen	Ajax	1-0	Strasbourg
1989	Barcelona	Sampdoria	2-0	Berne
1990	Sampdoria	Anderlecht	2-0 aet	Gothenburg
1991	Manchester United	Barcelona	2-1	Rotterdam
1992	Werder Bremen	Monaco	2-0	Lisbon
1993	Parma	Antwerp	3-1	London
1994	Arsenal	Parma	1-0	Copenhagen
1995	Real Zaragoza	Arsenal	2-1 aet	Paris
1996	Paris St Germain	Rapid Vienna	1-0	Brussels
1997	Barcelona	Paris St Germain	1-0	Rotterdam
1998	Chelsea	Stuttgart	1-0	Stockholm
1999	Lazio	Mallorca	2-1	Birmingham (Villa Park)

All goalies great and small

Alf Wight was struggling to find a catchy pseudonym for his soon-to-be-published memoirs about life as a vet in Yorkshire in the 30s, 40s, and 50s. But football came to his rescue. One night, while watching a televised match, he became enamoured with the name of the Hibernian goalkeeper Jim Herriot. Quick as a flash, Alf Wight became James Herriot, his memoirs sold in their millions, and the later TV series allowed Christopher Timothy to make a career out of putting his arm up a cow's backside.

FIFA World Player of the Year

1991	Lothar Matthäus (Germany)
1992	Marco Van Basten (Holland)
1993	Roberto Baggio (Italy)
1994	Romario (Brazil)
1995	George Weah (Liberia)
1996	Ronaldo (Brazil)
1997	Ronaldo (Brazil)
1998	Zinedine Zidane (France)
1999	Rivaldo (Brazil)
2000	Zinedine Zidane (France)

Football finance

Tottenham Hotspur was the first football club to float on the London Stock Exchange, where they are still listed. Currently there are eleven other British football clubs listed: Aston Villa, Celtic, Heart of Midlothian, Leeds United, Manchester United, Millwall, Newcastle United, Sheffield United, Southampton, Sunderland and Watford.

2001 Luis Figo (Portugal)
2002 Ronaldo (Brazil)
2003 Zinedine Zidane (France)
2004 Ronaldinho (Brazil)

A-Z

assist	a pass that results in the scoring of a goal, eg *Henry scored a goal and had two assists*
assistant referee	one of the two officials on either touchline who help the referee to officiate the game by using flags to indicate offsides, throw-ins, and corner kicks. They were formerly know as linesmen
association football	the official name for football, used especially in the past to distinguish it from other types of football such as rugby football
back	same as **defender**
back heel	a pass or shot made with the heel
back-pass rule	law approved in 1992 by FIFA which states that a goalkeeper may not handle the ball in the **penalty box** when it has been intentionally kicked back to him/her by a team-mate
bench	where a team's managers and substitutes sit, near the touchline of the pitch
bicycle kick	a kick by a player who is in mid-air with the feet above the head
booking	the entry of a player's name in the referee's notebook, when a serious foul has been committed. A booking is signalled by the showing of a yellow card to the offending player. Two yellow cards result in a red card and a **sending-off**
Bosman ruling	the result of a case won by the Belgian footballer Jean-Marc Bosman in 1995 which removed the limit on the number of foreign players any club within the European Union can field and which gave out-of-contract footballers the right to become free agents
box	short for **penalty box**
cap	commemorative cap given to a footballer every time he or she plays in an international match. It also refers to the number of appearances a player has made at international level, eg *he won 60 caps for Finland*
caution	same as **booking**
centre circle	the circle painted on the middle of the pitch, at the centre of which is the **centre spot**
centre forward	an attacking player who leads the line of attack
centre half, centre back	a defensive player who plays in the middle of the defence
centre spot	the painted spot in the middle of the pitch from which the **kick-off** is made at the start of each half and after a goal is scored
corner (kick)	a kick awarded to the attacking team at one of the four corners of the pitch as a result of a defending player putting the ball out of play beyond the **goal line**
corner flag	one of the four flags that mark the corners of the pitch where the **touchline** meets the **goal line**
crossbar	the wooden or metal bar that is supported by the two goal **posts**
D	the D-shaped area on the edge of the penalty box outside which players must stand when a penalty is being taken

International Records

	England	Wales	Northern Ireland	Republic of Ireland	Scotland	Worldwide
Most appearances	Peter Shilton 125	Neville Southall 92	Pat Jennings 119	Steve Staunton 102	Kenny Dalglish 102	Claudio Suarez (Mexico) 171
	Bobby Moore 108	Gary Speed 85		Niall Quinn 91	Jim Leighton 91	
	Bobby Charlton 106					
	Billy Wright 105					
Top scorers	Bobby Charlton 49	Ian Rush 28	David Healy 14	Niall Quinn 21	Dennis Law 30	Ali Daei (Iran) 89
	Gary Lineker 48	Ivor Allchurch 23		Robbie Keane 21	Kenny Dalglish 30	Ferenc Puskás (Hungary & Spain) 84
	Jimmy Greaves 44	Trevor Ford 23		Frank Stapleton 20		Pelé (Brazil) 77
Biggest victory	13-0 v Ireland, 1882	11-0 v Ireland, 1888	7-0 v Wales, 1930	8-0 v Malta, 1983	11-0 v Ireland, 1901	Australia 31-0 American Samoa, 2001

Supreme misses a sitter

Diana Ross was delighted when the organizers of the 1994 World Cup in the USA invited her to take part in the opening cermenony. During a choreographed routine she was supposed to take a penalty, the force of which would 'shatter' the frame of the tiny goal. However, when it came to the big moment the disco diva emulated Chris Waddle at the previous World Cup and put the penalty (from all of four yards) wide of the post. The goal frame still 'broke' though, much to the amazement of TV viewers.

Salad days

In 1993 goalkeeper Dave Beasant was the victim of an off-the-ball challenge that left him on the sidelines for a number of weeks. Much to Beasant's embarrassment the perpetrator of this foul was not an opponent or even a team-mate but a bottle of salad cream. The collision between garnish and foot resulted from the big keeper's attempts to stop the bottle hitting the ground following a fumble while making a sandwich. Dave's toe required medical attention but, thankfully, the bottle survived the fall.

dangerous play any play which is likely to cause injury to another player, especially play that involves raised feet to an opponent who is trying to head the ball

dead ball the ball when it is stationary but ready to be played, for example at a free kick or corner

defender a player whose duties are mainly defensive

direct free kick see **free kick**

dive a deliberate going to ground of a player when he or she has not been fouled by an opponent, in an attempt to win a penalty or free kick

double the winning of the Premiership and FA Cup in one season

dribble to run with the ball at one's feet, where control is maintained by a series of small kicks

eighteen-yard box same as **penalty area**

extra time a period of play, consisting of two halves of 15 minutes, used to decide cup matches that have been drawn

far post the post furthest away from where the ball is

five-a-side a form of the game played, usually indoors, on a smaller pitch than standard and with five players on each side

formation the arrangement of the players in a team into a certain pattern, for example a 4-4-2 formation features four defenders, four midfielders, and two attackers

forward an attacking player such as a **centre forward** or a **winger**

foul an infringement of the rules resulting in a **free kick**

fourth official official who assists the referee and assistant referees from the **technical area** and makes sure that substitutes, managers, trainers, etc maintain discipline off the pitch. The fourth official was introduced into the game in 1991, originally as cover in case one of the three other officials sustained an injury

free kick a kick, awarded after a foul or an offside, which is taken without interference from the opposing team. Free kicks can be direct or indirect, depending on the nature of the foul. A goal cannot be scored from an indirect free kick unless the ball is touched by another player first

friendly a match arranged between two teams outside normal competition, such as a player's testimonial or a warm-up match before the start of a season or competition

full back a defensive player who plays on either the left or right side of the pitch

futsal a form of the game played with five players on each side, a less bouncy ball, and a duration of 40 minutes. The word derives from Spanish *fútbol* football + *sala* room

give-and-go same as **one-two**

goal 1. the area bounded by crossbar, posts, and netting and defended by the goalkeeper 2. a successful attempt to score, in which the whole of the ball crosses the **goal line**

goal difference the difference between the number of goals scored and conceded by a team, used to separate teams tied on the same number of points in a league competition

goalie short for **goalkeeper**

goalkeeper the player who protects the goal and who is the only player allowed to handle the ball in the penalty area

goal kick a free kick awarded to the defending team in the **six-yard area** of the penalty box when the opposing team puts the ball behind

	the goal line. The kick is usually but not always taken by the goalkeeper
goal line	the line marking each end of the pitch, on which the goals stand
goalmouth	the area immediately in front of the goal
golden goal	a goal scored in **extra time** which settles a match immediately. The golden goal rule was first used in a major competition in the European Championship finals of 1996
half	one of the 45-minute periods of play into which each 90-minute match is divided
halfway line	the line separating the two halves of the pitch. At a kick-off the opposing team must stay outside the **centre circle** and in their own half
half time	the 15-minute period between halves during which players rest
half volley	a kick in which the player makes contact with the ball just as it starts to bounce up off the ground
hand ball	a foul committed when a player intentionally uses his or her hand or arm to play the ball. A goalkeeper is exempt from this inside his penalty box
hat trick	three goals scored by the same player in a single game
header	a pass or effort on goal using the head
indirect free kick	see **free kick**
injury time	see **stoppage time**
keeper	short for **goalkeeper**
kick-off	the start or resumption of a game, in which a player passes the ball from the **centre spot** to a team-mate. Kick-offs are taken at the start of each half and after a goal has been scored
left back	see **full back**
libero	same as **sweeper**. The word is Italian and means 'free'
linesman	a former name for **assistant referee**
loan	a temporary transfer of a player from one club to another with no transfer fee involved
lob	if a player lobs the goalkeeper, he or she lofts the ball gently over the goalkeeper
man marking	a defensive strategy in which a player is assigned an opposing player to mark and tackle throughout the game
mark	if a player marks an opposing player, he or she stays close to that player in order to prevent him/her being effective
midfield	the area in the middle of the pitch
midfielder	one of the three, four or five players who play in the middle of the pitch for a team
near post	the post nearest to where the ball is
net	the openwork fabric of string attached to the goalposts and crossbar
obstruction	a foul committed by a player who does not have control of the ball using his body to get in the way of his opponent
offside	if a player is offside, he or she is nearer the goal line than one or both of the last two defenders (the goalkeeper counting as a defender) when the ball is played forward to him/her by a member of his/her own team. An offside results in a free kick to the defending team
offside trap	a strategy that involves defensive players moving towards the half-way line in unison in order to catch attacking players **offside** when a forward pass is being made

off-the-ball an off-the-ball incident is a fight or argument between two or more players away from the play

one-two a series of two passes in which a player passes the ball to a team-mate, runs past an opponent, then receives the ball back again

onside not **offside**

outfield player any player other than the goalkeeper

overhead kick same as **bicycle kick**

own goal a goal scored inadvertently by a player in the defending team

pass a kick or header from one team-mate to another

penalty area an area in front of the goal within which a foul against the attacking team, if punishable by a direct free kick, leads to the award of a **penalty**

penalty box same as **penalty area**

penalty (kick) a direct free kick at goal taken from the penalty spot. Only the goalkeeper and penalty taker are allowed inside the penalty box as a penalty kick is taken

penalty spot the spot in the penalty box, 12yd from goal, from which a penalty kick is taken

pitch the rectangular surface, bounded by the goal lines and touchlines, on which the match is played

play-offs (in England) a series of knockout games involving the four teams finishing from third to sixth in a division, used to decide the third team to be promoted to a higher division

possession 1. the state of being in control of the ball 2. the amount of possession a team has is the amount of time they spend with the ball under their control

post one of the two pillars which support the crossbar and net of the goal

professional foul a cynical foul made with no attempt to play the ball, designed to foil a goal-scoring opportunity. It has been a **red-card** offence since 1990

promotion the elevation of a club from a lower division to a higher division at the end of a season in which the club has finished in a high position in the league

red card the red-coloured card shown by a referee to a player who is being sent off. A red card is given following two **yellow cards** or one very serious foul

referee the official in charge of a game who upholds the laws with the help of two **assistant referees** on the touchlines and a **fourth official** off the pitch

relegation demotion for a club from a higher division to a lower one following a season in which they have finished at the bottom or near the bottom of their division

relegation zone the positions at the bottom of the league which will result in relegation at the end of the season, eg *United are just three points above the relegation zone*

right back see **full back**

save a goalkeeper's successful attempt at stopping the ball from entering the goal

sending off dismissal from the pitch of a player by the referee following two **yellow cards** or one serious offence that merits a **straight red** card

set piece a rehearsed play from a corner kick or a free kick near the penalty area

shot	an attempt on goal struck with the foot
silver goal	a goal scored in **extra time** that, unlike a **golden goal**, does not decide the game immediately. If a team scores in the first period of extra time the match continues for the remainder of that period. If the opposition does not score then the match ends after the first period of extra time. If the goal is scored in the second period of extra time the match continues until the end of that period
six-yard area	the rectangular area in front of the goal, within which a **goal kick** may be taken
soccer	a name given to **association football** in Britain in the 19th century in order to distinguish it from other forms of football. It derives from the word *association*
stepover	a move where a player tries to throw his or her opponent off balance by stepping over the ball with one leg, without actually kicking the ball
stoppage time	the time added on to the regulation 90 minutes of a game to make up for time lost to injuries and time wasting
stopper	a defender renowned for his tackling ability
straight red	a **red card** given to a player for a very serious offence, which results in his or her immediate **sending off**
striker	an attacking player who is expected to score goals
substitute	a player who replaces a team-mate during a match. In most matches three substitutes are allowed
suspension	the temporary barring of a player from competitive football
sweeper	a player who plays behind the defenders in a free role without marking duties
tackle	an attempt to win the ball from an opponent using the leg or foot
tackle from behind	see **tackle**
technical area	the area, marked by white lines, at the side of the pitch to which managers, trainers and substitutes are restricted during play
throw-in	the throwing of the ball from behind the touchline to restart play when the ball is put out by an opposing player
time wasting	tactic of prolonging the time taken for throw-ins, corner kicks, goal kicks, etc by a team in a winning position which, if noticed by the referee, results in **stoppage time** added at the end of the match
touchline	the line around the pitch inside which play takes place
transfer	if a player is transferred from one team to another, he or she moves there, usually for a fee
trap	if a player traps the ball, he or she controls the ball and brings it to rest with the feet
treble	the winning of three trophies in one season
two-footed tackle	see **tackle**
upright	a goalpost
volley	a shot or pass in which the ball is struck before it hits the ground
wall	a formation of defensive players lined up to defend their goal against a free kick
wall pass	same as **one-two**
wingback	a **full back** who also has an attacking role on the wing when the team goes forward
winger	an attacking player who plays primarily on the touchline and whose main job is to supply crosses into the penalty box

Some football slang

custodian	the goalkeeper
handbags	handbags or 'handbags at ten paces' is sometimes used by commentators to describe incidents between players that involve pushing and threatening language but without much in the way of serious fisticuffs. The phrase implies that the confrontation is rather effeminate and not a proper man's fight
hole	the space between the midfielders and the attackers where attacking midfielders play
keepie-uppie	the practice of juggling the ball with feet, knees, chest and, if the player is appearing in a commercial for a soft drink or a sportswear manufacturer, the shoulders and the back of the neck
lollipop	same as **stepover**
nutmeg	when a player puts the ball through his opponent's legs and retrieves it on the other side
onion bag	the net behind the goals
woodwork	for the posts and the crossbar, usually in the phrase 'to hit the woodwork'

Some famous footballers and managers

Franz Beckenbauer, 1945–

Born in Munich, Germany, the 'Kaiser' is one of the greatest players and managers of all time. As a sweeper he captained West Germany to back-to-back major titles in the early 70s (1972 European Championships and 1974 World Cup) and led his Bayern Munich team to three successive European Cups (1974–6). He managed West Germany, during which time they were runners-up in the World Cup finals twice. He then went on to manage the newly re-united Germany side to World Cup success in 1990, becoming the first man to win the World Cup as a player and as a manager. He is President of Bayern Munich and led Germany's successful bid to host the 2006 World Cup.

David Beckham, 1975–

Born in London, England, he joined Manchester United as a youth and made his Old Trafford debut in 1995. His telegenic looks, soap-opera marriage to former Spice Girl Victoria Adams, lucrative advertising contracts, and undoubted skill as a right-sided midfielder and free-kick specialist mean that he is one of the most iconic – and highly paid – sportsmen on the planet. All this is a remarkable achievement for a man who was blamed for England's exit from the 1998 World Cup after he kicked an opponent and was sent off. His journey from zero to hero was complete four years after this disgrace when his vital goals as captain led England through the qualifying campaign and into the knockout stages of the 2002 World Cup finals. After a bust-up with Manchester United boss **Sir Alex Ferguson**, Beckham joined a star-studded Real Madrid in 2003. He was awarded the OBE in 2003.

George Best, 1946–

Born in Belfast, Northern Ireland, he is considered one of the most naturally talented players the UK has ever produced. In his early years at Manchester United in the late 60s, he scored many goals and showed flashes of footballing genius, helping the Old Trafford side in 1968 become the first English team to win the European Cup. For this he was voted European Footballer of the Year, but these early achievements proved the pinnacle of his career as he found it hard to cope with the temptations that his wealth, fame and good looks afforded. Although he went on playing until the 1980s, his career never reached the heights of 1968. Since his retirement he has regularly appeared on the front pages of tabloid newspapers, his battle with alcoholism being well documented. He appeared 37 times for Northern Ireland and scored nine goals.

Sir Matt Busby, 1909–94

Born in Bellshill, Lanarkshire, Scotland, he became Manchester United boss in 1945 after a modest playing career. His young side of the mid to late 50s (known as Busby's Babes) seemed destined for success in the European Cup but was largely wiped out in the Munich air crash of 1958. Recovering from severe injuries, he put together a formidable team containing players such as **Bobby Charlton**, **George Best** and Dennis Law. This side achieved success in the league and then, in 1968, crowned Busby's career by becoming the first English team to win the European Cup.

Sir Bobby Charlton, 1937–

Born in Ashington, Northumberland, England, he played with Manchester United throughout his career (1954-73). Surviving the Munich air disaster of 1958, he went on to become arguably England's greatest player. He captained Manchester United to European Cup success in 1968 and played 106 times for England, scoring a record 49 goals in the process. He also played for England during their finest hour, the 1966 World Cup campaign, along with his brother Jack. He was knighted in 1994 and is now a director of Manchester United.

Brian Clough, 1935–2004

Born in Middlesbrough, England, he became a manager when injury cut short a successful goal-scoring career with Middlesbrough and Sunderland. He was one of the few managers to take two clubs to the English First Division title (Derby County in 1974–5 and Nottingham Forest in 1977–8). His greatest achievement, however, is in managing Forest to back-to-back European Cup wins in 1979 and 1980. Opinionated and often eccentric, Cloughie was one of the English game's best-loved characters, and it is perhaps those traits that prevented him from becoming England manager. In 1991 he was awarded the OBE, which he claimed stood for 'Old Big 'Ead'.

Johann Cruyff, 1947–

Born in Amsterdam, the Netherlands, he was one of the stars of the golden age of Dutch soccer in the 70s. Voted European Footballer of the Year three times, he was part of the Ajax side that won the European Cup three years in succession (1971–3) and the Dutch national side that won many admirers with its brand of 'total football'. He also achieved notable success as a manager, winning the European Cup with both Barcelona and Ajax. His excellent goal-scoring record for Holland – 33 goals in 48 games – should have been even better but his disputes with footballing authorities led to his refusal to go to the 1978 World Cup in Argentina.

Alfredo di Stefano, 1926–

Born in Buenos Aires, Argentina, he was one of the stars of the near invincible Real Madrid team that dominated European football in the infancy of pan-European club competition. He scored a goal in each of Real Madrid's five successive European Cup wins, including a hat trick in the 7-3 win over Eintracht Frankfurt at Hampden Park. As an international he played for both Argentina and Spain, and he later managed Valencia to the Spanish league title in 1971. However, it is his career at Real Madrid for which he is best remembered, especially his partnership with **Ferenc Puskás**.

Sir Alex Ferguson, 1941–

Born in Govan, Glasgow, Scotland, he has become one of the most successful club managers in British football history. After a playing career which included a spell with Rangers, he achieved early managerial success with St Mirren before heading north to Pittodrie where his eight-year reign brought domestic and European success to Aberdeen and an end – albeit temporary – to the Old Firm's dominance. He left for Old Trafford in 1986, after a brief spell as Scotland manager, and, after a trying first few seasons, turned Manchester United into the dominant force in English football. Under his guidance United have so far won eight Premierships, the European Cup Winners' Cup, four FA Cups, and, most impressive of all, the European Cup in 1999.

Diego Maradona, 1960–

Born in Lanús, Argentina, the diminutive forward is one of the best players that has ever played the game. Despite his small stature, his pace, strength, vision and dazzling skill have lit up numerous matches in Argentina, Italy (with Napoli), and on the world stage. His greatest success came in 1986 when Argentina won the World Cup in Mexico, although it was marred by the 'hand of God' incident against England in which he fisted the ball into the net. He almost single-handedly dragged Argentina into the final of the next World Cup but experienced defeat at the hands of Germany. After that his career went into decline and he was suspended on a number of occasions for failing drugs tests, most notably during the 1994 World Cup which brought his international career to an end.

Bobby Moore, 1941–93

Born in Barking, Essex, England, he spent 18 years as a stylish defender with West Ham United, during which time the Hammers won the FA Cup and the European Cup Winners' Cup. His international record is almost peerless, playing 108 times for England, 90 of them as captain. He played in three successive World Cups for England, and lifted the Jules Rimet trophy as captain of the side in 1966. He finished his English playing career with Fulham but went on to play in the USA for Seattle and San Antonio. He was awarded the OBE in 1967.

Pelé, 1940–

Born in Três Corações, Brazil, as Edson Arantes do Nascimento, he is widely regarded as the greatest player of all time. Capped by Brazil at 16, he won his first World Cup medal in Sweden in 1958 when still a teenager, scoring twice in the final. He won another World Cup medal in 1970, playing in a Brazilian team that is often referred to as the greatest in World Cup history. As a club player, he played most of his career with Santos and scored an extraordinary 1,000 goals in first-class football. After bowing out from the international game, he made a fortune from US club football in the 70s and led the New York Cosmos to a league title in 1977.

Ferenc Puskás, 1927-

Born in Budapest, Hungary, the 'fat little chap' was one of the most skilful players and greatest goal scorers in football history. His Hungarian team's 6-3 win at Wembley in 1953 shattered the myth of English supremacy, and was just one of many internationals in which Puskás, who scored 83 goals in 84 games, excelled. He teamed up with **Alfredo di Stefano** at Real Madrid during that side's dominance of the European Cup, and his four goals in the 1960 final have still to be matched. He had limited success as a manager, although he did take Panathinaikos to the European Cup final in 1971.

Bill Shankly, 1913-81

Born in the mining village of Glenbuck, Lanarkshire, Scotland, he became one of the great triumvirate of Scottish managers – along with **Matt Busby** and **Jock Stein** – that dominated British football in the 1960s and 70s. As a player he won a Cup Final medal with Preston North End but it is as manager of Liverpool that he is best remembered. He turned the Anfield club from second-division strugglers into one of the most feared in Britain. When he retired in 1974 (the year in which he was awarded the OBE) the foundations had been laid for his successors – men such as Bob Paisley and Kenny Dalglish – to maintain Liverpool's position as one of the top teams in Europe.

Jock Stein, 1922-85

Born in Burnbank, Lanarkshire, Scotland, he became one of Scotland's greatest club and national managers. He led Dunfermline Athletic to success in the Scottish Cup in 1965, but it is as Celtic manager between 1965 and 1978 that his greatest achievements were made. During his tenure, the Old Firm duopoly became a Celtic monopoly, as the Parkhead side won nine championships in a row and became the first British team to win the European Cup (1967). After leaving Celtic he briefly joined Leeds United, but soon took over as Scotland boss, guiding Scotland to two World Cup qualifications. He tragically died at the end of Scotland's qualifying match with Wales in Cardiff. He was awarded the CBE in 1970.

Zinedine Zidane, 1972-

Born in Marseilles, France, of Algerian origin, the attacking midfielder is widely regarded as currently the world's best player. He is undoubtedly the most expensive, costing Real Madrid £45m when they bought him from Juventus in 2001. Zizou, as he is affectionately known, became a French national hero in 1998 when his two goals helped France beat Brazil 3-0 in the World Cup final on home ground. He was also Player of the Tournament at the European Championships of 2000, which France won, and has been voted FIFA World Player of the Year on three occasions.

What are the chances of that happening?

In the 63rd minute of the Ryman League match between Worthing and Bromley in January 2001, two players were sent off. Nothing odd there, you might think. However, both players – one from Bromley and one from Worthing – were called Danny Smith. After the game bookmakers William Hill estimated that the chances of this happening were 10,000-1.

GAELIC FOOTBALL

Origins

Gaelic football began life in the 16th century in Ireland. The early form of the game involved two teams from rival parishes attempting to drive a ball over the boundary line between the two settlements. The modern game was codified in 1884 by the Gaelic Athletic Association, the body that runs the game to this day.

Rules and description

A field game, popular in Ireland, played by teams of 15 men or (more recently) women with a round ball on a rectangular, grass playing surface resembling a rugby pitch. The aim is to score goals and points into or over the goals. The goals are H-shaped as in rugby, but the section beneath the crossbar has a net and is protected by a goalkeeper as in soccer. A goal is scored when the ball is kicked or punched under the crossbar and between the posts, and is worth three points. A point is scored when the ball is kicked or punched between the posts and over the crossbar, and is worth one point. The ball can be passed from one player to another by means of kicking and 'handpassing' (punching). Players can run with the ball but only while bouncing it or 'toe-tapping' the ball (dribbling the ball from hand to foot and back again). Carrying the ball for more than four steps without bouncing it or toe-tapping it is not permissible, and the ball can only be bounced once. The officials in charge of the game are one referee, two linesmen, and four umpires. Scores are expressed in points and goals. For example, a team scoring 0-9 (nine points) beats a team scoring 2-2 (two goals and two points).

Ruling body: Cumann Lúthchleas Gael, the English translation of which is Gaelic Athletic Association (abbreviated to GAA). The GAA was founded not only to support the traditional Irish sports of Gaelic football, hurling, camogie and handball, but also to conserve and nurture Ireland's cultural heritage

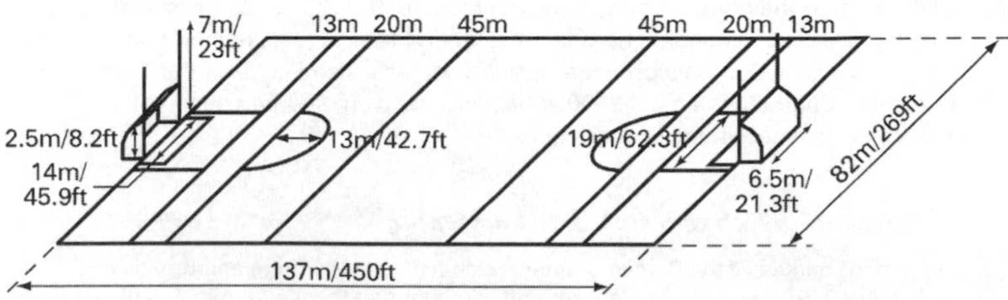

Note: Pitch size is approximate (length minimum 130m/426.5ft, maximum 145m/475.7ft; width minimum 80m/262.5ft, maximum 90m/295.3ft). The goalpost height of 7m/23ft is the minimum permitted.

All-Ireland Champions

The final of the game's premier competition in Ireland takes place at Croke Park, Dublin, on the third Sunday in September each year. First played in 1887, the senior championship trophy has been known as the Sam Maguire Cup since 1928.

* the tournament was not completed as a tour took place that year to the USA by hurlers, Gaelic footballers and athletes

** Louth won by default as their opponents, Kerry, refused to travel because they were in dispute with the Great Southern and Western Railway Company

1887	Limerick
1888	*Unfinished**
1889	Tipperary
1890	Cork
1891	Dublin
1892	Dublin
1893	Wexford
1894	Dublin
1895	Tipperary
1896	Limerick
1898	Dublin
1899	Dublin
1900	Tipperary
1901	Dublin
1902	Dublin
1903	Kerry
1904	Kerry
1905	Kildare
1906	Dublin
1907	Dublin
1908	Dublin
1909	Kerry
1910	Louth**
1911	Cork
1912	Louth
1913	Kerry
1914	Kerry
1915	Wexford
1916	Wexford
1917	Wexford
1918	Wexford
1919	Kildare
1920	Tipperary
1921	Dublin
1922	Dublin
1923	Dublin
1924	Kerry
1925	Galway
1926	Kerry
1927	Kildare
1928	Kildare
1929	Kerry
1930	Kerry
1931	Kerry
1932	Kerry
1933	Cavan
1934	Galway
1935	Cavan
1936	Mayo
1937	Kerry
1938	Galway
1939	Kerry
1940	Kerry
1941	Kerry
1942	Dublin
1943	Roscommon
1944	Roscommon
1945	Cork
1946	Kerry
1947	Cavan
1948	Cavan
1949	Meath
1950	Mayo
1951	Mayo
1952	Cavan
1953	Kerry
1954	Meath
1955	Kerry
1956	Galway
1957	Louth
1958	Dublin
1959	Kerry
1960	Down
1961	Down
1962	Kerry
1963	Dublin
1964	Galway
1965	Galway
1966	Galway
1967	Meath

1968	Down	**1987**	Meath
1969	Kerry	**1988**	Meath
1970	Kerry	**1989**	Cork
1971	Offaly	**1990**	Cork
1972	Offaly	**1991**	Down
1973	Cork	**1992**	Donegal
1974	Dublin	**1993**	Derry
1975	Kerry	**1994**	Down
1976	Dublin	**1995**	Dublin
1977	Dublin	**1996**	Meath
1978	Kerry	**1997**	Kerry
1979	Kerry	**1998**	Galway
1980	Kerry	**1999**	Meath
1981	Kerry	**2000**	Kerry
1982	Offaly	**2001**	Galway
1983	Dublin	**2002**	Armagh
1984	Kerry	**2003**	Tyrone
1985	Kerry	**2004**	Kerry
1986	Kerry		

From Croke Park to Central Park

The 1947 All-Ireland final was held not, as is traditional, at Croke Park but at the Polo Grounds in New York. The game, in which Cavan beat Kerry, was transmitted live by radio to Ireland. Fifty years later, teams from the two counties played a commemorative game in New York, in which Kerry were able to avenge their defeat.

A-Z

booking an instance of a player having his name taken by the referee for a serious foul. As in soccer, yellow cards are used for bookings and red cards for sendings off

bounce if a player bounces the ball, he bounces it from hand to ground and back to hand again. This is a way of a player retaining possession and gaining ground.

boundary line one of the lines surrounding the pitch, beyond which the ball is out of bounds and the play is stopped

forty-five metre kick a free kick awarded to an attacking team when the ball goes out of play beyond the goal line off a defender. It is taken from a line 45m from the goal and is the equivalent of a corner kick in soccer

foul a transgression of the rules. Technical fouls, such as throwing the ball instead of passing it, lifting the ball straight off the ground, **killing the ball**, and wrestling the ball from an opponent who has caught the ball, are punishable by free kicks. Aggressive fouls, such as kicking an opponent, are punished by **bookings** and sendings-off

goal a score of three points awarded to a team when the ball is kicked or punched under the crossbar and between the posts of the opponents' goal

handpass if a player handpasses the ball, he passes the ball to a team-mate by punching the ball

point a score of one point awarded to a team when the ball is kicked over the opponents' crossbar

punt if a player punts the ball, he releases it from his hand and kicks it before it bounces off the ground

side charge a shoulder charge on an opponent. Side charges must be done with one foot on the ground and only when the opponent is in possession of the ball or about to play the ball

sideline kick an unimpeded kick taken from the side of the pitch after the ball has gone out of play. The kick may be taken from the hands or from the ground. It is the equivalent of a throw-in in soccer

solo if a player solos the ball, he releases the ball from hand to foot and then kicks it back into his hands. This is a way of a player retaining possession and gaining ground

toe-tap same as **solo**

Some famous Gaelic footballers

Paddy Doherty, 1940–

Born in County Down, Ireland, he was an exceptionally talented left-sided (and left-footed) forward who played in the Down teams that won the All-Ireland finals of 1960, 1961 and 1968.

Kevin Heffernan, 1929–

Born in Dublin, Ireland, he distinguished himself as a player with his hometown team, winning the All-Ireland final as captain in 1958 and the National League in 1953, 1955 and 1958. 'Heffo', as he was known, knew even greater success, however, as manager of the same team, taking them to All-Ireland final victory in 1974, 1976 and 1977. He was the only Dublin player to be included in the GAA's Football Team of the Millennium in 1999.

Mick O'Connell, 1937–

Born on Valentia Island, off the coast of County Kerry, Ireland, he played as a midfielder for Kerry from 1956 to 1972. He was renowned for his long accurate kicking, balance and style. He played in nine All-Ireland finals, winning in 1959, 1962, 1969 and 1970. In 1999 he was selected as one of the GAA's Football Team of the Millennium.

GLIDING

Origins

In the late 19th century Otto Lilienthal in Germany and Percy Pilcher in Britain were leading innovators in creating heavier-than-air craft that flew without an engine. Their work was picked up by the Wright brothers, who achieved the first powered flight in 1903; but the desire to fly unencumbered by engines persisted and the sport of gliding became popular in the early 20th century – especially in Germany where the Treaty of Versailles outlawed the building of engined aircraft.

The Lilienthal Medal

The sport's highest award (instituted in 1938 and given at the discretion of the FAI) was named after Otto Lilienthal, a German inventor who studied aerodynamics. By 1877 he had invented a glider, a device that mimicked both a bird's wings and its flight pattern. Unfortunately, Lilienthal died from his injuries in 1896 after a glider he was piloting crashed.

Rules and description

Gliders are engineless aircraft that are towed to high elevations by powered aircraft then released, and use the rising air currents to maintain their altitude or to soar upwards. Endurance competitions are held for distance and altitude (where pilots seek out thermals in order to be able to soar higher); and courses, generally out and return or triangular in shape, are devised. Different categories of glider are used in competition, including one-seater and two-seater models. They are generally made from fibreglass, have streamlined cockpits in which pilots adopt a near-lying position, and have long slender wings measuring 15 to 20m/16.4 to 21.9yd.

Ruling body: Fédération Aéronautique Internationale (FAI)

World Championships

The World Championships were inaugurated in 1937. Various competitions are held, including those for distance, duration and altitude.

Open category

1937 Heini Dittmar (Germany)
1948 Per-Axel Persson (Sweden)
1950 Billy Nilsson (Sweden)
1952 Philip Wills (Great Britain)
1954 Gérard Pierre (France)
1956 Paul MacCready (USA)
1958 Ernst Haase (West Germany)
1960 Rudolfo Hossinger (Argentina)
1963 Edward Makula (Poland)
1965 Jan Wroblewski (Poland)
1968 Harro Wödl (Austria)
1970 George Moffat (USA)
1972 Göran Ax (Sweden)
1974 George Moffat (USA)
1976 George Lee (Great Britain)
1978 George Lee (Great Britain)
1981 George Lee (Great Britain)
1983 Ingo Renner (Austria)
1985 Ingo Renner (Austria)
1987 Ingo Renner (Austria)
1989 Claude Lopitaux (France)
1991 Janusz Centka (Poland)
1993 Janusz Centka (Poland)
1995 Ray Lynskey (New Zealand)
1997 Gérard Lherm (France)
1999 Holger Karow (Germany)
2001 Oscar Goudriaan (South Africa)
2003 Holger Karow (Germany)

> ***Those magnificent men in their flying machines***
>
> The first international gliding meeting was held at Itford Hill, near Brighton in East Sussex, in 1922. The prize money of £1,000 was put up by the *Daily Mail* and was won by Alexis Maneyrol of France, who completed a world-record flight in a Peyret tandem glider lasting 3 hours and 21 minutes and 7 seconds. As well as the £1,000, he also received the Légion d'honneur from the French government.

GOLF

Origins

The precise origins of golf are uncertain but it is believed to have evolved from different stick-and-ball games played centuries ago in countries such as Scotland and the Netherlands. What is certain is that the game we recognize today was developed in Scotland, where the landscape along the east coast provided ideal conditions. The earliest written reference to the game dates from 1457, when James II decreed that 'ye golf be utterly cryt done and not usyt' (because it was interfering with archery practice). The world's first golf club was the Gentlemen Golfers of Edinburgh, formed in 1744.

Rules and description

Outdoor sport played on a course normally 4,500–6,500m/5,000–7,000yd long, usually with 18 but sometimes nine holes. The object is to hit a small rubber-cored ball using a long-handled metal- or (formerly) wooden-faced club from a flat starting point or 'tee' along a 'fairway' to a hole positioned on an area of smooth grass or 'green'. Additional hazards include trees, bushes, streams, sand-filled 'bunkers' and the 'rough', or uncut grass beside the fairway. In a 'strokeplay' competition, the most common, the winner completes the course using the lowest number of strokes. A handicapping system allows players of differing abilities to compete against each other. No more than 14 clubs can be carried during a round and players must adhere to the many strict rules laid down by the R&A.

Ruling bodies: Royal and Ancient Golf Club of St Andrews (R&A); United States Golf Association (USGA)

> ***Good sports***
>
> Golf is characterized by good sportsmanship and etiquette. One of the greatest examples of the former came in the 1969 Ryder Cup in the deciding singles game between Tony Jacklin and Jack Nicklaus. Nicklaus conceded a two-foot putt on the 18th hole to Jacklin that meant the game was halved and the match tied. Nicklaus's captain Sam Snead was not impressed but Jack himself later said 'I believed good sportsmanship should be as much a part of the Ryder Cup as great competition'.

The Open Championship

Regarded as the world's leading golf tournament, players now compete for the claret jug trophy, although a red morocco belt was awarded between 1860 and 1870 when Young Tom Morris, having won for the third time in succession, was allowed to keep it. Between 1860 and 1891, it was played over 36 holes in one day; the championship was extended in 1892 to 72 holes.

(A) = amateur

	Champion	Venue
1860	Willie Park, Sr (Scotland)	Prestwick
1861	Tom Morris, Sr (Scotland)	Prestwick
1862	Tom Morris, Sr (Scotland)	Prestwick
1863	Willie Park, Sr (Scotland)	Prestwick
1864	Tom Morris, Sr (Scotland)	Prestwick
1865	Andrew Strath (Scotland)	Prestwick
1866	Willie Park, Sr (Scotland)	Prestwick
1867	Tom Morris, Sr (Scotland)	Prestwick
1868	Tom Morris, Jr (Scotland)	Prestwick
1869	Tom Morris, Jr (Scotland)	Prestwick
1870	Tom Morris, Jr (Scotland)	Prestwick
1871	*Not held*	
1872	Tom Morris, Jr (Scotland)	Prestwick
1873	Tom Kidd (Scotland)	St Andrews
1874	Mungo Park (Scotland)	Musselburgh
1875	Willie Park, Sr (Scotland)	Prestwick
1876	Bob Martin (Scotland)	St Andrews
1877	Jamie Anderson (Scotland)	Musselburgh
1878	Jamie Anderson (Scotland)	Prestwick
1879	Jamie Anderson (Scotland)	St Andrews
1880	Bob Ferguson (Scotland)	Musselburgh
1881	Bob Ferguson (Scotland)	Prestwick
1882	Bob Ferguson (Scotland)	St Andrews
1883	Willie Fernie (Scotland)	Musselburgh
1884	Jack Simpson (Scotland)	Prestwick
1885	Bob Martin (Scotland)	St Andrews
1886	David Brown (Scotland)	Musselburgh
1887	Willie Park, Jr (Scotland)	Prestwick
1888	Jack Burns (Scotland)	St Andrews
1889	Willie Park, Jr (Scotland)	Musselburgh
1890	John Ball, Jr (A) (England)	Prestwick
1891	Hugh Kirkaldy (Scotland)	Hoylake
1892	Harold Hilton (A) (England)	Muirfield
1893	Willie Auchterlonie (Scotland)	Prestwick
1894	J H Taylor (England)	Sandwich
1895	J H Taylor (England)	St Andrews
1896	Harry Vardon (England)	Muirfield
1897	Harold Hilton (A) (England)	Hoylake
1898	Harry Vardon (England)	Prestwick

Golfing royals

There have been six royal captains of the R&A at St Andrews: The Prince of Wales (later King Edward VII) in 1863; Prince Leopold in 1876; The Prince of Wales (later King Edward VIII) in 1922 (he was also captain of Royal St George's, Sandwich); The Duke of York (later King George VI) in 1930; The Duke of Kent in 1937; and Prince Andrew (who has a handicap in single figures) in 2003. As part of his inauguration, the captain has to make a ceremonial drive off the first tee of the Old Course. Further back in time, Mary Queen of Scots is also recorded as having played golf at St Andrews.

A licence to putt

Creator of James Bond, Ian Fleming was a keen golfer and member at Royal St George's, Sandwich, and set a scene from *Goldfinger* there (the course was renamed Royal St Mark's). Other small changes included the name of the pro (Albert Whiting became Alfred Blacking) and the name of the landmark sand dune (the Maiden mutated to the Virgin).

	Champion	Venue
1899	Harry Vardon (England)	Sandwich
1900	J H Taylor (England)	St Andrews
1901	James Braid (Scotland)	Muirfield
1902	Sandy Herd (Scotland)	Hoylake
1903	Harry Vardon (England)	Prestwick
1904	Jack White (Scotland)	Sandwich
1905	James Braid (Scotland)	St Andrews
1906	James Braid (Scotland)	Muirfield
1907	Arnaud Massy (France)	Hoylake
1908	James Braid (Scotland)	Prestwick
1909	J H Taylor (England)	Deal
1910	James Braid (Scotland)	St Andrews
1911	Harry Vardon (England)	Sandwich
1912	Ted Ray (England)	Muirfield
1913	J H Taylor (England)	Hoylake
1914	Harry Vardon (England)	Prestwick
1915-19	*Not held*	
1920	George Duncan (Scotland)	Deal
1921	Jock Hutchison (USA)	St Andrews
1922	Walter Hagen (USA)	Sandwich
1923	Arthur Havers (England)	Troon
1924	Walter Hagen (USA)	Hoylake
1925	Jim Barnes (England)	Prestwick
1926	Bobby Jones (A) (USA)	Royal Lytham & St Annes
1927	Bobby Jones (A) (USA)	St Andrews
1928	Walter Hagen (USA)	Sandwich
1929	Walter Hagen (USA)	Muirfield
1930	Bobby Jones (A) (USA)	Hoylake
1931	Tommy Armour (USA)	Carnoustie
1932	Gene Sarazen (USA)	Prince's, Sandwich
1933	Denny Shute (USA)	St Andrews
1934	Henry Cotton (England)	Sandwich
1935	Alf Perry (England)	Muirfield
1936	Alf Padgham (England)	Hoylake
1937	Henry Cotton (England)	Carnoustie
1938	Reg Whitcombe (England)	Sandwich
1939	Dick Burton (England)	St Andrews
1940-5	*Not held*	
1946	Sam Snead (USA)	St Andrews
1947	Fred Daly (Northern Ireland)	Hoylake
1948	Henry Cotton (England)	Muirfield
1949	Bobby Locke (South Africa)	Sandwich
1950	Bobby Locke (South Africa)	Troon
1951	Max Faulkner (England)	Royal Portrush
1952	Bobby Locke (South Africa)	Royal Lytham & St Annes
1953	Ben Hogan (USA)	Carnoustie
1954	Peter Thomson (Australia)	Birkdale
1955	Peter Thomson (Australia)	St Andrews
1956	Peter Thomson (Australia)	Hoylake

The duel in the sun

The 1977 British Open, held at Turnberry, became a head-to-head clash between two of the greatest modern golfers, Jack Nicklaus and Tom Watson, played out in a blisteringly hot summer. The 18th hole has recently been renamed 'The Duel in The Sun' in recognition of this classic Open battle.

	Champion	Venue
1957	Bobby Locke (South Africa)	St Andrews
1958	Peter Thomson (Australia)	Royal Lytham & St Annes
1959	Gary Player (South Africa)	Muirfield
1960	Kel Nagle (Australia)	St Andrews
1961	Arnold Palmer (USA)	Birkdale
1962	Arnold Palmer (USA)	Troon
1963	Bob Charles (New Zealand)	Royal Lytham & St Annes
1964	Tony Lema (USA)	St Andrews
1965	Peter Thomson (Australia)	Royal Birkdale
1966	Jack Nicklaus (USA)	Muirfield
1967	Roberto de Vicenzo (Argentina)	Hoylake
1968	Gary Player (South Africa)	Carnoustie
1969	Tony Jacklin (England)	Royal Lytham & St Annes
1970	Jack Nicklaus (USA)	St Andrews
1971	Lee Trevino (USA)	Royal Birkdale
1972	Lee Trevino (USA)	Muirfield
1973	Tom Weiskopf (USA)	Royal Troon
1974	Gary Player (South Africa)	Royal Lytham & St Annes
1975	Tom Watson (USA)	Carnoustie
1976	Johnny Miller (USA)	Royal Birkdale
1977	Tom Watson (USA)	Turnberry
1978	Jack Nicklaus (USA)	St Andrews
1979	Seve Ballesteros (Spain)	Royal Lytham & St Annes
1980	Tom Watson (USA)	Muirfield
1981	Bill Rogers (USA)	Sandwich
1982	Tom Watson (USA)	Royal Troon
1983	Tom Watson (USA)	Royal Birkdale
1984	Seve Ballesteros (Spain)	St Andrews
1985	Sandy Lyle (Scotland)	Sandwich
1986	Greg Norman (Australia)	Turnberry
1987	Nick Faldo (England)	Muirfield
1988	Seve Ballesteros (Spain)	Royal Lytham & St Annes
1989	Mark Calcavecchia (USA)	Royal Troon
1990	Nick Faldo (England)	St Andrews
1991	Ian Baker-Finch (Australia)	Royal Birkdale
1992	Nick Faldo (England)	Muirfield
1993	Greg Norman (Australia)	Sandwich
1994	Nick Price (Zimbabwe)	Turnberry
1995	John Daly (USA)	St Andrews
1996	Tom Lehman (USA)	Royal Lytham & St Annes
1997	Justin Leonard (USA)	Royal Troon
1998	Mark O'Meara (USA)	Royal Birkdale
1999	Paul Lawrie (Scotland)	Carnoustie
2000	Tiger Woods (USA)	St Andrews
2001	David Duval (USA)	Royal Lytham & St Annes
2002	Ernie Els (South Africa)	Muirfield
2003	Ben Curtis (USA)	Sandwich
2004	Todd Hamilton (USA)	Royal Troon
2005		St Andrews

	Champion	Venue
2006		Hoylake
2007		Carnoustie

Messing about in the river

When Frenchman Jean Van de Velde came to the par-four 72nd hole of the 1999 British Open at Carnoustie, he just needed a bogey to win the championship. After a wild drive and wilder second, his third shot finished in the Barry Burn that runs along the front of the green. He took his socks and shoes off and climbed in, before common sense took hold and he opted to take a drop. His two-over par six meant a three-way play-off that was won by Paul Lawrie. In the 1938 US Open, however, Ray Ainsley did play from a river. He was in contention until he hit his ball into the fast-moving stream bordering the par-four 16th hole. Ainsley repeatedly tried to chip the ball out of the water as it drifted downstream. He eventually succeeded but ended up with a 19 for the hole (a record).

US Open

Began in 1895 as a sideshow to the national amateur championship. The 1895-97 US Opens were played over 36 holes in one day; in 1898 the format changed to 72 holes over two days; and only in 1965 to the current 72 holes over four days. The latter change was prompted by Ken Venturi nearly expiring of heatstroke during the final 36 holes of his win the previous year.

(A) = amateur
* = non-homebred American

	Champion	Venue
1895	Horace Rawlins (England)*	Newport (RI)
1896	James Foulis (Scotland)*	Shinnecock Hills (NY)
1897	Joe Lloyd (England)*	Chicago Golf Club (IL)
1898	Fred Herd (Scotland)*	Myopia Hunt Club (MA)
1899	Willie Smith (Scotland)*	Baltimore (MD)
1900	Harry Vardon (England)	Chicago Golf Club (IL)
1901	Willie Anderson (Scotland)*	Myopia Hunt Club (MA)
1902	Laurie Auchterlonie (Scotland)*	Garden City (NJ)
1903	Willie Anderson (Scotland)*	Baltusrol (NJ)
1904	Willie Anderson (Scotland)*	Glen View (IL)
1905	Willie Anderson (Scotland)*	Myopia Hunt Club (MA)
1906	Alex Smith (Scotland)*	Onwentsia (IL)
1907	Alex Ross (Scotland)*	Philadelphia Cricket Club (PA)
1908	Fred McLeod (Scotland)*	Myopia Hunt Club (MA)
1909	George Sargent (England)*	Englewood (NJ)
1910	Alex Smith (Scotland)*	Philadelphia Cricket Club (PA)
1911	John McDermott (USA)	Chicago Golf Club (IL)
1912	John McDermott (USA)	Buffalo (NY)
1913	Francis Ouimet (A) (USA)	Brookline (MA)
1914	Walter Hagen (USA)	Midlothian Country Club (IL)
1915	Jerome Travers (A) (USA)	Baltusrol (NJ)
1916	Chick Evans (A) (USA)	Minikahda (MN)

	Champion	Venue
1917-18	*Not held*	
1919	Walter Hagen (USA)	Brae Burn Country Club (MA)
1920	Ted Ray (England)	Inverness (OH)
1921	Jim Barnes (England)	Columbia Country Club (MD)
1922	Gene Sarazen (USA)	Skokie (IL)
1923	Bobby Jones (A) (USA)	Inwood Country Club (NY)
1924	Cyril Walker (England)*	Oakland Hills (MI)
1925	Willie MacFarlane (Scotland)*	Worcester Country Club (MA)
1926	Bobby Jones (A) (USA)	Scioto Country Club (OH)
1927	Tommy Armour (Scotland)*	Oakmont (PA)
1928	John Farrell (USA)	Olympic Field Golf Club (IL)
1929	Bobby Jones (A) (USA)	Winged Foot (NY)
1930	Bobby Jones (A) (USA)	Interlachen Country Club (MN)
1931	William Burke (USA)	Inverness (OH)
1932	Gene Sarazen (USA)	Fresh Meadow Country Club (NY)
1933	John Goodman (A) (USA)	North Shore Golf Club (IL)
1934	Olin Dutra (USA)	Merion Cricket Club (PA)
1935	Sam Parks, Jr (USA)	Oakmont (PA)
1936	Tony Manero (USA)	Baltusrol (NJ)
1937	Ralph Guldahl (USA)	Oakland Hills (MI)
1938	Ralph Guldahl (USA)	Cherry Hills (CO)
1939	Byron Nelson (USA)	Philadelphia Cricket Club (PA)
1940	Lawson Little (USA)	Canterbury (OH)
1941	Craig Wood (USA)	Colonial Golf Club (TX)
1942-5	*Not held*	
1946	Lloyd Mangrum (USA)	Canterbury (OH)
1947	Lew Worsham (USA)	St Louis Country Club (MO)
1948	Ben Hogan (USA)	Riviera Country Club (CA)
1949	Cary Middlecoff (USA)	Medinah (IL)
1950	Ben Hogan (USA)	Merion Cricket Club (PA)
1951	Ben Hogan (USA)	Oakland Hills (MI)
1952	Julius Boros (USA)	Northwood Club (TX)
1953	Ben Hogan (USA)	Oakmont (PA)
1954	Ed Furgol (USA)	Baltusrol (NJ)
1955	Jack Fleck (USA)	Olympic Club, San Francisco (CA)
1956	Cary Middlecoff (USA)	Oak Hill (NY)
1957	Dick Mayer (USA)	Inverness (OH)
1958	Tommy Bolt (USA)	Southern Hills (OK)
1959	Billy Casper (USA)	Winged Foot (NY)
1960	Arnold Palmer (USA)	Cherry Hills (CO)
1961	Gene Littler (USA)	Oakland Hills (MI)
1962	Jack Nicklaus (USA)	Oakmont (PA)
1963	Julius Boros (USA)	Brookline (MA)
1964	Ken Venturi (USA)	Congressional Country Club (MD)
1965	Gary Player (South Africa)	Bellerive (MI)
1966	Billy Casper (USA)	Olympic Club, San Francisco (CA)
1967	Jack Nicklaus (USA)	Baltusrol (NJ)
1968	Lee Trevino (USA)	Oak Hill (NY)
1969	Orville Moody (USA)	Champion Golf Club (TX)

	Champion	Venue
1970	Tony Jacklin (England)	Hazeltine National (MN)
1971	Lee Trevino (USA)	Merion (PA)
1972	Jack Nicklaus (USA)	Pebble Beach (CA)
1973	Johnny Miller (USA)	Oakmont (PA)
1974	Hale Irwin (USA)	Winged Foot (NY)
1975	Lou Graham (USA)	Medinah (IL)
1976	Jerry Pate (USA)	Atlanta Athletic Club (GA)
1977	Hubert Green (USA)	Southern Hills (OK)
1978	Andy North (USA)	Cherry Hills (CO)
1979	Hale Irwin (USA)	Inverness (OH)
1980	Jack Nicklaus (USA)	Baltusrol (NJ)
1981	David Graham (Australia)	Merion (PA)
1982	Tom Watson (USA)	Pebble Beach (CA)
1983	Larry Nelson (USA)	Oakmont (PA)
1984	Fuzzy Zoeller (USA)	Winged Foot (NY)
1985	Andy North (USA)	Oakland Hills (MI)
1986	Raymond Floyd (USA)	Shinnecock Hills (NY)
1987	Scott Simpson (USA)	Olympic Club, San Francisco (CA)
1988	Curtis Strange (USA)	Brookline (MA)
1989	Curtis Strange (USA)	Oak Hill (NY)
1990	Hale Irwin (USA)	Medinah (IL)
1991	Payne Stewart (USA)	Hazeltine National (MN)
1992	Tom Kite (USA)	Pebble Beach (CA)
1993	Lee Janzen (USA)	Baltusrol (NJ)
1994	Ernie Els (South Africa)	Oakmont (PA)
1995	Corey Pavin (USA)	Shinnecock Hills (NY)
1996	Steve Jones (USA)	Oakland Hills (MI)
1997	Ernie Els (South Africa)	Bethesda (MD)
1998	Lee Janzen (USA)	Olympic Club, San Francisco (CA)
1999	Payne Stewart (USA)	Pinehurst (NC)
2000	Tiger Woods (USA)	Pebble Beach (CA)
2001	Retief Goosen (South Africa)	Southern Hills (OK)
2002	Tiger Woods (USA)	Bethpage State Park (NY)
2003	Jim Furyk (USA)	Olympia Fields (IL)
2004	Retief Goosen (South Africa)	Shinnecock Hills (NY)
2005		Pinehurst (NC)
2006		Winged Foot (NY)

Golf architects

Golf course architecture is big business nowadays but the older courses still rank as the greatest. Two of the best-known architects were Scottish-born: Alistair Mackenzie, who designed Cypress Point and the Augusta National (with Bobby Jones), and Donald Ross (one-time professional at Royal Dornoch) whose huge portfolio includes US courses Inverness, Oakland Hills and Pinehurst no 2, which have all staged the US Open. Two well-respected modern architects are Americans Tom Fazio (responsible for Pelican Hill and Barton Creek) and Pete Dye (TPC Sawgrass, Crooked Stick, Whistling Straits). Many famous players have turned their hands successfully to design, notably Jack Nicklaus and Arnold Palmer in recent years. Further back, Old Tom Morris (Carnoustie, Muirfield) and James Braid (Gleneagles, Dalmahoy) stand out as two of the greats.

The Masters

Takes place at the Augusta National course in Georgia every April. As well as a large cheque and a trophy, the winner receives a green jacket that is presented to him by the winner from the previous year. The green jacket was introduced in 1937 for members and was presented to a Masters champion (Sam Snead) for the first time in 1949.

1934 Horton Smith (USA)
1935 Gene Sarazen (USA)
1936 Horton Smith (USA)
1937 Byron Nelson (USA)
1938 Henry Picard (USA)
1939 Ralph Guldahl (USA)
1940 Jimmy Demaret (USA)
1941 Craig Wood (USA)
1942 Byron Nelson (USA)
1943-5 *Not held*
1946 Herman Keiser (USA)
1947 Jimmy Demaret (USA)
1948 Claude Harmon (USA)
1949 Sam Snead (USA)
1950 Jimmy Demaret (USA)
1951 Ben Hogan (USA)
1952 Sam Snead (USA)
1953 Ben Hogan (USA)
1954 Sam Snead (USA)
1955 Cary Middlecoff (USA)
1956 Jack Burke, Jr (USA)
1957 Doug Ford (USA)
1958 Arnold Palmer (USA)
1959 Art Wall, Jr (USA)
1960 Arnold Palmer (USA)
1961 Gary Player (South Africa)
1962 Arnold Palmer (USA)
1963 Jack Nicklaus (USA)
1964 Arnold Palmer (USA)
1965 Jack Nicklaus (USA)
1966 Jack Nicklaus (USA)
1967 Gay Brewer, Jr (USA)
1968 Bob Goalby (USA)
1969 George Archer (USA)
1970 Billy Casper (USA)
1971 Charles Coody (USA)
1972 Jack Nicklaus (USA)
1973 Tommy Aaron (USA)
1974 Gary Player (South Africa)
1975 Jack Nicklaus (USA)
1976 Ray Floyd (USA)
1977 Tom Watson (USA)
1978 Gary Player (South Africa)

The War on the Shore

This was the name given by journalists to the Ryder Cup of 1991, played at Kiawah Island in South Carolina. The rivalry was particularly intense during the 14½–13½ US victory, not helped by the behaviour of some spectators who shouted out as European players played shots. The 1999 competition at Brookline, Massachusetts, was characterized by similar events and, most notoriously, the incident at the 17th green where US players and their wives ran on to the green after Justin Leonard holed his putt and before José María Olazábal had a chance to hit his, which could have kept him in the match.

Nice jumper

Golf fashion (symbolized by the Pringle jumper) does not have a good reputation. Some recent Ryder Cup outfits have stood out, in particular the garish US polo shirts in 1999, but perhaps even they are eclipsed by the ensembles favoured by the late Payne Stewart, who wore a variety of brightly coloured plus fours and caps, or Swede Jesper Parnevik, who has been known to sport baby-pink slacks. The wearing of plus-fours (so called because they were cut four inches below the knee) and long socks for golf was popularized by the great Harry Vardon who was tired of the heavy woollen trousers and tweed jacket that was the standard dress in his day.

1979	Fuzzy Zoeller (USA)
1980	Seve Ballesteros (Spain)
1981	Tom Watson (USA)
1982	Craig Stadler (USA)
1983	Seve Ballesteros (Spain)
1984	Ben Crenshaw (USA)
1985	Bernhard Langer (West Germany)
1986	Jack Nicklaus (USA)
1987	Larry Mize (USA)
1988	Sandy Lyle (Scotland)
1989	Nick Faldo (England)
1990	Nick Faldo (England)
1991	Ian Woosnam (Wales)
1992	Fred Couples (USA)
1993	Bernhard Langer (Germany)
1994	José María Olazábal (Spain)
1995	Ben Crenshaw (USA)
1996	Nick Faldo (England)
1997	Tiger Woods (USA)
1998	Mark O'Meara (USA)
1999	José María Olazábal (Spain)
2000	Vijay Singh (Fiji)
2001	Tiger Woods (USA)
2002	Tiger Woods (USA)
2003	Mike Weir (Canada)
2004	Phil Mickelson (USA)

Eat your greens

On the Tuesday before the Masters begins, a meal is served for all previous winners, known as the 'Champions' dinner'. It began in 1952 at the instigation of Ben Hogan. Each year the defending champion selects the menu and acts as host for the dinner. Recent interesting menus have included cheeseburgers, chicken sandwiches, French fries and milkshakes (Tiger Woods's choice in 1998); haggis (Sandy Lyle in 1989); fish flown in from his home town of Pedrena (Seve Ballesteros in 1981); Welsh lamb (Ian Woosnam in 1992); south-west barbecue (Ben Crenshaw in 1996); and fish and chips (Nick Faldo in 1997).

European Tour

The European Tour is something of a misnomer as it includes tournaments played in such exotic locations as Thailand, South Africa, Malaysia, Qatar, Dubai, Hong Kong and Singapore.

US PGA Championship

A matchplay event until 1958.
* = non-homebred American

	Champion	**Venue**
1916	Jim Barnes (England)	Siwanoy Country Club (NY)
1917-18	*Not held*	
1919	Jim Barnes (England)	Engineers Country Club (NY)
1920	Jock Hutchinson (Scotland)*	Flossmoor Country Club (IL)
1921	Walter Hagen (USA)	Inwood Country Club (NY)
1922	Gene Sarazen (USA)	Oakmont (PA)
1923	Gene Sarazen (USA)	Pelham Golf Club (NY)
1924	Walter Hagen (USA)	French Lick Springs Golf Club (IN)
1925	Walter Hagen (USA)	Olympia Fields Country Club (IL)
1926	Walter Hagen (USA)	Salisbury Golf Links (NY)
1927	Walter Hagen (USA)	Cedar Crest Country Club (TX)
1928	Leo Diegel (USA)	Five Farms Country Club (MD)
1929	Leo Diegel (USA)	Hillcrest Country Club (CA)
1930	Tommy Armour (Scotland)*	Fresh Meadows Country Club (NY)
1931	Tom Creavy (USA)	Wannamoisett Country Club (RI)
1932	Olin Dutra (USA)	Keller Golf Club (MN)

	Champion	Venue
1933	Gene Sarazen (USA)	Blue Mound Country Club (WI)
1934	Paul Runyan (USA)	Blue Mound Country Club (WI)
1935	Johnny Revolta (USA)	Twin Hills Country Club (OK)
1936	Denny Shute (USA)	Hershey Country Club (PA)
1937	Denny Shute (USA)	Pittsburgh Field Club (PA)
1938	Paul Runyan (USA)	Shawnee Country Club (PA)
1939	Henry Picard (USA)	Pomonok Country Club (NY)
1940	Byron Nelson (USA)	Hershey Country Club (PA)
1941	Victor Ghezzi (USA)	Cherry Hills (CO)
1942	Sam Snead (USA)	Seaview Country Club (NJ)
1943	*Not held*	
1944	Bob Hamilton (USA)	Manito (WA)
1945	Byron Nelson (USA)	Moraine Country Club (OH)
1946	Ben Hogan (USA)	Portland (OR)
1947	Jim Ferrier (Australia)	Plum Hollow Country Club (MI)
1948	Ben Hogan (USA)	Norwood Hills Country Club (MO)
1949	Sam Snead (USA)	Hermitage Country Club (VA)
1950	Chandler Harper (USA)	Scioto Country Club (OH)
1951	Sam Snead (USA)	Oakmont (PA)
1952	James Turnesa (USA)	Big Spring Country Club (KY)
1953	Walter Berkerno (USA)	Birmingham Country Club (MI)
1954	Melvin Harbert (USA)	Keller Golf Club (MN)
1955	Doug Ford (USA)	Meadowbrook Country Club (MI)
1956	Jack Burke, Jr (USA)	Blue Hill (MA)
1957	Lionel Herbert (USA)	Miami Valley (OH)
1958	Dow Finsterwald (USA)	Llanerch Country Club (PA)
1959	Bob Rosburg (USA)	Minneapolis Golf Club (MN)
1960	Jay Herbert (USA)	Firestone Country Club (OH)
1961	Jerry Barber (USA)	Olympia Fields Country Club (IL)
1962	Gary Player (South Africa)	Aronimink (PA)
1963	Jack Nicklaus (USA)	Dallas Athletic Club (TX)
1964	Bob Nichols (USA)	Columbus Country Club (OH)
1965	Dave Marr (USA)	Laurel Valley (PA)
1966	Al Geiberger (USA)	Firestone Country Club (OH)
1967	Don January (USA)	Columbine Country Club (CO)
1968	Julius Boros (USA)	Pecan Valley Country Club (TX)
1969	Ray Floyd (USA)	NCR Country Club (OH)
1970	Dave Stockton (USA)	Southern Hills (OK)
1971	Jack Nicklaus (USA)	PGA National Golf Club (FL)
1972	Gary Player (South Africa)	Oakland Hills (MI)
1973	Jack Nicklaus (USA)	Canterbury (OH)
1974	Lee Trevino (USA)	Tanglewood (NC)
1975	Jack Nicklaus (USA)	Firestone Country Club (OH)
1976	Dave Stockton (USA)	Congressional Country Club (MD)
1977	Lanny Wadkins (USA)	Pebble Beach (CA)
1978	John Mahaffey (USA)	Oakmont (PA)
1979	David Graham (Australia)	Oakland Hills (MI)
1980	Jack Nicklaus (USA)	Oak Hill (NY)
1981	Larry Nelson (USA)	Atlanta Athletic Club (GA)

	Champion	Venue
1982	Raymond Floyd (USA)	Southern Hills (OK)
1983	Hal Sutton (USA)	Riviera Country Club (CA)
1984	Lee Trevino (USA)	Shoal Creek (AL)
1985	Hubert Green (USA)	Cherry Hills (CO)
1986	Bob Tway (USA)	Inverness (OH)
1987	Larry Nelson (USA)	PGA National Golf Club (FL)
1988	Jeff Sluman (USA)	Oak Tree (OK)
1989	Payne Stewart (USA)	Kemper Lakes (IL)
1990	Wayne Grady (Australia)	Shoal Creek (AL)
1991	John Daly (USA)	Crooked Stick (IN)
1992	Nick Price (Zimbabwe)	Bellerive (MI)
1993	Paul Azinger (USA)	Inverness (OH)
1994	Nick Price (Zimbabwe)	Southern Hills (OK)
1995	Steve Elkington (Australia)	Riviera Country Club (CA)
1996	Mark Brooks (USA)	Valhalla (KY)
1997	Davis Love III (USA)	Winged Foot (NY)
1998	Vijay Singh (Fiji)	Sahalee (WA)
1999	Tiger Woods (USA)	Medinah (IL)
2000	Tiger Woods (USA)	Valhalla (KY)
2001	David Toms (USA)	Atlanta Athletic Club (GA)
2002	Rich Beem (USA)	Hazeltine (MN)
2003	Shaun Micheel (USA)	Oak Hill (NY)
2004	Vijay Singh (Fiji)	Whistling Straits (WI)
2005		Baltusrol (NJ)
2006		Medinah (IL)

Grand Slammers

Only five players have achieved the golfing grand slam (winning each of the four Majors): Gene Sarazen (USA), Ben Hogan (USA), Gary Player (South Africa), Jack Nicklaus (USA) and Tiger Woods (USA).

World Matchplay Championship

Played at Wentworth Golf Club in Surrey, England, since its inception. Sponsored by Piccadilly (1964-76), Colgate (1977-8), Suntory (1979-90), Toyota (1991-7), Cisco (1998-2002) and now HSBC (from 2003). Now the second most valuable prize in world golf (after the Nedbank Challenge in Sun City, South Africa), players compete for a trophy that bears the name of the event founder Mark McCormack.

	Champion	Defeated finalist
1964	Arnold Palmer (USA)	Neil Coles (England)
1965	Gary Player (South Africa)	Peter Thomson (Australia)
1966	Gary Player (South Africa)	Jack Nicklaus (USA)
1967	Arnold Palmer (USA)	Peter Thomson (Australia)
1968	Gary Player (South Africa)	Bob Charles (New Zealand)
1969	Bob Charles (New Zealand)	Gene Littler (USA)
1970	Jack Nicklaus (USA)	Lee Trevino (USA)

	Champion	Defeated finalist
1971	Gary Player (South Africa)	Jack Nicklaus (USA)
1972	Tom Weiskopf (USA)	Lee Trevino (USA)
1973	Gary Player (South Africa)	Graham Marsh (Australia)
1974	Hale Irwin (USA)	Gary Player (South Africa)
1975	Hale Irwin (USA)	Al Geiberger (USA)
1976	David Graham (Australia)	Hale Irwin (USA)
1977	Graham Marsh (Australia)	Ray Floyd (USA)
1978	Isao Aoki (Japan)	Simon Owen (New Zealand)
1979	Bill Rogers (USA)	Isao Aoki (Japan)
1980	Greg Norman (Australia)	Sandy Lyle (Scotland)
1981	Seve Ballesteros (Spain)	Ben Crenshaw (USA)
1982	Seve Ballesteros (Spain)	Sandy Lyle (Scotland)
1983	Greg Norman (Australia)	Nick Faldo (England)
1984	Seve Ballesteros (Spain)	Bernhard Langer (Germany)
1985	Seve Ballesteros (Spain)	Bernhard Langer (Germany)
1986	Greg Norman (Australia)	Sandy Lyle (Scotland)
1987	Ian Woosnam (Wales)	Sandy Lyle (Scotland)
1988	Sandy Lyle (Scotland)	Nick Faldo (England)
1989	Nick Faldo (England)	Ian Woosnam (Wales)
1990	Ian Woosnam (Wales)	Mark McNulty (Zimbabwe)
1991	Seve Ballesteros (Spain)	Nick Price (Zimbabwe)
1992	Nick Faldo (England)	Jeff Sluman (USA)
1993	Corey Pavin (USA)	Nick Faldo (England)
1994	Ernie Els (South Africa)	Colin Montgomerie (Scotland)
1995	Ernie Els (South Africa)	Steve Elkington (Australia)
1996	Ernie Els (South Africa)	Vijay Singh (Fiji)
1997	Vijay Singh (Fiji)	Ernie Els (South Africa)
1998	Mark O'Meara (USA)	Tiger Woods (USA)
1999	Colin Montgomerie (Scotland)	Mark O'Meara (USA)
2000	Lee Westwood (England)	Colin Montgomerie (Scotland)
2001	Ian Woosnam (Wales)	Padraig Harrington (Ireland)
2002	Ernie Els (South Africa)	Sergio Garcia (Spain)
2003	Ernie Els (South Africa)	Thomas Bjorn (Denmark)
2004	Ernie Els (South Africa)	Lee Westwood (England)

Count your clubs

The rules of golf state that you can only carry 14 clubs in your bag. At the 2001 British Open at Royal Lytham & St Annes, Ian Woosnam was in contention starting the final round and scored a birdie two at the first hole. On the way to the second hole, his caddie Miles Byrne noticed that he had put an extra club in the bag. The mistake cost Woosnam a two-shot penalty, significant as he only finished four shots behind the winner David Duval. 'I give you one job to do and this is what happens', said Woosnam to Byrne. Byrne was sacked after making another mistake at a later tournament.

Ryder Cup

The leading international team tournament for male professional golfers. First held in 1927, it takes place every two years between teams from the USA and Europe (Great Britain 1927–71; Great Britain and Ireland 1973–7). The 2001 tournament was postponed because of the attacks on the World Trade Center.

	Winner	Score	Venue	GB/Europe captain	US captain
1927	USA	9½–2½	Worcester (MA)	Ted Ray	Walter Hagen
1929	GB	7–5	Moortown (England)	George Duncan	Walter Hagen
1931	USA	9–3	Scioto (OH)	Charles Whitcombe	Walter Hagen
1933	GB	6½–5½	Southport (England)	J H Taylor	Walter Hagen
1935	USA	9–3	Ridgewood (NJ)	Charles Whitcombe	Walter Hagen
1937	USA	8–4	Southport (England)	Charles Whitcombe	Walter Hagen
1939-45	*Not held*				
1947	USA	11–1	Portland (OR)	Henry Cotton	Ben Hogan
1949	USA	7–5	Ganton (England)	Charles Whitcombe	Ben Hogan
1951	USA	9½–2½	Pinehurst (NC)	Arthur Lacey	Sam Snead
1953	USA	6½–5½	Wentworth (England)	Henry Cotton	Lloyd Mangrum
1955	USA	8–4	Palm Springs (CA)	Dai Rees	Chick Harbert
1957	GB	7½–4½	Lindrick (England)	Dai Rees	Jack Burke, Jr
1959	USA	8½–3½	Palm Desert (CA)	Dai Rees	Sam Snead
1961	USA	14½–9½	Royal Lytham & St Annes (England)	Dai Rees	Jerry Barber
1963	USA	23–9	East Lake (GA)	John Fallon	Arnold Palmer
1965	USA	19½–12½	Royal Birkdale (England)	Harry Weetman	Byron Nelson
1967	USA	23½–8½	Champions Golf Club (TX)	Dai Rees	Ben Hogan
1969	Drawn	16-16	Royal Birkdale (England)	Eric Brown	Sam Snead
1971	USA	18½–13½	Old Warson (MO)	Eric Brown	Jay Hebert
1973	USA	19–13	Muirfield (Scotland)	Bernard Hunt	Jack Burke, Jr
1975	USA	21–11	Laurel Valley (PA)	Bernard Hunt	Arnold Palmer
1977	USA	12½–7½	Royal Lytham & St Annes (England)	Brian Huggett	Dow Finsterwald
1979	USA	17–11	The Greenbrier (WV)	John Jacobs	Billy Casper
1981	USA	18½–9½	Walton Heath (England)	John Jacobs	Dave Marr
1983	USA	14½–13½	Palm Beach (FL)	Tony Jacklin	Jack Nicklaus
1985	Europe	16½–11½	The Belfry (England)	Tony Jacklin	Lee Trevino
1987	Europe	15–13	Muirfield Village (OH)	Tony Jacklin	Jack Nicklaus
1989	Drawn	14–14	The Belfry (England)	Tony Jacklin	Ray Floyd
1991	USA	14½–13½	Kiawah Island (SC)	Bernard Gallacher	Dave Stockton
1993	USA	15–13	The Belfry (England)	Bernard Gallacher	Tom Watson
1995	Europe	14½–13½	Oak Hill (NY)	Bernard Gallacher	Lanny Wadkins
1997	Europe	14½–13½	Valderrama (Spain)	Seve Ballesteros	Tom Kite
1999	USA	14½–13½	Brookline (MA)	Mark James	Ben Crenshaw
2002	Europe	15½–12½	The Belfry (England)	Sam Torrance	Curtis Strange
2004	Europe	18½–9½	Oakland Hills (MI)	Bernhard Langer	Hal Sutton
2006			Kildare (Ireland)		Tom Lehman

	Winner	Score	Venue	GB/Europe captain	US captain
2008			Valhalla (KY)		
2010			Celtic Manor (Wales)		
2012			Medinah (IL)		
2014			Gleneagles (Scotland)		

PUT 3

Three putting, ie taking three putts to get the ball in the hole rather than the regulation two, is a cardinal sin for a golfer. English golfer and now renowned commentator Peter Alliss was an inveterate sufferer and so chose the number plate PUT 3 for his Rolls-Royce.

Solheim Cup

The women's equivalent of the Ryder Cup. The competition was founded in 1990 by Karsten Solheim, owner of Karsten Manufacturing Corporation (KMC).

	Winner	Score	Venue	Europe captain	US captain
1990	USA	11½–4½	Lake Nona (FL)	Mickey Walker	Kathy Whitworth
1992	Europe	11½–6½	Dalmahoy (Scotland)	Mickey Walker	Kathy Whitworth
1994	USA	13–7	Greenbrier (WV)	Mickey Walker	JoAnne Carner
1996	USA	17–11	St Pierre (Wales)	Mickey Walker	Judy Rankin
1998	USA	12–6	Muirfield Village (OH)	Pia Nilsson	Judy Rankin
2000	Europe	14½–11½	Loch Lomond (Scotland)	Dale Reid	Pat Bradley
2002	USA	15½–12½	Interlachen (MN)	Dale Reid	Patty Sheehan
2003	Europe	17½–10½	Barsebäck (Sweden)	Catrin Nilsmark	Patty Sheehan
2005			Crooked Stick (IN)	Catrin Nilsmark	Nancy Lopez

Walker Cup

The amateur equivalent of the Ryder Cup (although a Great Britain and Ireland still compete, instead of a European team), the competition is named after George Herbert Walker, the president of the United States Golf Association in 1920. The trophy was initially known as the International Trophy.

	Winner	Score	Venue
1922	USA	8–4	Long Island (NY)
1923	USA	6½–5½	St Andrews (Scotland)
1924	USA	9–3	Garden City (NY)
1926	USA	6½–5½	St Andrews (Scotland)
1928	USA	11–1	Chicago (IL)
1930	USA	10–2	Sandwich (England)
1932	USA	9½–2½	Brookline (MA)
1934	USA	9½–2½	St Andrews (Scotland)
1936	USA	10½–1½	Pine Valley (NJ)
1938	GB & I	7½–4½	St Andrews (Scotland)
1940-6	*Not held*		
1947	USA	8–4	St Andrews (Scotland)

Mucho formaggio

The winner of the Italian Open, in addition to a sizable cheque, receives his weight in Grana Padano, a cheese similar to parmesan.

	Winner	Score	Venue
1949	USA	10–2	Winged Foot (NY)
1951	USA	7½–4½	Royal Birkdale (England)
1953	USA	9–3	Kittansett (MA)
1955	USA	10–2	St Andrews (Scotland)
1957	USA	8½–3½	Minikahda (MN)
1959	USA	9–3	Muirfield (Scotland)
1961	USA	11–1	Seattle (WA)
1963	USA	12–8	Turnberry (Scotland)
1965	Drawn	11–11	Baltimore (MD)
1967	USA	13–7	Sandwich (England)
1969	USA	10–8	Milwaukee (WI)
1971	GB & I	13–11	St Andrews (Scotland)
1973	USA	14–10	Brookline (MA)
1975	USA	15½–8½	St Andrews (Scotland)
1977	USA	16–8	Shinnecock Hills (NY)
1979	USA	15½–8½	Muirfield (Scotland)
1981	USA	15–9	Pebble Beach (CA)
1983	USA	13½–10½	Hoylake (England)
1985	USA	13–11	Pine Valley (NJ)
1987	USA	16½–7½	Sunningdale (England)
1989	GB & I	12½–11½	Peachtree (GA)
1991	USA	14–10	Portmarnock (Ireland)
1993	USA	19–5	Interlachen Country Club (MN)
1995	GB & I	14–10	Royal Porthcawl (Wales)
1997	USA	18–6	Quaker Ridge (NY)
1999	GB & I	15–9	Nairn (Scotland)
2001	GB & I	15–9	Ocean Forest (GA)
2003	GB & I	12½–11½	Ganton (England)
2005			Chicago (IL)
2007			Royal County Down (Ireland)

Big John's big day

When John Daly (nickname 'Wild Thing') won the 1991 US PGA tournament and shot to stardom as a big-hitting, big-waisted and big-drinking golfer, he was only ninth reserve to play but a series of withdrawals saw him make a last-minute dash from his home in Arkansas to the Crooked Stick course where he shot a first-round 69 without even having time for a practice round.

Curtis Cup

The women's equivalent of the Walker Cup, the Curtis Cup was first played for in 1932, for a trophy donated by the Misses Harriot and Margaret Curtis from Boston. Harriot Curtis won the USGA Women's Amateur Championship in 1906 and Margaret was champion in 1907, 1911 and 1912.

	Winner	Score	Venue
1932	USA	5½–3½	Wentworth (England)
1934	USA	6½–2½	Chevy Chase (MD)
1936	Drawn	4½–4½	Gleneagles (Scotland)
1938	USA	5½–3½	Essex (MA)
1940-6	*Not held*		
1948	USA	6½–2½	Birkdale (England)
1950	USA	7½–1½	Buffalo (NY)
1952	GB & I	5–4	Muirfield (Scotland)
1954	USA	6–3	Merion (PA)

Sub-60

Americans Al Geiberger (1977), Chip Beck (1991), David Duval (1999) and Phil Mickelson (2004) are the only men to have shot 59 in a PGA Tour event. Geiberger was nicknamed 'Mr 59' afterwards. Swede Annika Sorenstam achieved the feat on the LPGA Tour in 2001.

	Winner	Score	Venue
1956	GB & I	5–4	Prince's, Sandwich (England)
1958	Drawn	4½–4½	Brae Burn (MA)
1960	USA	6½–2½	Lindrick (England)
1962	USA	8–1	Broadmoor (CO)
1964	USA	10½–7½	Royal Porthcawl (Wales)
1966	USA	13–5	Cascades (VA)
1968	USA	10½–7½	Royal County Down (N Ireland)
1970	USA	11½–6½	Brae Burn (MA)
1972	USA	10–8	Western Gailes (Scotland)
1974	USA	13–5	San Francisco (CA)
1976	USA	11½–6½	Royal Lytham & St Annes (England)
1978	USA	12–6	Apawamis (NY)
1980	USA	13–5	St Pierre (Wales)
1982	USA	14½–3½	Denver (CO)
1984	USA	9½–8½	Muirfield (Scotland)
1986	GB & I	13–5	Prairie Dunes (KS)
1988	GB & I	11–7	Sandwich (England)
1990	USA	14–4	Somerset Hills (NJ)
1992	GB & I	10-8	Hoylake (England)
1994	Drawn	9-9	The Honors Course (TN)
1996	GB & I	11½-6½	Killarney (Ireland)
1998	USA	10-8	Minikahda (MN)
2000	USA	10-8	Ganton (England)
2002	USA	11-7	Fox Chapel (PA)
2004	USA	10-8	Formby (England)
2006			Bandon Dunes (OR)
2008			St Andrews (Scotland)

Not a thing of beauty

US Open champion Jim Furyk has a very distinctive swing. David Feherty, from Northern Ireland, a former Ryder Cup golfer and now a pundit for American TV, has described it as looking like both 'an octopus falling out of a tree' and a 'one-armed man using a club to kill a snake in a phone booth'.

A-Z

address a player's **stance** in preparation for striking the ball

air shot a stroke that fails to connect with the ball

albatross a score of three under **par** on a hole

Amen Corner the 11th, 12th and 13th holes at the Augusta National course, home of The Masters; the name was coined in 1958 by journalist Herbert Warren Wind writing in *Sports Illustrated* to describe the part of the course at which the crucial action had taken place

approach (shot) a stroke when a player puts or attempts to put the ball onto the green

apron the part of the **fairway** just in front of the **green**

attend the flag to hold the flag whilst another player putts, removing it after the ball has been struck

away the player who is away is the player furthest from the hole

back nine the last nine holes on a course

backswing the movement when the hands and arms take the club away from the ball

baffy an old-fashioned club similar to a modern 3-wood

balata a resilient sap-like substance from the Balata tree used to cover balls, softer than other coverings and said to give greater feel but prone to cuts

belly putter a type of putter with a slightly longer than normal shaft; the top of the shaft is lodged in the player's midriff during the shot

bestball 1. a match in which one player plays against two or three players, the lowest score of the team being counted 2. sometimes used to mean the same as **fourball**

betterball a **strokeplay** or **matchplay fourball** game in which the lower score of each team is counted on each hole

birdie a score of one under **par** on a hole

blades clubs that do not have a **cavity back**

blaster same as **sand wedge**

bogey a score of one over **par** on a hole

borrow the allowance to be made for a slope on a **green**

bounce the projection at the bottom of the back of a **wedge**

brassie an old-fashioned name for a 2-wood, so called because it had a brass **sole**

break same as **borrow**

broomhandle putter a type of putter with a much longer than normal shaft; the top of the shaft is held in one hand, at chest height, and the other hand, which is the only one that moves during the stroke, holds the club at waist height

bump and run an **approach shot** played so that the ball runs a long distance after landing

bunker a hazard consisting of a sand-filled hollow

caddie someone who assists a golfer during a round, by carrying the clubs and advising on choice of club

card if a player cards a score, he or she returns that score on the scorecard, eg *he carded a level-par 72 to finish third*

carry the distance which a player has to hit the ball in the air over an obstacle (water, rough etc), eg *there's a carry of 180 yards over the lake*

casual water pools of water caused by rain or flooding etc; a ball in casual water can be dropped without penalty

cavity back a design of the **clubhead** with a depression on the back; this feature creates a bigger **sweet spot** and hence makes it easier to hit good shots

Challenge Tour lower-ranking part of the European Tour

chip a shot, usually from close to the green, giving the ball a low trajectory so that it runs forward on landing

chip-in when a player puts the ball in the hole directly from a **chip** shot

club face the striking surface of the club

clubhead the part of the club that strikes the ball

compression a measure of the resilience of a ball and hence how hard it feels when hit; ratings are usually between 80 and 100

course management if a player demonstrates good course management, he or she adapts his/her game to the demands of the particular course

cross-handed grip a style of putting grip where the right hand is below the left (for a right-handed player)

Crow's Nest an upper part of the clubhouse at the Augusta National course, where amateurs can stay during the Masters

cup the plastic or metal casing that lines a hole

cut 1. a shot in which the ball intentionally moves from left to right in the air (for a right-handed player) 2. the reduction of the field in a tournament after a set number of rounds (usually two), only those players with the better scores qualifying to play in the final round(s)

dimple small depression on a golf ball; golf ball manufacturers now produce balls with different sizes, shapes and arrangements of dimples

divot a small piece of turf dug up by the head of a club during a stroke

dog leg a hole with a **fairway** that bends

dormie if a player is dormie in a **matchplay** game, he or she is ahead by as many holes as there are still to play, eg *he was dormie 5*. The word may come from the Latin verb meaning to sleep as the player who is dormie cannot lose even by going to sleep

downswing the part of the swing where the club is moving down towards the ball

drain a putt same as **sink a putt**

draw if a player draws the ball, he or she hits it in such a way that, as intended, it moves from right to left in the air (if right-handed) or from left to right (if left-handed). A more extreme form of such movement produced unintentionally is a **hook**

drive a **tee shot** using a **driver**

driver a golf club with a metal or wooden head used to hit the ball a long way, usually from the **tee**

driving iron an **iron** that has an enlarged head and is used for **tee shots** when greater accuracy is required

drop when the ball is repositioned from an **unplayable** position by letting it fall from one's outstretched arm

duck hook a badly mishit shot that veers sharply and low to the left (for a right-handed player) as soon as it is hit

eagle a score of two under **par** on a hole

Eisenhower Tree a pine tree situated 195yd from the championship tee on the 17th hole at the Augusta National course; named after the former US president who hit his ball into it so many times that he campaigned (in vain) to have it cut down

explosion shot a stroke that sends the ball in a high trajectory out of a **bunker** by striking the sand behind the ball with a strong swing of the club

fade if a player fades the ball, he or she hits it in such a way that, as intended, it moves from left to right in the air (if right-handed) or from right to left (if left-handed). A more extreme form of such movement produced unintentionally is a **slice**

fairway the smooth turf between the **tee** and **green**, distinguished from the uncut **rough** and from **hazards**

fairway wood a wood other than a **driver** that is used for hitting shots from the **fairway**

fat if a player hits the ball fat, he or she mishits it, striking the ground before the ball, so that it does not travel very far

featherie an old-fashioned golf ball made from animal feathers, the predecessor of the **gutty**

first cut the area of rough closest to the **fairway**; the grass here will usually only be slightly longer than the fairway

flag, flagstick marks the position of the hole; 'flagstick' is more commonly used in US English

flier a mishit ball that travels further than intended

flop shot a short **pitch** shot with a very high trajectory

fore a warning cry to anybody in the way of the ball

fore caddie a caddie who formerly was posted up ahead so as to see where the balls went

fourball a match played between two pairs of players, in which only the lower score of each pair for each hole is counted

foursome a match played between two pairs of players, in which each pair plays only one ball, players taking alternate strokes

free drop a ruling allowing one to lift a golf ball from its resting place and drop it elsewhere without penalty

fringe the area bordering the **green**, where the grass is slightly longer

front nine the first nine holes on a course

gallery the spectators at a golf tournament

get down to manage to get the ball in the hole, eg *he got down in six*

gimme a short putt that one's opponent is sportingly excused from playing, there being little likelihood of missing it

grand slam the winning of all four major championships

green the area around a hole where the grass has been cut very short for putting

green in regulation if a player reaches the green in regulation, he or she takes two strokes fewer than par (two putts being assumed to be standard); this statistic is widely used in gauging performance

greensomes a type of **fourball** match in which all players drive and then each pair selects the ball with which they want to complete the hole

ground under repair any part of the course being repaired, often indicated by a sign with the letters GUR; a ball that lands in such an area must be removed (without penalty)

gutta-percha a strong waterproof substance, like rubber but harder and not extensible, used to make early golf balls

gutty an old-fashioned type of golf ball made from **gutta-percha**

handicap the number of strokes by which a golfer's average score exceeds **par** for the course, this number being subtracted from one's score in **strokeplay** competitions

hanging lie when the ball is resting on a slope

Haskell the rubber-cored ball that succeeded the **gutty** at the beginning of the 20th century, invented by American dentist Coburn Haskell

hazard a **bunker** or water obstacle

heel the lower part of the **clubhead**, nearest the player

Hell Bunker the biggest bunker on the Old Course at St Andrews, at the 14th hole; over 10ft deep, it is positioned across the fairway on this par-five and has caught many misjudged second shots

high side if a player misses a putt on the high side, it means that he or she has allowed too much **borrow**

hole out to successfully put the ball into the hole

honour if a player has the honour, he or she has the right to tee off first as the last player to win a hole

hood the clubhead to decrease the **loft** on the club by pressing the hands forward; this will make the ball fly at a lower trajectory than normal

hook if a player hooks the ball, he or she mishits it so that it inadvertently moves in the air from right to left (for a right-handed player), or from left to right (for a left-handed player); compare **slice**

hosel the socket for the shaft in the **clubhead**

iron a club with a thin metal head

jigger formerly, an iron with a narrow blade and moderate **loft**, equivalent to the modern 4-iron

lag a putt to play a putt with the intention of getting the ball near the hole but not necessarily in it

lateral water hazard a river, pond or ditch that runs parallel to the hole

lay up if a player lays up, he or she plays a shot deliberately short of a **hazard** or **green**

leaderboard the scoreboard that lists the names and scores of the current leaders in a competition

lie the position from which the ball has to be played

links sometimes used to describe any golf course, but properly one on low-lying ground by the sea

lob wedge a club with the greatest degree of **loft**, for playing **pitches** and **flop shots**

loft the degree of angle at which a **clubhead** is set

long iron an iron club (numbers 1 to 4) used to play long-range shots

low side if a player misses a putt on the low side, it means that he or she has not allowed enough **borrow**

the Maiden an enormous sand dune to the left of the par-3 6th green at Royal St George's, Sandwich

Major any one of the four most important golf competitions: The Open, the US Open, the US PGA and the Masters

mashie an old-fashioned club used for shots of medium length and **loft**, corresponding to a modern 5-iron

mashie-niblick an old-fashioned club between a **mashie** and a **niblick**, corresponding to a modern 7-iron

matchplay scoring according to holes won and lost rather than the overall total of strokes taken; compare **strokeplay**

medalplay same as **strokeplay**

midiron 1. an iron club (numbers 5 to 7) used to play medium-range shots 2. formerly, a long-shafted iron equivalent to the modern 2-iron

mulligan in friendly games, a free extra shot sometimes allowed to a player when he or she has played a bad shot

Nassau a type of informal game consisting of a given bet for the **front nine**, a given bet for the **back nine** and a total bet for the overall game

niblick an old-fashioned club for lofted shots, corresponding to a modern 8- or 9-iron

out of bounds (OB) if a ball goes into the area of the course designated as out of bounds (usually by white posts), the player must play again, incurring a stroke and distance penalty

overclub to use a club with too little **loft**, thus hitting the ball too far

overlapping grip the most common form of grip, in which the little finger of the right hand overlaps the index finger of the left hand (for a right-handed player)

overshoot if a player overshoots the green, he or she hits the ball beyond it

par the number of strokes that should be taken for a hole or a round by good play, two putts being allowed on each green

perimeter weighting modern irons often have extra metal around the edge of the **clubhead**, making the club more forgiving

pin — the rod of a golf flag, and more commonly, the flag itself

pin high — if an **approach shot** or **chip** finishes pin high, the ball is adjacent to the flag

pin position — the position of the flag on the green. In competitions, this will be changed from round to round

pitch — 1. a shot where the ball flies in a high arc and does not roll much on landing 2. when a ball pitches, it hits the ground, eg *the ball pitched next to the hole and rolled a few feet past*

pitch and run — a **pitch** shot played so that the ball runs on after landing

pitching wedge — a club with a lot of **loft** for playing **pitch** shots

pitch mark — a small depression left by the ball when it lands on the green; golf etiquette dictates that they should always be repaired

plug — If a ball plugs, it becomes embedded in wet ground or sand

preferred lies — if preferred lies are allowed on a course (eg during the winter), players are able to move their ball on the **fairway**

provisional — if a player thinks that he might not be able to find a ball or that it might be out of bounds, he or she can opt to take a provisional shot, the ball used then being played if the first ball is indeed lost or **out of bounds**

pull — if a player pulls a shot, he or she hits the ball too much to the left for a right-handed player, or to the right for a left-handed player; compare **push**

punch — a shot played so that the ball has a lower than normal trajectory, an effect created by placing the ball further back in one's **stance**

push — if a player pushes a shot, he or she hits the ball too much to the right for a right-handed player, or to the left for a left-handed player; compare **pull**

putt — to hit the ball with a **putter** so that it rolls along the ground and towards, ideally into, the hole

putt out — to complete a hole by putting the ball into the hole

putter — a usually short-handled club with an upright striking-face, used in putting. Modern varieties include the **belly putter** and the **broomhandle putter**

qualifying school — also known as Q school, a six-round competition held in November for players seeking one of 35 places available via this route on the European Tour

R&A — the Royal and Ancient Golf Club of St Andrews

Rae's Creek — the stream that runs in front of the 12th green and behind the 11th green at the Augusta National course

relief — the option of moving one's ball because a player is obstructed from making a normal stroke at it, eg if it is next to a staked tree

Road Hole — the par-four 17th hole on the Old Course, St Andrews, so called because of the road that runs behind the green. Famed as one of the hardest holes in golf

rough — rough ground, especially uncut grass, around a **fairway** or **green**

sand save — getting the ball in the hole from a **bunker** with a **wedge** shot and a single putt

sand trap — same as **bunker**; an especially American term

sand wedge — a club with a high degree of **loft** that is specially designed to hit the ball out of **bunkers**

scratch — a scratch golfer, or one who 'plays off scratch' is one who has a **handicap** of zero

shaft	the stick joined to the **clubhead**; modern shafts are made from steel or graphite and can have different stiffnesses; older shafts were made from hickory
shank	when a player hits the ball by mistake close to the heel of the club so that it makes contact with the **hosel**, causing the ball to fly to the right (for a right-handed player)
short game	play on and around the **green**
short iron	an iron club used to play shots from close to the green; an 8- or 9-iron and all **wedges**
sink a putt	to successfully get a putt in the hole
skins	a type of **matchplay** game in which each hole is worth a given amount of points or money
skull	same as **thin**
slice	if a player slices the ball, he or she mishits it so that it inadvertently moves in the air from left to right (for a right-handed player), or from right to left (for a left-handed player); compare **hook**
socket	the part of the **clubhead** that houses the shaft of a club
sole	the undersurface of a **clubhead**
spoon	an old-fashioned wooden-headed club with the face slightly hollowed, commonly used to refer to a 3-wood
Stableford	a competition in which points are awarded for scores achieved on each hole, the player's **handicap** and the **stroke index** being used to help calculate the points; named after Frank Stableford (1870–1959), an English doctor who devised it
stance	the standing position of a player at **address**
stimpmeter	a device that measures the speed of a green by rolling a golf ball down a ramp at a standard initial velocity and measuring how far it travels; named after its US inventor Edward Stimpson (died 1985)
stone dead	if a ball is stone dead, it is so close to the hole as to make a putt a mere formality
stroke index (SI)	a measure of the relative difficulty of the holes on a course, the holes being numbered 1 to 18, with 1 the hardest
strokeplay	scoring by counting the total number of strokes played rather than the number of holes won; compare **matchplay**
stymie	if a player is stymied, he or she does not have a direct route to the flag; previously referred to the situation on the green where an opponent's ball blocked the way to the hole, before the rules were changed (in 1951) to allow the obstructing ball to be lifted and its position marked
sweet spot	the spot on the **club face** where, for best effect and control, the ball should ideally make contact
swing	the way in which the club is moved back from the ball and then brought down and through to strike it
tap-in	a very short, light putt required to put the ball into the hole
tee	1. a small plastic or wooden support for the ball, with a concave top, used when it is first played at each hole 2. the strip of ground where this is done
tee box	a box containing sand for filling **divots** made on the **tee**
tee marker	a coloured marker on the ground indicating the forward limit of the **tee**
tee off	to start play with a shot from the **tee**
tee shot	the first stroke at a hole

Texas scramble — an informal game in which all of the players hit each shot from the same place, the best ball determining the location of the next shot

thin — if a player thins a shot, he or she hits the ball with the leading edge of the **club face**, causing it to fly further than intended with a low trajectory

toe — the part of the **clubhead** furthest from the player

top — if a player tops a shot, he or she hits the ball on the upper part, so that it only travels a short distance along the ground

trap — short for **sand trap**

turn — the halfway point on an 18-hole course, at which the players turn to begin the return nine holes, eg *she was two up at the turn*

two-ball putter — a modern type of putter with a large head featuring two white golf ball-sized discs; these help the player to align the putt

twosome — a game between two players

underclub — to use a club with too much **loft**, thus not hitting the ball far enough

unplayable — a ball is unplayable if it is in a position where the player cannot hit it; it can then be dropped no nearer the hole with one penalty stroke

up-and-down — getting the ball in the hole from close to the green with a **pitch** or **chip** shot and a single putt

Valley of Sin — a hollow in front of the 18th green on the Old Course at St Andrews, where an underhit **approach shot** will end up

Vardon grip — same as **overlapping grip**; so called because it was invented by Harry Vardon

wedge — any iron-headed club (**pitching wedge**, **sand wedge** or **lob wedge**) with a broad low-angled face and a high degree of **loft**

whipping — waxed thread that used to be wound around the **hosel** of wooden-headed woods

wood — a club with a bulky head, traditionally made of wood though now usually of metal, used for hitting the ball long distances

yips — nervous twitching caused by tension when putting

Some golfing slang

ace — a hole in one

back door — if a putt goes in by the back door, it falls into the hole by slowly dropping in from one side

bail out — if you bail out, you play safe by eg playing short of a green which has **bunkers** guarding it

bandit — an amateur player who has a higher **handicap** than his or her skill merits, thus giving him/her an advantage in competitions

cabbage — deep, thick **rough**

dance floor — the green; so called because it is flat and smooth

fried egg — when a ball lands in soft sand in a **bunker** and sits in a circular hollow

hacker — a poor amateur player

heavy artillery — the **driver**, eg *I'd better get the heavy artillery out for this tee shot*

jungle — tall rough, bushes or trees

legs — if a shot, usually a putt, has legs, it will run for a long distance

lip out — to hit the rim of the hole and not fall in

member's bounce — a favourable bounce that takes the ball on to the **fairway** or green; so called because it always seems to be the member rather than a visitor who benefits

never up, never in	a comment made by or to a frustrated putter when he or she has hit a putt too softly
nineteenth hole	the clubhouse
out of the screws	if a player hits a shot out of the screws, it is hit perfectly in the **sweet spot**
professional's side	the **high side**, so called because if a putt is missed on this side, the player has not underestimated the **break** (a common error by amateurs)
rabbit	a poor amateur player
reload	if a player reloads, he or she takes a second **tee shot** because the first may be lost or **out of bounds**
sclaff	a badly hit shot that does not travel very far
short stuff	the **fairway**, eg *that's not a good drive but at least it's on the short stuff*
spinach	same as **cabbage**
stiff	same as **stone dead**
Texas wedge	a putter, when it is used from off the green; so called because the ground is hard and dry in Texas and such shots are thus common there
tiger country	same as **jungle**
tiger line	the most direct, and hence risky, line for a **drive** or **approach shot**
watery grave	the fate of a shot hit into water
whiff	same as **air shot**
worker	a shot, especially a putt, that runs a long way, closer to the hole

Greenland golf

Every year golfers converge from all over the world to compete in the World Ice Golf Championships, held in Uummannaq, Greenland, in March. The green is the 'white', the ball is fluorescent pink or orange, the temperatures drop to –50°C/–58°F and the obstacles are icebergs and polar bears. The shape of the course, which is created anew each year, is dictated by the position of icebergs in the frozen fjord in which the Championships take place; however, the course changes constantly as the pack ice drifts and new icy outcrops are thrown up.

Some famous golfers

Seve(riano) Ballesteros, 1957–

Born in Pedrena, Spain, he was a highly combative, adventurous player, continually setting records and with an exceptional short game. When he won The Open in 1979 he was the youngest player in the 20th century to do so, and he took the title again in 1984 and 1988. He was the youngest player ever to win The Masters in 1980 (a record usurped by Tiger Woods in 1997). Although no longer successful as a player, in 1997 he captained the European team that won the Ryder Cup in Valderrama. Run-ins with officials have marred the latter part of his career.

James Braid, 1870–1950

Born in Earlsferry, Scotland, he trained as a joiner and went to work in St Andrews, where he became an impressive player. In 1893 he became a professional golfer. He won The Open five times between 1901 and 1910 (when he became the first player to break 300 for 72 holes at St Andrews), four News of the World matchplay championships between 1903 and 1911, and the French Championship in 1910. With **Harry Vardon** and **J H Taylor** he formed the so-called 'Great Triumvirate' of British golf in the Edwardian era.

Bob Charles, 1936–

Born in Carterton, New Zealand, he won the New Zealand Open championship in 1954 but did not turn professional until 1960. In 1963 he won five US Tour events and that same year also became the only left-handed player to triumph in The Open. He was awarded an OBE in 1972 and a CBE in 1982.

Sir Henry Cotton, 1907–87

Born at Holmes Chapel, Cheshire, England, in the 1930s and 1940s he almost single-handedly fought off the US challenge in The Open, winning in 1934, 1937 and 1948. He won many other titles, and played in the Ryder Cup against the USA four times between 1929 and 1953. He received his knighthood just a few days before he died.

Laura Davies, 1963–

Born in Coventry, Warwickshire, England, she turned professional in 1985. By 1994 she was ranked number one in the world and had achieved the distinction (unique in both the men's and women's game) of winning on five different tours. Her most significant victories include the British Women's Open (1986) and the US Women's Open (1987). She was awarded the MBE in 1987.

Ernie Els, 1969–

Born in Johannesburg, South Africa, he became junior World Champion at the age of 14 and established his reputation in 1992 by winning a hat-trick of the South African Open, PGA and Masters titles. In 1994 he became only the fourth foreign-born player since 1927 to win the US Open, a feat he repeated in 1997. 'The Big Easy''s other achievements have included a record six victories in the World Matchplay championship (1994–6, 2002–4) and victory in The Open in 2002.

Nick Faldo, 1957–

Born in Welwyn Garden City, Hertfordshire, England, he has six victories in Majors to his name: The Open (1987, 1990, 1996) and The Masters (1989, 1990, 1996), as well as two World Matchplay championships (1989, 1992). His greatest victory was perhaps the 1996 Masters when he overcame a six-stroke deficit to beat Greg Norman by five shots. Two partnerships have been important to him: with his long-term Swedish caddy Fanny Sunesson, and with coach David Leadbetter who rebuilt his swing in the early 1980s. He still holds the record as the leading points scorer in Ryder Cup history with 25 points. He was awarded the MBE in 1987.

Walter Hagen, 1892–1969

Born in Rochester, New York, USA, he was the first US-born winner of The Open, which he won four times (1922, 1924, 1928–9). He also won the US Open twice (1914, 1919), the US PGA championship five times (1921, 1924–7), a record since equalled by **Jack Nicklaus**, and captained the first six US Ryder Cup teams (1927–37). Nicknamed 'the Haig', he was a charismatic showman with a flamboyant dress sense and was the first sportsman to be given a tickertape parade down Broadway.

Ben Hogan, 1912–97

Born in Dublin, Texas, USA, in 1948 he became the first man in 26 years to win all three US Major titles. Despite a bad car accident in 1949 when he crashed head-on into a Greyhound bus and was told he might never walk again, he returned to win three of the four Majors in 1953 (US Open, The Masters and The Open). He won the US Open four times (1948, 1950–1, 1953) before retiring in 1970.

Tony Jacklin, 1944–

Born in Scunthorpe, Humberside, England, he became in 1969 the first Briton since 1951 to win The Open. Within eleven months he became the first Briton since **Harry Vardon** to have held the British and US Open titles in the same twelve months. His US Open victory by seven strokes was the biggest winning margin since that of Jim Barnes in 1921. In 1985 he captained the European team to its first Ryder Cup victory in 28 years, and in 1987 the team had its first victory on US soil. He was awarded the OBE in 1970 and was inducted into the World Golf Hall of Fame in 2002.

Bobby Jones, 1902–71

Born in Atlanta, Georgia, USA, he studied law and remained an amateur throughout his career. He won the US Open four times (1923, 1926, 1929, 1930), The Open three times (1926, 1927, 1930), the US Amateur championship five times and the British Amateur championship once. In 1930 he achieved the staggering feat of winning the Grand Slam of the US and British Open and Amateur championships in the same year. He retired at 28, regarded as one of the greatest golfers in the history of the game. He was responsible for the founding of The Masters in Augusta.

Bernhard Langer, 1957–

Born in Anhausen, Germany, he turned professional at the age of 15, won The Masters twice and by 2001 had amassed 39 victories on the European Tour. Regarded as the professional's professional, he recorded 68 tournaments without missing a cut, and in 2001 was selected for his tenth Ryder Cup team. He was widely praised for the dignity with which he reacted to missing a short putt on the last green at Kiawah Island in the 1991 Ryder Cup that would have drawn the match for Europe. He was captain of the victorious European 2004 Ryder Cup team.

Nancy Lopez, 1957–

Born in Torrance, California, USA, she won the last of her 48 LPGA victories in 1997 and retired in 2002. She was selected by the Associated Press as Female Athlete of the Year (1978, 1985), and she has been the LPGA Player of the Year four times – in 1978, 1979, 1985 and 1988. She was captain of the 2005 US Solheim Cup team.

Sandy Lyle, 1958–

Born in Shrewsbury, Shropshire, England, of Scottish parents, his major championship successes have been the European Open in 1979, the French Open in 1981, The Open in 1985 and The Masters in 1988. A straight hitter with an admirably phlegmatic temperament, with **Nick Faldo** he was largely responsible for the revival of British professional golf at world level. He was awarded the MBE in 1987.

Colin Montgomerie, 1963-

Born in Glasgow, Scotland, he grew up within sight of the first tee at Troon and turned professional in 1988. Although European Order of Merit winner from 1993 to 1999 inclusive and with numerous tournament wins, including three successive Volvo PGA Championships (1998–2000), he is yet to capture a Major (despite twice being runner-up in the US Open in 1994 and 1997). He has played in seven consecutive Ryder Cup teams since 1991, and has made a major contribution to European success (he has never lost a singles match). He was awarded the MBE in 1998 and the OBE in 2005.

Old Tom Morris, 1821-1908

Born in St Andrews, Scotland, he served an apprenticeship as a golfball-maker there. He went to Prestwick as a greenkeeper in 1851, returning to St Andrews as a professional in 1861. He won The Open four times (1861, 1862, 1864, 1867). His son, **Young Tom Morris**, became champion after him. He designed many courses, including Prestwick, Machrihanish and the New Course at St Andrews.

Young Tom Morris, 1851-75

Precociously brilliant, he won The Open three times in succession (1868–70), thereby winning the championship belt outright; there was no contest in 1871, but he won it again in 1872. He is the youngest ever winner at 17. His early death on Christmas Day 1875 was said to have been caused by grief at the loss of his young wife a few months earlier. He was the son of **Old Tom Morris**.

Jack Nicklaus, 1940-

Born in Columbus, Ohio, USA, his first professional victory was the US Open (1962), a tournament he won a further three times (1967, 1972, 1980). Of the other Majors, he won The Masters a record six times (1963, 1965–66, 1972, 1975, 1986); The Open championship three times (1966, 1970, 1978); and the US PGA a record-equalling five times (1963, 1971, 1973, 1975, 1980). His total of 20 Major victories (including his two US Amateurs) is also a record and he is arguably the greatest golfer in history. Nicknamed 'The Golden Bear', he is now a respected course designer.

Greg Norman, 1955-

Born in Mount Isa, Queensland, Australia, he started playing golf when he was 15 years old, and turned professional in 1976. Nicknamed the 'Great White Shark' because of his blond hair, he has won two Major titles – the 1986 and 1993 British Opens – and three World Matchplay championships (1980, 1983 and 1986) but has acquired the reputation of being the eternal runner-up. The only player of modern times to have competed in a Grand Slam of playoffs, unfortunately he lost them all.

Arnold Palmer, 1929-

Born in Youngstown, Pennsylvania, USA, he was one of the postwar golfing stars whose powerful, attacking golf introduced the game to millions throughout the world. He turned professional in 1955 after a brilliant amateur career, won the US Open in 1960 and the Masters in 1958, 1960, 1962 and 1964. One of the most popular golfers of all time, he was followed around the world by 'Arnie's Army', as his fans became known. His back-to-back British Open victories (1961–2) inspired his fellow Americans to travel and compete on British courses.

Gary Player, 1936–

He was born in Johannesburg, South Africa. Small and slightly built, he nonetheless won three British Opens (1959, 1968, 1974), The Masters three times (1961, 1974, 1978), the US Open once (1965), and the US PGA title twice (1962, 1972) in a prolific career. His trademark black clothes made him an instantly recognizable character. He also won the South African Open 13 times, and the Australian Open seven times. Since retiring he has been extremely successful on the seniors tour.

Gene Sarazen, 1902–99

Born in Harrison, New York, USA, he took up golf as a teenager on his doctor's recommendation to improve a lung condition. He won The Open (1932), the US Open (1922, 1932) and the US PGA Championship (1922, 1923, 1932), but it was his victory in the 1935 Masters (in only its second year), and his spectacular albatross at the 15th hole, which helped establish the event worldwide.

Sam Snead, 1912–2002

He was born in Ashwood, Virginia, USA. Of the Majors, he won The Open once (1946), The Masters three times (1949, 1952, 1954) and the US PGA championship three times (1942, 1949, 1951). He had 81 US Tour victories, the last of which came at the age of 52 years 10 months, making him the oldest winner on Tour.

Annika Sorenstam, 1970–

Born in Stockholm, Sweden, Sorenstam started playing golf at the age of twelve. A gifted amateur (she was World Amateur champion in 1992), she turned professional in 1994. She has achieved the women's grand slam of Majors with victories in the US Women's Open (1995, 1996), the British Women's Open (2003), the LPGA championship (2003) and the Nabisco championship (2001, 2002). She made history, and created controversy, in 2003 by becoming the first woman to compete in a men's PGA tour event (she missed the cut by four shots).

J(ohn) H(enry) Taylor, 1871–1963

Born in Northam, Devon, England, he won The Open five times (1894, 1895, 1900, 1909, 1913). He also won the French Open twice, and the German Open once. Along with **James Braid** and **Harry Vardon**, he formed the 'Great Triumvirate' of Edwardian golf. He was a founder and first president of the PGA (British Professional Golfers' Association).

Peter Thomson, 1929–

Born in Melbourne, Australia, he dominated The Open in the 1950s, winning it in 1954, 1955, 1956, 1958 and 1965 (becoming the only player to win the event three times in a row in modern times). He retired to concentrate upon golf architecture and writing but returned briefly to the senior game in 1984 and broke all the existing money-winning records before retiring once more.

Lee Trevino, 1939–

Born in Dallas, Texas, USA, he gained his nickname 'Supermex' from his Mexican origins. He won six Majors – the US Open twice (1968, 1971), The Open twice (1971,

1972) and the US PGA twice (1974, 1984) – and is the only man to have held the Open titles of America, Britain and Canada simultaneously. More than his victories, it was his ability to combine wisecracks with exciting and inventive golf that made him one of the game's most popular players.

Harry Vardon, 1870–1937

He was born in Grouville, Jersey, the Channel Islands, and began as a caddie. He won The Open six times, in 1896, 1898, 1899, 1903, 1911 and 1914, overcoming serious illness (TB) in mid-career. He also won the US Open in 1900. He turned professional in 1903, and is remembered for the fluency of his swing, his rigorous practice regime, and his overlapping grip which is still known as the 'Vardon grip'. Along with **James Braid** and **J H Taylor,** he formed the 'Great Triumvirate' of Edwardian golf. He was also the first golfer to wear plus fours.

Tom Watson, 1949–

He was born in Kansas City, Missouri, USA. Through the mid-1970s and early 1980s Watson, with **Jack Nicklaus**, dominated world golf, winning the US Open (1982), two Masters tournaments (1977, 1981) and five British Opens (1975, 1977, 1980, 1982, 1983). Four of the latter were on Scottish courses and he remains an extremely popular player in Britain.

Karrie Webb, 1974–

Born in Ayr, Queensland, Australia, she began playing golf aged eight and turned professional in 1994. She won the Women's British Open a year later and by the end of her first season had added another four Major tournament titles. She reclaimed the Women's British Open in 1997, among other titles, and was soon being described as women's golf's equivalent of **Tiger Woods.** In 2001 she became the youngest woman to complete a Grand Slam of all four of the modern-day Majors.

Tiger Woods, 1976–

Born in Cypress, California, USA, he was the first man to win both the US junior amateur and US amateur titles. The nickname 'Tiger' is a tribute to a Vietnam colleague of his father (his real name is Eldrick). He retained the amateur title for a record three years in a row, and his outstanding amateur career included a Walker Cup appearance in 1995. Having turned professional in August 1996, in 1997 he became the youngest, as well as the first black winner of The Masters. Since then he has won The Open (2000), the US Open (2000, 2002), the US PGA (1999, 2000) and The Masters (2001, 2002). When he won The Masters in 2001, he achieved the unique feat of holding all four Major titles at the same time. He has the superstition of always wearing a red shirt during the final round. His dominance of world golf was threatened in 2004 when his five-year reign as world number one came to an end.

Babe Zaharias, 1914–56

She was born Mildred Zaharias in Port Arthur, Texas, USA. A multi-talented sportswoman (she won two gold medals – for javelin and 80m sprint - at the 1932 Olympics in Los Angeles), she turned to golf in 1934, and won the US National Women's Amateur Championship in 1946 and the British Ladies' Amateur Championship in 1947. She went on to win the US Women's Open three times (1948, 1950, 1954).

GREYHOUND RACING

Origins

Greyhound racing has its origins in the sport of hare coursing. The first 'simulated coursing' event over a straight course took place in 1876 at Hendon, near London, but interest in the sport soon waned. However, the sport in its modern format of dogs racing around round or oval circuits after an artificial hare was pioneered by American Owen Smith in the early 20th century when he built a track near Salt Lake City. It was reintroduced into Britain in 1926 when the Belle Vue stadium in Manchester was opened and very soon tracks opened up all over the United Kingdom. The sport proved popular with working-class male audiences because of the urban venues, evening meetings, and on-course betting opportunities.

Rules and description

A racing sport in which a number of greyhounds, normally six, pursue a 'lure' in the form of an artificial hare, around a circular or oval track over distances of usually less than half a mile. The first dog to cross the finishing line is the winner. Gambling on the results of races is a key element of the sport.

Ruling bodies: World Greyhound Racing Federation; the National Greyhound Racing Club (NGRC) controls the sport in Great Britain

Evidently Barking

The owner of the winner (Entry Badge) of the first Greyhound Derby in 1927 was a butcher from Kent named Edwin Baxter. He also owned the second and third placed dogs (Ever Bright and Elder Brother), all given names with the same initials as him. Entry Badge was the first great greyhound champion, winning eleven out of its twelve races.

Greyhound Derby

British greyhound racing's premier event, run over 525yd/480m. Its venue between 1927 and 1984 was White City in London. It has been run at Wimbledon greyhound racing track since 1985.

1927	Entry Badge
1928	Boher Ash
1929	Mick The Miller
1930	Mick The Miller
1931	Seldom Led
1932	Wild Woolley
1933	Future Cutlet
1934	Davesland
1935	Greta Ranee
1936	Fine Jubilee
1937	Wattle Bark
1938	Lone Keel
1939	Highland Rum
1940	G R Archduke
1945	Ballyhennessy Seal
1946	Mondays News
1947	Trevs Perfection
1948	Priceless Border
1949	Narrogar Ann
1950	Ballymac Ball
1951	Ballylanigan Tanist
1952	Endless Gossip
1953	Daws Dancer
1954	Paul's Fun
1955	Rushton Mac
1956	Dunmore King
1957	Ford Spartan

1958	Pigalle Wonder	**1974**	Jimsun	**1990**	Slippy Blue
1959	Mile Bush Pride	**1975**	Tartan Khan	**1991**	Ballinderry Ash
1960	Duleek Dandy	**1976**	Mutts Silver	**1992**	Farloe Melody
1961	Palms Printer	**1977**	Ballinska Band	**1993**	Ringa Hustle
1962	The Grand Canal	**1978**	Lacca Champion	**1994**	Moral Standards
1963	Lucky Boy Boy	**1979**	Sarah's Bunny	**1995**	Moaning Lad
1964	Hack Up Chieftan	**1980**	Indian Joe	**1996**	Shanless Slippy
1965	Chittering Champ	**1981**	Parkdown Jet	**1997**	Some Picture
1966	Faithful Hope	**1982**	Lauries Panther	**1998**	Tom's The Best
1967	Tric Trac	**1983**	I'm Slippy	**1999**	Chart King
1968	Camira Flash	**1984**	Whisper Wishes	**2000**	Rapid Ranger
1969	Sand Star	**1985**	Pagan Swallow	**2001**	Rapid Ranger
1970	John's Silver	**1986**	Tico	**2002**	Allen Gift
1971	Dolores Rocket	**1987**	Signal Spark	**2003**	Droopys Hewitt
1972	Patricia's Hope	**1988**	Hit The Lid	**2004**	Droopys Scholes
1973	Patricia's Hope	**1989**	Lartigue Note		

Mick the Miller

Probably the most famous greyhound of all time, he was born in 1926 in Ireland, bred by a parish priest. In 1928 he won the first race in which he was entered, and went on to win 61 of his 81 starts, including the Derby in successive years (1929 and 1930), a feat only repeated twice since and which made him a hero in both Ireland and England. Throughout his career, he used guile as much as his speed to win races. He finished his racing career by winning the 1931 St Leger but had an active retirement making celebrity appearances and even appearing on-screen in the 1934 comedy-thriller *Wild Boy*, which also featured Bud Flanagan and Chesney Allen.

A-Z

blanket a cover worn by a greyhound during the **parade.** The blanket bears a colour and number corresponding to the dog's **post** position

card the list of races at a meeting

course the race's distance

dam the mother of a greyhound

dead heat an exact tie between two or more greyhounds in a race

draw the random process used to determine the greyhounds' starting positions

handicapper the official who grades greyhounds and decides weights to be carried in handicap events

head length of a dog's head; one of a number of terms used to indicate the distance between two dogs finishing a race

judge official responsible for determining the finishing order in a race

kennel business that owns and races greyhounds

lead-out a dog handler who parades the greyhounds in front of the public before a race and who retrieves the dogs after the race has finished

length length of a dog's body; one of a number of terms used to indicate the distance between two dogs finishing a race

lure — an object, resembling a hare, attached to a mechanical arm and electrically driven around the inside of the track ahead of the greyhounds. It is the object which the greyhounds chase during the race

maiden — a greyhound that has not won an official race

muzzle — plastic, leather, or wire device fitted over the greyhound's mouth to protect other greyhounds while racing and as an aid in a **photo finish**

nose — the smallest distance between two greyhounds finishing a race

paddock — the area on a track where the greyhounds are kept before the start of the race

parade — the showing of the dogs to the spectators before the start of the race

photo finish — the finish of a race in which the dogs are so close that a photograph is used to determine the winner and **places**

place — a position of second or third in a race. An each-way bet on a greyhound that finishes second or third in a race results in a return on the punter's stake but at odds usually a quarter of those at which the bet was placed

post — a greyhound's box or position number for the start. The number on a greyhound's back always corresponds to the number of his or her **starting box**

post weight — the greyhound's weight determined by officials before the dog enters the track

rail — the circular strip around which the mechanical **lure** moves

short head — distance between a **head** and a **nose**; one of a number of terms used to indicate the distance between two dogs finishing a race

sire — the father of a greyhound

starting boxes — the mechanical gates behind which the greyhounds are kept and which open simultaneously at the start of a race

tattoo — a number on the inside of a registered greyhound's ear used to identify the dog

trainer — a person responsible for training and preparing greyhounds for racing

traps — another name for **starting boxes**

wire — the finishing line in a race

GYMNASTICS

Origins

Gymnastics is an ancient pastime, evidence of which can be found on pottery and wall paintings from ancient Greece and Egypt. In ancient Greece there was a sport known as bull leaping in which the competitors would run towards a charging bull, grab hold of his horns and let the bull flip them into the air while performing twists and somersaults. Exercises such as rope climbing were part of the ancient Olympic Games. The first modern teacher of gymnastics was Friedrich Ludwig Jahn, who created a nationwide gymnastic society called the *Turnverein* in 1811 in Germany. He invented exercises to develop strength. Meanwhile, a Swedish gymnast called

Per Henrik Ling was developing exercises using hoops, clubs and balls that helped with coordination.

Rules and description

Gymnastics is an artistic sport but exponents also display great strength and flexibility. The term 'gymnastics' covers a variety of skills and events. The most recognizable branch of the sport is artistic gymnastics. This describes competition by men and women on various pieces of apparatus (see below). A sister form of the sport is rhythmic gymnastics.

At the Olympic Games trampolining has been part of the gymnastics programme since 2000. Likewise, aerobics, acrobatics and tumbling have the Fédération Internationale de Gymnastique as their ruling body.

Artistic gymnastics

Men's

In men's competition there are six events or pieces of 'apparatus' that are performed on. They are the 'horizontal bar' (also called the 'high bar'), the 'vault' (or 'longhorse vault'), the 'pommel horse', the 'rings', the 'parallel bars' and the 'floor' exercises. In major competitions there are also team events (usually composed of six members per team) and an all-around event, which combines the marks scored on the individual pieces of apparatus to give a total score.

Horizontal bar

The horizontal bar is made of steel, is 2.4m/7.9ft long and is suspended on a frame 2.57m/8.43ft above the ground. Originally, the bar was a wooden pole. Gymnasts are required to produce a rhythmic performance where swinging movements are delivered without a pause. Various elements such as turns, flights and 'giant' swings are included.

Vault

The vaulting horse is 1.35m/4.43ft high and is covered in leather. Male gymnasts vault along the length of the horse. A springboard is placed at one end and the gymnast runs and takes off from the board, placing both hands on the horse as he flies past. Each vault is marked according to various elements (flight, landing, and so on) and vaults are graded according to their difficulty (that is, the amount of twists and turns involved).

Pommel horse

The pommel horse stands 1.15m/3.77ft high and is 1.6m/5.25ft long. At the top of the stuffed leather body are two handrails or 'pommels'. Gymnasts need to perform a variety of swings, including 'leg circles', scissors, forward and backward splits and handstands. Gymnasts lose points if they lose momentum while performing or touch the horse with their legs.

Rings

A rings routine starts with the gymnast leaping up to catch a ring in each hand. He then executes a series of swings and handstands that show off upper-body strength. The two rings hang from wire cables 50cm/1.64ft apart and 2.75m/9ft above the floor. The whole apparatus is suspended from a 5.5m/18ft high frame.

Parallel bars

Parallel bars are 3.5m/11.48ft long and are arranged side by side, 1.95m/6.39ft from the ground. The routines are carried out both below and above the bars and include 'giant' swings, releasing and re-grasping movements and handstands.

Floor exercises

The men's floor exercises last from 50 to 70 seconds and are performed without music on a matted area that is $12m^2/39.37ft^2$. Gymnasts are expected to make use of all the space available but not to step off the mat. The floor exercises show artistic ingenuity and tumbling, acrobatics and handstand strength. The exercises contain both free and compulsory elements.

Women's

In women's competition there are four events. They are the 'vault' (or 'sidehorse vault'), the 'asymmetric' (or 'uneven') bars, the 'balance beam' and the 'floor' exercises. There are also team events and an all-round title.

Vault

Whereas the men's discipline sees gymnasts vaulting the horse along its length, women vault a 1.2m/3.94ft horse across its width. They are also marked on the distance they travel during flight. Vaults are graded according to difficulty.

Asymmetric bars

This event, also called the A-bars and the uneven bars to distinguish it from the men's parallel bar discipline, has gymnasts performing along and between two parallel bars, one 1.6m/5.25ft and the other 2.4m/7.87ft from the floor. Moves that feature on this piece of apparatus include pirouettes, handstands and swinging between the bars. Most spectacular are the routines where gymnasts release and fly before re-grasping either of the bars.

Balance beam

Another very skilled discipline is the balance beam. It is a suede-covered wooden beam that is 1.2m/3.94ft above the ground and measures 5m/16.4ft in length but only 10cm/3.93in in width. Each gymnast performs a routine on it (including a mount and dismount) that lasts 70 to 90 seconds and consists of a series of compulsory and optional elements, such as leaps, pirouettes, somersaults and handstands.

Floor exercises

Like the men, women perform a floor exercise. The routine is longer (at 70 to 90 seconds) and is accompanied by music. As in the men's routines, women gymnasts need to cover all the surface area of the mat. The floor exercises are the opportunity to be expressive and balletic, although tumbling routines are added for good measure.

Scoring and judging

Judges mark a gymnast's routine out of ten points and judge it according to difficulty as well as to how well executed it is. Until 1976 the best gymnasts scored marks ranging from around 9.0 to 9.9. However, at the Olympic Games of that year the Romanian gymnast Nadia Comaneci scored 10.0, the first 'perfect' score given in top-class competition.

Ruling body: Fédération Internationale de Gymnastique (FIG)

A nudity clause

The word 'gymnastics' comes from the ancient Greek 'gymnazein' and means 'to exercise naked'!

The man in the tight suit

Leotards are named after the French trapeze artist Jules Léotard, who wore a one-piece skin-tight garment when performing in the circus. Léotard is also credited with inventing the flying trapeze act. The music hall composer George Leybourne celebrated Léotard in verse with the tune, *The Flying Trapeze*:

He'd fly through the air with the greatest of ease,
That daring young man on the flying trapeze.
His movements were graceful, all girls he could please
And my love he purloined away.

Artistic Gymnastics World Championships

The first gymnastics World Championships were held in 1903 in Antwerp when only four countries competed. Women were first allowed to compete in 1934.

	Men's individual	**Team**
1903	Joseph Martinez (France)	France
1905	Marcel Lalu (France)	France

	Men's individual	**Team**
1907	Josef Cada (Czechoslovakia)	Czechoslovakia
1909	Marco Torrès (France)	France
1911	Ferdinand Steiner (Czechoslovakia)	Czechoslovakia
1913	Marco Torrès (France)	Czechoslovakia
1922	Peter Sumi (Yugoslavia)/ Frantisek Pechacek (Czechoslovakia)	Czechoslovakia
1926	Peter Sumi (Yugoslavia)	Czechoslovakia
1930	Josip Primozic (Yugoslavia)	Czechoslovakia
1934	Eugen Mack (Switzerland)	Switzerland
1938	Jan Gajdos (Czechoslovakia)	Czechoslovakia
1950	Walter Lehmann (Switzerland)	Switzerland
1954	Viktor Chukarin (USSR)	USSR
1958	Boris Shakhlin (USSR)	USSR
1962	Yuri Titov (USSR)	Japan
1966	Mikhail Voronin (USSR)	Japan
1970	Eizo Kenmotsu (Japan)	Japan
1974	Shigeru Kasamatsu (Japan)	Japan
1978	Nikolai Andrianov (USSR)	Japan
1979	Aleksandr Dityatin (USSR)	USSR
1981	Juri Korolev (USSR)	USSR
1983	Dimitri Bilozerchev (USSR)	China
1985	Yuri Korolev (USSR)	USSR
1987	Dimitri Bilozerchev (USSR)	USSR
1989	Igor Korobchinsky (USSR)	USSR
1991	Grigori Misyutin (USSR)	USSR
1993	Vitali Scherbo (Belarus)	*Not held*
1994	Ivan Ivankov (Belarus)	China
1995	Li Xiaoshuang (China)	China
1997	Ivan Ivankov (Belarus)	China
1999	Nikolai Krukov (Russia)	China
2001	Feng Jing (China)	Belarus
2003	Paul Hamm (USA)	China

	Women's individual	**Team**
1934	Vlasta Dekanová (Czechoslovakia)	Czechoslovakia
1938	Vlasta Dekanová (Czechoslovakia)	Czechoslovakia
1950	Helena Rakoczy (Poland)	Sweden
1954	Galina Roudiko (USSR)	USSR
1958	Larissa Latynina (USSR)	USSR
1962	Larissa Latynina (USSR)	USSR
1966	Vera Čáslavská (Czechoslovakia)	Czechoslovakia
1970	Lyudmila Tourischeva (USSR)	USSR
1974	Lyudmila Tourischeva (USSR)	USSR
1978	Yelena Mukhina (USSR)	USSR
1979	Nelli Kim (USSR)	Romania
1981	Olga Bicherova (USSR)	USSR
1983	Natalia Yurchenko (USSR)	USSR
1985	Oksana Omelianchik (USSR)/ Yelena Shushunova (USSR)	USSR

	Women's individual	Team
1987	Aurelia Dobre (Romania)	Romania
1989	Svetlana Boginskaya (USSR)	USSR
1991	Kim Zmeskal (USA)	USSR
1993	Shannon Miller (USA)	*Not held*
1994	Shannon Miller (USA)	Romania
1995	Lilia Podkopayeva (Ukraine)	Romania
1997	Svetlana Khorkina (Russia)	Romania
1999	Maria Olaru (Romania)	Romania
2001	Svetlana Khorkina (Russia)	Romania
2003	Svetlana Khorkina (Russia)	USA

Olympic Games

Gymnastics formed part of the programme of the first modern Olympic Games in 1896. Men took part in horizontal bar, parallel bars, vault, pommel horse and rings events, with German gymnasts dominating. The all-around competition was instituted at the 1900 Olympics, and the floor exercise made its first appearance as late as 1932. Women were first allowed to compete at the Olympics in 1928 in a team combined competition.

	Men's all-around	Women's all-around
1900	Gustave Sandras (France)	
1904	Julius Lenhart (Austria)	
1908	Alberto Braglia (Italy)	
1912	Alberto Braglia (Italy)	
1920	Giorgio Zampori (Italy)	
1924	Leon Štukelj (Yugoslavia)	
1928	Georges Miez (Switzerland)	
1932	Romeo Neri (Italy)	
1936	Alfred Schwarzmann (Germany)	
1948	Veikko Huhtanen (Finland)	
1952	Viktor Chukarin (USSR)	Maria Gorokhovskaya (USSR)
1956	Viktor Chukarin (USSR)	Larissa Latynina (USSR)
1960	Boris Shakhlin (USSR)	Larissa Latynina (USSR)
1964	Yukio Endo (Japan)	Vera Čáslavská (Czechoslovakia)
1968	Sawao Kato (Japan)	Vera Čáslavská (Czechoslovakia)
1972	Sawao Kato (Japan)	Lyudmila Tourischeva (USSR)
1976	Nikolai Andrianov (USSR)	Nadia Comăneci (Romania)
1980	Aleksandr Dityatin (USSR)	Yelena Davydova (USSR)
1984	Koji Gushiken (Japan)	Mary Lou Retton (USA)
1988	Vladimir Artemov (USSR)	Yelena Shushunova (USSR)
1992	Vitali Scherbo (Unified Team)	Tatiana Gutsu (Unified Team)
1996	Li Xiaoshuang (China)	Lilia Podkopayeva (Ukraine)
2000	Alexei Nemov (Russia)	Simona Amanar (Romania)
2004	Paul Hamm (USA)	Carly Patterson (USA)

Gymnastics

Team event

	Men	Women
1904	USA (Team Philadelphia)	
1908	Sweden	
1912	Italy	
1920	Italy	
1924	Italy	
1928	Switzerland	The Netherlands
1932	Italy	
1936	Germany	Germany
1948	Finland	Czechoslovakia
1952	USSR	USSR
1956	USSR	USSR
1960	Japan	USSR
1964	Japan	USSR
1968	Japan	USSR
1972	Japan	USSR
1976	Japan	USSR
1980	USSR	USSR
1984	USA	Romania
1988	USSR	USSR
1992	Unified Team	Unified Team
1996	Russia	USA
2000	China	Romania
2004	Japan	Romania

A-Z

aerial a manoeuvre where a gymnast completes a full rotation in the air without touching the **apparatus**

all-around a competition where the highest total score from all events is combined to give an all-around champion

apparatus the term applied to each piece of gymnastics equipment

back handspring a move in which the gymnast takes off from one or both feet, flips backwards onto his or her hands and then lands with both feet on the floor or **apparatus**

back-in, full-out a move comprised of a double **salto** with a full **twist** completed during the second salto

back walkover a move performed on the floor or beam in which the gymnast does a **bridge** and then brings each leg in succession forward, passing via a handstand position

bridge the position of the body with an arched back position

cartwheel a revolution through 360 degrees in which the hands touch the beam or floor one after the other and then the legs travel afterwards to complete the circle

compulsories routines that contain mandatory moves

cross on the rings, a move in which the gymnast holds his body at right angles to the floor and his arms stretched out at right angles to the body

Cuervo a vault that consists of a **handspring** off the springboard, and then a half-**twist** followed by a backward **salto** off the horse; named after the Cuban gymnast Jorge Cuervo who first performed it in 1973

dismount the move or end of a routine on leaving the piece of apparatus

double back a move with two consecutive back flips

double twist a single **layout** flip with two **twists**

element each move that makes up a routine

Endo on the high bar and asymmetric bars, a **Stalder** in a forward position; named after the Japanese gymnast Yukio Endo (1937–) who pioneered it

execution the technical ability with which a routine or element is performed

flair a move performed on the pommel horse or floor where the gymnast swings his open legs in front of or behind his arms, only the hands touching the horse or floor

flic-flac same as **back handspring**

flyaway on the high bar and asymmetric bars, when a gymnast swings down and releases, usually to do a back flip and land

front handspring a **handspring** that starts with a forward flip

front walkover a move in which the gymnast performs a **handstand** with legs split and then arches the back further to bring one foot down to the ground or beam, followed by the other foot

full-in, back-out a double **salto** with a full **twist** completed during the first salto

Gaylord on the high bar, a move that consists of a front **giant** and a one-and-a-half front **salto** over the bar, followed by the gymnast re-grabbing the bar; named after the US gymnast Mitch Gaylord (1961–), who first performed it in competition in 1981

giant a 360-degree swing around the high bar

Gienger on the high bar and asymmetric bars, a **flyaway** with a one-half **twist**, followed by a re-grasping of the bar. It is named after German gymnast Eberhard Gienger (1951–), who first performed it in competition in 1978

half-in, half-out a move that incorporates a double **salto** with a half **twist** on each salto

handspring a move in which the gymnast springs off the hands with a strong push from the shoulders

handstand a move in which the body is supported on both hands, with the arms straight and the body vertical

hip circle a move on the high bar or the asymmetric bars in which the gymnast performs a circle with the hips touching the bar. When the hips do not touch the bar, the move is called a **clear hip circle**

inverted cross a holding move performed on the rings in a **handstand** position, with the arms stretched out perpendicular to the body

Kovacs on the high bar and asymmetric bars, a flyaway with two back somersaults over the bar, followed by a re-grasping of the bar; named after Hungarian gymnast Peter Kovacs, who first performed it in competition in 1979

layout a position in which the body is fully extended lengthwise either straight or slightly arched

leg circle a move performed on the pommel horse where the gymnast keeps his legs together and swings them in complete circles around the horse. He lifts each hand in turn to allow the legs to pass

nail same as **stick**

pike a body position where the legs are kept straight but the torso is bent at the hips

pirouette a turn about the vertical axis. A gymnast can change direction by swivelling or stepping the foot in a 180-degree move; alternatively, a pirouette can be performed in a **handstand** position

rotation each of the periods during which groups or teams of gymnasts work on a specific piece of apparatus, eg *the next rotation for Myers is the vault*

round-off a movement that starts as a **cartwheel** but in which the gymnast lands on both feet simultaneously rather than one, facing the direction from which they have come

rudi a vault that consists of a **handspring** off the springboard, and then a forward **salto** with one-and-a half twists off the horse

salto an **aerial** flip or somersault in which the feet come up over the head and the body rotates around the waist. It does not use the hands

somersault same as **salto**

Stalder on the high bar and asymmetric bars, a 360-degree swing around the bar in a **straddle pike** position; named after the Swiss gymnast Josef Stalder who first performed it

stick if a gymnast sticks a landing, he or she lands perfectly, without any foot movement

straddle a position in which the legs are spread far apart to the side

Swedish fall in floor exercises, a move in which a gymnast does a free-fall drop straight onto the ground, with the hands shooting out to the floor at the last moment

tariff the degree of difficulty of a vault

tuck a position in which the body is folded at the waist, with the knees and hips bent and tucked up into the chest

Tsukahara a vault in which the gymnast does a half-twist before pushing off the horse backwards. It was invented by the Japanese gymnast Mitsuo Tsukahara (1947–)

twist a rotation of the body around the spine as the longitudinal axis

whip back a back **handspring** where the hands do not touch the floor

Yurchenko in the vault, a move consisting of a **roundoff** on to the springboard, then a **flic-flac** on to the vault, followed by a **back flip** dismount. It is named after the Soviet gymnast, Natalia Yurchenko (1965–), who first performed it in competition in 1982

Some famous gymnasts

Nikolai Andrianov, 1952–

Born in Vladimir, Russia, he was introduced to gymnastics aged twelve. He won 15 Olympic medals (seven gold) between 1972 and 1980. In addition, he won twelve World Championship medals, including the overall individual title in 1978.

Vera Čáslavská, 1942–

Born in Prague, Czechoslovakia, she switched from ice-skating to gymnastics as a 15-year-old, and went on to win 22 Olympic, World and European titles (1959–68), and ten silver and three bronze medals. She won three Olympic gold medals in 1964, and four in 1968.

Nadla Comaneci, 1961–

Born in Onesti, Romania, she was the star of the 1976 Olympic Games when, at the age of 14, she won gold medals in the parallel bars and beam disciplines, becoming the first gymnast to obtain a perfect score of 10.0 for both. She also won a gold medal in the beam at the 1978 World Championships. She won both the beam and floor exercise gold medals in the 1980 Olympics. She defected to the USA in 1989, married US gymnast Bart Conner in 1996 and is now involved in charity work.

Aleksandr Dityatin, 1957–

Born in Leningrad (now St Petersburg), Russia, he was the first person to win eight medals in one Olympic Games – in Moscow in 1980. He won three golds for overall, team and rings, four silvers for parallel bars, horizontal bar, pommel horse and vault, and one bronze for floor exercises. He was also the first male gymnast to receive a score of 10.0 in an Olympic event, with the horse vault.

Olga Korbut, 1956–

Born in Grodno, Belarus, she captivated the world at the 1972 Olympics at Munich with her supple grace and impish personality, and gave gymnastics a new lease of life. She won a gold medal as a member of the winning Soviet team, as well as individual golds in the beam and floor exercises and silver for the parallel bars.

Larissa Latynina, 1935–

Born in Kharson, Ukraine, she collected 18 Olympic medals for the USSR in 1956 and 1964, a record for any sport, winning nine golds (also a record). During her 13-year career she gained 24 Olympic, World and European titles, including individual world champion in 1958 and 1962. She was coach of the Soviet team from 1967 to 1977.

Vitali Scherbo, 1972–

Born in Minsk, Belarus, he became a member of the Soviet national team at the age of 15. He was part of the USSR team at the 1992 Olympics and was the first male gymnast to win six Olympic golds at a single games (four won on the same day). At the 1996 Atlanta Olympics, competing for Belarus, he won the all-round bronze medal and three more bronze medals to bring his total at all World and Olympic events to 33 medals (17 golds).

Rhythmic gymnastics

Origins

Rhythmic gymnastics can trace its origins to the teachings of Swedish gymnast Per Henrik Ling, who was less interested in the strength elements of gymnastics as by grace and 'free movement'.

Rules and description

Rhythmic gymnastics marries traditional floor exercises and classical ballet and female gymnasts perform with a ball, rope, ribbon or hoop or clubs. Only four of the five items are chosen for each competition. There are also team events. Traditionally, only girls and women compete in rhythmic gymnastics but it is a developing sport for men.

The Marias have it

At the World Championships the sport has been dominated by two gymnasts named Maria. The first, Maria Guigova, was a World all-round champion on three successive occasions (1969, 1971, 1973). The second, another Bulgarian gymnast, was Maria Petrova who also won three consecutive titles (1993–5).

Olympic Games

Rhythmic gymnastics made its debut at the 1984 Olympics with an all-around event.

	All-around individual	Team
1984	Lori Fung (Canada)	
1988	Marina Lobach (USSR)	
1992	Aleksandra Timoshenko (Unified Team)	
1996	Yekaterina Serebryanskaya (Ukraine)	Spain
2000	Yuliya Barsukova (Russia)	Russia
2004	Akina Kabaeva (Russia)	Russia

HANDBALL

Origins

Although some similarities exist with hand games played during Greek and Roman times (especially with a Greek game called 'harpaston' or other games described in Homer's *Odyssey*), handball in its current form stems from games created and played in countries such as Czechoslovakia ('hazena'), Denmark ('handbold'), Sweden and Germany at the end of the 19th century. In 1919, a German PE teacher, Karl Schelenz, drew up the first official rules for 'handball' with eleven players. Although the indoor seven-a-side version of this sport was also played at that time, it was the outdoor eleven-a-side game that was introduced at the Berlin Olympic Games in 1936. The outdoor form then declined in popularity in the 1950s, the indoor form taking over and becoming an official Olympic sport in 1972.

Rules and description

It is sometimes said that handball is a cross between basketball and water polo, or even hockey. Team handball is an indoor game played with seven players per side (six court players and a goalkeeper) on a court 40m/43.8yd long and 20m/21.9yd wide, with goals 2m/6ft 6in high and 3m/9ft 9in wide. A game consists of two 30-minute halves – with a ten-minute break – during which players pass, catch, dribble and throw – but never strike – a small ball (58-60cm/22.8-23.6in wide for men and 54-56cm/21.3-22in wide for women) with the aim of scoring as many goals as possible. An overtime period of two five-minute halves is played if the game is tied. Players play with their hands but the ball can touch any other part of the body except for the lower legs and feet, which is a foul. They are allowed a maximum of three steps while holding the ball but cannot keep the ball in their hands for more than three seconds. Handball is therefore a fast-paced game and is also a very physical sport as body contact is allowed.

Ruling bodies: International Handball Federation (IHF); European Handball Federation (EHF)

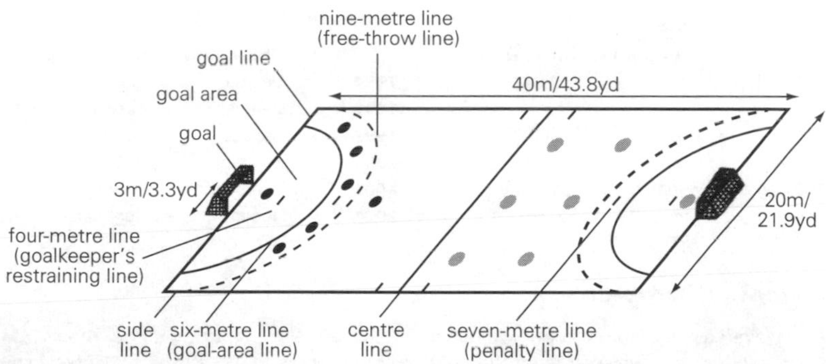

World Championships

The first men's championship was held in Germany in 1938, both indoor and outdoor (the latter was discontinued in 1966), with Germany winning both competitions. The first women's outdoor championship was held in 1949 (discontinued in 1960) and the first women's indoor championships held in 1957. The world championships now take place every two years. Only results for indoor handball are listed below.

	Men			Women	
	Champion	**Runner-up**		**Champion**	**Runner-up**
1954	Sweden	West Germany			
1958	Sweden	Czechoslovakia	**1957**	Czechoslovakia	Hungary
1961	Romania	Czechoslovakia	**1962**	Romania	Denmark
1964	Romania	Sweden	**1965**	Hungary	Yugoslavia
1967	Czechoslovakia	Denmark	**1971**	East Germany	Yugoslavia
1970	Romania	East Germany	**1973**	Yugoslavia	Romania
1974	Romania	East Germany	**1975**	East Germany	USSR

	Champion	Runner-up		Champion	Runner-up
1978	West Germany	USSR	**1978**	East Germany	USSR
1982	USSR	Yugoslavia	**1982**	USSR	Hungary
1986	Yugoslavia	Hungary	**1986**	USSR	Czechoslovakia
1990	Sweden	USSR	**1990**	USSR	Yugoslavia
1993	Russia	France	**1993**	Germany	Denmark
1995	France	Croatia	**1995**	South Korea	Hungary
1997	Russia	Sweden	**1997**	Denmark	Norway
1999	Sweden	Russia	**1999**	Norway	France
2001	France	Sweden	**2001**	Russia	Norway
2003	Croatia	Germany	**2003**	France	Hungary

European Championships

First held in Portugal for men and Germany for women in 1994, they take place every two years.

	Men			Women	
	Champion	**Runner-up**		**Champion**	**Runner-up**
1994	Sweden	Russia	**1994**	Denmark	Germany
1996	Russia	Spain	**1996**	Denmark	Norway
1998	Sweden	Spain	**1998**	Norway	Denmark
2000	Sweden	Russia	**2000**	Hungary	Ukraine
2002	Sweden	Germany	**2002**	Denmark	Norway
2004	Germany	Slovenia	**2004**	Norway	Denmark

Olympic Champions

First played as an Olympic sport in Berlin in 1936 as the eleven-a-side outdoor men's version (Germany beat Austria for the gold and Switzerland took the bronze). However, handball did not reappear until the 1972 Games as the seven-a-side indoor form. Women's handball was introduced in 1976.

	Men	Women
1972	Yugoslavia	
1976	USSR	USSR
1980	East Germany	USSR
1984	Yugoslavia	Yugoslavia
1988	USSR	South Korea
1992	Unified Team	South Korea
1996	Croatia	Denmark
2000	Russia	Denmark
2004	Croatia	Denmark

A-Z

court player — a player other than the goalkeeper

entering the goal area — a foul called when a court player encroaches the **six-metre line** or lands in the **goal area** before having thrown the ball; it can be penalized with a **free throw** or a **seven-metre throw**, and if a goal is scored, it will not be awarded

four-metre line — a 15cm-long mark, 4m in front of the goal, where the goalkeeper stands during a **seven-metre throw** but which he or she cannot cross; also called **goalkeeper's restraining line**

free throw — an advantage awarded to a team for a foul against them; when taken at the **nine-metre line**, the opponents can form a defensive wall by standing just outside the **six-metre line** with their arms in the air to try to prevent a goal

free-throw line — same as **nine-metre line**

goal area — a D-shaped area around the goal that nobody but the goalkeeper can enter

goal-area line — same as **six-metre line**

jump shot — a shot executed while jumping in the air; compare **running shot** and **standing shot**

line player — same as **pivot**

nine-metre line — an arcing dotted line parallel to the **six-metre line** and extending 9m from the goal, where offensive players resume play after a defender has made a foul inside it

passive play — a foul called when a team keeps the ball for too long without trying to attack or score

penalty line — same as **seven-metre line**

pivot — a player who tries to intercept the ball when defending but, when attacking, stays around the **six-metre line** from where he or she tries to score

referee throw — a throw into the air by the referee between two players who jump for the ball, usually taken when a foul is called for both teams

resin — a sticky substance applied to the hands to maintain a good grip of the ball and put extra spin on shots

running shot — a shot executed while running

seven-metre line — a 1m-long line, 7m from the goal, from where a **seven-metre throw** is taken

seven-metre throw — a penalty throw taken as a direct shot on goal by a player who must not touch or cross the **seven-metre line** before the ball leaves the hand

six-metre line — the arcing line outlining the **goal area**, 6m from the goal

6-0 defence — a defensive formation in which all players line up along the **six-metre line** to block the attackers; other formations are the **4-2 defence**, **3-2-1 defence**, or the very common **5-1 defence** when the pivot tries to intercept a pass while his or her teammates stay along the line

standing shot — a shot executed from a standing position

throw-off — a throw from the centre line of the court at the beginning of a game or after a goal; defenders must stand 3m away from the thrower

two-minute suspension — if a player receives a second warning by the referee or is guilty of faulty or unsportsmanlike conduct, he or she is given a suspension, hence reducing the court team to five players for two minutes

HEPTATHLON

Origins

The pentathlon of five events was the first combined event for women. The first pentathlon competition was held in Germany over two days and comprised the shot, long jump, 100m, high jump and javelin events. The pentathlon of 80m hurdles, shot, high jump, long jump and 200m was added to the Olympic Games in 1964. In 1984 it was superseded by the heptathlon of seven events.

Rules and description

The heptathlon is an athletics event for women consisting of seven separate contests held on two consecutive days. On day one is the 100m hurdles, shot put, high jump, 200m; on day two, the long jump, javelin and 800m. In the field events, each competitor has three throws or jumps. Points are awarded for each individual event according to a set of tables approved by the IAAF. Top heptathletes achieve more than 6,500 points.

Ruling body: International Association of Athletics Federations (IAAF).

Olympic Champions

The event was held for the first time in 1984.

	Winner	**Points**
1984	Glynis Nunn (Australia)	6,393
1988	Jackie Joyner-Kersee (USA)	7,291
1992	Jackie Joyner-Kersee (USA)	7,044
1996	Ghada Shouaa (Syria)	6,780
2000	Denise Lewis (Great Britain)	6,584
2004	Carolina Kluft (Sweden)	6,952

Men's magnificent seven

Men also compete in the heptathlon, but only in indoor competition when the two-day event comprises a 60m, long jump, shot put, high jump, 60m hurdles, pole vault and 1,000m.

Jackie Joyner-Kersee, 1962-

Born in East St Louis, Illinois, USA, she won silver in the heptathlon at the Los Angeles Olympics in 1984, missing out on gold by just five points, but returned to claim gold in the 1988 and 1992 Games. In 1987, she won gold in the world championships at both long jump and heptathlon. She also excelled in the long jump, winning Olympic gold in 1988 and bronze in 1992 and 1996. In 1991 she won her second world championships long jump gold, a feat she repeated in the heptathlon in 1993. Possessing more Olympic track and field medals than any other American woman, and the first woman to win an individual event and a multi-event in a major competition, she is one of the greatest female athletes of all time.

HOCKEY

Origins

Historical records reveal that a basic form of hockey was played in Egypt some 4,000 years ago. There is also evidence that a similar game was played by both the ancient Greeks and Romans. The Romans played a game called 'paganica', where a feather-filled ball was hit by a club; in South America the Araucano natives devised a game called 'cheuca', or 'the twisted one', which referred to the stick used. The modern game of hockey evolved in England in the mid-18th century. The first hockey club in England was the Blackheath Football and Hockey Club, founded some time around 1861. The word hockey itself is believed to come from the Old French 'hoquet', meaning a shepherd's crook.

Rules and description

Hockey is a stick-and-ball game played between two teams of eleven players each. Both men and women play hockey (sometimes, and especially in North America, called field hockey to distinguish it from ice hockey). The object is to move a hard ball by dribbling or striking it upfield, using a long wooden stick with a curved end, and to score in the opponent's goal. Only the front of the stick can be used to propel the ball. Games last for 70 minutes with a half-time break.

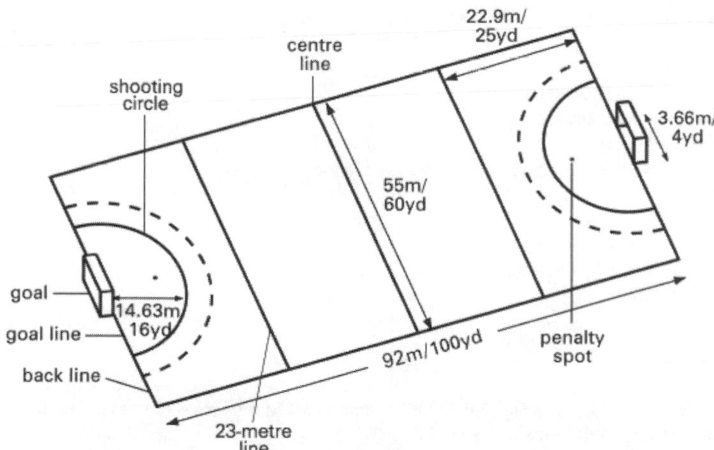

Originally played on grass, the modern game is more likely to be played on sand-based or water-based artificial surfaces, which make for faster, more skilful games. The pitch should measure about 92 x 55m/100 x 60yd with goals at either end. The goalposts are 2.13m/7ft high and 3.66m/4yd apart, with a crossbar between them. The goal is defended by a goalkeeper who wears a protective helmet, leg-pads and gloves, with which he or she can handle the ball. The wooden hockey stick should weigh between 340 and 793g/12 and 28oz and measure around 90cm/3ft long. The hard ball is white and weighs between 156 and 163g (around 5oz).

Ruling body: International Hockey Federation (IHF). The Federation was formed by an amalgamation of the International Hockey Federation and the International Federation of Women's Hockey Associations (IFWHA).

Olympic Games

Regarded as hockey's leading competition; the first Olympic Games matches were held in 1908. A hockey competition has been included at every Olympics since 1928. A women's competition was first held in 1980.

	Men	Women
1908	England	
1912	*Not held*	
1920	Great Britain	
1924	*Not held*	
1928	India	
1932	India	
1936	India	
1948	India	
1952	India	
1956	India	
1960	Pakistan	
1964	India	
1968	Pakistan	
1972	West Germany	
1976	New Zealand	
1980	India	Zimbabwe
1984	Pakistan	The Netherlands
1988	Great Britain	Australia
1992	Germany	Spain
1996	The Netherlands	Australia
2000	The Netherlands	Australia
2004	Australia	Germany

Commemorated in stained glass

Gloucester Cathedral features a stained-glass window from 1350 illustrating a man hitting a ball with a bent stick, representing a game of either golf or hockey. There is a similar memorial in stained glass at Canterbury Cathedral.

World Cup

A men's tournament was first held in 1971, and every four years since 1978. The first women's tournament took place in 1974.

Men

	Winner	Runner-up	Venue
1971	Pakistan	Spain	Barcelona, Spain
1973	The Netherlands	India	Amsterdam, The Netherlands
1975	India	Pakistan	Kuala Lumpur, Malaysia
1978	Pakistan	The Netherlands	Buenos Aires, Argentina

	Winner	Runner-up	Venue
1982	Pakistan	West Germany	Mumbai, India
1986	Australia	England	London, UK
1990	The Netherlands	Pakistan	Lahore, Pakistan
1994	Pakistan	Netherlands	Sydney, Australia
1998	The Netherlands	Spain	Utrecht, The Netherlands
2002	Germany	Australia	Bukit Jalil, Malaysia
2006			Monchengladbach, Germany

Women

	Winner	Runner-up	Venue
1974	The Netherlands	Argentina	Mandelieu, France
1976	West Germany	Argentina	Berlin, Germany
1978	The Netherlands	West Germany	Madrid, Spain
1981	West Germany	The Netherlands	Buenos Aires, Argentina
1983	The Netherlands	Canada	Kuala Lumpur, Malaysia
1986	The Netherlands	West Germany	Amsterdam, The Netherlands
1990	The Netherlands	Australia	Sydney, Australia
1994	Australia	Argentina	Dublin, Ireland
1998	Australia	The Netherlands	Utrecht, The Netherlands
2002	Argentina	The Netherlands	Perth, Australia
2006	Spain		

Champions Trophy

The tournament was first held in Lahore, Pakistan, in 1978 and is now held annually. Both the men's and the women's trophy is contested by the world's top six teams.

Men

	Winner	Runner-up	Venue
1978	Pakistan	Australia	Lahore, Pakistan
1980	Pakistan	West Germany	Karachi, Pakistan
1981	The Netherlands	Australia	Karachi, Pakistan
1982	The Netherlands	Australia	Amsterdam, The Netherlands
1983	Australia	Pakistan	Karachi, Pakistan
1984	Australia	Pakistan	Karachi, Pakistan
1985	Australia	Great Britain	Perth, Australia
1986	West Germany	Australia	Karachi, Pakistan
1987	West Germany	The Netherlands	Amsterdam, The Netherlands
1988	West Germany	Pakistan	Lahore, Pakistan
1989	Australia	The Netherlands	Berlin, Germany
1990	Australia	The Netherlands	Melbourne, Australia
1991	Germany	Pakistan	Berlin, Germany
1992	Germany	Australia	Karachi, Pakistan
1993	Australia	Germany	Kuala Lumpur, Malaysia
1994	Pakistan	Germany	Lahore, Pakistan
1995	Germany	Australia	Berlin, Germany

	Winner	Runner-up	Venue
1996	The Netherlands	Pakistan	Madras, India
1997	Germany	Australia	Adelaide, Australia
1998	The Netherlands	Pakistan	Lahore, Pakistan
1999	Australia	South Korea	Brisbane, Australia
2000	The Netherlands	Germany	Amstelveen, The Netherlands
2001	Germany	Australia	Rotterdam, The Netherlands
2002	The Netherlands	Germany	Cologne, Germany
2003	The Netherlands	Australia	Amsterdam, The Netherlands
2004	Spain	The Netherlands	Lahore, Pakistan
2005			Chennai, India

The barefoot maestro

The great Indian player Dhyan Chand was probably at the height of his powers during the Berlin Olympics of 1936. India played Germany in the final. In order to stifle the talent of this barefoot maestro, the Germans employed rough tactics, which led to Dhyan Chand having a tooth knocked out.

Women

	Winner	Runner-up	Venue
1987	The Netherlands	Australia	Amsterdam, The Netherlands
1989	South Korea	Australia	Frankfurt, Germany
1991	Australia	Germany	Berlin, Germany
1993	Australia	The Netherlands	Amstelveen, The Netherlands
1995	Australia	South Korea	Mar del Plata, Argentina
1997	Australia	Germany	Berlin, Germany
1999	Australia	The Netherlands	Brisbane, Australia
2000	The Netherlands	Germany	Amstelveen, The Netherlands
2001	Argentina	The Netherlands	Amstelveen, The Netherlands
2002	China	Argentina	Macao, China
2003	Australia	China	Sydney, Australia
2004	The Netherlands	Germany	Rosario, Argentina
2005			Canberra, Australia

A-Z

back line the line marking the limit of either end of the pitch

bully-off the term used to describe a way of restarting the game after play has been stopped for an injury; also formerly to start the game and restart it after each goal. One player from each team hits the ground and the opponent's stick once above the ball, before attempting to be the first to strike the ball lying between them

centre forward an attacking position in the centre of the field

centre half a position in the centre of midfield

centre pass the pass that starts the game (or restarts it after a goal), made by a centre from the centre spot, backwards to a team-mate

corner hit same as **long corner**

D same as **shooting circle**

dribble to move the ball forward little by little, keeping it under close control with the stick

feet an infringement that occurs when the ball either deliberately or accidentally comes into contact with the player's foot

field goal a goal scored from open play

field player a player other than the goalkeeper

flick same as **scoop**

free hit a shot taken when an offence has been committed outside the **shooting circle** or by an attacker within the opposition's **23-metre line**

goal circle same as **shooting circle**

green card a card shown by the referee as an official warning to a player after a relatively minor offence

hit to propel the ball across the pitch surface. The hands are gripped near the top of the stick

inside left an attacking position on the left side

inside right an attacking position on the right side

left back a position on the left side of defence

left half a position on the left side of midfield

left wing an attacking position on the extreme left

long corner a free stroke taken on the **back line** 5m from the corner flag after a defender has unintentionally hit the ball over the back line

obstruction penalty given when players turn in front of the opposition or use a stick to bar the opponent's way

penalty corner a free stroke taken on the **back line** 9m from the goalpost for an offence committed within the **shooting circle** or **23-metre line**. The ball is pushed back to a player on the edge of the shooting circle to shoot on goal

penalty spot a spot 6.4m/7yd from goal, from which **penalty strokes** are taken

penalty stroke a free shot at goal. It is taken from the **penalty spot**, with only the goalkeeper allowed to attempt to stop it

push if a player pushes the ball, he or she propels it in a continuous movement with the stick across the pitch surface without the ball leaving the ground. The right-hand grip is lower down the handle of the stick than in a **hit**

red card a card shown by the referee to send a player off the pitch permanently

reverse sticks a legal move where the player turns the stick so that the flat blade faces to the right and hence can make a shot in the opposite direction

right back a position on the right side of defence

right half a position on the right side of midfield

right wing an attacking position on the extreme right

scoop to propel the ball through the air using a lifting motion of the stick

shooting circle the D-shaped area in front of goal from within which the ball must be hit in order to score

short corner same as **penalty corner**

striking circle same as **shooting circle**

tackle a move attempting to take away the ball from the possession of another player using the stick

23-metre line a line marked horizontally across the field, 22.9m/25yd from each **back line**

yellow card a card signifying that the referee has suspended a player. The referee usually indicates the length of the suspension

Some famous hockey players

Dhyan Chand, 1905–79

Born in Allahabad, India, this centre-forward formed part of three consecutive Olympic gold medal-winning sides (1928, 1932, 1936) and is revered as hockey's most prolific goalscorer and most masterful player. By occupation an army captain, he scored 38 goals in twelve Olympic matches. His brother Roop Singh also won two gold medals and his son Ashok Kumar won an Olympic bronze in 1972.

Ric Charlesworth, 1952–

Born in Suniaco, Perth, Australia, he followed parallel careers as a state cricketer and a hockey player. He played 234 times for Australia and took part in four Olympic Games (1972, 1976, 1984 and 1988), winning a silver medal in 1976. Charlesworth won two further Olympic Games gold medals (1996 and 2000) as coach to the Australian women's hockey team – the Hockeyroos.

Rechelle Hawkes, 1967–

Born in Albany, Australia, she is the most decorated women's player in history with three Olympic Games gold medals (1988, 1996, 2000) and two World Cups (1994, 1998). She represented Australia in 279 internationals. At the 2000 Olympics, her last before retirement, she recited the Olympic Oath at the opening ceremony.

Sean Kerly, 1960–

Born in Tankerton, Kent, England, Kerly won a bronze medal at the 1984 Olympic Games and a gold medal at the 1988 Olympics. He played for England 79 times (scoring 45 goals) and for Great Britain 99 times, becoming the side's record goalscorer with 64 goals. He also has a silver medal from the 1986 World Cup. He received an MBE in 1992.

Richard Leman, 1959–

Born in East Grinstead, West Sussex, Leman is England's most-capped international with 158 caps. He also represented Great Britain on 70 occasions. He won a gold medal at the 1988 Olympic Games, and a bronze in 1984 as well as a silver at the 1986 World Cup.

Nova Perris-Kneebone

This Australian hockey player won a gold medal at the 1996 Atlanta Olympics. In doing so she became the first Australian Aborigine to win an Olympic Games gold. She later turned to sprinting and won a gold medal at the 200m event at the 1998 Commonwealth Games.

HORSE RACING

Origins

The 'sport of kings' is well named as the racing of horses has long associations with royalty. During the Crusades of the 12th century English knights returned from the Middle East with Arab horses, animals whose speed and stamina made them ideal for racing. Charles II was keen on the sport and during his reign racing for prize money took place. Newmarket, still known in the British racing world as 'headquarters', became Britain's first racecourse. In the early 18th century Queen Anne founded Ascot racecourse, the sport became professionalized, and spectators started to bet on the races. The governing body of the sport in Britain, the Jockey Club, was founded in 1750 and within the next 60 years all the English classic races had become established. Horse racing over fences and hurdles evolved from the hunting of stags and foxes, pastimes which involved the surmounting of many natural obstacles. Steeplechasing developed from the 'pounding matches' held in Ireland in the late 17th century, the loser being 'pounded' to a standstill by the winner's superior stamina over rough country terrain. Eventually races over set distances developed, with the winning post often being a church steeple, hence the word 'steeplechase'. Britain's first steeplechase over a course took place at Bedford in 1810 and within 30 years the Grand National was first run at Aintree. The sport required a governing body so the National Hunt committee, as it later became known, was formed and then formally recognized by the Jockey Club in 1866.

Rules and description

An equestrian sport in which horses ridden by jockeys compete over set distances. The sport exists in two forms: National Hunt, in which obstacles must be jumped, and flat racing, in which there are no obstacles. Flat races, for thoroughbred horses, are over distances of between five furlongs and two and a half miles. National Hunt races are longer, up to a distance of four and a half miles. National Hunt has two types of race: hurdling races over short, flexible obstacles called hurdles; and steeplechases, over larger, more rigid obstacles called fences. In handicap races horses are given extra weight to carry according to their recent form, age and gender. Horses are entered into races by owners on the advice of professional trainers who look after and train the horses. The sport is professional and supported mainly by the gambling industry, which provides punters with odds for each horse in every race run. Steeplechasing for amateur riders and trainers is known as 'point-to-point'.

Ruling bodies: the British Horseracing Board (BHB) and the Jockey Club regulate British horse racing.

Wonder horse

Golden Miller must be a strong candidate for the title of the greatest horse of the 20th century. As well as winning five consecutive Cheltenham Gold Cups (1932–6) – a record still to be matched – he also found time to win the 1934 Grand National. This remarkable double is unique.

Beginner's luck

In March 2003 a Welsh woman, who still wishes to remain anonymous, went into a betting shop and placed her first ever bet, a £2 treble on three horses running at Doncaster. The horses all won and the first-time punter went to collect her winnings, which she thought would be in the region of £600. Not bad for a novice gambler. She handed over her ticket and nearly fainted when told that she had in fact netted nearly £40,000. Her accumulator was on three horses all at 33–1, and that added up to combined odds of 39,303–1 which, Coral reckoned, was a world record for a treble. The three horses were selected for a variety of reasons: Intellibet One because the punter's grandmother is called Bet; Zucchero because she is a big fan of John Travolta's character Danny Zuko in *Grease*; and, finally, Lady of Gdansk because she stuck a pin in its name.

Two Thousand Guineas

The second youngest of the English classics is run over the Rowley Mile course at Newmarket in May for three-year-old colts and fillies. The race's name derives from the fact that in the early years the winning prize was a guaranteed 2,000 guineas regardless of the number of entrants.

	Winner (Jockey)
1809	Wizard (Bill Clift)
1810	Hephestion (Frank Buckle)
1811	Trophonius (Sam Barnard)
1812	Cwrw (Sam Chifney, Jr)
1813	Smolensko (H Miller)
1814	Olive (Bill Arnull)
1815	Tigris (Bill Arnull)
1816	Nectar (Bill Arnull)
1817	Manfred (Will Wheatley)
1818	Interpreter (Bill Clift)
1819	Antar (Edward Edwards)
1820	Pindarrie (Frank Buckle)
1821	Reginald (Frank Buckle)
1822	Pastille (Frank Buckle)
1823	Nicolo (Will Wheatley)
1824	Schahriar (Will Wheatley)
1825	Enamel (Jem Robinson)
1826	Dervise (John Barham Day)
1827	Turcoman (Frank Buckle)
1828	Cadland (Jem Robinson)
1829	Patron (Frank Boyce)
1830	Augustus (Patrick Conolly)
1831	Riddlesworth (Jem Robinson)
1832	Archibald (Arthur Pavis)
1833	Clearwell (Jem Robinson)
1834	Glencoe (Jem Robinson)
1835	Ibrahim (Jem Robinson)
1836	Bay Middleton (Jem Robinson)
1837	Achmet (Edward Edwards)

	Winner (Jockey)
1838	Grey Momus (John Barham Day)
1839	The Corsair (Bill Wakefield)
1840	Crucifix (John Barham Day)
1841	Ralph (John Barham Day)
1842	Meteor (Bill Scott)
1843	Cotherstone (Bill Scott)
1844	The Ugly Buck (John Day)
1845	Idas (Nat Flatman)
1846	Sir Tatton Sykes (Bill Scott)
1847	Conyngham (Jem Robinson)
1848	Flatcatcher (Jem Robinson)
1849	Nunnykirk (Frank Butler)
1850	Pitsford (Alfred Day)
1851	Hernandez (Nat Flatman)
1852	Stockwell (John Norman)
1853	West Australian (Frank Butler)
1854	The Hermit (Alfred Day)
1855	Lord of the Isles (Tom Aldcroft)
1856	Fazzoletto (Nat Flatman)
1857	Vedette (John Osbourne)
1858	Fitz-Roland (John Wells)
1859	The Promised Land (Alfred Day)
1860	The Wizard (Tom Ashmall)
1861	Diophantus (Arthur Edwards)
1862	The Marquis (Tom Ashmall)
1863	Macaroni (Tom Chaloner)
1864	General Peel (Tom Aldcroft)
1865	Gladiateur (Harry Grimshaw)
1866	Lord Lyon (R Thomas)

	Winner (Jockey)
1867	Vauban (George Fordham)
1868	Moslem (Tom Chaloner)
	Formosa (George Fordham) *(dead heat)*
1869	Pretender (John Osborne)
1870	MacGregor (John Daley)
1871	Bothwell (John Osborne)
1872	Prince Charlie (John Osborne)
1873	Gang Forward (Tom Chaloner)
1874	Atlantic (Fred Archer)
1875	Camballo (John Osborne)
1876	Petrarch (Harry Luke)
1877	Chamant (Jem Goater)
1878	Pilgrimage (Tom Cannon)
1879	Charibert (Fred Archer)
1880	Petronel (George Fordham)
1881	Peregrine (Fred Webb)
1882	Shotover (Tom Cannon)
1883	Galliard (Fred Archer)
1884	Scot Free (Billy Platt)
1885	Paradox (Fred Archer)
1886	Ormonde (George Barrett)
1887	Enterprise (Tom Cannon)
1888	Ayrshire (John Osborne)
1889	Enthusiast (Tom Cannon)
1890	Surefoot (John Liddiard)
1891	Common (George Barrett)
1892	Bona Vista (Jack Robinson)
1893	Isinglass (Tom Loates)
1894	Ladas (Jack Watts)
1895	Kirkonnel (Jack Watts)
1896	St Frusquin (Tom Loates)
1897	Galtee More (Charlie Wood)
1898	Disraeli (Sam Loates)
1899	Flying Fox (Morny Cannon)
1900	Diamond Jubilee (Herbert Jones)
1901	Handicapper (William Halsey)
1902	Sceptre (Herbert Randall)
1903	Rock Sand (Skeets Martin)
1904	St Amant (Kempton Cannon)
1905	Vedas (Herbert Jones)
1906	Gorgos (Herbert Jones)
1907	Slieve Gallion (Billy Higgs)
1908	Norman III (Otto Madden)
1909	Minoru (Herbert Jones)
1910	Neil Gow (Danny Maher)
1911	Sunstar (George Stern)
1912	Sweeper II (Danny Maher)
1913	Louvois (Johnny Reiff)
1914	Kennymore (George Stern)
	Winner (Jockey)
1915	Pommern (Steve Donoghue)
1916	Clarissimus (Jimmy Clark)
1917	Gay Crusader (Steve Donoghue)
1918	Gainsborough (Joe Childs)
1919	The Panther (Dick Cooper)
1920	Tetratema (Brownie Carslake)
1921	Craig an Eran (Jack Brennan)
1922	St Louis (George Archibald)
1923	Ellangowan (Charlie Elliott)
1924	Diophon (George Hulme)
1925	Manna (Steve Donoghue)
1926	Colorado (Tommy Weston)
1927	Adam's Apple (Jack Leach)
1928	Flamingo (Charlie Elliott)
1929	Mr Jinks (Harry Beasley)
1930	Diolite (Freddy Fox)
1931	Cameronian (Joe Childs)
1932	Orwell (Bobby Jones)
1933	Rodosto (Roger Brethes)
1934	Colombo (Rae Johnstone)
1935	Bahram (Freddy Fox)
1936	Pay Up (Bobby Dick)
1937	Le Ksar (Charles Semblat)
1938	Pasch (Gordon Richards)
1939	Blue Peter (Eph Smith)
1940	Djebel (Charlie Elliott)
1941	Lambert Simnel (Charlie Elliott)
1942	Big Game (Gordon Richards)
1943	Kingsway (Sam Wragg)
1944	Garden Path (Harry Wragg)
1945	Court Martial (Cliff Richards)
1946	Happy Knight (Tommy Weston)
1947	Tudor Minstrel (Gordon Richards)
1948	My Babu (Charlie Smirke)
1949	Nimbus (Charlie Elliott)
1950	Palestine (Charlie Smirke)
1951	Ki Ming (Scobie Breasley)
1952	Thunderhead II (Roger Poincelet)
1953	Nearula (Edgar Britt)
1954	Darius (Manny Mercer)
1955	Our Babu (Doug Smith)
1956	Gilles de Retz (Frank Barlow)
1957	Crepello (Lester Piggott)
1958	Pall Mall (Doug Smith)
1959	Taboun (George Moore)
1960	Martial (Ron Hutchinson)
1961	Rockavon (Norman Stirk)
1962	Privy Councillor (Bill Rickaby)
1963	Only For Life (Jimmy Lindley)

	Winner (Jockey)		Winner (Jockey)
1964	Baldric II (Bill Pyers)	**1985**	Shadeed (Lester Piggott)
1965	Niksar (Duncan Keith)	**1986**	Dancing Brave (Greville Starkey)
1966	Kashmir II (Jimmy Lindley)	**1987**	Don't Forget Me (Willie Carson)
1967	Royal Palace (George Moore)	**1988**	Doyoun (Walter Swinburn)
1968	Sir Ivor (Lester Piggott)	**1989**	Nashwan (Willie Carson)
1969	Right Tack (Geoff Lewis)	**1990**	Tirol (Michael Kinane)
1970	Nijinsky (Lester Piggott)	**1991**	Mystiko (Michael Roberts)
1971	Brigadier Gerard (Joe Mercer)	**1992**	Rodrigo de Triano (Lester Piggott)
1972	High Top (Willie Carson)	**1993**	Zafonic (Pat Eddery)
1973	Mon Fils (Frankie Durr)	**1994**	Mister Baileys (Jason Weaver)
1974	Nonoalco (Yves Saint-Martin)	**1995**	Pennekamp (Thierry Jarnet)
1975	Bolkonski (Gianfranco Dettori)	**1996**	Mark of Esteem (Frankie Dettori)
1976	Wollow (Gianfranco Dettori)	**1997**	Entrepreneur (Michael Kinane)
1977	Nebbiolo (Gabriel Curran)	**1998**	King of Kings (Michael Kinane)
1978	Roland Gardens (Frankie Durr)	**1999**	Island Sands (Frankie Dettori)
1979	Tap On Wood (Steve Cauthen)	**2000**	King's Best (Kieren Fallon)
1980	Known Fact (Willie Carson)	**2001**	Golan (Kieren Fallon)
1981	To-Agori-Mou (Greville Starkey)	**2002**	Rock of Gibraltar (Johnny Murtagh)
1982	Zino (Freddie Head)	**2003**	Refuse To Bend (Pat Smullen)
1983	Lomond (Pat Eddery)	**2004**	Haafhd (Richard Hills)
1984	El Gran Senor (Pat Eddery)		

Arise, Sir Peter

Sir Peter Teazle was certainly an extraordinary horse. As well as winning the Derby in 1787 he sired a number of sons, three of whom took the first three places in the 1803 running of the Epsom classic.

One Thousand Guineas

The youngest of the English classics is run over the Rowley Mile course at Newmarket in May for three-year-old fillies. The Rowley Mile is named after King Charles II (Old Rowley) who founded the Newmarket meetings.

	Winner (Jockey)		Winner (Jockey)
1814	Charlotte (Bill Clift)	**1828**	Zoe (Jem Robinson)
1815	*Filly by Selim* (Bill Clift)	**1829**	Young Mouse (Bill Arnull)
1816	Rhoda (Sam Barnard)	**1830**	Charlotte West (Jem Robinson)
1817	Neva (Bill Arnull)	**1831**	Galantine (Patrick Conolly)
1818	Corinne (Frank Buckle)	**1832**	Galata (Bill Arnull)
1819	Catgut (*Unknown*)	**1833**	Tarantella (E Wright)
1820	Rowena (Frank Buckle)	**1834**	May-Day (John Barnham Day)
1821	Zeal (Frank Buckle)	**1835**	Preserve (Nat Flatman)
1822	Whizgig (Frank Buckle)	**1836**	Destiny (John Barham Day)
1823	Zinc (Frank Buckle)	**1837**	Chapeau d'Espagne (John Barham Day)
1824	Cobweb (Jem Robinson)	**1838**	Barcarolle (Edward Edwards)
1825	Tontine (*Unknown*)	**1839**	Cara (George Edwards)
1826	Problem (John Barnham Day)	**1840**	Crucifix (John Barham Day)
1827	Arab (Frank Buckle)		

	Winner (Jockey)
1841	Potentia (Jem Robinson)
1842	Firebrand (Sam Rogers)
1843	Extempore (Sam Chifney, Jr)
1844	Sorella (Jem Robinson)
1845	Picnic (William Abdale)
1846	Mendicant (Sam Day)
1847	Clementina (Nat Flatman)
1848	Canezou (Frank Butler)
1849	The Flea (Alfred Day)
1850	Lady Orford (Frank Butler)
1851	Aphrodite (Job Marson)
1852	Kate (Alfred Day)
1853	Mentmore Lass (Jack Charlton)
1854	Virago (John Wells)
1855	Habena (Sam Rogers)
1856	Manganese (John Osbourne)
1857	Imperieuse (Nat Flatman)
1858	Governess (Tom Ashmall)
1859	Mayonaise (George Fordham)
1860	Sagitta (Tom Aldcroft)
1861	Nemesis (George Fordham)
1862	Hurricane (Tom Ashmall)
1863	Lady Augusta (Arthur Edwards)
1864	Tomato (John Wells)
1865	Siberia (George Fordham)
1866	Repulse (Tom Cannon)
1867	Achievement (Mark Pearson)
1868	Formosa (George Fordham)
1869	Scottish Queen (George Fordham)
1870	Hester (Jeremy Grimshaw)
1871	Hannah (Charlie Maidment)
1872	Reine (Henry Parry)
1873	Cecilia (Jack Morris)
1874	Apology (John Osborne, Jr)
1875	Spinaway (Fred Archer)
1876	Camelia (Tom Glover)
1877	Belphoebe (Harry Jeffrey)
1878	Pilgrimage (Tom Cannon)
1879	Wheel of Fortune (Fred Archer)
1880	Elizabeth (Charlie Wood)
1881	Thebais (George Fordham)
1882	St Marguerite (Charlie Wood)
1883	Hauteur (George Fordham)
1884	Busybody (Tom Cannon)
1885	Farewell (George Barrett)
1886	Miss Jummy (Jack Watts)
1887	Reve d'Or (Charlie Wood)
1888	Briar Root (Billy Warne)
1889	Minthe (Jimmy Woodburn)

	Winner (Jockey)
1890	Semolina (Jack Watts)
1891	Mimi (Fred Rickaby)
1892	La Fleche (George Barrett)
1893	Siffleuse (Tom Loates)
1894	Amiable (Walter Bradford)
1895	Galeottia (Fred Pratt)
1896	Thais (Jack Watts)
1897	Chelandry (Jack Watts)
1898	Nun Nicer (Sam Loates)
1899	Sibola (Tod Sloan)
1900	Winifreda (Sam Loates)
1901	Aida (Danny Maher)
1902	Sceptre (Herbert Randall)
1903	Quintessence (Herbert Randall)
1904	Pretty Polly (Willie Lane)
1905	Cherry Lass (George McCall)
1906	Flair (Bernard Dillon)
1907	Witch Elm (Barrington Lynham)
1908	Rhodora (Lucien Lyne)
1909	Electra (Bernard Dillon)
1910	Winkipop (Barrington Lynham)
1911	Atmah (Freddy Fox)
1912	Tagalie (Les Hewitt)
1913	Jest (Fred Rickaby, Jr)
1914	Princess Dorrie (Bill Huxley)
1915	Vaucluse (Fred Rickaby, Jr)
1916	Canyon (Fred Rickaby, Jr)
1917	Diadem (Fred Rickaby, Jr)
1918	Ferry (Brownie Carslake)
1919	Roseway (Albert Whalley)
1920	Cinna (William Griggs)
1921	Bettina (George Bellhouse)
1922	Silver Urn (Brownie Carslake)
1923	Tranquil (Ted Gardner)
1924	Plack (Charlie Elliott)
1925	Saucy Sue (Frank Bullock)
1926	Pillion (Dick Perryman)
1927	Cresta Run (Arthur Balding)
1928	Scuttle (Joe Childs)
1929	Taj Mah (Wally Sibbritt)
1930	Fair Isle (Tommy Weston)
1931	Four Course (Charlie Elliott)
1932	Kandy (Charlie Elliott)
1933	Brown Betty (Joe Childs)
1934	Campanula (Harry Wragg)
1935	Mesa (Rae Johnstone)
1936	Tide-Way (Dick Perryman)
1937	Exhibitionist (Steve Donoghue)
1938	Rockfel (Sam Wragg)

	Winner (Jockey)		Winner (Jockey)
1939	Galatea II (Bobby Jones)	**1972**	Waterloo (Eddie Hide)
1940	Godiva (Doug Marks)	**1973**	Mysterious (Geoff Lewis)
1941	Dancing Time (Dick Perryman)	**1974**	Highclere (Joe Mercer)
1942	Sun Chariot (Gordon Richards)	**1975**	Nocturnal Spree (Johnny Roe)
1943	Herringbone (Harry Wragg)	**1976**	Flying Water (Yves Saint-Martin)
1944	Picture Play (Charlie Elliott)	**1977**	Mrs McArdy (Eddie Hide)
1945	Sun Stream (Harry Wragg)	**1978**	Enstone Spark (Ernie Johnson)
1946	Hypericum (Doug Smith)	**1979**	One in a Million (Joe Mercer)
1947	Imprudence (Rae Johnstone)	**1980**	Quick As Lighning (Brian Rouse)
1948	Queenpot (Gordon Richards)	**1981**	Fairy Footsteps (Lester Piggott)
1949	Musidora (Edgar Britt)	**1982**	On The House (John Reid)
1950	Camaree (Rae Johnstone)	**1983**	Ma Biche (Freddie Head)
1951	Belle of All (Gordon Richards)	**1984**	Pebbles (Philip Robinson)
1952	Zabara (Ken Gethin)	**1985**	Oh So Sharp (Steve Cauthen)
1953	Happy Laughter (Manny Mercer)	**1986**	Midway Lady (Ray Cochrane)
1954	Festoon (Scobie Breasley)	**1987**	Miesque (Freddie Head)
1955	Meld (Harry Carr)	**1988**	Ravinella (Gary Moore)
1956	Honeylight (Edgar Britt)	**1989**	Musical Bliss (Walter Swinburn)
1957	Rose Royale II (Charlie Smirke)	**1990**	Salsabil (Willie Carson)
1958	Bella Paola (Serge Boullenger)	**1991**	Shadayid (Willie Carson)
1959	Petite Etoile (Doug Smith)	**1992**	Hatoof (Walter Swinburn)
1960	Never Too Late II (Roger Poincelet)	**1993**	Sayyedati (Walter Swinburn)
1961	Sweet Solera (Bill Rickaby)	**1994**	Las Meninas (John Reid)
1962	Abermaid (Bill Williamson)	**1995**	Harayir (Richard Hills)
1963	Hula Dancer (Roger Poincelet)	**1996**	Bosra Sham (Pat Eddery)
1964	Pourparler (Garnie Bougoure)	**1997**	Sleepytime (Kieren Fallon)
1965	Night Off (Bill Williamson)	**1998**	Cape Verdi (Frankie Dettori)
1966	Glad Rags (Paul Cook)	**1999**	Wince (Kieren Fallon)
1967	Fleet (George Moore)	**2000**	Lahan (Richard Hills)
1968	Caergwrle (Sandy Barclay)	**2001**	Ameerat (Philip Robinson)
1969	Full Dress II (Ron Hutchinson)	**2002**	Kazzia (Frankie Dettori)
1970	Humble Duty (Lester Piggott)	**2003**	Russian Rhythm (Kieren Fallon)
1971	Altesse Royal (Yves Saint-Martin)	**2004**	Attraction (Kevin Darley)

One lady trainer

Jenny Pitman is the only woman to have trained a Grand National winner, doing so in 1983 when Ben de Haan rode Corbiere to victory at Aintree. She would have completed a notable double a decade later when Esha Ness crossed the line first but this was the year of the infamous void race when the field was not recalled after a false start.

The Oaks

The Oaks is for three-year-old fillies and is run at Epsom Downs in June over one and a half miles. The race gets its name from Lord Derby's estate at Epsom.

* = held at Newmarket

	Winner (Jockey)
1779	Bridget (Dick Goodisson)
1780	Teetotum (Dick Goodisson)
1781	Faith (Dick Goodisson)
1782	Ceres (Sam Chifney)
1783	Maid of the Oaks (Sam Chifney)
1784	Stella (Charles Hindley)
1785	Trifle (J Bird)
1786	Yellow Filly (James Edwards)
1787	Annette (Dennis Fitzpatrick)
1788	Nightshade (Dennis Fitzpatrick)
1789	Tag (Sam Chifney)
1790	Hippolyta (Sam Chifney)
1791	Portia (John Singleton, Jr)
1792	Volante (Charles Hindley)
1793	Celia/Caelia (John Singleton, Jr)
1794	Hermione (Sam Arnull)
1795	Platina (Dennis Fitzpatrick)
1796	Parissot/Parisot (John Arnull)
1797	Nike (Frank Buckle)
1798	Bellissima (Frank Buckle)
1799	Bellina (Frank Buckle)
1800	Ephemera (Dennis Fitzpatrick)
1801	Eleanor (John Saunders)
1802	Scotia (Frank Buckle)
1803	Theophania (Frank Buckle)
1804	Pelisse (Bill Clift)
1805	Meteora (Frank Buckle)
1806	Bronze (William Edwards)
1807	Briseis (Sam Chifney, Jr)
1808	Morel (Bill Clift)
1809	Maid of Orleans (Ben Moss)
1810	Oriana (Bill Peirse)
1811	Sorcery (Sam Chifney, Jr)
1812	Manuella (Bill Peirse)
1813	Music (Tom Goodisson)
1814	Medora (Sam Barnard)
1815	Minuet (Tom Goodisson)
1816	Landscape (Sam Chifney, Jr)
1817	Neva (Frank Buckle)
1818	Corinne (Frank Buckle)
1819	Shoveler (Sam Chifney, Jr)
1820	Caroline (Harry Edwards)
1821	Augusta (Jem Robinson)
1822	Pastille (Harry Edwards)
1823	Zinc (Frank Buckle)
1824	Cobweb (Jem Robinson)
1825	Wings (Sam Chifney, Jr)
1826	Lilias (Tommy Lye)

	Winner (Jockey)
1827	Gulnare (Frank Boyce)
1828	Turquoise (John Barham Day)
1829	Green Mantle (George Dockeray)
1830	Variation (George Edwards)
1831	Oxygen (John Barham Day)
1832	Galata (Patrick Conolly)
1833	Vespa (Jem Chapple)
1834	Pussy (John Barham Day)
1835	Queen of Trumps (Tommy Lye)
1836	Cyprian (Bill Scott)
1837	Miss Letty (John Holmes)
1838	Industry (Bill Scott)
1839	Deception (John Barham Day)
1840	Crucifix (John Barham Day)
1841	Ghuznee (Bill Scott)
1842	Our Nell (Tommy Lye)
1843	Poison (Frank Butler)
1844	The Princess (Frank Butler)
1845	Refraction (Henry Bell)
1846	Mendicant (Sam Day)
1847	Miami (Sim Templeman)
1848	Cymba (Sim Templeman)
1849	Lady Evelyn (Frank Butler)
1850	Rhedycina (Frank Butler)
1851	Iris (Frank Butler)
1852	Songstress (Frank Butler)
1853	Catherine Hayes (Charlie Marlow)
1854	Mincemeat (Jack Charlton)
1855	Marchioness (Sim Templeman)
1856	Mincepie (Alfred Day)
1857	Blink Bonny (Jack Charlton)
1858	Governess (Tom Ashmall)
1859	Summerside (George Fordham)
1860	Butterfly (Jim Snowden)
1861	Brown Duchess (Luke Snowden)
1862	Feu de Joie (Tom Chaloner)
1863	Queen Bertha (Tom Aldcroft)
1864	Fille de l'Air (Arthur Edwards)
1865	Regalia (John Norman)
1866	Tormentor (Jimmy Mann)
1867	Hippia (John Daley)
1868	Formosa (George Fordham)
1869	Brigantine (Tom Cannon)
1870	Gamos (George Fordham)
1871	Hannah (Charlie Maidment)
1872	Reine (George Fordham)
1873	Marie Stuart (Tom Cannon)
1874	Apology (John Osborne)

	Winner (Jockey)
1875	Spinaway (Fred Archer)
1876	Camelia (Tom Glover)
	Enguerrande (J Hudson) *(dead heat)*
1877	Placida (Harry Jeffrey)
1878	Jannette (Fred Archer)
1879	Wheel of Fortune (Fred Archer)
1880	Jenny Howlet (Jim Snowden)
1881	Thebais (George Fordham)
1882	Geheimniss (Tom Cannon)
1883	Bonny Jean (Jack Watts)
1884	Busybody (Tom Cannon)
1885	Lonely (Fred Archer)
1886	Miss Jummy (Jack Watts)
1887	Reve d'Or (Charlie Wood)
1888	Seabreeze (Jack Robinson)
1889	L'Abbesse de Jouarre (Jimmy Woodburn)
1890	Memoir (Jack Watts)
1891	Mimi (Fred Rickaby)
1892	La Fleche (George Barrett)
1893	Mrs Butterwick (Jack Watts)
1894	Amiable (Walter Bradford)
1895	La Sagesse (Sam Loates)
1896	Canterbury Pilgrim (Fred Rickaby)
1897	Limasol (Walter Bradford)
1898	Airs and Graces (Walter Bradford)
1899	Musa (Otto Madden)
1900	La Roche (Morny Cannon)
1901	Cap and Bells (Milton Henry)
1902	Sceptre (Herbert Randall)
1903	Our Lassie (Morny Cannon)
1904	Pretty Polly (Willie Lane)
1905	Cherry Lass (Herbert Jones)
1906	Keystone (Danny Maher)
1907	Glass Doll (Herbert Randall)
1908	Signorinetta (Billy Bullock)
1909	Perola (Frank Wootton)
1910	Rosedrop (Charlie Trigg)
1911	Cherimoya (Fred Winter)
1912	Mirska (Joe Childs)
1913	Jest (Fred Rickaby, Jr)
1914	Princess Dorrie (Bill Huxley)
1915*	Snow Marten (Walter Griggs)
1916*	Fifinella (Joe Childs)
1917*	Sunny Jane (Otto Madden)
1918*	My Dear (Steve Donoghue)
1919	Bayuda (Joe Childs)
1920	Charlebelle (Albert Whalley)
1921	Love in Idleness (Joe Childs)

	Winner (Jockey)
1922	Pogrom (Ted Gardner)
1923	Brownhylda (Vic Smyth)
1924	Straitlace (Frank O'Neill)
1925	Saucy Sue (Frank Bullock)
1926	Short Story (Bobby Jones)
1927	Beam (Tommy Weston)
1928	Toboggan (Tommy Weston)
1929	Pennycomequick (Henri Jelliss)
1930	Rose of England (Gordon Richards)
1931	Brulette (Charlie Elliott)
1932	Udaipur (Michael Beary)
1933	Chatelaine (Sam Wragg)
1934	Light Brocade (Brownie Carslake)
1935	Quashed (Henri Jelliss)
1936	Lovely Rosa (Tommy Weston)
1937	Exhibitionist (Steve Donoghue)
1938	Rockfel (Harry Wragg)
1939	Galatea (Bobby Jones)
1940*	Godiva (Doug Marks)
1941*	Commotion (Harry Wragg)
1942*	Sun Chariot (Gordon Richards)
1943*	Why Hurry (Charlie Elliott)
1944*	Hycilla (George Bridgland)
1945*	Sun Stream (Harry Wragg)
1946	Steady Aim (Harry Wragg)
1947	Imprudence (Rae Johnstone)
1948	Masaka (Billy Nevett)
1949	Musidora (Edgar Britt)
1950	Asmena (Rae Johnstone)
1951	Neasham Belle (Stan Clayton)
1952	Frieze (Edgar Britt)
1953	Ambiguity (Joe Mercer)
1954	Sun Cap (Rae Johnstone)
1955	Meld (Harry Carr)
1956	Sicarelle (Freddie Palmer)
1957	Carrozza (Lester Piggott)
1958	Bella Paola (Max Garcia)
1959	Petite Etoile (Lester Piggott)
1960	Never Too Late (Roger Poincelet)
1961	Sweet Solera (Bill Rickaby)
1962	Monade (Yves Saint-Martin)
1963	Noblesse (Gamie Bougoure)
1964	Homeward Bound (Greville Starkey)
1965	Long Look (Jack Purtell)
1966	Valoris (Lester Piggott)
1967	Pia (Eddie Hide)
1968	La Lagune (Gerard Thiboeuf)
1969	Sleeping Partner (John Gorton)
1970	Lupe (Sandy Barclay)

	Winner (Jockey)
1971	Altesse Royale (Geoff Lewis)
1972	Ginevra (Tony Murray)
1973	Mysterious (Geoff Lewis)
1974	Polygamy (Pat Eddery)
1975	Juliette Marny (Lester Piggott)
1976	Pawneese (Yves Saint-Martin)
1977	Dunfermline (Willie Carson)
1978	Fair Salinia (Greville Starkey)
1979	Scintillate (Pat Eddery)
1980	Bireme (Willie Carson)
1981	Blue Wind (Lester Piggott)
1982	Time Charter (Billy Newnes)
1983	Sun Princess (Willie Carson)
1984	Circus Plume (Lester Piggott)
1985	Oh So Sharp (Steve Cauthen)
1986	Midway Lady (Ray Cochrane)
1987	Unite (Walter Swinburn)
1988	Diminuendo (Steve Cauthen)
1989	Snow Bride (Steve Cauthen)
1990	Salsabil (Willie Carson)
1991	Jet Ski Lady (Christy Roche)
1992	User Friendly (George Duffield)
1993	Intrepidity (Michael Roberts)
1994	Balanchine (Frankie Dettori)
1995	Moonshell (Frankie Dettori)
1996	Lady Carla (Pat Eddery)
1997	Reams of Verse (Kieren Fallon)
1998	Shahtoush (Micheal Kinane)
1999	Ramruma (Kieren Fallon)
2000	Love Divine (Richard Quinn)
2001	Imagine (Micheal Kinane)
2002	Kazzia (Frankie Dettori)
2003	Casual Look (Martin Dwyer)
2004	Ouija Board (Kieren Fallon)

Come on, Aussie, come on

1853 was a historic year for the English classics as, for the first time, the elusive triple crown of the Two Thousand Guineas, the Derby, and the St Leger was won. The horse that broke the record was called West Australian. Since then only another 14 horses have completed the ultimate achievement in English flat racing, Nijinsky being the last to do so in 1970.

The Derby

The Derby Stakes is for three-year-olds and is run at Epsom Downs in June over one and a half miles. Lord Derby won the honour of having the race named after him following the toss of a coin with Sir Charles Bunbury, although the latter's horse won the first race. The first four races were held over one mile.

* = held at Newmarket

	Winner (Jockey)
1780	Diomed (Sam Arnull)
1781	Young Eclipse (Charles Hindley)
1782	Assassin (Sam Arnull)
1783	Saltram (Charles Hindley)
1784	Serjeant (John Arnull0
1785	Aimwell (Charles Hindley)
1786	Noble (J White)
1787	Sir Peter Teazle (Sam Arnull)
1788	Sir Thomas (William South)
1789	Skyscraper (Sam Chifney, Sr)
1790	Rhadamanthus (John Arnull)
1791	Eager (Matt Stephenson)
1792	John Bull (Frank Buckle)
1793	Waxy (Bill Clift)
1794	Daedulus (Frank Buckle)
1795	Spread Eagle (Anthony Wheatley)
1796	Didelot (John Arnull)
1797	*Unnamed colt by* Fidget (John Singleton)
1798	Sir Harry (Sam Arnull)
1799	Archduke (John Arnull)
1800	Champion (Bill Clift)
1801	Eleanor (John Saunders)
1802	Tyrant (Frank Buckle)
1803	Ditto (Bill Clift)
1804	Hannibal (Bill Arnull)

	Winner (Jockey)
1805	Cardinal Beaufort (Denni Fitzpatrick)
1806	Paris (John Shepherd)
1807	Election (John Arnull)
1808	Pan (Frank Collinson)
1809	Pope (Tom Goodisson)
1810	Whalebone (Bill Clift)
1811	Phantom (Frank Buckle)
1812	Octavius (Bill Arnull)
1813	Smolensko (Tom Goodisson)
1814	Blücher (Bill Arnull)
1815	Whisker (Tom Goodisson)
1816	Prince Leopold (Will Wheatley)
1817	Azor (Jem Robinson)
1818	Sam (Sam Chifney, Jr)
1819	Tiresias (Bill Clift)
1820	Sailor (Sam Chifney, Jr)
1821	Gustavus (Sam Day)
1822	Moses (Tom Goodisson)
1823	Emilius (Frank Buckle)
1824	Cedric (Jem Robinson)
1825	Middleton (Jem Robinson)
1826	Lap-Dog (George Dockeray)
1827	Mameluke (Jem Robinson)
1828	Cadland (Jem Robinson)
1829	Frederick (John Forth)
1830	Priam (Sam Day)
1831	Spaniel (Will Wheatley)
1832	St Giles (Bill Scott)
1833	Dangerous (Jem Chapple)
1834	Plenipotentiary (Patrick Conolly)
1835	Mündig (Bill Scott)
1836	Bay Middleton (Jem Robinson)
1837	Phosphorous (George Edwards)
1838	Amato (Jem Chapple)
1839	Bloomsbury (Sim Templeman)
1840	Little Wonder (William Macdonald)
1841	Coronation (Patrick Conolly)
1842	Attila (Bill Scott)
1843	Cotherstone (Bill Scott)
1844	Orlando (Nat Flatman)
1845	The Merry Monarch (Foster Bell)
1846	Pyrrhus the First (Sam Day)
1847	Cossack (Sim Templeman)
1848	Surplice (Sim Templeman)
1849	The Flying Dutchman (Charlie Marlow)
1850	Voltigeur (Job Marson)
1851	Teddington (Job Marson)
1852	Daniel O'Rourke (Frank Butler)

	Winner (Jockey)
1853	West Australian (Frank Butler)
1854	Andover (Alfred Day)
1855	Wild Dayrell (Robert Sherwood)
1856	Ellington (Tom Aldcroft)
1857	Blink Bonny (Jack Charlton)
1858	Beadsman (John Wells)
1859	Musjid (John Wells)
1860	Thormanby (Harry Custance)
1861	Kettledrum (Ralph Bullock)
1862	Caractacus (John Parsons)
1863	Macaroni (Tom Chaloner)
1864	Blair Athol (Jim Snowden)
1865	Gladiateur (Harry Grimshaw)
1866	Lord Lyon (Harry Custance)
1867	Hermit (John Daley)
1868	Blue Gown (John Wells)
1869	Pretender (John Osbourne)
1870	Kingcraft (Tom French)
1871	Favonius (Tom French)
1872	Cremorne (Charlie Maidment)
1873	Doncaster (Fred Webb)
1874	George Frederick (Harry Custance)
1875	Galopin (Jack Morris)
1876	Kisber (Charlie Maidment)
1877	Silvio (Fred Archer)
1878	Sefton (Harry Constable)
1879	Sir Bevys (George Fordham)
1880	Bend Or (Fred Archer)
1881	Iroquois (Fred Archer)
1882	Shotover (Tom Cannon)
1883	St Blaise (Tom Cannon)
1884	St Gatien (Charlie Wood) Harvester (Samuel Loates) *(dead heat)*
1885	Melton (Fred Archer)
1886	Ormonde (Fred Archer)
1887	Merry Hampton (Jack Watts)
1888	Ayrshire (Fred Barrett)
1889	Donavon (Tommy Loates)
1890	Sainfoin (Jack Watts)
1891	Common (George Barrett)
1892	Sir Hugo (Fred Allsopp)
1893	Isinglass (Tommy Loates)
1894	Ladas II (Jack Watts)
1895	Sir Visto (Sam Loates)
1896	Persimmon (Jack Watts)
1897	Galtee More (Charlie Wood)
1898	Jeddah (Otto Madden)
1899	Flying Fox (Morny Cannon)

	Winner (Jockey)
1900	Diamond Jubilee (Herbert Jones)
1901	Volodyovski (Lester Reiff)
1902	Ard Patrick (Skeets Martin)
1903	Rock Sand (Danny Maher)
1904	St Amant (Kempton Cannon)
1905	Cicero (Danny Maher)
1906	Spearmint (Danny Maher)
1907	Orby (Johnny Reiff)
1908	Signorinetta (Billy Bullock)
1909	Minoru (Herbert Jones)
1910	Lemberg (Bernard Dillon)
1911	Sunstar (George Stern)
1912	Tagalle (Johnny Reiff)
1913	Aboyeur (Edwin Piper)
1914	Durbar II (Matt MacGee)
1915*	Pommern (Steve Donoghue)
1916*	Fifinella (Joe Childs)
1917*	Gay Crusader (Steve Donoghue)
1918*	Gainsborough (Joe Childs)
1919	Grand Parade (Fred Templeman)
1920	Spion Kop (Frank O'Neill)
1921	Humorist (Steve Donoghue)
1922	Captain Cuttle (Steve Donoghue)
1923	Papyrus (Steve Donoghue)
1924	Sansovino (Tommy Weston)
1925	Manna (Steve Donoghue)
1926	Coronach (Joe Childs)
1927	Call Boy (Charlie Elliot)
1928	Felstead (Harry Wragg)
1929	Trigio (Joe Marshall)
1930	Blenheim (Harry Wragg)
1931	Cameronian (Freddie Fox)
1932	April the Fifth (Fred Lane)
1933	Hyperion (Tommy Weston)
1934	Windsor Lad (Charlie Smirke)
1935	Bahram (Freddie Fox)
1936	Mahmoud (Charlie Smirke)
1937	Mid-Day Sun (Michael Beary)
1938	Bois Roussel (Charlie Elliot)
1939	Blue Peter (Eph Smith)
1940*	Pont L'Eveque (Sam Wragg)
1941*	Owen Tudor (Billy Nevett)
1942*	Watling Street (Harry Wragg)
1943*	Straight Deal (Tommy Carey)
1944*	Ocean Swell (Billy Nevett)
1945*	Dante (Billy Nevett)
1946	Airborne (Tommy Lowrey)
1947	Pearl Diver (George Bridgland)
1948	My Love (Rae Johnstone)

	Winner (Jockey)
1949	Nimbus (Charlie Elliot)
1950	Galcador (Rae Johnstone)
1951	Arctic Prince (Chuck Spares)
1952	Tulyar (Charlie Smirke)
1953	Pinza (Gordon Richards)
1954	Never Say Die (Lester Piggott)
1955	Phil Drake (Freddie Palmer)
1956	Lavandin (Rae Johnstone)
1957	Crepello (Lester Piggott)
1958	Hard Ridden (Charlie Smirke)
1959	Parthia (Harry Carr)
1960	St Paddy (Lester Piggott)
1961	Psidium (Roger Poincelet)
1962	Larkspur (Neville Sellwood)
1963	Relko (Yves Saint-Martin)
1964	Santa Claus (Scobie Breasley)
1965	Sea Bird II (Pat Glennon)
1966	Charlottown (Scobie Breasley)
1967	Royal Palace (George Moore)
1968	Sir Ivor (Lester Piggott)
1969	Blakeney (Ernie Johnson)
1970	Nijinsky (Lester Piggott)
1971	Mill Reef (Geoff Lewis)
1972	Roberto (Lester Piggott)
1973	Morston (Eddie Hide)
1974	Snow Knight (Brian Taylor)
1975	Grundy (Pat Eddery)
1976	Empery (Lester Piggott)
1977	The Minstrel (Lester Piggott)
1978	Shirley Heights (Greville Starkey)
1979	Troy (Willie Carson)
1980	Henbit (Willie Carson)
1981	Shergar (Walter Swinburn)
1982	Golden Fleece (Pat Eddery)
1983	Teenoso (Lester Piggott)
1984	Secreto (Christy Roche)
1985	Slip Anchor (Steve Cauthen)
1986	Shahrastani (Walter Swinburn)
1987	Reference Point (Steve Cauthen)
1988	Kahyasi (Ray Cochrane)
1989	Nashwan (Willie Carson)
1990	Quest For Fame (Pat Eddery)
1991	Generous (Alan Munro)
1992	Dr Devious (John Reid)
1993	Commander In Chief (Michael Kinane)
1994	Erhaab (Willie Carson)
1995	Lammtarra (Walter Swinburn)
1996	Shaamit (Michael Hills)

	Winner (Jockey)		Winner (Jockey)
1997	Benny The Dip (Willie Ryan)	**2001**	Galileo (Michael Kinane)
1998	High-Rise (Olivier Peslier)	**2002**	High Chapparal (Johnny Murtagh)
1999	Oath (Kieren Fallon)	**2003**	Kris Kin (Kieren Fallon)
2000	Sinndar (Johnny Murtagh)	**2004**	North Light (Kieren Fallon)

Stout-hearted horse is the punters' favourite

In February 2004 the *Racing Post* published the winners of a readers' poll to find Britain and Ireland's favourite racehorse. Arkle, the Irish chaser who won three consecutive Cheltenham Gold Cups in the 1960s, was top with 21.9% of the vote. Perhaps his success was down to the two bottles of Guinness he was fed with his oats every day. The other nine horses in the list were, in order of popularity: Desert Orchid; Red Rum; Istabraq; Brigadier Gerard; One Man; Persian Punch; Dancing Brave; Sea Pigeon; and Nijinsky.

St Leger

The oldest of the English classic races, the St Leger is for three-year-olds and is run over 1 mile, 6 furlongs and 132 yards in September at Doncaster, Yorkshire. The race is named after Anthony St Leger, an Army officer and member of Parliament, whose idea it was for the race. From 1915–18 the race was held at Newmarket, in 1940 at Thirsk, in 1941 at Manchester, from 1942–4 at Newmarket, in 1945 at York, and in 1989 at Ayr.

	Winner (Jockey)		Winner (Jockey)
1776	Allabaculia (John Singleton)	**1800**	Champion (Francis Buckle)
1777	Bourbon (John Cade)	**1801**	Quiz (John Shepherd)
1778	Hollandaise (George Herring)	**1802**	Orville (John Singleton, Jr)
1779	Tommy (George Lowry, Sr)	**1803**	Remembrancer (Ben Smith)
1780	Ruler (John Mangle)	**1804**	Sancho (Francis Buckle)
1781	Serina (Richard Foster)	**1805**	Stavely (John Jackson)
1782	Imperatrix (George Searle)	**1806**	Fyldener (Tom Carr)
1783	Phenomenon (Anthony Hall)	**1807**	Paulina (Bill Clift)
1784	Omphale (John Kirton)	**1808**	Petronius (Ben Smith)
1785	Cowslip (George Searle)	**1809**	Ashton (Ben Smith)
1786	Paragon (John Mangle)	**1810**	Octavian (Bill Clift)
1787	Spadille (John Mangle)	**1811**	Soothsayer (Ben Smith)
1788	Young Flora (John Mangle)	**1812**	Otterington (Bob Johnson)
1789	Pewett (William Wilson)	**1813**	Altisidora (John Jackson)
1790	Ambidexter (George Searle)	**1814**	William (John Shepherd)
1791	Young Traveller (John Jackson)	**1815**	Filho da Puta (John Jackson)
1792	Tartar (John Mangle)	**1816**	The Duchess (Ben Smith)
1793	Ninety-Three (Bill Peirse)	**1817**	Ebor (Bob Johnson)
1794	Beningbrough (John Jackson)	**1818**	Reveller (Bob Johnson)
1795	Hambletonian (Dixon Boyce)	**1819**	Antonio (Tom Nicholson)
1796	Ambrosio (John Jackson)	**1820**	St Patrick (Bob Johnson)
1797	Lounger (John Shepherd)	**1821**	Jack Spigot (Bill Scott)
1798	Symmetry (John Jackson)	**1822**	Theodore (John Jackson)
1799	Cockfighter (Tom Fields)	**1823**	Barefoot (Dick Goodisson)

	Winner (Jockey)
1824	Jerry (Ben Smith)
1825	Memnon (Bill Scott)
1826	Tarrare (George Nelson)
1827	Matilda (Jem Robinson)
1828	The Colonel (Bill Scott)
1829	Rowton (Bill Scott)
1830	Birmingham (Patrick Conolly)
1831	Chorister (John Barham Day)
1832	Margrave (Jem Robinson)
1833	Rockingham (Sam Darling)
1834	Touchstone (George Calloway)
1835	Queen of Trumps (Tommy Lye)
1836	Elis (John Barham Day)
1837	Mango (Sam Day, Jr)
1838	Don John (Bill Scott)
1839	Charles XII (Bill Scott)
1840	Launcelot (Bill Scott)
1841	Satirist (Bill Scott)
1842	Blue Bonnet (Tommy Lye)
1843	Nutwith (Job Marson)
1844	Faugh-A-Ballagh (Henry Bell)
1845	The Baron (Frank Butler)
1846	Sir Tatton Sykes (Bill Scott)
1847	Van Tromp (Job Marson)
1848	Surplice (Nat Flatman)
1849	The Flying Dutchman (Charlie Marlow)
1850	Voltigeur (Job Marson)
1851	Newminster (Sim Templeman)
1852	Stockwell (John Norman)
1853	West Australian (Frank Butler)
1854	Knight of St George (Robert Basham)
1855	Saucebox (John Wells)
1856	Warlock (Nat Flatman)
1857	Imperieuse (Nat Flatman)
1858	Sunbeam (Luke Snowden)
1859	Gamester (Tom Aldcroft)
1860	St Albans (Luke Snowden)
1861	Caller Ou (Tom Chaloner)
1862	The Marquis (Tom Chaloner)
1863	Lord Clifden (Johnny Osbourne)
1864	Blair Athol (Jim Snowden)
1865	Gladiateur (Harry Grimshaw)
1866	Lord Lyon (Harry Custance)
1867	Achievement (Tom Chaloner)
1868	Formosa (Tom Chaloner)
1869	Pero Gomez (John Wells)
1870	Hawthornden (Jemmy Grimshaw)

	Winner (Jockey)
1871	Hannah (Charlie Maidment)
1872	Wenlock (Charlie Maidment)
1873	Marie Stuart (Tom Osbourne)
1874	Apology (John Osbourne)
1875	Craig Millar (Tom Chaloner)
1876	Petrarch (Jem Goater)
1877	Silvio (Fred Archer)
1878	Jannette (Fred Archer)
1879	Rayon d'Or (Jem Goater)
1880	Robert the Devil (Tom Cannon)
1881	Iroquois (Fred Archer)
1882	Dutch Oven (Fred Archer)
1883	Ossian (Jack Watts)
1884	The Lambkin (Jack Watts)
1885	Melton (Fred Archer)
1886	Ormonde (Fred Archer)
1887	Kilwarlin (Jack Robinson)
1888	Seabreeze (Jack Robinson)
1889	Donovan (Fred Barrett)
1890	Memoir (Jack Watts)
1891	Common (George Barrett)
1892	La Fleche (Jack Watts)
1893	Isinglass (Tommy Loates)
1894	Throstle (Morny Cannon)
1895	Sir Visto (Sam Loates)
1896	Persimmon (Jack Watts)
1897	Galtee More (Charlie Wood)
1898	Wildflower (Charlie Wood)
1899	Flying Fox (Morny Cannon)
1900	Diamond Jubilee (Herbert Jones)
1901	Doricles (Kempton Cannon)
1902	Sceptre (Fred Hardy)
1903	Rock Sand (Danny Maher)
1904	Pretty Polly (Willie Lane)
1905	Challacombe (Otto Madden)
1906	Troutbeck (George Stern)
1907	Wool Winder (Bill Halsey)
1908	Your Majesty (Wal Griggs)
1909	Bayardo (Danny Maher)
1910	Swynford (Frank Wootton)
1911	Prince Palatine (Frank O'Neill)
1912	Tracery (George Bellhouse)
1913	Night Hawk (Elijah Wheatley)
1914	Black Jester (Wal Griggs)
1915	Pommern (Steve Donoghue)
1916	Hurry On (Charlie Childs)
1917	Gay Crusader (Steve Donoghue)
1918	Gainsborough (Joe Childs)
1919	Keysoe (Brownie Carslake)

	Winner (Jockey)
1920	Caligula (Arthur Smith)
1921	Polemarch (Joe Childs)
1922	Royal Lancer (Bobby Jones)
1923	Tranquil (Tommy Weston)
1924	Salmon-Trout (Brownie Carslake)
1925	Solario (Joe Childs)
1926	Coronach (Joe Childs)
1927	Book Law (Henri Jelliss)
1928	Fairway (Tommy Weston)
1929	Trigo (Micheal Beary)
1930	Singapore (Gordon Richards)
1931	Sandwich (Harry Wragg)
1932	Firdaussi (Freddy Fox)
1933	Hyperion (Tommy Weston)
1934	Windsor Lad (Charlie Smirke)
1935	Bahram (Charlie Smirke)
1936	Boswell (Pat Beasley)
1937	Chulmleigh (Gordon Richards)
1938	Scottish Union (Brownie Carslake)
1939	*Not run*
1940	Turkhan (Gordon Richards)
1941	Sun Castle (George Bridgland)
1942	Sun Chariot (Gordon Richards)
1943	Herringbone (Harry Wragg)
1944	Tehran (Gordon Richards)
1945	Chamossaire (Tommy Lowrey)
1946	Airborne (Tommy Lowrey)
1947	Sayajirao (Edgar Britt)
1948	Black Tarquin (Edgar Britt)
1949	Ridge Wood (Michael Beary)
1950	Scratch (Rae Johnstone)
1951	Talma (Rae Johnstone)
1952	Tulyar (Charlie Smirke)
1953	Premonition (Eph Smith)
1954	Never Say Die (Charlie Smirke)
1955	Meld (Harry Carr)
1956	Cambremer (Freddie Palmer)
1957	Ballymoss (Tommy Burns)
1958	Alcide (Harry Carr)
1959	Cantelo (Eddie Hide)
1960	St Paddy (Lester Piggott)
1961	Aurelius (Lester Piggott)
1962	Hethersett (Harry Carr)

	Winner (Jockey)
1963	Ragusa (Garnie Bougoure)
1964	Indiana (Jimmy Lindley)
1965	Provoke (Joe Mercer)
1966	Sodium (Frankie Durr)
1967	Ribocco (Lester Piggott)
1968	Ribero (Lester Piggott)
1969	Intermezzo (Ron Hutchinson)
1970	Nijinsky (Lester Piggott)
1971	Athens Wood (Lester Piggott)
1972	Boucher (Lester Piggott)
1973	Peleid (Frankie Durr)
1974	Bustino (Joe Mercer)
1975	Bruni (Tony Murray)
1976	Crow (Yves Saint-Martin)
1977	Dunfermline (Willie Carson)
1978	Julio Mariner (Eddie Hide)
1979	Son of Love (Alain Lequeux)
1980	Light Cavalry (Joe Mercer)
1981	Cut Above (Joe Mercer)
1982	Touching Wood (Paul Cook)
1983	Sun Princess (Willie Carson)
1984	Commanche Run (Lester Piggott)
1985	Oh So Sharp (Steve Cauthen)
1986	Moon Madness (Pat Eddery)
1987	Reference Point (Steve Cauthen)
1988	Minister Son (Willie Carson)
1989	Michelozzo (Steve Cauthen)
1990	Snurge (Richard Quinn)
1991	Toulon (Pat Eddery)
1992	User Friendly (George Duffield)
1993	Bob's Return (Philip Robinson)
1994	Moonax (Pat Eddery)
1995	Classic Cliche (Frankie Dettori)
1996	Shantou (Frankie Dettori)
1997	Silver Patriarch (Pat Eddery)
1998	Nedawi (John Reid)
1999	Mutafaweq (Richard Hills)
2000	Millenary (Richard Quinn)
2001	Milan (Michael Kinane)
2002	Bollin Eric (Kevin Darley)
2003	Brian Boru (Jamie Spencer)
2004	Rule of Law (Kerrin McEvoy)

Sport of kings

Ambush II holds a noble position in the ranks of Grand National winners. So far he is the only royal-owned horse to win the Aintree race, doing so in 1900 for the man who became, a year later, King Edward VII.

The Grand National

Britain's most famous steeplechase is run over 4 miles and 856 yards in early April at Aintree, Liverpool. The two circuits include 16 fences, 14 of which are jumped twice. The named fences are: Becher's Brook, Foinavon, Canal Turn, Valentine's, and The Chair.

	Winner (Jockey)
1839	Lottery (Jem Mason)
1840	Jerry (Mr B Bretherton)
1841	Charity (Mr A Powell)
1842	Gay Lad (Tom Olliver)
1843	Vanguard (Tom Olliver)
1844	Discount (Mr H Crickmere)
1845	Cure-All (Mr William Loft)
1846	Pioneer (W Taylor)
1847	Matthew (Denis Wynne)
1848	Chandler (Capt. Joseph Little)
1849	Peter Simple (T Cunningham)
1850	Abd-El-Kader (Chris Green)
1851	Abd-El-Kader (T Abbot)
1852	Miss Mowbray (Mr Alec Goodman)
1853	Peter Simple (Tom Olliver)
1854	Bourton (J Tasker)
1855	Wanderer (J Hanlon)
1856	Freetrader (George Stevens)
1857	Emigrant (Charlie Boyce)
1858	Little Charley (William Archer)
1859	Half Caste (Chris Green)
1860	Anatis (Mr Tommy Pickernell)
1861	Jealousy (J Kendall)
1862	The Huntsman (Harry Lamplugh)
1863	Emblem (George Stevens)
1864	Emblematic (George Stevens)
1865	Alcibiade (Capt. Henry Coventry)
1866	Salamander (Mr Alec Goodman)
1867	Cortolvin (John Page)
1868	The Lamb (Mr George Ede)
1869	The Colonel (George Stevens)
1870	The Colonel (George Stevens)
1871	The Lamb (Mr Tommy Pickernell)
1872	Casse Tête (John Page)
1873	Disturbance (Mr John Richardson)
1874	Reugny (Mr John Richardson)
1875	Pathfinder (Mr Tommy Pickernell)
1876	Regal (Joe Cannon)
1877	Austerlitz (Mr Fred Hobson)
1878	Shifnal (J Jones)
1879	The Liberator (Mr Garry Moore)
1880	Empress (Mr Tommy Beasley)
1881	Woodbrook (Mr Tommy Beasley)

	Winner (Jockey)
1882	Seaman (Lord Manners)
1883	Zoëdone Count (Charles Kinsky)
1884	Voluptuary (Mr Ted Wilson)
1885	Roquefort (Mr Ted Wilson)
1889	Frigate (Mr Tommy Beasley)
1890	Ilex (Arthur Nightingall)
1891	Come Away (Mr Harry Beasley)
1892	Father O'Flynn (Capt. Roddy Owen)
1893	Cloister (Bill Dollery)
1894	Why Not (Arthur Nightingall)
1895	Wild Man (Mr Joe Widger)
1896	The Soarer (Mr David Campbell)
1897	Manifesto (Terry Kavanagh)
1898	Drogheda (John Gourley)
1899	Manifesto (George Williamson)
1900	Ambush II (Algy Anthony)
1901	Grudon (Arthur Nightingall)
1902	Shannon Lass (David Read)
1903	Drumcree (Percy Woodland)
1904	Moifaa (Arthur Birch)
1905	Kirkland (Frank Mason)
1906	Ascetic's Silver (Mr Aubrey Hastings)
1907	Eremon (Alf Newey)
1908	Rubio (Henry Bletsoe)
1909	Lutteur III (Georges Parfrement)
1910	Jenkinstown (Robert Chadwick)
1911	Glenside (Mr Jack Anthony)
1912	Jerry M (Ernie Piggott)
1913	Covertcoat (Percy Woodland)
1914	Sunloch (Bill Smith)
1915	Ally Sloper (Mr Jack Anthony)
1916–18	*Not run*
1919	Poethlyn (Ernie Piggott)
1920	Troytown (Mr Jack Anthony)
1921	Shaun Spadah (Fred Rees)
1922	Music Hall (Lewis Rees)
1923	Sergeant Murphy (Capt. Geoffrey Bennett)
1924	Master Robert (Bob Trudgill)
1925	Double Chance (Major John Wilson)
1926	Jack Horner (William Watkinson)
1927	Sprig (Ted Leader)

	Winner (Jockey)		Winner (Jockey)
1928	Tipperary Tim (Mr Bill Dutton)	**1969**	Highland Wedding (Eddie Harty)
1929	Gregalach (Robert Everett)	**1970**	Gay Trip (Pat Taaffe)
1930	Shaun Goilin (Tommy Cullinan)	**1971**	Specify (John Cook)
1931	Grakle (Bob Lyall)	**1972**	Well To Do (Graham Thorner)
1932	Forbra (Tim Hamey)	**1973**	Red Rum (Brian Fletcher)
1933	Kellsboro' Jack (Dudley Williams)	**1974**	Red Rum (Brian Fletcher)
1934	Golden Miller (Gerry Wilson)	**1975**	L'Escargot (Tommy Carberry)
1935	Reynoldstown (Mr Frank Furlong)	**1976**	Rag Trade (John Burke)
1936	Reynoldstown (Mr Fulke Walwyn)	**1977**	Red Rum (Tommy Stack)
1937	Royal Mail (Evan Williams)	**1978**	Lucius (Bob Davies)
1938	Battleship (Bruce Hobbs)	**1979**	Rubstic (Maurice Barnes)
1939	Workman (Tim Hyde)	**1980**	Ben Nevis (Mr Charlie Fenwick)
1940	Bogskar (Mervyn Jones)	**1981**	Aldaniti (Bob Champion)
1941–5	*Not run*	**1982**	Grittar (Mr Dick Saunders)
1946	Lovely Cottage (Capt. Bobby Petre)	**1983**	Corbiere (Ben de Haan)
1947	Caughoo (Eddie Dempsey)	**1984**	Hallo Dandy (Neale Doughty)
1948	Sheila's Cottage (Arthur Thompson)	**1985**	Last Suspect (Hywel Davies)
1949	Russian Hero (Leo McMorrow)	**1986**	West Tip (Richard Dunwoody)
1950	Freebooter (Jimmy Power)	**1987**	Maori Venture (Steve Knight)
1951	Nickel Coin (John Bullock)	**1988**	Rhyme 'n' Reason (Brendan Powell)
1952	Teal (Arthur Thompson)	**1989**	Little Polveir (Jimmy Frost)
1953	Early Mist (Bryan Marshall)	**1990**	Mr Frisk (Mr Marcus Armytage)
1954	Royal Tan (Bryan Marshall)	**1991**	Seagram (Nigel Hawke)
1955	Quare Times (Pat Taaffe)	**1992**	Party Politics (Carl Llewellyn)
1956	ESB (Dave Dick)	**1993***	*Void race*
1957	Sundew (Fred Winter)	**1994**	Minnehoma (Richard Dunwoody)
1958	Mr What (Arthur Freeman)	**1995**	Royal Athlete (Jason Titley)
1959	Oxo (Michael Scudamore)	**1996**	Rough Quest (Mick Fitzgerald)
1960	Merryman II (Gerry Scott)	**1997**	Lord Gyllene (Tony Dobbin)
1961	Nicolaus Silver (Bobby Beasley)	**1998**	Earth Summit (Carl Llewellyn)
1962	Kilmore (Fred Winter)	**1999**	Bobbyjo (Paul Carberry)
1963	Ayala (Pat Buckley)	**2000**	Papillon (Ruby Walsh)
1964	Team Spirit (George Robinson)	**2001**	Red Marauder (Richard Guest)
1965	Jay Trump (Mr Tommy Smith)	**2002**	Bindaree (Jim Culloty)
1966	Anglo (Tim Norman)	**2003**	Monty's Pass (Barry Geraghty)
1967	Foinavon (John Buckingham)	**2004**	Amberleigh House (Graham Lee)
1968	Red Alligator (Brian Fletcher)		

*Esha Ness, ridden by John White, first past the post but race voided because of false start

Frankie's magnificent seven

28 September 1996 was a black day for British bookies. At the staggering odds of 25,095–1, Frankie Dettori won all seven races on the card at Ascot, costing the betting industry £30m and netting one lucky punter winnings on an accumulator of more than £500,000. Dettori's winners were as follows: Wall Street (2–1); Diffident (12–1); Mark of Esteem (100–30); Decorated Hero (7–1); Fatefully (7–4); Lochangel (5–4); and Fujiyama Crest (2–1).

Cheltenham Festival

The Cheltenham Festival, which takes place each year in March, is the climax of the National Hunt season in Britain and the Gold Cup is considered to be the sport's greatest prize. Queen Elizabeth the Queen Mother, a great supporter of National Hunt, was honoured in 1980 in her 80th year by having the Champion Chase named after her. The Gold Cup is run over 3 miles, 2 furlongs and 110 yards; the Champion Hurdle over 2 miles and 110 yards; and the Queen Mother Champion Chase over 2 miles.

	Gold Cup winner	Champion Hurdle winner	Queen Mother Champion Chase winner
1924	Red Spash (Dick Rees)		
1925	Ballinode (Ted Leader)		
1926	Koko (Tim Hamey)		
1927	Thrown In (Mr Hugh Grosvenor)	Blaris (George Duller)	
1928	Patron Saint (Dick Rees)	Brown Jack (Bilbie Rees)	
1929	Easter Hero (Dick Rees)	Royal Falcon (Dick Rees)	
1930	Easter Hero (Tommy Cullinan)	Brown Tony (Tommy Cullinan)	
1931	*Not run because of frost*		
1932	Golden Miller (Ted Leader)	Insurance (Ted Leader)	
1933	Golden Miller (Billy Stott)	Insurance (Billy Stott)	
1934	Golden Miller (Gerry Wilson)	Chenango (Danny Morgan)	
1935	Golden Miller (Gerry Wilson)	Lion Courage (Gerry Wilson)	
1936	Golden Miller (Evan Williams)	Victor Norman (Frenchie Nicholson)	
1937	*Not run because of snow*	Free Fare (Georges Pellerin)	
1938	Morse Code (Danny Morgan)	Our Hope (Capt. Perry Harding)	
1939	Brendan's Cottage (George Owen)	African Sister (Keith Piggott)	
1940	Roman Hackle (Evan Williams)	Soliford (Sean Magee)	
1941	Poet Prince (Roger Burford)	Seneca (Ron Smyth)	
1942	Medoc II (Frenchie Nicholson	Forestation (Ron Smyth)	
1943–4	*Not run*		
1945	Red Rower (Davy Jones)	Brains Trust (Fred Rimell)	
1946	Prince Regent (Tim Hyde)	Distel (Bobby O'Ryan)	
1947	Fortina (Mr Dick Black)	National Spirit (Danny Morgan)	
1948	Cottage Rake (Aubrey Brabazon)	National Spirit (Ron Smyth)	
1949	Cottage Rake (Aubrey Brabazon)	Hatton's Grace (Aubrey Brabazon)	
1950	Cottage Rake (Aubrey Brabazon)	Hatton's Grace (Aubrey Brabazon)	
1951	Silver Fame (Martin Molony)	Hatton's Grace (Tim Molony)	
1952	Mont Tremblant (Dave Dick)	Sir Ken (Tim Molony)	
1953	Knock Hard (Tim Molony)	Sir Ken (Tim Molony)	
1954	Four Ten (Tommy Cusack)	Sir Ken (Tim Molony)	
1955	Gay Donald (Tony Grantham)	Clair Soliel (Fred Winter)	
1956	Limber Hill (Jimmy Power)	Doorknocker (Harry Sprague)	
1957	Linwell (Michael Scudamore)	Merry Deal (Grenville Underwood)	

	Gold Cup winner	Champion Hurdle winner	Queen Mother Champion Chase winner
1958	Kerstin (Stan Hayhurst)	Bandalore (George Slack)	
1959	Roddy Owen (Bobby Beasley)	Fare Time (Fred Winter)	Quita Que (Bunny Cox)
1960	Pas Seul (Bill Rees)	Another Flash (Bobby Beasley)	Fortria (Pat Taaffe)
1961	Saffron Tartan (Fred Winter)	Ebomeezer (Fred Winter)	Fortria (Pat Taaffe)
1962	Mandarin (Fred Winter)	Anzio (Willie Robinson)	Piperton (Dave Dick)
1963	Mill House (Willie Robinson)	Winning Fair (Mr Alan Lillingston)	Sandy Abbot (Stan Mellor)
1964	Arkle (Pat Taaffe)	Magic Court (Pat McCarron)	Ben Stack (Pat Taaffe)
1965	Arkle (Pat Taaffe)	Kirriemuir (Willie Robinson)	Dunkirk (Dave Dick)
1966	Arkle (Pat Taaffe)	Salmon Spray (Johnny Haine)	Flyingbolt (Pat Taaffe)
1967	Woodland Venture (Terry Biddlecombe)	Saucy Kit (Roy Edwards)	Drinny's Double (Frank Nash)
1968	Fort Leney (Pat Taaffe)	Persian War (Jimmy Uttley)	Drinny's Double (Frank Nash)
1969	What a Myth (Paul Kelleway)	Persian War (Jimmy Uttley)	Muir (Ben Hannon)
1970	L'Escargot (Tommy Carberry)	Persian War (Jimmy Uttley)	Straight Fort (Pat Taaffe)
1971	L'Escargot (Tommy Carberry)	Bula (Paul Kelleway)	Crisp (Paul Kelleway)
1972	Glencaraig Lady (Frank Berry)	Bula (Paul Kelleway)	Royal Relief (Bill Smith)
1973	The Dikler (Ron Barry)	Comedy of Errors (Bill Smith)	Inkslinger (Tommy Carberry)
1974	Captain Christy (Bobby Beasley)	Lanzarote (Richard Pitman)	Royal Relief (Bill Smith)
1975	Ten Up (Tommy Carberry)	Comedy of Errors (Ken White)	Lough Inagh (Sean Barker)
1976	Royal Frolic (John Burke)	Night Nurse (Paddy Broderick)	Skymas (Mouse Morris)
1977	Davy Lad (Dessie Hughes)	Night Nurse (Paddy Broderick)	Skymas (Mouse Morris)
1978	Midnight Court (John Francome)	Monksfield (Tommy Kinane)	Hilly Way (Tommy Carmody)
1979	Alverton (Jonjo O'Neill)	Monksfield (Dessie Hughes)	Hilly Way (Mr Ted Walsh)
1980	Master Smudge (Richard Hoare)	Sea Pigeon (Jonjo O'Neill)	Another Dolly (Sam Morshead)
1981	Little Owl (Mr Jim Wilson)	Sea Pigeon (John Francome)	Drumgora (Frank Berry)
1982	Silver Buck (Robert Earnshaw)	For Auction (Mr Colin Magnier)	Rathgorman (Kevin Whyte)
1983	Bregawn (Graham Bradley)	Gaye Brief (Richard Linley)	Badsworth Boy (Robert Earnshaw)
1984	Burrough Hill Lad (Phil Tuck)	Dawn Run (Jonjo O'Neill)	Badsworth Boy (Robert Earnshaw)
1985	Forgive 'n' Forget (Martin Dwyer)	See You Then (Steve Smith-Eccles)	Badsworth Boy (Robert Earnshaw)
1986	Dawn Run (Jonjo O'Neill)	See You Then (Steve Smith-Eccles)	Buck House (Tommy Carmody)
1987	The Thinker (Ridley Lamb)	See You Then (Steve Smith-Eccles)	Pearlyman (Peter Scudamore)
1988	Charter Party (Richard Dunwoody)	Celtic Shot (Peter Scudamore)	Pearlyman (Tom Morgan)
1989	Desert Orchid (Simon Sherwood)	Beech Road (Richard Guest)	Barnbrook Again (Simon Sherwood)
1990	Norton's Coin (Graham McCourt)	Kribensis (Richard Dunwoody)	Barnbrook Again (Hywel Davies)
1991	Garrison Savannah (Mark Pitman)	Morley Street (Jimmy Frost)	Katabatic (Simon McNeill)
1992	Cool Ground (Adrian Maguire)	Royal Gait (Graham McCourt)	Remittance Man (Jamie Osborne)

	Gold Cup winner	Champion Hurdle winner	Queen Mother Champion Chase winner
1993	Jodami (Mark Dwyer)	Granville Again (Peter Scudamore)	Deep Sensation (Declan Murphy)
1994	The Fellow (Adam Kondrat)	Flakey Dove (Mark Dwyer)	Viking Flagship (Adrian Maguire)
1995	Master Oats (Norman Williamson)	Alderbrook (Norman Williamson)	Viking Flagship (Charlie Swan)
1996	Imperial Call (Conor O'Dwyer)	Collier Bay (Graham Bradley)	Klairon Davis (Francis Woods)
1997	Mr Mulligan (Tony McCoy)	Make a Stand (Tony McCoy)	Martha's Son (Rodney Farrant)
1998	Cool Dawn (Andrew Thornton)	Istabraq (Charlie Swan)	One Man (Brian Harding)
1999	See More Business (Mick Fitzgerald)	Istabraq (Charlie Swan)	Call Equiname (Mick Fitzgerald)
2000	Looks Like Trouble (Richard Johnson)	Istabraq (Charlie Swan)	Edredon Bleu (Tony McCoy)
2001	*Not held because of foot and mouth disease restrictions on the movement of animals*		
2002	Best Mate (Jim Culloty)	Hors La Loi III (Dean Gallagher)	Flagship Uberalles (Richard Johnson)
2003	Best Mate (Jim Culloty)	Rooster Booster (Richard Johnson)	Moscow Flyer (Barry Geraghty)
2004	Best Mate (Jim Culloty)	Hardy Eustace (Conor O'Dwyer)	Azertyuiop (Ruby Walsh)

What's in a name?

Becher's Brook, one of the most difficult obstacles to jump successfully at Aintree, gets its name from one Captain Martin Becher (1797–1864). Riding in the first Grand National in 1839, Becher was deposited by his mount into the water at the fence that now bears his name. The experience did not agree with the gallant captain as, after remarking 'how dreadful water tastes without the benefit of whisky', he decided never to compete in the Grand National again.

Prix de l'Arc de Triomphe

Europe's richest horse race is run on the first Sunday in October at Longchamp, Paris. It is open to colts and fillies and is run over a mile and a half.

* = held at Le Tremblay

	Winner (Jockey)		Winner (Jockey)
1920	Comrade (Frank Bullock)	**1930**	Motrico (Marcel Fruhinsholtz)
1921	Ksar (George Stem)	**1931**	Pearl Cap (Charles Semblat)
1922	Ksar (Frank Bullock)	**1932**	Motrico (Charles Semblat)
1923	Parth (Frank O'Neill)	**1933**	Crapom (Paolo Caprioli)
1924	Massine (Fred Sharpe)	**1934**	Brantome (Charles Bouillon)
1925	Priori (Marcel Allemand)	**1935**	Samos (Wally Sibbritt)
1926	Biribi (Domingo Torterolo)	**1936**	Corrida (Charlie Elliott)
1927	Mon Talisman (Charles Semblat)	**1937**	Corrida (Charlie Elliott)
1928	Kantar (Arthur Esling)	**1938**	Eclair au Chocolat (Charles Bouillon)
1929	Ortello (Paolo Caprioli)	**1939–40**	*Not run*

	Winner (Jockey)		Winner (Jockey)
1941	La Pacha (Paul Francolon)	**1973**	Rheingold (Lester Piggott)
1942	Djebel (Jacko Doyasbère)	**1974**	Allez France (Yves Saint-Martin)
1943*	Verso II (Guy Duforez)	**1975**	Star Appeal (Greville Starkey)
1944*	Ardan (Jacko Doyasbère)	**1976**	Ivanjica (Freddie Head)
1945	Nikellora (Rae Johnstone)	**1977**	Alleged (Lester Piggott)
1946	Caracalla (Charlie Elliott)	**1978**	Alleged (Lester Piggott)
1947	Le Paillon (Femand Rochetti)	**1979**	Three Troikas (Freddie Head)
1948	Migoli (Charlie Smirke)	**1980**	Detroit (Pat Eddery)
1949	Coronation (Roger Poincelet)	**1981**	Gold River (Gary Moore)
1950	Tantième (Jacko Doyasbère)	**1982**	Akiyda (Yves Saint-Martin)
1951	Tantième (Jacko Doyasbère)	**1983**	All Along (Walter Swinburn)
1952	Nuccio (Roger Poincelet)	**1984**	Sagace (Yves Saint-Martin)
1953	La Sorellina (Maurice Larraun)	**1985**	Rainbow Quest (Pat Eddery)
1954	Sica Boy (Rae Johnstone)	**1986**	Dancing Brave (Pat Eddery)
1955	Ribot (Enrico Camici)	**1987**	Trempolino (Pat Eddery)
1956	Ribot (Enrico Camici)	**1988**	Tony Bin (John Reid)
1957	Oroso (Serge Boullenger)	**1989**	Carroll House (Michael Kinane)
1958	Ballymoss (Scobie Breasley)	**1990**	Saumarez (Gerald Masse)
1959	Saint Crespin (George Moore)	**1991**	Suave Dancer (Cash Asmussen)
1960	Puissant Chef (Max Garcia)	**1992**	Subotica (Thierry Jarnet)
1961	Molvedo (Enrico Camici)	**1993**	Urban Sea (Eric Saint-Martin)
1962	Soltikoff (Marcel Depalmas)	**1994**	Camegie (Thierry Jarnet)
1963	Exbury (Jean Deforge)	**1995**	Lammtarra (Frankie Dettori)
1964	Prince Royal (Roger Poincelet)	**1996**	Helissio (Olivier Peslier)
1965	Sea Bird (Pat Glennon)	**1997**	Peintre Célèbre (Olivier Peslier)
1966	Bon Mot (Freddie Head)	**1998**	Sagamix (Olivier Peslier)
1967	Topyo (Bill Pyers)	**1999**	Montjeu (Michael Kinane)
1968	Vaguely Noble (Bill Williamson)	**2000**	Sinndar (Johnny Murtagh)
1969	Levmoss (Bill Williamson)	**2001**	Sakhee (Frankie Dettori)
1970	Sassafras (Yves Saint-Martin)	**2002**	Marienbard (Frankie Dettori)
1971	Mill Reef (Geoff Lewis)	**2003**	Dalakhani (Christophe Soumillon)
1972	San San (Freddie Head)	**2004**	Bago (Thierry Gillet)

Shergar eats up Epsom

1981 was certainly Shergar's year. Not only did he trounce the second-place horses by four lengths apiece in the Irish Derby and King George VI and Queen Elizabeth Diamond Stakes, he also managed to beat the record in the Derby for the biggest winning margin. With Walter Swinburn on board, the Aga Khan's pride and joy passed the winning post a clear ten lengths ahead of the field. A few years later he was kidnapped and was never seen again: a sad end for a truly great horse.

Kentucky Derby

The USA's premier horse race is run by three-year-olds over one and a quarter miles at Churchill Downs, Louisville, Kentucky each May. Between 1875 and 1895 the race was run over one and a half miles.

	Winner (Jockey)
1875	Aristides (Oliver Lewis)
1876	Vagrant (Bobby Swim)
1877	Baden-Baden (Billy Walker)
1878	Day Star (Jimmy Carter)
1879	Lord Murphy (Charlie Shauer)
1880	Fonso (George Lewis)
1881	Hindoo (Jim McLaughlin)
1882	Apollo (Babe Hurd)
1883	Leonatus (Billy Donohue)
1884	Buchanan (Isaac Murphy)
1885	Joe Cotton (Babe Henderson)
1886	Ben Ali (Paul Duffy)
1887	Montrose (Isaac Lewis)
1888	Macbeth II (George Covington)
1889	Spokane (Thomas Kiley)
1890	Riley (Isaac Murphy)
1891	Kingman (Isaac Murphy)
1892	Azra (Alonzo Clayton)
1893	Lookout (Eddie Kunze)
1894	Chant (Frank Goodale)
1895	Halma (James Perkins)
1896	Ben Brush (Willie Simms)
1897	Typhoon II (Buttons Garner)
1898	Plaudit (Willie Simms)
1899	Manuel (Fred Taral)
1900	Lieutenant Gibson (Jimmy Boland)
1901	His Eminence (Jimmy Winkfield)
1902	Alan-a-Dale (Jimmy Winkfield)
1903	Judge Himes (Hal Booker)
1904	Elwood (Shorty Prior)
1905	Agile (Jack Martin)
1906	Sir Huon (Roscoe Troxler)
1907	Pink Star (Andrew Minder)
1908	Stone Street (Arthur Pickens)
1909	Wintergreen (Vincent Powers)
1910	Donau (Fred Herbert)
1911	Meridian (George Archibald)
1912	Worth (C H Shilling)
1913	Donerail (Roscoe Goose)
1914	Old Rosebud (John McCabe)
1915	Regret (Joe Notter)
1916	George Smith (Johnny Loftus)
1917	Omar Khayham (Charles Borel)
1918	Exterminator (William Knapp)
1919	Sir Barton (Johnny Loftus)
1920	Paul Jones (Ted Rice)
1921	Behave Yourself (Charles Thompson)
1922	Morvich (Albert Johnson)
1923	Zev (Earl Sande)

	Winner (Jockey)
1924	Black Gold (John Mooney)
1925	Flying Ebony (Earl Sande)
1926	Bubbling Over (Albert Johnson)
1927	Whiskery (Linus McAtee)
1928	Reigh Count (Chick Lang)
1929	Clyde Van Dusen (Linus McAtee)
1930	Gallant Fox (Earl Sande)
1931	Twenty Grand (Charles Kurtsinger)
1932	Burgoo King (Eugene James)
1933	Brokers Tip (Don Meade)
1934	Cavalcade (Mack Garner)
1935	Omaha (Willie Saunders)
1936	Bold Venture (Ira Hanford)
1937	War Admiral (Charles Kurtsinger)
1938	Lawrin (Eddie Arcaro)
1939	Johnstown (James Stout)
1940	Gallahadion (Carroll Bierman)
1941	Whirlaway (Eddie Arcaro)
1942	Shut Out (Wayne Wright)
1943	Count Fleet (Johnny Longden)
1944	Pensive (Conn McCreary)
1945	Hoop Jr (Eddie Arcaro)
1946	Assault (Warren Mehrtens)
1947	Jet Pilot (Eric Guerin)
1948	Citation (Eddie Arcaro)
1949	Ponder (Steve Brooks)
1950	Middleground (William Boland)
1951	Count Turf (Conn McCreary)
1952	Hill Gail (Eddie Arcaro)
1953	Dark Star (Hank Moreno)
1954	Determine (Raymond York)
1955	Swaps (Willie Shoemaker)
1956	Needles (David Erb)
1957	Iron Leige (Bill Hartack)
1958	Tim Tam (Ismael Valenzuela)
1959	Tomy Lee (Willie Shoemaker)
1960	Venetian Way (Bill Hartack)
1961	Carry Back (John Sellers)
1962	Decidedly (Bill Hartack)
1963	Chateaugay (Braulio Baeza)
1964	Northern Dancer (Bill Hartack)
1965	Lucky Debonair (Willie Shoemaker)
1966	Kauai King (Don Brumfield)
1967	Proud Clarion (Bobby Ussery)
1968	Forward Pass (Ismael Valenzuela)
1969	Majestic Prince (Bill Hartack)
1970	Dust Commander (Mike Manganello)
1971	Canonero II (Gustavo Avila)
1972	Riva Ridge (Ron Turcotte)

	Winner (Jockey)		Winner (Jockey)
1973	Secretariat (Ron Turcotte)	**1989**	Sunday Silence (Pat Valenzuela)
1974	Cannonade (Angel Cordero, Jr)	**1990**	Unbridled (Craig Perret)
1975	Foolish Pleasure (Jacinto Vasquez)	**1991**	Strike The Gold (Chris Antley)
1976	Bold Forbes (Angel Cordero, Jr)	**1992**	Lil E Tee (Pat Day)
1977	Seattle Slew (Jean Cruguet)	**1993**	Sea Hero (Jerry Bailey)
1978	Affirmed (Steve Cauthen)	**1994**	Go For Gin (Chris McCarron)
1979	Spectacular Bird (Ron Franklin)	**1995**	Thunder Gulch (Gary Stevens)
1980	Genuine Risk (Jacinto Vasquez)	**1996**	Grindstone (Jerry Bailey)
1981	Pleasant Colony (Jorge Velasquez)	**1997**	Silver Charm (Gary Stevens)
1982	Gato Del Sol (Eddie Delahoussaye)	**1998**	Real Quiet (Kent Desormeaux)
1983	Sunny's Halo (Eddie Delahoussaye)	**1999**	Charismatic (Chris Antley)
1984	Swale (Laffit Pincay, Jr)	**2000**	Fusaichi Pegasus (Kent Desormeaux)
1985	Spend A Buck (Angel Cordero, Jr)	**2001**	Monarchos (Jorge Chavez)
1986	Ferdinand (Willie Shoemaker)	**2002**	War Emblem (Victor Espinoza)
1987	Alysheba (Chris McCarron)	**2003**	Funny Cide (Jose Santos)
1988	Winning Colors (Gary Stevens)	**2004**	Smarty Jones (Stewart Elliott)

How did they get them all into the parade ring?

The race caller at Aintree in 1926 must have had a tough time remembering the names and colours of the horses during the Grand National. In that year an amazing 66 horses went under starter's orders for the highlight of the steeplechase season, a record field that stands to this day. The field is now restricted to 40 horses for safety reasons.

A-Z

accumulator a bet on four or more races, where the original stake and any money won on the first race are bet on the next race and then, if the second selection wins, on the third selection, and so on. All the selections in an accumulator must win for the bet to pay out

all-weather a synthetic surface intended to allow racing to take place in any weather conditions

ante-post (of a bet) placed before the day of the race

blinkers the leather sidepieces attached to a horse's bridle to prevent the horse from seeing to the side

bookmaker an individual or company that sets odds and takes bets

bumper race a **National Hunt** flat race for horses that have not yet competed in **flat racing** or over **National Hunt** jumps

chaser a horse that competes in **steeplechases**

classic one of the principal flat races for three-year-old horses. In Britain the five classics are the Two Thousand Guineas, the One Thousand Guineas, the Oaks, the Derby, and the St Leger

colt a male horse under the age of four

conditions race the most prestigious type of flat race. Conditions races are divided into pattern races and listed races. Pattern races consist of three groups: group 1 consists of classics and other important international races; group 2 races are the less important international races; group 3 races are mainly domestic. Listed races are less important than pattern races but are still highly prized

connections the people associated with a horse, such as the owner(s) and the trainer

dam	the mother of a **foal**
evens	if a horse's odds are evens, the amount staked on it is equal to the amount won if the horse wins. As with all winning bets, the stake is also returned
faller	a horse that falls at a fence or hurdle and fails to complete the race
favourite	the horse on which most money has been wagered, giving it the shortest odds
fence	an obstacle to be jumped in a **steeplechase**
field	the horses in a race, eg *she led the field with two furlongs to go*
filly	a female horse under the age of four
firm	see **going**
flat racing	racing over relatively short distances on **turf** or **all-weather** surfaces with no hurdles, fences, or other obstacles. The introduction of all-weather surfaces has meant that flat racing now takes place all year round in Britain, but the traditional flat season is still from March to November
foal	a young horse
form	the performances of a horse in its most recent races
furlong	a distance used in British horse racing. A furlong is equal to one eighth of a mile (220yd)
gelding	a castrated male horse
going	the state of the ground at a racecourse in terms of the amount of moisture it holds and how much give it has. In increasing order of firmness the going conditions are as follows: heavy, yielding, soft, good-to-soft, good, good-to-firm, firm, standard and hard
good	see **going**
group race	same as **pattern race**
handicap	a weight that a horse must carry in a **handicap race** according to its previous performances, gender, age, and the quality of the horses it is racing against
handicap race	a race, less important than a **conditions race**, that involves a **handicapper** giving horses different weights according to their ability. Theoretically, each horse in a handicap race should have a chance of winning it
handicapper	the official body in charge of assigning handicaps to horses
hard	see **going**
head	the length of a horse's head, used to describe a short winning margin
heavy	see **going**
hunter chase	a **steeplechase** for amateur riders riding horses that have been used in hunting
hurdling	racing over hurdles over distances of between two to three and a half miles. The hurdles are a minimum of three and a half feet high and are more flexible than fences
jockey	the rider of a horse in a race
juvenile	a two-year-old racehorse
length	the length of a horse, as used in reporting the distances between horses at the finishing post, eg *Silver Patriarch won by two lengths*
listed race	see **conditions race**
maiden	a horse that has yet to win a race
mare	a female horse over the age of four

meeting a day's racing at a particular course

National Hunt the British term for racing over hurdles and fences. National Hunt racing takes place all year round although the main season is between October and April

non-runner a horse that was originally entered but which has been pulled out shortly before the race

nose in USA, the narrowest winning margin

novice a horse which has not won a race under a particular code (hurdling or chasing) before the start of the season

odds the chances a horse has of winning a race, as determined by the amount of money placed on it by punters

odds-on odds of better than even, such that the winnings are less than the amount staked

outsider a horse whose long odds before the start of a race suggest that it has little chance of winning

owner the person who owns a particular racehorse and who decides, on the advice of the trainer, which races it should run

pacemaker a horse put into a race in order to set the early pace to benefit a stable mate

paddock, parade ring the area where the horses are displayed for the benefit of spectators before the start of a race

pattern race see **conditions race**

photo finish a finish that is so close that a photograph is required to identify the winner and **places**

place the positions of second, third, and sometimes fourth in a race

pull up if a horse pulls up, it stops running during a race

racecard a programme for a day of racing at a meeting

scratch if a horse is scratched, it is removed from a race after it has been entered

short head the narrowest winning margin in British racing, shorter than a **head** but a longer than a **nose**

silks the shirt and cap worn by a jockey, made in the racing colours of the horse's owner

sire the father of a **foal**

soft see **going**

sprint a short race of five or six furlongs on the flat

stable all the racehorses of a single trainer, eg *the Dickinson stable had three winners at the meeting*

stake the money wagered in a bet

stakes race a race in which the horses are usually of the same age, sex and class

stallion a male horse used for breeding

standard see **going**

starting stalls a mechanical device in which the horses are kept briefly before the start of the race, the gates of which open for each horse simultaneously to ensure that the horses start racing at the same time

stayer a horse that does not tire as quickly as others over longer distances

steeplechase racing over fences that are a minimum of four and a half feet high. Steeplechases are run over distances of between two to four and a half miles. In steeplechases the **fences** are larger and more rigid than **hurdles**

stewards	the officials on the racecourse that uphold the rules of the sport
stewards' enquiry	an investigation by the stewards into the conduct of a race
stud	1. a male horse used for breeding. 2. a breeding farm
thoroughbred	a horse breed developed in Britain in the 18th century for the purposes of racing. All the sport's thoroughbreds are descended from the three Arabian **stallions** – Darley Arabian, Byerly Turk, and Godolphin Barb – which were mated with English **mares**
tic-tac	a sign language used on the racecourse to transmit changes in the betting market to bookmakers as quickly as possible. Most of the terms relate to how the odds are signed or are corrupted backward spellings
tipster	person who offers racing tips to punters
tote	a ticketed betting system where the odds are calculated once all bets have been taken. The payout is decided by taking the total amount of money bet (minus an administration charge) and dividing it by the number of winning tickets bought
trainer	the person employed to school racehorses and prepare them for races
trip	1. the distance of a race 2. if a horse 'gets the trip', it is able to complete the distance comfortably
triple crown	in Great Britain, the Two Thousand Guineas, the Derby, and the St Leger
turf	1. the grass surface used in horse racing, as distinct from **all-weather** surfaces. 2. the turf is the sport of horse racing
weight	the weight that the **handicapper** assigns a horse to carry based on its recent performances
weighing room	the room in which the jockeys and their saddles are weighed before and after a race
winning post	the post marking the finishing line on a racecourse
yearling	a racehorse that is officially one year old
yard	the stables, grounds and facilities owned by a trainer
yielding	see **going**

Some horse racing and betting slang

Bismarck	a favourite that bookmakers do not expect to win. It derives from the German WWII pocket battleship of the same name which was sent to the bottom of the Atlantic by the Royal Navy despite being considered 'unsinkable'
bottle	in **tic-tac**, odds of 2–1
Burlington Bertie	in **tic-tac**, odds of 100–30. 'Burlington Bertie' was a popular music hall song
carpet	in **tic-tac**, odds of 3–1. It derives from the criminal slang for a three-month stretch in prison
double carpet	in **tic-tac**, odds of 33–1
earhole	in **tic-tac**, odds of 6–4
hand	in **tic-tac**, odds of 5–1
face	in **tic-tac**, odds of 5–2
levels you devils	in **tic-tac**, odds of evens
mudlark	an informal name for a horse that performs well over heavy or soft ground
nap	the horse a tipster reckons has the best chance of winning out of all his tips

net	in **tic-tac**, odds of 10–1. Net is 'ten' spelt backwards
neves	in **tic-tac**, odds of 7–1
raider	a horse brought over from abroad to run in a particular race, eg *there are two Irish raiders in this race*
rouf	in **tic-tac**, odds of 4–1. Rouf is 'four' backwards
shoulder	in **tic-tac**, odds of 7–4
shoulders	in **tic-tac**, odds of 9–2
steamer	a horse whose odds shorten rapidly because a large amount of money has been unexpectedly placed on it
tips	in **tic-tac**, odds of 11–10
top of the head	in **tic-tac**, odds of 9–4
wrist	in **tic-tac**, odds of 5–4

Some famous horse racing personalities

Willie Carson, 1942–

Born in Stirling, Scotland, he was a top flat jockey during a long career that was brought to an end in 1997 following a serious accident in 1996. In 1972 he became the first Scottish champion jockey and also won his first English classic, the Two Thousand Guineas, on High Top. He made Queen Elizabeth II's silver jubilee year (1977) extra special for Her Majesty by riding her horse Dunfermline to the Oaks and the St Leger. He won the Derby four times, in 1979, 1980, 1989 and 1994. Since his retirement he has been a mainstay of the BBC's flat racing commentary team. He has received an OBE.

Frankie Dettori, 1970–

Born in Milan, Italy, the son of Gianfranco (also a notable jockey), he is one of the most popular figures in horse racing. He started his career in impressive fashion when he became the first teenager since Lester Piggott to ride 100 winners in a season. In 1995 he had a remarkable season, winning two English classics (the Oaks and the St Leger) and the Prix de l'Arc de Triomphe. The next year he hit the headlines again by winning all seven races on the card at Ascot, a unique feat and one that cost the British bookmaking industry a fortune. In 2000 he was involved in the crash of a light aircraft at Newmarket in which the pilot died. An injured Dettori was rescued from the burning wreckage by fellow jockey Ray Cochrane and, just nine weeks later, was back in the saddle. He delights racegoers with his 'flying dismount' whenever he wins a race. He received an MBE in 2001.

John Francome, 1952–

Born in Swindon, England, he has one of the best records in National Hunt. In a career spanning over a quarter of a century he established a then record of 1,138 wins and was champion jockey seven times. Since his retirement in 1985 he has published several racing-related novels, received an MBE and now works as a racing commentator for Channel 4.

Tony McCoy, 1974–

Born in County Antrim, Northern Ireland, he is well on his way to becoming the greatest National Hunt jockey of all time. McCoy has already eclipsed the career achievements of **John Francome** and beaten Richard Dunwoody's record of 1,699 winners over jumps. He then created racing history in 2001–2 by beating Sir Gordon Richards' 1947 record of 269 winners in a season. In season 2003–4 he became champion jockey for the ninth time, despite missing two months of the season through injury. He was awarded the MBE in 2003.

Vincent O'Brien, 1917–

Born in County Cork, Ireland, he is one of the greatest trainers in history. Concentrating on jump racing initially, he achieved great success in the big races in English National Hunt in the 1940s and 50s. Hat-tricks were achieved in the Cheltenham Gold Cup (1948–50), the Cheltenham Champion Hurdle (1949–51), and, in a record that has still to be matched, the Grand National (1953–5). He later tried his hand at flat racing and was rewarded with yet more success. His career on the flat yielded 16 English classics (including six Derbies) and 25 wins at Royal Ascot. He also won a staggering 27 Irish classics and had three wins in the Prix de l'Arc de Triomphe.

Lester Piggott, 1935–

Born in Wantage, England, he is one of the sport's legends and certainly the greatest flat jockey of the post-war era. Known as the 'Long Fellow' because of his relatively tall stature (5ft 9in), he rode a total of 30 classics over five decades. His first of nine Derbies was in 1954, his last in 1983. He retired from riding in the 1980s and became a trainer but was jailed for tax irregularities in 1987 (hence losing his OBE). On his release he resumed his training career but found himself yearning for the saddle again. In his second spell as a jockey he won his final classic, the Two Thousand Guineas in 1992. He finally retired from riding in 1995, having had 4,493 winners in Great Britain.

Martin Pipe, 1945–

Born in Somerset, England, he is one of the most successful National Hunt trainers of all time and has received the CBE for his achievements. He has dominated jump racing since the late 1980s and been champion trainer in terms of winners every year since 1989. Although many of his successes have come at relatively unfashionable courses, he has also enjoyed an enviable number of wins in big races. He has been very successful at the Cheltenham Festival and, most memorably, trained Minnehoma to victory in the 1994 Grand National. Pipe, working from his yard in Somerset, had a long and successful partnership with rider **Tony McCoy**, although that came to an end in 2004. He has also had some success training winners on the flat.

Sir Gordon Richards, 1904–86

Born in Oakengates, Shropshire, England, he was one of the greatest jockeys of the 20th century. In 34 seasons (1921–54) he was champion jockey 26 times. During his career he rode 4,870 winners including, in 1933, a record 12 consecutive winners. He won 14 classics, although it is surprising that he rode only one Derby winner. That was on Pinza in 1953, the year he received his knighthood. He retired in 1954 following a serious injury when a horse fell on him in the paddock. After hanging up his riding boots he became a trainer, finally retiring from the sport in 1969.

Willie Shoemaker, 1931–

Born in Fabens, Texas, USA, he was one of the USA's greatest jockeys. His career spanned a remarkable seven decades, during which time he won 8,833 races. His record in America's premier races is impressive and includes four Kentucky Derbies and five

Belmont Stakes. Towards the end of his career he crossed the Atlantic and found some success racing in Europe. He retired in 1990.

Fred Winter, 1926–2004

Born in Hampshire, England, he is a National Hunt legend, achieving great success as both a jockey and a trainer (for which he received a CBE in 1963). During a great career in the saddle he was champion jump jockey four times and had 923 winners. He retired from riding in 1964 and embarked on an equally successful career as a trainer, during which he won eight championships, including five in a row between 1971 and 1975. His peerless record of wins in National Hunt includes the Grand National twice as both trainer and jockey, the Cheltenham Gold Cup twice as a jockey and once as a trainer, and the Cheltenham Champion Hurdle four times as a jockey and three times as a trainer.

Happy Birthday one and all

Just like the Queen, every horse has an official birthday as well as an actual one. The age of a horse is important in racing so it makes sense to have a simple system for dealing with birthdays. The solution is that all horses are given 1 January in the year they are born as their official date of birth. Since foals born near the start of the calendar year have a growth advantage, the breeding industry is set up to try to achieve January or February foaling. Pity the premature Christmas foal who becomes a yearling at just one week old.

HURLING

Origins

Hurling is mentioned first in a description of the mythical 13th-century BC Battle of Moytura, where the Tuatha dé Danann, Irish descendants of the mother goddess, defeated the Firbolg invaders in a game of hurling, and later in battle. Legend also tells that the ancient warrior chieftain Cú Chulainn was a skilled hurler. Despite being outlawed by the 14th-century Statutes of Kilkenny, the game survived and the Gaelic Athletic Association formalized the rules in 1884.

Rules and description

Hurling is a 15-a-side, stick-and-ball field game played almost exclusively in Ireland. The wooden stick or 'hurley' has a curved wide blade and is used to both hit and carry the ball, the 'sliotar'. Unlike in the game of hockey, which it resembles, players can carry the ball in the hand for four steps before transferring it back to the hurley for a further carry or strike. At each end of the playing field are H-shaped goalposts. A single point is scored when the ball passes over the crossbar; three points are scored for a goal. Hurling is regarded as the fastest-moving field game. The version of the game played by women is known as 'camogie'.

Ruling body: The Gaelic Athletic Association (GAA)

	Winner
1887	Tipperary
1888	*Unfinished**
1889	Dublin
1890	Cork
1891	Kerry
1892–4	Cork
1895–6	Tipperary
1897	Limerick
1898–1900	Tipperary
1901	London Irish
1902–3	Cork
1904–5	Kilkenny
1906	Tipperary
1907	Kilkenny
1908	Tipperary
1909	Kilkenny
1910	Wexford
1911–13	Kilkenny
1914	Clare
1915	Laois
1916	Tipperary
1917	Dublin
1918	Limerick
1919	Cork
1920	Dublin
1921	Limerick
1922	Kilkenny
1923	Galway
1924	Dublin
1925	Tipperary
1926	Cork
1927	Dublin
1928–9	Cork
1930	Tipperary
1931	Cork
1932–3	Kilkenny
1934	Limerick
1935	Kilkenny
1936	Limerick
1937	Tipperary
1938	Dublin
1939	Kilkenny
1940	Limerick
1941–4	Cork
1945	Tipperary

	Winner
1946	Cork
1947	Kilkenny
1948	Waterford
1949–51	Tipperary
1952–4	Cork
1955–6	Wexford
1957	Kilkenny
1958	Tipperary
1959	Waterford
1960	Wexford
1961–2	Tipperary
1963	Kilkenny
1964–5	Tipperary
1966	Cork
1967	Kilkenny
1968	Wexford
1969	Kilkenny
1970	Cork
1971	Tipperary
1972	Kilkenny
1973	Limerick
1974–5	Kilkenny
1976–8	Cork
1979	Kilkenny
1980	Galway
1981	Offaly
1982–3	Kilkenny
1984	Cork
1985	Offaly
1986	Cork
1987–8	Galway
1989	Tipperary
1990	Cork
1991	Tipperary
1992–3	Kilkenny
1994	Offaly
1995	Clare
1996	Wexford
1997	Clare
1998	Offaly
1999	Cork
2000	Kilkenny
2001	Tipperary
2002–3	Kilkenny
2004	Cork

All-Ireland Hurling Final

The final of this inter-county cup takes place at Dublin's Croke Park in September each year. The winning team receives the McCarthy Cup, named after Liam McCarthy who donated it in 1921.

* the tournament was not completed, as a tour took place that year to the USA by hurlers, Gaelic footballers and athletes

A-Z

bas — the flat blade of the **hurley**

bos — same as **bas**

camán — Gaelic variant name for the **hurley**

Croke Park — venue for the All-Ireland final and headquarters of the GAA, located in Dublin. It is named after its patron, Dr Croke, the Roman Catholic Archbishop of Cashel

cúl — a goal, scored when the ball is played under the crossbar and worth three points

hurley — the wooden stick with a flat blade, traditionally made of ash

sliotar — the leather-covered ball

From Croke Park to Leinster House

Jack Lynch won five All-Ireland hurling medals (1941–4, 1946), as well as an All-Ireland medal in Gaelic football (1945), before becoming the prime minister (Taoiseach) of the Republic of Ireland in 1966.

Some famous hurlers

Mick Mackey, 1912-82

Born in Castleconnell, County Limerick, Ireland, he first played for the senior Limerick side at the age of 18. Six years later he scored a record five goals and three points as he captained Limerick to victory in the All-Ireland final. Other All-Ireland final wins came in 1934 and 1940.

Rackard brothers

Nicky (1922–90), Bobby (1927–) and Billy (1930–) Rackard were born in Killane, County Wexford, Ireland, and were all in the Wexford side that won the All-Ireland finals of 1955 and 1956. They all played for the Rathnure club and knew success, although Nicky was perhaps the star performer, a prolific forward who finished as leading points scorer in the country in the cup-winning years. Billy picked up a further All-Ireland medal in 1960.

Christy Ring, 1920-79

Born in Cloyne, County Cork, Ireland, he is widely regarded as the greatest hurler of all time. In a 24-year career he won two Minor All-Ireland and eight Senior All-Ireland medals. He was the season's top scorer three times – in 1959 (when he became the only player to average over ten points a game), 1961 and 1962.

ICE HOCKEY

Origins

A game played on a frozen pond or lake by men with sticks has been depicted in drawings, especially in The Netherlands, as far back as the 16th century, though its origins have been traced as far back as the second century. The sport as we know it today has Canadian roots, being generally recognized to stem from a game played by British soldiers on the frozen expanse of Kingston Harbour, Ontario, in 1860. The first organized game took place at Montreal's Victoria Skating Rink in 1875, and the first recognized team (still in existence today) was McGill University (Montreal) Hockey Club, which was founded in 1880.

Rules and description

A fast game played on an ice surface measuring a minimum of 56 x 26m/184 x 85ft and a maximum of 61 x 30m/200 x 98ft, divided into three equal parts by two blue lines and surrounded by boards and protective glass or netting. Teams are composed of six players (usually two defenders, three forwards and a goal-tender), who may be changed at any time to ensure that the game is played at a constant high speed. Players wear ice skates and protective clothing. Games are 60 minutes long, timed by a clock that is stopped whenever play is halted. The aim is to score goals by using a stick to propel the puck into the opposing team's goal. Players are credited with one point for each goal or assist. The player gaining most points is declared the scoring champion.

Ruling bodies: The world governing body is the International Ice Hockey Federation (IIHF), founded in 1908 and based in Zurich, Switzerland. The ruling body of the major professional league is the National Hockey League (NHL), founded in 1917 and based in New York, USA.

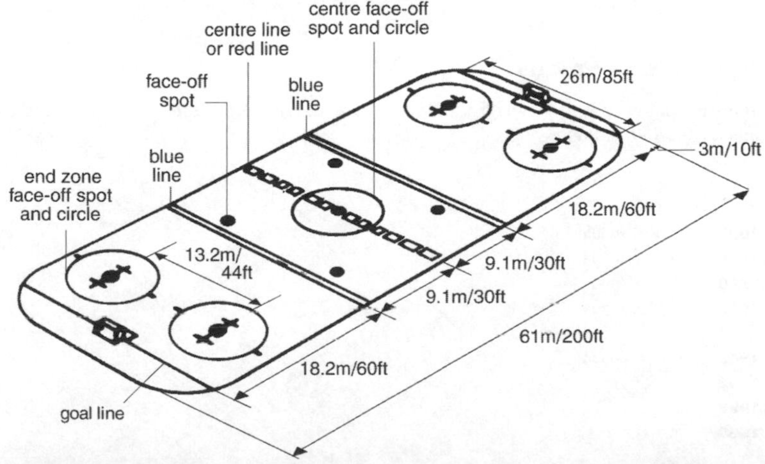

World Championships

Organized by the IIHF and played annually since 1930 (the winners of the Winter Olympic ice hockey tournaments in 1920, 1924 and 1928 were also recognized as world champions). Since 1998, the world's leading 16 nations have competed for the title. The remaining nations compete in three qualifying groups (Divisions I, II and III) with promotion and relegation between them. Many NHL professionals are unable to compete in the World Championships, as the competition coincides with the Stanley Cup play-offs in North America.

Men

1980	*Not held* (Olympics)	**1993**	Russia
1981	USSR	**1994**	Canada
1982	USSR	**1995**	Finland
1983	USSR	**1996**	Czech Republic
1984	*Not held* (Olympics)	**1997**	Canada
1985	Czechoslovakia	**1998**	Sweden
1986	USSR	**1999**	Czech Republic
1987	Sweden	**2000**	Czech Republic
1988	*Not held* (Olympics)	**2001**	Czech Republic
1989	USSR	**2002**	Slovakia
1990	USSR	**2003**	Canada
1991	Sweden	**2004**	Canada
1992	Sweden		

Women

1990	Canada	**1999**	Canada
1992	Canada	**2000**	Canada
1994	Canada	**2001**	Canada
1997	Canada	**2004**	Canada

Olympic Champions

The world's best professionals from the NHL did not compete in the Winter Olympics ice hockey tournament until 1998.

Men

1920	Canada
1924	Canada
1928	Canada
1932	Canada
1936	Great Britain
1948	Canada
1952	Canada
1956	USSR
1960	USA

1964	USSR
1968	USSR
1972	USSR
1976	USSR
1980	USA
1984	USSR
1988	USSR
1992	Unified Team
1994	Sweden
1998	Czech Republic
2002	Canada

Britain's finest hour

The 1930s produced what is considered to be the British game's finest hour. In February 1936, Britain upset the ice hockey world in Garmisch-Partenkirchen, Bavaria, by winning the triple crown of Olympic, world and European titles. Their five victories (there were also two draws) included a 2–1 defeat of Canada, the reigning world champions. The players – though born in Britain, all but two lived and learned the game in Canada – were hand-picked by the Canadian coach, Percy Nicklin, and John F 'Bunny' Ahearne, the secretary of the British Ice Hockey Association.

Women

1998	USA
2002	Canada

National Hockey League World Championships

The NHL was formed in 1917 with four teams: Montreal Canadiens and Wanderers, Ottawa Senators and Toronto Arenas. Since season 2000–1 there have been 30 teams playing in two conferences (Eastern and Western) with six divisions (Atlantic, Northeast and Southeast in the Eastern; Central, Northwest and Pacific in the Western). Each team plays 82 games (until 2003–4) and the team with the best overall record is awarded the Presidents' Trophy. A players' strike meant that there was a 48-game schedule in season 1994–5.

	Winners	**Runners-up**
1979–80	Philadelphia Flyers	Buffalo Sabres
1980–1	New York Islanders	St Louis Blues
1981–2	New York Islanders	Edmonton Oilers
1982–3	Boston Bruins	Philadelphia Flyers
1983–4	Edmonton Oilers	New York Islanders
1984–5	Philadelphia Flyers	Edmonton Oilers
1985–6	Edmonton Oilers	Philadelphia Flyers
1986–7	Edmonton Oilers	Philadelphia Flyers
1987–8	Calgary Flames	Montreal Canadiens
1988–9	Calgary Flames	Montreal Canadiens
1989–90	Boston Bruins	Calgary Flames
1990–1	Chicago Blackhawks	St Louis Blues
1991–2	New York Rangers	Washington Capitals
1992–3	Pittsburgh Penguins	Boston Bruins
1993–4	New York Rangers	New Jersey Devils
1994–5	Detroit Redwings	Quebec Nordiques
1995–6	Detroit Redwings	Colorado Avalanche
1996–7	Colorado Avalanche	Dallas Stars
1997–8	Dallas Stars	New Jersey Devils

Ice Hockey

	Winners	Runners-up
1998–9	Dallas Stars	New Jersey Devils
1999–2000	St Louis Blues	Detroit Redwings
2000–1	Colorado Avalanche	Detroit Redwings
2001–2	Detroit Redwings	Boston Bruins
2002–3	Ottawa Senators	Dallas Stars
2003–4	Detroit Redwings	Tampa Bay Lightning

Stanley Cup

The oldest trophy for which professional athletes in North America still compete. The Stanley Cup was donated in 1892 by Sir Frederick Arthur, Lord Stanley of Preston. At first it was awarded to the amateur hockey champions of Canada. Since 1910, when the National Hockey Association (the forerunner of the NHL) took possession of the trophy, it has been symbolic of professional hockey supremacy. With the demise of first the National Hockey Association and then the rival Pacific Coast Hockey League, the Stanley Cup became in 1926 the sole preserve of the NHL.

Sixteen NHL teams qualify for the Stanley Cup play-offs: the league's six divisional winners, and the five best teams in each conference, based on their points totals within their conference.

	Winners	Defeated finalists
1980	New York Islanders	Philadelphia Flyers
1981	New York Islanders	Minnesota North Stars
1982	New York Islanders	Vancouver Canucks
1983	New York Islanders	Edmonton Oilers
1984	Edmonton Oilers	New York Islanders
1985	Edmonton Oilers	Philadelphia Flyers
1986	Montreal Canadiens	Calgary Flames
1987	Edmonton Oilers	Philadelphia Flyers
1988	Edmonton Oilers	Boston Bruins
1989	Calgary Flames	Montreal Canadiens
1990	Edmonton Oilers	Boston Bruins
1991	Pittsburgh Penguins	Minnesota North Stars
1992	Pittsburgh Penguins	Chicago Blackhawks
1993	Montreal Canadiens	Los Angeles Kings
1994	New York Rangers	Vancouver Canucks
1995	New Jersey Devils	Detroit Red Wings
1996	Colorado Avalanche	Florida Panthers
1997	Detroit Red Wings	Philadelphia Flyers
1998	Detroit Red Wings	Washington Capitals
1999	Dallas Stars	Buffalo Sabres
2000	New Jersey Devils	Dallas Stars
2001	Colorado Avalanche	New Jersey Devils
2002	Detroit Red Wings	Carolina Hurricanes
2003	New Jersey Devils	Anaheim Mighty Ducks
2004	Tampa Bay Lightning	Calgary Flames

World Cup of Hockey

An invitational tournament for the world's leading ice hockey nations, organized jointly by the IIHF and the NHL. The competition is played in September so that professionals from the National Hockey League can take part. Originally known as the Canada Cup, it was renamed in 1996.

1976	Canada
1981	USSR
1984	Canada
1987	Canada
1991	Canada
1996	USA
2004	Canada

Continental Cup

The major European club championship, organized by the IIHF. Originally the European Cup, it was renamed after the formation of the short-lived European League (1996–2000).

1966–8	ZKL Brno
1969–74	CSKA Moscow
1975	Krylja Sovjetov (Moscow)
1976	CSKA Moscow
1977	Poldi Kladno
	CSKA Moscow
1991–2	Djurgardens Stockholm
1993	Malmo IF
1994	TPS Turku
1995–6	Jokerit Helsinki
1997	Lada Togliatti
1998	HC Kosice
1999–2000	HC Ambri-Piotta
2001–2	Zurich SC Lions
2003	Jokerit Helsinki
2004	Slovan Bratislava

The sin-bin

Dave 'Tiger' Williams is the NHL's most penalized player. He spent an average of 4.12 minutes in the penalty box for each of the 962 games he played during his 14 seasons – easily the highest in league history. His total of 3,966 minutes is also an all-time record. Dave 'The Hammer' Schultz was put in the 'cooler' for a record 42 minutes while playing for Philadelphia Flyers against Toronto Maple Leafs in a Stanley Cup game on 22 April 1976. He was assessed a minor, two majors, a ten-minute misconduct and two game misconducts.

British Champions (Modern Era)

The modern era is generally accepted as beginning with the sponsorship in 1983 of the mostly amateur British League by the Whitbread Company, under the Heineken banner. The finals of the (Heineken) British Championship were played at Wembley Arena from 1984 to 1996.

	Winners	**Defeated finalists**
1983	Dundee Rockets	Durham Wasps
1984	Dundee Rockets	Murrayfield Racers
1985	Fife Flyers	Murrayfield Racers
1986	Murrayfield Racers	Dundee Rockets
1987	Durham Wasps	Murrayfield Racers

	Winners	Defeated finalists
1988	Durham Wasps	Fife Flyers
1989	Nottingham Panthers	Ayr Bruins
1990	Cardiff Devils	Murrayfield Racers
1991	Durham Wasps	Peterborough Pirates
1992	Durham Wasps	Nottingham Panthers
1993	Cardiff Devils	Humberside Seahawks
1994	Cardiff Devils	Sheffield Steelers
1995	Sheffield Steelers	Edinburgh Racers
1996	Sheffield Steelers	Nottingham Panthers

Recent UK League Winners

The British League was replaced in 1996 by the professional Superleague, which relied heavily on overseas players. When this became too costly and collapsed in 2003, the Elite League was formed.

	Superleague
1997	Cardiff Devils
1998	Ayr Scottish Eagles
1999	Manchester Storm
2000	Bracknell Bees
2001	Sheffield Steelers
2002	Belfast Giants
2003	Sheffield Steelers
	Elite League
2004	Sheffield Steelers

NHL Individual Award Winners

	Art Ross Trophy (Leading Points Scorer)	Hart Memorial Trophy (Most Valuable Player)
1980	Marcel Dionne (Los Angeles)	Wayne Gretzky (Edmonton)
1981	Wayne Gretzky (Edmonton)	Wayne Gretzky (Edmonton)
1982	Wayne Gretzky (Edmonton)	Wayne Gretzky (Edmonton)
1983	Wayne Gretzky (Edmonton)	Wayne Gretzky (Edmonton)
1984	Wayne Gretzky (Edmonton)	Wayne Gretzky (Edmonton)
1985	Wayne Gretzky (Edmonton)	Wayne Gretzky (Edmonton)
1986	Wayne Gretzky (Edmonton)	Wayne Gretzky (Edmonton)
1987	Wayne Gretzky (Edmonton)	Wayne Gretzky (Edmonton)
1988	Mario Lemieux (Pittsburgh)	Mario Lemieux (Pittsburgh)
1989	Mario Lemieux (Pittsburgh)	Wayne Gretzky (Edmonton)
1990	Wayne Gretzky (Edmonton)	Mark Messier (Edmonton)
1991	Wayne Gretzky (Edmonton)	Brett Hull (St Louis)
1992	Mario Lemieux (Pittsburgh)	Mark Messier (NY Rangers)
1993	Mario Lemieux (Pittsburgh)	Mario Lemieux (Pittsburgh)
1994	Wayne Gretzky (Edmonton)	Sergei Fedorov (Detroit)
1995	Jaromir Jagr (Pittsburgh)	Eric Lindros (Philadelphia)

	Art Ross Trophy (Leading Points Scorer)	Hart Memorial Trophy (Most Valuable Player)
1996	Mario Lemieux (Pittsburgh)	Mario Lemieux (Pittsburgh)
1997	Mario Lemieux (Pittsburgh)	Dominik Hasek (Buffalo Sabres)
1998	Jaromir Jagr (Pittsburgh)	Dominik Hasek (Buffalo Sabres)
1999	Jaromir Jagr (Pittsburgh)	Jaromir Jagr (Pittsburgh)
2000	Jaromir Jagr (Pittsburgh)	Chris Pronger (St Louis)
2001	Jaromir Jagr (Pittsburgh)	Joe Sakic (Colorado)
2002	Jarome Iginla (Calgary)	Jose Theodore (Montreal)
2003	Peter Forsberg (Colorado)	Peter Forsberg (Colorado)
2004	Martin St-Louis (Tampa Bay)	Martin St-Louis (Tampa Bay)

On the loneliness of being a hockey goalie

'If you make a mistake, they turn on a red light, a siren goes off and thousands of people scream.' Hockey Hall of Fame goal-tender Jacques Plante, who led Montreal Canadiens to six Stanley Cups.

A-Z

assist a pass that leads directly or indirectly to a goal. Players score one point for each assist; up to two assists may be credited on each goal

blue line one of the two lines, each 30cm wide, that divide the playing area into three equal parts

boarding **bodychecking** an opponent violently into the **boards**; the offender is assessed a **penalty** at the referee's discretion

boards the wooden or plastic wall surrounding the playing area, not less than 1.17m and not more than 1.22m in height above the level of the ice, and usually topped with protective glass or netting

body-check same as **check**

centre line same as **red line**

centreman the forward playing between the two wingers; responsible for the central part of the ice, from his or her own **blue line** up to the opposition's goal

check the legitimate blocking of an opponent's progress by use of the shoulder or hip

cross-check illegal check delivered with both hands on the stick and no part of the stick on the ice; the offender is assessed a **penalty** at the referee's discretion

defenceman the player whose prime duty is to defend against the opposition; each team normally uses two on the ice at any one time

face-off the way in which play is started or re-started: a linesman drops the **puck** between two opposing players

goal-tender a player who wears special leg pads and gloves and whose job is to stop the **puck** from entering the net

icing (the puck) when a player ices the **puck**, he or she shoots it from their side of the **red line** to beyond the opposing team's goal line. Play is stopped, and a **face-off** takes place in the offending team's zone on the face-off spot nearest to where they last touched the puck (this does not apply if the offending player's team is **short-handed**)

linesman	in addition to the referee (two referees in the NHL), there are two linesmen on the ice who are responsible for calling any rules infraction concerning the lines, eg **offside**, **icing**. They are also responsible for **facing-off** the puck in most circumstances, and for assisting the referee
netminder	same as **goal-tender**
offside	when a player precedes the **puck** over the opposition's **blue line**. The player is judged to be offside only if both his or her skates are completely over the line
overtime	when a game requires a clear result, it may be extended by **sudden-death** extra time. Under IIHF rules, this is ten minutes' actual time. In the NHL, teams play an extra five minutes in the league and unlimited overtime in the Stanley Cup play-offs
penalty	suspension from play for unruly behaviour for a statutory length of time, depending on the severity of the offence. Penalties are minor (two minutes), misconduct (ten minutes), major, game misconduct and match penalty. For the latter three offences, the player is ruled out of the remainder of the game, though in the case of a major penalty he or she can be replaced by a team-mate after five minutes. Offenders who receive a game misconduct or match penalty are referred to the appropriate authority for further disciplinary action
penalty bench, penalty box	the enclosed area situated at the side of the rink opposite the players' benches, where players who have violated the rules serve their **penalties**
penalty shot	a free shot on the goal-tender, awarded for specific infringements of the rules; also used for deciding the results of games that remain drawn after **overtime**
period	one of the three periods that makes up a game, each of 20 minutes' actual time, with two 15-minute intervals; teams change ends for each period
power play	when one team is **short-handed** through penalties, the opposing team is said to be on the power play
puck	a hard disc which slides easily on ice, usually made of vulcanized rubber, measuring 7.62cm in diameter and 2.54cm in thickness
red line	the line, 30cm wide, which divides the playing area in two
short-handed	when a team has one or more players on the **penalty bench**
shutout	when a team concedes no goals in a game; officially credited to the goal-tender
sin-bin	same as **penalty bench**
slap shot	a fast powerful shot by a player taking his stick back above his or her head
slashing	an illegal attempt by a player to stop, slow or intimidate an opponent by swinging the stick at him or her or at the **puck**; the offender is assessed a **penalty** at the referee's discretion
spearing	stabbing an opponent with the point of the stick blade; the offender is assessed a **penalty** at the referee's discretion
sudden-death	the goal scored in **overtime** to decide a result
Zamboni	tractor-like machine used for cleaning the ice, invented in 1949 by Frank Zamboni; the term is now used to describe any similar machine
zones	the three equal parts of the playing area: the centre or neutral zone, the attacking zone and the defending zone

Some ice hockey slang

bluellner a **defenceman**
cage the goal net. The goal-tender is sometimes known as the **cageman**
five-hole the space between the goal-tender's leg pads, through which a goal may be scored
going top shelf hitting the puck into the roof of the goal net
one-timer receiving a pass and hitting the puck towards the goal in one movement

Some famous ice hockey players

Peter Forsberg, 1973–

A centreman, rated as the best player in the world, he is one of the select group in the Triple Gold Club (see below). Born in Ornskoldsvik, Sweden, he won his gold medal in the 1994 Winter Olympics, the Stanley Cup with Colorado Avalanche in 1996 and 2001 and the World Championship in 1998. He damaged his spleen in a collision with an opponent in May 2001 and missed the next season; on his return, he won the Art Ross trophy as the league's top points scorer and the Hart Memorial trophy as its most valuable player.

The Triple Gold Club

Only 14 players have won an Olympic gold medal, the Stanley Cup and a World Championship. In 2004, this unique group comprised: Rob Blake (Canada), Viacheslav Fetisov (Russia), Peter Forsberg (Sweden), Alexei Gusarov (Russia), Tomas Jonsson (Sweden), Valeri Kamenski (Russia), Igor Larionov (Russia), Hakan Loob (Sweden), Vladimir Malakhov (Russia), Alexander Mogilny (Russia), Mats Naslund (Sweden), Scott Niedermayer (Canada), Joe Sakic (Canada) and Brendan Shanahan (Canada).

Wayne Gretzky, 1961–

Universally known as 'The Great One' or simply '99' after his shirt number, the centreman was the finest player ever to play the game. Born in Brantford, Ontario, Canada, he played 19 seasons in the NHL and one in the rival World Hockey Association (WHA) from 1978 until his retirement in 1999. He played for five professional teams, notably Edmonton Oilers, with whom he won four Stanley Cups in the 1980s. He still holds the league scoring records for points (2,857), assists (1,963) and goals (894) by wide margins; he set 62 NHL records, a figure that may never be broken. He remains actively involved in the sport, as managing partner of the NHL's Phoenix Coyotes and general manager of Team Canada.

Tony Hand, 1967–

The Scottish forward broke into senior ice hockey at the age of 13 with his hometown team, Murrayfield Racers, and in 1986 became the first British player to be drafted by an NHL club, Edmonton Oilers. He also played for Sheffield Steelers, Ayr Scottish Eagles and Dundee Stars. In 2001–2, as player-coach of Dundee, he became the first player to score over 1,000 goals in the British leagues. He is also Britain's top points scorer, with

119 in 59 internationals. In 2004 he received an MBE in the New Year's Honours for 'services to ice hockey', and joined Belfast Giants as their player-coach.

Gordie Howe, 1928–

Dubbed 'Mr Hockey', the powerful right-winger turned pro at the age of 18 and only retired reluctantly at the age of 52. Born in Floral, Saskatchewan, Canada, he played 26 seasons in the NHL, all but one of them with the Detroit Redwings, with whom he won four Stanley Cups in the 1950s. He joined the NHL's rival league, the World Hockey Association (WHA), in 1973, playing six seasons with the Houston Aeros and the New England (Hartford) Whalers. On his retirement, he held the NHL records for the most seasons (26) and most games played (1,767) and for scoring with 801 goals, 1,049 assists and 1,850 points.

Mr Hockey

Gordie Howe created the legend of the 'Gordie Howe hat-trick': a goal, an assist and a fight. When he retired holding the league's scoring records, a rival paid tribute by describing him as 'everything you expect an ideal athlete to be. He is soft-spoken, self-deprecating and thoughtful. He is also one of the most vicious, cruel and mean men I have ever met in a hockey game.'

Jaromir Jagr, 1972–

The right-winger is probably the greatest Czech ever to play in the NHL. As well as winning two Stanley Cups with Pittsburgh Penguins in 1991 and 1992, he was the first European player to win the Art Ross trophy as the league's leading points scorer. He went on to win it four more times. He signed a record long-term contract for $77 million with the Washington Capitals in 2001, and was traded to New York Rangers in 2004. He played for the Czech Republic in two Winter Olympics, 1998 and 2002, winning a gold medal in Nagano.

Mario Lemieux, 1965–

The Montreal, Quebec-born forward won two Stanley Cups with Pittsburgh in 1991 and 1992, six Art Ross trophies as the league's leading points scorer and three Hart Memorial trophies as its most valuable player. He won an Olympic gold medal at Salt Lake City in 2002. Poor health forced him into retirement in 1997, but he came back to the Penguins in 2000 and at the end of the 2003–4 season had taken his goals total to 683 in 889 games, an average of 0.768 goals per game – an all-time league best by a comfortable margin.

Mario the Magnificent

Mario Lemieux, a 6ft 4in giant nicknamed 'The Magnificent', twice saved his club, Pittsburgh Penguins, from going under. When he joined the near-bankrupt team in 1984, he scored in his first game and then led them to two Stanley Cups. In 1999 the Penguins owed him so much in back salary that he had to buy the club in order to save it. A year later, he emerged from premature retirement to become the sport's first player-owner. His battles against cancer and chronic back problems are also legendary. His remarkable powers of recovery were most memorably displayed in 1993 when he returned from his brush with cancer (Hodgkin's disease) and scored only hours after having his last radiation treatment.

Bobby Orr, 1948–

The greatest defenceman in NHL history revolutionized the game in the 1960s by showing how defenders could score as prolifically as forwards while still playing their position effectively. Born in Parry Sound, Ontario, Canada, he spent ten of his twelve NHL seasons with Boston Bruins and won two Stanley Cups in 1970 and 1972. Chronic knee problems forced him into premature retirement in 1979, three years after joining Chicago Back Hawks. His 915 career points included 645 assists for an average of 0.982 assists per game, third in the all-time list.

ICE SKATING

Origins

The origins of ice skating are uncertain but probably date from many thousands of years ago when hunters used pieces of wood or bone as blades to travel faster across icy landscapes. In the 17th century the Great Frost Fairs on the River Thames made ice skating popular.

Rules and description

There are separate figure skating competitions for men, women and pairs, as well as 'ice dance' (sometimes likened to ballroom dancing on ice). The individuals and pairs perform a 'short programme', which requires them to perform preset movements and then a longer, 'free programme'. In the ice dance competition there are three sections: compulsory dance, set pattern dance (to a same tempo dance such as tango or waltz) and a free dance. The most obvious difference between pairs and ice dance is that the former includes major lifts of the female partner and in the ice dance the couple need to spend most of their routines in close contact with each other. All performances are skated to music. Since the mid-1990s there has been a fifth discipline, synchronized skating, in which teams of 12 to 20 skaters perform complicated routines in formation.

Scoring underwent a revolution after the cheating at the 2002 Olympic Games and performances are now scored by 14 judges; then nine are chosen at random by computer with the top and bottom two results being excluded. Judges score according to a code of points.

Ruling body: International Skating Union (ISU); a counter-organization, The World Skating Federation, was set up in 2003 in the light of the cheating at the 2002 Winter Olympics.

World Championships

The first men's championships were held in 1896; the first women's event in 1906; and the pairs first contested in 1908. Ice dance was officially recognized in 1952.

	Men's figures	Women's figures
1980	Jan Hoffmann (East Germany)	Anett Pötzsch (East Germany)
1981	Scott Hamilton (USA)	Denise Biellmann (Switzerland)
1982	Scott Hamilton (USA)	Elaine Zayak (USA)
1983	Scott Hamilton (USA)	Rosalynn Sumners (USA)
1984	Scott Hamilton (USA)	Katarina Witt (East Germany)
1985	Aleksandr Fadeyev (USSR)	Katarina Witt (East Germany)
1986	Brian Boitano (USA)	Debbie Thomas (USA)
1987	Brian Orser (Canada)	Katarina Witt (East Germany)
1988	Brian Boitano (USA)	Katarina Witt (East Germany)
1989	Kurt Browning (Canada)	Midori Ito (Japan)
1990	Kurt Browning (Canada)	Jill Trenary (USA)
1991	Kurt Browning (Canada)	Kristi Yamaguchi (USA)
1992	Viktor Petrenko (CIS)	Kristi Yamaguchi (USA)
1993	Kurt Browning (Canada)	Oksana Baiul (Ukraine)
1994	Elvis Stojko (Canada)	Yuka Sato (Japan)
1995	Elvis Stojko (Canada)	Lu Chen (China)
1996	Todd Eldredge (USA)	Michelle Kwan (USA)
1997	Elvis Stojko (Canada)	Tara Lipinski (USA)
1998	Alexei Yagudin (Russia)	Michelle Kwan (USA)
1999	Alexei Yagudin (Russia)	Maria Butyrskaya (Russia)
2000	Alexei Yagudin (Russia)	Michelle Kwan (USA)
2001	Yevgeny Plushenko (Russia)	Michelle Kwan (USA)
2002	Alexei Yagudin (Russia)	Irina Slutskaya (Russia)
2003	Yevgeny Plushenko (Russia)	Michelle Kwan (USA)
2004	Yevgeny Plushenko (Russia)	Shizuka Arakawa (Japan)

Pairs

1980	Marina Cherkasova & Sergei Shakhrai (USSR)
1981	Irina Vorobieva & Igor Lisovsky (USSR)
1982	Sabine Baess & Tassilo Thierbach (East Germany)
1983	Yelena Valova & Oleg Vasilyev (USSR)
1984	Barbara Underhill & Paul Martini (Canada)
1985	Yelena Valova & Oleg Vasilyev (USSR)
1986	Yekaterina Gordeyeva & Sergei Grinkov (USSR)
1987	Yekaterina Gordeyeva & Sergei Grinkov (USSR)
1988	Yelena Valova & Oleg Vasilyev (USSR)
1989	Yekaterina Gordeyeva & Sergei Grinkov (USSR)
1990	Yekaterina Gordeyeva & Sergei Grinkov (USSR)
1991	Natalia Mishkutienok & Artur Dmtriev (USSR)
1992	Natalia Mishkutienok & Artur Dmtriev (USSR)
1993	Isabelle Brasseur & Lloyd Eisler (Canada)
1994	Evgenia Shishkova & Vadim Naumov (Russia)
1995	Radka Kovarikova & Rene Novotny (Czech Republic)
1996	Marina Eltsova & Andrei Bushkov (Russia)
1997	Mandy Woetzel & Ingo Steuer (Germany)
1998	Elena Berezhnaya & Anton Sikharulidze (Russia)
1999	Elena Berezhnaya & Anton Sikharulidze (Russia)
2000	Maria Petrova & Alexei Tikhonov (Russia)

Pairs

2001 Jamie Sale & David Pelletier (Canada)
2002 Xue Shen & Zhao Hongbo (China)
2003 Xue Shen & Zhao Hongbo (China)
2004 Tatiana Totmianina & Maxim Marinin (Russia)

Ice dance

1980 Krisztina Regöczy & András Sallay (Hungary)
1981 Jayne Torvill & Christopher Dean (Great Britain)
1982 Jayne Torvill & Christopher Dean (Great Britain)
1983 Jayne Torvill & Christopher Dean (Great Britain)
1984 Jayne Torvill & Christopher Dean (Great Britain)
1985 Natalia Bestemianova & Andrei Bukin (USSR)
1986 Natalia Bestemianova & Andrei Bukin (USSR)
1987 Natalia Bestemianova & Andrei Bukin (USSR)
1988 Natalia Bestemianova & Andrei Bukin (USSR)
1989 Marina Klimova & Sergei Ponomarenko (USSR)
1990 Marina Klimova & Sergei Ponomarenko (USSR)
1991 Isabelle Duchesnay & Paul Duchesnay (France)
1992 Marina Klimova & Sergei Ponomarenko (CIS)
1993 Maya Usova & Aleksandr Zhulin (Russia)
1994 Oksana Gritschuk & Yevgeny Platov (Russia)
1995 Oksana Gritschuk & Yevgeny Platov (Russia)
1996 Oksana Gritschuk & Yevgeny Platov (Russia)
1997 Oksana Gritschuk & Yevgeny Platov (Russia)
1998 Anjelika Krylova & Oleg Ovsyannikov (Russia)
1999 Anjelika Krylova & Oleg Ovsyannikov (Russia)
2000 Marina Anissina & Gwendal Peizerat (France)
2001 Barbara Fusar-Poli & Maurizio Margaglio (Italy)
2002 Irina Lobacheva & Ilia Averbukh (Russia)
2003 Shae-Lynn Bourne & Victor Kraatz (Canada)
2004 Tatiana Navka & Roman Kostomarov (Russia)

Judging scandal

Skating judge Marie-Reine Le Gougne was banned from the sport following the scandal of the 2002 Olympic Games pairs result. Much to the surprise of everyone, Russians Elena Berezhnaya and Anton Sikharulidze were awarded the gold medal. French judge Le Gougne claimed pressure had been put on her in a vote-swapping deal with the Russians. The Canadian couple denied a gold medal at the outset – Jamie Sale and David Pelletier – were also given first place and the sport went through a change in the rules to prevent future rigging.

A-Z

axel a jump where the skater takes off from the forward outside edge of one skate and lands on the back outside edge of the opposite skate. There are single axel, double axel and triple axel variations. The jump is named after Norwegian skater Axel Paulsen (1855–1938)

Biellmann spin	a spin, similar to the **layback spin**, where the skater arches his or her back and pulls up the free leg over the head. Named after Swiss skater Denise Biellmann (1962–) who made the move famous
bracket	a half-turn that takes the skater from one edge to the opposite edge of the blade
camel spin	a one-legged spin where one leg is extended horizontally behind the skater, parallel to the ice
choctaw	a two-footed turn performed from outside edge to inside edge (or inside to outside edge); compare **mohawk**
crossover	a basic move where the skater crosses one skate over the other when turning corners and increasing speed
death spiral	a move in pairs skating where the male skater spins the female skater around him in a circle as she skates on one foot and with her body laid nearly horizontal to the ice
flip	a jump where the take-off is from the back inside edge of one skate and the landing on the back outside edge of the other
flying camel	a jump-and-spin combination that ends in a **camel spin**
flying sit spin	a jump-and-spin combination that ends in a **sit spin**
headless spin	a spin like the **upright spin** but with the head tilted away
Ina Bauer	a move similar to the **spread eagle** but performed with a bent knee and the other leg stretched out behind. Named after the German skater Ina Bauer who first performed it
inside edge	the inner of the two edges of the blade of an ice skate. It is further divided into two sections: forward and back
layback spin	an **upright spin** where the skater leans over with an arched back
loop	a jump where the skater takes off and then lands on the same back outside edge
lutz	a jump performed while travelling backwards where the skater takes off from the back outside edge of one skate and lands on the back outside edge of the other. It is named after the Austrian skater Alois Lutz (1898–1918) who invented it
mohawk	a two-footed turn performed from one inside edge to the inside edge of the opposite skate (or outside edge to outside edge); compare **choctaw**
outside edge	the outer of two edges of the blade of an ice skate. It is further divided into two sections: forward and back
rocker	a one-footed turn with no change of edge
salchow	a jump where the skater takes off from the back inside edge of one skate, spins in the air and lands on the back outside edge of the other skate. It is named after the Swedish skater Ulrich Salchow (1877–1949) who first performed it
sit spin	a spin performed in a sitting position close to the ice, with one leg bent and the other fully extended
spread eagle	a manoeuvre performed on both skates (on either inside edges or outside edges) where the skates point in opposite directions
stag leap	a leaping jump performed with the leading leg tucked under the skater and the trailing leg kicked out straight behind
toe jump	a jump where the skater pushes off with the toe of his or her free foot
toe loop	a jump where the skater takes off and lands on the same back outside edge
toe pick	the serrated teeth at the front of the blade. The toe pick is used in certain jumps and spins

upright spin a spin where the skater stands and rotates on one foot

walley a jump that starts from a back inside edge and lands on the back outside edge of the same blade

waltz a jump executed by taking off from a front outside edge, performing a half-revolution and landing on the back outside edge of the other skate

Some famous figure skaters

Christopher Dean, 1958–

Born in Nottingham, England, he was a policeman before taking up skating full time. He formed a skating partnership with **Jayne Torvill** in 1975. They were six times British champions (1978–83) and won World, Olympic and European ice-dance titles in 1984, with a haunting interpretation of Ravel's 'Bolero'.

Sonja Henie, 1912–69

Born in Oslo, Norway, she won three consecutive women's figures gold medals at the Winter Olympics of 1928, 1932 and 1936. In 1927 she won the first of ten consecutive World championships. After retiring from competitive skating she starred in ice shows and in the 1940s and 1950s graduated to become a Hollywood actress.

Michelle Kwan, 1980–

Born in Torrance, California, USA, she began skating aged five and in 1992 was a reserve for the US Olympic team, aged just 13. She was world champion in 1996, 1998, 2000, 2001 and 2003.

Irina Rodnina, 1949–

Born in Moscow, Russia, she began skating aged seven and with her first partner Alexei Ulanov won four consecutive World pairs titles (1969–72) as well as the 1972 Olympic Games gold medal. She changed partners in 1973 and she and Aleksandr Zaitsev won six World Championships (1973–8) and Olympic gold medals in 1976 and 1980. She and Zaitsev married in 1975.

Jayne Torvill, 1957–

Born in Nottingham, England, she started skating at the age of ten, and met **Christopher Dean** in 1975. The pair were six times British champions, and won World, Olympic and European ice-dance titles in 1984. In total they received a record 136 perfect 'sixes'.

Katarina Witt, 1965–

Born in Chemnitz, East Germany, she starting skating aged five and was twice Olympic champion (1984 and 1988) and won four World titles (1984–5, 1987–8).

JUDO

Origins

The Japanese martial art of judo ('the gentle way') is derived from ju-jitsu, the hand-to-hand combat technique of the samurai warriors, and was devised and codified by Dr Jigoro Kano in the 1880s. Kano opened his first school, or 'dojo', in 1882. The sport took a while to find a worldwide audience and was not admitted into the Olympic Games until 1964.

Rules and description

Judo matches are held on rectangular, vinyl-coated foam mats called 'tatami' and last five minutes (four minutes for women at the major championships). The contest area is between 8 and $10m^2$ with a safety zone outside it. Players win a match by scoring an 'ippon', the highest score in judo, which ends a bout. Other lesser scores include a 'waza-ari', a 'yuko' and a 'koka'. If a bout does not end with an ippon, the winner is decided by who has scored most points via these cumulative other scores. Judo players (also known as 'judoka') score points in three main ways: by winning throws in which their opponents are thrown to the floor, making holds, and gaining points through penalties given against the opponent. Judo players wear loose trousers and jackets. A coloured belt tied around the jacket denotes the skill level of the judo player.

Ruling body: International Judo Federation (IJF)

World Championships

First held in 1956, they are now contested every two years; the women's championships were instituted in 1980.

Men

	Open	**Heavyweight (over 100kg)***
1991	Naoya Ogawa (Japan)	Sergei Kosorotov (USSR)
1993	Rafael Kubacki (Poland)	David Douillet (France)
1995	David Douillet (France)	David Douillet (France)
1997	Rafael Kubacki (Poland)	David Douillet (France)
1999	Shinichi Shinohara (Japan)	Shinichi Shinohara (Japan)
2001	Aleksandr Michailin (Russia)	Aleksandr Michailin (Russia)
2003	Keiji Suzuki (Japan)	Yauyuki Muneta (Japan)

* Until 1999 over 95kg

	Half-heavyweight (under 100kg)*	**Middleweight (under 90kg)****
1991	Stéphane Traineau (France)	Hirotaka Okada (Japan)
1993	Antal Kovacs (Hungary)	Yoshio Nakamura (Japan)
1995	Pawel Nastula (Poland)	Jeon Ki-young (South Korea)
1997	Pawel Nastula (Poland)	Jeon Ki-young (South Korea)

	Half-heavyweight (under 100kg)*	Middleweight (under 90kg)**
1999	Kosei Inoue (Japan)	Hidehiko Yoshida (Japan)
2001	Kosei Inoue (Japan)	Frédéric Demontfaucon (France)
2003	Kosei Inoue (Japan)	Hwang Hee-tae (South Korea)
	* Until 1999 under 95kg	** Until 1999 under 86kg

	Half-middleweight (under 81kg)*	Lightweight (under 73kg)**
1991	Daniel Lascau (Germany)	Toshihiko Koga (Japan)
1993	Chun Ki-young (South Korea)	Chung Hoon (South Korea)
1995	Toshihiko Koga (Japan)	Daisuke Hideshima (Japan)
1997	Cho In-chul (South Korea)	Kenzo Nakamura (Japan)
1999	Graeme Randall (Great Britain)	Jimmy Pedro (USA)
2001	Cho In-chul (South Korea)	Vitali Makarov (Russia)
2003	Florian Wanner (Germany)	Lee Won-hee (South Korea)
	* Until 1999 under 78kg	**Until 1999 under 71kg

	Half-lightweight (under 66kg)*	Extra lightweight (under 60kg)
1991	Udo Quellmalz (Germany)	Tadanori Koshino (Japan)
1993	Yukimasa Nakamura (Japan)	Ryuji Sonoda (Japan)
1995	Udo Quellmalz (Germany)	Nikolai Ojeguine (Russia)
1997	Hyuk Kim (South Korea)	Tadahiro Nomura (Japan)
1999	Larbi Benboudaoud (France)	Manolo Poulot (Cuba)
2001	Arash Miresmaeili (Iran)	Anis Lounifi (Tunisia)
2003	Arash Miresmaeili (Iran)	Min Ho-choi (South Korea)
	* Until 1999 under 65kg	

Women

	Open	Heavyweight (over 78kg)*
1991	Zhuang Xiaoyan (China)	Moon Ji-yoon (South Korea)
1993	Beata Maksymow (Poland)	Johanna Hagn (Germany)
1995	Monique van der Lee (The Netherlands)	Angelique Seriese (The Netherlands)
1997	Daina Beltran (Cuba)	Christine Cicot (France)
1999	Daina Beltran (Cuba)	Beata Maksymow (Poland)
2001	Céline Lebrun (France)	Yuan Hua (China)
2003	Tong Wen (China)	Sun Fuming (China)
		* Until 1999 over 72kg

	Half-heavyweight (under 78kg)*	Middleweight (under 70kg)**
1991	Kim Mi-jung (South Korea)	Emanuela Pierantozzi (Italy)
1993	Leng Chunhui (China)	Cho Min-sun (South Korea)
1995	Diadenis Luna (Cuba)	Cho Min-sun (South Korea)
1997	Noriko Anno (Japan)	Kate Howey (Great Britain)
1999	Noriko Anno (Japan)	Sibelis Veranes (Cuba)
2001	Noriko Anno (Japan)	Masae Ueno (Japan)
2003	Noriko Anno (Japan)	Masae Ueno (Japan)
	* Until 1999 under 72kg	** Until 1999 under 66kg

	Half-middleweight (under 63kg)*	Lightweight (under 57kg)**
1991	Frauke Eickhoff (Germany)	Miriam Blasco (Spain)
1993	Gella van de Caveye (Belgium)	Nicola Fairbrother (Great Britain)
1995	Jung Sung-sook (South Korea)	Driulis González-Morales (Cuba)
1997	Séverine Vandenhende (France)	Isabel Fernandez (Spain)
1999	Keiko Maeda (Japan)	Driulis González-Morales (Cuba)
2001	Gella van de Caveye (Belgium)	Yurisleidis Lupetey (Cuba)
2003	Daniela Krukower (Argentina)	Sun Hui-kye (North Korea)
	* Until 1999 under 61kg	** Until 1999 under 56kg

	Half-lightweight (under 52kg)	Extra lightweight (under 48kg)
1991	Alessandra Giungi (Italy)	Cécile Nowak (France)
1993	Legna Verdecia-Rodriguez (Cuba)	Ryoko Tamura (Japan)
1995	Marie-Claire Restoux (France)	Ryoko Tamura (Japan)
1997	Marie-Claire Restoux (France)	Ryoko Tamura (Japan)
1999	Noriko Narasaki (Japan)	Ryoko Tamura (Japan)
2001	Sun Hui-kye (North Korea)	Ryoko Tamura (Japan)
2003	Amarilis Savon (Cuba)	Ryoko Tamura (Japan)

A-Z

armlock the use of pressure on an opponent's elbow joint to gain a submission

awasewaza an **ippon** made by scoring two **waza-ari**

body drop a common throw where a **judoka** throws the opponent forward over an outstretched leg

bout a judo contest

choke hold a move that involves choking or strangling an opponent by encircling the neck with an arm, or the legs, or the lapels of the jacket of the **judogi**

chui a penalty awarded against a **judoka** for a more serious violation. The opponent is awarded a **yuko**; compare **keikoku** and **shido**

dan a grade of black belt

dojo a place or school where judo is taught or practised

hajime the command with which the referee starts a judo **bout**

hanso-kumake a disqualification for an offence. The opponent is awarded an **ippon** and thereby the **bout**

harai goshi a sweeping hip throw

ippon a winning score, awarded for a perfectly executed move, either by throwing the opponent onto his or her back with 'force, speed and control', by holding an opponent for 25 seconds or by gaining submission through a **choke hold** or **armlock**

judogi the costume (loose-fitting jacket and trousers secured by a belt) worn by a **judoka**

judoist same as **judoka**

judoka a person who practises, or is expert in, judo

juji-gatame same as **armlock**

keikoku a penalty awarded against a **judoka** for a very serious violation. The opponent is awarded a **wazi-ari**; compare **chui** and **shido**

koka	the lowest score, an 'almost **yuko**', awarded for a throw or hold or by a ten-second hold-down
kyo	a set of throws
kyu	one of the six novice grades, the least experienced being sixth kyu
matte	the command with which the referee stops the action in a judo **bout**
non-combativity	failure of a **judoka** to make an attack, penalized by **shido** or **chui**
obi	the belt worn by a **judoka**
passivity	same as **non-combativity**
seoi-nage	a shoulder throw
shido	a penalty awarded against a **judoka** for a minor violation. The opponent is awarded a **koka**; compare **chul** and **keikoku**
sono-mama	the referee's command to freeze, with the **judoka** stopping all action and holding their positions
sore matte	the command with which the referee brings a judo **bout** to an end
stranglehold	same as **choke hold**
tai-otoshi	same as **body drop**
throw	a move that casts one's opponent to the ground
uchi mata	an inner thigh throw
waza-ari	a score, an 'almost ippon', awarded for a throw or hold not quite worthy of a maximum score of an **ippon** or by a 25-second hold-down. If a competitor gains two **waza-ari** in a match it is equal to an ippon and is called an **awasewaza**
yoshi	the command with which the referee restarts a bout after a stop-page
yuko	a score, an 'almost waza-ari', awarded for a throw or hold not worthy of **waza-ari** or by a 20-second hold-down

Some famous judo players

Ingrid Berghmans, 1961–

Born in Koersel, Belgium, she is perhaps the most successful woman judo fighter in history. She won six world titles: the Open class in 1980, 1982, 1984 and 1986, and the under 72kg class in 1984 and 1989. In 1988, when judo was a demonstration event, she took the Olympic under 72kg class gold medal.

Karen Briggs, 1963–

Born in Kingston-upon-Hull, England, she was a four-times world champion (1984, 1986, 1989). She also won a gold medal at the 1990 Commonwealth Games but was unable to complete her event at the inaugural Olympic Games event in 1992 because of injury. She was awarded an MBE in 1990.

David Douillet, 1969–

Born in Rouen, France, he first competed in the Olympics in 1992, earning a bronze medal in the heavyweight category. He took gold four years later and again at the Sydney Olympics in 2000 despite having been seriously injured in a motorcycle accident. Douillet also has four world titles (1993, 1995, 1997) to his name.

Anton Geesink, 1934–

Born in Utrecht, the Netherlands, this outstanding judo player was the first non-Japanese to win a judo world title. He won the 1961 world title and followed it with a gold medal in the Open class at the 1964 Olympic Games and further world titles in 1964 and 1965. He also won European titles in 1953 and 1954, 1957–60, 1962–4 and 1967. He was promoted 10th dan in 1997.

Ryoko Tamura, 1975–

Born in Fukuoka, Japan, she won a silver medal as a 16-year-old at the 1992 Barcelona Olympics and was then undefeated for four years, winning 84 matches. Her first loss was in the Olympic final of 1996 and she again had to settle for a silver medal. Once more she went four years undefeated before finally securing a gold medal at the Sydney Olympics of 2000. Tamura also has six world titles (1993, 1995, 1997, 1999, 2001 and 2003).

The clue is in the colour

There are two ranks in judo: the kyu rank for novices and the dan rank for senior players. Each grade is indicated by the colour of the belt worn by the judoka.

Rank	Belt colour
6th kyu	white
5th kyu	yellow
4th kyu	orange
3rd kyu	green
2nd kyu	blue
1st kyu	purple (juniors)/brown (seniors)
1st–5th dan	black
6th–8th dan	black or chequered red and white
9th–10th dan	black or red

JU-JITSU

Origins

Ju-jitsu is derived from the combat techniques used by the 'bushi' (knights) during the Japanese Kamakura period (1185–1333). It was used by unarmed knights against their armed foes. It was formalized during the Edo period (1603–1868), an era of relative peace in Japan's history. Various 'ryu' (schools) developed, such as 'wa-jutsu', 'yawara', 'kogu-soku', 'hakuda', 'shubaku' and 'kempo'.

Rules and description

Ju-jitsu, from the Japanese 'ju' meaning 'gentle or soft' and 'jitsu' meaning 'art', is a martial art that includes throws, strangleholds, wristholds, kicks, chops and punches. Unlike other forms of Japanese martial arts, the aggression is not tempered with a spiritual aspect. Ju-jitsu consists of five major elements: 'ukemi waza' (break-falling techniques), 'nage waza' (throwing techniques), 'katame waza' (grappling techniques), 'atemi waza' (striking techniques), and 'katsu waza' (revival techniques). From jujitsu, Dr Kano Jigoro developed judo – 'the gentle way'.

Ruling bodies: Ju-jitsu International Federation (JJIF); International Sport Ju-jitsu Association (ISJA)

World Championships

The fighting system consists of one round of combat with different phases: in the first phase striking is allowed, in the next grappling and throwing, in the final phase ground fighting is permitted.

Men

	Up to 62kg	Up to 69kg*	Up to 77kg**
1994	Jonatan Vega (Spain)	Philippe Taurines (France)	Bertrand Amoussou (France)
1996	Kelly Molinari (France)	Johan Blomdahl (Sweden)	Bertrand Amoussou (France)
1998	Jörn Meiners (Germany)	Gerhard Ableidinger (Austria)	Marc Marie-Louise (France)
2000	Kelly Molinari (France)	Gerhard Ableidinger (Austria)	Jan Henningsen (Denmark)
2002	Francisco Garcia (Spain)	Cyril Juffroy (France)	Gregory Vallarino (Uruguay)
2004	André Hötzel (Germany)	Julien Boussuge (France)	Marek Krajewski (Poland)
		*Until 1998, 72kg	**Until 1998, 82kg

	Up to 94kg*	Over 94kg**
1994	Lionel Hugonnier (France)	Marcelo Figueiredo (Brazil)
1996	Lionel Hugonnier (France)	Christophe Julve (France)
1998	Joachim Göhrmann (Germany)	Grzegorz Zimolag (Poland)
2000	Eduardo Figueiredo (Brazil)	Marcelo Figueiredo (Brazil)
2002	Fernando Segovia (Spain)	Marcelo Figueiredo (Brazil)
2004	Fernando Segovia (Spain)	Dariusz Zimolag (Poland)
	*Until 1998, 92kg	**Until 1998, 92kg

Women

	Up to 55kg*	Up to 62kg**	Over 70kg***
1994	Esther Oostlander (The Netherlands)	Anna Dimberg (Sweden)	Laurence Sionneal (France)
1996	Laurence Delvingt (France)	Anna Dimberg (Sweden)	Pia Larsen (Denmark)
1998	Florence Baily (France)	Patricia Hekkens (The Netherlands)	Jennie Brolin (Sweden)
2000	Annabelle Reydy (France)	Katrin Berger (Germany)	Sabine Felser (Germany)
2002	Annabelle Reydy (France)	Isabelle Bacon (France)	Sabine Felser (Germany)
2004	Monika Dikow (Poland)	Maria Merino (Spain)	Eila Günther (Germany)
	*Until 1998, 58kg	**Until 1998, 68kg	***Until 1998, 68kg

KABADDI

Origins

Kabaddi, also sometimes spelt kabbadi or kabardee, is a game that originated in India. It is thought to be about 4,000 years old. In the ancient Indian epic poem known as the *Mahabharata*, a famous battle is described where the young hero Abhimanyu, son of the Pandava hero Arjuna, went into battle against seven warriors. They created a barricade against him but he managed to breach it. However, the seven warriors surrounded him and he was captured and killed. The tactics of this battle are mimicked in kabaddi and the themes of 'raiding', 'fighting' and 'killing' are well to the fore in the sport.

Rules and description

Kabaddi is a team pursuit game a little like tag. Each team comprises twelve players but only seven are allowed on the field of play at any one time. The field is a pitch measuring 13 x 10m/42ft 6in x 33ft that is marked into two halves, known as courts. The side that wins the toss sends a 'raider' into the opponents' court to try to tag as many players as possible. Only one is sent at a time. And then each side sends one alternately until the end of the game.

The added difficulty is that as the raider crosses the halfway line he has to start chanting 'kabaddi', loudly enough for everyone within 10m/33ft to hear and continuously until the raid is over. This is called the cant; if a player runs out of breath he is said to have 'lost his cant' and he is out. The object of the game is to touch as many opponents as possible. Meanwhile, the opponents try to touch him and also to hem him in to prevent him from returning to his own court. If he gets back to his court successfully, then all players touched by him are out – and the team scores a point. If a team puts out all of the opposition it scores an 'iona' (bonus points). The team with the most points at the end of 40 minutes' play wins.

Ruling bodies: Amateur Kabaddi Federation; World Kabaddi Federation

Asian Games

Kabaddi is very popular in India and is also played in Pakistan, Myanmar (Burma), Sri Lanka and China. The game has been part of the Asian Games since 1990.

	Winner	**Venue**
1990	India	Beijing, China
1994	India	Hiroshima, Japan
1998	India	Bangkok, Thailand
2002	India	Pusan, South Korea

A-Z

anti, anti-raiders	members of the opposing side
baulk lines	lines on the pitch parallel to the centre line and 3m/9ft 10in from it
cant	the chanting of 'kabaddi'
court	each of the two equal areas into which the pitch is divided
iona	bonus points score achieved by putting out the entire opposition
losing cant	losing breath and failing to chant 'kabaddi'
raider	player who moves into the opponents' half
waiting blocks	area where non-playing members of team wait as reserves or where players go when out

KARATE

Origins

An unarmed Japanese martial art, karate's origins can be traced to the 6th-century Chinese art of shaolin boxing. This was developed on the island of Okinawa into a form called 'tang hand' around 1500. It was introduced to Japan in the 1920s by Gichin Funakoshi and the name of the sport was coined in the 1930s. Karate spread to the West in the 1950s.

Rules and description

Karate, Japanese for 'empty hand', is a form of self-defence in which blows of the hands and feet are accompanied by special breathing and shouts. The physical actions are delivered from poised positions or stances. Each competitor aims blows at specific parts of the body: the spine, face, kidneys, chest and so on. The most common blows used are chops or knife hands, knuckle punches, hammer blows, finger jabs, and front, side, back, round, jump, and stamping kicks. Deep breathing and sudden shouts accompany the movements.

Competitive karate takes two forms: 'kata' and 'kumite'. The former is a performance of movements and is assessed by five judges. In kumite two fighters stand on a mat between 8 and 10m^2, known as the contest area, attempting to aim blows at each other. They are also judged on their technique. There are a number of different styles, but the five major ones are 'shotokan', 'wado-ryu', 'kyokushinkai', 'shito-ryu' and 'gojo-ryu'.

Each competitor, or 'karateka', rises through the grades from 'kyu' or student to 'dan' or graduate. As in judo, coloured belts denote the level of attainment reached.

Ruling body: World Karate Federation (WKF)

Karate

World Championships

First held in Tokyo in 1970, the World Championships have taken place every two years since 1980. There are team competitions and individual competitions at kumite and kata.

	Venue		Venue
1970	Tokyo, Japan	**1990**	Mexico City, Mexico
1972	Paris, France	**1992**	Grenada, Spain
1975	Long Beach, USA	**1994**	Kota Kinabalu, Malaysia
1977	Tokyo, Japan	**1996**	Sun City, South Africa
1980	Madrid, Spain	**1998**	Rio de Janeiro, Brazil
1982	Taipei, Taiwan	**2000**	Munich, Germany
1984	Maastricht, The Netherlands	**2002**	Madrid, Spain
1986	Sydney, Australia	**2004**	Monterrey, Mexico
1988	Cairo, Egypt		

Men

Kumite

	Team		Team
1970	Japan	**1990**	Great Britain
1972	France	**1992**	Spain
1975	Great Britain	**1994**	France
1977	The Netherlands	**1996**	France
1980	Spain	**1998**	France
1982	Great Britain	**2000**	France
1984	Great Britain	**2002**	Spain
1986	Great Britain	**2004**	France
1988	Great Britain		

	Under 60kg	Under 65kg	Under 70kg
1980	Ricardo Abad (Spain)	Toshiaki Maeda (Japan)	Damian Gonzales (Spain)
1982	Jukka-Pekka Väyrinen (Finland)	Yuichi Suzuki (Japan)	Seiji Nishimura (Japan)
1984	Dirk Betzien (West Germany)	Ramon Malavé (Sweden)	Jim Collins (Great Britain)
1986	Hideto Nakano (Japan)	Eizou Kondo (Japan)	Thierry Masci (France)
1988	Abdu Shaher (Great Britain)	Tim Stephens (Great Britain)	Thierry Masci (France)
1990	Stewin Widar Rönning (Norway)	Toshikatsu Azumi (Japan)	Haldun Alagas (Turkey)
1992	Veysel Bugur (Turkey)	Jesús Juan Rubio (Spain)	Willie Thomas (Great Britain)
1994	Damien Dovy (France)	Teruchika Ito (Japan)	Shisua Shiina (Japan)
1996	David Luque (Spain)	Mahdi Amouzadeh (Iran)	A Goubachiev (Russia)
1998	David Luque (Spain)	Alexandre Biamonti (France)	Haldun Alagas (Turkey)
2000	Cécil Boulesnane (France)	Lazaar Boskovic (Germany)	Gustaff Lefevre (Croatia)
2002	Damien Dovy (France)	George Kotaka (USA)	Giuseppe di Domenico (Italy)
2004	Paul Newby (England)	Luis Plumacher (Venezuela)	Shinji Nagaki (Japan)

	Under 75kg	Under 80kg	Over 80kg
1980	Sadao Tajima (Japan)	Tokey Hill (USA)	Jean-Luc Montana (France)
1982	Javier Gomez (Switzerland)	Pat McKay (Great Britain)	Geoff Thompson (Great Britain)

	Under 75kg	Under 80kg	Over 80kg
1984	Toon Stelling (The Netherlands)	Pat McKay (Great Britain)	Jerome Atkinson (Great Britain)
1986	Kenneth Leewin (The Netherlands)	Jacques Tapol (France)	Vic Charles (Great Britain)
1988	Kyo Hayashi (Japan)	Dudley Josepa (The Netherlands)	Emmanuel Pinda (France)
1990	Hideo Tamaru (Japan)	José Manuel Egea (Spain)	Marc Pyrée (France)
1992	Wayne Otto (Great Britain)	José Manuel Egea (Spain)	Brian Peakall (Australia)
1994	Daniel Devigli (Austria)	David Benetello (Italy)	Alain Le Hetet (France)
1996	Wayne Otto (Great Britain)	Gilles Cherdieu (France)	Yasumasa Shimizu (Japan)
1998	David Felix (France)	Gilles Cherdieu (France)	Marc Haubold (France)
2000	Ivan Leal (Spain)	Daniel Sabanovic (The Netherlands)	Mamadou Aly Ndiaye (Senegal)
2002	Ivan Leal (Spain)	Yann Baillon (France)	Leon Walters (England)
2004	David Santana Vega (Spain)	Zeynel Celik (Turkey)	Aleksandr Guerunov (Russia)

	No weight limit
1970	Kouji Wada (Japan)
1972	Luiz Tasuke Watanabe (Brazil)
1975	Kazusada Murakami (Japan)
1977	Otti Roethoff (The Netherlands)

Open	
1980	Giovanni Ricciardi (Italy)
1982	Hisao Murase (Japan)
1984	Emmanuel Pinda (France)
1986	Karl Doggfeldt (Sweden)
1992	Hiroshi Hayashi (Japan)
1994	Manabu Takenouchi (Japan)
1996	Paul Alderson (Great Britain)
1998	Konstantinos Papadopoulos (Greece)
2000	Christophe Pinna (France)
2002	Predrag Stojadinov (Yugoslavia)
2004	Rory Daniels (England)

Kata

	Individual	Team
1977	Keiji Okada (Japan)	
1980	Keiji Okada (Japan)	
1982	Masashi Koyama (Japan)	
1984	Tsuguo Sakumoto (Japan)	
1986	Tsuguo Sakumoto (Japan)	Japan
1988	Tsuguo Sakumoto (Japan)	Japan
1990	Tomojuki Aihara (Japan)	Italy
1992	Luis-Maria Sanz (Spain)	Japan
1994	Michaël Milon (France)	Japan
1996	Michaël Milon (France)	Japan
1998	Ryoki Abe (Japan)	Japan
2000	Michaël Milon (France)	Japan
2002	Takashi Katada (Japan)	Japan
2004	Luca Valdesi (Italy)	Italy

Women

Kumite

	Team
1992	Great Britain
1994	Spain
1996	Great Britain
1998	Turkey
2000	France
2002	Spain
2004	Turkey

	Under 53kg	Under 60kg	Over 60kg
1982	Sophie Berger (France)	Yukari Yamakawa (Japan)	Guus van Mourik (The Netherlands)
1984	Sophie Berger (France)	Tomoko Kinishi (Japan)	Guus van Mourik (The Netherlands)
1986	Johanna Kauri (Finland)	Rita Virelius (Finland)	Guus van Mourik (The Netherlands)
1988	Yuko Hasama (Japan)	Akimi Kimura (Japan)	Guus van Mourik (The Netherlands)
1990	Yuko Hasama (Japan)	Monique Amghar (France)	Catherine Belrhiti (France)
1992	Charlene Machin (Australia)	Mollie Samuels (Great Britain)	Catherine Belrhiti (France)
1994	Sari Laine (Finland)	Mayumi Baba (Japan)	Sandra Louw (South Africa)
1996	Teresia Larsson (Sweden)	Jillian Toney (Great Britain)	Patricia Duggin (Great Britain)
1998	Hiromi Masama (Japan)	Jillian Toney (Great Britain)	Laurence Fischer (France)
2000	Hiromi Masama (Japan)	Alexandra Witteborn (Germany)	Natsu Yamaguchi (Japan)
2002	Kora Knuhmann (Germany)	Nathalie Leroy (France)	Elisa Au (USA)
2004	Tomoko Araga (Japan)	Yadira Lira (Mexico)	Elisa Au (USA)

Kata

	Individual	Team
1980	Suzuko Okamura (Japan)	
1982	Mie Nakayama (Japan)	
1984	Mie Nakayama (Japan)	
1986	Mie Nakayama (Japan)	Taiwan
1988	Yuki Mimura (Japan)	Japan
1990	Yuki Mimura (Japan)	Italy
1992	Yuki Mimura (Japan)	Japan
1994	Hisami Yokoyama (Japan)	Japan
1996	Yuki Mimura (Japan)	Japan
1998	Atsuko Wakai (Japan)	Japan
2000	Atsuko Wakai (Japan)	France
2002	Atsuko Wakai (Japan)	France
2004	Atsuko Wakai (Japan)	Japan

What the coloured belts mean

There are two ranks in karate: the kyu rank for novices and the dan rank for senior players. The number of levels varies according to the style but the general system in Britain is described below.

Rank	Belt colour
novice	white
9th kyu	orange
8th kyu	red
7th kyu	yellow
6th kyu	green
5th kyu	purple
4th kyu	purple with white stripe
3rd kyu	brown
2nd kyu	brown with white stripe
1st kyu	brown with two white stripes
1st–10th dan	black

A-Z

cat stance same as **neko-ashi-dachi**

chop to strike with a sharp blow

dachi any stance taken up by the **karateka**

dan the highest proficiency grade

dojo a place or school where karate is taught or practised

encho-sen an extension of play to determine the winner of a tied match

gargu kamae a stance with raised arms ready to defend the body

gie, gi a karate costume

ippon a winning score, awarded for a perfectly executed move

karateka a karate practitioner

kata a formal sequence of practice exercises and movements; kata competitors are marked for their routines rather than for fighting

kentsui the 'hammer fist' strike

kiai the shout delivered with a movement

kumite competitive karate bouts

kyu student **karateka**

neko-ashi-dachi a position or stance where the front foot is raised ready for kicking

reclining dragon same as **gargu kamae**

seiken the forefist

sensei a karate master

tzuki a punch

uraken the inverted fist

waza-ari a half-point, two being required for an **ippon**

KENDO

Origins

Kendo, Japanese for 'way of the sword', is an ancient Japanese martial art practised by the warrior class in the 12th century – the samurai. The first references to 'kenjitsu' (swordsmanship), the forerunner of kendo, appear in the written history, the *Kojiki*, from AD 712.

Rules and description

The object of kendo is to land two scoring blows on the opponent using either cuts or thrusts from a bamboo sword. The contest area ranges from $9m^2$ to $11m^2$. Kendo is a system of mental and physical training and each strike of the sword must be accompanied by the correct posture and a shout.

Ruling body: International Kendo Federation (IKF)

World Championships

First held in 1970, and subsequently every three years. A women's championship was inaugurated in 1997.

Men

	Champion	Team	Venue
1970	Mitsuru Kobayashi (Japan)	Japan	Tokyo, Japan
1973	Tatsushi Sakuragi (Japan)	Japan	San Francisco, USA
1976	Eijo Yoko (Japan)	Japan	Milton Keynes, UK
1979	Hironori Yamada (Japan)	Japan	Sapporo, Japan
1982	Minoru Makita (Japan)	Japan	Sao Paulo, Brazil
1985	Kunishide Koda (Japan)	Japan	Paris, France
1988	Isawu Okido (Japan)	Japan	Seoul, South Korea
1991	Shizuo Muto (Japan)	Japan	Toronto, Canada
1994	Hideaki Takahashi (Japan)	Japan	Paris, France
1997	Masahiro Miyazaki (Japan)	Japan	Kyoto, Japan
2000	Naoki Eiga (Japan)	Japan	Santa Clara, USA
2003	Hiromitsu Sato (Japan)	Japan	Glasgow, UK

Women

	Champion	Team	Venue
1997	Mike Kimura (Japan)	Japan	Kyoto, Japan
2000	Tomoko Kawano (Japan)	Japan	Santa Clara, USA
2003	Keiko Baba (Japan)	Japan	Glasgow, UK

A-Z

bogu armour worn by a **kendoka**, consisting of the **men**, **do**, **kote** and **tare**

do 1. the **kendoka**'s breastplate, made of bamboo or plastic and covered in leather 2. the shout made when aiming a cut at the torso

hakama flowing trousers

keikogi the kendo jacket. The colour of the keikogi denotes the competitor's grade

kendoka a kendo practitioner

kiai the yell or shout that accompanies a cut or thrust. Competitors must give the appropriate shout to score

kote 1. padded gloves 2. the shout made when aiming a cut at the wrists

men 1. the **kendoka**'s padded helmet, which includes a metal face grille 2. the shout made when aiming a cut at the face

reigi the etiquette required for kendo

shiai a kendo contest or match

shinai a bamboo sword made from four lengths of bamboo tied together with a waxed cord. The shinai is around 1.2m long and weighs 450g

tare the padded apron that covers the hips and stomach

tsuki a thrust to the throat

KICKBOXING

Origins

Derived from karate, kickboxing is a combat sport that blends the foot techniques of that sport with western-style boxing. It was devised in the USA in the 1970s as a counterpart to non-contact martial arts competitions. The sport was first known as full-contact karate.

Rules and description

Competitors use sparring, kicks, punches, kick blocks, foot sweeps and shadow boxing. All kicks must be performed above the waist. Fights can be sanctioned to last for anything between three and twelve rounds of two minutes per round. There are four different types of competitive boxing: semi-contact, light contact, full contact and low contact. Fighters must wear protective boots, shin pads, groin protector, gum shield, boxing gloves and hand wrappings. In the full-contact version of the sport long trousers rather than shorts are worn.

Judges score the match on a points system where the winner of each round takes ten points and the opponent a score less than ten. As in regular boxing, a bout can be won with a knockout or by failing to beat the count.

Ruling bodies: World Association of Kickboxing Associations (WAKO). There are also three fur-

ther bodies that have their own rules and world rankings: International Sport Karate Association (ISKA); International Kickboxing Federation (IKF); World Kickboxing Association (WKA)

WAKO World Championships 2003 (Paris, France)

First held in 1978, it is now held usually every two years.

Men Full Contact

51kg	Anq Arsayev (Russia)
54kg	Mirbek Susumbayev (Kyrgyzstan)
57kg	Fouad Habbani (France)
60kg	Artur Tasleyan (Russia)
63.5kg	Aleksandr Pogorelov (Moldova)
67kg	Jere Reinikainen (Finland)
71kg	Igor Kulbayjev (Russia)
75kg	Nermin Basovic (Bosnia-Herzegovina)
81kg	Maxim Voronov (Russia)
86kg	Muamer Hukic (Germany)
91kg	Ruslan Karayev (Russia)
+91kg	Jaroslav Zavorotny (Ukraine)

Women Full Contact

48kg	Alesia Gladkova (Russia)
52kg	Oksana Vassilieva (Ukraine)
56kg	Lydia Andreyeva (Russia)
60kg	Anna Kasprzak (Poland)
65kg	Maria Karlova (Russia)
70kg	Karolina Lukasik (Poland)
+70kg	Aissoui Ilhame (Germany)

KORFBALL

Origins

Korfball was first developed in 1902 in Amsterdam, the Netherlands, by a schoolteacher named Nico Broekhuysen who had been inspired by a game he had watched in Näs, Sweden. Broekhuysen drew up rules for his new game and it was played by mixed teams of boys and girls at his school. Korf in Dutch means 'basket'.

Rules and description

Korfball is an indoor game played on a court measuring 40 x 20m (or can also be played outdoors on a larger pitch of up to 60 x 30m); the court is divided into two zones. The game is played by two teams of eight, generally mixed teams of four men and four women. Each team has two men and two women in the attacking zone and two each in the defence zone. The aim is to score goals in baskets suspended 3.5m high. After every two goals the attackers and defenders change zones. Running with the ball is not permitted. A game lasts 60 minutes with a half-time interval.

Ruling body: International Korfball Federation (IKF)

Korfball and the Olympic Games

Korfball has not as yet been admitted to the Olympic Games programme but it was a demonstration sport in 1920 and 1928, appropriately at the Games of Antwerp and Amsterdam.

World Korfball Championships

The World Korfball Championships were first held in 1978. The inaugural competition celebrated the 75th anniversary of the founding of the Royal Netherlands Korfball Association. The cup is named after the founder of the game, Nico Broekhuysen.

	Winner	Runner-up	Host country
1978	The Netherlands	Belgium	The Netherlands
1984	The Netherlands	Belgium	Belgium
1987	The Netherlands	Belgium	The Netherlands
1991	Belgium	The Netherlands	Belgium
1995	The Netherlands	Belgium	India
1999	The Netherlands	Belgium	Australia
2003	The Netherlands	Belgium	The Netherlands

The true basketball game

While basketball is the better-recognized sport, it cannot claim to use a real basket as in korfball. In basketball the faux basket is a metal ring from which suspends wide-meshed white netting. In korfball the basket is made from woven rattan or wicker.

KUNG FU

Origins

Kung Fu, known as 'wushu' in international competition, is derived from a wide variety of ancient Chinese martial arts dating back as far as 3000 BC.

Rules and description

Wushu covers both armed and unarmed combat techniques and can include kicks and punches as well as holds, locks, blocks and throws. There are many hundreds of different styles practised. For many it is more than simply a sport or form of combat, often being tightly bound to philosophical, mystical and religious traditions. It has been argued that other forms of martial art performed today are ultimately descended from kung fu, such as taekwondo and karate, through Chinese migrants taking their art abroad. For competition purposes, the sport of wushu was standardized in the 20th century, creating two distinct disciplines, 'taolu' and 'sanshou'. In 'taolu' various routines are performed and judged on style, whereas the 'sanshou' form of the sport, also commonly known as 'sanda', comprises combat events in a number of weight categories.

Ruling body: International Wushu Federation

The 7th World Wushu Championships (2003)

Sanshou

Men

48kg	Rene Catalan (Philippines)
52kg	Li Bijin (China)
56kg	Zhang Shuaike (China)
60kg	Kim Gwee-jong (South Korea)
65kg	Jung Sung-hoon (South Korea)
70kg	Tai Puqing (China)
75kg	Dzhanhuvat Beletov (Russia)
80kg	Liu Hailong (China)
85kg	Mohammad Reza Jafari Khorasani (Iran)
90kg	Moursi Attia Wael (Egypt)
90kg+	Ataev Bozigit (Russia)

Women

48kg	Li Yonghong (China)
52kg	Qin Lizi (China)
56kg	Thi Ha Ngo (Vietnam)
60kg	Huang Zhifang (China)
65kg	Wu Chaolai (China)
70kg	Elaina Maxwell (USA)

Taolu

Routine	Men	Women
Changquan (Long fist)	Zhao Qingjian (China)	Cao Jing (China)
Nanquan (Southern fist)	Cheng Ka Ho (Hong Kong)	Luo Hao (China)
Daoshu (Broadsword)	Arvin Ting (Philippines)	Thi Thuy Hien Nguyen (Vietnam)
Jianshu (Straight sword)	Wei Jian (China)	Han Jing (Macao)
Nandao (Southern broadsword)	Trong Tuan Tran (Vietnam)	Thi Ngoc Oanh Nguyen (Vietnam)
Gunshu (Long staff)	Fei Baoxian (The Netherlands)	Dasha Tarasova (Russia)
Qiangshu (Spear)	Chow Ting Yu (Hong Kong)	Zhao Yangyang (China)
Nangun (Southern long staff)	Huang Shaoxiong (China)	Thantma Swe Swe (Myanmar)
Taijiquan (Taiji hand form)	Yi Peng (China)	Guo Yina (China)
Taijijian (Taiji straight sword)	Toshiya Watanabe (Japan)	Khaing Khaing Maw (Myanmar)
Duilian (Dual event*)	Zhao Qingjian/Yi Peng/Wei Jian (China)	Jing Han/Sao Lan Chong (Macao)

* for two- or three-person teams

LACROSSE

Origins

The name 'la crosse' is the French word for a bishop's crozier or a hooked staff, and was given by French settlers in Canada to the game played by the Iroquois people there. The Iroquois called it 'baggataway' and it is thought they had been playing the game since the end of the 15th century. They played on an immense pitch some 500m long. However, there were many variations on rules played by the different tribes: the Cherokee called it 'the little brother of war' and with games running up to hundreds of people per side, It must have look like some gigantic battle. The first organized club was the Montreal Lacrosse Club, which was founded in 1856. Lacrosse was introduced to England by the Caughnawaga people in 1867.

Rules and description

Lacrosse is a ball-and-stick field game played by both men and women. Men's lacrosse is a ten-a-side game played on a field that measures about 100 x 55m; the women's version is twelve a side, and is played on a pitch with minimum dimensions of around 110 x 60m. The aim of both forms of the game is to score more goals than the opposition. In men's lacrosse the goals measure 1.8m wide with a 1.8m-high crossbar; a pyramid-shaped net is affixed behind. The goals are placed 14m forward of each end line and lie within a circle (the 'goal crease') that has a radius of 2.74m. The pitch is divided into two halves, with a 'restraining line' marked 18m from the centre line in each half (one becomes the attack restraining line, the other the defending restraining line). Fouls are conceded when players move offside, or when there is dangerous play with the crosse.

The ball may be carried, thrown or batted with the crosse, the distinctive stick with a basket carried by the players. There are short crosses (around 100cm in length) and long crosses (130 to 180cm long); only four long sticks per team are permitted, with the goalkeeper having a stick of any length. The netting of the crosse is of gut or synthetic materials and the ball is made from rubber and is white, yellow or orange. The match is divided into four periods of 20 minutes each. Teams comprise a goalkeeper, three defenders (traditionally called 'point', 'cover point' and 'third man'), three midfielders (two wings and a 'centre'; five in the women's game) and three attackers (first, second and third 'home'). Each team must keep at least four players, including the goalkeeper, within the defensive restraining line. Men's lacrosse begins with a 'face-off'. The ball is placed between the sticks of two squatting players at the centre of the field and each tries to gain possession of the ball. Only the goalkeeper can touch the ball with the hand.

Women's lacrosse shares more similarities with field hockey and, unlike the men's game, body contact is outlawed. There are goal circles at each end of the pitch and a centre circle with a radius of 9m. A 'draw' starts the game and is the equivalent of the face-off in the men's game.

Lacrosse

Ruling bodies: International Lacrosse Federation (ILF) for the men's game; International Federation of Women's Lacrosse Associations for the women's

World Championships

Men

	Winner	Venue
1967	USA	Toronto, Canada
1974	USA	Melbourne, Australia
1978	Canada	Manchester, UK
1982	USA	Baltimore, USA
1986	USA	Toronto, Canada
1990	USA	Perth, Australia
1994	USA	Manchester, UK
1998	USA	Baltimore, USA
2002	USA	Perth, Australia
2006		London, Canada

Women

First held in 1969 and discontinued in 1978. The World Championships were succeeded by a World Cup tournament.

	Winner
1969	Great Britain
1974	USA
1978	Canada

World Cup

First held in 1982 when it replaced the World Championships.

	Winner	Venue
1982	USA	Nottingham, UK
1986	Australia	Philadelphia, USA
1989	USA	Perth, Australia
1993	USA	Edinburgh, UK
1997	USA	Tokyo, Japan
2001	USA	High Wycombe, UK
2005		Annapolis, USA

Indoor lacrosse

An indoor version of lacrosse, known as box lacrosse or 'boxla' was developed in Canada during the early 1930s. It is played in hockey rinks with six-man teams.

Olympic Games

A men's tournament was held between club sides in 1904 and between countries in 1908. The third-placed side in 1904 was named the Mohawk Indians and team members included Snake Eater, Black Eagle, Spotted Tail, and, more unexpectedly, Man Afraid Soap. Lacrosse was also a demonstration sport in 1928, 1932 and 1948.

1904 Canada (Shamrock Lacrosse Team, Winnipeg)
1908 Canada

A-Z

body-check a deliberate obstruction of an opposing player's movements that is a permitted part of the rules in the men's game. Body-checking does not form part of the women's game

centre midfield player who competes in the **draw** and links play between defence and attack

cover point defensive player whose role is to mark the opposing team's **second home**

cradle the gently rocking movement of keeping the ball near the lip of the net of the **crosse** so that a player can quickly throw the ball when necessary

crosse the playing stick, it has a pocket at the end for catching, carrying and throwing the ball

draw the method of starting and restarting the women's game. The ball is balanced on the backs of the two **centres**' sticks, held horizontally, and is flung in the air as the **crosses** are pulled up and away

face-off the method of starting and restarting the men's game. The players squat down and the ball is placed between their **crosses**. The aim is to capture or fling the ball away to a player on the same side

first home attacking player, usually the main goalscorer

goal crease the circle around the goal into which only defensive players may enter

pocket the strung part of the head of the stick which holds the ball

point defensive player whose role is to mark the opposing team's **first home**

second home attacking player

third home attacking player

third man defensive player whose role is to mark the opposing team's **third home**

LUGE

Origins

Luge is the French word for sledge, though the origins of sledging appear to focus on Viking communities in Norway around 1,200 years ago. Historians believe that the Vikings had sledges with two runners that resemble their modern-day counterparts. The first organized competition took place in 1883 in Davos, Switzerland.

Rules and description

Regarded as one of the world's most dangerous sports, competitors in the luge lie on their backs on specially designed fibreglass sledges and slide down fabricated, twisting, ice-covered tracks. Lugers descend feet first and therefore have difficulty in seeing where they are going. (A similar sport, the skeleton bob, has sliders going headfirst on their sledges.) They steer by means of shifting the weight of their legs and shoulders. The luge has no brakes.

Competition is for single lugers or for doubles – a spectacular event with one slider lying on his or her partner. The sledges for singles can weigh no more than 23kg; for doubles, 27kg. There are two runs in singles events (four at the Olympic Games) and two runs in doubles. The win is decided by the best cumulative time to descend the course. As well as competitions held on artificially built tracks, luging also takes place on natural tracks.

Ruling body: International Luge Federation (Féderation Internationale de Luge, FIL)

Olympic champions

The luge became an Olympic sport in 1964.

Singles

	Men	Women
1964	Thomas Köhler (East Germany)	Ortrun Enderlein (East Germany)
1968	Manfred Schmid (Austria)	Erica Lechner (Italy)
1972	Wolfgang Scheidel (East Germany)	Anna-Maria Müller (East Germany)
1976	Dettlef Günther (East Germany)	Margit Schumann (East Germany)
1980	Bernhard Glass (East Germany)	Vera Zozula (USSR)
1984	Paul Hildgartner (Italy)	Steffi Martin (East Germany)
1988	Jens Müller (East Germany)	Steffi Walter, née Martin (East Germany)
1992	Georg Hackl (Germany)	Doris Neuner (Austria)
1994	Georg Hackl (Germany)	Gerda Weissensteiner (Italy)
1998	Georg Hackl (Germany)	Silke Kraushaar (Germany)
2002	Armin Zoeggeler (Italy)	Sylke Otto (Germany)

Doubles

1964	Austria (Josef Feistmantl & Manfred Stengl)
1968	East Germany (Klaus Bonsack & Thomas Köhler)
1972	East Germany (Horst Hörnlein & Reinhard Bredow)
1976	East Germany (Hans Rinn & Norbert Hahn)
1980	East Germany (Hans Rinn & Norbert Hahn)
1984	West Germany (Hans Stanggassinger & Franz Wembacher)
1988	East Germany (Jörg Hoffmann & Jochen Pietzsch)
1992	Germany (Stefan Krausse & Jan Behrendt)
1994	Italy (Kurt Brugger & Wilfried Huber)
1998	Germany (Stefan Krausse & Jan Behrendt)
2002	Germany (Patric-Fritz Leitner & Alexander Resch)

And when you don't have access to ice ...

... you can invent the new sport of street luge. An extreme sport that originated in California, street luging evolved from skateboarding. Competitors race each other over steep mountain roads with speeds of 130kph being reached.

MARATHON RUNNING

Origins

The marathon race was first run at the 1896 Olympic Games in Athens, Greece. It was a 40,000m race that commemorated the legend of the Greek messenger Pheidippides. In 490 BC he ran to Athens carrying the news of a great Greek victory over the Persians at the Battle of Marathon. On reaching Athens he cried out 'Be joyful, we win' and promptly dropped dead from exhaustion. The first city marathon was the Boston Marathon of 1897. The modern distance of the marathon was established at the 1908 London Olympic Games.

Rules and description

The popularity of city marathon running is evidenced by the fact that there is scarcely a weekend on the calendar when one is not being held. The first was held in Boston, USA, which with London, New York, Rotterdam, Berlin, Amsterdam and Chicago is among the most famous. All courses measure 42km, 195m/26mi, 385yd but because each city has variations in elevation there were previously no world records, only 'world bests'. This stand was reversed by the International Association of Athletics Federations (IAAF) in early 2004.

Royal prerogative

The distance for the marathon was changed for the 1908 London Olympics as King Edward VII requested that the race begin at Windsor Castle so he could watch the start. The distance between the castle and the Olympic stadium was 26 miles; the extra 385 yards accounted for the distance round the track so the race would finish beneath the royal box.

Olympic Champions

	Men	Women
1896	Spyridon Louis (Greece)	
1900	Michel Theato (Luxembourg)	
1904	Thomas Hicks (USA)	
1908	John Hayes (USA)	
1912	Kennedy Mcarthur (South Africa)	
1920	Hannes Kolehmainen (Finland)	
1924	Albin Stenroos (Finland)	
1928	Mohamed El Ouafi (France)	
1932	Juan Carlos Zabala (Argentina)	
1936	Kitei Son (Japan)	
1948	Delfo Cabrera (Argentina)	
1952	Emil Zatopek (Czechoslovakia)	
1956	Alain Mimoun (France)	
1960	Abebe Bikila (Ethiopia)	
1964	Abebe Bikila (Ethiopia)	
1968	Mamo Wolde (Ethiopia)	
1972	Frank Shorter (USA)	
1976	Waldemar Cierpinski (East Germany)	
1980	Waldemar Cierpinski (East Germany)	
1984	Carlos Lopes (Portugal)	Joan Benoit (USA)
1988	Gelindo Borlin (Italy)	Rosa Mota (Portugal)
1992	Hwang Young-cho (South Korea)	Valentina Yegorova (Unified Team)
1996	Josia Thugwane (South Africa)	Fatima Roba (Ethiopia)
2000	Gezahng Abera (Ethiopia)	Naoko Takahashi (Japan)
2004	Stefano Baldini (Italy)	Mizuki Noguchi (Japan)

Hitting the wall

Hitting the wall is what marathoners call the sudden loss of energy that can happen around the 20th mile of the race. US marathon runner Dick Beardsley described the first time he hit the wall as follows: 'It felt like an elephant had jumped out of a tree onto my shoulders and was making me carry it the rest of the way in.'

London Marathon

The race was first run in March 1981, the brainchild of former middle-distance runner Chris Brasher who was inspired by running the New York marathon. The course runs from Greenwich in south-east London to a finishing line on Birdcage Walk by Buckingham Palace. By 2004 more than 570,000 people had completed the annual race.

	Men	Women
1981	Dick Beardsley (US) and Inge Simonsen (Norway)	Joyce Smith (Great Britain)
1982	Hugh Jones (Great Britain)	Joyce Smith (Great Britain)
1983	Mike Gratton (Great Britain)	Grete Waitz (Norway)

	Men	Women
1984	Charlie Spedding (Great Britain)	Ingrid Kristiansen (Norway)
1985	Steve Jones (Great Britain)	Ingrid Kristiansen (Norway)
1986	Toshihiko Seko (Japan)	Grete Waitz (Norway)
1987	Hiromi Taniguchi (Japan)	Ingrid Kristiansen (Norway)
1988	Henrik Jørgensen (Denmark)	Ingrid Kristiansen (Norway)
1989	Douglas Wakiihuri (Kenya)	Véronique Marot (Great Britain)
1990	Allister Hutton (Great Britain)	Wanda Panfil (Poland)
1991	Yakov Tolstikov (USSR)	Rosa Mota (Portugal)
1992	António Pinto (Portugal)	Katrin Dörre (Germany)
1993	Eamonn Martin (Great Britain)	Katrin Dörre (Germany)
1994	Dionicio Cerón (Mexico)	Katrin Dörre (Germany)
1995	Dionicio Cerón (Mexico)	Malgorzata Sobanska (Poland)
1996	Dionicio Cerón (Mexico)	Liz McColgan (Great Britain)
1997	António Pinto (Portugal)	Joyce Chepchumba (Kenya)
1998	Abel Antón (Spain)	Catherina McKiernan (Ireland)
1999	Abdelkader El Mouaziz (Morocco)	Joyce Chepchumba (Kenya)
2000	António Pinto (Portugal)	Tegla Loroupe (Kenya)
2001	Abdelkader El Mouaziz (Morocco)	Derartu Tulu (Ethiopia)
2002	Khalid Khannouchi (USA)	Paula Radcliffe (Great Britain)
2003	Gezahegne Abera (Ethiopia)	Paula Radcliffe (Great Britain)
2004	Evans Rutto (Kenya)	Margaret Okayo (Kenya)

New York Marathon

The course begins on Staten Island and finishes in Central Park, Manhattan, after passing through all five New York boroughs. The race is held each year in November and was first run in 1970.

	Men	Women
1970	Gary Muhrcke (USA)	
1971	Norman Higgins (USA)	Beth Bonner (USA)
1972	Sheldon Karlin (USA)	Nina Kuscsik (USA)
1973	Tom Fleming (USA)	Nina Kuscsik (USA)
1974	Norbert Sander (USA)	Kathrine Switzer (USA)
1975	Tom Fleming (USA)	Kim Merritt (USA)
1976	Bill Rodgers (USA)	Miki Gorman (USA)
1977	Bill Rodgers (USA)	Miki Gorman (USA)
1978	Bill Rodgers (USA)	Grete Waitz (Norway)
1979	Bill Rodgers (USA)	Grete Waitz (Norway)
1980	Alberto Salazar (USA)	Grete Waitz (Norway)
1981	Alberto Salazar (USA)	Allison Roe (New Zealand)
1982	Alberto Salazar (USA)	Grete Waitz (Norway)
1983	Rod Dixon (New Zealand)	Grete Waitz (Norway)
1984	Orlando Pizzolato (Italy)	Grete Waitz (Norway)
1985	Orlando Pizzolato (Italy)	Grete Waitz (Norway)
1986	Gianni Poli (Italy)	Grete Waitz (Norway)
1987	Ibrahim Hussein (Kenya)	Priscilla Welch (Great Britain)
1988	Steve Jones (Great Britain)	Grete Waitz (Norway)

Marathon Running

	Men	Women
1989	Juma Ikangaa (Tanzania)	Ingrid Kristiansen (Norway)
1990	Douglas Wakiihuri (Kenya)	Wanda Panfil (Poland)
1991	Salvador Garcia (Mexico)	Liz McColgan (Great Britain)
1992	Willie Mtolo (South Africa)	Lisa Ondieki (Australia)
1993	Andres Espinosa (Mexico)	Uta Pippig (Germany)
1994	German Silva (Mexico)	Tegla Loroupe (Kenya)
1995	German Silva (Mexico)	Tegla Loroupe (Kenya)
1996	Giacomo Leone (Italy)	Anuta Catuna (Romania)
1997	John Kagwe (Kenya)	Franziska Rochat-Moser (Switzerland)
1998	John Kagwe (Kenya)	Franca Fiacconi (Italy)
1999	Joseph Chebet (Kenya)	Adriana Fernandez (Mexico)
2000	Abdelkader El Mouaziz (Morocco)	Ludmila Petrova (Russia)
2001	Tesfaye Jifar (Ethiopia)	Margaret Okayo (Kenya)
2002	Rodgers Rop (Kenya)	Joyce Chepchumba (Kenya)
2003	Martin Lel (Kenya)	Margaret Okayo (Kenya)
2004	Hendrik Ramaala (South Africa)	Paula Radcliffe (Great Britain)

Keeping the women out

In the 1960s women in the USA were not allowed to compete in many long-distance running events, so the marathon was totally out of bounds. Roberta Gibb was the first woman known to have run the Boston Marathon (in 1966) but she had to resort to hiding in bushes before the start so as not to be spotted. Kathrine Switzer ran the following year, but identified herself merely as 'K Switzer' and was not discovered until part-way through the race, when officials attempted to carry her away from the course. In Britain it was all a bit different: Violet Piercy was the first woman to be officially timed in the marathon, when setting a time of 3h 40min 22s in a British race on 3 October 1926.

Boston Marathon

The marathon was first run in 1897, following the inaugural Olympic Games event in Athens the previous year. The first run had 15 competitors of whom only 10 finished the race, the winner being John McDermott. In 2004 there were 20,344 runners (the biggest field was the 36,748 who ran in the centenary race of 1996). The event was traditionally held on the Patriots Day holiday in April. Women were first officially allowed to run in the race in 1972.

	Men	Women
1972	Olavi Suomalainen (Finland)	Nina Kuscsik (USA)
1973	Jon Anderson (USA)	Jacqueline Hansen (USA)
1974	Neil Cusack (Ireland)	Michiko Gorman (USA)
1975	Bill Rodgers (USA)	Liane Winter (West Germany)
1976	Jack Fultz (USA)	Kim Merritt (USA)
1977	Jerome Drayton (Canada)	Michiko Gorman (USA)
1978	Bill Rodgers (USA)	Gayle Barron (USA)
1979	Bill Rodgers (USA)	Joan Benoit (USA)
1980	Bill Rodgers (USA)	Jacqueline Gareau (Canada)
1981	Toshihiko Seko (Japan)	Allison Roe (New Zealand)

	Men	Women
1982	Alberto Salazar (USA)	Charlotte Teske (West Germany)
1983	Greg Meyer (USA)	Joan Benoit (USA)
1984	Geoff Smith (Great Britain)	Lorraine Moller (New Zealand)
1985	Geoff Smith (Great Britain)	Lisa Larsen Weidenbach (USA)
1986	Robert de Castella (Australia)	Ingrid Kristiansen (Norway)
1987	Toshihiko Seko (Japan)	Rosa Mota (Portugal)
1988	Ibrahim Hussein (Kenya)	Rosa Mota (Portugal)
1989	Abebe Mekonnen (Ethiopia)	Ingrid Kristiansen (Norway)
1990	Gelindo Bordin (Italy)	Rosa Mota (Portugal)
1991	Ibrahim Hussein (Kenya)	Wanda Panfil (Poland)
1992	Ibrahim Hussein (Kenya)	Olga Markova (CIS)
1993	Cosmas Ndeti (Kenya)	Olga Markova (CIS)
1994	Cosmas Ndeti (Kenya)	Uta Pippig (Germany)
1995	Cosmas Ndeti (Kenya)	Uta Pippig (Germany)
1996	Moses Tanui (Kenya)	Uta Pippig (Germany)
1997	Lameck Aguta (Kenya)	Fatuma Roba (Ethiopia)
1998	Moses Tanui (Kenya)	Fatuma Roba (Ethiopia)
1999	Joseph Chebet (Kenya)	Fatuma Roba (Ethiopia)
2000	Elijah Lagat (Kenya)	Catherine Ndereba (Kenya)
2001	Lee Bong-ju (South Korea)	Catherine Ndereba (Kenya)
2002	Rodgers Rop (Kenya)	Margaret Okayo (Kenya)
2003	Robert Cheruiyot (Kenya)	Svetlana Zakharova (Russia)
2004	Timothy Cherigat (Kenya)	Catherine Ndereba (Kenya)

MODERN PENTATHLON

Origins

As founder of the modern Olympic Games, Baron Pierre de Coubertin asked for the inclusion of a modern pentathlon at the 1912 Games in Stockholm. The event was modelled on a fanciful scenario of the exploits of a Napoleonic cavalry officer. His mission was to deliver an urgent despatch. He rides across a rugged terrain, stops to fight a duel with swords, then fires his pistol at his pursuers before swimming a river and then running a final leg to his destination. Back in 1912 the five events were held over five days; since the 1996 Games the modern pentathlon has been completed in a single day.

Rules and description

Each of the five events is scored on points, either against scoring tables or other competitors. At its inception, the modern pentathlon was decided by the placing in each individual event. Today, the first event is the shooting. Competitors use an air pistol to fire 20 shots at a 17cm^2 target from 10m. They have a time limit of 40s per shot. Next is the fencing element, with each competitor facing each other in a round-robin event where épées are used. The swimming comprises a 200m swim.

The showjumping part of modern pentathlon has each rider introduced to an unfamiliar horse (drawn by lots) 20min before they ride; this event more than any other introduces an element of unpredictability. The final event is the running; competitors set off at intervals over a 3,000m cross-country run.

Ruling body: L'Union Internationale de Pentathlon Moderne (UIPM)

Scoring system

Each of the five events is scored on a 1,000-point scale as follows:

Shooting The maximum score achievable on each of the 20 shots is 10. 1,000 pentathlon points are assessed as 172 (out of 200) shooting points. Each scoring point above or below this 172-point level gains or loses a further 12 points. Therefore a maximum 200 shooting points convert to a modern pentathlon score of 1,336.

Fencing The 1,000-point score equates to winning 70 per cent of the matches. Additional points are achieved for winning more matches but these are determined on the number of competitors.

Swimming The 1,000-point score equates to swimming the 200m in 2min 30s (for men) or 2min 40s (for women). Every extra 0.33s under or over this measure scores at +/-4 points.

Riding A ride without faults within the time limit gains 1,200 points. Deductions to this perfect score are made for knocking down fences (28 points) and going over the time limit (4 points per second).

Running The 1,000-point score equates to running the 3,000m in 10min (for men) or 11min 20s (for women). Each further second incurs a 4-point deduction, or bonus if within the time limit.

Poor shot for a general

One of the competitors in the inaugural Olympic event in 1912 was a young American cavalryman Lieutenant George Patton. Patton finished behind four Swedish competitors, largely because he could only manage 21st place in the shooting, but he went on to lead the US Third Army in World War II.

Olympic Games

The team event was introduced in 1952 and discontinued after 1992. A women's individual event was instituted at the 2000 Sydney Games.

Men

	Team	Individual
1912		Gösta Lilliehöök (Sweden)
1920		Gustaf Dyrssen (Sweden)
1924		Bo Lindman (Sweden)
1928		Sven Thofelt (Sweden)

	Team	Individual
1932		Johan Oxenstierna (Sweden)
1936		Gotthardt Handrick (Germany)
1948		Willie Grut (Sweden)
1952	Hungary	Lars Hall (Sweden)
1956	USSR	Lars Hall (Sweden)
1960	Hungary	Ferenc Németh (Hungary)
1964	USSR	Ferenc Török (Hungary)
1968	Hungary	Björn Ferm (Sweden)
1972	USSR	András Balczó (Hungary)
1976	Great Britain	Janusz Pyciak-Peciak (Poland)
1980	USSR	Anatoli Starostin (USSR)
1984	Italy	Daniele Masala (Italy)
1988	Hungary	János Martinek (Hungary)
1992	Poland	Arkadiusz Skrzypaszek (Poland)
1996		Aleksandr Parygin (Kazakhstan)
2000		Dmitri Svatkovski (Russia)
2004		Andrei Moiseev (Russia)

Women

	Individual
2000	Stephanie Cook (Great Britain)
2004	Zsuzsanna Vörös (Hungary)

Ancient Olympian Games

The pentathlon was a sport at the ancient Olympian Games in 708 BC. It comprised a discus throw, a javelin throw, a jumping event, a running race and a wrestling bout.

Some famous modern pentathletes

András Balczó, 1938–

Born in Kondoros, Hungary, he won five individual world championships as part of his domination of the sport in the 1960s (he also won two titles in the early 1970s). In addition, he won five World team titles. At the Olympic Games, Balczó, a typewriter mechanic by trade, finished fourth at his first attempt in 1960, and won a silver medal in 1968 before finally securing a gold in 1972. He formed part of the Hungarian gold-winning team in 1960 and 1968 as well as achieving a team silver medal in 1972.

Lars Hall, 1927–91

Born in Karlskrone, Sweden, he was a carpenter by trade. Unlike many of his rivals, Hall did not have a military background but to date he is the only back-to-back winner of the modern pentathlon at the Olympic Games. At the 1952 Helsinki Games he won both the swimming and the riding on his way to the overall title. Four years later he finished only 24th in the shooting but still won the gold medal.

MOTORCYCLE RACING

Origins

The first motorcycle races were held in conjunction with car races, usually between major cities (see **Motor racing**). Some races were held on velodromes as early motorcycles were little more than bicycles with low-powered engines attached. The first race on a closed circuit was organized in 1904 by the Automobile Club de France, featuring teams from Austria, Denmark, France, Germany and Great Britain. 1907 saw the building of Brooklands in England (see **Motor racing**) and the introduction of the TT races on the Isle of Man.

Trials riding was a popular early form of the sport, one of the first events being the Scott Trial, sponsored by engineer and designer of the Scott motorcycle Alfred Angus Scott, founded in 1909 and held in Yorkshire, England.

Speedway is said to have originated in 1923 in New South Wales, Australia, when a young New Zealander called Johnny Hoskins organized motorcycle races around the trotting track at the annual show of the near-bankrupt West Maitland Agricultural Society in order to raise funds.

Motocross developed from trials riding in 1924 when a motorcycle club in Camberly, Surrey, England, hosted a cross-country event (called the Southern Scott Scramble) over a 2.5mi course but where speed was the only factor and with no observed sections. This form of the sport caught on in France where it was given the name motocross.

Rules and description

Races held on tracks are speed competitions for motorcycles, which for the annual season-long grand prix are categorized by the engine sizes 80cc, 125cc, 250cc, 500cc, Superbike and Sidecar. Other forms include 'speedway', 'motocross' and 'trials riding' (see A-Z section).

Ruling body: International Motorcycling Federation (FIM; Fédération Internationale de Motocyclisme)

Motorcycling World Championships

First organized in 1949; current titles for Superbike, 500cc, 250cc, 125cc, 80cc and Sidecar; Formula One and Endurance world championships also held annually; the most prestigious title is the 500cc category, known since 2002 as the MotoGP.

500cc/MotoGP

	Champion	Bike	Constructor's championship
1979	Kenny Roberts (USA)	Yamaha	Suzuki
1980	Kenny Roberts (USA)	Yamaha	Suzuki

	Champion	Bike	Constructor's championship
1981	Marco Lucchinelli (Italy)	Suzuki	Suzuki
1982	Franco Uncini (Italy)	Suzuki	Suzuki
1983	Freddie Spencer (USA)	Honda	Honda
1984	Eddie Lawson (USA)	Yamaha	Honda
1985	Freddie Spencer (USA)	Honda	Honda
1986	Eddie Lawson (USA)	Yamaha	Yamaha
1987	Wayne Gardner (Australia)	Honda	Yamaha
1988	Eddie Lawson (USA)	Yamaha	Yamaha
1989	Eddie Lawson (USA)	Honda	Honda
1990	Wayne Rainey (USA)	Yamaha	Yamaha
1991	Wayne Rainey (USA)	Yamaha	Yamaha
1992	Wayne Rainey (USA)	Yamaha	Honda
1993	Kevin Schwantz (USA)	Suzuki	Yamaha
1994	Michael Doohan (Australia)	Honda	Honda
1995	Michael Doohan (Australia)	Honda	Honda
1996	Michael Doohan (Australia)	Honda	Honda
1997	Michael Doohan (Australia)	Honda	Honda
1998	Michael Doohan (Australia)	Honda	Honda
1999	Alex Criville (Spain)	Honda	Honda
2000	Kenny Roberts, Jr (USA)	Suzuki	Yamaha
2001	Valentino Rossi (Italy)	Honda	Honda
2002	Valentino Rossi (Italy)	Honda	Honda
2003	Valentino Rossi (Italy)	Honda	Honda
2004	Valentino Rossi (Italy)	Yamaha	Honda

World Superbikes Championship

	Champion	Bike	Constructor's championship
1988	Fred Merkel (USA)	Honda	Honda
1989	Fred Merkel (USA)	Honda	Honda
1990	Raymond Roche (France)	Ducati	Honda
1991	Doug Polen (USA)	Ducati	Ducati
1992	Doug Polen (USA)	Ducati	Ducati
1993	Scott Russell (USA)	Kawasaki	Ducati
1994	Carl Fogarty (Great Britain)	Ducati	Ducati
1995	Carl Fogarty (Great Britain)	Ducati	Ducati
1996	Troy Corser (USA)	Ducati	Ducati
1997	John Kocinski (USA)	Honda	Honda
1998	Carl Fogarty (Great Britain)	Ducati	Ducati
1999	Carl Fogarty (Great Britain)	Ducati	Ducati
2000	Colin Edwards (USA)	Honda	Ducati
2001	Troy Bayliss (Australia)	Ducati	Ducati
2002	Colin Edwards (USA)	Honda	Ducati
2003	Neil Hodgson (Great Britain)	Ducati	Ducati
2004	James Toseland (Great Britain)	Ducati	Ducati

Motorcycle Racing

Isle of Man TT Races

The most famous of all motorcycle races, they take place each June on a road circuit; first held 1907; principal race is the Senior TT.

Senior TT

1979	Mike Hailwood (Great Britain)
1980	Graeme Crosby (New Zealand)
1981	Mick Grant (Great Britain)
1982	Norman Brown (Great Britain)
1983	Rob McElnea (Great Britain)
1984	Rob McElnea (Great Britain)
1985	Joey Dunlop (Northern Ireland)
1986	Roger Burnett (Great Britain)
1987	Joey Dunlop (Northern Ireland)
1988	Joey Dunlop (Northern Ireland)
1989	Steve Hislop (Great Britain)
1990	Carl Fogarty (Great Britain)
1991	Steve Hislop (Great Britain)
1992	Steve Hislop (Great Britain)
1993	Phil McCallen (Northern Ireland)
1994	Steve Hislop (Great Britain)
1995	Joey Dunlop (Northern Ireland)
1996	Phil McCallen (Northern Ireland)
1997	Phil McCallen (Northern Ireland)
1998	Ian Simpson (Great Britain)
1999	David Jefferies (Great Britain)
2000	David Jefferies (Great Britain)
2001	*Not held*
2002	David Jefferies (Great Britain)
2003	Adrian Archibald (Northern Ireland)
2004	Adrian Archibald (Northern Ireland)

Road Racing

The TT takes place over temporarily closed public roads in the Isle of Man. The island became the home of road racing in the early 1900s, when racing on public roads in the UK was forbidden by an Act of Parliament, and a strict 20mph/32kph speed limit was enforced. However, the ban did not apply to the Isle of Man, and after some persuasion by early racing enthusiasts, the Tynwald – the island's Parliament – passed a Bill allowing road racing in 1904.

Motocross World Championship

500cc first held in 1957; called Motocross GP as of 2003.

	Champion	Bike
1979	Graham Noyce (Great Britain)	Honda
1980	André Malherbe (Belgium)	Honda
1981	André Malherbe (Belgium)	Honda
1982	Brad Lackey (USA)	Suzuki
1983	Hakan Carlqvist (Sweden)	Yamaha
1984	André Malherbe (Belgium)	Honda
1985	David Thorpe (Great Britain)	Honda
1986	David Thorpe (Great Britain)	Honda
1987	Georges Jobe (Belgium)	Kawasaki
1988	Eric Geboers (Belgium)	Honda
1989	David Thorpe (Great Britain)	Honda
1990	Eric Geboers (Belgium)	Honda
1991	Georges Jobe (Belgium)	Honda
1992	Georges Jobe (Belgium)	Honda

	Champion	Bike
1993	Jacky Martens (Belgium)	Husqvarna
1994	Marcus Hansson (Sweden)	Honda
1995	Joël Smets (Belgium)	Husaberg
1996	Shayne King (New Zealand)	KTM
1997	Joël Smets (Belgium)	Husaberg
1998	Joël Smets (Belgum)	Husaberg
1999	Andrea Bartolini (Italy)	Yamaha
2000	Joël Smets (Belgium)	KTM
2001	Stefan Everts (Belgium)	Yamaha
2002	Stefan Everts (Belgium)	Yamaha
2003	Stefan Everts (Belgium)	Yamaha
2004	Stefan Everts (Belgium)	Yamaha

Speedway World Championship

First competed for in 1936 when it was won by Lionel van Praag (Australia); no championship from 1939 to 1948.

1979	Ivan Mauger (New Zealand)
1980	Michael Lee (Great Britain)
1981	Bruce Penhall (USA)
1982	Bruce Penhall (USA)
1983	Egon Müller (West Germany)
1984	Erik Gundersen (Denmark)
1985	Erik Gundersen (Denmark)
1986	Hans Nielsen (Denmark)
1987	Hans Nielsen (Denmark)
1988	Erik Gundersen (Denmark)
1989	Hans Nielsen (Denmark)
1990	Per Jonsson (Sweden)
1991	Jan Pedersen (Denmark)
1992	Gary Havelock (Great Britain)
1993	Sam Ermolenko (USA)
1994	Tony Rickardsson (Sweden)
1995	Hans Nielsen (Denmark)
1996	Billy Hamill (USA)
1997	Greg Hancock (USA)
1998	Tony Rickardsson (Sweden)
1999	Tony Rickardsson (Sweden)
2000	Mark Loram (Great Britain)
2001	Tony Rickardsson (Sweden)
2002	Tony Rickardsson (Sweden)
2003	Nicki Pedersen (Denmark)
2004	Jason Crump (Australia)

Speedway World Cup

First competed for in 1960 in Gothenburg, when it was won by Sweden.

	Winner	Venue
1979	New Zealand	London, UK
1980	Great Britain	Wroclaw, Poland
1981	Denmark	Olching, Denmark
1982	USA	London, UK
1983	Denmark	Vojens, Denmark
1984	Denmark	Leszno, Poland
1985	Denmark	Long Beach, USA
1986	Denmark	Vetlanda (Sweden)/Vojens/Bradford
1987	Denmark	Fredericia (Denmark)/Coventry/Prague
1988	Denmark	Long Beach, USA

	Winner	Venue
1989	Great Britain	Bradford, UK
1990	USA	Pardubice, Czech Republic
1991	Denmark	Vojens, Denmark
1992	USA	Kumla, Sweden
1993	USA	Coventry, UK
1994	Sweden	Broksted, Denmark
1995	Denmark	Bydgoszcz, Poland
1996	Poland	Diedenbergen, Germany
1997	Denmark	Pila, Poland
1998	USA	Vojens, Denmark
1999	Australia	Pardubice, Czech Republic
2000	Sweden	Coventry, UK
2001	Australia	Wroclaw, Poland
2002	Australia	Peterborough, UK
2003	Sweden	Vojens, Denmark
2004	Sweden	Poole, UK

A-Z

broadsiding same as **powersliding**

enduro long-distance cross-country racing that tests reliability and endurance; events include the ISDE (International Six Days Enduro) and the Paris-Dakar rally. Riders travel between check-points and incur penalties if they arrive late

foot in **trials**, if a rider foots, he touches the ground and hence incurs a penalty

grass-track racing a form of speedway over grass tracks of varying length, usually laid out in fields although some dedicated tracks also exist

hare and hounds an **enduro** but with no checkpoints, the winner being the rider who has ridden the most laps in a given time

long-track racing a form of **speedway** over 1,000m-long tracks with larger bikes and heats of eight

motocross racing (solo motorbikes, bikes with sidecars or quad bikes) on a cross-country circuit with natural obstacles such as jumps

parade in **speedway**, when the riders are introduced to the public

pits in **speedway** and track racing, the area where teams can make repairs to bikes

podium finish if a rider has a podium finish, he finishes in first, second or third place, and hence stands on the winner's podium

powersliding in **speedway**, the method used to take a corner: sliding the back wheel out while maintaining acceleration

road racing racing on closed-off public roads

scrutineering the inspection of bikes by the officials before the race to ensure that technical regulations have not been broken

snowcross racing snowmobiles over a **motocross** circuit

speedway racing motorbikes without brakes or gears round an oval dirt circuit in a stadium; events are usually held in the evening under floodlights with a series of heats (four riders in each) lasting four laps

starting gate in **motocross**, a board across the starting area that drops down to start the race

superbike either a 750cc four-cylinder or 1000cc twin-cylinder machine

supercross racing **motocross** bikes in a stadium on a temporary dirt or sand track with obstacles such as jumps

supermoto racing (solo motorbikes or quad bikes) on a circuit that is partly tarmac and partly natural with obstacles such as jumps

trials an event held over a cross-country circuit with a series of sections in which riders have to negotiate obstacles, penalties being incurred if the rider touches the ground; riders can also fail sections, for example if they exceed the allowed time

washboard in **motocross**, a succession of hillocks

wheelie a trick in which the front wheel is lifted off the ground, traditionally performed as the winner crosses the finishing line

Some famous motorcycle racers

Giacomo Agostini, 1943–

Born in Lovere, Bergamo, Italy, he won a record 15 world titles between 1966 and 1975, including the 500cc title a record eight times (1966–72, 1975). He won ten Isle of Man TT Races (1966–75), including the Senior TT five times (1968–72).

Michael Doohan, 1965–

Born in Brisbane, Australia, he made his Grand Prix debut for Honda on a 500cc motorcycle in 1989. He recovered from a serious crash in 1992 that nearly resulted in the amputation of one of his legs and returned to win five consecutive 500cc world championships on a Honda between 1994 and 1998. In 1999, he had another accident, again breaking his leg and forcing him to retire.

Joey Dunlop, 1952–2000

Born in Ballymoney, Londonderry, Northern Ireland, he was an outstanding rider at Isle of Man TT races, winning 26 races between 1977 and 2000, including the Senior Tourist Trophy in 1985, 1987–8 and 1995. He won the Formula One TT for the sixth successive season in 1988, and was Formula One world champion (1982–6). In 1988, he set the TT lap record at 118.54mph/190.73kph. He died after crashing in a road race in Estonia. He was awarded the MBE in 1986 and the OBE in 1996.

Carl Fogarty, 1966–

Born in Blackburn, England, he started his career in motocross before progressing to road racing. He won the Senoir TT in 1990 and set an incredibly fast lap record in 1992, before turning his back on the race. 'Foggy' excelled, however, in the World Superbikes Championship, winning in 1994, 1995, 1998 and 1999 and clocking up 59 wins in all before he retired in 2001.

Mike Hailwood, 1940–81

He was born in Oxford, England. He took nine world titles: the 250cc in 1961 and 1966–7, the 350cc in 1966–7, and the 500cc in 1962–5, all riding Honda or MV Augusta machines.

In addition, he won 14 Isle of Man TT races between 1961 and 1979, and during the 1960s he also had a career in motor racing. He was killed in a car accident shortly after retiring.

Ivan Mauger, 1939–

Born in Christchurch, New Zealand, Mauger (pronounced 'major') raced for most of his speedway life in England, appearing for Newcastle Diamonds, Belle Vue, Exeter Falcons and Hull Vikings, among others. Probably the greatest speedway rider of all time, he dominated the sport in 1970s and was world champion six times (1968–70, 1972, 1977 and 1979). He was awarded the MBE in 1976 and the OBE in 1989.

Valentino Rossi, 1979–

Born in Urbino, Italy, he started racing 125cc bikes in 1996 for Aprilia, winning the championship the following year. He also won the 250cc championship in 1999 before graduating to the 500cc class, where he has taken the title for four consecutive years (2001–4), on a Honda in 2001–3 and a Yamaha in 2004. A charismatic individual with a cavalier riding style, he is famous for using the number 46.

Barry Sheene, 1950–2003

Born in London, England, he made his racing debut in 1968, and won the British 125cc title in 1970. Despite a bad crash in 1975 at Daytona, which left him with fractures and a pin in his leg, he won the 500cc world championship in 1976 to give Suzuki their first victory. He repeated it in 1977 and was runner-up in 1978. After another crash in 1982 at Silverstone he retired to take up a career in broadcasting and business in Australia. He was awarded the MBE in 1978.

John Surtees, 1934–

Born in Westerham, Kent, England, he became the only man to win world titles on two and four wheels. He won the 350cc motorcycling world title in 1958–60, and the 500cc title in 1956, and 1958–60 (all on an MV Augusta). He then turned to car racing, and won the 1964 world title driving a Ferrari. He later became a racing-car manufacturer. He was awarded the MBE in 1959.

MOTOR RACING

Origins

The first race between cars was held in 1894, between Paris and Rouen, and was organized by the Parisian daily newspaper *Le Petit Journal*. Although a De Dion steam-powered car completed the course in the fastest time, the organizers gave the prizes to Peugeot and Panhard cars with internal-combustion engines, deemed to be more practical. The following year, a group of enthusiasts founded the Automobile Club de France, the first motor racing club. Further races between Paris and other cities followed. The first car race in the United States took place in Chicago, Illinois, in 1895.

The first race to be called a Grand Prix was held in 1901 at Le Mans. This race, like all other previous ones, was held on private roads. The first purpose-built racetrack was at Brooklands in Surrey, England, which held its first race on 6 July 1907. The 3.25mi circuit was built by wealthy car enthusiast Hugh Locke King on his own land and had large concrete banked curves.

Rules and description

The racing of finely-tuned motor cars, either purpose-built or modified production vehicles, over a tarmac track. Strict specifications of vehicle design are applied at all levels. Different forms of the sport are categorized by the type of car and the size of the engine. The 'Formula One' world championship (March–November) involves usually 16 (as of 2004, 18, and 2005, 19) races at different venues worldwide. Less highly-powered cars compete in Formula Three, Formula Ford and Formula 3000 (which replaced Formula Two in 1984 and was so named because engines were 3000cc, but ended in 2004). Similar cars to those in Formula One but with smaller engines and fuelled by methanol take part in Indy car racing (as of 2004 known as the ChampCar series) in the USA. In stock car racing such as Nascar® (National Association for Stock Car Auto Racing) in the USA, modified production cars are raced on usually oval tracks; in touring car racing (in Europe), similar cars race on the same circuits as purpose-built racing cars. With a few exceptions (notably the Le Mans and Daytona 24-hour races), races in all of these forms of motor racing last for a specified number of laps.

Ruling body: Fédération Internationale d'Automobile (FIA)

What the flags mean

Flags were first used in motor racing in 1899.
Red flag: the race has been stopped (eg because a car is lying in a dangerous position or because of poor weather conditions).
Yellow flag: danger ahead; no overtaking.
Blue flag: shown to a driver to indicate that a faster car is trying to overtake.
Black flag: shown with a car number to indicate that the driver must enter the pits immediately.
Red- and yellow-striped flag: the track is slippery (usually because of oil or water).
Green flag: a hazard has been cleared up and the cars can proceed at racing speed.
Black flag with an orange disc: shown with a car number to indicate that the car has a mechanical problem and the driver must come into the pits.
White and black diagonal halves: shown with a car number to indicate a warning for unsportsmanlike behaviour.
White flag: a slow-moving vehicle is on the track, eg the safety car.
Chequered flag: the race has ended. Shown to the winner, and then to every subsequent car to cross the line.

Formula One World Championship

Formula One drivers' world championship instituted in 1950; constructor's championship instituted in 1958.

Motor Racing

	Driver	Car	Constructor
1950	Guiseppe Farina (Italy)	Alfa Romeo	
1951	Juan Manuel Fangio (Argentina)	Alfa Romeo	
1952	Alberto Ascari (Italy)	Ferrari	
1953	Alberto Ascari (Italy)	Ferrari	
1954	Juan Manuel Fangio (Argentina)	Maserati	
1955	Juan Manuel Fangio (Argentina)	Mercedes-Benz	
1956	Juan Manuel Fangio (Argentina)	Ferrari	
1957	Juan Manuel Fangio (Argentina)	Maserati	
1958	Mike Hawthorn (Great Britain)	Ferrari	Vanwall
1959	Jack Brabham (Australia)	Cooper	Cooper
1960	Jack Brabham (Australia)	Cooper	Cooper
1961	Phil Hill (USA)	Ferrari	Ferrari
1962	Graham Hill (Great Britain)	BRM	BRM
1963	Jim Clark (Great Britain)	Lotus	Lotus
1964	John Surtees (Great Britain)	Ferrari	Ferrari
1965	Jim Clark (Great Britain)	Lotus	Lotus
1966	Jack Brabham (Australia)	Brabham	Brabham
1967	Denny Hulme (New Zealand)	Brabham	Brabham
1968	Graham Hill (Great Britain)	Lotus	Lotus
1969	Jackie Stewart (Great Britain)	Matra	Matra
1970	Jochen Rindt (Austria)	Lotus	Lotus
1971	Jackie Stewart (Great Britain)	March	Tyrell
1972	Emerson Fittipaldi (Brazil)	Lotus	Lotus
1973	Jackie Stewart (Great Britain)	Tyrell	Lotus
1974	Emerson Fittipaldi (Brazil)	McLaren	McLaren
1975	Niki Lauda (Austria)	Ferrari	Ferrari
1976	James Hunt (Great Britain)	McLaren	Ferrari
1977	Niki Lauda (Austria)	Ferrari	Ferrari
1978	Mario Andretti (USA)	Lotus	Lotus
1979	Jody Scheckter (South Africa)	Ferrari	Ferrari
1980	Alan Jones (Australia)	Williams	Williams
1981	Nelson Piquet (Brazil)	Brabham	Williams
1982	Keke Rosberg (Finland)	Williams	Ferrari
1983	Nelson Piquet (Brazil)	Brabham	Ferrari
1984	Niki Lauda (Austria)	McLaren	McLaren
1985	Alain Prost (France)	McLaren	McLaren
1986	Alain Prost (France)	McLaren	Williams
1987	Nelson Piquet (Brazil)	Williams	Williams
1988	Ayrton Senna (Brazil)	McLaren	McLaren
1989	Alain Prost (France)	McLaren	McLaren
1990	Ayrton Senna (Brazil)	McLaren	McLaren
1991	Ayrton Senna (Brazil)	McLaren	McLaren
1992	Nigel Mansell (Great Britain)	Williams	Williams
1993	Alain Prost (France)	Williams	Williams
1994	Michael Schumacher (Germany)	Benetton	Williams
1995	Michael Schumacher (Germany)	Benetton	Benetton
1996	Damon Hill (Great Britain)	Williams	Williams
1997	Jacques Villeneuve (Canada)	Williams	Williams
1998	Mika Hakkinen (Finland)	McLaren	McLaren

	Driver	Car	Constructor
1999	Mika Hakkinen (Finland)	McLaren	Ferrari
2000	Michael Schumacher (Germany)	Ferrari	Ferrari
2001	Michael Schumacher (Germany)	Ferrari	Ferrari
2002	Michael Schumacher (Germany)	Ferrari	Ferrari
2003	Michael Schumacher (Germany)	Ferrari	Ferrari
2004	Michael Schumacher (Germany)	Ferrari	Ferrari

Put 'em up!

Tempers can flare when drivers fail to follow racing etiquette. The most famous example of this was in the German Grand Prix at Hockenheim in 1982. Nelson Piquet was leading and closed up on back marker Eliseo Salazar at the Ostkurve chicane. Instead of giving way, Salazar's car went into the side of Piquet's BMW as Piquet tried to overtake and both cars crashed. An irate Piquet got out of his car and started to punch the hapless Chilean, landing several useful hooks.

Le Mans 24-Hour Race

The greatest of all endurance races. The first race, on 26/27 May 1923, was over a 10.726mi/17.25km circuit. The length of the circuit has been successively reduced and since 1987 has been 8.45mi/13.6km. The last time drivers started by running across the track to their cars was in 1969.

	Drivers	Car
1923	André Lagache, René Leonard (both France)	Chenard & Walcker
1924	John Duff, Frank Clement (both Great Britain)	Bentley
1925	Gérard de Courcelles, André Rossignol (both France)	Lorraine-Dietrich
1926	Robert Bloch, André Rossignol (both France)	Lorraine-Dietrich
1927	John Benjafield, Sammy Davis (both Great Britain)	Bentley
1928	Woolf Barnato, Bernard Rubin (both Great Britain)	Bentley
1929	Woolf Barnato, Sir Henry Birkin (both Great Britain)	Bentley
1930	Woolf Barnato, Glen Kidston (both Great Britain)	Bentley
1931	Earl Howe, Sir Henry Birkin (both Great Britain)	Alfa Romeo
1932	Raymond Sommer (France), Luigi Chinetti (Italy)	Alfa Romeo
1933	Raymond Sommer (France), Tazio Nuvolari (Italy)	Alfa Romeo
1934	Luigi Chinetti (Italy), Philippe Etancelin (France)	Alfa Romeo
1935	John Hindmarsh, (Great Britain), Luis Fontes (Argentina)	Lagonda
1936	*Not held*	
1937	Jean-Pierre Wimille, Robert Benoist (both France)	Bugatti
1938	Eugène Chaboud, Jean Tremoulet (both France)	Delahaye
1939	Jean-Pierre Wimille, Pierre Veyron (both France)	Bugatti
1940–8	*Not held*	
1949	Luigi Chinetti (USA), Lord Peter Seldson (Great Britain)	Ferrari
1950	Louis Rosier, Jean-Louis Rosier (both France)	Talbot-Lago
1951	Peter Walker, Peter Whitehead (both Great Britain)	Jaguar
1952	Hermann Lang, Fritz Reiss (both West Germany)	Mercedes
1953	Tony Rolt, Duncan Hamilton (both Great Britain)	Jaguar
1954	José Froilan Gonzalez (Argentina), Maurice Trintignant (France)	Ferrari

	Drivers	Car
1955	Mike Hawthorn, Ivor Bueb (both Great Britain)	Jaguar
1956	Ron Flockhart, Ninian Sanderson (both Great Britain)	Jaguar
1957	Ron Flockhart, Ivor Bueb (both Great Britain)	Jaguar
1958	Olivier Gendebein (Belgium), Phil Hill (USA)	Ferrari
1959	Carroll Shelby (USA), Roy Salvadori (Great Britain)	Aston Martin
1960	Olivier Gendebein, Paul Frère (both Belgium)	Ferrari
1961	Olivier Gendebein (Belgium), Phil Hill (USA)	Ferrari
1962	Olivier Gendebein (Belgium), Phil Hill (USA)	Ferrari
1963	Ludovico Scarfiotti, Lorenzo Bandini (both Italy)	Ferrari
1964	Jean Guichet (France), Nino Vaccarella (Italy)	Ferrari
1965	Jochen Rindt (Austria), Masten Gregory (USA)	Ferrari
1966	Bruce McLaren, Chris Amon (both New Zealand)	Ford
1967	Dan Gurney, A J Foyt, Jr (both USA)	Ford
1968	Pedro Rodriguez (Mexico), Lucien Bianchi (Belgium)	Ford
1969	Jacky Ickx (Belgium), Jackie Oliver (Great Britain)	Ford
1970	Hans Herrmann (West Germany), Richard Attwood (Great Britain)	Porsche
1971	Helmut Marko (Austria), Gijs van Lennep (The Netherlands)	Porsche
1972	Henri Pescarolo (France), Graham Hill (Great Britain)	Matra-Simca
1973	Henri Pescarolo, Gérard Larrousse (both France)	Matra-Simca
1974	Henri Pescarolo, Gérard Larrousse (both France)	Matra-Simca
1975	Jacky Ickx (Belgium), Derek Bell (Great Britain)	Mirage
1976	Jacky Ickx (Belgium), Gijs van Lennap (The Netherlands)	Porsche
1977	Jacky Ickx (Belgium), Hurley Haywood (USA), Jürgen Barth (West Germany)	Porsche
1978	Jean-Pierre Jaussaud, Didier Pironi (both France)	Renault-Alpine
1979	Klaus Ludwig (West Germany), Bill Whittington (USA), Don Whittington (USA)	Porsche
1980	Jean-Pierre Jaussaud, Jean Rondeau (both France)	Ford
1981	Jacky Ickx (Belgium), Derek Bell (Great Britain)	Porsche
1982	Jacky Ickx (Belgium), Derek Bell (Great Britain)	Porsche
1983	Al Holbert (USA), Hurley Haywood (USA), Vern Schuppan (Australia)	Porsche
1984	Henri Pescarolo (France), Klaus Ludwig (West Germany)	Porsche
1985	Klaus Ludwig (West Germany), John Winter (West Germany), Paolo Barilla (Italy)	Porsche
1986	Hans Stück (West Germany), Derek Bell (Great Britain), Al Holbert (USA)	Porsche
1987	Hans Stück (West Germany), Derek Bell (Great Britain), Al Holbert (USA)	Porsche
1988	Jan Lammers (The Netherlands), Johnny Dumfries (Great Britain), Andy Wallace (Great Britain)	Jaguar
1989	Jochen Mass (West Germany), Manuel Reuter (West Germany), Stanley Dickens (Sweden)	Sauber-Mercedes
1990	John Nielsen (Denmark), Price Cobb (USA), Martin Brundle (Great Britain)	Jaguar
1991	Volker Weidler (Germany), Johnny Herbert (Great Britain), Bertrand Gachot (Belgium)	Mazda
1992	Derek Warwick (Great Britain), Mark Blundell (Great Britain), Yannick Dalmas (France)	Peugeot

	Drivers	Car
1993	Geoff Brabham (Australia), Christophe Bouchut (France), Eric Hélary (France)	Peugeot
1994	Yannick Dalmas (France), Hurley Haywood (USA), Mauro Baldi (Italy)	Porsche
1995	Yannick Dalmas (France), J J Lehto (Finland), Masanori Sekiya (Japan)	McLaren
1996	Manuel Reuter (Germany), Davy Jones (USA), Alexander Würz (Austria)	Porsche
1997	Michele Alboreto (Italy), Stefan Johansson (Sweden), Tom Kristensen (Denmark)	Porsche
1998	Allan McNish (Great Britain), Laurent Aiello (France), Stéphane Ortelli (France)	Porsche
1999	Pierluigi Martini (Italy), Joachim Winkelhock (Germany), Yannick Dalmas (France)	BMW
2000	Frank Biela (Germany), Tom Kristensen (Denmark), Emanuele Pirro (Italy)	Audi
2001	Frank Biela (Germany), Tom Kristensen (Denmark), Emanuele Pirro (Italy)	Audi
2002	Frank Biela (Germany), Tom Kristensen (Denmark), Emanuele Pirro (Italy)	Audi
2003	Tom Kristensen (Denmark), Rinaldo Capello (Italy), Guy Smith (Great Britain)	Bentley
2004	Tom Kristensen (Denmark), Rinaldo Capello (Italy), Seiji Ara (Japan)	Audi

ChampCar Championship

Was known as the CART (Championship Auto Racing Teams) championship from 1979 to 2004.

1979	Rick Mears (USA)
1980	Johnny Rutherford (USA)
1981	Rick Mears (USA)
1982	Rick Mears (USA)
1983	Al Unser (USA)
1984	Mario Andretti (USA)
1985	Al Unser (USA)
1986	Bobby Rahal (USA)
1987	Bobby Rahal (USA)
1988	Danny Sullivan (USA)
1989	Emerson Fittipaldi (Brazil)
1990	Al Unser, Jr (USA)
1991	Michael Andretti (USA)
1992	Bobby Rahal (USA)
1993	Nigel Mansell (Great Britain)
1994	Al Unser, Jr (USA)
1995	Jacques Villeneuve (Canada)
1996	Jimmy Vasser (USA)
1997	Alex Zanardi (Italy)
1998	Alex Zanardi (Italy)

It could have been so different

Three Formula One world champions almost chose a career in a different sport. Jackie Stewart is an excellent shot and nearly made the British Olympic team before concentrating on motor racing. Alain Prost could have been a professional footballer, and Nigel Mansell is an accomplished golfer. Mansell owns his own course in the UK and competed as an amateur in the Australian Open. He recently narrowly failed in an attempt to qualify for the European Seniors Tour.

1999	Juan Montoya (Colombia)
2000	Gil de Ferran (Brazil)
2001	Gil de Ferran (Brazil)
2002	Cristiano da Matta (Brazil)
2003	Paul Tracy (Canada)
2004	Sébastien Bourdais (France)

Indianapolis 500

Often known as the Indy 500; first held in 1911; raced over the Indianapolis Raceway as part of the Memorial Day celebrations at the end of May each year.

1911	Ray Harroun (USA)
1912	Joe Dawson (USA)
1913	Jules Goux (France)
1914	René Thomas (France)
1915	Ralph De Palma (Italy)
1916	Dario Resta (Italy)
1917–18	*Not held*
1919	Howdy Wilcox (USA)
1920	Gaston Chevrolet (France)
1921	Tommy Milton (USA)
1922	Jimmy Murphy (USA)
1923	Tommy Milton (USA)
1924	L L Corum (USA) and Joe Boyer (USA)
1925	Pete De Paolo (USA)
1926	Frank Lockhart (USA)
1927	George Souders (USA)
1928	Louis Meyer (USA)
1929	Ray Keech (USA)
1930	Billy Arnold (USA)
1931	Louis Schneider (USA)
1932	Fred Frame (USA)
1933	Louis Meyer (USA)
1934	Bill Cummings (USA)
1935	Kelly Petillo (USA)
1936	Louis Meyer (USA)
1937	Wilbur Shaw (USA)
1938	Floyd Roberts (USA)
1939	Wilbur Shaw (USA)
1940	Wilbur Shaw (USA)
1941	Floyd Davis (USA) and Mauri Rose (USA)
1942–5	*Not held*
1946	George Robson (Great Britain)
1947	Mauri Rose (USA)
1948	Mauri Rose (USA)
1949	Bill Holland (USA)
1950	Johnnie Parsons (USA)
1951	Lee Wallard (USA)

Winning by a whisker

Some Indy 500 races have been won by the slenderest of margins. The closest ever finish took place in 1992, when Al Unser beat Scott Goodyear by just 0.043 of a second. Other close races have been in 1982 (0.16 of a second separating the winner from the runner, up), 1997 (0.57 of a second) and 1996 (0.695 of a second).

A word from our sponsor

Advertising and motor racing are now inextricably linked (with adverts for banks, drinks, condoms etc emblazoning the cars) but it was only in 1968 that the first sponsorship deal was struck. Colin Chapman signed up with Imperial Tobacco and decked out his Lotus cars in the company's Gold Leaf colours (red, white and gold). As of 2006, however, the EU have banned cigarette advertising on cars for races held in Europe.

Fewest finishers

Only four cars completed the Monaco Grand Prix of 1966, the fewest ever. Three of the cars were BRMs, including the race winner Jackie Stewart and third place Graham Hill. Two other drivers did finish but were unclassified as they had not completed at least 90 of the 100 laps.

1952	Troy Ruttman (USA)
1953	Bill Vukovich (USA)
1954	Bill Vukovich (USA)
1955	Bob Sweikert (USA)
1956	Pat Flaherty (USA)
1957	Sam Hanks (USA)
1958	Jimmy Bryan (USA)
1959	Rodger Ward (USA)
1960	Jim Rathmann (USA)
1961	A J Foyt, Jr (USA)
1962	Rodger Ward (USA)
1963	Parnelli Jones (USA)
1964	A J Foyt, Jr (USA)
1965	Jim Clark (Great Britain)
1966	Graham Hill (Great Britain)
1967	A J Foyt, Jr (USA)
1968	Bobby Unser (USA)
1969	Mario Andretti (USA)
1970	Al Unser (USA)
1971	Al Unser (USA)
1972	Mark Donohue (USA)
1973	Gordon Johncock (USA)
1974	Johnny Rutherford (USA)
1975	Bobby Unser (USA)
1976	Johnny Rutherford (USA)
1977	A J Foyt, Jr (USA)
1978	Al Unser (USA)
1979	Rick Mears (USA)
1980	Johnny Rutherford (USA)
1981	Bobby Unser (USA)
1982	Gordon Johncock (USA)
1983	Tom Sneva (USA)
1984	Rick Mears (USA)
1985	Danny Sullivan (USA)
1986	Bobby Rahal (USA)
1987	Al Unser (USA)
1988	Rick Mears (USA)
1989	Emerson Fittipaldi (Brazil)
1990	Arie Luyendyk (The Netherlands)
1991	Rick Mears (USA)
1992	Al Unser, Jr (USA)
1993	Emerson Fittipaldi (Brazil)
1994	Al Unser, Jr (USA)
1995	Jacques Villeneuve (Canada)
1996	Buddy Lazier (USA)
1997	Arie Luyendyk (The Netherlands)
1998	Eddie Cheever (USA)
1999	Kenny Brack (Sweden)
2000	Juan Montoya (Colombia)
2001	Helio Castroneves (Brazil)

Winning from beyond the grave

The only posthumous Formula One world champion was the Austrian Jochen Rindt. He died in a crash at the Parabolica curve in 1970 in the last qualifying session before the Monza Grand Prix. He already had a huge lead in the world championship over his closest rival Jacky Ickx.

Who's had all the caviar?

Nigel Mansell clearly enjoyed his life out of the driving seat. It was widely reported that when he returned to Formula One in 1995, he was unable to squeeze into the cockpit of his McLaren car, which had to be widened to fit him.

2002	Helio Castroneves (Brazil)
2003	Gil de Ferran (Brazil)
2004	Buddy Rice (USA)

Nascar Nextel Cup

Known as Grand National from 1949 to 1971, and the Winston Cup from 1972 to 2003. Awarded to the driver who has accumulated the most points in a season. As of 2004, there is a ten-race 'play-off' at the end of the season in which the top ten drivers complete.

	Driver	**Car**
1949	Red Byron	Oldsmobile
1950	Bill Rexford	Oldsmobile
1951	Herb Thomas	Hudson
1952	Tim Flock	Hudson
1953	Herb Thomas	Hudson
1954	Lee Petty	Chrysler
1955	Tim Flock	Chrysler
1956	Buck Baker	Chrysler
1957	Buck Baker	Chevrolet
1958	Lee Petty	Oldsmobile
1959	Lee Petty	Plymouth
1960	Rex White	Chevrolet
1961	Ned Jarrett	Chevrolet
1962	Joe Weatherly	Pontiac
1963	Joe Weatherly	Pontiac
1964	Richard Petty	Plymouth
1965	Ned Jarrett	Ford
1966	David Pearson	Dodge
1967	Richard Petty	Plymouth
1968	David Pearson	Ford
1969	David Pearson	Ford
1970	Bobby Isaac	Dodge
1971	Richard Petty	Plymouth
1972	Richard Petty	Plymouth
1973	Benny Parsons	Chevrolet
1974	Richard Petty	Dodge
1975	Richard Petty	Dodge
1976	Cale Yarborough	Chevrolet
1977	Cale Yarborough	Chevrolet
1978	Cale Yarborough	Oldsmobile
1979	Richard Petty	Chevrolet
1980	Dale Earnhardt	Chevrolet
1981	Darrell Waltrip	Buick
1982	Darrell Waltrip	Buick
1983	Bobby Allison	Buick
1984	Terry Labonte	Chevrolet
1985	Darrell Waltrip	Chevrolet

Driving into history

With his win in 2004, Tom Kristensen became the first driver to achieve five consecutive Le Mans wins. Kristensen now shares the record of six career wins with Belgian racing driver Jacky Ickx, who won the race in 1969, 1975, 1976, 1977, 1981 and 1982.

	Driver	Car
1986	Dale Earnhardt	Chevrolet
1987	Dale Earnhardt	Chevrolet
1988	Bill Elliott	Ford
1989	Rusty Wallace	Pontiac
1990	Dale Earnhardt	Chevrolet
1991	Dale Earnhardt	Chevrolet
1992	Alan Kulwicki	Ford
1993	Dale Earnhardt	Chevrolet
1994	Dale Earnhardt	Chevrolet
1995	Jeff Gordon	Chevrolet
1996	Terry Labonte	Chevrolet
1997	Jeff Gordon	Chevrolet
1998	Jeff Gordon	Chevrolet
1999	Dale Jarrett	Ford
2000	Bobby Labonte	Pontiac
2001	Jeff Gordon	Chevrolet
2002	Tony Stewart	Pontiac
2003	Matt Kenseth	Ford
2004	Kurt Busch	Ford

Cars on film

It's not surprising that the flamboyant world of motor racing has attracted film-makers. Motor sport-themed films include *Grand Prix* (1966) starring James Garner, the Nascar-themed *Days of Thunder* (1990) with Tom Cruise as the improbably named Cole Trickle, and the 1969 *Winning* with Paul Newman attempting to take the Indy 500. In the latter, real-life drivers Bobby Unser and Dan Gurney appeared alongside Newman and his wife Joanne Woodward. Paul Newman subsequently raced in many events and set up his own Indy car team in 1983 with Carl Haas. The best of the bunch, however, is probably *Le Mans* (1971), starring Steve McQueen, which manages to capture accurately what it feels like to drive a Gulf Porsche 917 at 200mph. McQueen did a lot of the actual driving, although the wisdom of this may be questionable as during the making of the film he managed to crash a hire car, and put himself and a co-star through the windscreen.

Most Grand Prix Wins

Driver	Wins	Starts
Michael Schumacher	83	213
Alain Prost	51	199
Ayrton Senna	41	161
Nigel Mansell	31	186
Jackie Stewart	27	99
Jim Clark	25	72
Niki Lauda	25	171
Juan Manuel Fangio	24	51
Nelson Piquet	23	204
Damon Hill	22	115
Mika Hakkinen	20	165

A-Z

apex the centre point of a corner

apron in Indy car and Nascar racing, the paved portion of a racetrack that separates the racing surface from the infield

Armco metal crash barriers designed to absorb the impact of cars and protect spectators, now rarely used

back marker a driver at the back of the field

barge board a vertical piece of bodywork behind the front wheels of a Formula One car that directs airflow into the **sidepods** and away from the car

braking zone the area of track preceding a corner in which drivers apply the brakes

Brickyard the name given to the Indianapolis circuit; so called because of the 3.2 million bricks laid in 1909. They are now covered with asphalt, except for the symbolic yard-wide strip left at the start/finish line

chicane two bends, one immediately after another

cockpit the space where the driver sits

diffuser the rear part of a car's underbody, designed to channel the air-flow and generate **down force**

dirty air turbulent air, created by a car in front, which affects the aero-dynamics of a following car

down force the aerodynamic force that is applied in a downwards direction as a car travels forwards

drafting driving close behind a car in order to benefit from the vacuum created

drive-through penalty a penalty where a driver must enter the **pit lane**, drive through it complying with the speed limit, and then rejoin the race

fishtail if a car fishtails, the back moves erratically from side to side because of lack of grip

formation lap the lap that the cars make prior to the start of a race to allow them to warm up their tyres

fuel load the amount of fuel on board a car; teams will modify this depending on their race strategy, ie how many **pit stops** they plan to make

gravel trap an area of gravel near a corner, which will slow cars down if they run off the track

grid the staggered arrangement of the cars before the start of a race

ground effect the extra adhesion to the track created by the car design; ground-effect cars have been banned in some forms of racing

hairpin a tight corner that turns back on itself and must therefore be taken slowly; two of the most famous hairpins are at Monte Carlo: the Mirabeau (before the tunnel) and the Rascasse (near the end of the lap)

in lap the lap done before a driver makes a **pit stop**

intermediates tyres that have more grooves and tread than dry-weather tyres, but fewer than wet-weather tyres; used when the weather is changeable

lap 1. a completed circuit of a racetrack. 2. if a driver laps another one, he overtakes him so that he is ahead of him by one or more laps

launch control the electronic technology that performs a fully automatic start for a car; now banned

lollipop — the sign on a stick held in front of the car during a **pit stop**; one side tells the driver to apply the brakes and the other to engage first gear before the car is lowered from the jacks

marshal — one of the officials posted around the racetrack whose job is to ensure the safety of drivers and spectators

monocoque — a one-piece, light but strong structure that houses the **cockpit**

Nomex® — synthetic fire-resistant material used to make drivers' protective clothing and gloves

outbrake — if a driver outbrakes another driver, he brakes later going into a corner and so is able to overtake

out lap — 1. the lap done after a driver has made a **pit stop** 2. in **qualifying**, the lap done after leaving the pits and before doing the measured lap

oval — in Indy car and Nascar racing, an oval-shaped circuit with gentle bends that can be taken at high speed

oversteer — if a car has oversteer, the front wheels have more traction than the rear, making the rear of the car unstable and likely to slide when taking corners

pace car — a saloon car behind which the racing cars drive at its pace during the **formation lap**

paddock — the closed-off area behind the **pits** where teams park their transporters and motor homes

parade lap — same as **formation lap**

parc fermé — a cordoned-off area into which cars are driven after **qualifying** and the race itself; teams can then only work on them under the strict supervision of race officials

pit — 1. the area of the **pits** assigned to an individual team 2. if a driver pits, he comes into the pits, eg *Button pitted on lap 46*

pit board — a board held out from the **pit wall** and which tells a driver his position, the time gap to the car ahead or behind, and the number of laps remaining

pit lane — the lane that leads to the **pits** from the circuit and by which a driver can rejoin the circuit

pits — the area close to the circuit in which teams service their cars; the word originates from the below ground-level pits dug next to the track in Sicily in 1908 to allow mechanics to replace the detachable tyre rims that were used at that time

pit stop — when a driver comes into the **pits** in order to refuel, change tyres or have repairs made to his car

pit straight — same as **start/finish straight**

pit wall — the wall that separates the pit area from the **start/finish straight**; on larger circuits it houses the technical members of teams and their electronic equipment

plank — a 10mm-thick wooden board fitted to the underside of Formula One cars to check that they are not too low to the ground; if the plank wears by more than 1mm, the car is disqualified

podium finish — if a driver has a podium finish, he finishes in first, second or third place, and hence stands on the winner's podium

pole (position) — the front position on the **grid**

qualifying — the period, usually on the day preceding the race, when drivers try to record fast lap times, the results determining their position on the **grid**

racing line — the optimum line on which to drive between one corner and the next

run-off area an area of gravel or other material near a corner, which will slow cars down if they run off the track

safety car a saloon car that comes out onto the track and behind which the racing cars must drive at its pace after an accident has occurred that requires **marshals** to be on the track

scrutineering the inspection of cars by the officials to ensure that technical regulations have not been broken

scuderia a name used to refer to the Ferrari team; this Italian word literally means 'stable'

sidepods the parts of the car body on each side of the **monocoque**, containing the radiator and impact-absorbing structures

slicks tyres with no tread, used in dry-weather conditions; since 1998 these have had to have grooves

slipstream 1. the area of decreased wind resistance behind a moving car 2. if a driver slipstreams another driver, he takes advantage of the reduced wind resistance in order to close up and attempt to pass

stagger in Indy car racing, when the right-hand tyre has a larger diameter than the left-hand one, in order to aid in taking turns in races on **ovals**

start/finish straight the straight section of track where the **grid** is and where races begin and end

steward a high-ranking official who makes decisions about the running of a race, including the awarding of penalties

stop-go penalty if a driver exceeds the speed limit in the **pit lane**, he has to return to the pit lane and remain stationary for a period of time (ten seconds in Formula One; one second in Nascar) before rejoining the race

straight a straight section of track

straightaway US term for a **straight**

superspeedway in Nascar and Indy car racing, a track over one mile long

T-car a team's spare car; so called because it used to be known as the training car and had a T on it rather than a number

team orders when teams have more than one driver in a race, team orders may apply, whereby it is agreed that drivers should allow another member of their team to win if they are leading themselves and their team-mate is in second place

telemetry the system by which information on the car's performance is relayed back to the technical crew in the pit area

tifosi Italian for 'fans', it is applied to Ferrari followers, renowned for their passionate attachment to their team

traction control the computerized system by which the output of the engine can be controlled in order to achieve the optimum grip and hence avoid wheel spin; now banned

tyre blanket covers used to warm tyres up before a race as they function better at a higher temperature

tyre wall crash barrier consisting of two to six rows of car tyres bolted together

understeer if a car has understeer, the rear wheels have more traction then the front and so the car is less willing to turn

victory lane in Nascar, the place on the racetrack's infield where the race winner parks for the prize giving

warm-up lap same as **formation lap**

Some motor racing slang

off an accident in which the car leaves the track, eg *he had a massive off*
pit babe an attractive young woman employed by a team to adorn its pit area and promote the team
shunt an accident in which one car crashes into another
shut the door if a driver shuts the door on another one, he moves over sharply to prevent a passing move
traffic cars that are further back in the field and going more slowly than the leading cars, eg *Schumacher was held up by traffic*

Some famous racing drivers

Mario Andretti, 1940–

Born in Montona, Italy, he emigrated with his family to Nazareth, Pennsylvania, USA, in 1955 and began his career in stock car and midget car racing, then progressed to the US Auto Club circuit, in which he was champion three times (1965, 1966, 1969). He gained pole position in his first Formula One race (1968 at Watkins Glen) and, in a long career stretching to 1982, he competed in 128 Grand Prix, winning 16. His most successful year was 1978 when, in a Lotus, he became only the second American to win the world championship. He continued racing into his fifties, taking his last Indycar victory in 1993. His son Michael (1962–) followed him into motor racing.

Alberto Ascari, 1918–55

Born in Milan, Italy, he was the son of Antonio Ascari, a successful driver himself who died in a racing accident when Alberto was six. He shared his father's passion for motor racing. His first race was in a Ferrari and his name became closely associated with the car. It was in a Ferrari that he won the championship in 1952 and 1953, before switching to Lancia in 1954. He died in a practice accident, just four days after a spectacular crash in the Monaco Grand Prix, where he had to be fished out of the harbour. The Ascari Curve at Monza is named after him.

Sir Jack Brabham, 1926–

Born in Sydney, Australia, after service with the Royal Australian Air Force he started his racing career in 1947, in midget cars. He won the Australian Grand Prix in 1955 (and again in 1963 and 1964), then went to the UK where he joined the successful Cooper team. His aggressive style saw him win his first Formula One world championship at Sebring, Florida, in 1959 (when had to he push his car over the finishing line) and repeat the feat in 1960. In 1966 he won his third world title, and also the constructor's championship, with a car of his own design, the Repco-Brabham. He was awarded the OBE in 1966 and knighted in 1979.

Jim Clark, 1936–68

Born in Kilmany, Scotland, he won his first motor race in 1956, and became Scottish Speed Champion in 1958 and 1959. In 1960 he joined the Lotus team as a Formula One driver and, after narrowly losing out in 1962 to **Graham Hill**, won the world championship in 1963 and 1965. Also in 1965 he became the first non-American since

1916 to win the Indianapolis 500, leading for 190 of the 200 laps. Of his 72 Grand Prix races, he won 25, breaking the record of 24 held by **Juan Manuel Fangio**. He was killed during practice for a Formula Two race at Hockenheim in Germany (where a chicane was named after him for many years). A quiet and unassuming man, he was happiest when on his farm near Duns in the Scottish Borders (where there is now a museum celebrating his life).

Dale Earnhardt, 1951–2001

Born in Kannapolis, North Carolina, USA, he was nicknamed 'The Intimidator' for his aggressive driving style. He shares the honour with **Richard Petty** of being the only driver to win seven championships, all driving a Chevrolet. He died in an accident on the final lap of the 2001 Daytona 500, leaving his two sons, also Nascar drivers, to continue the Earnhardt tradition.

Juan Manuel Fangio, 1911–95

Born in Balcarce, Argentina, of Italian descent, his first motor racing experience was in long-distance racing in South America and it was not until 1949, at the age of 37, that he took part in European Grand Prix racing. In 1951 he won the first of his five world championships and, after recovering from a near-fatal accident in 1952, he won four consecutive championships between 1954 and 1957. His record of Grand Prix wins to starts will probably never be beaten. Such was the respect in which he was held by his peers (who called him 'the maestro') that, in his last race in 1958, leader Mike Hawthorn slowed down so as not to lap him.

Janet Guthrie, 1938–

Born in Iowa City, Iowa, USA, she began building and racing cars in 1962. In 1976 she became the first woman to race in a Nascar Winston Cup event, and the following year she became the first woman to compete in the Indianapolis 500, though she did not finish. In 1978 she competed and finished ninth. Her 1978 Indianapolis 500 driver's suit and helmet are in the Smithsonian Institution in Washington DC, and she is in the International Women's Sports Hall of Fame.

Graham Hill, 1929–75

Born in London, England, he won the world championship in 1962 in a BRM, and was runner-up twice in the following three years. In 1967 he rejoined Lotus and won the world championship for a second time (1968). He won the Monaco Grand Prix five times (1963–5, 1968–9). In 1975 he started his own racing team, Embassy Racing, but was killed when the plane he was piloting crashed near London. His son Damon Hill also became a championship-winning racing driver.

James Hunt, 1947–93

Born in London, he drove with the Hesketh and McLaren teams (1973–9), and was Formula One world champion in 1976 when he managed to come third in the last race of the season, the rain-soaked Japanese Grand Prix, and hence pip his rival **Niki Lauda**. He was a flamboyant and adventurous driver who had so many crashes that he earned the nickname 'Hunt the Shunt'. He retired in 1979 and was a BBC television broadcaster from 1980 until his death.

Niki Lauda, 1949–

He was born in Vienna, Austria. World-champion racing driver in 1975 with Ferrari, he suffered horrific burns and injuries in the German Grand Prix at the Nürburgring (1976) but incredibly, after a series of operations, he returned to racing just six weeks later. He won his second championship with Ferrari in 1977 before moving to Brabham and then retiring to set up his own airline Lauda-Air. He returned to racing in 1982 with McLaren and won his third and last championship in 1984 (by just half a point), before finally retiring in 1985. An undemonstrative character and a determined rather than talented driver, the contrast in styles with rival **James Hunt** was marked.

Nigel Mansell, 1953–

Born in Solihull, West Midlands, England, he worked as a window cleaner to fund his Formula Three career and had to follow a long, hard road to Formula One. However, he made his debut in 1980, and had his first win in 1985, with the Williams team, having started with Lotus. Following a spell with Ferrari, he returned to Williams in 1991, and in 1992 won the world championship. He did not defend his title, preferring to drive in the Indy car circuit in the USA, and in 1993 became the first man to win the Indy car world series championship in his rookie year. An aggressive, sometimes reckless but always committed driver, he had a brief Formula One swansong with McLaren before retiring for good in 1995.

Sir Stirling Moss, 1929–

Born in London, England, he won many major races in the 1950s, including the British Grand Prix (1955, 1957), the Mille Miglia, and the Targa Florio. Between 1951 and 1961, he won 16 races from 66 starts but is probably the greatest driver never to win a Formula One world championship. He came closest in 1958, losing out by just one point to Mike Hawthorn. He retired in 1962 after a crash at Goodwood. He then became a journalist and broadcaster, and returned to saloon car racing in 1980. He was knighted in 2000.

Richard Petty, 1937–

Probably the most famous Nascar driver of all time, he chalked up an unprecedented 200 wins during a career in which he competed in 1,185 races. Known as 'The King', he took a record seven championships (a feat equalled by **Dale Earnhardt**). His father Lee was also a Nascar champion and his son Kyle is a driver too.

Nelson Piquet, 1952–

Born in Rio de Janeiro, Brazil, he changed his name so that his parents would not find out about his racing exploits. He was British Formula Three champion in 1978, and Formula One world champion in 1981, 1983 (both with Brabham), and 1987 (with Williams). He won 20 races from 157 starts between 1978 and 1988.

Alain Prost, 1955–

Born in St Chamond, France, he won his first Grand Prix in 1981 in a Renault. He switched to McLaren and with them won the world championship three times (1985, 1986, 1989); then to Ferrari for a brief, unhappy period; and finally to Williams with whom he won his fourth championship in 1993. In 1987 'the Professor', as he was nicknamed, surpassed **Jackie Stewart**'s record of 27 Grand Prix wins (he went on to record 51 wins). He retired in 1994.

Michael Schumacher, 1969–

Born in Hürth-Hermuhlheim, Germany, after starting his career in karting he made a remarkable Formula One debut in the 1991 Belgium Grand Prix when he unexpectedly qualified in seventh place in a Jordan, and he joined the Benetton team two weeks later. He won the Formula One world championship in 1994, 1995, 2000, 2001, 2002, 2003 and 2004, becoming the first man to win five consecutive titles. In 1996 he signed a $26 million contract with Ferrari. He has dominated the sport since **Ayrton Senna**'s death with his clinical, determined and exceptionally smooth style of driving and has beaten almost all Formula One records (including most wins in a season – 13 in 2004).

Ayrton Senna, 1960–94

Born in São Paulo, Brazil, he made his Grand Prix debut in Brazil in 1984 with the Toleman team after graduating through karts, Formula Ford and Formula Three. He later drove for Lotus (1985–7), McLaren (1988–93) and Williams (1994). One of the fastest and most gifted drivers of all time, he was Formula One world champion in 1988, 1990 and 1991, and was a national hero in Brazil. He was killed after crashing at the Tamburello corner at Imola during the San Marino Grand Prix. A statue commemorating him stands there today, and an S-bend at the Interlagos circuit in his home town is named after him.

Sir Jackie Stewart, 1939–

Born in Dunbartonshire, Scotland, he won 27 Grand Prix in his career. He had been third in the world championship in 1965 with BRM, his first season of Grand Prix racing, but won the world title in 1969, 1971 and 1973 with the Tyrrell team, retiring after his last victory. He was knighted in 2001. In 1997 he returned to Formula One as joint team owner, with his son, of Stewart Racing, which was bought by Jaguar in 2000.

Al Unser, 1939–

Born in Albuquerque, New Mexico, he has won the Indianapolis 500 four times – 1970, 1971, 1978 and 1987. He was three times Indy car champion (1970, 1983 and 1985), was International Race of Champions (IROC) champion in 1978 and won the 24-hour Daytona race in 1985. His brother, Bobby Unser (1934–), was twice Indy car champion (1968 and 1974) and IROC champion in 1975, and his son, Al Unser Jr, (1962–), was Indy car champion in 1990 and 1994 and IROC champion in 1986 and 1988, and won the Indianapolis 500 in 1992 and 1994.

MOUNTAIN BIKING

Origins

Riding and racing bicycles off-road began shortly after people began riding bicycles. Organized off-road cycling events have been documented in France as far back as the 1920s. However, it was the riding of the 'Repack' riders in Marin County, California, USA, which popularized the sport.

Rules and description

Whilst the term 'mountain biking' covers any off-road cycling, the sport can be divided into various disciplines:

Cross-country

Generally raced over loops of several miles. Depending on the category, these races can last from 1h 45min to 2h 30min. The tracks comprise gradients and may include a variety of off-road terrain, including wide smooth tracks, narrower tracks, paths through forests, rocky paths and even stream crossings.

Downhill

This has become the blue riband event of the sport owing to the spectacular speeds and the terrain involved. The competition takes place over a marked course on a hillside, with riders setting off at intervals. The rider with the fastest time down the course is the winner. Tracks feature a variety of terrain, including fast open sections, slower more technical sections over rocks and roots, and often a range of jumps. Descents last between two and five minutes with up to 3km being covered in this time.

4-cross

Downhill BMX for mountain bikes. Four riders race over jumps and banked curves.

Freeriding

A new form of competition where riders negotiate a track with obstacles including huge drops and jumps. Judged on style and bravado rather than time.

Trials

Riders negotiate a course of obstacles grouped into 'sections', without putting their feet on the ground (or they incur penalties). After negotiating a series of sections, the rider who has collected the fewest penalty points is declared the winner.

Ruling body: Union Cycliste Internationale (UCI)

Olympic Champions

Mountain biking became an Olympic sport in 1996. Only a cross-country event is held.

	Men	Women
1996	Bart Brentjens (The Netherlands)	Paula Pezzo (Italy)
2000	Miguel Martinez (France)	Paula Pezzo (Italy)
2004	Julien Absalon (France)	Gunn-Rita Dahle (Norway)

Mountain Bike World Cup

An annual series of races (currently six for downhill, seven for cross-country) held at venues around the world and introduced in 1991. The winner is the rider with the greatest number of points over the series.

Mountain Biking

Downhill

	Men	Women
1999	Nicolas Vouilloz (France)	Anne-Caroline Chausson (France)
2000	Nicolas Vouilloz (France)	Anne-Caroline Chausson (France)
2001	Greg Minnaar (South Africa)	Anne-Caroline Chausson (France)
2002	Steve Peat (Great Britain)	Anne-Caroline Chausson (France)
2003	Nathan Rennie (Australia)	Sabrina Jonnier (France)
2004	Steve Peat (Great Britain)	Céline Gros (France)

Cross-country

	Men	Women
1999	Cadel Evans (Australia)	Alison Sydor (Canada)
2000	Miguel Martinez (France)	Barbara Blatter (Switzerland)
2001	Roland Green (Canada)	Barbara Blatter (Switzerland)
2002	Filip Meirhaege (Belgium)	Alison Dunlap (USA)
2003	Julien Absalon (France)	Gunn-Rita Dahle (Norway)
2004	Christophe Sauser (Switzerland)	Gunn-Rita Dahle (Norway)

World Championships

An annual one-race competition first held in 1990.

Downhill

	Men	Women	Venue
1999	Nicolas Vouilloz (France)	Anne-Caroline Chausson (France)	Are, Sweden
2000	Myles Rockwell (USA)	Anne-Caroline Chausson (France)	Sierra Nevada, Spain
2001	Nicolas Vouilloz (France)	Anne-Caroline Chausson (France)	Vail, USA
2002	Nicolas Vouilloz (France)	Anne-Caroline Chausson (France)	Kaprun, Austria
2003	Greg Minnaar (South Africa)	Anne-Caroline Chausson (France)	Lugano, Switzerland
2004	Fabien Barel (France)	Vanessa Quin (New Zealand)	Les Gets, France

Cross-country

	Men	Women
1999	Michael Rasmussen (Denmark)	Margarita Fullana Riera (Spain)
2000	Miguel Martinez (France)	Margarita Fullana Riera (Spain)
2001	Roland Green (Canada)	Alison Dunlap (USA)
2002	Roland Green (Canada)	Gunn-Rita Dahle (Norway)
2003	Filip Meirhaege (Belgium)	Sabine Spitz (Germany)
2004	Julien Absalon (France)	Gunn-Rita Dahle (Norway)

MOUNTAINEERING & CLIMBING

Origins

The urge to explore new places and to conquer high mountains provided the impetus to the sports of mountaineering and climbing. Mont Blanc in the Alps was successfully scaled at the end of the 18th century and was the stimulus for climbers (many of them British) to set their sights on other Alpine peaks. The 19th century was a boom period in the growth of mountaineering clubs and by the 20th century many climbers were turning their attention to the Himalayan peaks, the world's tallest. Climbing as a competitive sport derived from mountaineering and traces its origins to the former USSR, where the skills of individual climbers were pitted against each other in speed and technical tests.

Rules and description

Rock climbing and mountaineering involve ropework – ropes being used to secure climbers in pairs and groups, and to provide a method for both ascending and descending. Depending on conditions, equipment can vary from the lightest leisure gear to complete protection against extreme wintry conditions. Footwear also varies according to conditions from light climbing shoes to heavy boots. In icy conditions crampons (devices with rows of metal teeth) are strapped to boots to provide a grip on the ice and climbers carry ice axes to embed into the ice to provide stability. Some daring rock climbers dispense totally with tools and equipment and climb without back-up support. This traditional climbing is carried out according to agreed style and ethics (the climbers' bible being *Games Climbers Play*) and has no ruling body.

Competitive or sport climbing is regulated by the UIAA, which created the first World Cup series in 1989 to compare the skills of climbers in three disciplines: 'difficulty', where the person who climbs highest is the winner; 'speed', in which climbers compete head-to-head on parallel routes on a knockout basis; and 'bouldering', where climbers attempt to overcome the most obstacles on a route without the use of ropes. Most competitions take place on specially erected climbing walls. A recently introduced discipline is ice climbing – a World Cup event was instituted in 2000.

Ruling body: International Mountaineering and Climbing Federation (Union Internationale des Associations d'Alpinisme, UIAA)

UIAA World Championships

	Venue
2001	Winterthur (Switzerland)
2003	Chamonix (France)
2005	Munich (Germany)

	Men	Women
Difficulty		
2001	Gérôme Pouvreau (France)	Martina Cufar (Slovenia)
2003	Tomás Mrázek (Czech Republic)	Muriel Sarkany (Belgium)
Speed		
2001	Maxim Stenkovoi (Ukraine)	Olena Ryepko (Ukraine)
2003	Maxim Stenkovoi (Ukraine)	Olena Ryepko (Ukraine)
Bouldering		
2001	Mauro Calibani (Italy)	Myriam Motteau (France)
2003	Christian Core (Italy)	Sandrine Levet (France)

World Cup

A series of competitions held at various venues around the world (mostly in Europe) throughout the year at which points are accrued towards the title. Bouldering was introduced in 1999, speed in 1998.

	Men	Women
Difficulty		
1989	Simon Nadin (Great Britain)	Nanette Raybaud (France)
1990	François Legrand (France)	Isabelle Patissier (France)
1991	François Legrand (France)	Isabelle Patissier (France)
1992	François Legrand (France)	Robyn Erbesfield (USA)
1993	François Legrand (France)	Robyn Erbesfield (USA)
1994	François Legrand (France)	Robyn Erbesfield (USA)
1995	François Petit (France)	Robyn Erbesfield (USA)
1996	Arnaud Petit (France)	Liv Sansoz (France)
1997	François Legrand (France)	Muriel Sarkany (Belgium)
1998	Yuji Hirayama (Japan)	Liv Sansoz (France)
1999	François Petit (France)	Muriel Sarkany (Belgium)
2000	Yuji Hirayama (Japan)	Liv Sansoz (France)
2001	Alexandre Chabot (France)	Muriel Sarkany (Belgium)
2002	Alexandre Chabot (France)	Muriel Sarkany (Belgium)
2003	Patxi Usobiaga (Spain)	Sandrine Levet (France)
2004	Tomáš Mrázek (Czech Republic)	Angela Eiter (Austria)
Bouldering		
1999	Christian Core (Italy)	Stéphanie Bodet (France)
2000	Pedro Pons (Spain)	Sandrine Levet (France)
2001	Jérôme Meyer (France)	Sandrine Levet (France)
2002	Christian Core (Italy)	Natalia Perlova (Ukraine)
2003	Jérôme Meyer (France)	Sandrine Levet (France)
2004	Daniel Du Lac (France)	Sandrine Levet (France)
Speed		
1998	Andrei Vedenmeer (Ukraine)	Olga Zakharova (Ukraine)
1999	Tomasz Oleksy (Poland)	Olga Zakharova (Ukraine)

Speed		
2000	Andrei Vedenmeer (Ukraine)	Olena Ryepko (Ukraine)
2001	Maxim Stenkovoi (Ukraine)	Olga Zakharova (Ukraine)
2002	Aleksandr Pechekhonov (Russia)	Olena Ryepko (Ukraine)
2003	Tomasz Oleksy (Poland)	Valentina Yurina (Russia)
2004	Sergei Sinitsyne (Russia)	Tatiana Rouiga (Russia)

Ice Climbing

World Championships

	Venue
2002	Pitztal, Austria
2003	Kirov, Russia
2004	Saas Fee, Switzerland

	Men	**Women**
Difficulty		
2002	Evgeni Krivosheitsev (Ukraine)	Ines Papert (Germany)
2003	Evgeni Krivosheitsev (Ukraine)	Ines Papert (Germany)
2004	Harald Berger (Austria)	Ines Papert (Germany)
Speed		
2003	Aleksandr Matveev (Russia)	Natalia Koulikova (Russia)
2004	Aleksandr Matveev (Russia)	Natalia Koulikova (Russia)

World Cup

	Men	**Women**
2000	Will Gadd (Canada)	Kim Csizmazia (Canada)
2001	Daniel Du Lac (France)	Ines Papert (Germany)
2002	Harald Berger (Austria)/ Dimitri Bychkov (Russia)	Ksenia Sdobnikova (Russia)
2003	Harald Berger (Austria)	Ines Papert (Germany)
2004	*Cancelled; only one round completed*	

A-Z

abseil to descend on a fixed rope by means of sliding and braking mechanisms

ascender a sliding metal grip threaded on a rope as a foothold or aid to climbing

belay a safety technique in which a stationary climber provides protection, by means of ropes, anchors and braking devices, to an ascending partner

bouldering a discipline in which climbers attempt to overcome obstacles on a short route without the use of ropes, acquiring points for each obstacle negotiated

cam mechanical device with protrusions which grip into a crack in the rock

carabiner — aluminium or steel ring device with spring-loaded gates through which a rope can be threaded. They are used in **abseiling**, **belaying** and **prusiking**

chimney — a cleft in a rockface just large enough for a climber to enter and climb

climbing wall — a specially constructed wall with hand- and foot-holds for practising mountaineering and rock climbing techniques

cornice — a dangerous overhanging mass of wind-sculpted snow that projects beyond the crest of a ridge.

crampons — metal devices with spikes that are attached to climbing boots to provide grip on snow and ice

dead hang — to hang limp from a handhold with straightened arms so that the body weight is supported by the skeleton rather than arm muscles

descender — a device for controlling the descent on a rope

dyno — (short for dynamic), an athletic leap for a distant hold

expansion bolt — a bolt that expands within a hole or crack in the rockface to provide firm support

fixed rope — a rope anchored to a route by the lead climber and left in place for those that follow

free climbing — climbing without aids

glissade — the act of sliding down a slope in a standing or squatting position, often with the aid of an ice axe for braking

jam — the act of twisting a part of the body (fist, hand, foot or finger) in a crack to secure it

karabiner — same as **carabiner**

nut — a tapered piece of metal that fits into a crack in a rockface to provide protection

pitch — a section of rock or ice between two **belay** points

piton — an iron peg that can be hammered into the rock and to which a rope may be attached

prusik — a type of rope sling attached to a climbing rope, which grips firmly when carrying weight but when unweighted can be moved up the rope. Named after Karl Prusik (1895–1961), an Austrian climber

quickdraw — a short loop with a **carabiner** at each end, used to connect the climbing rope to a bolt, **piton** or **cam**

rappel — same as **abseil**

running belay — a device attached to the rockface through which a rope runs freely

topo — (short for topographic map), a map of a climbing route with obstacles marked

top out — if a climber tops out, he or she successfully reaches the top of the route

toprope — a rope fixed at the top of a route

traverse — to climb in a horizontal (rather than a vertical) direction

wall — a very steep smooth rockface

wire — same as **nut**

NETBALL

Origins

Netball is regarded as the sister sport to basketball, a game that was invented in the USA in 1891. Basketball was taken to England and was immediately modified: a ring with a suspended net replaced the basket, and the playing area was divided into zones, with each player being restricted to certain zones of play. Played almost exclusively by women, netball is popular in countries of the Commonwealth.

Martina Bergman Österberg

A Swedish fitness instructor named Martina Bergman Österberg was largely responsible for the early development of netball. She founded a physical training college in 1885 in Hampstead, north London, England, and the game was introduced to the curriculum at the end of the century by an American visitor. In the Victorian era, when women were tightly bound by corsets and rigid rules regarding their behaviour, the pioneering Mrs Österberg led a sporting revolution.

Rules and description

Netball is a seven-a-side ball game with great emphasis placed on the skills of passing and shooting. The aim of the game is to score more goals than the opposition. Netball is played on a hard-surface court (either indoors or outdoors) that measures 30.5 x 15.25m/100 x 50ft. The court is divided into three equal areas: a defending third, a centre third and an attacking third. At each end of the court there is a goal – a ring and net suspended on a post 3.05m/10ft high. Marked on the court around the base of the goal is a shooting (or goal) circle, from within which goals are scored. Only two attacking players are allowed in the circle: the 'goal shooter' and 'goal attack'; similarly, only two defenders are permitted in the circle: the goalkeeper and the 'goal defence'.

Players advance the ball by passing it. They are not allowed to travel with the ball, only to take a single step while pivoting on the other foot. They also need to release the ball within three seconds. Netball is a non-contact sport and penalties are given for obstruction and other infringements. A game normally lasts an hour, divided into four 15-minute quarters. Players wear bibs with abbreviations to identify their position.

Ruling body: International Federation of Netball Associations (IFNA)

World Championships

World championships have been held every four years since 1963.

	Winner	Runner-up	Venue
1963	Australia	New Zealand	Eastbourne, England
1967	New Zealand	Australia	Perth, Australia

Netball

	Winner	Runner-up	Venue
1971	Australia	New Zealand	Kingston, Jamaica
1975	Australia	England	Auckland, New Zealand
1979	Australia/New Zealand/ Trinidad & Tobago		Port of Spain, Trinidad
1983	Australia	New Zealand	Singapore
1987	New Zealand	Australia/Trinidad & Tobago	Glasgow, Scotland
1991	Australia	New Zealand	Sydney, Australia
1995	Australia	South Africa	Birmingham, England
1999	Australia	New Zealand	Christchurch, New Zealand
2003	New Zealand	Australia	Kingston, Jamaica

A-Z

airborne throw a throw made while the player is in midair

centre a player (who wears the abbreviation C) who can play in all areas of the court except the **shooting circles**

centre pass the throw from the centre of the court that starts or restarts the game

free pass a pass awarded as the result of an infringement

goal attack an attacking player (who wears the abbreviation GA) restricted to the **shooting circle**, attacking third and centre third

goal circle same as **shooting circle**

goal defence a defensive player (who wears the abbreviation GD) restricted to the **shooting circle**, defending third and centre third

goalkeeper a defensive player (who wears the abbreviation GK) restricted to the **shooting circle** and defending third

goal shooter an attacking player (who wears the abbreviation GS and is skilled at shooting) restricted to the **shooting circle** and attacking third

obstruction an infringement that involves an opposition player blocking or interfering with a pass or shot. A **penalty pass** or **penalty shot** is awarded to the obstructed team

offside the offence committed by a player when she leaves the zone to which she is restricted

penalty pass a **free pass** awarded when a team has been fouled

penalty shot as for a **penalty pass**, but taken when the infringement occurs in the **shooting circle**

pivoting grounding one foot while stepping with the free foot any number of times. Pivoting can last no longer than three seconds before the ball has to be released

shooting circle the semicircular area drawn around the goalpost that indicates the scoring zone

transverse lines the lines dividing the court into thirds

travelling the offence of running with the ball

wing attack an attacking player (who wears the abbreviation WA) restricted to the attacking third and centre third

wing defence a defensive player (who wears the abbreviation WD) restricted to the attacking third and centre third

OCTOPUSH

Origins

Octopush was devised by subaqua divers in Southsea, England, in August 1954. Originally, it was to be played by eight team members (hence the 'octo' part of the name) and to use a stick called a 'pusher'. (The pun on the word octopus was also appealing.) Before long, the sport surfaced in the USA, South Africa and Australasia.

Rules and description

Also known as underwater hockey, octopush is played by teams of ten, only six of whom are in the water at any time. Games are held in 25m swimming pools and the water needs to be at least 2m deep. The object is to hit a circular 2kg lead puck, called a 'squid', into the opponent's goal – a 2m-long tray known as the 'gulley'. Players wear mask, snorkel and fins, and with a single gloved hand they hold the spatula-shaped piece of equipment known as the pusher that moves the squid into the gulley.

Players take a breath above the water's surface and then descend to pass, tackle and score before returning to the surface to breathe again. Substitutions are common and octopush resembles tag wrestling in that respect. Games last for 30 minutes with a three-minute half-time break and are run by two water referees and an out-of-water referee.

Ruling body: Confédération Mondiale des Activités Subaquatiques (CMAS)

World Octopush Championships

Held every two years since 1980. Women's event introduced in 1984.

	Men	Women	Venue
1980	The Netherlands		Vancouver, Canada
1982	Australia		Brisbane, Australia
1984	Australia	Australia	Chicago, USA
1986	Canada	Australia	Adelaide, Australia
1988	Australia	New Zealand	Amersfoort, The Netherlands
1990	Australia	Australia	Montreal, Canada
1992	Australia	South Africa	Wellington, New Zealand
1994	Australia	Australia	Grand-Couronne, France
1996	Australia	South Africa	Durban, South Africa
1998	France	South Africa	San José, USA
2000	Australia	Australia	Hobart, Australia
2002	Australia	Australia	Calgary, Canada
2004	New Zealand	The Netherlands	Christchurch, New Zealand

OLYMPIC GAMES

Origins

The modern Olympic Games first took place in 1896 in Athens, Greece. They were the brainchild of the French educationalist Baron Pierre de Coubertin (1863–1937), who wanted to revive the spirit of competition from the ancient Greek Olympian Games of the 8th century BC. In 1894 he helped set up the International Olympic Committee (IOC), which still formulates policy and decides on venues. The Olympics have been held every four years, except during the two world wars. Women first competed in 1900. The first separate Winter Olympics were held in 1924.

Rules and description

The IOC chooses the city to host the Olympic Games roughly seven years in advance of competition. At the closing ceremony of every Games the Olympic flag is passed to the host of the forthcoming Games. The flag has a white ground and five interlocking coloured rings – representing the five continents. Other symbols of the Games include the torch, a lighted flame that is carried from venue to venue and which stays lit during the course of the Games. There are also an Olympic hymn; an Olympic motto – '*citius*, *altius*, *fortius*' ('swifter, higher, stronger'); and an Olympic creed: 'The important thing in these Olympics is not so much winning as taking part'.

The Olympic Games last two to three weeks; at the beginning of the 20th century the events were spread over a number of months. The winners of events are presented with a gold medal (the runner-up receives a silver medal and the third-placed competitor a bronze medal) at a ceremony that sees the raising of the medallists' national flags and the playing of the winner's national anthem.

Ruling body: International Olympic Committee (IOC)

Olympic Venues

Olympic Summer Games

1896	Athens, Greece	**1928**	Amsterdam, the Netherlands
1900	Paris, France	**1932**	Los Angeles, USA
1904	St Louis, USA	**1936**	Berlin, Germany
1906*	Athens, Greece	**1940**	*Not held*
1908	London, UK	**1944**	*Not held*
1912	Stockholm, Sweden	**1948**	London, UK
1916	*Not held*	**1952**	Helsinki, Finland
1920	Antwerp, Belgium	**1956****	Melbourne, Australia
1924	Paris, France	**1960**	Rome, Italy

1964 Tokyo, Japan
1968 Mexico City, Mexico
1972 Munich, West Germany
1976 Montreal, Canada
1980 Moscow, USSR
1984 Los Angeles, USA
1988 Seoul, South Korea
1992 Barcelona, Spain
1996 Atlanta, USA
2000 Sydney, Australia
2004 Athens, Greece
2008 Beijing, China

* Special Olympic Games were held to commemorate the tenth anniversary of the birth of the modern Games. They are called the Intercalated Games.

** The 1956 equestrian events were held at Stockholm, Sweden, because of quarantine laws in Australia.

Olympic Winter Games

1924 Chamonix, France
1928 St Moritz, Switzerland
1932 Lake Placid, USA
1936 Garmisch-Partenkirchen, Germany
1940 *Not held*
1944 *Not held*
1948 St Moritz, Switzerland
1952 Oslo, Norway
1956 Cortina, Italy
1960 Squaw Valley, USA
1964 Innsbruck, Austria
1968 Grenoble, France
1972 Sapporo, Japan
1976 Innsbruck, Austria
1980 Lake Placid, USA
1984 Sarajevo, Yugoslavia
1988 Calgary, Canada
1992 Albertville, France
1994* Lillehammer, Norway
1998 Nagano, Japan
2002 Salt Lake City, USA
2006 Turin, Italy
2010 Vancouver, Canada

* In 1994 the Olympic Winter Games celebrations were readjusted to take place in cycles two years in advance of the Summer Olympics rather than in the same year.

Leading Medal Winners at Olympic Summer Games

Includes medals won in 2004.

	Gold	Silver	Bronze	Total
USA	897	691	605	2,193
Russia*	526	437	407	1,370
Germany**	231	274	304	809
Great Britain	189	242	234	665
France	183	191	213	587
Italy	182	147	164	493
Sweden	141	155	173	469
Hungary	156	136	156	448
East Germany	153	129	127	409
Australia	120	126	152	398

* Includes medals won by the former USSR team, and by the Unified Team (Armenia, Azerbaijan, Belarus, Georgia, Kazakhstan, Kyrgyzstan, Moldova, Russia, Tajikistan, Turkmenistan, Ukraine and Uzbekistan) in 1992.

** Includes medals won as West Germany (1968–88).

Olympic Games

Olympic Winter Games

Includes medals won in 2002.

	Gold	Silver	Bronze	Total
Russia*	113	83	78	274
Norway	94	92	75	261
USA	69	72	51	192
Germany**	68	68	52	188
Austria	42	57	64	163
Finland	41	52	49	142
East Germany	39	36	35	110
Sweden	36	30	38	104
Switzerland	33	33	38	104
Canada	30	28	37	95

* Includes medals won by the former USSR team, and by the Unified Team (Armenia, Azerbaijan, Belarus, Georgia, Kazakhstan, Kyrgyzstan, Moldova, Russia, Tajikistan, Turkmenistan, Ukraine and Uzbekistan) in 1992.
** Includes medals won as West Germany (1968–88).

Discontinued Sports and Events

Some sports appear at one or a few Olympic Games and then disappear from view. Other events reach the Olympic programme because they appeal particularly to the host city. Here are some of the stranger sports and events that form part of Olympic history.

	Sports
1900	Cricket, Croquet, Golf, Pelota Basque, Polo, Rugby union
1904	Lacrosse, Roque
1908	Jeu de Paume, Motor boating, Rackets

	Events
1896	12-hour cycling race
1896, 1924, 1932	Rope-climbing
1900	Equestrian long jump
1900	Underwater swimming
1900–12	Standing high jump
1908–24	Running deer shooting
1912	Javelin (both hands)
1920	Fixed bird target archery

Recognized Sports

To become an Olympic sport, a sport's governing body needs to gain official recognition by the IOC. Here are the sports that have achieved recognition and could conceivably become part of Olympic Games in the future.

Air sports
Automobile
Karate
Korfball
Racquetball
Roller sports

Bandy	Life-saving	Rugby
Billiard sports	Motorcycle racing	Squash
Boules	Mountaineering and climbing	Sumo
Bowling	Netball	Surfing
Bridge	Orienteering	Tug-of-war
Chess	Pelota	Underwater sports
Dance sport	Polo	Water-skiing
Golf	Powerboating	Wushu

Most Gold Medals

Summer Olympics

	Men		Women
9	Paavo Nurmi (Finland), Athletics	9	Larissa Latynina (USSR), Gymnastics
9	Mark Spitz (USA), Swimming	8	Jenny Thompson (USA), Swimming
9	Carl Lewis (USA), Athletics	8	Birgit Fischer/Schmidt (Germany), Canoeing
8	Sawao Kato (Japan), Gymnastics	7	Vera Caslavska (Czechoslovakia), Gymnastics
8	Matt Biondi (USA), Swimming		

Winter Olympics

	Men		Women
8	Bjorn Dählie (Norway), Cross-country skiing	6	Lyubov Yegoreva (Russia), Cross-country skiing
5	Clas Thunberg (Finland), Speed skating	6	Lydia Skoblikova (USSR), Speed skating
5	Ole Einar Björndalen (Norway), Biathlon	5	Larissa Lazutina (Russia), Cross-country skiing
5	Eric Heiden (USA), Speed skating	5	Bonnie Blair (USA), Speed skating

How much gold is there in a gold medal?

A gold medal actually contains at least 92.5% silver, with a gilded covering of just six grams of gold applied.

ORIENTEERING

Origins

The sport's origins can be traced to Scandinavia, where in October 1897 the Tjalve Sports Club, based near Oslo, Norway, staged the first public orienteering competition. In 1918, seeking to stimulate interest in cross-country running, a Swede named Major Ernst Killander encouraged competitors to run a course with map and compass and to use map-reading and navigational skills as well as purely athletic ones.

Rules and description

The sport of orienteering is a blend of cross-country running and map-reading skills for individuals and relay teams. Runners need to reach their destination via various control points that are marked on a map they carry with them. Control points on the course are marked by white and orange flags and at each control point the runners get their cards punched to prove that they passed by. Latterly, electronic chip technology has been used for the same purpose. Runners also use a compass to establish their location. There are three basic forms of the sport: in 'line orienteering' runners follow a set circuit shown on a master map at the start – the control points are found by skilled map and compass work; in 'route orienteering' competitors mark on their own maps the exact position of the control points – the route is marked on the ground but not on the map; and in 'score orienteering' a number of control points are established, each having a different points value: high-value ones are a long way from the start and are difficult to find, whereas low-value ones may be nearby and easier to find.

Ski orienteering (Ski-O as opposed to Foot-O) is especially popular in Scandinavia and world championships were inaugurated in 1975. It is held over classic and sprint distances. Mountain bike orienteering (Bike-O) and trail orienteering (Trail–O), a competition that places more emphasis on map interpretation and is therefore suitable for physically disabled competitors, are other variations on the sport.

Ruling body: International Orienteering Federation

World Championships

The championships were inaugurated in 1966. The classic event for men is 17.5km (the short event, added since 1991, is 5.8km). The women's equivalent distances are 10.5km and 5.5km.

	Men	**Women**	**Venue**
1987	Kent Olsson (Sweden)	Arja Hannus (Sweden)	Gérardmer, France
1989	Petter Thoresen (Norway)	Marita Skogum (Sweden)	Skaraborg, Sweden
1991	Jörgen Mårtensson (Sweden)	Katalin Olah (Hungary)	Mariánské Lázně, Czechoslovakia
1993	Allan Mogensen (Denmark)	Marita Skogum (Sweden)	West Point, USA
1995	Jörgen Mårtensson (Sweden)	Katalin Olah (Hungary)	Detmold, Germany
1997	Petter Thoresen (Norway)	Hanne Staff (Norway)	Grimstad, Norway
1999	Bjornar Valstad (Norway)	Kirsi Bostrom (Finland)	Inverness, UK
2001	Jörgen Rostrup (Norway)	Simone Luder (Switzerland)	Tampere, Finland
2003	Thomas Bührer (Switzerland)	Simone Luder (Switzerland)	Rapperswil/Jona, Switzerland
2004	Bjørnar Valstad (Norway)	Karolina Höjsgaard (Sweden)	Västerås, Sweden

PADDLEBALL

Origins

Modern paddleball is basically two games: one-wall paddleball and four-wall paddleball. Legend has it that the one-wall version of the game was invented in the 1850s by Irish immigrants, who used a wooden paddle to hit a ball against a wall. The Irish game had begun as a version of handball, but the inclement New York weather encouraged players to adopt paddles. Earl Riskey, a physical education instructor from the University of Michigan, USA, devised the second version of the game in 1930. He used indoor racquetball courts to give a four-wall version of the game that could also be played during cold winters.

Rules and description

Both forms of the game can be played by either two or four players and to modified handball rules. The object is to win the rally by serving or returning the ball so the opponent is unable to return the ball to the front wall before it touches the floor twice. Points are only scored by the serving player or side. Once exclusively wooden, paddles are nowadays being developed in the newer materials of graphite and titanium.

One-wall paddleball:
The ball used is similar to a squash ball and the paddle is 18in/46cm in length and 8¼in/21cm wide. Players can elect to play for the best of 11, 15, 21 or 25 points.

Four-wall paddleball:
Each game is scored to 21 points. A match is the best of three games. The dimensions of the court are generally 20 x 40ft/6 x 12m. The ball is smaller than a tennis ball with a maximum bounce of 42in/1m.

Ruling body: National Paddleball Association (NPA)

Great balls of fire

While the game was still evolving, tennis balls were considered, but they proved too heavy for the short-handled bats. The spongy rubber ball that was used in paddle tennis proved to be too slow. Earl Riskey experimented: his novel approach, according to rumour, was to soak tennis balls in petrol, which removed the fuzzy layer and left the balls considerably lighter while still retaining their bounce. A potential danger to players, the idea did not last long.

PADDLE TENNIS

Origins

Paddle tennis dates from the end of the 19th century, when an American named Frank P Beal created a new form of lawn tennis as a way of teaching young children the game. When Beal moved to New York in the 1920s he took the game with him, and in 1923 the US Paddle Tennis Association was formed. The rules were revised in 1959 by Murray Geller, who introduced, among other rule changes, enlarged courts.

Rules and description

Paddle tennis is today played by both children and adults, on smaller courts than lawn tennis. The dimensions are generally 50 x 20ft/15.25 x 6m. Both doubles and singles matches are played. Players aim to win the best of three sets.

Originally the ball was spongy and made from rubber, but nowadays players use a deadened tennis ball (deflated using a hypodermic needle, which means that its bounce is restricted to between 31 and 33in/79 and 84cm). The racket is in fact a wooden paddle measuring no more than 17½in/44cm long and 8½in/21.5cm wide with a short handle. Usually, the surface of the paddle is perforated. The net is 31in/79cm high.

In most respects the rules of the game are as for lawn tennis, but unlike that game the serves are made underarm, with only one serve rather than two. The scoring follows the sequence 'love', 15, 30, 40. The sport remains largely concentrated in New York and in the tennis states of California and Florida, USA.

Ruling body: US Paddle Tennis Association

Althea Gibson

American player Althea Gibson won a series of Grand Slam lawn tennis titles in the 1950s. She was regarded as a role model for future generations of black tennis players, especially for sisters Venus and Serena Williams at the turn of the 21st century. She began her interest in sport by playing paddle tennis in New York's streets and playgrounds, and won several national titles.

PARACHUTING

See also **Skydiving**

Origins

The French aeronaut Jean Pierre Blanchard reportedly dropped a dog attached to a parachute from a balloon in 1785, possibly the first deliberate parachutist! During

World War II, armies used paratroopers to convey troops beyond enemy lines, and after the war these same military parachutes were utilized to provide the basic equipment of the sport.

Rules and description

A parachute is a large, fabric, umbrella-shaped canopy that provides resistance to the air and therefore slows down the speed at which a falling object travels. The parachutist carries the parachute in a pack on his or her back; the parachute is activated once the jumper leaves the aircraft. In this way the parachutist has a relatively gentle and slow drift to the ground. Strictly speaking, skydiving and free-falling are disciplines where the parachutist does not immediately open the parachute and literally falls towards earth before pulling the ripcord, the device for opening the parachute.

Modern parachutes are made from nylon or silk and consist of around 25 panels, or 'gores'. A canopy is typically 7–8m in diameter. A parachutist dives, jumps or steps from the plane and pulls the ripcord after an interval of about three seconds. This interval enables the parachutist to fall far enough to ensure that the parachute will be clear of the plane when it opens because of the way the parachute momentarily pulls the parachutist upwards. Once the parachute has opened, jumpers descend at a rate of about 5.2m per second. In competition parachuting the classic disciplines are style, and accuracy landing where jumpers attempt to hit the centre of a target laid out below. Style is judged by referees on the ground.

Ruling body: Fédération Aéronautique Internationale (FAI)

World Championships

The first World Parachuting Championships were held in Yugoslavia in 1951.

Accuracy landing

	Men	Women	Venue
1990	Branco Mirt (Yugoslavia)	Alla Vinogradova (USSR)	Bled, Yugoslavia
1992	Jindrich Vedmoch (Czechoslovakia)	Ortai Nuntarom (Thailand)	Trieben, Austria
1994	Alessandro Ruggeri (Italy)	Sheng Jun (China)	Chengdu, China
1996	Paolo Filippini (Italy)	Denise Bär (Germany)	Békéscsaba, Hungary
1998	Paolo Filippini (Italy)	Tatiana Ossipova (Russia)	Vrsar, Croatia
2000	Borut Erjavec (Slovenia)	Monika Filipowska (Poland)	Ise-Shima, Japan
2001	Sergei Vertiprakhov (Russia) (Czech Republic)	Katerina Papeziková	Granada, Spain
2003	Roman Karun (Slovenia)	Lyudmila Zintchenko (Russia)	Gap, France
2004	Damir Sladetic (Croatia)	Wang Keqing (China)	Rijeka, Croatia
	Men's team	**Women's team**	
1990	France	Czechoslovakia	

	Men's team	Women's team
1992	Czechoslovakia	Germany
1994	Italy	China
1996	Czech Republic	China
1998	Italy	China
2000	Germany	Russia
2001	Slovenia	China
2003	Slovenia	China
2004	Italy	Russia

Overall style and accuracy

	Men	Women
1990	Sergei Rasomasov (USSR)	Denise Bär (East Germany)
1992	Josef Pavlata (Czechoslovakia)	Nadezhda Kotova (Russia)
1994	Jan Wantula (Czech Republic)	Cheryl Stearns (USA)
1996	Eric Lauer (France)	Tatiana Ossipova (Russia)
1998	Philippe Valois (France)	Tatiana Ossipova (Russia)
2000	Marco Pflüger (Germany)	Irena Avbelj (Slovenia)
2001	Philippe Valois (France)	Irena Avbelj (Slovenia)/ Marika Kraav (Russia)
2003	Philippe Valois (France)	Lyudmila Zintchenko (Russia)
2004	Philippe Valois (France)	Irena Avbelj (Slovenia)
	Men's Team	**Women's Team**
1992	Czechoslovakia	Germany
1994	Russia	China
1996	Czech Republic	Russia
1998	France	Russia
2000	France	Russia
2001	Russia	Russia
2003	Russia	Russia
2004	Russia	Russia

PARAGLIDING

Origins

Parachutes were first used regularly in World War I as a means of escape from observation balloons. Paragliding as a sport emerged later in the 1960s following the development of steerable square (as opposed to mushroom-shaped) parachutes or canopies.

Rules and description

A paraglider can be described as a flexible wing, rather than a form of parachute, as the pilot is able to use forward momentum to inflate an aerofoil that generates lift. Pilots use thermals to keep their craft airborne and the correct weather conditions are vital. The sport is also often referred to as cross-country gliding. Pilots carry the glider in a backpack and wear boots, helmet, flight suit and harness. Paragliding, as well as being a recreational sport, sees pilots engaging in competitions that include acrobatics, distance contests and accuracy events where the challenge is to land as close to a target as possible.

Tow launching using an engine-driven winch allows paragliders to take off where there is no access to high ground. Parascending flyers use vehicles to tow them to heights before descending on a pre-determined spot. Paragliders are also launched over water, towed by motor boats.

Ruling bodies: The British Hang Gliding and Paragliding Association (BHPA); Fédération Aéronautique Internationale (FAI)

World Paragliding Championship

The championships were inaugurated in 1989.

	Men	Women	Venue
1989	*	Lucy McSwinney (Great Britain)	Kössen, Austria
1991	Robert Whittal (Great Britain)	Andrea Amann (Austria)	Dignes-les-Bains, France
1993	Hans Bollinger (Switzerland)	Camilla Perner (Austria)	Verbier, Switzerland
1995	Stefan Stieglair (Austria)	Judy Leden (Great Britain)	Kitakyushu, Japan
1997	John Pendry (Great Britain)	*	Castejon de Sos, Spain
1999	Christian Heinrich (Austria)	Louise Crandal (Denmark)	Bramberg-Neukirchen, Austria
2001	Luca Donini (Italy)	Louise Crandal (Denmark)	Granada, Spain
2003	Alex Hofer (Switzerland)	Petra Krausova (Czech Republic)	Montalegre, Portugal

*Event not concluded because of poor weather conditions

PARALYMPIC GAMES

Origins

The modern Paralympic Games can trace their origins to Stoke Mandeville Hospital in Aylesbury, Buckinghamshire, UK, a centre with a worldwide reputation for treating patients with spinal injuries. In the 1940s an eminent neurologist, Dr Ludwig Guttman (1899–1980), pioneered the use of sports as a means of rehabilitation for injured World War II servicemen. In 1948 (the same year as the London Olympic Games) he organized a set of games that were known as the International Wheelchair Games. Wheelchair competitors took part in a number of disciplines. Four years later, Dutch ex-servicemen travelled to the games. By 1960 the Paralympic Games (from 'Parallel Olympics') had become associated with the Olympic Games; in 1976 the first Paralympic Winter Games attracted 250 athletes from 14 countries; and since 1988 the Paralympic Winter and Summer Games have been hosted by the same city as for the Olympic Games.

Rules and description

The Paralympics are a series of sporting events for people with physical and learning disabilities. The first Summer Games were held in 1952, solely for competitors from the UK and the Netherlands. Since 1960 they have been held every four years; the Winter Games were first held in 1976, then once every four years until 1992, after which time they were held once every four years from 1994, to coincide with the Winter Olympic Games.

Athletes are graded according to the severity of their disabilities to ensure that they compete fairly against other athletes with a similar degree of disability. So, for example, in athletics events classes T11–13 are for track athletes with different degrees of visual impairment (who run with a 'guide runner'), whereas T31–8 covers track athletes with cerebral palsy. Originally, wheelchair users were the only competitors but in 1976 the visually impaired, amputees and those of mixed disabilities (classed as 'les autres') were admitted and the wider classification as outlined was introduced. Many of the sports are recognizable from the Olympic Games but others are held uniquely at the Paralympics, such as boccia (a bowling game) for athletes with cerebral palsy who compete from a wheelchair, and goalball for visually impaired athletes. Other sports have modified rules: for example, wheelchair rugby and wheelchair football.

Ruling bodies: International Paralympic Committee (IPC)

Paralympic Venues

Since 1988 (Summer Paralympic Games) and 1992 (Winter Paralympic Games) the Paralympics have taken place at the same venue as the Olympic Games; this will become obligatory for Olympic host cities from 2012 onwards.

Paralympic Summer Games

1952 Stoke Mandeville, UK
1960 Rome, Italy
1964 Tokyo, Japan
1968 Tel Aviv, Israel
1972 Heidelberg, West Germany
1976 Toronto, Canada
1980 Arnhem, The Netherlands
1984 Stoke Mandeville, UK and New York, USA
1988 Seoul, South Korea
1992 Barcelona, Spain
1996 Atlanta, USA
2000 Sydney, Australia
2004 Athens, Greece
2008 Beijing, China

Deaflympics

Deaf athletes are not usually involved in the Paralympic Games. Instead, the International Committee of Sports for the Deaf (CISS) holds World Games for the Deaf (known as Deaflympics). More than 2,400 athletes from 71 countries took part in the Deaflympic Summer Games in 2001.

Numbers game

Wheelchair basketball is one of the most popular Paralympic sports, but there is one significant difference from the able-bodied game. Players are classified according to their disability and given a grading (1.0, 1.5, 2.0, 2.5, 3.0, 3.5, 4.0 and 4.5) – the higher the number, the less the impairment. At any time the points score of the five players on the court must not add up to more than 14, so coaches have to do some quick mental arithmetic when making substitutions.

Paralympic Winter Games

1976 Örnsköldsvik, Sweden
1980 Geilo, Norway
1984 Innsbruck, Austria
1988 Innsbruck, Austria
1992 Albertville, France
1994* Lillehammer, Norway
1998 Nagano, Japan
2002 Salt Lake City, USA
2006 Turin, Italy
2010 Vancouver, Canada

* In 1994 the Paralympic Winter Games celebrations were readjusted to take place every four years between the Paralympic Summer Games years.

Leading Medal Winners

Totals are for the years 1984–2004.

Paralympic Summer Games

	Gold	Silver	Bronze	Total
USA	408	374	403	1,185
Great Britain	319	335	321	975
Germany	293	315	299	907
Canada	255	210	222	687
France	235	235	217	687
Australia	225	229	220	674
Spain	171	140	164	475
Sweden	153	130	86	369
The Netherlands	129	119	104	352
Poland	115	129	101	345

Paralympic Winter Games

	Gold	Silver	Bronze	Total
Germany	89	80	78	247
Austria	92	76	76	244
Norway	102	74	62	238
USA	85	91	61	237

Paralympic Games

	Gold	Silver	Bronze	Total
Switzerland	35	53	47	135
Finland	54	31	39	124
France	36	39	37	112
Russia[1]	39	39	27	105
Canada	19	30	33	82
Sweden	13	22	22	57

[1] Includes medals won by the former USSR team, and by the Unified Team (Armenia, Azerbaijan, Belarus, Georgia, Kazakhstan, Kyrgyzstan, Moldova, Russia, Tajikistan, Turkmenistan, Ukraine and Uzbekistan) in 1992.

Data source: International Paralympic Committee.

Summer Paralympic Sports

Archery
Athletics
Boccia
Cycling
Equestrian
Football
Goalball
Judo
Powerlifting
Sailing
Shooting
Swimming
Table tennis
Volleyball
Wheelchair basketball
Wheelchair fencing
Wheelchair rugby
Wheelchair tennis

Winter Paralympic sports

Alpine skiing
Biathlon
Cross-country
Sledge hockey
Wheelchair curling

The Special Olympics

The Special Olympics are motivational games for people with mental and developmental difficulties. They were first held in Chicago, USA, in 1968. They were inspired by the day camps organized by Eunice Kennedy Shriver (sister of President John F Kennedy and mother-in-law of Arnold Schwarzenegger) in the early 1960s. More than 6,500 competitors took part in the 2003 Special Olympics held in Dublin.

Some famous Paralympians

Dame Tanni Grey-Thompson, 1969–

Born in Cardiff, Wales, she was a wheelchair user from the age of eight and emerged as a promising athlete while still at school. After the 2004 Paralympics she has now amassed eleven gold medals from five Games, including four at Sydney in 2000 (in the 100m, 200m, 400m and 800m). Her other triumphs have included six wins in the London marathon and many British and world records. She has received both the MBE (1993) and the OBE (2000) in recognition of her achievements and was made a Dame in 2005.

Simon Jackson, 1972–

Born in Rochdale, England, he is a visually impaired judo player. His first Paralympics were in Seoul, South Korea, in 1988 and he won a gold medal. He repeated the feat at the next two Games before being defeated at Sydney and having to settle for a bronze medal on that occasion. It was his first loss in 163 fights – a run stretching over twelve years. In 2004 he was eliminated on a controversial refereeing decision and finished medalless for the first time. He has received an MBE.

Nathalie du Toit, 1984–

Born in Cape Town, South Africa, she was a promising young swimmer and competed at the Commonwealth Games in 1998. At 17 she lost her left leg at the knee after a scooter accident but continued to compete, winning gold medals in the 50m and 100m freestyle multi-disability events and making the final of the 800m able-bodied event at the 2002 Commonwealth Games. She holds world records as a disabled freestyle swimmer and took five gold and one silver at the 2004 Paralympics in Athens. In 2002 she was awarded the South African Sportswoman of the Year award.

PELOTA

Origins

The game of pelota is derived from the medieval French handball game called 'jeu de paume'. Its direct origins are from a game called 'longue paume' (long palm or long glove) that used a glove or racket. Over time, pelota developed and what was essentially an outdoor game moved indoors to enclosed courts. The game became most popular in the Basque country of Spain and France but also spread, in time, to Latin America and Florida in the USA.

Rules and description

Pelota (also known as pilota in Basque, pelote in French, and pallone in Italian) describes a number of related court games in which players hurl a ball against a marked wall using, variously, their hands, a glove, racket, bat or basket depending on the variant of the game. There are two ways of playing: direct play ('jeu direct' in French, 'juego directo' in Spanish), where two players face each other; and indirect play ('jeu indirect' in French, 'juego indirecto' in Spanish), where players face a wall and play off that. There are two direct-play games: 'rebot' (or 'rebote') and 'pasaka'. The former is a five-a-side game where the players use a 'cesta' or 'chistera' (a slim basket attached to the hand) to throw and catch the ball; one side leads by defending the wall before they swap over. 'Pasaka' is a doubles game, played on a covered court with galleries (similar to real tennis). Players use bare hands or gloves.

The list of indirect-play games includes 'pelota pala', 'grand chistera' and 'cesta punta' (pointed basket). Pelota pala is a two-a-side game played with a long wooden bat and a leather handgrip. Grand chistera uses chisteras on a 'place libre' (French) or 'plaza libre' (Spanish) (outdoor court). Cesta punta is also known as 'jai alai', the major alternative name for pelota. Jai alai ('merry festival' in the Basque language) is played as singles and doubles with players alternately bouncing a small, hard ball against one, two or three walls and catching it upon its return. The ball or 'pelota' is caught and propelled at high speeds in the scoop-shaped wicker basket – the cesta. Singles matches are usually played to 30 points and doubles to 40 points. Gambling is heavily associated with the sport and 'quiniela' and 'perfecta' are types of bet where gamblers need to pick the winners and runners-up.

Pelota balls come in various shapes and sizes but are generally of hard construction with a goatskin cover. In jai alai the ball is about 5cm in diameter. The dress code is important to pelota players. The regulation uniform consists of white trousers and coloured shirts, generally red or blue, bearing a number. Players also wear helmets for protection, although traditionally in the Basque country dark-blue berets were worn.

Ruling bodies: Federación Internacional de Pelota Vasca (FIPV); Fédération Française de Pelote Basque (FFPB)

The inventors of the cesta

In 1857, Gantchiki Dithurbide, a 14-year-old boy, improvised a glove by using an oblong, shallow, curved basket that had been used for fruit and vegetables and so invented the cesta. Alberto Alcorta Tellechea, a Basque priest, added some improvements, namely an attached glove which meant that the cesta could be worn rather than held in the hand.

A-Z

casco — a helmet. Frontcourt players wear yellow helmets and backcourt players wear red helmets

cesta — the wicker-woven basket used to propel the ball. It is made from reeds woven over a chestnut frame. They are custom-made but are usually about 60cm long. A leather glove is attached for the player's hand

chistera — same as **cesta**

cinta — the string that ties the **cesta** to the player's hand

delantero — a frontcourt player

faja — a fringed red sash worn as part of the standard uniform

frontis — the front wall of a court

frontón — 1. a two- or three-walled court of variable dimensions 2. the wall against which the game of pelota is played

jai alai — a form of pelota. In the Basque language jai alai means 'merry festival'

main nue — a form of pelota played with the bare hand

pasaka — a form of pelota played in pairs on covered courts

pelotari — a pelota player

perfecta — a wager on **jai alai** where the first two players or teams must finish in the order chosen

place libre a single-walled, open, outdoor court of variable dimensions

quiniela a wager that requires the gambler to pick the two players or teams that finish first and second in any order

rebote 1. a form of pelota with five players per side and in which a **cesta** is used 2. the back wall of a court

trinquet a small covered court

zaguero a backcourt player

Pelota at the Olympics

Only two teams competed at the 1900 Olympic Games in Paris: one from France and one from Spain. The Spanish pair of Villota/Amezola defeated the French team of Durguetty/Etchegaray. Pelota reappeared as a demonstration sport in 1924 (Paris), 1968 (Mexico City) and 1992 (Barcelona).

POLO

Origins

Polo is an ancient Asian sport dating back several thousand years, possibly first developed as training for the cavalry of nomadic warriors. It was first recorded in Persia in 500 BC and it is known that Alexander the Great was a keen player. Genghis Khan also encouraged his Mongol warriors to take up the sport. The British Army started playing polo in the mid 19th century, learning it from tribesmen in the north-eastern Indian state of Manipur. The locals called the game Kangjai but the British preferred polo (derived from Tibetan 'pulu' meaning willow, from which the balls were originally made). The first official game in Britain was played between the 10th Hussars and the 9th Lancers on Hounslow Heath in 1869, and the Hurlingham Club (still responsible for governing the game in Britain, Ireland and the Commonwealth) was founded in 1875.

Rules and description

A team game played on horseback on a grass field 300 x 160yd. Each team has four team members and the game is officiated by two umpires on horseback (one in each half of the field) and a 'third man' seated on the sideline who adjudicates when the umpires are in disagreement. The object of the game is to score goals by using a mallet to propel a small hard ball between the opponent's goalposts. Goalposts are at either end of the field and are set 8yd apart. The game is divided into six seven-and-a-half minute periods known as 'chukkers'. Play starts at the beginning of each chukker and after each goal with a 'throw-in' at the centre of the field by one of the umpires.

Ruling bodies: Federation of International Polo (FIP); the Hurlingham Polo Association is the governing body for the sport in the UK, Ireland, and a number of Commonwealth countries

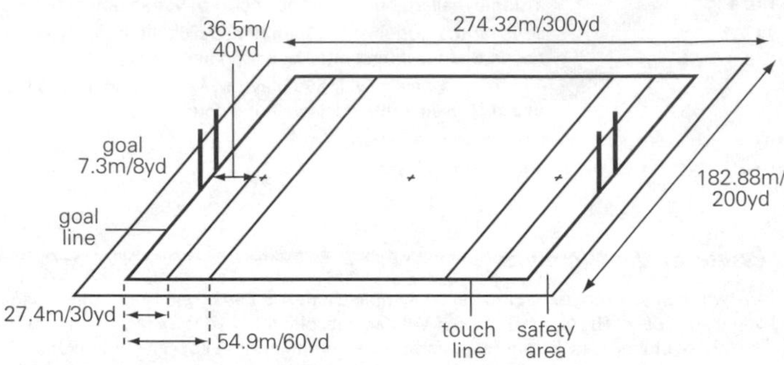

World Cup

The game's premier international tournament, organized by the FIP, is played usually every three years.

	Winner	Runner-up	Score	Host country
1987	Argentina	Mexico	14–14*	Argentina
1989	USA	England	7–6	Germany
1992	Argentina	Chile	12–7	Chile
1995	Brazil	Argentina	11–10	France
1998	Brazil	Argentina	13–8	USA
2001	Brazil	Australia	10–9	Australia
2004	Brazil	England	10–9	France

*Argentina won, as they secured more victories against other nations than Mexico

Elephant polo

Polo is also played on rather less agile animals – elephants. The World Elephant Polo Association has held a world championship since 1982. The 2004 winners of the competition held in Meghauly, Nepal, were, surprisingly, Scotland (a country not known for its elephants) who beat the Nepalese National Parks team in the final. The game has similar rules to horse polo, except that only two ten-minute chukkers are played, the elephants are 'driven' by a mahout who sits in front of the player, and the pitch is smaller. Two of the most serious fouls are if the elephant sits down in front of goal, and if it picks the ball up with its trunk.

A-Z

back line one of two lines at each end of the field beyond which the ball is out of play

back shot a shot played in the opposite direction to the flow of play

bowl-in same as **throw-in**

chukker one of the six seven-and-a-half minute periods into which a game of polo is divided

flagman an official who signals a goal by waving a flag over his head, or under the waist if a shot does not pass over the line and between the posts

forehand the hitting of the ball forwards or sideways to a team-mate

handicap a value assigned to each player in a polo team based on previous performances. The combined values for each team in a game are taken into account and the team with the highest handicap value has to concede points, based on the handicap difference between the two teams, to their opponents before the match has started. Unlike in golf, the higher the handicap the better the player

hook the catching of an opponent's mallet, below the level of the horse's back, in mid-shot or pass

knock in if the defending team knocks the ball in, they put the ball back into play from their own **back line**

made pony an experienced polo pony

mallet a long stick with a bamboo shaft and a hammer-shaped head with which the players propel the ball

nearside the left-hand side of the horse

neck shot the hitting of the ball under the horse's neck

offside the right-hand side of the horse

penalty a free hit awarded for a foul. Penalties are numbered from 1 to 10 according to the severity of the foul committed

pony goal a goal resulting from the ball contacting a pony

sideboards the short boards along the sidelines of the field which help keep the ball in play

stick same as **mallet**

tail shot the hitting of the ball behind and under the pony's rump

third man an official who sits on the sidelines and who makes final decisions when the two mounted **umpires** are in disagreement

throw-in the start or resumption of a match in which an **umpire** rolls the ball down the centre of a line-up of players

umpire one of two mounted referees, one on each side of the field

wraps the protective bandages worn on the ponies' legs

POOL

Origins

Although a table-and-ball game called 'life pool' was played in England in the early 19th century (a multi-player betting game involving coloured balls), the game of pool that we know today was derived from billiards in the USA in the 1840s. Its first manifestation was as 15-ball pool with balls numbered 1 to 15. 'Eight-ball pool' was invented around the turn of the 19th century, 'straight pool' in 1910, and 'nine-ball pool' in the 1920s, all in the USA.

Rules and description

There are three common modern games that go under the name of pool. All are games played with a cue and balls on a baize-covered table smaller than that used for snooker, and with pockets (hence the alternative name 'pocket billiards').

Nine-ball pool is played with nine differently-coloured object balls numbered 1 to 9 (racked in a diamond formation with the number-9 ball in the centre and the number-1 ball at the top), and a 'cue ball'. Each shot must always hit the lowest numbered ball on the table first and then pocket a ball, but the balls need not be pocketed in order. A player remains at the table until he or she misses, commits a foul, or wins the game by legally pocketing the 9-ball.

Eight-ball pool is played with 15 object balls, numbered 1 to 15, and a cue ball. Balls numbered 1 to 7 are differently-coloured solid colours (or 'spots'), 9 to 15 have differently-coloured stripes, and 8 is solid black. Players must pocket only one group; the first to do so, and then legally pocket the 8-ball, wins the game.

'Straight pool' is a version of the eight-ball game in which any object ball can be pocketed in any order, a point being scored for each pocketed ball. If 14 of the 15 balls have been potted, the balls are reracked and the break continues.

Ruling bodies: World Pool-Billiard Association (WPA), Women's Professional Billiard Association (WPBA)

I'll wager you didn't know that ...

The game of pool gets its name from the collective bet of that name that used to be placed on games. Each player would put in a sum and the winner would scoop the 'pool'. Somewhat confusingly, 'pool rooms' are also named after this type of bet as in the 19th century they were places for betting on horse races. Billiards (and then pool) tables were installed to give punters something to occupy their time between races, even though playing pool was not the primary aim of the establishment.

WPA World 9-ball Championship

First held in 1990.

Men

	Champion	Defeated finalist	Venue
1990	Earl Strickland (USA)	Jeff Carter (USA)	Bergheim, Germany
1991	Earl Strickland (USA)	Nick Varner (USA)	Las Vegas, USA
1992	Johnny Archer (USA	Bob Hunter (USA)	Taipei, Taiwan
1993	Chao Fong-Pang (Taiwan)	Thomas Hasch (Germany)	Königswinter, Germany
1994	Takeshi Okumura (Japan)	Itsuzaki Yasunati (Japan)	Arlington Heights, USA
1995	Oliver Ortmann (Germany)	Dallas West (USA)	Taipei, Taiwan
1996	Ralf Souquet (Germany)	Tom Storm (Sweden)	Borlange, Sweden
1997	Johnny Archer (USA)	Lee Kun-Fang (Taiwan)	Arlington Heights, USA
1998	Kunihiko Takahashi (Japan)	Johnny Archer (USA)	Taipei, Taiwan
1999	Nick Varner (USA)	Jeremy Jones (USA)	Alicante, Spain
1999	Efren Reyes (Philippines)	Chang Hao-Ping (Taiwan)	Cardiff, Wales
2000	Chao Fong-Pang (Taiwan)	Ismael Paez (Mexico)	Cardiff, Wales
2001	Mika Immonen (Finland)	Ralf Souquet (Germany)	Cardiff, Wales

	Champion	Defeated finalist	Venue
2002	Earl Strickland (USA)	Francisco Bustamante (Philippines)	Cardiff, Wales
2003	Thorsten Hohmann (Germany)	Alex Pagulayan (Canada)	Cardiff, Wales
2004	Alex Pagulayan (Canada)	Chang Pei-Wei (Taiwan)	Taipei, Taiwan

Women

	Champion	Defeated finalist	Venue
1990	Robin Bell (USA)	Loree Jon Jones (USA)	Bergheim, Germany
1991	Robin Bell (USA)		Las Vegas, USA
1992	Franziska Stark (Germany)	Vivian Villarreal (USA)	Taipei, Taiwan
1993	Loree Jon Jones (USA)	Jeanette Lee (USA)	Königswinter, Germany
1994	Ewa Mataya Laurance (USA)	Jeanette Lee (USA)	Arlington Heights, USA
1995	Gerda Hofstätter (Austria)	Vivian Villarreal (USA)	Taipei, Taiwan
1996	Allison Fisher (Great Britain)	Helena Thornfeldt (Sweden)	Borlange, Sweden
1997	Allison Fisher (Great Britain)	Chen Chun-Chen (Taiwan)	Arlington Heights, USA
1998	Allison Fisher (Great Britain)	Franziska Stark (Germany)	Taipei, Taiwan
1999	Liu Hsin-Mei (Taiwan)	Allison Fisher (Great Britain)	Alicante, Spain
2000	Julie Kelly (Ireland)	Karen Corr (Northern Ireland)	Quebec, Canada
2001	Allison Fisher (Great Britain)	Karen Corr (Northern Ireland)	Amagasaki, Japan
2002	Liu Hsin-Mei (Taiwan)	Karen Corr (Northern Ireland)	Kao Hsiung, Taiwan
2003	*Not held*		
2004	Kim Ga Young (South Korea)	Liu Hsin-Mei (Taiwan)	Rankveil, Austria

The pool table on platform 7 ...

Commuters rushing through the ornate splendour of New York's Grand Central Station may well have been surprised to find that a major pool tournament was taking place. The inaugural competition of the World Summit of Pool in 2003, and the 2004 event, were held there in Vanderbilt Hall.

WPA World 8-ball Championship

First held in 2004.

	Champion	Defeated finalist	Venue
2004	Efren Reyes (Philippines)	Marlon Manalo (Philippines)	Fujairah, UAE

Minnesota Fats

Minnesota Fats (1913–96), whose real name was Rudolph Wanderone, Jr (he took his name from *The Hustler*), was famous for his large personality as much as his large frame. He said of his pool career, 'When I played pool I was like a good psychiatrist. I cured 'em of all their daydreams and delusions'.

Nicknames

Johnny Archer	'The Scorpion'
Francisco Bustamente	'Django' (from his resemblance to Franco Nero, who played the character Django in 1960s westerns)
Marcus Chamat	'Napoleon' (because of his short stature)
Karen Corr	'The Irish Invader'
Allison Fisher	'The Duchess of Doom'
Thorsten Hohmann	'The Hitman'
Ewa Mataya Laurance	'The Striking Viking' (because of her good looks and because she was born in Sweden)
Jeanette Lee	'Black Widow' (because of her habit of wearing black clothes and her black hair)
Alex Pagulayan	'The Lion'
Efren Reyes	'The Magician'
Ralf Souquet	'The Kaiser'
Earl Strickland	'The Pearl'
Nick Varner	'Kentucky Colonel'

A-Z

bank	a US term for **double**
break	the first shot of a game
break cue	a cue with a hard tip that is used specifically for **breaking**
check side	see **side**
combination	a shot that hits more than one ball and pockets the last one hit
cue	a long tapered wooden shaft with a leather tip, used to propel the **cue ball**
cue ball	the white ball struck by the cue and used to propel the **object ball**
cushion	the padded lining of the inner side of a pool table
diamonds	diamond-shaped inlays on the top surfaces of **cushions** (three between each pocket) that are used as reference points when playing **doubles**
double	a shot in which the **object ball** is played off a cushion back towards the player
English	a US term for **side**
foot spot	in 9-ball pool, the spot on the surface of the table on which the number-1 ball (and in 8-ball pool the ball at the apex of the **rack**) is positioned at the beginning of a game
head string	a line one-quarter of the length of the table from the top, from behind which a player must play when breaking
jump cue	a cue used for making the **cue ball** jump
kick shot	a shot in which the **cue ball** bounces off one or more **cushions** before hitting the **object ball**
lag for break	a way of deciding who has **break** in the first game by both players hitting the **cue ball** off the bottom **cushion** and back towards the head of the table. The player whose ball finishes nearest to the head cushion wins the right to break
object ball	the ball that the player intends to strike with the **cue ball**
open table	a situation in 8-ball pool in which a player can hit either **solid** or **stripe**
power break	a **break** shot hit with a lot of force

push out — a shot allowed after the **break** in 9-ball pool where a player can hit the **cue ball** anywhere on the table (it does not need to hit a ball) and the opponent can either take the next shot from where it finishes or ask the first player to play again

rack — the arrangement of the balls (in a diamond or triangle shape) at the beginning of the game

rail — same as **cushion**

running side — see **side**

side — side spin imparted by the cue causing the cue ball to swerve and altering its angle of rebound; **check side** causes the cue ball to rebound off a cushion at less of an angle than a normally struck shot, while **running side** causes the cue ball to rebound off a cushion at more of an angle

solid — a coloured ball with a number in a small white circle on it

spot — 1. same as **solid** 2. same as **diamond**

stripe — a ball with a broad coloured stripe and a number on it

wing balls — the two balls adjacent to the 9-ball (towards the side **cushions**) in a 9-ball **rack**

Some pool slang

kitchen — the area behind the **head string**

on the hill — a player is on the hill if he or she has one more game to win for victory

POWERBOAT RACING

Origins

Powerboat racing became possible as a sport with the invention of the internal combustion engine at the end of the 19th century. The first recorded race was held in 1888. The leading promoter of powerboat racing was the British newspaper magnate Sir Alfred Harmsworth (later Lord Northcliffe). In 1903 he presented the Harmsworth Cup, a team trophy for boats under 40ft/12m powered by any means. In the following year the Gold Cup Race, the premier US competition, was first organized. Early races were held in England's inland waters but the desire to head for offshore waters was soon satisfied.

Rules and description

Powerboat racing is the sport of navigating a motor-powered vessel on water. The craft may have inboard or outboard engines. The sport takes two basic forms: circuit racing and offshore racing. Races are held on inland stretches of water such as lakes and rivers on courses marked by buoys. The offshore version of powerboat racing is generally for higher-powered craft. International competition calls for a driver and a throttleman. Famous classic offshore races include the Miami–Nassau, Cowes–Torquay–Cowes Classic, and Viareggio–Bastia–Viareggio.

There are also speed tests, held on straight courses over a measured mile (or similar distance), where a craft makes an outward and inward pass and the average speed is taken. Endurance competition includes challenges such as the Round Britain race and the fastest transatlantic crossing.

Ruling bodies: Royal Yachting Association; Union Internationale Motonautique; American Powerboat Association (APBA)

Powerboating at the Olympics

Motorboating was an Olympic event for the one and only time at the London Games in 1908. Held at Southampton Water, two of the classes were won by the British vessel *Gyrinus II*, piloted by Thomas Thornycroft. He took along Bernard Redwood and Captain John Field-Richards who, hearsay has it, came in useful for bailing out the craft.

Class 1 World Powerboat Championships

The premier competition in world offshore powerboating. The champion receives the Sam Griffith trophy, named after a driver who dominated the early days of the sport, winning four Miami–Nassau races, before his death in 1963. In the table below the driver is given first and then the throttle man.

1966 Jim Wynne (USA)
1967 Don Aronow & Knocky House (both USA)
1968 Vincenzo Balestrieri (Italy) & J Stuteville (USA)
1969 Don Aronow & Knocky House (both USA)
1970 Vincenzo Balestrieri (Italy) & J Stuteville (USA)
1971 Bill Wishnick & Bobby Moore (both USA)
1972 Bobby Rautbord & Bobby Moore (both USA)
1973 Carlo Bonomi (Italy) & R Powers (USA)
1974 Carlo Bonomi (Italy) & R Powers (USA)
1975 Wally Franz (Brazil) & Bobby Moore (USA)
1976 Tom Gentry (USA) & R Powers (USA)
1977 Betty Cook (USA) & John Connor (USA)
1978 Francesco Cosentino & A Diridoni (both Italy)
1979 Betty Cook (USA) & John Connor (USA)
1980 Michel Meynard & Bob Idoni (both USA)
1981 Jerry Jacoby & K Hazell (both USA)
1982 Renato della Valle (Italy) & Gianfranco Rossi (Monaco)
1983 Tony Garcia & K Hazell (both USA)
1984 Alberto Petri & F Statua (both Italy)
1985 Anthony Roberts (USA) & Steve Curtis (Great Britain)
1986 Antonio Gioffredi & J Di Meglio (both Italy)
1987 Steve Curtis (Great Britain) & W Falcon (USA)
1988 Fabio Buzzi & Romeo Ferraris (both Italy)
1989 Stefano Casiraghi (Monaco) & Romeo Ferraris (Italy)
1990 *Not awarded**
1991 Angelo Spelta & M Ambrogetti (Italy)

Big money

Powerboating is a very expensive sport and many of the competitors are successful businessmen. Class 1 offshore world champion in 1998, 2002, 2003 and 2004 Bjorn Gjelsten is no exception. He has also dipped his toe into British football by owning Wimbledon FC during a traumatic period of the club's history.

1992 Walter Ragazzi (Italy) & Jukka Mattila (Finland)
1993 Khalfan Harib (UAE) & Ed Colyer (USA)
1994 Norberto Ferretti (Italy) & Luca Ferrari (Italy)
1995 Saeed al Tayer (UAE) & Felix Serrales (Puerto Rico)
1996 Saeed al Tayer (UAE) & Felix Serrales (Puerto Rico)
1997 Laith Pharaon (Saudi Arabia) & John Tomlinson (USA)
1998 Bjorn Gjelsten (Norway) & Steve Curtis (Great Britain)
1999 Ali Nasser (UAE) & Randy Scism (USA)
2000 Khalfan Harib (UAE) & Ali Nasser (UAE)
2001 Saeed al Tayer (UAE) & Mohammed al Marri (UAE)
2002 Bjorn Gjelsten (Norway) & Steve Curtis (Great Britain)
2003 Bjorn Gjelsten (Norway) & Steve Curtis (Great Britain)
2004 Bjorn Gjelsten (Norway) & Steve Curtis (Great Britain)

* The 1990 Class 1 World Championship was not awarded as a mark of respect after the death of Stefano Casiraghi, the winner the previous year, in an accident. Casiraghi was the husband of Princess Caroline of Monaco.

RACKETS

Origins

Rackets (also spelt racquets) had a highly unusual start: it was played between inmates at the Fleet and the King's Bench debtors' prisons in London, who hit balls against the prison walls. Gentlemen debtors received concessions and were allowed to take their real tennis rackets in with them. Competitions were also held on courts attached to local London public houses. By the 1820s the game had been adopted mainly by public schools in England and shortly afterwards was taken up by Oxford and Cambridge universities. Rackets has also proved popular in the USA.

Rules and description

Rackets is a racquet-and-ball game for two or four players. The racket is similar to a squash racket but longer and more slender; the ball is white and hard. A standard court measures 18 x 9m/60 x 30ft; there are front and side walls that are 18m/30ft high and a back wall around 4.5m/15ft high. The serve must hit the front wall above the service line and must then land in the opposite backcourt before a rally can commence. To win a game players generally need to score 15 points (or 'aces') but if the score reaches 13 all, then the player that lost the last point can elect to set the game to 15, 16 or 18 points. Singles matches are the best of five games and doubles the best of seven.

Ruling body: The Tennis and Rackets Association

World Rackets Championship

The first world champion, Robert Mackay, was an inmate of Fleet prison. Normally the championship changes hands when the defending champion accepts and loses a challenge from a contender. All the winners have been British except where indicated.

1820	Robert Mackay
1825–34	Thomas Pittman
1834–8	John Pittman
1838–40	John Lamb
1840–6	*Vacant*
1846–60	L C Mitchell
1860	Francis Erwood
1862–3	Sir William Hart-Dyke
1863–6	Henry Gray
1866–75	William Gray
1876–8	H B Fairs
1878–87	Joseph Gray
1887–1902	Peter Latham
1903–11	J Jamsetji (India)
1911–13	Charles Williams
1913–28	Jock Soutar (USA)
1929–35	Charles Williams
1937–47	David Milford
1947–54	James Dear
1954–71	Geoffrey Atkins
1972–3	William Surtees (USA)
1973–4	Howard Angus
1975–81	William Surtees (USA)
1981–4	John Prenn
1984–6	William Boone
1986–8	John Prenn
1988–99	James Male
1999–2001	Neil Smith
2001–	James Male

RACQUETBALL

Origins

Racquetball was developed by American Joe Sobek in 1949 on a handball court at the Greenwich YMCA in Connecticut, USA. He blended elements of both handball and squash into a fast-paced racquet-and-ball game that he originally termed 'paddle rackets'.

Rules and description

Racquetball is played on an enclosed, indoor court. The racquet resembles a tennis racquet but is shorter and lighter. The ball is hollow and made from rubber. The rules follow closely those of handball, played on courts that measure 12.2 x 6.1m/40 x 20ft, but the ball can be played off the ceiling. Matches are for singles and doubles. The first player or side to 15 points wins the game; the first to two games wins the match. A tie-breaking game, played to eleven points, is introduced at one game all.

Ruling body: International Racquetball Federation (IRF)

World Racquetball Championships

	Men	Women	Venue
1981	Ed Andrews (USA)	Cindy Baxter (USA)	Santa Clara, USA
1984	Ross Harvey (Canada)	Mary Dee (USA)	Sacramento, USA
1986	Egan Inoue (USA)	Cindy Baxter (USA)	Orlando, USA
1988	Andy Roberts (USA)	Heather Stupp (Canada)	Hamburg, Germany
1990	Egan Inoue (USA)	Heather Stupp (Canada)	Caracas, Venezuela
1992	Chris Cole (USA)	Michelle Gould (USA)	Montreal, Canada
1994	Sherman Greenfeld (Canada)	Michelle Gould (USA)	San Luis Potosi, Mexico
1996	Todd O'Neil (USA)	Michelle Gould (USA)	Phoenix, USA
1998	Sherman Greenfeld (Canada)	Christie Van Hees (Canada)	Cochabamba, Bolivia
2000	Alvaro Beltran (Mexico)	Cheryl Gudinas (USA)	San Luis Potosi, Mexico
2002	Jack Huczek (USA)	Cheryl Gudinas (USA)	San Juan, Puerto Rico
2004	Jack Huczek (USA)	Cheryl Gudinas (USA)	Anyang, South Korea

	Men's doubles	Women's doubles
1981	Mark Malowitz & Jeff Kwartler (USA)	Mary Ann Cluess & Karen Borga (USA)
1984	Stan Wright & Steve Trent (USA)	Carol French & Malia Kamahoahoa (USA)
1986	Jack Nolan & Todd O'Neil (USA)	Carol McFetridge & Marion Sicotte (Canada)
1988	Doug Ganim & Dan Obremski (USA)	Diane Green & Trina Rasmussen (USA)
1990	Doug Ganim & Dan Obremski (USA)	Malia Bailey & Jackie Paraiso (USA)
1992	Doug Ganim & Eric Muller (USA)	Malia Bailey & Robin Levine (USA)
1994	John Ellis & Eric Muller (USA)	Laura Fenton & Jackie Paraiso (USA)
1996	Adam Karp & Bill Sell (USA)	Joy MacKenzie & Jackie Paraiso (USA)
1998	Adam Karp & Bill Sell (USA)	Joy MacKenzie & Jackie Paraiso (USA)
2000	Luis Bustillos & Javier Moreno (Mexico)	Kersten Hallander & Kim Russell (USA)
2002	Polo Gutierrez & Gilberto Mejia (Mexico)	Jackie Paraiso Rice & Kim Russell (USA)
2004	Shane Vanderson & Mike Dennison (USA)	Jackie Paraiso Rice & Kim Russell (USA)

British racketball

The British game of racketball (sic) was invented in 1976 by Ian Wright. It is played on a smaller court than its American relative – a standard squash court – and with a slower and less bouncy ball.

RALLY DRIVING

Origins

See **Motor Racing**.

Most early car races were tests of endurance as much as speed and a useful method of testing the latest technical improvements and innovations. The Monte Carlo Rally, first held in 1911 at the instigation of Prince Albert, was one of the first such races.

Rules and description

Racing specially adapted cars over testing conditions, with terrain varying from gravel to tarmac to snow. Most rallies last several days and consist of a number of timed sections or 'stages', the accumulated time for the stages being used to determine the winner.

Ruling body: Fédération Internationale de l'Automobile (FIA)

Co-drivers

The co-driver performs an unglamorous but essential role in a rally team and his relationship with the driver is similar to that of the professional golfer and his caddy. The driver relies on him to carry out a lot of the organizational and administrative work, including handling mundane tasks such as arranging insurance and the competition licence. Famous partnerships include the Welsh/Scottish pairing of Nicky Grist and Colin McRae, and the Spanish duo Luis Moya and Carlos Sainz who were together for 14 years until they split in 2002.

World Rally Championship (WRC)

First held in 1979; now comprises a series of races in 16 different countries over a variety of terrains, between January and November.

	Driver	Car	Manufacturer's championship
1979	Bjorn Waldegard (Sweden)	Ford	Ford
1980	Walter Rohrl (West Germany)	Fiat	Fiat
1981	Ari Vatanen (Finland)	Ford	Talbot
1982	Walter Rohrl (West Germany)	Opel	Audi
1983	Hannu Mikkola (Finland)	Audi	Lancia
1984	Stig Blomqvist (Sweden)	Audi	Audi
1985	Timo Salonen (Finland)	Peugeot	Peugeot
1986	Juha Kankkunen (Finland)	Peugeot	Peugeot
1987	Juha Kankkunen (Finland)	Lancia	Lancia
1988	Miki Biasion (Italy)	Lancia	Lancia
1989	Miki Biasion (Italy)	Lancia	Lancia
1990	Carlos Sainz (Spain)	Toyota	Lancia
1991	Juha Kankkunen (Finland)	Lancia	Lancia
1992	Carlos Sainz (Spain)	Toyota	Lancia
1993	Juha Kankkunen (Finland)	Toyota	Toyota
1994	Didier Auriol (France)	Toyota	Toyota
1995	Colin McRae (Great Britain)	Subaru	Subaru
1996	Tommi Mäkinen (Finland)	Mitsubishi	Subaru
1997	Tommi Mäkinen (Finland)	Mitsubishi	Subaru
1998	Tommi Mäkinen (Finland)	Mitsubishi	Mitsubishi
1999	Tommi Mäkinen (Finland)	Mitsubishi	Toyota
2000	Marcus Gronholm (Finland)	Peugeot	Peugeot
2001	Richard Burns (Great Britain)	Subaru	Peugeot
2002	Marcus Gronholm (Finland)	Peugeot	Peugeot
2003	Petter Solberg (Norway)	Subaru	Citroen
2004	Sebastien Loeb (France)	Citroen	Citroen

The Dakar Rally

Founded in 1979 by Thierry Sabine after he was lost in the Sahara Desert when participating in another rally. Usually around 7,000 miles long, routes have varied. Originally starting in Paris, France, in recent years it has begun in other parts of France and even in Spain, although it does still usually end in Dakar, Senegal. Motorcycles and trucks also compete in separate races.

	Winners	**Car**
1979	Genestier & Lemordant (both France)	Range Rover
1980	Freddy Kottulinsky (Sweden) & Gerd Löffleman (West Germany)	Volkswagen
1981	René Metge & Bernard Giroux (both France)	Range Rover
1982	Bernard Marreau & Claude Marreau (both France)	Renault
1983	Jacky Ickx & Claude Brasseur (both Belgium)	Mercedes
1984	René Metge & Dominique Lemoine (both France)	Porsche
1985	Patrick Zanirola & Jean Da Silva (both France)	Mitsubishi
1986	René Metge & Dominique Lemoine (both France)	Porsche
1987	Ari Vatanen (Finland) & Bernard Giroux (France)	Peugeot
1988	Juha Kankkunen & Juha Piironen (both Finland)	Peugeot
1989	Ari Vatanen (Finland) & Bruno Berglund (Sweden)	Peugeot
1990	Ari Vatanen (Finland) & Bruno Berglund (Sweden)	Peugeot
1991	Ari Vatanen (Finland) & Bruno Berglund (Sweden)	Citroen
1992	Hubert Auriol & Philippe Monnet (both France)	Mitsubishi
1993	Bruno Saby & Dominique Serieys (both France)	Mitsubishi
1994	Pierre Lartigue & Michel Perin (both France)	Citroen
1995	Pierre Lartigue & Michel Perin (both France)	Citroen
1996	Pierre Lartigue & Michel Perin (both France)	Citroen
1997	Kenjiro Shinozuka (Japan) & Henri Magne (Andorra)	Mitsubishi
1998	Jean-Pierre Fontenay & Gilles Picard (both France)	Mitsubishi
1999	Jean-Louis Schlesser (France) & Henri Magne (Andorra)	Renault
2000	Jean-Louis Schlesser (France) & Henri Magne (Andorra)	Renault
2001	Jutta Kleinschmidt & Andreas Schulz (both Germany)	Mitsubishi
2002	Hiroshi Masuoka (Japan) & Pascal Maimon (France)	Mitsubishi
2003	Hiroshi Masuoka (Japan) & Andreas Schulz (Germany)	Mitsubishi
2004	Stéphane Peterhansel & Jean-Pierre Cottret (both France)	Mitsubishi

Flying Finns

Scandinavians have dominated modern rally driving and the Finns have shown themselves to be particularly adept, having won the championship no fewer than 13 times. In the late 1960s, a film was made of the 1968 Rally of 1000 Lakes in Finland called *The Flying Finns*. It featured the rivalry between veteran driver Timo Mäkinen in a Mini Cooper and newcomer Hannu Mikola in a Ford Escort. Since then, the nickname has been widely used for any fast Finnish rally driver. Flying Finn was also the name of a short-lived (2002–4) low-cost Finnish airline which included rally driver Juha Kankkunen as one of its shareholders.

A-Z

co-driver	the navigator whose job is to read the **pace notes**
flying finish	the end of a stage when the car crosses the finish line at speed
pace notes	notes used by the **co-driver** to alert the driver to bends and hazards ahead and instruct him on the recommended speed
parc fermé	a cordoned-off area into which cars are driven after each day's rallying; teams are unable to carry out any servicing
recce	inspection of the course by the driver and co-driver in advance of the rally in order to draw up the **pace notes**
road book	a book of instructions, timings, directions and maps for the whole rally issued to each crew by the rally organizers
scrutineering	the inspection of cars by rally officials to ensure that technical regulations have not been broken
service park	the area where a crew has 20 minutes to make any running repairs to a car
shakedown	the day before the rally starts, when teams can test their cars on roads similar to those used in the rally
special stage	one of the timed competitive sections of the rally, over closed public or private roads
super special stage	a short stage with two parallel tracks, allowing pairs of rally cars to race against each other without actually being on the same road
time control	location where cars must stop in order to have their time recorded by rally officials
yump	when a car leaves the ground after a crest in the road

Some famous rally drivers

Juha Kankkunen, 1959–

Born on the family farm in Laukaa, Finland, he took part in his first rally in 1978 and then, the following year, made a spectacular entrance onto the WRC scene by winning his first championship rally (the Safari Rally). He won 23 of his 162 WRC races and took the title four times (twice with Lancia and once each with Peugeot and Toyota), an achievement equalled only by **Tomi Mäkinen**.

Colin McRae, 1968–

Born in Lanark, Scotland, he started his motorsport career early, winning the Scottish schoolboy motocross and trials championships when just 13. He made his rally debut in 1986 and soon earned the nickname 'The Flying Scotsman'. Driving for Subaru (1991–8) and subsequently (from 1999) for Ford, he won the British Rally Championship in 1991, 1992 and 1998 and the World Rally Championship in 1995, becoming the youngest driver ever to win the title. He won 25 of 143 WRC rallies in his career. Since retirement from the WRC in 2003, he has competed in endurance races and the Paris–Dakar rally. He was awarded the MBE in 1996.

Tommi Mäkinen, 1964–

Born in Puuppola, Finland, he started his motorsport career racing tractors (he won the Finnish national ploughing title in 1982 and 1985). He took up rallying in 1985 and was almost unbeatable in the late 1990s, winning a record-equalling four WRC titles in successive years between 1996 and 1999, all driving a Mitsubishi. He has 24 WRC victories to his name, including four Monte Carlo rallies.

Hannu Mikkola, 1942-

Born in Joensuu on the eastern borders of Finland, he launched himself and the Ford Escort to popular status when he won a hat-trick of rallies in 1970: the 16,000-mile London–Mexico rally, the Arctic and the 1,000 Lakes. His immense versatility was proved through a career of 19 wins (1970–94) in cars that included Ford, Mercedes and Audi, and in rallies as varied as the Safari (winner 1972) to the Lombard RAC rally, which Mikkola has won four times. He won the title only once, however, in 1983.

Carlos Sainz, 1962-

Born in Madrid, Spain, he abandoned his law studies to dedicate himself to rallying, making his debut in 1980. He made his first WRC appearance in 1987 with Ford, and won the championship in 1990 in a Toyota, repeating the feat two years later. He has also been runner-up four times, and third four times, in a long and consistent career (he retired in 2004) in which he has raced (and won) more WRC rallies than any other driver.

REAL TENNIS

Origins

Also known as 'royal tennis', the name is probably a corruption of the Spanish for royal: 'real'. It is regarded as the predecessor of most racket-and-ball games. First played by the French as jeu de paume in monastery cloisters, it was soon being played by English and Scottish royalty and was favoured by Henry VIII, who built a court at Hampton Court Palace. Real tennis is also popular in Australia, and the USA, where it is known as 'court tennis'.

Rules and description

Real tennis is a racquet-and-ball game played between either two or four players. The racquets are pear-shaped with an upward curved head; the balls are solid and cloth-covered. There is no standard size of court and measurements are approximate, courts being about 110 x 39ft/33.5m x 11.8m. The court is split into two halves separated by a net: the 'service' side and the 'hazard' side. The design of the court retains the look of monastery cloisters. There are 'penthouses' running along one long wall and the two shorter sides of the court. They resemble sheds with sloping roofs. Other obstacles on the court include a 'tambour' obstruction on one side and galleries, doors and other openings built into the penthouses. Unlike in lawn tennis, the net is higher at the sides (5ft/1.5m) than at the centre (3ft/1m). Players serve and receive, hitting the ball against the walls and penthouses to gain an advantage.

The scoring generally resembles lawn tennis, following the love, 15, 30, 40, deuce system. The first to six games wins the set; matches can be best of three or five sets. The special feature of the game is the 'chase', a system of setting points in abeyance. If the ball enters a gallery a chase is made; if a ball drops twice a chase is also laid, its quality depending on where on the court it drops. When two chases are made, or if there is one chase and game point is reached, players change ends and the chases are then 'played off' to achieve a winning point.

Ruling body: The Tennis and Racquets Association

Real Tennis World Championship (Men)

The competition is believed to date from 1740 when a Monsieur Clerge of France won the first title. The title changes hands when a challenger beats the defending champion.

1740	Monsieur Clerge (France)
1765	Raymond Masson (France)
1785	Joseph Barcellon (France)
1816	Marchesio (Italy)
1819	Philip Cox (Great Britain)
1829	Edmond Barre (France)
1862	Edmund Tomkins (Great Britain)
1871	George Lambert (Great Britain)
1885	Tom Pettitt (USA)
1890	Charles Saunders (Great Britain)
1895	Peter Latham (Great Britain)
1905	Cecil Fairs (Great Britain)
1907	Peter Latham (Great Britain)
1908	Cecil Fairs (Great Britain)
1912	Fred Covey (Great Britain)
1914	Jay Gould (USA)
1916	Fred Covey (Great Britain)
1928	Pierre Etchebaster (France)
1955	James Dear (Great Britain)
1957	Albert Johnson (Great Britain)
1959	Northrup Knox (USA)
1969	Pete Bostwick (USA)
1972	Jimmy Bostwick (USA)
1976	Howard Angus (Great Britain)
1981	Chris Ronaldson (Great Britain)
1987	Wayne Davies (Australia)
1994	Robert Fahey (Australia)

Original sport of kings

The real tennis court at Falkland Palace in Fife, Scotland, was built in 1539 for James V of Scotland and is believed to be the world's oldest court still in use today. Reputedly, both French kings Louis X and Charles VIII died while playing the game.

A-Z

chase a point which is held in abeyance. It is made when a ball enters a **gallery** (except the **winning gallery**) or falls on the floor (bounces a second time). Lines measured in yards and marked

	on the court floor indicate the quality of the chase. The nearer the ball drops to the end wall the better the chase. The opponent needs to make a better chase to win the point
dead ball	a ball is dead after a point is won or lost
dedans	an opening in the short wall behind the server; a shot played into this wins a point. Spectators generally view the action through the dedans
drop ball	a ball is said to drop when, after passing the net, it bounces for the first time on the floor
fault line	the line parallel to the **main wall** in the **hazard** end. With the **service line**, which meets it at right angles, it delineates the area into which a server must get the ball to drop
galleries	a series of small openings in the side **penthouse**. Shots into the galleries count as **chases**. On the service side of the net the sequence is: first gallery, door, second gallery, last gallery; on the **hazard** side, hazard the first gallery, hazard the door, hazard the second gallery and the **winning gallery**
grille	a 3ft/1m square window in the short wall above the **tambour**. The opening is covered by a net. A shot played into the grille wins a point
hazard	the half of the court into which the ball is served
main wall	the long wall with no **penthouse**
marker	the umpire
pass line	same as **fault line**
penthouse	a roofed corridor that runs along one long wall and the two shorter ends of the court. They are around 7ft 6in/2.28m deep and slope from 10ft 7in/3.22m to around 7ft/2.1m.
play line	the line positioned around the court at 18ft/5.48m high and above which the ball must not be hit
rest	a series of strokes concluding with the **dead ball**
service line	a line about 21ft/6.4m from the **grille** wall
tambour	a feature that buttresses into the court at the **hazard** end and narrows the court to around 30ft 2in/9.19m
winning gallery	the **gallery** furthest away from the net at the **hazard** end of the court; a shot played into this wins a point
winning openings	the **dedans**, the **grille** and the **winning gallery**

ROLLER HOCKEY

Origins

The invention of roller skates is usually attributed to Joseph Merlin of Huy, Belgium, in 1760. The basic design was improved upon by the American inventor Joseph Plympton in 1863 and by the early 20th century organized stick-and-ball games on skates were being devised.

Rules and descriptions

Originally called rink hockey, and also known as 'hardball' or traditional hockey, it uses a short hockey stick and a hard ball (rather than the puck used in ice hockey).

The game is played on a rink and the object of the game is to score more goals than the opposition. Each team has five members, including a goalkeeper. Inline hockey, played on inline skates, was introduced in the 1990s.

Ruling body: Fédération Internationale de Roller Sports (FIRS)

World Hardball Championships

Men's competition first held in Stuttgart, Germany, in 1936 when England won. Women's championship first held in 1992.

	Men	Venue
1991	Portugal	Porto, Portugal
1993	Portugal	Lodi Bassano, Italy
1995	Argentina	Recife, Brazil
1997	Italy	Wuppertal, Germany
1999	Argentina	Réus, Spain
2001	Spain	San Juan, Argentina
2003	Portugal	Oliveira de Azeméis, Portugal

	Women	Venue
1992	Canada	Springe, Germany
1994	Spain	Algarve, Portugal
1996	Spain	Sertãozinho, Brazil
1998	Argentina	Buenos Aires, Argentina
2000	Spain	Marl, Germany
2002	Argentina	Paços de Ferreira, Portugal
2004	Argentina	Wuppertal, Germany

Inline Hockey World Championships

First held for men in 1995 and women in 2002.

	Men	Women	Venue
2002	Sweden	Canada	Rochester, USA
2003	USA	USA	Pisek, Czech Republic
2004	USA	Canada	London, Canada

ROLLER SKATING

Origins

See **Roller hockey**

Rules and description

Roller skating has three major forms: roller speed skating, roller figure skating and roller dancing. The first world speed skating events took place in 1937. Roller figure skating is modelled on figure skating on ice. Rollerblading, also known as inline speed skating, is a recent offshoot of roller skating where the wheels are arranged in a single line rather than being in a rectangular arrangement.

Ruling body: Fédération Internationale de Roller Sports (FIRS)

World Figure Skating Championships

First held in 1947.

Men's combined

1970–2	Michael Obrecht (West Germany)
1973	Randy Dayney (USA)
1974	Michael Obrecht (West Germany)
1975	Leonardo Lienhard (Switzerland)
1990	Samo Kokorovec (Italy)
1991–2	Sandro Guerra (Italy)
1993	Samo Kokorovec (Italy)
1994	Lee Taylor (Great Britain)
1995	Jason Sutcliffe (Australia)
1996	Francesco Cerisola (Italy)
1997	Mauro Mazzoni (Italy)
1998	Daniele Tofani (Italy)
1999–2000	Adrian Stoltzenberg (Germany)
2001	Leonardo Pancani (Italy)
2002	Frank Albiez (Germany)
2003–4	Luca D'Alisera (Italy)

Women's combined

1988–92	Rafaella Del Vinaccio (Italy)
1993–5	Letizia Tinghi (Italy)
1996	Giusy Locane (Italy)
1997	Sabrina Tomassini (Italy)
1998	Elke Dederichs (Germany)
1999–2001	Elisa Facciotti (Italy)
2002–4	Tanja Romano (Italy)

ROUNDERS

Origins

Thought to have been played in England since Tudor times, the bat-and-ball game called rounders is mentioned in publisher John Newbery's *A Little Pretty Pocketbook* (1744), where it is termed 'Base-ball'. *The Boy's Own Book* (1828) devoted a chapter to rounders. The first rounders association was formed in 1889 – the Liverpool and Scottish Rounders Association.

Rules and description

Rounders is an outdoors bat-and-ball game that is generally played by children and young adults of both sexes and is therefore played mostly in schools. Although international interest has been shown in the sport, its main centre of activity is in the British Isles. Each side has nine players and two innings, and attempts to score more rounders than the opposition. The field is set out in a diamond formation similar to baseball, with posts to mark the four 'bases'. The bowler bowls three balls underarm at each batter. If the bowler bowls an illegal ball ('no ball'), the batter advances to the first post. When a batter hits the ball out of the reach of the fielders and manages to run around all four bases non-stop a 'rounder' is scored. A lesser hit allows the batter to reach first, second or third base before the opposition retrieves the ball. The aim of the opposition is to get the batters out by running the player out before he or she reaches any of the four bases (by touching the base with the ball before the batter has made his or her ground) and by catching the ball.

A 'half-rounder' is scored if the batter completes the circuit without hitting the ball (ie following a 'no ball'), or if second post is reached after hitting the ball. A batter cannot overtake another nor may there be two of them at the same post.

The wooden or aluminium bats have a maximum length of 46cm/18in and a maximum weight of 370g/13oz.

Ruling body: National Rounders Association (NRA)

The mother game

Unhappily for Americans, it has been proved that the children's game of rounders is the precursor of baseball and not the other way around. The name originally coined for it was baseball, and 'rounders' appears not to have made an appearance until the 1850s. While rounders has remained a game played almost exclusively in the British Isles it has found its way abroad in other guises, most notably in the Finnish game pesäpello.

ROWING

Origins

Ancient Greek and Roman literature refers to races between oared galleys. In its modern form, competitive rowing dates from 1715 when Thomas Doggett, an Irish comedian and actor, instituted a race for Thames watermen. It subsequently became known as Doggett's Coat and Badge and is the oldest rowing contest in the world. The first known regatta was held on the River Thames at Putney in 1775.

Doggett's Coat and Badge

In the early 18th century there were more than 10,000 watermen licensed to work on the Thames above London Bridge, ferrying passengers between the northern and southern sides of the city before the grand era of bridge-building began. Doggett instituted the race for Thames watermen in 1715 to commemorate the anniversary of George I's accession to the throne. The Doggett's Coat is a scarlet uniform of full-skirted coat and knee-breeches and the badge a huge silver adornment worn above the left elbow.

Rules and description

Rowing is the propulsion of a boat through water using oars. Rowers face backwards to the direction of the moving boat. The stroke begins with the placing of the oar in the water and ends when the oar has re-emerged and is poised to begin another cycle. The stroke comprises four elements: the 'catch', 'drive', 'finish' and 'recovery'. The vessel is sometimes steered by a non-rowing crew member called the 'coxswain' or 'cox'. Competitions are held over river courses (such as the River Thames) or on lakes (such as Lake Lucerne). International and Olympic races are rowed over a standard course of 2,000m; women row over 1,000m. The water course is generally inshore and divided into six lanes; each boat must stay within its designated lane.

There are numerous classes of rowing. The 'eights' are rowed by eight oarsmen or oarswomen, steered by a cox. There are two types of 'fours': one version is coxed and the other is coxless. In the coxless boat, the steering is done by one of the oarsmen, generally the bowman, using steering lines or rudder lines attached to his shoes. The 'pairs', for two rowers, are also both coxed and coxless.

In 'sculling' the scullers have two oars each, rather than just the one oar used by rowers. The individual event is the single sculls; there are also double sculls and quadruple sculls. In women's quadruple sculls there is a cox.

In addition, there are competitions for lightweight crews (generally rowers weighing less than 70kg/154lb), who weigh less than their heavier counterparts and are therefore handicapped in terms of the power they can generate.

All international rowing competitions start with qualifying heats. The fastest qualifiers go into the semi-finals and the losers have a second chance to qualify via a 'repechage' round. The top repechage finishers also advance to the semi-final. Finals are contested by six crews. Often there is a B final for those that finish in seventh to twelfth places.

Ruling body: FISA (Fédération Internationale des Sociétés d'Aviron)

University Boat Race of 1912

In the history of the University Boat Race there have been only six sinkings. In 1912 both the Cambridge and the Oxford boat sank; Oxford won the re-rowed race two days later. By a strange coincidence only two weeks after that the magnificent 'unsinkable' luxury ocean-going liner the *Titanic* also sank, after colliding with an iceberg.

University Boat Race

An annual contest between the crews from Oxford and Cambridge universities. It was first contested in 1829; not held in some years in the early history of the race and held twice in 1849 (March and December). The current course runs from Putney to Mortlake.

1829	Oxford	**1909–13**	Oxford
1836	Cambridge	**1914**	Cambridge
1839–41	Cambridge	**1915–19**	*Not held*
1842	Oxford	**1920–2**	Cambridge
1845–6	Cambridge	**1923**	Oxford
1849	Cambridge	**1924–36**	Cambridge
1849	Oxford	**1937–8**	Oxford
1852	Oxford	**1939**	Cambridge
1854	Oxford	**1940–5**	*Not held*
1856	Cambridge	**1946**	Oxford
1857	Oxford	**1947–51**	Cambridge
1858	Cambridge	**1952**	Oxford
1859	Oxford	**1953**	Cambridge
1860	Cambridge	**1954**	Oxford
1861–9	Oxford	**1955–8**	Cambridge
1870–4	Cambridge	**1959–60**	Oxford
1875	Oxford	**1961–2**	Cambridge
1876	Cambridge	**1963**	Oxford
1877	*Dead heat*	**1964**	Cambridge
1878	Oxford	**1965–7**	Oxford
1879	Cambridge	**1968–73**	Cambridge
1880–3	Oxford	**1974**	Oxford
1884	Cambridge	**1975**	Cambridge
1885	Oxford	**1976–85**	Oxford
1886–9	Cambridge	**1986**	Cambridge
1890–8	Oxford	**1987–92**	Oxford
1899–1900	Cambridge	**1993–9**	Cambridge
1901	Oxford	**2000**	Oxford
1902–4	Cambridge	**2001**	Cambridge
1905	Oxford	**2002–3**	Oxford
1906–8	Cambridge	**2004**	Cambridge

Easy as child's play

Dr Benjamin Spock (1903–98), author of *The Common Sense Book of Baby and Child Care* (1946), the tome that transformed the attitudes of the postwar generation to parenthood, was also an Olympic rower. He won a gold medal in the USA eight in the 1924 Olympic Games.

The Oxford and Cambridge Bumps

The 'bumps', rowed at the universities of Oxford and Cambridge, is a form of rowing where competing boats start simultaneously but at fixed distances apart. The aim is to 'bump' the boat in front (that is to touch or overtake it) before being 'bumped' by the boat behind. Once bumped, the crew has to drop out. Racing takes place over four days. Unlucky crews that get 'bumped' on all four days are awarded a wooden spoon or are said to be 'getting spoons'.

Olympic Games

Rowing has been held at the Olympic Games since 1900. Women's events were introduced in 1976.

Men's single sculls

1900	Hermann Barrelet (France)
1904	Frank Greer (USA)
1908	Harry Blackstaffe (Great Britain)
1912	William Kinnear (Great Britain)
1920	John Kelly, Sr (USA)
1924	Jack Beresford, Jr (Great Britain)
1928	Henry Pearce (Australia)
1932	Henry Pearce (Australia)
1936	Gustav Schäfer (Germany)
1948	Mervyn Wood (Australia)
1952	Yuri Tyukalov (USSR)
1956	Vyacheslav Ivanov (USSR)
1960	Vyacheslav Ivanov (USSR)
1964	Vyacheslav Ivanov (USSR)
1968	Henri Jan Wienese (The Netherlands)
1972	Yuri Malishev (USSR)
1976	Pertti Karppinen (Finland)
1980	Pertti Karppinen (Finland)
1984	Pertti Karppinen (Finland)
1988	Thomas Lange (East Germany)
1992	Thomas Lange (Germany)
1996	Xeno Müller (Switzerland)
2000	Rob Waddell (New Zealand)
2004	Olaf Tufte (Norway)

Women's single sculls

1976	Christine Scheiblich (East Germany)
1980	Sanda Toma (Romania)
1984	Valeria Račilă (Romania)
1988	Jutta Behrendt (East Germany)
1992	Elisabeta Lipă (Romania)
1996	Yekaterina Khodotovich (Belarus)
2000	Yekaterina Karsten (née Khodotovich) (Belarus)
2004	Katrin Rutschow-Stromporowski (Germany)

Men's Eight

1900	USA
1904	USA
1908	Great Britain
1912	Great Britain
1920	USA
1924	USA
1928	USA
1932	USA
1936	USA
1948	USA
1952	USA
1956	USA

1960	Germany	**1984**	Canada
1964	USA	**1988**	West Germany
1968	West Germany	**1992**	Canada
1972	New Zealand	**1996**	The Netherlands
1976	East Germany	**2000**	Great Britain
1980	East Germany	**2004**	USA

Women's Eight

1976	East Germany	**1992**	Canada
1980	East Germany	**1996**	Romania
1984	USA	**2000**	Romania
1988	East Germany	**2004**	Romania

Henley Royal Regatta

The Henley Royal Regatta, held each June at Henley-upon-Thames, England, dates from 1839. The Straight Course, of about 1⅓ miles, was instituted in 1924 and is still in use today. The following competitions are held:

The Grand Challenge Cup	First presented in 1839. An open event for amateur eights
The Ladies' Challenge Plate	Instituted in 1845. An event for intermediate men's eights
The Thames Challenge Cup	Instituted in 1868, the Cup is competed for by club rather than student eights
The Temple Challenge Cup	Instituted in 1990 for student eights
The Princess Elizabeth Challenge Cup	Competition for eights. Instituted in 1946 for public schools
The Remenham Challenge Cup	Founded as the The Henley Prize in 2000 for open women's eights
The Stewards' Challenge Cup	First awarded in 1841. Event open to amateur crews in four-oared boats
The Visitors' Challenge Cup	For coxed fours, the Cup is competed for by academic institutions around the world
The Wyfold Challenge Cup	For coxless fours, the Cup was instituted in 1847
The Queen Mother Challenge Cup	First awarded in 1981. Event instituted for quadruple sculls
The Men's Quadruple Sculls	For club and university crews below Queen Mother Challenge Cup standard
The Fawley Challenge Cup	Competitions for quadruple sculls, first rowed at the 1992 Henley Regatta. Crews need to be under 19 years of age
The Princess Grace Challenge Cup	Founded as the Women's Quadruple Sculls in 2001, The Princess Grace Challenge Cup was first presented in 2003 in memory of Princess Grace of Monaco
Men's Student Coxed Fours	Event open for coxed fours. Student crews only
The Britannia Challenge Cup	First presented in 1969 for coxed fours. It replaced the Henley Prize and from 2004 was restricted to club crews
The Silver Goblets & Nickalls'	The Silver Goblets was instituted in 1850 for pairs.

Challenge Cup	Tom Nickalls, father of Guy and Vivien, added the Nickalls' Cup in 1895
The Double Sculls Challenge Cup	The inaugural race was run in 1939, with the Cup being first presented in 1946
The Diamond Challenge Sculls	First presented in 1844. The blue riband event for amateur single scullers
The Princess Royal Challenge Cup	Presented to women's single scullers for the first time in 1997. The event had been rowed at Henley since 1993

A-Z

blade — the flat part of the oar or **scull** that enters the water during the rowing **stroke**

Boat Race — the annual boat race between crews from Oxford and Cambridge universities. It is held each spring on the River Thames in London between Putney and Mortlake and is also known variously as the University Boat Race and the Varsity Race

bow — 1. the front end of the boat 2. the rower who sits in the bow (also termed a bowman)

bowside — the left-hand side of the boat from the rowers' point of view. The bowman's oar is on this side; compare **strokeside**

button — a plastic or metal fitting tightened on the oar to keep it from slipping through the **rowlock**

canvas — the covered front or back of a racing boat. In a close race it is used to describe the measure of lead between two boats. If a crew 'wins by a canvas' it is a margin of victory of about 5 to 6 feet; see also **length**

catch — when the **blade** enters the water at the beginning of the rowing **stroke**

collar — same as **button**

cox — (short for coxswain); the steersman who sits opposite the **stroke** and gives instructions during a race

coxed/coxless — having/not having a cox. In coxless boats the steering is generally done by the bowman using steering lines attached to his or her shoes

coxswain — see **cox**

crew — the oarsmen or oarswomen (and cox, where appropriate) of a racing boat

double scull — a two-manned boat in which each crew member has a pair of **sculls**

drive — the action of pulling the oar through the water

easy — a command to stop rowing

eight — an eight-oared boat with eight rowers and a cox

ergometer — (usually shortened to ergo); a land-based rowing machine, used mainly for winter training and fitness testing

feathering — holding the oars so that the **blade** is parallel to the water (in order to reduce wind resistance) when they are being swung forward as the rower prepares to take a **stroke**

finish — when the **blade** is brought out of the water at the end of the **stroke**

four — a four-oared boat with four rowers

gate the U-shaped attachment at the outer end of the **rigger** that holds the oar in place at the pivot point

give way instruction given to begin rowing

gunwale, gunnel the top section on the sides of a **shell**, to which the **riggers** are secured

head races (also known as head-of-the-river races); these differ from straight races in that crews are sent off at intervals and are timed over the course

jumping the slide problem that affects rowers when the **slide seat** becomes derailed from the track

keel the structure of the bottom of the boat running along the centre from **bow** to **stern**

length the length of a boat used to judge the distance between boats. At the race's completion a boat may be said to have won by '6 lengths' or '4½ lengths', for example; see also **canvas**

loom the long section of the oar between the handle and the **blade**

missing water problem that occurs when the rower starts the **drive** before the **catch** has been completed

outrigger same as **rigger**

paddling rowing at less than full speed

pair a two-oared racing boat

pitch the angle at which the **blade** enters the water

puddle the whirlpool effect of the water after the oar comes out of the water at the end of a **stroke**

quad (or quadruple scull); a four-manned boat in which each crew member has a pair of **sculls**

rating the number of strokes rowed per minute. It is often used to advise a crew of its work rate. Generally, 32–40 strokes a minute are achieved in full race mode. Over 40 strokes means a crew is rowing flat out

recovery the rest phase in the **stroke** cycle where the rower is swinging forward to take the next **catch**

regatta an organized programme of races

repechage a supplementary heat or competition that gives crews that have been eliminated in the first heat or earlier competitions a second chance to go on to the final or semi-final. Originates from a French word meaning 'fishing out again'

rig a description of all the adjustable elements involved in fine-tuning a boat prior to racing it

rigger the adjustable device that connects the **rowlocks** to the **shell**

rowlocks U-shaped swivels that hold the oars in place. They are mounted at the end of the **rigger** and rotate around a metal pin. A **gate** closes across the top to keep the oar secure. The US term is **oarlocks**

row over if a crew or a rower rows over, they win a heat by rowing the course unopposed

scull 1. a light boat that is propelled by an oarsman or oarswoman with an oar in each hand 2. a short oar used by scullers

sculler someone who sculls

shell a racing boat, formerly made from wood but nowadays constructed from carbon fibre. Shells vary in length from 8.2m/27ft for a single scull to 19.9m/62ft for an eight

shortening up rowing too fast at too high a **rating** and not pulling the oar fully through the water

single scull a one-manned boat in which the rower has a pair of **sculls**

skeg a small fin attached to the **stern** section of the hull. It helps to stabilize the **shell** during rowing

skying a problem caused by the hands being too low during the **recovery** phase

slide seat a seat that slides backwards and forwards along a track with the swing of the rower's body

span the distance from the pin or pivot point of the **gate** to the centre line of the boat (in **sculls**, to the pin of the other gate)

stern the back end of the boat

stretcher an adjustable support for the rowers' feet, to which are attached flexible shoes

stroke 1. the rower whose stroke sets the rhythm for the rest of the rowers. The stroke sits in the **stern** of the boat facing the **cox** 2. the complete single movement of the oars in and out of the water

strokeside the right-hand side of the boat from the rowers' point of view; compare **bowside**

wash 1. the rough water left behind by a boat that can affect the progress of competing boats 2. the water disturbed by an oar

Some rowing slang

boatie a rowing enthusiast, a term used especially in university rowing circles

catch a crab if a rower catches a crab, he or she sinks the oar too deeply (or not deeply enough) into the water. The jolt can affect the progress of the boat or even stop it dead in its tracks

getting spoons a crew being overtaken in four consecutive races in the Oxford and Cambridge University rowing 'bumps' has its failure called 'getting spoons'

toss the oars a successful crew might toss the oars by raising them vertically, resting them on the handles. It is a form of winning salute

Some famous rowers

Jack Beresford, 1899–1977

Born in London, England, he competed for Great Britain at five Olympic Games (1920–36) as a sculler and an oarsman, winning three gold and two silver medals. He won the Diamond Sculls at Henley Royal Regatta four times, and was elected president of the Thames Rowing Club in 1971. He received a CBE in 1960. His father won a silver medal in the eights at the 1912 Olympics.

Guy Nickalls, 1866–1935

Born in Horton Kirby, Kent, England, he won the Diamond Sculls at Henley Royal Regatta five times and had a total of 23 wins at Henley between 1885 and 1907. When he was nearly 42 he rowed in the Leander eight which won the Olympic title at the 1908 Games. His father Tom presented the Nickalls' Challenge Cup to the Henley Regatta in 1895 to commemorate Guy's, and his brother Vivian's, successes there.

Sir Matthew Pinsent, 1970-

Born in Holt, Norfolk, England, he dominated world rowing throughout the 1990s in partnership with **Steve Redgrave**. An Oxford Blue, he also has ten world titles to his name. Pinsent has four Olympic gold medals: two with Redgrave in the coxless pairs (1992 and 1996), a third with Redgrave, Tim Foster and James Cracknell in the coxless fours (2000), and a fourth with James Cracknell, Ed Coode and Steve Williams (again in the coxless fours in 2004). He was awarded an MBE in 1993 and a CBE in 2001 and was knighted in 2005.

Sir Steve Redgrave, 1962-

Born in Marlow, Buckinghamshire, England, he became in 2000 Britain's greatest Olympian ever after winning his fifth successive gold medal at the Olympic Games. Redgrave won his first Olympic gold in 1984 in the coxed four, followed it with successive wins in 1988, 1992 and 1996 in the coxless pairs (the final two triumphs partnering **Matthew Pinsent**) and then remarkably formed part of a coxless four crew that took gold in the Sydney Games. Nine times a world champion, Redgrave was knighted in 2001.

RUGBY LEAGUE

Origins

A precise date can be given for the origins of rugby league: 28 August 1895, the day on which 21 clubs from Lancashire and Yorkshire broke away from the Rugby Football Union in a dispute over compensation for players who had to take time off work. Originally called the Northern Union, the organization renamed itself the Rugby Football League in 1921. A series of innovations was introduced to differentiate the sport from rugby union, notably reducing each side to 13 players and allowing the ball-carrier to retain possession after a tackle, and professional players were accepted. The first international rugby league game was held in 1904, when England lost to an Other Nationalities team 9–3.

Rules and description

Rugby league is played with an oval ball between two teams of 13 players. Each team may also use four substitutes, with a maximum of six interchanges of players allowed over the course of a game. The playing area has a standard length of 100m/110yd and a maximum width of 68m/74 yd, with an H-shaped goal in the centre of the line at each end (the 'goal line'). In addition, there is an area known as the 'in-goal' at each end of the pitch, extending back 6–11m/6.5–12yd from the goal line. The main playing area is divided into two equal halves, with further lines across the pitch every 10m/11yd. Games last for 80 minutes, divided into two halves, between which the teams change ends.

Upon gaining possession of the ball, a side has six attempts or 'tackles' to move the ball up the field by running, passing and kicking (forward passing is not allowed). If it fails to score in these six attempts, possession is awarded to the opposing team. The object is to score a 'try' by grounding the ball in the opposing team's in-goal area. The scoring system awards four points for a try, two points for a 'conversion' (kicking the ball between the posts and over the crossbar following a try), two points for a 'penalty' (a successful kick through the posts following an infringement by the opposition), and one point for a 'drop goal' (a successful kick through the posts from open play in which the ball bounces before being struck).

Ruling bodies: Rugby Football League (RFL) administers the game in the UK, Australian Rugby League (ARL) in Australia, and the New Zealand Rugby League (NZRL) in New Zealand

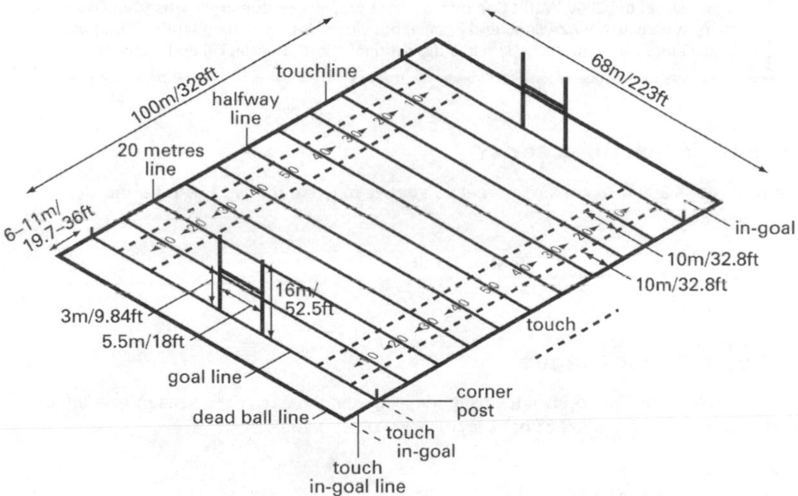

World Cup

First held in 1954 between Great Britain, France, Australia and New Zealand; played intermittently since, and now with the inclusion of other countries. In 1957, 1960 and 1975 (when it was renamed the World Championship) it was played on a league basis. The 1975 tournament stretched over eight months, whereas the winners in 1988 and 1992 lifted the trophy after rounds of games played over three years.

	Winner	Beaten finalist	Venue
1954	Great Britain	France	France
1957	Australia		Australia
1960	Great Britain		England
1968	Australia	France	Australia & New Zealand
1970	Australia	Great Britain	England
1972	Great Britain	Australia	France
1975	Australia		Worldwide
1977	Australia	Great Britain	Australia & New Zealand

Rugby League

	Winner	Beaten finalist	Venue
1988	Australia	New Zealand	Worldwide
1992	Australia	Great Britain	Worldwide
1995	Australia	England	England & Wales
2000	Australia	New Zealand	Great Britain, Northern Ireland & France
2005			Great Britain

> ***Global warming***
>
> In spite of many attempts to spread the game to other parts, passion for rugby league has seldom spread far beyond its heartlands in Northern England, New South Wales and Queensland. However, there are signs that the rest of the world is starting to warm to the game: the 2000 World Cup included not only the customary teams from Great Britain, Australia, New Zealand and France, but also sides from such far-flung outposts as Papua New Guinea (where it is the national sport), Russia, Fiji and Lebanon.

Gillette Tri-Nations series

Introduced in 2004. Triangular competition between Great Britain, Australia and New Zealand.

	Winner	Beaten finalist
2004	Australia	Great Britain

Tetley's Super League

First held in 1996. The top five teams in the league at the end of the season play off for the title; known as the JJB Super League from 1996 to 1999.

1996	St Helens
1997	Bradford Bulls
1998	Wigan Warriors
1999	St Helens
2000	St Helens
2001	Bradford Bulls
2002	St Helens
2003	Bradford Bulls
2004	Leeds Rhinos

> ***It's a jungle out there***
>
> With the introduction of the Super League in 1996, many teams took on American-style club nicknames. As a result rugby league watchers can now enjoy watching a whole menagerie of animals, including Rhinos (Leeds), Wolves (Warrington), Wildcats (Wakefield), Tigers (Castleford) and Cougars (Keighley), at some distance from their natural habitats.

Challenge Cup

Leading British cup competition. The first final to be held at Wembley Stadium was in 1929. Since 2001 finals have been played at Murrayfield (Edinburgh), Twickenham and the Millennium Stadium (Cardiff). The Lance Todd trophy (named in memory of a New Zealand-born player and administrator killed in a road accident during World War II) is awarded to the man of the match.

* = player on losing side

	Winner	Beaten finalist	Lance Todd trophy winner
1897	Batley	St Helens	
1898	Batley	Bradford	
1899	Oldham	Hunslet	
1900	Swinton	Salford	
1901	Batley	Warrington	
1902	Broughton Rangers	Salford	
1903	Halifax	Salford	
1904	Halifax	Warrington	
1905	Warrington	Hull Kingston Rovers	
1906	Bradford	Salford	
1907	Warrington	Oldham	
1908	Hunslet	Hull	
1909	Wakefield Trinity	Hull	
1910	Leeds	Hull	
1911	Broughton	Wigan	
1912	Dewsbury	Oldham	
1913	Huddersfield	Warrington	
1914	Hull	Wakefield Trinity	
1915	Huddersfield	St Helens	
1915-19	*Not held*		
1920	Huddersfield	Wigan	
1921	Leigh	Halifax	
1922	Rochdale Hornets	Hull	
1923	Leeds	Hull	
1924	Wigan	Oldham	
1925	Oldham	Hull Kingston Rovers	
1926	Swinton	Oldham	
1927	Oldham	Swinton	
1928	Swinton	Warrington	
1929	Wigan	Dewsbury	
1930	Widnes	St Helens	
1931	Halifax	York	
1932	Leeds	Swinton	
1933	Huddersfield	Warrington	
1934	Hunslet	Widnes	
1935	Castleford	Huddersfield	
1937	Widnes	Keighley	
1938	Salford	Barrow	
1939	Halifax	Salford	
1941	Leeds	Halifax	

	Winner	Beaten finalist	Lance Todd trophy winner
1942	Leeds	Halifax	
1943	Dewsbury	Leeds	
1944	Bradford Northern	Wigan	
1945	Huddersfield	Bradford Northern	
1946	Wakefield Trinity	Wigan	Billy Stott
1947	Bradford Northern	Leeds	Willie Davies
1948	Wigan	Bradford Northern	Frank Whitcombe*
1949	Bradford Northern	Halifax	Ernest Ward
1950	Warrington	Widnes	Gerry Helme
1951	Wigan	Barrow	Cec Mountford
1952	Workington Town	Featherstone Rovers	Billy Ivison
1953	Huddersfield	St Helens	Peter Ramsden
1954	Warrington	Halifax	Gerry Helme
1955	Barrow	Workington Town	Jack Grundy
1956	St Helens	Halifax	Alan Prescott
1957	Leeds	Barrow	Jeff Stevenson
1958	Wigan	Workington Town	Rees Thomas
1959	Wigan	Hull	Brian McTigue
1960	Wakefield Trinity	Hull	Tommy Harris*
1961	St Helens	Wigan	Dick Huddart
1962	Wakefield Trinity	Huddersfield	Neil Fox
1963	Wakefield Trinity	Wigan	Harold Poynton
1964	Widnes	Hull KR	Frank Collier
1965	Wigan	Hunslet	Ray Ashby/Brian Gabbitas*
1966	St Helens	Wigan	Len Killeen
1967	Featherstone Rovers	Barrow	Carl Dooler
1968	Leeds	Wakefield Trinity	Don Fox*
1969	Castleford	Salford	Malcolm Reilly
1970	Castleford	Wigan	Bill Kirkbride
1971	Leigh	Leeds	Alex Murphy
1972	St Helens	Leeds	Kel Coslett
1973	Featherstone Rovers	Bradford Northern	Steve Nash
1974	Warrington	Featherstone Rovers	Derek Whitehead
1975	Widnes	Warrington	Ray Dutton
1976	St Helens	Widnes	Geoff Pimblett
1977	Leeds	Widnes	Steve Pitchford
1978	Leeds	St Helens	George Nicholls*
1979	Widnes	Wakefield Trinity	David Topliss*
1980	Hull Kingston Rovers	Hull	Brian Lockwood
1981	Widnes	Hull Kingston Rovers	Mick Burke
1982	Hull	Widnes	Eddie Cunningham*
1983	Featherstone Rovers	Hull	David Hobbs
1984	Widnes	Wigan	Joe Lydon
1985	Wigan	Hull	Brett Kenny
1986	Castleford	Hull Kingston Rovers	Bob Beardmore
1987	Halifax	St Helens	Graham Eadie
1988	Wigan	Halifax	Andy Gregory
1989	Wigan	St Helens	Ellery Hanley
1990	Wigan	Warrington	Andy Gregory

	Winner	Beaten finalist	Lance Todd trophy winner
1991	Wigan	St Helens	Denis Betts
1992	Wigan	Castleford	Martin Offiah
1993	Wigan	Widnes	Dean Bell
1994	Wigan	Leeds	Martin Offiah
1995	Wigan	Leeds	Jason Robinson
1996	St Helens	Bradford Bulls	Robbie Paul*
1997	St Helens	Bradford Bulls	Tommy Martyn
1998	Sheffield Eagles	Wigan Warriors	Mark Aston
1999	Leeds Rhinos	London Broncos	Leroy Rivett
2000	Bradford Bulls	Leeds Rhinos	Henry Paul
2001	St Helens	Bradford Bulls	Sean Long
2002	Wigan Warriors	St Helens	Kris Radlinski
2003	Bradford Bulls	Leeds Rhinos	Gary Connolly*
2004	St Helens	Wigan Warriors	Sean Long

Poor lad

The most memorable of all Challenge Cup finals was the 1968 match, in which Wakefield Trinity scored a try in the last minute to narrow the score to 11–10 and leave Don Fox with the apparently simple task of kicking a conversion from in front of the posts to secure victory. However, the pitch was saturated, and Fox managed to miss the kick, meaning that Wakefield lost the game. Commentator Eddie Waring could only feel sympathy for the kicker, repeating the words 'Poor lad' as Fox slumped down in the Wembley mud, never to play rugby again.

Man of Steel

A prestigious award made by the Super League (previously the English Premiership) to the player or personality who has made the biggest impact on the season.

1977	David Ward (Leeds)
1978	George Nicholls (St Helens)
1979	Doug Laughton (Widnes)
1980	George Fairbairn (Wigan)
1981	Ken Kelly (Warrington)
1982	Mick Morgan (Carlisle)
1983	Allan Agar (Featherstone Rovers)
1984	Joe Lydon (Widnes)
1985	Ellery Hanley (Bradford Northern)
1986	Gavin Miller (Hull Kingston Rovers)
1987	Ellery Hanley (Wigan)
1988	Martin Offiah (Widnes)
1989	Ellery Hanley (Wigan)
1990	Shaun Edwards (Wigan)
1991	Garry Schofield (Leeds)
1992	Dean Bell (Wigan)
1993	Andy Platt (Wigan)
1994	Jonathan Davies (Warrington)
1995	Denis Betts (Wigan)
1996	Andy Farrell (Wigan Warriors)
1997	James Lowes (Bradford Bulls)
1998	Iestyn Harris (Leeds Rhinos)
1999	Adrian Vowles (Castleford Tigers)
2000	Sean Long (St Helens)
2001	Paul Sculthorpe (St Helens)
2002	Paul Sculthorpe (St Helens)
2003	Jamie Peacock (Bradford Bulls)
2004	Andy Farrell (Wigan Warriors)

State of Origin series winners

The Australian states of Queensland and New South Wales have been playing each other since 1908. The State of Origin series (in which players represent their home state) was introduced in 1980 to make games fairer as more and more players were playing for clubs in New South Wales. Usually three (but sometimes two or four) games are played, and the state teams are selected from local clubs.

1980	Queensland
1981	Queensland
1982	Queensland
1983	Queensland
1984	Queensland
1985	New South Wales
1986	New South Wales
1987	Queensland
1988	Queensland
1989	Queensland
1990	New South Wales
1991	Queensland
1992	New South Wales
1993	New South Wales
1994	New South Wales
1995	Queensland
1996	New South Wales
1997	New South Wales
1998	Queensland
1999	Drawn
2000	New South Wales
2001	Queensland
2002	Drawn
2003	New South Wales
2004	New South Wales

We'll see if it stands up

Much of rugby league's popularity outside its Northern English heartlands must be ascribed to the commentaries of Eddie Waring in the 1960s and 1970s. Faced with the problem of describing events on a wet afternoon when players became so covered in mud that it was impossible to identify them, Waring resorted to colourful terminology to entertain the viewers, coining the term 'early bath' when a player was sent off and 'up and under' for a high kick. During one particularly muddy game, with the camera focusing on an indeterminate spherical object, he uttered the memorable words, 'I don't know if that is his head or the ball. We'll see if it stands up.'

A-Z

acting halfback the player who picks up the ball immediately after a **play-the-ball**; often this is the hooker

advantage if the referee plays advantage, he allows a period of time following an infringement to determine whether the other team will be better served by the award of a **penalty**, or by allowing play to continue

back any of the seven players who do not participate in the **scrum**

blind side the side of the pitch with less space between the **scrum** or **play-the-ball** and the touchline; compare **open side**

blood bin if a player is sent to the blood bin, he leaves the pitch because he has a bleeding wound; a replacement player must be used until the wound has been attended to

centre either of the two **three-quarters** in the centre of the pitch; centres wear the number 3 and 4 shirts

charge down if a player charges down a kick, he blocks it using his hands or body

conversion the opportunity to score a further two points after a **try** by kicking the ball between the posts and over the bar; conversions are taken from the **twenty-metre line** in line with where the try was scored

dead-ball line the line at the end of the **in-goal** area

drop goal a means of scoring, worth one point, in which the ball is dropped to the floor, kicked as it bounces, and sent through the posts and over the bar

dropout a drop kick taken from between the goalposts or from the centre of the **twenty-metre line**, when restarting play

dummy to feign to pass the ball in order to distract and run past an opponent

dummy half same as **acting halfback**

feed same as **put-in** (sense 1)

field goal same as **drop goal**

five-eighth an Antipodean term for **stand-off**

40/20 rule a newly introduced rule whereby if a player kicks the ball from inside his own forty-metre line, and it goes into touch between the opposition's **twenty-metre line** and the **try line** on the bounce, then that player's side are awarded the **put-in** at the scrum

forward any of the six players who participate in the **scrum**

forward pass an illegal pass where the ball travels forward

free kick a kick taken 10m in from the touchline that restarts play following a kick into touch from a **penalty**. The ball may be kicked in any manner in any direction, but it may not be kicked for goal

front row the three powerfully built forwards, the two **props** and the **hooker**, who push (or more usually lean) directly against their opponents in a **scrum**

full back the player who normally stands furthest back on the pitch in a defensive situation; as well as being the last line of defence, he is used as an attacking runner; wears the number 1 shirt

gain line if a player or team gets beyond the gain line, they move the ball beyond an the imaginary line on which the preceding **play-the-ball** or **scrum** has taken place

goal line same as **try line**

grubber kick a ball dropped from hand and kicked along the ground

halfback either the **scrum-half** or **standoff**

handoff a legal move in which a player with the ball pushes away a tackler

handover the change in possession after the **sixth tackle**

hooker the forward who binds between the two **props** in a **scrum**; wears the number 9 shirt

in-goal the area between the **goal line** and the **dead-ball line**, in which a **try** may be scored

knock on if a player knocks the ball on, he touches or drops it forward with the hand or arm; punished by a **scrum** with opposition **put-in**

lock same as **loose forward**

loose forward the forward who binds at the back of the **scrum**, behind the two **second-row forwards**; wears the number 13 shirt

loose-head prop the **prop** on the left-hand side of a team's **front row**, whose head is not completely inside the **scrum**; the scrum-half puts the ball into the scrum through his legs

offload a very short pass made to a team-mate running past

offside players are generally expected to stay on their own side of the ball; deliberately or negligently being further forward than the rules allow is termed as offside, and is punished by a penalty

open side the side of the pitch with more space between the **scrum** or **play-the-ball** and the touchline; compare **blind side**

pack a team's forwards

penalty a punishment for foul play. If kicked for goal, a successful attempt gains two points

penalty try a **try** awarded by the referee if an incident of foul play has prevented the opposition from scoring a try

place kick a kick taken with the ball placed on the ground, ie the kick-off, a **penalty** kick or a **conversion**

play-the-ball the means of restarting play after a tackle, in which the tackled player rolls the ball back behind him with his foot

prop one of the two strongly built players who push (or more usually lean) directly against their opponents; together with the **hooker** the props form the **front row**; props wear the number 8 and 10 shirts

punt a kick in which the ball is dropped from the hands and struck before it hits the ground

put-in 1. the introduction of the ball to a **scrum** 2. the right to do so

scissors a move in which the ball is **offloaded** by a player running diagonally across the pitch to a team-mate running behind him at a different angle

scrum the formation, in three rows, of the two teams' forwards, who then push (or more usually lean) against each other, while the **scrum-half** puts the ball in between the legs of his **loose-head prop**. Following rule changes, scrums are now virtually uncontested and never won by the team not putting the ball in

scrum-half the player, often slightly built and agile, who initiates plays, puts the ball into the **scrum** and moves it away from the **pack** to the **backs**; wears the number 7 shirt

second-row forward either of the two tall, powerfully built forwards who form the second row in the **scrum**; second-row forwards wear the number 11 and 12 shirts

sidestep a sudden change of direction used to beat an opponent

sin-bin to send a player temporarily from the field of play following repeated or particularly serious foul play

sixth tackle the last tackle in the allowable set, resulting in a **handover**

standoff (half) a **back** who stands next to the **scrum-half** and links play with the centres; wears the number 6 shirt

tackle 1. stopping a player by using one's arms to bring him down. Unlike in rugby union, a tackled player may hold on to the ball 2. a successful attempt to do so, following which there is a **play-the-ball**

Test an international game between two of the major rugby league-playing nations

three-quarter one of the four **backs**, two **centres** and two **wingers**, who aim to run with the ball and prevent their opposites from doing so

touch in-goal the touchline in the **in-goal** area

try touching the ball down in the **in-goal** area; worth four points

try line the line on which the goalposts stand and over which the ball must be touched down to score a try

turnover the loss of possession of the ball

twenty-metre line a line marked across the pitch 20m from the **try line** at each end

up-and-under a very high kick, after which the kicker and his team-mates rush to catch it or tackle the catcher

video referee an official in the stands who has access to TV replays and whose opinion the referee may ask when he is unsure if a try has been legally scored

winger often the fastest players in a team, the wingers try to run with the ball at pace down the sides of the pitch; wingers wear the number 2 and 5 shirts

yellow card a card shown to a player which sends him to the **sin-bin**

zero tackle additional tackle at the beginning of the standard set of six, awarded after a **knock-on** or **forward pass**

Some famous rugby league players

Brian Bevan, 1924–91

Born in Sydney, Australia, he settled in England after World War II and played as a winger for Warrington from 1945 to 1962 and Blackpool Borough from 1962 to 1964. He belied his spindly frame and premature baldness with extreme pace and a mazy running style that enabled him to score a record 796 tries in 688 first-class matches, over 200 tries more than any other player in the game's history.

Shaun Edwards, 1966–

Born in Wigan, England, he signed for Wigan at the age of 17 for £35,000 – then the world's biggest fee paid for a schoolboy. A tenacious scrum-half, he went on to become the youngest player to appear in a Challenge Cup final and was the youngest international when he played against France at the age of 18. He played in 43 consecutive winning Challenge Cup games, as Wigan won the trophy for a record eight successive seasons (1988–95).

Andy Farrell, 1975–

Born in Wigan, England, he made his debut for the local club in 1991 and soon established himself as a fixture at loose forward both for Wigan and Great Britain. He has gone on to establish a record for most tests as Great Britain captain, has twice won the prestigious Man of Steel award, and was voted international player of the year in 2004. He received an OBE in 2005.

Neil Fox, 1939–

Born in Sharlston, England, he played for Wakefield Trinity, Bradford Northern, Hull Kingston Rovers, York, Bramley and Huddersfield, starting as a centre, but later playing as a forward. He made his debut in 1956 and went to accumulate 6,220 points, more than any other player in the history of the game, before retiring in 1979.

Ellery Hanley, 1961–

Born in Leeds, England, he played for a Leeds amateur club and signed for Bradford Northern in 1978. He transferred to Wigan in 1985 for the record fee of £150,000, and transferred to Leeds in 1991 for £250,000. He was contemplating retirement when he was offered a job by the Australian Rugby League and signed as coach for a reputed £433,000 in May 1995.

Mal Meninga, 1960–

Born in Bundaberg, Australia, he made his debut in 1979 and played club rugby for Southern Suburbs, St Helens and Canberra Raiders before retiring in 1994. He also played for Australia in 45 tests (23 as captain), scoring a world record 270 points, and represented Queensland 38 times. He was noted as a tough competitor who combined formidable physical power with deft handling skills, and for his resilience in recovering from four broken arms during the course of his career.

Roger Millward, 1948–

Born in Castleford, England, he played for the local club from 1964 to 1966, but lack of first-team opportunities led to a £6,000 move to Hull Kingston Rovers, for whom he went on to play 406 matches before retiring in 1980. Nicknamed 'Roger the Dodger' for his unorthodox halfback play, he made 47 international appearances, scoring 20 tries. After his retirement he became a successful coach for Rovers, and was awarded the MBE in 1983.

Alex Murphy, 1939–

Born in St Helens, England, he played as a scrum-half for St Helens, Leigh and Warrington, scoring 275 tries in a 19-year career that also brought him 27 caps for Great Britain and four Challenge Cup winner's medals. He possessed great acceleration and pace, but was also noted for his ability to read the game and his use of gamesmanship to secure any advantage for his side. After his retirement in 1975, he turned to coaching (for clubs including Warrington, Wigan and St Helens) and became a television commentator.

Martin Offiah, 1966–

Born in London, England, he began as a rugby union player with Rosslyn Park, representing England Students in the amateur code. He made the move to rugby league by signing for Widnes in September 1987, and by the following January had played for Great Britain. In January 1992 he joined Wigan, reinforcing that club's dominant position in the British game, and later played for London Broncos and Salford City Reds. A winger whose searing pace earned him the nickname 'Chariots' Offiah, he scored over 500 tries in his career.

Jim Sullivan, 1903–77

Born in Cardiff, Wales, he began playing rugby union but switched to play rugby league as full-back for Wigan in 1921, thus beginning a career that lasted 25 years. In that time he amassed 6,022 points, including 2,867 goals, in a world-record 928 games. He went on three Lions tours to Australia in 1924, 1928 and 1932 and finished as leading points scorer each time. He was coach (initially player coach) at Wigan from 1932 to 1952 before moving to St Helens where he did much to further the career of **Alex Murphy** and won the team its first Challenge Cup.

Dramatic moments

In spite of its no-nonsense cloth-cap image, rugby league has more than once provided inspiration for the performing arts. Lindsay Anderson's 1963 film *This Sporting Life* (adapted from the novel by David Storey) won an Oscar nomination for actor Richard Harris and was voted among the best 100 British films of the 20th century, while John Godber's play *Up and Under* proved a long-running success in the theatre before being filmed in 1998.

RUGBY UNION

Origins

The most common explanation for the origin of the sport is that, while playing association football at Rugby School in central England in 1823, William Webb Ellis picked up the ball and ran with it. The accuracy of this legend is disputed, although the game certainly developed at the school at around that time. The first rugby club was founded in 1843 at Guy's Hospital, London, and the first rules were published in 1845 by Rugby School.

Rules and description

Rugby union is a form of football played with an oval ball, in which (unlike association football) the handling of the ball is permitted. The game is played by two teams of 15 players each. The playing area has a maximum length of 100m/110yd and a maximum width of 70m/77yd, with an H-shaped goal in the centre of the line at each end (the 'goal line'). In addition, there is an area known as the 'in-goal' at each end of the pitch, extending back generally 10m/11yd from the goal line. The main playing area is divided into two equal halves, and further lines cross the pitch 5m/6yd (broken), and 22m/25yd (solid) from each goal line and 10m/11yd (broken) from the centre line. Broken lines run parallel to the side lines, at 5m/6yd and 15m/17yd, ending 5m from each goal line. Games last for 80 minutes, divided into two halves, between which the teams change ends.

The object of the game is to accumulate more points than the opposing team. Five points are awarded for scoring a 'try', which is done by advancing the ball and pressing it to the playing surface on or over the opponents' goal line. The other three means of scoring involve kicking the ball between the posts and over the bar. An attempt from the ground is awarded following the scoring of a try (a 'conversion'), and is worth two points if successful. A 'penalty goal' may be attempted from the ground following certain infringements by the opposition (three points), and a 'drop goal', also worth three points, involves a player dropping the ball and kicking it as it bounces, so that it passes over the bar.

The ball may be moved by running with it, by passing it to another player, by kicking, or, in certain circumstances, by advancing when bound to a team-mate. Forward passing is not allowed. Players of the team without the ball are allowed to tackle the ball-carrier with their arms. Minor infringements, such as dropping the ball forwards, or making a forward pass, are penalized by the award of a 'scrum' to the opposition. In a scrum, eight players from each side, the 'forwards', bind together in rows and push against each other. The ball is put into the passage between the two front rows. The team putting the ball in is usually able to use the feet to direct the ball to the rear of its formation, where it is removed from the scrum and often passed to the remaining members of the team (the 'backs'). Forwards generally compete for possession of the ball and tend to be taller, heavier and stronger players, while backs tend to be faster, with greater technical skill, and concentrate on elusive running and precise kicking.

The game was strictly amateur for most of its history, with payments to players not permitted. During this time, talented players would often be tempted to sign professional contracts with clubs from the other code of rugby, rugby league, in order to earn money from their talent. The highest levels of rugby union embraced professionalism in 1995, since which time many players have been 'converted' from rugby league.

Ruling bodies: International Rugby Board (IRB). The game in each playing country is governed by an individual union, of which the oldest is England's Rugby Football Union (RFU)

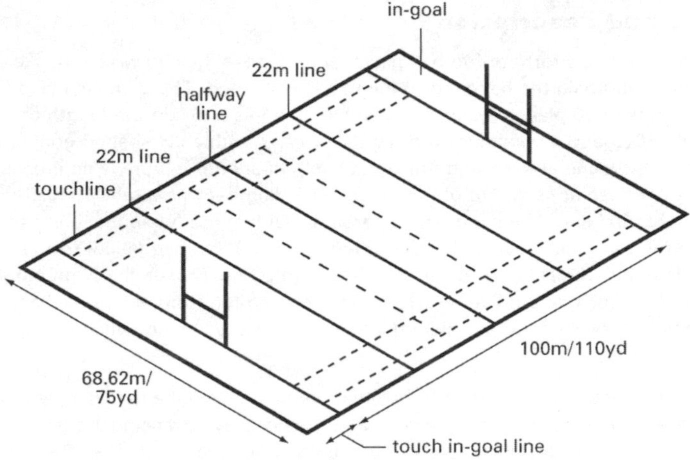

> ***A gentleman's game***
>
> Because of rugby's public school origins, class is often mentioned in connection with the sport, especially in the UK. Two well-known descriptions of the game emphasize this: 'a game played by gentlemen with odd-shaped balls', and 'a game for hooligans played by gentlemen' (soccer being vice versa).

World Cup

The first Rugby Union World Cup was staged in 1987. The competition now takes place every four years and teams compete for the Webb Ellis trophy.

	Winner	Beaten finalist	Score	Host country
1987	New Zealand	France	29–9	Australia & New Zealand
1991	Australia	England	12–6	England, Wales, Scotland, Ireland & France
1995	South Africa	New Zealand	15–12	South Africa

	Winner	Beaten finalist	Score	Host country
1999	Australia	France	35–12	England, Wales, Scotland, Ireland & France
2003	England	Australia	20–17	Australia
2007				France

Sing up, sing up

Singing before and during games has long been a part of rugby union. As well as the national anthems sung when the teams line up, other unofficial anthems have caught on and are sung with gusto by the fans. Welsh fans have adopted the hymn 'Bread of Heaven', while the English have made the Negro spiritual 'Swing Low, Sweet Chariot' their own. The Scottish Rugby Union chose to have 'Flower of Scotland', written by the folk singer Roy Williamson from the band The Corries and a long-time fans' favourite, as the pre-match anthem instead of the traditional 'Scotland the Brave'. It is always sung with particular relish at Scotland vs England games as it refers to the victory of Robert the Bruce over Edward II at Bannockburn in 1314, and to 'sending home' the English 'to think again'.

Six Nations Championship

A round-robin competition involving England, Ireland, Scotland, Wales, France (from 1910–32 and from 1947 onwards when it was known as the Five Nations), and from 2000, Italy. First contested in 1882.

* = Grand Slam

1882	England
1883	England
1884–5	*Not held*
1886	Scotland/England
1887	Scotland
1888–9	*Not held*
1890	England/Scotland
1891	Scotland
1892	England
1893	Wales
1894	Ireland
1895	Scotland
1896	Ireland
1897–8	*Not held*
1899	Ireland
1900	Wales
1901	Scotland
1902	Wales
1903	Scotland
1904	Scotland
1905	Wales
1906	Ireland/Wales
1907	Scotland
1908	Wales*
1909	Wales*
1910	England
1911	Wales*
1912	England/Ireland
1913	England*
1914	England*
1915–19	*Not held*
1920	England/Scotland/Wales
1921	England*
1922	Wales
1923	England*
1924	England*
1925	Scotland*
1926	Scotland/Ireland
1927	Scotland/Ireland
1928	England*
1929	Scotland
1930	England
1931	Wales
1932	England/Wales/Ireland
1933	Scotland
1934	England
1935	Ireland
1936	Wales

1937	England
1938	Scotland
1939	England/Wales/Ireland
1940–6	*Not held*
1947	Wales/England
1948	Ireland*
1949	Ireland
1950	Wales*
1951	Ireland
1952	Wales*
1953	England
1954	England/France/Wales
1955	France/Wales
1956	Wales
1957	England*
1958	England
1959	France
1960	France/England
1961	France
1962	France
1963	England
1964	Scotland/Wales
1965	Wales
1966	Wales
1967	France
1968	France*
1969	Wales
1970	France/Wales
1971	Wales*
1972	*Not held*
1973	England/France/Ireland/ Scotland/Wales
1974	Ireland
1975	Wales
1976	Wales*
1977	France*
1978	Wales*
1979	Wales
1980	England*
1981	France*
1982	Ireland
1983	France/Ireland
1984	Scotland*
1985	Ireland
1986	France/Scotland
1987	France*
1988	France/Wales
1989	France
1990	Scotland*
1991	England*
1992	England*
1993	France
1994	Wales
1995	England*
1996	England
1997	France*
1998	France*
1999	Scotland
2000	England
2001	England
2002	France*
2003	England*
2004	France*

Whipping boys

The World Cup can be an opportunity for the smaller rugby-playing nations to take on the big boys. Sometimes, however, this results in very one-sided games. In their 1995 game against Japan, New Zealand racked up 145 points (including 21 tries, a record 45 points from Simon Culhane, and a record six tries from Marc Ellis), while their opponents scored just 17. In 2003 Australia scored one more try in defeating Namibia 142–0, the biggest winning margin in international rugby.

Tri-Nations Championship

Established in 1996 and contested by the national teams of Australia, New Zealand and South Africa.

1996	New Zealand
1997	New Zealand
1998	South Africa
1999	New Zealand
2000	Australia
2001	Australia
2002	New Zealand
2003	New Zealand
2004	South Africa

Powergen Cup

An annual knockout competition for English club sides; first held in the 1971–2 season; known as the John Player Special Cup until 1988, the Pilkington Cup until 1997, and the Tetley's Bitter Cup until 2000.

	Winner	Beaten finalist
1972	Gloucester	Moseley
1973	Coventry	Bristol
1974	Coventry	London Scottish
1975	Bedford	Rosslyn Park
1976	Gosforth	Rosslyn Park
1977	Gosforth	Waterloo
1978	Gloucester	Leicester
1979	Leicester	Moseley
1980	Leicester	London Irish
1981	Leicester	Gosforth
1982	Gloucester/Moseley	
1983	Bristol	Leicester
1984	Bath	Bristol
1985	Bath	London Welsh
1986	Bath	Wasps
1987	Bath	Wasps
1988	Harlequins	Bristol
1989	Bath	Leicester
1990	Bath	Gloucester
1991	Harlequins	Northampton
1992	Bath	Harlequins
1993	Leicester	Harlequins
1994	Bath	Leicester
1995	Bath	Wasps
1996	Bath	Leicester
1997	Leicester	Sale
1998	Saracens	Wasps
1999	Wasps	Newcastle Falcons
2000	Wasps	Northampton
2001	Newcastle Falcons	Harlequins
2002	London Irish	Northampton
2003	Gloucester	Northampton
2004	Newcastle Falcons	Sale Sharks

Power in a union

A team's forwards are a tight-knit group, both figuratively speaking and literally when in a scrum. However, the two props and the hooker often form their own subgroup, which is informally referred to as the front-row union. Its members are not only broad of beam but usually of a tough, dour character. Their head-to-head encounters with their opposite numbers in a scrum allow many opportunities for banter and foul play. Exactly what goes on is a well-kept secret.

What a score!

Most rugby fans would choose Gareth Edwards's try in 1973 for the Barbarians against the All Blacks as the best try ever scored. Cliff Morgan's TV commentary of the try still brings out the goose pimples today: 'This is great stuff! Phil Bennett covering, chased by Alistair Scown. Brilliant, oh that's brilliant. John Williams. Pullin. John Dawes... great dummy. To David. Tom David. The halfway line. Brilliant by Quinnell. This is Gareth Edwards... a dramatic start... what a score!'

English League (Zurich Premiership)

Known as the Courage League until 1997 and the Allied Dunbar Premier League until 2000. From 2003 the champion was decided by play-off rather than being awarded to the team finishing first in the league table.

1988	Leicester	**1994**	Bath	**2000**	Leicester
1989	Bath	**1995**	Leicester	**2001**	Leicester
1990	Wasps	**1996**	Bath	**2002**	Leicester
1991	Bath	**1997**	Wasps	**2003**	Wasps
1992	Bath	**1998**	Newcastle Falcons	**2004**	Wasps
1993	Bath	**1999**	Leicester		

Welsh Rugby Union Challenge Cup (Konica Minolta Cup)

The knockout tournament for Welsh clubs; first held in 1971–2; formerly known as the Schweppes Welsh Cup, the Swalec Cup and the Principality Cup.

	Winner	Beaten finalist		Winner	Beaten finalist
1972	Neath	Llanelli	**1989**	Neath	Llanelli
1973	Llanelli	Cardiff	**1990**	Neath	Bridgend
1974	Llanelli	Aberavon	**1991**	Llanelli	Pontypool
1975	Llanelli	Aberavon	**1992**	Llanelli	Swansea
1976	Llanelli	Swansea	**1993**	Llanelli	Neath
1977	Newport	Cardiff	**1994**	Cardiff	Llanelli
1978	Swansea	Newport	**1995**	Swansea	Pontypridd
1979	Bridgend	Pontypridd	**1996**	Pontypridd	Neath
1980	Bridgend	Swansea	**1997**	Cardiff	Swansea
1981	Cardiff	Bridgend	**1998**	Llanelli	Ebbw Vale
1982	Cardiff	Bridgend	**1999**	Swansea	Llanelli
1983	Pontypool	Swansea	**2000**	Llanelli	Swansea
1984	Cardiff	Neath	**2001**	Newport	Neath
1985	Llanelli	Cardiff	**2002**	Pontypridd	Llanelli
1986	Cardiff	Newport	**2003**	Llanelli	Newport
1987	Cardiff	Swansea	**2004**	Neath	Caerphilly
1988	Llanelli	Neath			

Welsh Premiership

Premiership begun in 1991 and revived in 1998; from 1992–7 title taken by Division 1 Welsh League champions.

1991	Neath	**1996**	Neath	**2001**	Swansea
1992	Swansea	**1997**	Pontypridd	**2002**	Llanelli
1993	Llanelli	**1998**	Swansea	**2003**	Bridgend
1994	Swansea	**1999**	Llanelli	**2004**	Newport
1995	Cardiff	**2000**	Cardiff		

Let us sing of hairy men

The haka is the Maori war dance that the All Blacks perform before the start of each game, involving much waving of hands and stamping of feet and designed to intimidate the opposition. Opposing teams handle the haka in different ways – some link arms just feet away and eyeball the chanting Kiwis, while others affect complete indifference. The words to the song are: 'Ka mate Ka mate/Ka ora Ka ora/Ka mate Ka mate/Ka ora Ka ora/Tenei Te Tangata Puhuruhuru/Nana i tiki mai whakawhiti te ra/Upane Upane/Upane Kaupane/Whiti te ra', which can be translated as: 'It is death It is death/It is life It is life/It is death It is death/It is life It is life/This is the hairy man/Who caused the sun to shine again for me/Up the ladder Up the ladder/Up to the top/The sun shines!'

Scottish Club Championship (BT Premiership)

First held in 1973–4.

1974	Hawick	**1985**	Hawick	**1996**	Melrose
1975	Hawick	**1986**	Hawick	**1997**	Melrose
1976	Hawick	**1987**	Hawick	**1998**	Watsonians
1977	Hawick	**1988**	Kelso	**1999**	Heriot's FP
1978	Hawick	**1989**	Kelso	**2000**	Heriot's FP
1979	Heriot's FP	**1990**	Melrose	**2001**	Hawick
1980	Gala	**1991**	Boroughmuir	**2002**	Hawick
1981	Gala	**1992**	Melrose	**2003**	Boroughmuir
1982	Hawick	**1993**	Melrose	**2004**	Glasgow Hawks
1983	Gala	**1994**	Melrose		
1984	Hawick	**1995**	Stirling County		

Celtic League

Introduced in 2001–2 and competed for by the major Irish, Welsh and Scottish teams. Originally two pools and then a final knockout stage but as of 2004 played on a league basis.

	Winner	**Beaten finalist**
2002	Leinster	Munster
2003	Neath	Munster
2004	Llanelli Scarlets	

Celtic Cup

Introduced in 2003-4 when the Celtic League ceased to have a knockout stage.

	Winner	**Beaten finalist**
2004	Ulster	Edinburgh

Rugby Union

Heineken European Cup

Established in 1996 as a cup competition for major European clubs and provincial teams. English clubs did not take part in 1996 or 1999.

	Winner	Beaten finalist
1996	Stade Toulousain	Cardiff
1997	Brive	Leicester
1998	Bath	Brive
1999	Ulster	Colomiers
2000	Northampton	Munster
2001	Leicester	Stade Français
2002	Leicester	Munster
2003	Stade Toulousain	Perpignan
2004	Wasps	Stade Toulousain

Super 12

A competition established in 1996 for the leading state and provincial teams in Australia, New Zealand and South Africa. Super 10 games were played 1994–6.

	Winner	Beaten finalist
1996	Auckland Blues	Natal Coastal Sharks
1997	Auckland Blues	ACT Brumbies
1998	Canterbury Crusaders	Auckland Blues
1999	Canterbury Crusaders	Otago Highlanders
2000	Canterbury Crusaders	ACT Brumbies
2001	ACT Brumbies	Natal Coastal Sharks
2002	Canterbury Crusaders	ACT Brumbies
2003	Auckland Blues	Canterbury Crusaders
2004	ACT Brumbies	Canterbury Crusaders

Roe stops play

One of the most famous streaking incidents in sport happened when 24-year-old bookshop assistant Erica Roe came onto the pitch at Twickenham in 1982 at half-time during an England vs Australia game. England captain Bill Beaumont was in the middle of his team talk and couldn't understand why so many of his players were gazing distractedly over his shoulder. The well-endowed Ms Roe became a minor celebrity in the UK for a time and made several TV appearances. She seemed to enjoy herself: 'I had a moment of really feeling what it was like to be the Rolling Stones or Genesis up there on the stage. It was marvellous!'

A-Z

advantage — if the referee plays advantage, he allows a period of time following an infringement to determine whether the other team will be better served by the award of a **penalty**, **free kick** or **scrum**, or by allowing play to continue

against the head — if a pack wins the ball against the head, it gains possession of the ball from a scrum to which the opposition had the advantage of the **put-in**

All Blacks the nickname of the New Zealand rugby team

Baa-Baas same as **Barbarians**

back any of the seven players who do not participate in the **scrum**

back row the three forwards attached at the back of a team's **scrum**, the two **flankers** and the **number eight**

back three the **wingers** and **full back**, who are usually the three players furthest back in a defensive situation

Barbarians an invitational team, formed in 1890, that plays friendly games and whose players wear shirts with black-and-white hoops

binding holding on to another player; players must be bound at **scrums**, **rucks** and **mauls**

Bledisloe Cup the cup for which Australia and New Zealand have competed since 1931; presented by Lord Bledisloe, Governor-General of New Zealand

blind side 1. the side of the pitch with less space between the **scrum**, **ruck** or **maul** and the touchline; compare **open side** 2. the flanker binding on that side of the scrum

blood bin if a player is sent to the blood bin, he leaves the pitch because he has a bleeding wound; a replacement player must be used until the wound has been attended to

box kick a high kick, usually by the **scrum-half**, into the area (the box) behind the **scrum** or **line-out**

breakdown the termination of a run, causing a competition for the ball, usually following a **tackle**

Calcutta Cup the cup for which Scotland and England have competed, now as part of the Six Nations Championship, since 1877; so called because it was made from the rupees in the funds of the Calcutta Football Club after it was wound up

centre either of the two **three-quarters** in the centre of the pitch

charge down if a player charges down a kick, he blocks it using his hands or body

cite if a player is cited, an official complaint is made by the opposition team after a game about foul play by him

collapse if a set of forwards collapses a **scrum**, they deliberately cause the **front rows** to fall towards each other

conversion the opportunity to score a further two points after a try by kicking the ball between the posts and over the bar; conversions are taken from the **twenty-two** in line with where the try was scored

cover tackle a tackle made by a player running across the field behind his team-mates, on a player who has managed to break through the defensive line

crash ball if a player passes or receives a pass 'on the crash ball', he does it at the same time as he is tackled from the front

crossing an illegal move in which a player crosses in front of the ball-carrier, thus obstructing the defensive team from making a tackle

dead-ball line the line at the end of the **in-goal** area

drive the pushing forward by one team of a **maul**

drop goal a means of scoring, worth three points, in which the ball is dropped to the floor, kicked as it bounces, and sent through the posts and over the bar

dropout a drop kick from the defending team's **twenty-two**, awarded when the attacking team has sent the ball over the **dead-ball line**, or when the defending team has touched the ball down after the attacking side has put it in the **in-goal** area

dummy to feign to pass the ball in order to distract and run past an opponent

dummy scissors a move in which the attacking team **dummies** to play a **scissors** move

feed 1. same as **put-in** (sense 1) 2. if a **scrum-half** feeds the scrum he puts the ball in favouring his own team, an offence punished by a **free kick**

flanker a forward bound loosely on either side of the **scrum**; flankers wear the number 6 and 7 shirts

fly hack a kick forward of a ball lying loose on the ground

fly-half the back who usually stands one player out from the **scrum-half** at a **scrum** or **line-out**, usually an elusive runner and good kicker; wears the number 10 shirt

forward any of the eight players who participate in the **scrum**

forward pass an illegal pass where the ball travels forward

free kick a punishment for a technical offence. Less serious than a penalty, it may not be kicked for goal

front five same as **tight five**

front row the three powerfully built forwards, the two **props** and the **hooker**, who push directly against their opponents in a **scrum**

full back the player who normally stands furthest back on the pitch in a defensive situation and is a skilled kicker and tackler; wears the number 15 shirt

gain line if a player or team gets beyond the gain line, they move the ball beyond the imaginary line on which the preceding **set piece**, **ruck** or **maul** has taken place

garryowen same as **up and under**; the word derives from the Garryowen club in Limerick, Ireland

goal line same as **try line**

grand slam the feat of defeating all the other teams in the Six Nations Championship

grubber kick a ball dropped from hand and kicked along the ground

hack same as **fly hack**

halfback either of the two players, the **scrum-half** and **fly-half**, providing a link between the **forwards** and the **three-quarters**

handoff a legal move in which a player with the ball pushes away a tackler

hooker the **front-row** forward who specializes in using feet to move the ball back in a **scrum**, and usually the player who throws the ball in at a **line-out**; wears the number 2 shirt

in-goal the area between the **goal line** and the **dead-ball line**, in which a **try** may be scored

inside centre the **centre** who plays between the **fly-half** and the **outside centre**; wears the number 12 shirt

jumper a player who jumps to win the ball in a **line-out**

knock on if a player knocks the ball on, he touches or drops it forward with the hand or arm; punished by a **scrum** with opposition **put-in**

lifting the (now legal) boosting and supporting of a **jumper** in a **line-out** by other players

line-out the means of restarting the game after the ball has gone into **touch**. The two sets of forwards stand in file perpendicular to the touchline. A player from the team not responsible for the ball leaving the field throws the ball in, and the **jumpers** attempt to win possession

Lions a touring side (formerly the British Lions) made up of players from the British Isles

lock a **second-row** forward, often the tallest and heaviest players in a team; locks wear the number 4 and 5 shirts

loose the loose is forward play not involving **scrums** or **line-outs**; compare **tight**

loose-head prop the **prop** on the left-hand side of a team's **front row**, whose head is not completely inside the scrum

loose forward a member of the **back row**

mark a player in his own **twenty-two** may shout 'mark' at the time of catching a ball kicked by an opponent. If the catch is successful, a **free kick** is awarded to the player

maul a formation in which players, chiefly forwards, bind on to each other following a tackle in which the ball-carrier has not been brought to ground. They attempt to secure the ball for their team while pushing the formation forward; compare **ruck**

miss move a manoeuvre in which the attacking **three-quarters** miss out a back in order to move the ball more quickly to a player in a wider position

number eight the **back-row** forward who binds at the back of the **scrum**; wears the number 8 shirt

offload a very short pass made by a player being tackled to a team-mate running past

offside players are generally expected to stay on their own side of the ball; deliberately or negligently being further forward than the rules allow is termed as offside, and is punished by a penalty

open side 1. the side of the pitch with more space between the **scrum**, **ruck** or **maul** and the touchline; compare **blind side** 2. the **flanker** binding on that side of the scrum

outside centre the **centre** who plays between the **inside centre** and the **winger**; wears the number 13 shirt

outside half same as **fly-half**

pack a team's forwards

pack leader a forward designated to organize and motivate the **pack**

penalty a punishment for foul play. If kicked for goal, a successful attempt gains three points

penalty try a **try** awarded by the referee if an incident of foul play has prevented the opposition from scoring a try

phase a passage of play. First-phase play develops from a **set piece**; second and subsequent phases develop from the **breakdown** of the first phase, often following a **ruck** or **maul**

place kick a kick taken with the ball placed on the ground, ie a **penalty** kick or **conversion**

prop one of the two strongly built players who push directly against their opponents; together with the **hooker** the props form the **front row**; props wear the number 1 and 3 shirts

Pumas the nickname of the Argentine rugby team

pushover try a try scored after a **maul** or **scrum** close to the **try line** has been pushed over the line and the ball is able to be touched down

put-in 1. the introduction of the ball to a **scrum** 2. the right to do so

recycle to maintain possession of the ball following a **breakdown**

restart a drop kick from the halfway line to recommence play after the scoring of points by the other team

ruck a formation in which players bind with team-mates and attempt to push opponents backwards, with the ball on the ground below. It is the most usual result of a successful tackle; compare **maul**

scissors a move in which the ball is **passed** by a player running diagonally across the pitch to a team-mate running behind him at a different angle

scrum the formation, in three rows, of the two teams' forwards, who then push against each other, while the **scrum-half** puts the ball into the gap between the two **front rows**. The ball is usually hooked back by the side putting the ball in

scrum cap protective headgear worn by forwards

scrum-half the player, often slightly built and agile, who follows the forwards, putting the ball into the **scrum** and moving it away from the **pack** to the **backs**; wears the number 9 shirt

second row the two tall, powerfully built forwards, **locks**, who push behind the **front row** in a scrum

set piece a **scrum** or **line-out**

sevens a version of the game played by teams of seven players, with the emphasis on speed and ball-handling

sidestep a sudden change of direction used to beat an opponent

sin-bin to send a player temporarily from the field of play following repeated or particularly serious foul play

Springboks the nickname of the South African rugby team

standoff same as **fly-half**

tackle stopping a player by using one's arms to bring him down. A tackled player must release the ball. See also **breakdown**

tap penalty a penalty where the ball is merely tapped with the foot prior to being run with or passed, rather than being kicked towards goal or touch

tap tackle a tackle made by diving and touching the ankle of the player running with the ball, such that he trips over

tee a plastic device used to hold the ball stationary for **place kicks**

three-quarter one of the four **backs** (two **centres** and two **wingers**) who aim to run with the ball and prevent their opposites from doing so

tight forward play in **set pieces**, especially scrums; compare **loose**

tight five the **front row** and **second row**, generally the biggest players

tight-head prop the **prop** on the right-hand side of a team's **front row**, whose head is completely inside the scrum

touch the area off the side of the field

touch in-goal the touchline in the **in-goal** area

touch judge one of two officials, each with a flag, who assist the referee in the administration of the game. They are normally positioned on each touchline

touchline the line along the side of the field marking its edge, from which **line-outs** are taken

triple crown the defeat of the three other British teams by one team in the Six Nations Championship

truck and trailer an illegal move in which the ball-carrier (the 'trailer') moves forwards in loose play behind a team-mate (the 'truck') who shields him

try touching the ball down in the **in-goal** area; worth five points

try line the line on which the goalposts stand and over which the ball must be touched down to score a try

turnover the loss of possession of the ball

twenty-two 1. the area up to 22m from a team's own **goal line**, in which **marks** may be made and from which kicks direct to touch without bouncing may gain ground 2. the line marking the boundary of this area 3. same as **drop-out**

up-and-under a very high kick, after which the kicker and his team-mates rush to catch it or tackle the catcher

video referee an official in the stands who has access to TV replays and whose opinion the referee may ask when he is unsure if a try has been legally scored

Wallabies the nickname of the Australian rugby team

wheel to push the scrum unevenly, resulting in it twisting

wing forward same as **flanker**

winger often the fastest players in a team, the wingers try to run with the ball at pace down the sides of the pitch; wingers wear the number 11 and 14 shirts

Some rugby union slang

girls a term used by forwards to denote backs

handbags a term for a minor fight between players

ping to penalize a player for infringing the rules

ten-man rugby a style of play relying on the dominance of the forwards and kicking by either the **scrum-half** or the **fly-half**

third half the drinking following a game

Twickers Twickenham, where England plays its home games

uglies a term used by backs to denote forwards

up the jumper a style of play involving the advance of the ball through the forwards, with little passing and much **mauling** and **driving**

Some famous rugby union players

Rob Andrew, 1963–

Born in Richmond, Yorkshire, England, he is the world record holder, with 21, for international drop goals. As England's most capped fly-half he played 69 times between 1985 and 1995 and scored a record 396 points. He was one of the first players to embrace union's professionalism when he left his club Wasps and signed for the newly renamed Newcastle Falcons. He retired from international rugby in 1995 to concentrate on his player-coach role at Newcastle, and remained as coach after the end of his playing career.

Phil Bennett, 1948–

Born in Felin Foel, Wales, he had the difficult job of succeeding **Barry John** as Wales's fly-half but managed to form a successful half-back partnership with **Gareth Edwards** in the all-conquering team of the 1970s. He picked up 29 caps for his home country and captained the British Lions on their 1977 tour to New Zealand. He was awarded the OBE in 1978, the year in which he retired.

Serge Blanco, 1958–

Born in Caracas, Venezuela, he grew up in France and represented Biarritz at club level. He played 93 times for France and became the second most capped international player behind **Philippe Sella**. His position as full back allowed him to score 38 international tries, many the result of exciting counterattacking runs. He retired in 1991.

David Campese, 1962–

Born in Queanbeyan, New South Wales, Australia, he established a reputation as one of the fastest wingers in modern rugby, making his debut for Australia in 1982. He was the captain and undisputed star of the World-Cup-winning Australia side in 1991 and went on to represent Australia a record 101 times before his retirement in 1999, becoming in the process the leading try scorer in international rugby.

Will Carling, 1965–

Born in Bradford-on-Avon, he was England's most capped centre (60) and also held the world record for the most international wins as captain (40 in 53 games). He made his senior debut for England in 1988 and at 22 was made England's captain. He played a vital role in England's Grand Slam wins in 1991, 1992 and 1995, but was sacked in 1995 when he called Rugby Football Union administrators 'old farts', only to be reinstated two days later. Press exposure over his friendship with Princess Diana coincided with the break-up of his marriage and he announced his retirement as captain of the England team later in 1995. He made a brief comeback in the late 1990s before concentrating on a media career. He has been awarded the OBE and is now a motivational speaker.

Jonathan Davies, 1962–

Born in Trimsaran, Carmarthenshire, he first played for Wales in 1985, won 27 caps and then left to join rugby league in 1988, and set a record of 13 drop goals. He made headlines with his transfer to Widnes in January 1989 and scored 1,000 points in 109 matches. He moved to Warrington in 1993, and led Wales in league games. He returned to rugby union at the end of 1995, playing for Cardiff until his retirement in 1997.

Gareth Edwards, 1947–

Born in Gwaun-cae-Gurwen, near Swansea, he was first capped for Wales in 1967 at the age of 19, and became their youngest-ever captain a year later. With **Barry John** and **Phil Bennett** he created the most famous Welsh halfback partnerships, and he also played full back or centre. His 53 consecutive caps set a Welsh record. An MBE, he is a keen fisherman and is a former holder of the British pike record.

Sean Fitzpatrick, 1963–

Born in Auckland, he is New Zealand's most capped player. From 1986 he was a mainstay of the All Black front row, becoming the world's most capped hooker, and setting a further world record of 63 consecutive caps (1986–95). He first captained New Zealand in 1992 and went on to play a total of 128 games, with 51 caps as captain (1992–7).

Mike Gibson, 1947–

He was born in Belfast, Northern Ireland. A brilliant centre-threequarter and fly-half, he established a worldwide reputation while still at Cambridge University, and became

Ireland's most capped player with a total of 69 caps. He had an extremely long career at the highest level: he holds the record for the most appearances in Six Nations games with 67 between 1964 and 1977 and shares with **Willie John McBride** the record for most Lions tours (five). He was awarded the MBE.

Gavin Hastings, 1962–

Born in Edinburgh, Scotland, he made his debut for Scotland in 1986. A powerful attacking full back, he played in the 1987, 1991 and 1995 World Cups, and was an indispensable member of the Scotland team which won the Grand Slam in 1990. He also played on three tours for the British Lions and captained them in the 1993 tour of New Zealand. He became captain of Scotland for the first time in the 1992–3 season. Having broken Andy Irvine's record number of points scored for Scotland in international matches, he stood down after the 1995 World Cup in South Africa. His younger brother Scott (1965–) also had a long international career at centre, gaining 65 caps (a Scottish record).

Barry John, 1945–

Born in Cefneithin, Gwynedd, Wales, despite a relatively short international career of just 25 games, he took the art of the fly-half to a new level. His skilful running and adroit kicking, and his partnership with **Gareth Edwards**, were key to Wales's grand slam success in 1971, and the British Lions victory in New Zealand in the same year. He retired from international rugby at 27.

Martin Johnson, 1970–

Born in Solihull, England, he joined Leicester in 1988 as a lock-forward and made his full England debut in 1993. He was made captain of Leicester in 1997 and a year later succeeded Lawrence Dallaglio as captain of England. He led the British Lions to a historic victory on tour against South Africa (1997) and was reappointed in 2001 to lead a Lions tour of Australia. He retired from the international game, having won 84 caps, shortly after leading England to success in the 2003 World Cup in Australia. He was awarded the CBE in 2004.

Jonah Lomu, 1975–

Born in Mangere, New Zealand, he became the youngest-ever capped All Black. He made his international debut for New Zealand against France in 1994. A winger built more like a lock-forward, he scored four tries against England in the semi-finals of the 1995 Rugby World Cup, becoming a household name. Diagnosed with a serious kidney disorder in 1996, he fought his way back to fitness and won a gold medal in the rugby sevens at the 1998 Commonwealth Games. A superstar in international rugby union, he has remained there despite lucrative offers from rugby league. He suffered a recurrence of his illness in 2003, however, and underwent a kidney transplant in 2004.

Michael Lynagh, 1963–

Born in Brisbane, Australia, he gained 72 caps, mostly as a fly-half, between 1984 and 1995, and at the time of his retirement held the record for the most points scored (911), the most conversions (140) and the most penalty goals in international rugby (177). He retired from the competitive international scene as Australia's captain after the 1995 World Cup and played for Saracens in England at the end of his career.

Willie John McBride, 1940–

Born in Toomebridge, County Antrim, Northern Ireland, he played mostly with the Ballymena team from 1962. A tough lock-forward, he made a record 17 test appearances for the British Lions over the course of five tours, and played for Ireland 63 times. His greatest moment came when he captained the Lions to South Africa in 1974. The team went through the tour unbeaten, with McBride leading his men in a series of very physical encounters with the opposition. He also coached Ireland, managed the Lions team of 1983 and was awarded the MBE in 1971.

François Pienaar, 1967–

Born in Vereeniging, South Africa, he played for the South African Under 20s (1987) and subsequently joined the South African Barbarians (1990). Having been appointed captain of Transvaal and of the South African rugby side in 1993, he led the national team to a famous victory on home soil in the Rugby World Cup in 1995. He left to play and coach in England shortly afterwards.

Philippe Sella, 1962–

He was born in Clairac, France, and his home club was Agen. In 1993–4 he succeeded fellow Frenchman **Serge Blanco** as the most capped international player of all time with a record 111 caps. He was an attacking, flamboyant centre and scored 30 international tries. He retired from international tests after the 1995 World Cup.

Rory Underwood, 1963–

Born in Middlesbrough, he held the record for the most England caps, with 85, from 1985 to 1996, until it was surpassed by Jason Leonard (1968–) in 2000. As a British Lion he toured Australia in 1989 and New Zealand in 1993, although his service in the RAF sometimes restricted his availability. At club level he represented Middlesbrough, Durham, Leicester and Newcastle. His younger brother Tony (1969–) was also an international player before becoming a commercial pilot.

Jonny Wilkinson, 1979–

Born in Frimley, Surrey, England, he began playing rugby at the age of four and emerged as an exceptional talent in the English schools system. In 1998, aged just 18 and after only one complete game of professional club rugby, he made his England debut as a substitute. Under the guidance of his mentor at Newcastle Falcons, **Rob Andrew**, he developed into a key figure of the successful England team of the 2000s, combining precise goal-kicking with hard tackling and strong running and passing. He scored a drop goal in the last minute of extra time to win the 2003 World Cup for England, and following the tournament received a level of media attention unprecedented for a rugby union player, as well as an MBE.

J(ohn) P(eter) R(hys) Williams, 1949–

Born in Ogmore, Mid Glamorgan, Wales, he was a talented all-round athlete and won the Wimbledon Junior tennis championships, before studying medicine. He joined the London Welsh rugby team, won 55 caps and as a full back was a star of the highly successful British Lions tours to New Zealand in 1971 and to South Africa in 1974. He subsequently became an orthopaedic surgeon and has been a consultant at the Princess of Wales Hospital in Bridgend, Wales, since 1986.

Sir Clive Woodward, 1956–

Born in Ely, Cambridgeshire, he won 21 England caps as a centre before leaving to play for the Australian club, Manly. He began coaching while in Australia and, following a break from the game after his return to England, during which he built up a successful business, he became coach of Henley and then of two premiership clubs, London Irish and Bath. He was appointed England coach in 1997. He led his team to Six Nations Championships in 2000 and 2001, and won a grand slam in 2003. However, he will be remembered for coaching the team in its victorious World Cup campaign in Australia in 2003. He was knighted for services to rugby upon his return.

SAILING

Origins

It is thought that sailing as a sport originated in 17th-century Holland and was introduced to England by Charles II following his return from exile. Changes in boat-building methods over the years have made the sport more affordable, allowing a wider range of people to participate. Competitive sailing was often officially known as 'yachting' until the 2000 Sydney Olympics, when a name change was made in order to more accurately reflect the characteristics of the modern sport.

Rules and description

Many types of boat are used for both record-breaking attempts and racing. Suitable crafts include small single- or double-sided dinghies, sometimes with outboard motors or auxiliary engines for use in windless conditions; small, light sailing vessels with crews of one, two or three; and large ocean-going yachts of 25m/80ft or more in length. Within the two main types of sailing boat racing – offshore racing and harbour racing – there are three recognized disciplines: 'fleet', 'match' and 'team racing'. Competitions can take place between dissimilar boats with appropriate handicaps, or between boats of technically identical design (thereby emphasizing the importance of the skill of each boat's crew in determining the outcome). Finishing positions in each type of race determine the scores.

Ruling bodies: International Sailing Federation (ISAF); Royal Ocean Racing Club (RORC)

Cowes Week

The week of competitive racing that takes place annually at Cowes on the Isle of Wight dates back to 1826, making it the world's longest-running regular regatta. Around 8,000 competitors and 1,000 boats (split into 40 classes) typically participate in the week's races, which are held in the tricky tidal waters of the Solent.

America's Cup

One of sport's oldest and most famous trophies, the America's Cup (named after the boat that won the original race and affectionately known as 'the Auld Mug') is now held approximately every four years. Challengers compete in a series of races (the Challenger Selection Series, for which the Louis Vuitton Cup is awarded) to determine which of them races against the holder.

	Winner	Skipper	Challenger
1851	America (USA)	Dick Brown	
1870	Magic (USA)	Andrew Comstock	Cambria (Great Britain)
1871	Columbia & Sappho (USA)	Nelson Comstock	Livonia (Great Britain)
1876	Madeline (USA)	Josephus Williams	Countess of Dufferin (Canada)
1881	Mischief (USA)	Nathaniel Clock	Atlanta (Canada)
1885	Puritan (USA)	Aubrey Crocker	Genesta (Great Britain)
1886	Mayflower (USA)	Martin Stone	Galatea (Great Britain)
1887	Volunteer (USA)	Henry Haff	Thistle (Great Britain)
1893	Vigilant (USA)	William Hansen	Valkyrie II (Great Britain)
1895	Defender (USA)	Henry Haff	Valkyrie III (Great Britain)
1899	Columbia (USA)	Charlie Barr	Shamrock (Ireland)
1901	Columbia (USA)	Charlie Barr	Shamrock II (Ireland)
1903	Reliance (USA)	Charlie Barr	Shamrock III (Ireland)
1920	Resolute (USA)	Charles Adams	Shamrock IV (Ireland)
1937	Enterprise (USA)	Harold Vanderbilt	Shamrock V (Ireland)
1934	Rainbow (USA)	Harold Vanderbilt	Endeavour (Great Britain)
1937	Ranger (USA)	Harold Vanderbilt	Endeavour II (Great Britain)
1958	Columbia (USA)	Briggs Cunningham	Sceptre (Great Britain)
1962	Weatherly (USA)	Bus Mosbacher	Gretel (Australia)
1964	Constellation (USA)	Robert N Bavier	Sovereign (Great Britain)
1967	Intrepid (USA)	Bus Mosbacher	Dame Pattie (Australia)
1970	Intrepid (USA)	Bill Ficker	Gretel II (Australia)
1974	Courageous (USA)	Ted Hood	Southern Cross (Australia)
1977	Courageous (USA)	Ted Turner	Australia (Australia)
1980	Freedom (USA)	Dennis Conner	Australia (Australia)
1983	Australia II (Australia)	John Bertrand	Liberty (USA)
1987	Stars & Stripes (USA)	Dennis Conner	Kookaburra III (Australia)
1988	Stars & Stripes (USA)	Dennis Conner	KZ1 (New Zealand)
1992	America (USA)	Bill Koch	Il Moro di Venezia (Italy)
1995	Black Magic (New Zealand)	Russell Coutts	Young America (USA)
2000	Team New Zealand (New Zealand)	Russell Coutts	Luna Rossa (Italy)
2003	Alinghi (Switzerland)	Russell Coutts	Team New Zealand (New Zealand)

Captain Outrageous

Media mogul Ted Turner, better known as the founder of CNN, is also an accomplished yachtsman, having skippered Courageous to America's Cup victory in 1977. It seems that his sailing style was as flamboyant as his approach to business, as he acquired the nickname 'Captain Outrageous'.

Admiral's Cup

A biennial series of offshore races first held in 1957, originally in the English Channel, around Fastnet Rock and at Cowes; for national teams of three boats per team (excepting the 2003 race, when two-boat teams represented clubs).

	Winner	Boats
1957	Great Britain	Myth of Malham, Uomie, Jocasta
1959	Great Britain	Griffin II, Ramod, Myth of Malham
1961	USA	Windrose, Figaro, Cyane
1963	Great Britain	Clarion of Wight, Outlaw, Noryema
1965	Great Britain	Quiver IV, Noryema IV, Firebrand
1967	Australia	Mercedes III, Balandra, Caprice of Huon
1969	USA	Red Rooster, Carina, Palawan
1971	Great Britain	Prospect of Whitby, Morning Cloud, Cervates IV
1973	West Germany	Saudade, Rubin, Carina III
1975	Great Britain	Noryema X, Yeoman XX, Battlecry
1977	Great Britain	Moonshine, Yeoman XX, Marionette
1979	Australia	Impetuous, Police Car, Ragamuffin
1981	Great Britain	Dragon, Victory of Burnham, Yeoman XXIII
1983	West Germany	Outsider, Pinta, Sabina
1985	West Germany	Diva, Outsider, Rubin G VIII
1987	New Zealand	Goldcorp, Kiwi, Propaganda
1989	Great Britain	Indulgence VII, Jamarella, Juno IV
1991	France	Corum Diamant, Corum Rubis, Corum Saphir
1993	Germany	Container, Pinta, Rubin XII
1995	Italy	Brava Q8, Capricorno, Mumm a Mia
1997	USA	Flash Gordon 3, Jameson, MK Café
1999	The Netherlands	Innovision 7, Mean Machine, Trust Computer
2001	*Not held*	
2003	Australia	Aftershock, Wild Oats

Deep six that scuttlebutt

Many English slang words and phrases have a nautical origin. Among them are the US terms 'deep six' (meaning to get rid of something), which comes from the nautical term for a depth of between six and seven fathoms; and 'scuttlebutt' (meaning rumour or gossip), which originally referred to a water cask on board ship that served as a gathering place where gossip was exchanged (much like a modern-day water cooler).

Vendée Globe

A solo, non-stop round-the-world race held every four years, sailing westwards to and from Les Sables d'Olonne in France. Notoriously difficult and dangerous, it has been described as 'the Everest of the sea'.

	Winner	Skipper
1990	Écureuil d'Aquitaine II (France)	Titouan Lamazou
1993	Bagages Superior (France)	Alain Gautier
1997	Géodis (France)	Christophe Auguin
2001	PRB (France)	Michel Desjoyaux

Yngling

When Britain's 2004 Olympic team won its first gold medal for the women's Yngling event, interest in this relatively little-known class of boat soared. The Yngling (pronounced 'ing-ling') is a small craft with a keel and three sails. It was designed in 1967 by Norwegian Jan Linge, and was originally intended for his young son; hence its unusual name, which means 'youngster' in Norwegian.

Volvo Ocean Race

A round-the-world, one-design race. Until 1997 it was a handicap race, and until 2001 it was known as the Whitbread Round the World Race.

	Handicap winner	**Fastest yacht**
1973–4	Sayula II (Mexico)	Great Britain II (Great Britain)
1977–8	Flyer (The Netherlands)	Great Britain II (Great Britain)
1981–2	Flyer II (The Netherlands)	Flyer II (The Netherlands)
1985–6	L'Esprit d'Équipe (France)	UBS (Switzerland)
1989–90	Steinlager II (New Zealand)	Steinlager II (New Zealand)
1993–4	NZ Endeavour (New Zealand)	NZ Endeavour (New Zealand)
	Winner	
1997–8	EF Language (Sweden)	
2001–2	Illbruck (Germany)	

Red socks

During New Zealand's successful America's Cup challenge in 1995, skipper Peter Blake wore the same pair of red socks every day. The wearing of 'lucky' red socks was swiftly adopted by thousands of fans as a symbol of support for their team, and over 100,000 pairs were sold during the competition, providing Team New Zealand with a much-needed financial boost.

Route du Rhum

A solo transatlantic race from St Malo in France to Pointe-à-Pitre in Guadeloupe (5697km/3540mi). Two classes of boat, multihulls and monohulls, compete.

Multihulls

	Winner	**Skipper**
1978	Olympus Photo (Canada)	Mike Birch
1982	Elf Aquitaine (France)	Marc Pajot
1986	Fleury Michon (France)	Philippe Poupon
1990	Pierre 1 (France)	Florence Arthaud
1994	Primagaz (Switzerland)	Laurent Bourgnon
1998	Primagaz (Switzerland)	Laurent Bourgnon
2002	Géant (France)	Michel Desjoyeaux

Monohulls

	Winner	Skipper
1978	Kriter V (France)	Michel Malinovsky
1982	Kriter VIII (France)	Michel Malinovsky
1986	Macif (France)	Pierre Lenormand
1990	Écureuil d'Aquitaine (France)	Titouan Lamazou
1994	Cacolac d'Aquitaine (France)	Yves Parlier
1998	Aquitaine Innovations (France)	Thomas Coville
2002	Kingfisher (Great Britain)	Ellen MacArthur

Olympic Sailing Medals

Sailing (then officially known as yachting) was first included as an Olympic sport at the Paris Games of 1900. Olympic sailing events have varied over the past century; the modern games include eleven sailing disciplines in nine classes of boat. The ten nations that have won the most Olympic sailing medals in total are listed below.

Country	Gold	Silver	Bronze	Total
USA	17	23	17	57
Great Britain	19	15	11	45
Sweden	9	12	11	32
Norway	17	11	3	31
France	13	6	10	29
Denmark	11	8	6	25
Australia	5	3	8	16
Spain	10	4	1	15
New Zealand	6	4	5	15
Brazil	6	2	6	14

Around the world in 73 days

In February 2004, the Frenchman Francis Joyon set a new record of 72 days, 22 hours and 22 seconds – a remarkable 20 days fewer than the previous record – for solo circumnavigation of the world. He completed the 26,000-mile journey in a trimaran designed for a crew of ten, persevering despite difficult weather conditions and a collision that damaged his boat.

A-Z

aft towards the **stern** of a boat

amidships the middle part of a boat, between the **bow** and the **stern**

boom a pole that controls the position of a sail

bow 1. the forepart of a boat 2. one side of the forepart of the boat (the **starboard** and **port** bows meet at the **stem**)

catamaran a boat with two **hulls**

dinghy any small open boat

fleet race a race in which a number of single boats race the same course, starting and finishing at the same points

fore	towards the front of a boat
fore-and-aft sail	any sail that is not set on **yards** and lies fore-and-aft when not in use
gaff	a **spar** to which the head of a **fore-and-aft sail** is fastened
gybe	if a sailor gybes, he or she swings a sail over from one side of a vessel to the other, usually to alter course
halyard, halliard	a rope used for hoisting or lowering a sail, **yard** or **flag**
harbour race	a race in which competing boats sail a course marked out by buoys, generally making several laps
hull	the structural frame or body of a boat
jibe	same as **gybe**
keel	the part of a boat that extends along the bottom from **stem** to **stern**, serving as a 'backbone' upon which the **hull** is built
leeward	towards the direction in which the wind blows; compare **windward**
mast	a long upright pole supported by **rigging**, for carrying the sail of a boat
match race	a **one-design race** between two boats
monohull	a boat with one **hull**
multihull	a boat with two or more **hulls** (such as a **catamaran** or **trimaran**), generally able to reach higher speeds than a **monohull** craft
ocean race	same as **offshore race**
offshore race	a race in which competing boats sail at a distance from the shore, usually from one port to another
one-design race	race in which all competing boats must conform to detailed class specifications to ensure that they are evenly matched
port	a boat's left side when facing forward
regatta	an organized programme of races
rigging	the wires and ropes that support a boat's **masts** and can be used to extend its sails
round-the-cans	same as **harbour race**
spar	a general term for a **boom**, **gaff**, **mast** or **yard**
starboard	a boat's right side when facing forward
stem	the curved timber at the **bow** of a boat
stern	the after or hind part of a boat
tack	1. the course of a boat with respect to the side of the sail against which the wind is blowing 2. a zigzag course, to take advantage of wind blowing from the side when sailing to **windward**
team race	a race in which two or more teams of multiple, evenly matched boats compete against each other
trimaran	a boat with three **hulls**
windward	towards the direction from which the wind blows; compare **leeward**
yard	a long beam suspended on a mast for spreading sails

Some famous sailors

Sir Peter Blake, 1948–2001

Born in Auckland, New Zealand, he made his name in the Whitbread Round the World Race, which he won on his fifth attempt in 1989–90. In 1994 he was co-skipper with **Robin Knox-Johnston** on a record-breaking circumnavigation, and in 1995, for only the second time in its 144-year history, he took the America's Cup away from America with a non-US crew (Team New Zealand). He also assembled the successful team that defended the title in 2000. In 2001, he was killed by pirates on the River Amazon.

Sir Chay Blyth, 1940–

Born in Hawick, Scotland, in 1966 he rowed across the North Atlantic with John Ridgeway, and in 1970–1 became the first person to sail solo round the world in the westwards direction (against the prevailing winds). He circumnavigated the globe again in the 1973–4 Whitbread Round the World Race, sailed the Atlantic from Cape Verde to Antigua in record-breaking time (1977), and organized the British Steel Challenge Round The World Yacht Race (1992–3) and the BT Global Challenge Round The World Yacht Race (1996–7) with which he continues to be associated.

Sir Francis Chichester, 1901–72

Born in Barnstaple, Devon, England, he emigrated to New Zealand in 1919. He took up flying, and made a solo flight to Australia in a Gipsy Moth plane. In 1953 he turned to yacht racing, and in 1960 won the first solo transatlantic yacht race, with his boat *Gipsy Moth III*, sailing from Plymouth to New York in 40 days. He made a successful solo circumnavigation of the world in 119 days (1966–7) in *Gipsy Moth IV*, and was knighted in 1967.

Dennis Conner, 1942–

Born in San Diego, USA, Conner won the 1974 America's Cup as co-skipper in *Courageous*, and was Star Class world champion twice. However, after 1983 he became the only US skipper to lose the America's Cup in 132 years, when *Liberty* was beaten by *Australia II*. He regained the Cup from the Australians in *Stars and Stripes* in Perth (1987). After putting up a successful defence against New Zealand in 1988 (see box below), he lost to them in 1995.

A legal storm

Controversy struck the America's Cup in 1988, when the 60ft catamaran *Stars & Stripes* won a special challenge match against the 120ft monohull *New Zealand*. Infuriated by what they regarded as 'a gross mismatch', the New Zealand team instigated a legal battle, which led to the Cup passing temporarily into their possession. However, this decision was reversed by the New York Appeals Court in 1989, and the Cup was returned to *Stars & Stripes*.

Russell Coutts, 1962–

Born in Wellington, New Zealand, he first learned to sail aged six, and in 1980 became the single-handed world youth sailing champion. An Olympic gold medal in the Finn class followed in 1984. Ranked the best match racer in the world in 1993, he led New Zealand to victory in the 1995 America's Cup. He repeated his triumph in 2000 with New Zealand's successful defence of the title, and in 2003 when he led Switzerland's Team Alinghi to become the first European winners of the competition. He holds the record for captaining most America's Cup race wins, with 14 race victories under his belt. He has been awarded the CBE.

Sir Robin Knox-Johnston, 1939–

Born in London, England, he was the first person to sail non-stop and single-handed around the world in *Suhaili*, in 312 days from 14 June 1968 to 22 April 1969. He has since competed in and won many international races. In 1994, with **Peter Blake**, he broke the record for the world's fastest circumnavigation under sail – in 74 days, 22 hours, 17 minutes and 22 seconds. He has written several books, and was knighted in 1995.

Dame Ellen MacArthur, 1977–

Born in the village of Whatstandwell, Derbyshire, England, she sailed single-handed around Britain at the age of 18. Following success in the Route du Rhum transatlantic race in 1998, she was named Yachtsman of the Year. In 2000 she finished second in the Vendée Globe round-the-world event, in the process becoming the youngest ever competitor to finish the race, the fastest woman to sail around the globe and only the second person to complete a solo circumnavigation in fewer than 100 days. In 2005 she set a new record for the fastest solo circumnavigation of the world, and was created a Dame.

SHINTY

Origins

Played almost exclusively in the Scottish Highlands, the game is believed to have been introduced to the country by Irish missionaries around 2,000 years ago. The modern form of the game, which resembles hurling, dates from when the rules were drawn up by the Camanachd Association in 1893 ('camanachd' literally 'driving', is Gaelic for shinty).

Rules and description

Shinty is a stick-and-ball game played by teams of 12 players (men and women compete separately). The large pitch has maximum dimensions of 73 x 155m/80 x 170yd, with penalty areas marked around the goals. The stick is curved like a hockey stick; the ball is leather covered. The object of shinty is to score more goals than the opposition. The unusual start to the game features the referee throwing the ball high in the air with the opposing forwards ready to hit it on its descent. The reputation the game has for dangerous play comes from the number of strikes of the ball that are taken from above head level. Infringements incur free hits and penalty shots.

An international match between the hurlers of Ireland and the shinty players of Scotland is held each year, using a composite set of rules.

Ruling body: The Camanachd Association

Shinty stateside

The first competitive shinty match in the USA was held on 7 August 2004 at Monterey, California, as part of the Monterey Scottish Society Games. Northern California Camanachd Club beat San Luis Obispo 2–1 to win the Glenfarclas Cup.

Camanachd Association Challenge Cup

First competed for in 1896. The Camanachd Cup involves 16 teams, the eight members of the Premier League and another eight teams that qualify by way of a separate knockout cup competition.

	Winner	Defeated finalist	Score	Venue
1896	Kingussie	Glasgow Cowal	2–0	Inverness
1897	Beauly	Brae-Lochaber	5–0	Inverness
1898	Beauly	Inverary	2–1	Inverness
1899	Ballachulish	Kingussie	2–1	Perth
1900	Kingussie	Furnace	1–0	Perth
1901	Ballachulish	Kingussie	2–1	Inverness
1902	Kingussie	Ballachulich	3–1	Inverness
1903	Kingussie	Inverary	w/o	Inverness
1904	Kyles Athletic	Laggan	4–1	Kingussie
1905	Kyles Athletic	Newtonmore	2–0	Inverness
1906	Kyles Athletic	Newtonmore	4–2	Inverness
1907	Newtonmore	Kyles Athletic	7–2	Kingussie
1908	Newtonmore	Furnace	5–2	Inverness
1909	Newtonmore	Furnace	11–3	Glasgow
1910	Newtonmore	Furnace	6–1	Kingussie
1911	Ballachulish	Newtonmore	3–1	Lochaber
1912	Ballachulish	Newtonmore	4–2	Perth
1913	Beauly	Kyles Athletic	3–1	Kingussie
1914	Kingussie	Kyles Athletic	6–1	Glasgow
1915–19	*Not held*			
1920	Kyles Athletic	Kingussie	0–0, 2–1	Inverness/Glasgow
1921	Kingussie	Kyles Athletic	2–1	Inverness
1922	Kyles Athletic	Beauly	6–3	Oban
1923	Furnace	Newtonmore	2–0	Inverness
1924	Kyles Athletic	Newtonmore	3–3, 2–1	Glasgow/Kingussie
1925	Inverary	Lovat	2–0	Inverness
1926	Inverary	Spean Bridge	3–2	Oban
1927	Kyles Athletic	Newtonmore	2–1	Inverness
1928	Kyles Athletic	Boleskine	6–2	Glasgow
1929	Newtonmore	Kyles Athletic	5–3	Spean Bridge
1930	Inverary	Caberfeidh	2–1	Oban

	Winner	Defeated finalist	Score	Venue
1931	Newtonmore	Inverary	4–1	Inverness
1932	Newtonmore	Oban	1–0	Glasgow
1933	Oban	Newtonmore	1–1, 3–2	Fort William/Lochaber
1934	Caberfeidh	Kyles Athletic	3–0	Inverary
1935	Kyles Athletic	Caberfeidh	6–4	Inverness
1936	Newtonmore	Kyles Athletic	2–2, 1–0	Inverness/Spean Bridge
1937	Oban Celtic	Newtonmore	2–2, 2–1	Inverness/Keppoch
1938	Oban	Inverness	4–2	Oban
1939	Caberfeidh	Kyles Athletic	2–1	Inverness
1940–6	*Not held*			
1947	Newtonmore	Lochfyneside	4–0	Oban
1948	Newtonmore	Ballachulich	4–1	Inverness
1949	Oban Celtic	Newtonmore	1–0	Glasgow
1950	Newtonmore	Lochfyneside	4–2	Oban
1951	Newtonmore	Oban Camanachd	8–2	Inverness
1952	Inverness	Oban Celtic	3–2	Glasgow
1953	Lovat	Kyles Athletic	2–2, 4–1	Oban/Fort William
1954	Oban Celtic	Newtonmore	4–1	Inverness
1955	Newtonmore	Kyles Athletic	5–2	Glasgow
1956	Kyles Athletic	Kilmallie	4–1	Oban
1957	Newtonmore	Kyles Athletic	3–1	Spean Bridge
1958	Newtonmore	Oban Camanachd	3–1	Inverness
1959	Newtonmore	Kyles Athletic	7–3	Glasgow
1960	Oban Celtic	Newtonmore	4–1	Oban
1961	Kingussie	Oban Celtic	2–1	Fort William
1962	Kyles Athletic	Kilmallie	3–1	Inverness
1963	Oban Celtic	Kingussie	3–2	Glasgow
1964	Kilmallie	Inverary	4–1	Fort William
1965	Kyles Athletic	Kilmallie	4–1	Oban
1966	Kyles Athletic	Newtonmore	3–2	Inverness
1967	Newtonmore	Inverary	3–0	Glasgow
1968	Kyles Athletic	Kingussie	3–3, 2–1	Fort William/Oban
1969	Kyles Athletic	Kilmallie	3–1	Oban
1970	Newtonmore	Kyles Athletic	7–1	Kingussie
1971	Newtonmore	Kyles Athletic	7–1	Inverness
1972	Newtonmore	Oban Celtic	6–3	Glasgow
1973	Glasgow Mid Argyll	Kingussie	4–2	Fort William
1974	Kyles Athletic	Kingussie	4–1	Oban
1975	Newtonmore	Kyles Athletic	3–3, 1–0	Kingussie/Fort William
1976	Kyles Athletic	Newtonmore	4–2	Inverness
1977	Newtonmore	Kyles Athletic	5–3	Glasgow
1978	Newtonmore	Kyles Athletic	3–2	Fort William
1979	Newtonmore	Kyles Athletic	4–3	Oban
1980	Kyles Athletic	Newtonmore	6–5	Kingussie
1981	Newtonmore	Oban Camanachd	4–1	Glasgow
1982	Newtonmore	Oban Celtic	8–2	Inverness
1983	Kyles Athletic	Strachur & District	3–2	Fort William
1984	Kingussie	Newtonmore	4–1	Oban
1985	Newtonmore	Kingussie	4–2	Kingussie

	Winner	Defeated finalist	Score	Venue
1986	Newtonmore	Oban Camanachd	5–1	Glasgow
1987	Kingussie	Newtonmore	4–3	Fort William
1988	Kingussie	Glenurquhart	4–2	Inverness
1989	Kingussie	Newtonmore	5–1	Oban
1990	Skye	Newtonmore	4–1	Fort William
1991	Kingussie	Fort William	3–1	Inverness
1992	Fort William	Kingussie	1–0	Glasgow
1993	Kingussie	Oban Camanachd	4–0	Fort William
1994	Kyles Athletic	Fort William	3–1	Inverness
1995	Kingussie	Oban Camanachd	3–2	Oban
1996	Oban Camanachd	Kingussie	3–2	Inverness
1997	Kingussie	Newtonmore	12–1	Fort William
1998	Kingussie	Oban Camanachd	7–3	Oban
1999	Kingussie	Oban Camanachd	3–0	Kingussie
2000	Kingussie	Kyles Atletic	3–1	Fort William
2001	Kingussie	Oban Camanachd	2–0	Glasgow
2002	Kingussie	Inverary	3–2	Inverness
2003	Kingussie	Fort William	6–0	Fort William
2004	Inverary	Fort William	1–0	Oban

w/o = walkover

A-Z

camán a stick with a narrow curved end that is used to strike the ball. It is about 1m/3ft 6in long and made of laminated hickory or ash

cleek the shot If a player cleeks the shot he stops or blocks it

free hit a hit awarded following an infringement committed outside the area

goal-hit the method of re-entering the ball in play after it has gone over the goal line after last being touched by an attacker

hail goal

hailkeeper goalkeeper

hit-in the method of re-entering the ball in play after it has gone over the sidelines, or the goal line when it was last touched by a defender. The player throws the ball in the air and hits it with the heel of the **camán**

penalty a free shot on goal, taken 20yd/18.2m from goal, after an infringement has been committed in the penalty area

SHOOTING

Origins

The sport of competitive small-arms target shooting dates from the invention of the pistol and the rifle. The first shooting club was the Lucerne Shooting Guild, in Switzerland. It was formed around 1466 and the first recorded shooting match was at Zurich in 1472. The sport became popular in Europe and North America in the 19th century. Trapshooting dates from the late 18th century and skeet is a more modern form of the sport, dating from around 1915, invented by a Mr Foster, editor of the *National Sportsman* magazine, and developed by a group of hunting enthusiasts in Massachusetts, USA.

Rules and description

Competitive shooting can be divided into four main disciplines. They are pistol, rifle, running target and shotgun events. The pistol is a relatively small, hand-held gun that is used to hit targets at varying distances. All the targets have ten concentric rings with different points values, the inner ring or 'bull' being worth ten points. The shooter with the greatest total of points wins. Men shoot at targets set 10m, 25m and 50m away; women 10m and 25m. Events include an air pistol competition (air weapons use compressed air to fire lead pellets), a rapid-fire pistol and a free or sport pistol. Rifle events include the air rifle and the small-bore rifle. Competitions are held on shooting ranges and shooters aim at targets at distances of 10m and 50m. There are two small-bore rifle competitions: the 'prone' (lying down) and the 'three positions' (prone, kneeling and standing). The moving or running target sees the shooters firing from a distance of 10m at a moving target as it passes across a 2m opening.

The shotgun events are the 'trap' (and 'double trap') and the 'skeet'. Instead of concentric-ring targets, the shooters aim at saucer-shaped targets made of clay that weigh around 100g/3.5oz and are catapulted into the air by a device known as a 'trap'. The alternative name for the sport is clay-pigeon shooting. In trap, double trap and skeet events the competitors stand in shooting stations, make a call and the clays are released. The winner is the person who breaks most targets. In the trap event one of three traps at random fires the clay; 200 clays are released in total in the competition. In double trap two targets are released simultaneously. In skeet the range is semicircular and one or two targets are released from a 'high house' and 'low house', sending targets in opposite directions and at different elevations. The event is intended to mimic game shooting and is also called 'round-the-clock shooting'.

Ruling body: International Shooting Sport Federation (ISSF)

Sisters are shooting for themselves

Canadian Susan Nattrass (1950–) appeared in her first Olympic Games in 1976 as the only woman competitor alongside men in the trap event. After the 1992 Olympics, when women were barred from the event, she campaigned for a separate trap competition for women, which was achieved in 2000. Chinese shooter Zhang Shan (1968–) created history by winning gold in the skeet at the 1992 Olympic Games, becoming the first woman to win a mixed-sex shooting event. Women were then barred from competing in the event and she was unable to defend her title (a women's skeet was introduced at the 2000 Olympic Games when she finished eighth).

Olympic Games

Currently there are 17 different shooting events. Many events have been discontinued over the years, including the military revolver, the duelling pistols (when dummies dressed in frock coats were the 'victims') and the running deer shooting.

Men

The rapid-fire pistol and free pistol events were first held in 1896. The small-bore rifle from a prone position was added in 1908, from three different positions in 1952, the air rifle in 1984 and the air pistol in 1988. The trap and moving target events were introduced in 1900 (running target was included again in 1908 but then discontinued until 1972), double trap was first held in 1906 but discontinued until 1992, and the skeet event was first held in 1968.

	Rapid-fire pistol	**Free pistol**
1980	Corneliu Ion (Romania)	Aleksandr Melentyev (USSR)
1984	Takeo Kamachi (Japan)	Xu Haifeng (China)
1988	Afanasijs Kuzmins (USSR)	Sorin Babii (Romania)
1992	Ralf Schumann (Germany)	Konstantin Lukashik (Belarus)
1996	Ralf Schumann (Germany)	Boris Kokorev (Russia)
2000	Sergei Alifirenko (Russia)	Tanyu Kiryakov (Bulgaria)
2004	Ralf Schumann (Germany)	Mikhail Nestruev (Russia)

	Small-bore rifle – prone	**Small-bore rifle – three positions**
1980	Károly Varga (Hungary)	Viktor Vlasov (USSR)
1984	Edward Etzel (USA)	Malcolm Cooper (Great Britain)
1988	Miroslav Varga (Czechoslovakia)	Malcolm Cooper (Great Britain)
1992	Lee Eun-chul (Korea)	Hrachya Petikyan (Armenia)
1996	Christian Klees (Germany)	Jean-Pierre Amal (France)
2000	Jonas Edman (Sweden)	Rajmond Debevec (Slovenia)
2004	Matthew Emmons (USA)	Jia Zhanbo (China)

	Air pistol	**Air rifle**
1984	Philippe Héberlé (France)	
1988	Taniu Kiryakov (Bulgaria)	Goran Maksimović (Yugoslavia)
1992	Wang Yifu (China)	Yuri Fedkin (Russia)
1996	Roberto Di Donna (Italy)	Artem Khadzhibekov (Russia)
2000	Franck Dumoulin (France)	Cai Yalin (China)
2004	Wang Yifu (China)	Zhu Qinan (China)

	Running target	**Trap**
1980	Igor Sokolov (USSR)	Luciano Giovannetti (Italy)
1984	Li Yuwei (China)	Luciano Giovannetti (Italy)
1988	Tor Heiestad (Norway)	Dmitri Monakov (USSR)
1992	Michael Jakosits (Germany)	Petr Hrdlička (Czechoslovakia)
1996	Yang Ling (China)	Michael Diamond (Australia)
2000	Yang Ling (China)	Michael Diamond (Australia)
2004	Manfred Kurzer (Germany)	Alexei Alipov (Russia)

Shooting

	Double trap	Skeet
1980	Hans Kjeld Rasmussen (Denmark)	
1984	Matthew Dryke (USA)	
1988	Axel Wegner (East Germany)	
1992	Zhang Shan (China)	
1996	Russell Mark (Australia)	Ennio Falco (Italy)
2000	Richard Faulds (Great Britain)	Mikola Milchev (Ukraine)
2004	Ahmed Almaktoum (UAE)	Andrea Benelli (Italy)

Women

The sport pistol, small-bore rifle and air rifle events were first held in 1984, the air pistol was added in 1988, double trap in 1996 and trap and skeet in 2000.

	Sport pistol	Air pistol
1984	Linda Thom (Canada)	
1988	Nino Salukvadze (USSR)	Jasna Šekarić (Yugoslavia)
1992	Marina Logvinenko (Russia)	Marina Logvinenko (Russia)
1996	Li Duihong (China)	Olga Klochneva (Russia)
2000	Maria Grozdeva (Bulgaria)	Tao Luna (China)
2004	Maria Grozdeva (Bulgaria)	Olena Kostevych (Ukraine)

	Small-bore rifle – three positions	Air rifle
1984	Wu Xiaoxuan (China)	Pat Spurgin (USA)
1988	Sylvia Sperber (West Germany)	Irina Shilova (USSR)
1992	Launi Meili (USA)	Yeo Kab-soon (South Korea)
1996	Aleksandra Ivošev (Yugoslavia)	Renate Mauer (Poland)
2000	Renate Mauer-Rozanska (Poland)	Nancy Johnson (USA)
2004	Lioubov Galkina (Russia)	Du Li (China)

	Trap	Double trap
1996		Kimberly Rhode (USA)
2000	Daina Gudzineviciuté (Lithuania)	Pia Hansen (Sweden)
2004	Suzanne Balogh (Australia)	Kimberly Rhode (USA)

	Skeet
2000	Zemfira Meftakhetdinova (Azerbaijan)
2004	Diana Igaly (Hungary)

Ambidextrous aiming

Born in Budapest, Hungary, Károly Takacs (1910–76) was a member of the Hungarian pistol shooting team. He shot with his right hand but his career was seemingly ended in 1938 when, while he was serving as a sergeant in the army, a grenade exploded in his right hand. However, he taught himself to shoot left-handed and won the rapid-fire pistol event at the Olympic Games in both 1948 and 1952. He also won a rapid-fire pistol world team title in 1939.

A-Z

air-gun a pistol or rifle that uses compressed air or carbon dioxide to discharge its lead pellets

bull('s eye) the centre circle of the target, worth ten points

double trap a **trapshooting** event where two targets are released simultaneously at different heights and angles and the shooter must fire a shot at each target

down the line same as **trapshooting**

firing line the line from where competitors shoot

high house in **skeet** events, the higher trap house from where targets are catapulted

low house in **skeet** events, the lower trap house from where targets are catapulted

Olympic trench same as **trapshooting**

pull the command given by a shooter in **trapshooting** to release the clay pigeon

running target a target that moves across a track to simulate a moving animal or other target

shoot-off a form of tie-breaker in a shooting competition

sighter a practice shot fired at the beginning of a match to check sight adjustments; they are not counted toward the final score

skeet a form of clay-target shooting where targets are thrown from two traps about 40m apart and the shooter moves in an arc to different stations, firing from various angles

three-position rifle a shooting competition where shooters fire rifles from the prone, standing and kneeling positions

trap a mechanical device that releases clay targets at a set speed and trajectory

trapshooting the sport of shooting at clay targets thrown into the air by a **trap**

trench a long concrete structure in front of a **firing line** from where **traps** throw clay targets in **trap shooting**

Beware men with tall hats!

In the earliest days of trap shooting live pigeons were used instead of clays. The pigeons were hidden under tall hats; when the hats were removed they flew away and then – unfortunately for them – were shot. Later, more sophisticated substitute targets were devised, including using glass balls (filled with feathers to achieve the same effect when shattering in mid-air).

SKATEBOARDING

Origins

The pastime of skateboarding was invented in California in the 1950s as an alternative to surfing at sea and it was thus initially dubbed 'sidewalk surfing'. It gained in popularity throughout the 1960s and 1970s, before peaking at the end of that decade. Skateboarding went through a resurgence in the mid-1990s.

Rules and description

The skateboard is a narrow board made of wood or fibreglass, similar to a small surfboard, which is mounted on a set of axles (called 'trucks') that bear small wheels. Riders can turn the skateboard by shifting their weight on it. The skateboarder balances and rides on the board, which is curved slightly upwards at both ends, and also performs tricks and stunts on it by using specially designed bowl-shaped ramps, circuits, tracks, kerbs and other obstacles to help provide momentum and lift. Other courses provide obstacles for the skateboarder to manoeuvre around. The design of the skateboard differs according to the discipline, with slalom boards being more flexible than high-speed boards. Protective equipment is worn, including kneepads, elbow pads, wrist guards, gloves and a helmet.

Skateboard competition is divided into several disciplines, including 'freestyle', 'street' and 'vert' (short for vertical skating). Judges grade skaters' routines, awarding points for tricks based upon difficulty, variety, continuity, speed, control and style. Freestyle competition takes place on flat surfaces, usually without obstacles, and the skater performs stunts and tricks using only the skateboard. Street competitions involve manoeuvres performed on kerbs, benches, stairs, ramps, 'quarter-pipes' etc arranged in a skatepark, and performances are marked for creativity as well as jumps and landings. Vert competitions are held in 'half-pipes' – U-shaped large concrete or wooden bowls – and are the most spectacular events, with skateboarders doing aerial tricks. Another competition is slalom racing, where skaters glide between a set of cones.

A-Z

aerials tricks performed in mid-flight. Aerials are generally performed by launching the skateboard off a ramp, a **quarter-pipe** or a **half-pipe**

alley-oop a trick that is performed in the opposite direction to which the skater is travelling

blunt any move in which the tail area behind the rear **truck** is in contact with a surface

deck the board

drop in if a skateboarder drops in, he or she enters a **half-pipe** or obstacle from the top

fakie any move in which the skateboarder rides backwards

grind a move in which one of the **trucks** is scraped along a rail, wall edge or other surface

griptape a rough adhesive tape used on the board to provide extra grip

half-pipe a curved trough that ends with a vertical wall and lip and from where the skateboarder launches the board to perform **aerial** manoeuvres

kick-nose the curved front end of the skateboard. When the skateboarder applies downwards pressure on it the back or tail of the skateboard rises

kick-tail curved back end of the skateboard. When the skateboarder applies downwards pressure on it the front or nose of the skateboard rises

kick turn a turn on the skateboard through 180 degrees

McHawk a 720-degree rotational flip, named after US skateboarder Tony Hawk

McTwist a 540-degree rotational flip, named after US skateboarder Mike McGill

nollie an aerial manoeuvre where the front foot pushes down on the **kick-nose** and then the feet stay close to the board in flight before the back foot guides the board back to the ground

ollie an aerial manoeuvre where the back foot pushes down on the **kick-tail** and then the feet stay close to the board in flight before the front foot guides the board back to the ground. It was invented by Alan 'Ollie' Gelfland from Florida in the 1970s

quarter-pipe half of a **half-pipe**, a curved ramp

street an event held in a skatepark with a series of obstacles in which skateboarders are marked for creativity and technical skill

truck axle and wheel set

vert an event held in a **half-pipe** in which skateboarders perform **aerials**

SKIING

Origins

Competitive skiing began in the late 19th century but there is evidence from Stone Age artefacts that early mankind was using skis as a form of transport and a means to hunt animals many thousands of years ago. By the 15th century there are references to 'ski troops' being used in military campaigns by the Scandinavians and Russians. The sport of skiing developed rapidly after the invention by a Norwegian named Søndre Nordheim in the 1840s of a device to hold the heel steady on a ski, which gave the skier the ability to turn the ski and perform more complicated manoeuvres. In the 19th century the British popularized skiing in Alpine regions.

Rules and description

Skiing is divided into two main categories: 'Alpine' and 'Nordic'. Alpine consists of racing down specially prepared courses against the clock. There are five events. In 'downhill' each skier makes a single run down a course, with the fastest skier winning. In 'slalom' each skier makes two runs on a differently set-up course; each time the skier needs to negotiate a zigzag series of 'gates'. The slalom is the shortest course and features the quickest turns. The times of both runs are combined to give an overall winner. The 'giant slalom' is similar but run over a longer course with wider, smoother turns. Each skier has two turns on the course and again the winning time is the best combined score. The most recently introduced event is the 'Super-G' (short for super giant slalom). It is a fusion of downhill and giant slalom. Skiers run the Super-G course once. Finally, there is a 'combined' event, which comprises one downhill followed by two slalom runs. The times are added together and the fastest total time determines the winner.

Skiing

Nordic skiing includes cross-country skiing, on lighter skis over distances ranging from 10km/6.2mi to 50km/31mi, and ski-jumping. Ski-jumping is the most spectacular event, with male skiers launching themselves from an artificially built hill or slope and then flying through the air to distances of more than 100m/109yd. The Nordic combination is an event for cross-country skiers and ski-jumpers. The most recent departure for the sport of skiing are the 'freestyle' events, recognized only since 1979 and including 'aerials' (acrobatic manoeuvres performed in mid-air) and 'moguls' (a speed challenge over a steeply bumped descent during which two jumps must be made from specially designed ramps). In 'dual moguls' skiers race head-to-head over an identical course.

Skis differ in length and width according to the event but are made of synthetic materials and are curved upwards at the tips. Skiers maintain balance with the aid of ski poles in descending events and use them for pushing themselves forward in cross-country races. There are two varying styles in cross-country skiing: the classic style is a kick-off and glide forward slide (the 'diagonal slide') where the skier does not deviate from two parallel tracks; the freestyle takes its influences and movements from skating.

Ruling body: International Ski Federation (FIS; Fédération Internationale de Ski)

Alpine Skiing

World Championships

	Venues
1931	Mürren, Switzerland
1932	Cortina d'Ampezzo, Italy
1933	Innsbruck, Austria
1934	St Moritz, Switzerland
1935	Mürren, Switzerland
1936	Innsbruck, Austria
1937	Chamonix, France
1938	Engelberg, Switzerland
1939	Zakopane, Poland
1950	Aspen, USA
1954	Åre, Sweden
1958	Badgastein, Austria
1962	Chamonix, France
1966	Portillo, Chile
1970	Val Gardena, Italy
1974	St Moritz, Switzerland
1978	Garmisch-Partenkirchen, West Germany
1982	Schladming, Austria
1985	Bormio, Italy
1987	Crans Montana, Switzerland
1989	Vail, USA
1991	Saalbach, Austria
1993	Morioka, Japan
1995–6	Sierra Nevada, Spain
1997	Sestrière, Italy
1999	Vail, USA
2001	St Anton/Arlberg, Austria
2003	St Moritz, Switzerland
2005	Bormio, Italy

Men

	Downhill	Slalom	Combined
1931	Walter Prager (Switzerland)	David Zogg (Switzerland)	*Not awarded*
1932	Gustav Lantschner (Austria)	Friedl Dauber (Germany)	Otto Furrer (Switzerland)
1933	Walter Prager (Switzerland)	Anton Seelos (Austria)	Anton Seelos (Austria)

	Downhill	Slalom	Combined
1934	David Zogg (Switzerland)	Franz Pfnur (Germany)	David Zogg (Switzerland)
1935	Franz Zingerle (Austria)	Anton Seelos (Austria)	Anton Seelos (Austria)
1936	Rudolf Rominger (Switzerland)	Rudolf Matt (Austria)	Rudolf Rominger (Switzerland)
1937	Emile Allais (France)	Emile Allais (France)	Emile Allais (France)
1938	James Couttet (France)	Rudolf Rominger (Switzerland)	Emile Allais (France)
1939	Hermuth Lantschner (Germany)	Rudolf Rominger (Switzerland)	Josef Jannewein (Germany)
1950	Zeno Colò (Italy)	Georges Schneider (Switzerland)	*Not awarded*
1954	Christian Pravda (Austria)	Stein Eriksen (Norway)	Stein Eriksen (Norway)
1958	Toni Sailer (Austria)	Josi Rieder (Austria)	Toni Sailer (Austria)
1962	Karl Schranz (Austria)	Charles Bozon (France)	Karl Schranz (Austria)
1966	Jean-Claude Killy (France)	Carlo Senoner (Italy)	Jean-Claude Killy (France)
1970	Bernhard Russi (Switzerland)	Jean-Noël Augert (France)	Bill Kidd (USA)
1974	David Zwilling (Austria)	Gustavo Thoeni (Italy)	Franz Klammer (Austria)
1978	Josef Walcher (Austria)	Ingemar Stenmark (Sweden)	Andreas Wenzel (Liechtenstein)
1982	Harti Weirather (Austria)	Ingemar Stenmark (Sweden)	Michel Vion (France)
1985	Pirmin Zurbriggen (Switzerland)	Jonas Nilsson (Sweden)	Pirmin Zurbriggen (Switzerland)
1987	Peter Müller (Switzerland)	Frank Wörndl (West Germany)	Marc Girardelli (Luxembourg)
1989	Hansjörg Tauscher (West Germany)	Rudolf Nierlich (Austria)	Marc Girardelli (Luxembourg)
1991	Franz Heinzer (Switzerland)	Marc Girardelli (Luxembourg)	Stefan Eberharter (Austria)
1993	Urs Lehmann (Switzerland)	Kjetil André Aamodt (Norway)	Lasse Kjus (Norway)
1995–6	Patrick Ortlieb (Austria)	Alberto Tomba (Italy)	Marc Girardelli (Luxembourg)
1997	Bruno Kernan (Switzerland)	Tom Stiansen (Norway)	Kjetil André Aamodt (Norway)
1999	Hermann Maier (Austria)	Kalle Palander (Finland)	Kjetil André Aamodt (Norway)
2001	Hannes Trinkl (Austria)	Mario Matt (Austria)	Kjetil André Aamodt (Norway)
2003	Michael Walchhofer (Austria)	Ivica Kostelic (Croatia)	Bode Miller (USA)

	Giant slalom	Super-G
1954	Stein Eriksen (Norway)	
1958	Toni Sailer (Austria)	
1962	Egon Zimmermann (Austria)	
1966	Guy Périllat (France)	
1970	Karl Schranz (Austria)	
1974	Gustavo Thoeni (Italy)	
1978	Ingemar Stenmark (Sweden)	
1982	Steve Mahre (USA)	
1985	Markus Wasmaier (West Germany)	
1987	Pirmin Zurbriggen (Switzerland)	Pirmin Zurbriggen (Switzerland)
1989	Rudolf Nierlich (Austria)	Martin Hangl (Switzerland)
1991	Rudolf Nierlich (Austria)	Stephan Eberharter (Austria)
1993	Kjetil André Aamodt (Norway)	*Race cancelled*
1995–6	Alberto Tomba (Italy)	Atle Skaardal (Norway)
1997	Michael von Gruenigen (Switzerland)	Atle Skaardal (Norway)
1999	Lasse Kjus (Norway)	Hermann Maier (Austria)

	Giant slalom	Super-G
2001	Michael von Gruenigen (Switzerland)	Daron Rahlves (USA)
2003	Bode Miller (USA)	Stephan Eberharter (Austria)

Women

	Downhill	Slalom	Combined
1931	Esmé McKinnon (Great Britain)	Esmé McKinnon (Great Britain)	*Not awarded*
1932	Paola Wiesinger (Italy)	Rösli Streiff (Switzerland)	Rösli Streiff (Switzerland)
1933	Inge Wersin-Lantschner (Austria)	Inge Wersin-Lantschner (Austria)	Inge Wersin-Lantschner (Austria)
1934	Anny Rüegg (Switzerland)	Christl Cranz (Germany)	Christl Cranz (Germany)
1935	Christl Cranz (Germany)	Anny Rüegg (Switzerland)	Christl Cranz (Germany)
1936	Evelyn Pinching (Great Britain)	Gerda Paumgarten (Austria)	Evelyn Pinching (Great Britain)
1937	Christl Cranz (Germany)	Christl Cranz (Germany)	Christl Cranz (Germany)
1938	Lisa Resch (Germany)	Christl Cranz (Germany)	Christl Cranz (Germany)
1939	Christl Cranz (Germany)	Christl Cranz (Germany)	Christl Cranz (Germany)
1950	Trude Beiser-Jochum (Austria)	Dagmar Rom (Austria)	*Not awarded*
1954	Ida Schöpfer (Switzerland)	Trude Klecker (Austria)	Ida Schöpfer (Switzerland)
1958	Lucille Wheeler (Canada)	Inger Björnbakken (Norway)	Frieda Dänzer (Switzerland)
1962	Heidi Biebl (West Germany)	Anne Heggveit (Canada)	Anne Heggveit (Canada)
1966	Erika Schinegger (Austria)	Annie Famose (France)	Marielle Goitschel (France)
1970	Annerösli Zyrd (Switzerland)	Ingrid Lafforgue (Switzerland)	Michelle Jacot (France)
1974	Annemarie Moser-Pröll (Austria)	Hanni Wenzel (Liechtenstein)	Fabienne Serrat (France)
1978	Annemarie Moser-Pröll (Austria)	Lea Soelkner (Austria)	Annemarie Moser-Pröll (Austria)
1982	Gerry Sorensen (Canada)	Erika Hess (Switzerland)	Erika Hess (Switzerland)
1985	Michela Figini (Italy)	Perrine Pelen (France)	Erika Hess (Switzerland)
1987	Maria Walliser (Switzerland)	Erika Hess (Switzerland)	Erika Hess (Switzerland)
1989	Maria Walliser (Switzerland)	Mateja Svet (Yugoslavia)	Tamara McKinney (USA)
1991	Petra Kronberger (Austria)	Vreni Schneider (Switzerland)	Chantal Bournissen (Switzerland)
1993	Kate Pace (Canada)	Karin Buder (Austria)	Miriam Vogt (Germany)
1995–6	Picabo Street (USA)	Pernilla Wiberg (Sweden)	Pernilla Wiberg (Sweden)
1997	Hilary Lindh (USA)	Deborah Compagnoni (Italy)	Renate Goetschl (Austria)
1999	Renate Goetschl (Austria)	Zali Steggal (Australia)	Pernilla Wiberg (Sweden)
2001	Michaela Dorfmeister (Austria)	Anja Paerson (Sweden)	Martina Ertl (Germany)
2003	Melanie Turgeon (Canada)	Janica Kostelic (Croatia)	Janica Kostelic (Croatia)

	Giant slalom	Super-G
1950	Dagmar Rom (Austria)	
1954	Lucienne Schmith (France)	
1958	Lucille Wheeler (Canada)	
1962	Marianne Jahn (Austria)	
1966	Marielle Goitschel (France)	
1970	Betsy Clifford (Canada)	
1974	Fabienne Serrat (France)	
1978	Maria Epple (West Germany)	

	Giant slalom	Super-G
1982	Erika Hess (Switzerland)	
1985	Diann Roffe (USA)	
1987	Vreni Schneider (Switzerland)	Maria Walliser (Switzerland)
1989	Vreni Schneider (Switzerland)	Ulrike Maier (Austria)
1991	Pernilla Wiberg (Sweden)	Ulrike Maier (Austria)
1993	Carole Merle (France)	Katja Saizinger (Germany)
1995–6	Isolde Kostner (Italy)	Pernilla Wiberg (Sweden)
1997	Deborah Compagnoni (Italy)	Isolde Kostner (Italy)
1999	Alexandra Meissnitzer (Austria)	Alexandra Meissnitzer (Austria)
2001	Sonja Nef (Switzerland)	Regine Cavagnoud (France)
2003	Anja Paerson (Sweden)	Michaela Dorfmeister (Austria)

The bells, the bells

Swiss skiing fans are some of the most passionate. In their battle to make more noise than their great rivals, the Austrians, they unhitch the enormous bells from their cows and jangle them with gusto whenever a Swiss skier is on the course.

World Cup

The World Cup is a season-long competition first organized in 1967.

Overall

	Men	Women
1967	Jean-Claude Killy (France)	Nancy Greene (Canada)
1968	Jean-Claude Killy (France)	Nancy Greene (Canada)
1969	Karl Schranz (Austria)	Gertrud Gabl (Austria)
1970	Karl Schranz (Austria)	Michelle Jacot (France)
1971	Gustavo Thoeni (Italy)	Annemarie Moser-Pröll (Austria)
1972	Gustavo Thoeni (Italy)	Annemarie Moser-Pröll (Austria)
1973	Gustavo Thoeni (Italy)	Annemarie Moser-Pröll (Austria)
1974	Piero Gros (Italy)	Annemarie Moser-Pröll (Austria)
1975	Gustavo Thoeni (Italy)	Annemarie Moser-Pröll (Austria)
1976	Ingemar Stenmark (Sweden)	Rosi Mittermaier (West Germany)
1977	Ingemar Stenmark (Sweden)	Lise-Marie Morerod (Switzerland)
1978	Ingemar Stenmark (Sweden)	Hanni Wenzel (Liechtenstein)
1979	Peter Luescher (Switzerland)	Annemarie Moser-Pröll (Austria)
1980	Andreas Wenzel (Liechtenstein)	Hanni Wenzel (Liechtenstein)
1981	Phil Mahre (USA)	Marie-Thérèse Nadig (Switzerland)
1982	Phil Mahre (USA)	Erika Hess (Switzerland)
1983	Phil Mahre (USA)	Tamara McKinney (USA)
1984	Pirmin Zurbriggen (Switzerland)	Erika Hess (Switzerland)
1985	Marc Girardelli (Luxembourg)	Michela Figini (Switzerland)
1986	Marc Girardelli (Luxembourg)	Maria Walliser (Switzerland)
1987	Pirmin Zurbriggen (Switzerland)	Maria Walliser (Switzerland)
1988	Pirmin Zurbriggen (Switzerland)	Michela Figini (Switzerland)
1989	Marc Girardelli (Luxembourg)	Vreni Schneider (Switzerland)

	Men	Women
1990	Pirmin Zurbriggen (Switzerland)	Petra Kronberger (Austria)
1991	Marc Girardelli (Luxembourg)	Petra Kronberger (Austria)
1992	Paul Accola (Switzerland)	Petra Kronberger (Austria)
1993	Marc Girardelli (Luxembourg)	Anita Wachter (Austria)
1994	Kjetil André Aamodt (Norway)	Vreni Schneider (Switzerland)
1995	Alberto Tomba (Italy)	Vreni Schneider (Switzerland)
1996	Lasse Kjus (Norway)	Katja Seizinger (Germany)
1997	Luc Alphand (France)	Pernilla Wiberg (Sweden)
1998	Hermann Maier (Austria)	Katja Seizinger (Germany)
1999	Lasse Kjus (Norway)	Alexandra Meissnitzer (Austria)
2000	Hermann Maier (Austria)	Renate Götschl (Austria)
2001	Hermann Maier (Austria)	Janica Kostelic (Croatia)
2002	Stephan Eberharter (Austria)	Michaela Dorfmeister (Austria)
2003	Stephan Eberharter (Austria)	Janica Kostelic (Croatia)
2004	Hermann Maier (Austria)	Anja Paerson (Sweden)

Olympic Games

Alpine skiing

Men

	Downhill	Slalom	Combined
1936			Franz Pfnür (Germany)
1948	Henri Oreiller (France)	Edi Reinalter (Switzerland)	Henri Oreiller (France)
1952	Zeno Colò (Italy)	Othmar Schneider (Austria)	
1956	Toni Sailer (Austria)	Toni Sailer (Austria)	
1960	Jean Vuarnet (France)	Ernst Hinterseer (Austria)	
1964	Egon Zimmermann (Austria)	Josef Stiegler (Austria)	
1968	Jean-Claude Killy (France)	Jean-Claude Killy (France)	
1972	Bernhard Russi (Switzerland)	Francisco Fernández Ochoa (Spain)	
1976	Franz Klammer (Austria)	Piero Gros (Italy)	
1980	Leonhard Stock (Austria)	Ingemar Stenmark (Sweden)	
1984	William Johnson (USA)	Phil Mahre (USA)	
1988	Pirmin Zurbriggen (Switzerland)	Alberto Tomba (Italy)	Hubert Strolz (Austria)
1992	Patrik Ortlieb (Austria)	Finn Christian Jagge (Norway)	Josef Polig (Italy)
1994	Tommy Moe (USA)	Thomas Stangassinger (Austria)	Lasse Kjus (Norway)
1998	Jean-Luc Crétier (France)	Hans Petter Buraas (Norway)	Mario Reitner (Austria)
2002	Fritz Ströbl (Austria)	Jean-Pierre Vidal (France)	Kjetil André Aamodt (Norway)

	Giant slalom	Super-G
1952	Stein Eriksen (Norway)	
1956	Toni Sailer (Austria)	
1960	Roger Staub (Switzerland)	
1964	François Bonlieu (France)	
1968	Jean-Claude Killy (France)	
1972	Gustavo Thoeni (Italy)	

	Giant slalom	Super-G
1976	Heini Hemmi (Switzerland)	
1980	Ingemar Stenmark (Sweden)	
1984	Max Julen (Switzerland)	
1988	Alberto Tomba (Italy)	Franck Piccard (France)
1992	Alberto Tomba (Italy)	Kjetil André Aamodt (Norway)
1994	Markus Wasmeier (Germany)	Markus Wasmeier (Germany)
1998	Hermann Maier (Austria)	Hermann Maier (Austria)
2002	Stephan Eberharter (Austria)	Kjetil André Aamodt (Norway)

Women

	Downhill	Slalom	Combined
1936	Christl Cranz (Germany)		
1948	Hedy Schlunegger (Switzerland)	Gretchen Fraser (USA)	Trude Beiser (Austria)
1952	Trude Beiser-Jochum (Austria)	Andrea Mead-Lawrence (USA)	
1956	Madeleine Berthod (Switzerland)	Renée Colliard (Switzerland)	
1960	Heidi Biebl (West Germany)	Anne Heggtveit (Canada)	
1964	Christl Haas (Austria)	Christine Goitschel (France)	
1968	Olga Pall (Austria)	Marielle Goitschel (France)	
1972	Marie-Thérèse Nadig (Switzerland)	Barbara Ann Cochran (USA)	
1976	Rosi Mittermaier (West Germany)	Rosi Mittermaier (West Germany)	
1980	Annemarie Moser-Pröll (Austria)	Hanni Wenzel (Liechtenstein)	
1984	Michaela Figini (Switzerland)	Paoletta Magnoni (Italy)	
1988	Marina Kiehl (West Germany)	Vreni Schneider (Switzerland)	Anita Wachter (Austria)
1992	Kerrin Lee-Gartner (Canada)	Petra Kronberger (Austria)	Petra Kronberger (Austria)
1994	Katja Seizinger (Germany)	Vreni Schneider (Switzerland)	Pernilla Wiberg (Sweden)
1998	Katja Seizinger (Germany)	Hilde Gerg (Germany)	Katja Seizinger (Germany)
2002	Carole Montillet (France)	Janica Kostelic (Croatia)	Janica Kostelic (Croatia)

	Giant slalom	Super-G
1952	Andrea Mead-Lawrence (USA)	
1956	Ossi Reichert (West Germany)	
1960	Yvonne Rügg (Switzerland)	
1964	Marielle Goitschel (France)	
1968	Nancy Greene (Canada)	
1972	Marie-Thérèse Nadig (Switzerland)	
1976	Kathy Kreiner (Canada)	
1980	Hanni Wenzel (Liechtenstein)	
1984	Debbie Armstrong (USA)	
1988	Vreni Schneider (Switzerland)	Sigrid Wolf (Austria)
1992	Pernilla Wiberg (Sweden)	Deborah Compagnoni (Italy)
1994	Deborah Compagnoni (Italy)	Diann Roffe (USA)
1998	Deborah Compagnoni (Italy)	Picabo Street (USA)
2002	Janica Kostelic (Croatia)	Daniela Ceccarelli (Italy)

Ski-Jumping

World Championships

	Normal hill	Large hill
1925	Willi Dick (Czechoslovakia)	
1926	Jacob Tullin Thams (Norway)	
1927	Tore Edman (Sweden)	
1929	Sigmund Ruud (Norway)	
1930	Gunnar Andersen (Norway)	
1931	Birger Ruud (Norway)	
1933	Marcel Reymond (Switzerland)	
1934	Kristian Johansson (Norway)	
1935	Birger Ruud (Norway)	
1937	Birger Ruud (Norway)	
1938	Asbjørn Ruud (Norway)	
1939	Josef Bradl (Germany)	
1950	Hans Bjornstad (Norway)	
1954	Matti Pietikäinen (Finland)	
1958	Juhani Kärkinen (Finland)	
1962	Toralf Engan (Norway)	Helmut Recknagel (East Germany)
1966	Björn Wirkola (Norway)	Björn Wirkola (Norway)
1970	Gari Napalkov (USSR)	Gari Napalkov (USSR)
1974	Hans-Georg Aschenbach (East Germany)	Hans-Georg Aschenbach (East Germany)
1978	Mathias Buse (East Germany)	Tapio Räisänen (Finland)
1982	Armin Kogler (Austria)	Matti Nykänen (Finland)
1985	Jens Weissflog (East Germany)	Per Bergerud (Norway)
1987	Jiri Parma (Czechoslovakia)	Andreas Felder (Austria)
1989	Jens Weissflog (East Germany)	Jari Puikkonen (Finland)
1991	Heinz Kuttin (Austria)	Franci Petek (Yugoslavia)
1993	Masahiko Harada (Japan)	Espen Bredesen (Norway)
1995	Takanobu Okabe (Japan)	Tommy Ingebrigtsen (Norway)
1997	Janne Ahonen (Finland)	Masahiko Harada (Japan)
1999	Kazuyoshi Funaki (Japan)	Martin Schmitt (Germany)
2001	Adam Malysz (Poland)	Martin Schmitt (Germany)
2003	Adam Malysz (Poland)	Adam Malysz (Poland)

Olympic Games

	Large hill	Large hill team	Normal hill
1924	Jacob Tullin Thams (Norway)		
1928	Alf Andersen (Norway)		
1932	Birger Ruud (Norway)		
1936	Birger Ruud (Norway)		
1948	Petter Hugsred (Norway)		
1952	Amfinn Bergmann (Norway)		
1956	Antti Hyvärinen (Finland)		
1960	Helmut Recknagel (East Germany)		
1964	Toralf Engan (Norway)		Veikko Kankkonen (Finland)

	Large hill	Large hill team	Normal hill
1968	Vladimir Belousov (USSR)		Jiří Raška (Czechoslovakia)
1972	Wojciech Fortuna (Poland)		Yukio Kasaya (Japan)
1976	Karl Schnabl (Austria)		Hans-Georg Aschenbach (East Germany)
1980	Jouko Törmänen (Finland)		Anton Innauer (Austria)
1984	Matti Nykänen (Finland)		Jens Weissflog (East Germany)
1988	Matti Nykänen (Finland)	Finland	Matti Nykänen (Finland)
1992	Toni Nieminen (Finland)	Finland	Ernst Vettori (Austria)
1994	Jens Weissflog (Germany)	Germany	Espen Bredesen (Norway)
1998	Kazuyoshi Funaki (Japan)	Japan	Jani Soininen (Finland)
2002	Simon Ammann (Switzerland)	Germany	Simon Ammann (Switzerland)

Cross-country Skiing

Olympic Games

Men

	15km classical	50km classical
1924	Thorleif Haug (Norway)	Thorleif Haug (Norway)
1928	Johann Grøttumsbråten (Norway)	Per Erik Hedlund (Sweden)
1932	Sven Utterström (Sweden)	Veli Saarinen (Finland)
1936	Erik-August Larsson (Sweden)	Elis Wiklund (Sweden)
1948	Martin Lundström (Sweden)	Nils Karlsson (Sweden)
1952	Hallgeir Brenden (Norway)	Veikko Hakulinen (Finland)
1956	Hallgeir Brenden (Norway)	Sixten Jernberg (Sweden)
1960	Håkon Brusveen (Norway)	Kalevi Hämäläinen (Finland)
1964	Eero Mäntyranta (Finland)	Sixten Jernberg (Sweden)
1968	Harald Grønningen (Norway)	Ole Ellesfsaeter (Norway)
1972	Sven-Åke Lundbäck (Sweden)	Pål Tyldum (Norway)
1976	Nikolai Bazhukov (USSR)	Ivar Formo (Norway)
1980	Thomas Wassberg (Sweden)	Nikolai Zimyatov (USSR)
1984	Gunde Svan (Sweden)	Thomas Wassberg (Sweden)
1988	Mikhail Devyatyarov (USSR)	Gunde Svan (Sweden)
1992	Vegard Ulvang (Norway)*	Björn Daehlie (Norway)
1994	Björn Daehlie (Norway)*	Vladimir Smirnov (Kazakhstan)
1998	Björn Daehlie (Norway)*	Björn Daehlie (Norway)
2002	Andrus Veerpalu (Estonia)	Mikhail Ivanov (Russia)

* a 10km classical event

	30km freestyle	4x10km relay
1936	Finland	
1948	Sweden	
1952	Finland	
1956	Veikko Hakulinen (Finland)	USSR
1960	Sixten Jernberg (Sweden)	Finland
1964	Eero Mäntyranta (Finland)	Sweden

	30km freestyle	4x10km relay
1968	Franco Nones (Italy)	Norway
1972	Vyacheslav Vedenine (USSR)	USSR
1976	Sergei Savelyev (USSR)	Finland
1980	Nikolai Zimyatov (USSR)	USSR
1984	Nikolai Zimyatov (USSR)	Sweden
1988	Alexei Prokurorov (USSR)	Sweden
1992	Vegard Ulvang (Norway)	Norway
1994	Thomas Alsgaard (Norway)	Italy
1998	Mika Myllylä (Finland)	Norway
2002	Johann Muehlegg (Spain)	Norway

Women

	10km classical	30km classical	4x5km relay
1952	Lydia Wideman (Finland)		
1956	Lyubov Kozreva (USSR)		Finland**
1960	Maria Gusakova (USSR)		Sweden**
1964	Klavdia Boyarskikh (USSR)		USSR**
1968	Toini Gustafsson (Sweden)		Norway**
1972	Galina Kulakova (USSR)		USSR**
1976	Raisa Smetanina (USSR)		USSR
1980	Barbara Petzold (East Germany)		East Germany
1984	Marja-Liisa Hämäläinen (Finland)		Norway
1988	Vida Venciené (USSR)		USSR
1992	Lyubov Yegorova (USSR)*	Stefania Belmondo (Italy)	USSR
1994	Manuela Di Centa (Italy)*	Manuela Di Centa (Italy)	Russia
1998	Olga Danilova (Russia)*	Yulia Chepalova (Russia)	Russia
2002	Bente Skari (Norway)	Gabriella Paruzzi (Italy)	Germany

* a 15km classical event

** 3x5km relay

Freestyle Skiing

Olympic Games

Men

	Aerials	Moguls
1992	Edgar Grospiron (France)	
1994	Andreas Schönbächler (Switzerland)	Jean-Luc Brassard (Canada)
1998	Eric Bergoust (USA)	Jonny Moseley (USA)
2002	Aleš Vaneta (Czech Republic)	Janne Lahtela (Finland)

Women

	Aerials	Moguls
1992	Donna Weinbrecht (USA)	
1994	Lina Cheryazova (Uzbekistan)	Stine Lise Hattestad (Norway)
1998	Nikki Stone (USA)	Tae Satoya (Japan)
2002	Alisa Camplin (Australia)	Kari Traa (Norway)

A-Z

backscratcher a manoeuvre in aerial skiing where the skier touches his or her back with the tails of both skis. The legs are together with the knees bent under the body

basket a circular-shaped part of the ski pole near its base that prevents the pole from going too far into the snow

big air a freestyle event where skiers perform aerial tricks after jumping from a variety of jumps, scores being awarded for height, execution and the degree of difficulty of the trick

carving skis used for recreational skiing, they are narrower at the centre and wide at the top and tail, and allow a skier to make carving turns similar to a snowboarder

classic technique in Nordic skiing, the traditional ski racing technique. Skiers use a diagonal stride in which both skis stay parallel to each other

critical point same as **k point**

daffy a manoeuvre in aerial skiing where the skier spreads his or her legs apart with one in front of the body and one behind

edging the technique of tilting the skis so that the edges dig into the snow to provide stronger grip

egg position same as **tuck position**

fall line the most direct route down a slope

four-point landing a landing in aerial skiing where both poles plant on the snow when the skier lands from a jump

freestyle technique in Nordic skiing, the skating-style technique that closely resembles ice skating. It is usually faster than the **classic technique**

gate two flagged poles in matching colours that must be skied between in slalom events

glide if a downhill skier glides, he or she travels smoothly without any **edging**

glide wax the substance used to decrease the friction between the skis and the snow. It is applied to the entire ski in **freestyle technique** races, but to only the front and rear tips of the skis in **classic technique** races

grip wax the substance applied to skis and used to increase friction and thereby traction. It is applied to the middle part of the skis for **classic technique** races

Hahnenkamm hill and course in Kitzbühel that is renowned as the most difficult on the World Cup circuit

hairpin two **vertical gates** in succession on a slalom course

harries a preparation for skis in **classic technique** skiing where a wire brush is used to roughen the base of the skis

helicopter in aerial skiing, an upright aerial spin of 360 degrees

herringboning a technique for climbing in cross-country skiing where the tips of the skis are turned outwards

inrun — the portion of the jump in ski-jumping during which the skier travels down the ramp

kicker — the steep ramp used in aerial skiing

kick turn — a standing turn in which one ski is lifted so that its tail touches the ground and is then pivoted to point in the desired direction, the body and other ski then turning together to complete the manoeuvre

k point — in ski-jumping, the point at which the hill flattens out. For a **large hill**, the k point is 120m from the **takeoff**; for the **normal hill** it is 90m. The k point determines the amount of distance points awarded to a jump. A jump to the k point is worth 60 points; each metre over or under that distance decreases or increases the score by 2.0 points

kick wax — same as **grip wax**

large hill — the larger of the two Olympic ski jump hills; it measures 120m and is sometimes known as K120

mass start — a competition start in cross-country skiing where all the skiers start together and the first to pass the finish line is the winner

normal hill — the smaller of the two Olympic ski jump hills; it usually measures 90m or 95m and is sometimes known as K90/K95

outjump the hill — in ski-jumping, to jump beyond the **k point**

outrun — the flat area at the bottom of the hill in ski-jumping where skiers slow down and stop

piste — a prepared downhill trail

p point — the expected landing point in ski-jumping. It is marked in blue on the landing hill

safety bindings — the accident prevention devices that hold the foot to the ski and that release automatically when the skier falls to help prevent injury

safety netting — plastic mesh that is used to stop skiers who have lost control and prevent serious accident

schuss — a German word meaning a section of a downhill course with no bends

scramble leg — the first leg of a relay race in cross-country skiing; it describes a bunched **mass start**

ski blades — very short skis, often wider than normal skis and turned up at the edges – a cross between a ski and a snowboard

ski mountaineering — a combination of skiing and mountaineering using lighter, broader skis

skins — fabric coverings (previously made of sealskin) attached to the undersides of skis and used to allow skiers to walk uphill (the direction of the fibres preventing the skis from sliding back downhill)

split — a skier's intermediate time during a run

spread eagle — an aerial manoeuvre where the skier extends his or her arms and legs to the side while keeping the skis parallel and perpendicular to the body. The upper body remains straight and upright

staggered start — a competition start in cross-country skiing where the skiers leave the start at timed intervals. The winner is the skier with the best time

start hut — the building from which skiers start in downhill and all types of slalom

starting gate — the place from which skiers start their run in downhill and all types of slalom

Steilhang a steep, technically very difficult slope on the **Hahnenkamm** course with a long right-hand turn at the bottom

table top 1. a large jump constructed with a flattish surface before it and a big drop after it 2. a freestyle event held using this jump

takeoff in ski-jumping, the point at the end of the **inrun**, the moment where the jumper takes flight

Telemark position the position which a ski-jumper must adopt when landing, with one ski in front of the other

traverse to ski across a slope

tuck position the crouching stance adopted by downhill skiers to increase their aerodynamic shape, arms in front with hands together and poles tucked under the arms

vertical gate on a slalom course, when the two poles that make up the **gate** are placed vertically rather than horizontally

V-position the position of the skis adopted by most skiers in ski-jumping while in the air. The skis are touching or nearly touching at the tail and spread apart at the tips, forming a 'V'. Previously, ski-jumpers kept their skis parallel in flight

Some famous skiers

Christl Cranz, 1914–2004

Born in Brussels, Belgium, to German parents, she won her first German Alpine title in the combined event in 1934 and in 1936 at the Garmisch-Partenkirchen Olympic Games she won the combined gold medal. In total she won twelve world titles before World War II: in the slalom (1934, 1937, 1938 and 1939), the downhill (1935, 1937 and 1939) and the combined (1934, 1935, 1937, 1938 and 1939).

Bjørn Daehlie, 1967–

Born in Raholt, Norway, he achieved legendary status as a cross-country skier. Nicknamed 'The Rocketman', he dominated international competition through the 1990s, winning numerous medals. He also shattered the record for medals won by an individual in the Winter Olympics, winning three gold medals and one silver at Albertville in 1992, two golds and two silvers at Lillehammer in 1994 and three golds and a silver at Nagano in 1998.

Marc Girardelli, 1963–

Born in Laustenau, Austria, he has won the overall World Cup title a record five times (1985–6, 1989, 1991 and 1993). Regarded as a classic all-rounder, he skied all the disciplines – downhill, slalom, giant slalom and super-G. He won the 44th victory of his long career at Kitzbühel where he won the combined event. After a disagreement with his Austrian coaches, he chose to compete for Luxembourg.

Jean-Claude Killy, 1944–

Born in St-Cloud, France, but raised in Val d'Isère, his early career was disrupted by injury and military service but he returned to the slopes in 1966 to take gold in the downhill and combined in the world championships, going one better at the 1968 Olympics when he won slalom, giant slalom and downhill. He was the winner of the first

World Cup overall title in 1967, a year in which he won 12 out of 17 races, and repeated the feat the following year. He was a major driving force in bringing the 1992 Olympic Games to Albertville.

Franz Klammer, 1953–

Born in Mooswald, Austria, he took Olympic gold in the downhill, his specialist event, in 1976 in a spectacular run on his home slope of Innsbruck. He was World Cup downhill champion a record five times (1975–8 and 1983), winning eight out of the nine races in the 1975 season. A hugely popular skier, there was a national outcry when he was omitted from the 1980 Austrian Olympic team. After retiring in 1985 he set up a foundation to help athletes whose careers are curtailed by injury.

Hermann Maier, 1972–

Born in Flachau, Austria, he rose rapidly to the top of the sport and acquired the nickname 'The Herminator' from his dominance and aggressive style. He won his first World Cup race in 1997 and two gold medals in the slalom at the Winter Olympics at Nagano in 1998, going on to capture the overall World Cup title that year and again in 2000 and 2001. Despite a very serious motorbike accident in 2001 after which he required extensive reconstructive surgery, he returned to win the 2004 World Super-G title.

Annemarie Moser-Pröll, 1953–

Born in Kleinarl, Austria, she won a women's record 62 World Cup races (1970–9), and was overall World Cup champion (1971–5, 1979). She was also downhill world champion (1974, 1978), and took the world combined title (1978). Additionally, she was Olympic downhill champion (1980) before retiring that same year.

Ingemar Stenmark, 1956–

Born in Tärnaby, Sweden, he won the World Cup three years in succession (1976–8) and went on to become the most successful competitor in slalom and grand slalom ever. He won the Olympic gold medal at Lake Placid in 1980 and between 1974 and 1989 won a record 86 World Cup races. He retired in 1989.

Alberto Tomba, 1966–

Born in Bologna, Italy, he became the superstar of slalom skiing, characteristically winning from seemingly impossible positions. He regularly attracted thousands of chanting Italian fans to watch his phenomenal final runs. In his determination to win he could make costly mistakes but always seemed able to make up the time. His many victories include being world champion (1996), Olympic champion (1988, 1992) and World Cup champion (1995). Tomba was nicknamed 'La Bomba' ('The Bomb').

SKYDIVING

Origins

Although Leonardo da Vinci is believed to have been the first to design a parachute, the first parachute drop was made by a Frenchman, André Jacques Garnerin, in 1797. Leslie Irvin, an American, made the first free-fall jump near Dayton, Ohio, in 1919 using his own hand-operated parachute. In the years following World War II the sport developed using, at first, military parachutes.

Rules and description

The modern sport of skydiving involves individuals and groups jumping from aeroplanes (between about 3,200 and 4,200m/10,500 and 13,800ft high) with parachutes, the sport differing from parachuting in that the participants free-fall for a significant distance before the parachutes are deployed.

The governing body currently sanctions six skydiving disciplines. The classic categories are accuracy landing – trying to land on a target a mere 3cm/1in square – and free-fall style. In the latter, competitors perform set acrobatic manoeuvres such as turns and somersaults. Team competitions are formation skydiving, where teams of up to 350 flyers create geometric patterns, and the canopy formation, where skydivers form themselves into stacks once their canopies have opened. Finally, there are the newer disciplines of freestyle skydiving and skysurfing. In freestyle there are no pre-arranged manoeuvres. Skysurfing is similar but the competitors are attached to skyboards (like terrestrial skateboards). Free flying, a brand-new discipline, sees competitors taking up all sorts of positions, including head-down. Skydivers generally fly with video-camera flyers who record the jumps and who are marked according to the quality of their camera work.

Ruling body: Fédération Aéronautique Internationale (FAI)

Freestyle Skydiving World Champions

The second-named competitors in a grouping indicate the video-camera flyer.

	Men	**Mixed**
1994	Marco Manna/Bruno Brokken (Italy/Belgium)	Dale Stuart/Ray Cottingham (USA)
1995	Scott Smith/Richard Stuart (USA)	Carol Dorner/Troy Hahn (USA)
1997	Omar Alhegelan/Olly King (Saudia Arabia/USA)	Luci Manni-Hunold/Andy Duff (Switzerland)
1999	Ashley Crick/Jonathan King (Australia)	Emmanuelle Celicout/Alexandre Gillard (France)
2001	Nils Predstrup/Martin Kristensen (Denmark)	Stefania Martinengo/Filippo Fabbi (Italy)
2003	Nils Predstrup/Martin Kristensen (Denmark)	Emmanuelle Celicout/Alistair Marsh (France)

Skysurfing World Champions

	Men	Mixed
1994	Rob Harris/Joe Jennings (USA)	
1995	Rob Harris/Joe Jennings (USA)	Vivian Wegrath/Sjareis Boons (Switzerland/ Belgium)
1997	Oliver Furrer/Christian Schmid (Switzerland)	Vivian Wegrath/Marcus Heggli (Switzerland)
1999	Valery Rozov/Clif Burch (Russia/USA)	Tanya Garcia-O'Brien/Craig O'Brien (USA)
2001	Eric Fradet/Alessandro Iodice (France)	Tanya Garcia-O'Brien/Craig O'Brien (USA)
2003	Valery Rozov/Igor Kalinin (Russia)	Maria Ryabikova/Vassily Rodin (Russia)

Freeflying World Champions

The third-named competitor indicates the video-camera flyer.

2001 USA (Matt Nelson, Michael Swanson, Olav Zipser)
2003 USA (Matt Nelson, Michael Swanson, Jon Devore)

SLED DOG RACING

Origins

Sled dog racing developed from native peoples using dogs and sledges to move themselves and their goods around Arctic wastelands. The Alaskan gold rush era of the 19th century popularized the use of Alaskan malamute and Siberian husky dogs for the purpose. The first recognized race between teams of harnessed dogs driven by a 'musher' was the All-Alaska Sweepstakes race of 1908.

Rules and description

The number of dogs and type of sledge used depend on the type of racing. Relatively short distances (say 40km/25mi) are competed over at the world championships, whereas more famous events, such as the long-trail Iditarod, cover more than 1,800km/1,000mi. Events are mixed, and there have been a number of famous women mushers.

Ruling body: The International Dog Sled Racing Association

Iditarod Dog Sled Race

The most famous dog sled race is the 1,825–1,870km/1,135–1,165mi Iditarod race run from Anchorage to Nome in Alaska. It was inspired by a true-life dog-sled relay when a diphtheria serum was carried between the two towns in 1925 to save the community of Nome stricken by the disease. All mushers are American except as indicated.

	Musher	Lead dog(s)
1973	Dick Wilmarth	Hotfoot
1974	Carl Huntington	Nugget
1975	Emmitt Peters	Nugget and Digger
1976	Jerry Riley	Puppy and Sugar
1977	Rick Swenson	Andy and Old Buddy
1978	Dick Mackey	Skipper and Shrew
1979	Rick Swenson	Andy and Old Buddy
1980	Joe May	Wilbur and Cora Gray
1981	Rick Swenson	Andy and Slick
1982	Rick Swenson	Andy
1983	Rick Mackey	Preacher and Jody
1984	Dean Osmar	Red and Bullet
1985	Libby Riddles	Axle and Dugan
1986	Susan Butcher	Granite and Mattie
1987	Susan Butcher	Granite and Mattie
1988	Susan Butcher	Granite and Tolstoi
1989	Joe Runyan	Rambo and Ferlin the Huskey
1990	Susan Butcher	Sluggo and Lightning
1991	Rick Swenson	Goose
1992	Martin Buser	Tyrone and D2
1993	Jeff King	Herbie and Kitty
1994	Martin Buser	D2 and Dave
1995	Doug Swingley	Vic and Elmer
1996	Jeff King	Jake and Booster
1997	Martin Buser	Blondie and Fearless
1998	Jeff King	Red and Jenna
1999	Doug Swingley	Stormy, Cola and Elmer
2000	Doug Swingley	Stormy and Cola
2001	Doug Swingley	Stormy and Pepi
2002	Martin Buser	Bronson
2003	Robert Sørlie (Norway)	Tipp
2004	Mitch Seavey	Tread

Mushing Commands

come gee!	turn through 180 degrees to the right
come haw!	turn through 180 degrees to the left
easy!	slow down
gee!	turn right
haw!	turn left
hike!	command used to get the dogs moving
line out!	tells the lead dog to pull the rest of the team out of the sled
mush!	same as **hike!**
on by!	command used to overtake another team of dogs or pass an obstruction
whoa!	stop

SNOOKER

Origins

We have bored British Army officers serving in the Indian subcontinent to thank for the game of snooker. In 1875 Neville Chamberlain (no relation of the later British Prime Minister) and his associates at the Officers' Mess in Jubbalpore created an early form of snooker from gambling games such as pyramids, black pool, and life pool (see **Pool** section). It was played with fifteen reds and four colours – yellow, green, pink, and black – with the brown and blue balls added later. The name comes, it is believed, from military slang for a new recruit; although for some years it was believed that the game had been invented by a 'Colonel Snooker' of the Royal Artillery.

Rules and description

An indoor game played on a standard billiard table by two (or occasionally four) players. The aim is to 'pot' the 21 coloured balls (arranged on the table at the start) by hitting them with the white 'cue ball', itself hit using a tapered pole or 'cue', into one of the six holes or 'pockets' arranged at the corners and mid-point of the table. Fifteen of the balls are red; these must be potted alternately with the coloured ones. This sequence is called a 'break' and continues until a mistake is made. The reds remain in the pockets but coloured balls are returned to their designated 'spots' on the table until no reds are left, when they are potted in ascending order.

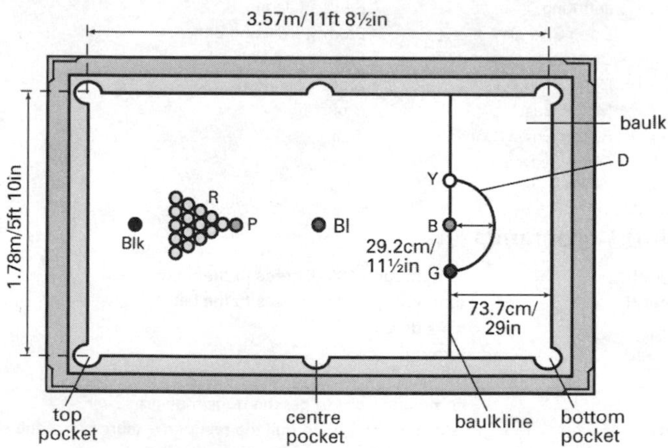

Note: The snooker table is 85–88cm/2ft 9½in–2ft 10½in high.

Y	yellow	P	pink
G	green	R	red
Br	brown	Blk	black
Bl	blue		

The game ends when the black is finally potted. Points 1–7 relate to the colours, in order: red, yellow, green, brown, blue, pink, black. The maximum break possible is 147.

Ruling bodies: International Billiards and Snooker Federation (IBSF) governs non-professional snooker and billiards; World Professional Billiards & Snooker Association (WPBSA) governs the professional game and organizes tours through its subsidiaries, World Snooker and the World Billiards Association. The women's game is governed by the World Ladies Billiards & Snooker Association (WLBSA)

I can't believe I just said that

BBC commentator 'Whispering' Ted Lowe was the voice of snooker for many years. He was prone to the occasional gaffe though: 'That's inches away from being millimetre perfect'; 'Fred Davis, the doyen of snooker, now 67 years of age and too old to get his leg over, prefers to use his left hand'; and the classic 'For those of you watching in black and white, the pink is behind the green'.

World Championship

Snooker's most prestigious tournament was first played in 1927. It has been staged at a number of venues but always in the UK and its home since 1977 has been the Crucible Theatre in Sheffield. Between 1964 and 1968 the championship was decided by challenge matches. The world championship has been sponsored by Embassy since 1976.

	Champion	Defeated finalist	Score
1927	Joe Davis (England)	Tom Dennis (England)	20–11
1928	Joe Davis (England)	Fred Lawrence (England)	16–13
1929	Joe Davis (England)	Tom Dennis (England)	19–14
1930	Joe Davis (England)	Tom Dennis (England)	25–12
1931	Joe Davis (England)	Tom Dennis (England)	25–21
1932	Joe Davis (England)	Clark McConachy (New Zealand)	30–19
1933	Joe Davis (England)	Willie Smith (England)	25–18
1934	Joe Davis (England)	Tom Newman (England)	25–23
1935	Joe Davis (England)	Willie Smith (England)	25–20
1936	Joe Davis (England)	Horace Lindrum (Australia)	34–27
1937	Joe Davis (England)	Horace Lindrum (Australia)	32–29
1938	Joe Davis (England)	Sidney Smith (England)	37–24
1939	Joe Davis (England)	Sidney Smith (England)	43–30
1940	Joe Davis (England)	Fred Davis (England)	37–36
1941–5	*Not held*		
1946	Joe Davis (England)	Horace Lindrum (Australia)	78–68
1947	Walter Donaldson (Scotland)	Fred Davis (England)	82–63
1948	Fred Davis (England)	Walter Donaldson (Scotland)	84–61
1949	Fred Davis (England)	Walter Donaldson (Scotland)	80–65
1950	Walter Donaldson (Scotland)	Fred Davis (England)	51–46
1951	Fred Davis (England)	Walter Donaldson (Scotland)	58–39
1952	Horace Lindrum (Australia)	Clark McConachy (New Zealand)	94–49
1952	Fred Davis (England)	Walter Donaldson (Scotland)	38–35
1953	Fred Davis (England)	Walter Donaldson (Scotland)	37–34

	Champion	Defeated finalist	Score
1954	Fred Davis (England)	Walter Donaldson (Scotland)	39–21
1955	Fred Davis (England)	John Pulman (England)	37–34
1956	Fred Davis (England)	John Pulman (England)	38–35
1957	John Pulman (England)	John Rea (Northern Ireland)	39–34
1958–63	*Not held*		
1964	John Pulman (England)	Fred Davis (England)	19–16
	John Pulman (England)	Rex Williams (England)	40–33
1965	John Pulman (England)	Fred Davis (England)	37–36
	John Pulman (England)	Rex Williams (England)	25–22
	John Pulman (England)	Fred Van Rensburg (South Africa)	39–12
1966	John Pulman (England)	Fred Davis (England)	5–2
1967	*Not held*		
1968	John Pulman (England)	Eddie Charlton (Australia)	39–34
1969	John Spencer (England)	Gary Owen (Wales)	37–24
1970	Ray Reardon (Wales)	John Pulman (England)	37–33
1971	John Spencer (England)	Warren Simpson (Australia)	37–29
1972	Alex Higgins (Northern Ireland)	John Spencer (England)	37–32
1973	Ray Reardon (Wales)	Eddie Charlton (Australia)	38–32
1974	Ray Reardon (Wales)	Graham Miles (England)	22–12
1975	Ray Reardon (Wales)	Eddie Charlton (Australia)	31–30
1976	Ray Reardon (Wales)	Alex Higgins (Northern Ireland)	27–16
1977	John Spencer (England)	Cliff Thorburn (Canada)	25–12
1978	Ray Reardon (Wales)	Perrie Mans (South Africa)	25–18
1979	Terry Griffiths (Wales)	Dennis Taylor (Northern Ireland)	24–16
1980	Cliff Thorburn (Canada)	Alex Higgins (Northern Ireland)	18–16
1981	Steve Davis (England)	Doug Mountjoy (Wales)	18–12
1982	Alex Higgins (Northern Ireland)	Ray Reardon (Wales)	18–15
1983	Steve Davis (England)	Cliff Thorburn (Canada)	18–6
1984	Steve Davis (England)	Jimmy White (England)	18–16
1985	Dennis Taylor (Northern Ireland)	Steve Davis (England)	18–17
1986	Joe Johnson (England)	Steve Davis (England)	18–12
1987	Steve Davis (England)	Joe Johnson (England)	18–14
1988	Steve Davis (England)	Terry Griffiths (Wales)	18–11
1989	Steve Davis (England)	John Parrott (England)	18–3
1990	Stephen Hendry (Scotland)	Jimmy White (England)	18–12
1991	John Parrott (England)	Jimmy White (England)	18–11
1992	Stephen Hendry (Scotland)	Jimmy White (England)	18–14
1993	Stephen Hendry (Scotland)	Jimmy White (England)	18–5
1994	Stephen Hendry (Scotland)	Jimmy White (England)	18–17
1995	Stephen Hendry (Scotland)	Nigel Bond (England)	18–9
1996	Stephen Hendry (Scotland)	Peter Ebdon (England)	18–12
1997	Ken Doherty (Ireland)	Stephen Hendry (Scotland)	18–12
1998	John Higgins (Scotland)	Ken Doherty (Ireland)	18–12
1999	Stephen Hendry (Scotland)	Mark Williams (Wales)	18–11
2000	Mark Williams (Wales)	Matthew Stevens (Wales)	18–16
2001	Ronnie O'Sullivan (England)	John Higgins (Scotland)	18–14
2002	Peter Ebdon (England)	Stephen Hendry (Scotland)	18–17
2003	Mark Williams (Wales)	Ken Doherty (Ireland)	18–16
2004	Ronnie O'Sullivan (England)	Graham Dott (Scotland)	18–8

Criminal records

A number of snooker stars have swapped cues for microphones and released pop singles. 'Snooker Loopy' by Chas 'n' Dave and the Matchroom Mob (Willie Thorne, Tony Meo, Dennis Taylor, Terry Griffiths and Steve Davis) reached number six in May 1986. Peter Ebdon deserves a gold disc for persistence, if not for musical ability. The 2002 world champion has released not one but two singles: 'I Am A Clown' and 'The Fall of Paradise'. And it's not just players who have come to the attention of music lovers. 1985's 'The Len Ganley Stance', by Half Man Half Biscuit, immortalized a rotund referee from Northern Ireland.

United Kingdom Championship

From 1977 to 1983 the UK Championship was open only to players holding a British passport, but since 1984 the tournament has been open to all nationalities. It is widely regarded as the second most important ranking tournament after the world championship. The event has had a number of venues, the latest being the Barbican Centre in York which has hosted the tournament since 2001.

	Champion	Defeated finalist	Score
1977	Patsy Fagan (Ireland)	Doug Mountjoy (Wales)	12–9
1978	Doug Mountjoy (Wales)	David Taylor (England)	15–9
1979	John Virgo (England)	Terry Griffiths (Wales)	14–13
1980	Steve Davis (England)	Alex Higgins (Northern Ireland)	16–6
1981	Steve Davis (England)	Terry Griffiths (Wales)	16–3
1982	Terry Griffiths (Wales)	Alex Higgins (Northern Ireland)	16–5
1983	Alex Higgins (Northern Ireland)	Steve Davis (England)	16–15
1984	Steve Davis (England)	Alex Higgins (Northern Ireland)	16–8
1985	Steve Davis (England)	Willie Thorne (England)	16–14
1986	Steve Davis (England)	Neal Foulds (England)	16–7
1987	Steve Davis (England)	Jimmy White (England)	16–14
1988	Doug Mountjoy (Wales)	Stephen Hendry (Scotland)	16–12
1989	Stephen Hendry (Scotland)	Steve Davis (England)	16–12
1990	Stephen Hendry (Scotland)	Steve Davis (England)	16–15
1991	John Parrott (England)	Jimmy White (England)	16–13
1992	Jimmy White (England)	John Parrott (England)	16–9
1993	Ronnie O'Sullivan (England)	Stephen Hendry (Scotland)	10–6
1994	Stephen Hendry (Scotland)	Ken Doherty (Ireland)	10–5
1995	Stephen Hendry (Scotland)	Peter Ebdon (England)	10–3
1996	Stephen Hendry (Scotand)	John Higgins (Scotland)	10–9
1997	Ronnie O'Sullivan (England)	Stephen Hendry (Scotland)	10–6
1998	John Higgins (Scotland)	Matthew Stevens (Wales)	10–6
1999	Mark Williams (Wales)	Matthew Stevens (Wales)	10–8
2000	John Higgins (Scotland)	Mark Williams (Wales)	10–4
2001	Ronnie O'Sullivan (England)	Ken Doherty (Ireland)	10–1
2002	Mark Williams (Wales)	Ken Doherty (Ireland)	10–9
2003	Matthew Stevens (Wales)	Stephen Hendry (Scotland)	10–8
2004	Stephen Maguire (Scotland)	David Gray (England)	10–1

A really interesting fact

Not only has Steve Davis won more trophies than most players, he has also garnered more nicknames. Over the years he has been called the Nugget, the Essex Executioner, the Romford Robot, the Ginger Magician, Golden Balls, and, courtesy of satirical TV show *Spitting Image*, Steve 'Interesting' Davis.

The Masters

The Masters is an invitational non-ranking tournament but is regarded as one of the game's majors. It has been played at the Wembley Conference Centre since 1979 and was sponsored between 1975 and 2003 by Benson & Hedges.

	Champion	Defeated finalist	Score
1975	John Spencer (England)	Ray Reardon (Wales)	9–8
1976	Ray Reardon (Wales)	Graham Miles (England)	7–3
1977	Doug Mountjoy (Wales)	Ray Reardon (Wales)	7–6
1978	Alex Higgins (Northern Ireland)	Cliff Thorburn (Canada)	7–5
1979	Perrie Mans (South Africa)	Alex Higgins (Northern Ireland)	8–4
1980	Terry Griffiths (Wales)	Alex Higgins (Northern Ireland)	9–5
1981	Alex Higgins (Northern Ireland)	Terry Griffiths (Wales)	9–6
1982	Steve Davis (England)	Terry Griffiths (Wales)	9–5
1983	Cliff Thorburn (Canada)	Ray Reardon (Wales)	9–7
1984	Jimmy White (England)	Terry Griffiths (Wales)	9–5
1985	Cliff Thorburn (Canada)	Doug Mountjoy (Wales)	9–6
1986	Cliff Thorburn (Canada)	Jimmy White (England)	9–5
1987	Dennis Taylor (Northern Ireland)	Alex Higgins (Northern Ireland)	9–8
1988	Steve Davis (England)	Mike Hallett (England)	9–0
1989	Stephen Hendry (Scotland)	John Parrott (England)	9–6
1990	Stephen Hendry (Scotland)	John Parrott (England)	9–4
1991	Stephen Hendry (Scotland)	Mike Hallett (England)	9–8
1992	Stephen Hendry (Scotland)	John Parrott (England)	9–4
1993	Stephen Hendry (Scotland)	James Wattana (Thailand)	9–5
1994	Alan McManus (Scotland)	Stephen Hendry (Scotland)	9–8
1995	Ronnie O'Sullivan (England)	John Higgins (Scotland)	9–3
1996	Stephen Hendry (Scotland)	Ronnie O'Sullivan (England)	10–5
1997	Steve Davis (England)	Ronnie O'Sullivan (England)	10–8
1998	Mark Williams (Wales)	Stephen Hendry (Scotland)	10–9
1999	John Higgins (Scotland)	Ken Doherty (Ireland)	10–8
2000	Matthew Stevens (Wales)	Ken Doherty (Ireland)	10–8
2001	Paul Hunter (England)	Fergal O'Brien (Ireland)	10–9
2002	Paul Hunter (England)	Mark Williams (Wales)	10–9
2003	Mark Williams (Wales)	Stephen Hendry (Scotland)	10–4
2004	Paul Hunter (England)	Ronnie O'Sullivan (England)	10–9

Most Maximum Breaks in Professional Competitions

A maximum break – a break of 147 points – is the ultimate achievement in snooker.

Stephen Hendry (Scotland)	8
Ronnie O'Sullivan (England)	6
John Higgins (Scotland)	5
James Wattana (Thailand)	3

Fastest cue in the west

Ronnie O'Sullivan compiled a 147 maximum break in 5 minutes and 20 seconds at the world championship in April 1997.

A-Z

angle when the cue ball is angled by a pocket, it is so close to the corner of the cushion that it cannot be hit in a straight line towards the desired object ball

backspin the backward motion imparted on the **cue ball** when the cue strikes it under the centre

baize the green woollen cloth used to cover the slate **bed** of a table

baulk the part of the table behind the **baulk line**

baulk line the line near the bottom of the table. The brown spot is at the centre of this line and the yellow and green spots are at either side of the brown spot at the points where the **D** meets the baulk line

bed the flat surface, made of slate, on which the **baize** cloth is laid

break 1. a consecutive series of pots, eg *it looks like his break is about to come to an end* 2. the score made at the end of such a series of pots, eg *a break of seventeen; a century break* 3. same as **break-off**

break-off the first shot of a frame, when the **cue ball** is hit from the **D** to break the formation of reds

bridge 1. the support for the cue made by the player placing his fingers on the table and raising his thumb 2. a metal support performing a similar function at one end of a **rest**

butt the thicker end of the cue

cannon if the cue ball cannons into a ball, it deflects from the **object ball** into another ball

century a break of 100 or more points

chalk a small cube of coloured chalk used to rub the tip of the cue to ensure a good contact when the cue strikes the **cue ball**

check side see **side**

colour any of the six coloured balls – yellow, green, brown, blue, pink and black – which are potted after a red and which must be potted in sequence after the 15 reds have been potted

cue a long tapered wooden shaft with a leather tip, used to propel the **cue ball**

cue ball the white ball struck by the cue and used to propel the **object ball**

cushion the padded lining of the inner side of a table

D the semi-circular area adjoining the **baulk line** at the bottom end of the table

double if a player doubles a ball, the **object ball** rebounds off a **cushion** back towards the player

drag the slightly retarded motion of the **cue ball**, caused by **backspin**, when it is struck just under the centre

English a North American term for **side**

extension a shaft extension attached to the end of a one-piece cue or screwed into the middle of a two-piece cue, used when a shot is not possible with a standard-size cue

feather if a player feathers the cue ball, he touches it lightly with his cue tip unintentionally while lining up a shot

fluke 1. a fortuitous pot usually resulting from an unintended collision or rebound 2. if a player flukes a shot he pots a ball in this way, eg *he fluked the green off three cushions*

follow-through the forward motion of the cue after the cue ball has been struck

foul an illegal shot that results in points awarded to one's opponent

frame a single game, completed when all the balls have been potted or when one player has conceded

free ball a situation where one's opponent plays a foul shot but leaves the cue ball in a position where one does not have a direct shot to the desired object ball. The referee awards a free ball, giving one the opportunity to nominate and then play another ball, which is then regarded as having the same points value as the desired object ball

full ball to hit a ball full ball is to strike the cue ball against the full face of the **object ball**; compare **half ball**

half ball to hit a ball half ball is to strike the cue ball against the edge of the **object ball**; compare **full ball**

half-butt a cue, longer than the standard cue, usually used with a long **rest**

half-century a break of between 50 and 99 points

in-off an instance of the cue ball going into a pocket, resulting in a foul and one's opponent taking his next shot from the **D**

jaws the jaws of a pocket are the corners of the **cushion**

kick a bad contact between cue ball and **object ball** caused by dust, chalk, etc, resulting in both balls slowing down or deviating from the intended path

kiss a light contact between two balls

massé a stroke made with the cue vertical or nearly so, in order to make the cue ball swerve sharply. The word derives from the French *masser* meaning to hit from above with a hammer

maximum (break) a break of 147 points, comprising 15 reds and 15 blacks followed by all six colours

miscue when a player miscues while playing a shot, there is a poor contact between the tip of the cue and the cue ball

miss if the referee judges that a player's failed attempt to escape from a **snooker** was deliberate, he calls a foul and a miss, penalizes the player, and either asks him to play the shot again, with the balls replaced in their original positions if they moved, or invites the player's opponent to play the next shot

object ball the ball the player intends to strike with the **cue ball**

pack the reds when gathered closely between the pink and black spots

plant a shot where the cue ball strikes the **object ball** which then strikes another ball into a pocket

pocket any of the six holes with pouches or nets into which the balls are potted

pot when a ball is potted it goes into one of the pockets

push stroke an illegal stroke in which the cue is still in contact, or comes into contact again, with the **cue ball** when the cue ball touches the **object ball**

rail same as **cushion**

rest a long wooden pole with a metal **bridge** at one end on which a player's cue is rested when he cannot bridge with his hand. See **half-butt** and **spider**

running side see **side**

safety a period of play in which both players attempt to prevent their opponent from scoring points by keeping the cue ball in positions from which pots are unlikely to be attempted, eg *a long spell of safety brought to an end by a fluked red*

safety shot a defensive shot the intention of which is not to give one's opponent an opportunity of potting a ball

screw if a player screws the **cue ball** back, he imparts backspin on it such that it recoils after striking the **object ball**

screw shot a shot in which **backspin** is imparted on the **cue ball** such that it spins backwards towards the player

set same as **plant**

shot to nothing an attempt to pot a ball played in such way that, if the shot is missed, one's opponent will not be left with an easy opportunity

side side spin imparted on the cue ball causing it to swerve and alter its angle of rebound; **check side** causes the cue ball to rebound off a cushion at less of an angle than a normally struck shot, while **running side** causes the cue ball to rebound off a cushion at more of an angle

sink same as **pot**

snooker 1. a situation where the path from cue ball to object ball is blocked, forcing an indirect shot to be played 2. if a player requires snookers there are insufficient points left on the table for him to win the frame without laying successful snookers

spider a **rest** with legs arched wide and offering several cueing positions

spot 1. any of the six marked points on the table on which the colours are placed at the start of a frame and after they are potted while there are still reds on the table 2. if a referee spots a colour, he places it back on its spot after it has been potted

stun if a player stuns the ball or plays a stun shot he imparts a small amount of **backspin** onto the **cue ball** such that its forward momentum is checked

tip the small circular surface made of leather at the narrow end of the **cue**. The tip is the part of the cue that comes into contact with the cue ball

topspin if a player plays a shot with topspin he strikes the **cue ball** above centre such that it moves forward with greater momentum after it strikes the **object ball**

touching ball a situation where the **cue ball** is touching another ball and must be played away from that ball without moving it

Some snooker slang

Chinese snooker	a position where the **cue ball** is awkwardly placed, usually very close to or touching another ball, rather than actually snookered, making cueing awkward
cocked hat	a shot in which the **object ball**, lying close to a side cushion, is hit off three cushions towards a middle pocket, the trajectory of the shot following a triangular shape like that of an old-fashioned three-cornered hat
wiped its feet	if a ball rattles off the jaws of the pocket before going in it can be said to have wiped its feet

Some famous snooker players

Fred Davis, 1913–98

Born in Whitwell, Derbyshire, England, the younger brother of **Joe Davis** has a unique place in the sport, straddling the early era of professional snooker, when he won eight world titles, and the modern age, when his skill and charm helped make snooker a mainstay of the television schedules. Remarkably, he competed professionally until 1992 when, at the age of 78 and with arthritis restricting his mobility, he finally retired.

Joe Davis, 1901–78

Born in Whitwell, Derbyshire, England, he completely dominated the early years of professional snooker, winning the first 15 world professional championships and remained unbeaten until he retired from world championship snooker after winning his last world title in 1946. He continued to play professionally and achieved the game's first 147 maximum break in an exhibition match at Leicester Square in 1955.

Steve Davis, 1957–

Born in London, England, he dominated snooker in the 1980s, winning in 1981 the first of six world championships and finishing the decade as number one in the world rankings for the seventh consecutive year. His dedication on the practice table and remorselessness in competition put him in a class of his own for most of his early career. The resulting financial rewards – he became snooker's first millionaire – changed the game's image from the sign of a 'misspent youth' to a respectable career option. As well as winning 28 ranking events, he recorded the first televised 147 break (1982). Although he now works as a TV commentator, Davis is still a formidable player.

Stephen Hendry, 1969–

Born in Edinburgh, Scotland, he is widely regarded as the game's greatest ever player, having become world number one and winner of all snooker's major tournaments before turning 22. As well as winning seven world championships – a record for the modern era – and being the youngest ever world champion, Hendry has also recorded many more century breaks than anyone else (over 600) and more maximum breaks too. His 16 centuries in the 2002 world championship is also a record. He is the game's leading money earner and, although his total dominance of the game is now at an end, is still one of the world's top players.

Alex Higgins, 1949–

Born in Belfast, Northern Ireland, 'The Hurricane' brought snooker to life in the 1970s with his flamboyant play and lifestyle. He trained as a jockey but decided snooker would be more lucrative and turned professional in 1971. He made an immediate impact, winning the world championship at his first attempt the following year. Throughout the 70s and early 80s he was snooker's biggest box-office draw, his restless energy and bold potting attracting a new generation of fans. His career reached its high point in 1982 when he won the world title for a second time. In the 90s his career began to decline and he appeared more on the front page of newspapers than on the back. He no longer plays at the highest level but is still fondly remembered, his turbulent career being dramatized in the play 'Hurricane' in 2003.

Ronnie O'Sullivan, 1975–

Born in Chigwell, Essex, England, 'The Rocket' is regarded as snooker's most naturally gifted player. He turned professional in 1992 and became the youngest player ever to win a ranking event when he won the UK championship in 1993, just before he turned 18. Although his talent ought to make him favourite for every match, his temperament has let him down and in his early twenties he threatened several times to retire. Fortunately, he has not done so and has achieved much since, including winning the world championship in 2001 and 2004 and becoming world number one in the rankings in 2002/03. Although right-handed, he can also play to a high standard as a left-hander.

Ray Reardon, 1932–

Born in Tredegar, Wales, the former miner and policeman is one of snooker's all-time greats. His relaxed manner masked a steely determination which, allied to a big-match temperament and an outstanding safety game, brought him six world titles in the70s. Nicknamed 'Dracula', because of his black, slicked-back hair, Reardon did much to make snooker a popular television sport. He was world number one from seasons 76/77 to 80/81 and is the only player so far to lose and then regain this status, doing so in season 82/83. More recently, he has acted as an advisor to **Ronnie O'Sullivan**.

Jimmy White, 1962–

Born in London, England, 'The Whirlwind' is one of snooker's most exciting and popular players. Left-handed, naturally gifted, and fast around the table, White has always been one of snooker's biggest draws. Although career winnings total over £4 million, he is known as snooker's nearly man, having so far failed to win the world championship despite appearing in the final six times between 1984 and 1994.

SOFTBALL

Origins

Softball was invented by George Hancock in Chicago, USA, in 1887 as an impromptu indoor version of baseball. It was described by a number of names, including 'ladies' baseball', 'cornball', 'kitten-ball', 'diamond ball', 'pumpkin ball' and 'mush-ball', before the term softball was coined by Walter Hakanson in 1926.

Rules and description

Softball is a nine-a-side ball game played by men and women. It can be played both indoors and outdoors. Like baseball, the aim is to earn runs by hitting the ball with the bat and running past all three bases before returning to the 'home plate'. The biggest difference is that softball uses an underarm rather than overarm pitching style. The bat and ball are larger and the bases are closer together. An orange safety base is attached to the normal white first base; the hitter runs to the orange base and the baseman to the white base in an attempt to avoid collisions. The left, centre, and right fielder play in the outfield, while the pitcher, catcher, first baseman, second baseman, third baseman, and shortstop play in the infield. Each side has seven innings. There are three 'outs' per side before the batting team becomes the pitching team and vice versa. Outs can be achieved by catching the ball, by tagging the runner between bases or when the batter makes three 'strikes' (missing the ball).

There are two major types of softball – slow-pitch and fast-pitch softball. In the slow-pitch version the pitched ball must be thrown in an arc between 12ft/3.66m and 6ft/1.83m minimum. Because of the requirement for an arc, the pitcher must throw the ball relatively slowly. There is no such restriction in fast-pitch softball. In order for a strike to be called, the ball must cross the home plate between the batter's shoulders and knees.

Ruling body: International Softball Federation (ISF)

World Championships

Men

	Winner	Runner-up	Venue
1966	USA	Mexico	Mexico City, Mexico
1968	USA	Canada	Oklahoma City, USA
1972	Canada	USA	Manila, Philippines
1976	Canada/New Zealand/USA		Lower Hutt, New Zealand
1980	USA	Canada	Tacoma, USA
1984	New Zealand	Canada	Midland, USA
1988	USA	New Zealand	Saskatoon, Canada
1992	Canada	New Zealand	Manila, Philippines
1996	New Zealand	Canada	Midland, USA
2000	New Zealand	Japan	East London, South Africa
2004	New Zealand	Canada	Christchurch, New Zealand

Women

	Winner	Runner-up	Venue
1965	Australia	USA	Melbourne, Australia
1970	Japan	USA	Osaka, Japan
1974	USA	Japan	Stratford, USA

	Winner	Runner-up	Venue
1978	USA	Canada	San Salvador, El Salvador
1982	New Zealand	Taiwan	Taipei, Taiwan
1986	USA	China	Auckland, New Zealand
1990	USA	New Zealand	Normal, USA
1994	USA	China	St John's, Canada
1998	USA	Australia	Fujinomiya, Japan
2002	USA	Japan	Saskatoon, Canada
2006			Beijing, China

Olympic Champions

At the Olympics softball is a women-only sport and the format is fast-pitch. The USA has won each time since its introduction in 1996.

SPEED SKATING

Origins

As a recreational sport skating became popular on frozen Dutch canals in the 17th century; the first recorded race, however, dates from 1763 and took place in the East Anglian Fens in England. By the end of the 19th century skaters from northern Europe and North America were competing in the first world championships. Short-track speed skating made its debut as a demonstration sport at the 1988 Winter Olympics.

Rules and description

An outdoor speed skating rink is a 400m oval. Skaters race in pairs against the clock. They cross over lanes along the back straight of each lap to even out the advantage of starting in the inner lane. Competition ranges from sprints of 500m to 1,000m up to a 10,000m race for men.

In short-track speed skating, racers compete around an oval track that measures 111.12m/121.52yd in circumference. The course is marked by rubber blocks and skaters have to skate outside the line of the blocks. Four to eight skaters engage in a mass start and race over distances ranging from 500m to 3,000m. Elimination heats lead to finals and semi-finals. Skaters wear hard-shell helmets as falls are commonplace.

Ruling body: International Skating Union (ISU)

Get on your bike

Many of the same muscle groups are used in speed skating and cycling, so it is not really surprising that a number of skaters have gone on to become talented cyclists. Eric Heiden retired at 22 to become a professional cyclist and competed in the 1986 Tour de France; Connie Carpenter was seventh at the 1972 Winter Games 1,500m and won the 1984 cycling road race title; and Christa Rothenberger, loath to give up either sport, won the gold medal at 1,000m at the 1988 Winter games and followed it up with a silver on two wheels in the 1,000m sprint in the Summer Games in Seoul.

Speed Skating World Championships – Overall Champion

The men's event has been held annually since 1889 and has been recognized by the ISU since 1893. The overall championship is contested over four distances: 500m, 1,000m, 5,000m and 10,000m. The women's event has been contested since 1936. The women's distances are 500m, 1,000m, 1,500m and 3,000m.

	Men	**Women**
1976	Piet Kleine (The Netherlands)	Sylvia Burka (Canada)
1977	Eric Heiden (USA)	Vera Bryndzei (USSR)
1978	Eric Heiden (USA)	Tatiana Averina (USSR)
1979	Eric Heiden (USA)	Beth Heiden (USA)
1980	Hilbert van der Duim (The Netherlands)	Natalia Petrussheva (USSR)
1981	Amund Sjøbrend (Norway)	Natalia Petrussheva (USSR)
1982	Hilbert van der Duim (The Netherlands)	Karin Busch (East Germany)
1983	Rolf Falk-Larssen (Norway)	Andrea Schöne (East Germany)
1984	Oleg Bozhev (USSR)	Karin Enke (née Busch) (East Germany)
1985	Hein Vergeer (The Netherlands)	Andrea Schöne (East Germany)
1986	Hein Vergeer (The Netherlands)	Karin Kania (née Busch) (East Germany)
1987	Nikolai Gulyayev (USSR)	Karin Kania (née Busch) (East Germany)
1988	Eric Flaim (USA)	Karin Kania (née Busch) (East Germany)
1989	Leo Visser (The Netherlands)	Constanze Moser (East Germany)
1990	Johann Olav Koss (Norway)	Jacqueline Börner (East Germany)
1991	Johann Olav Koss (Norway)	Gunda Niemann (Germany)*
1992	Roberto Sighel (Italy)	Gunda Niemann (Germany)
1993	Falko Zandstra (The Netherlands)	Gunda Niemann (Germany)
1994	Johann Olav Koss (Norway)	Emese Hunyady (Austria)
1995	Rintje Ritsma (The Netherlands)	Gunda Niemann (Germany)
1996	Rintje Ritsma (The Netherlands)	Gunda Niemann (Germany)
1997	Ids Postma (The Netherlands)	Gunda Niemann (Germany)
1998	Ids Postma (The Netherlands)	Gunda Niemann-Stirnemann (Germany)
1999	Rintje Ritsma (The Netherlands)	Gunda Niemann-Stirnemann (Germany)
2000	Gianni Romme (The Netherlands)	Claudia Pechstein (Germany)
2001	Rintje Ritsma (The Netherlands)	Anni Friesinger (Germany)
2002	Jochem Uytdehaage (The Netherlands)	Anni Friesinger (Germany)
2003	Gianni Romme (The Netherlands)	Cindy Klassen (Canada)
2004	Chad Hedrick (USA)	Renate Groenewold (The Netherlands)

* As Gunda Kleemann

Short-Track Speed Skating World Championships – Overall Champion

The world championships were unofficial until recognized by the ISU in 1981.

	Men	Women
1976	Alan Rattray (Canada)	Celeste Chiapaty (USA)
1977	Gaétan Boucher (Canada)	Brenda Webster (Canada)
1978	Jim Lynch (Australia)	Sarah Docter (Canada)
1979	Hiroshi Toda (Japan)	Sylvie Daigle (Canada)
1980	Gaétan Boucher (Canada)	Miyoshi Kato (Japan)
1981	Benoît Baril (Canada)	Miyoshi Kato (Japan)
1982	Guy Daigneault (Canada)	Maryse Perreault (Canada)
1983	Louis Grenier (Canada)	Sylvie Daigle (Canada)
1984	Guy Daigneault (Canada)	Mariko Kinoshita (Japan)
1985	Toshinobu Kawai (Japan)	Eiko Shishii (Japan)
1986	Tatsuyoshi Ishihara (Japan)	Bonnie Blair (USA)
1987	Michel Daigneault (Canada)/ Toshinobu Kawai (Japan)	Eiko Shishii (Japan)
1988	Paul van der Velde (The Netherlands)	Sylvie Daigle (Canada)
1989	Michel Daigneault (Canada)	Sylvie Daigle (Canada)
1990	Lee Joon-ho (South Korea)	Sylvie Daigle (Canada)
1991	Wilf O'Reilly (Great Britain)	Nathalie Lambert (Canada)
1992	Kim Ki-hoon (South Korea)	Kim So-hee (South Korea)
1993	Marc Gagnon (Canada)	Nathalie Lambert (Canada)
1994	Marc Gagnon (Canada)	Nathalie Lambert (Canada)
1995	Chae Ji-hoon (South Korea)	Chun Lee-kyung (South Korea)
1996	Marc Gagnon (Canada)	Chun Lee-kyung (South Korea)
1997	Kim Dong-sung (South Korea)	Chun Lee-kyung (South Korea)/ Yang Yang (A) (China)
1998	Marc Gagnon (Canada)	Yang Yang (A) (China)
1999	Li Jiajun (China)	Yang Yang (A) (China)
2000	Rioung Min (South Korea)	Yang Yang (A) (China)
2001	Li Jiajun (China)	Yang Yang (A) (China)
2002	Kim Dong-sung (South Korea)	Yang Yang (A) (China)
2003	Ahn Hyun-soo (South Korea)	Choi Eun-kyung (South Korea)
2004	Ahn Hyun-soo (South Korea)	Choi Eun-kyung (South Korea)

Happy clappy skaters

The introduction of the clap skate in the 1990s has seen speed records tumble. Designed in the Netherlands, its blade is hinged at the front to allow it to detach from the heel of the skate, thus staying in contact with the ice for longer. These skates are sometimes also known as 'slap skates'.

Some famous speed skaters

Ivar Ballangrud, 1904–69

Born in Lunner, Norway, he was one of the most successful early speed skaters and dominated the sport in the 1920s and 30s. He took four world championships (1926, 1932, 1936, 1938), four Olympic gold medals (for the 5,000m in 1928; and for the 10,000m, 5,000m and 500m in 1936) and four European championships (1929, 1930, 1933 and 1936).

Bonnie Blair, 1964–

Born in Cornwall, New York, USA, she started speed skating at just four years old. She became a specialist in sprints, winning Olympic gold at 500m in 1988, 1992 and 1994 and at 1,000m in 1992 and 1994, these five gold medals being a record for a female US athlete. She also took four world championship golds (in 1986, 1989, 1994 and 1995). She was elected to the US Olympic Hall of Fame in 2004.

Eric Heiden, 1958–

Born in Madison, Wisconsin, USA, he made sporting history at the 1980 Lake Placid Games by winning gold in all five speed-skating disciplines, from 500m to 10,000m, breaking the Olympic record in each. The most dramatic was in the 1,500m when, despite almost falling after hitting a rut, he recovered to win by 0.37s. He won the world championships for three consecutive years between 1977 and 1979. After retirement he became a successful cyclist and is now an orthopaedic surgeon.

Johann Olav Koss, 1968–

He was born in Drammen, Norway. Despite being in a hospital bed on the day of the opening ceremony of the 1992 Games, recovering from an operation on an inflamed pancreas, just days later he won gold in the 1,500m and silver in the 10,000m. Two years later on home ice at Lillehammer he took three golds (at 10,000m, 5,000m and 1,500m), breaking the world record each time. He won three overall world championship golds in 1990, 1991 and 1994 (he took silver in 1992 and bronze in 1993) during a period of dominance in which he broke ten world records. After retirement he pursued a career in medicine and became a Unicef ambassador.

Gunda Niemann-Stirnemann, 1966–

Born in Sondershausen, Germany, she dominated women's speed skating in the 1990s, winning the overall World Championships title no fewer than eight times (1991–3 and 1995–9). She took three Olympic golds (at 3,000m and 5,000m in 1992, and 3,000m in 1998) as well as four silvers.

Yang Yang, 1975–

Born in Heilongjiang province in the north of China, she is the most successful female short-track skater of all time and dominated the world championships between 1997 and 2002 with 14 individual and team golds. Her gold medal at the 2002 Games in the 500m was China's first ever in the Winter Olympics. She is usually known as Yang Yang (A) to distinguish her from another successful Chinese female short-track skater Yang Yang (S). The 'A' and 'S' appended to their names are for the benefit of non-Chinese speakers as their names are written differently in Chinese. The letters stand for 'August' and 'September', the months of their birth.

SQUASH

Origins

Squash can trace its origins via a series of racket-and-ball games that were played in England from the Middle Ages onwards. They include real tennis, fives and rackets. Squash developed in the middle of the 19th century at Harrow School and the first rules were described in 1886. It was probably played by young schoolboys as an introductory game before they graduated to rackets. The slower and softer ball was squeezable or 'squashable' – hence the derivation of the name.

Rules and description

Squash is a demanding indoor racket-and-ball game played by singles or doubles players. More properly called squash rackets, the game is played within an enclosed court that measures 9.75 x 6.4m/32 x 21ft; doubles courts are 1.22m/4ft wider. US courts are 5.4m/18ft wide and players use a harder ball. Previously made of wood and painted white, many squash court walls are now made of Perspex to allow spectators to view the action. A front wall line is marked on the front of the court 4.57m/15ft high; a back wall line 2.13m/7ft at the back, with the side wall lines sloping downward from front to back. If the ball goes above these lines it is out and the point lost. A 'cut line' or 'service line', 1.82m/6ft high, also appears on the front wall. The server stands in either 'service box' and needs to hit the serve so that the ball hits the wall above the cut line and then bounces back further than the 'short line' – a horizontal line marked on the floor of the court.

Shots are made alternately and players can return the shots on the volley or after a first bounce. A strip, generally made of metal, runs across the front wall, 48cm/19in high, and is known as the 'tin'. When the ball hits this it is 'out' and the point lost. In the usual international scoring system, the first player to nine points wins the game and the best of five games wins the match. Points can only be won by the server. When a rally is lost the serve transfers to the opponent. At eight-all the receiver (non-server) has to choose to play either to nine points (known as 'set one') or to ten points (known as 'set two'). In the American scoring system, which is also used in some international competitions, points are won regardless of who is serving and games are to 15 points.

The racket measures no more than 68.5cm/27in and the round head must not exceed 21.5cm/8.5in in length or 18.4cm/7.25in in width. The ball is black, squashy and light, weighing around 24g (less than an ounce).

Ruling body: World Squash Federation (WSF). The forerunners of the organization were the International Squash Rackets Federation (ISRF) and the Women's International Squash Rackets Federation

World Open

The World Amateur Individual Championship was inaugurated by the ISRF. However, players turned professional during the 1970s and an Open title for men was inaugurated in 1976 with a women's event being first held in 1979.

Men

	Winner	Runner-up	Venue
1976	Geoff Hunt (Australia)	Mohibullah Khan (Pakistan)	London, UK
1977	Geoff Hunt (Australia)	Qamar Zaman (Pakistan)	Adelaide, Australia
1978	*Not held*		
1979	Geoff Hunt (Australia)	Qamar Zaman (Pakistan)	Toronto, Canada
1980	Geoff Hunt (Australia)	Qamar Zaman (Pakistan)	Adelaide, Australia
1981	Jahangir Khan (Pakistan)	Geoff Hunt (Australia)	Toronto, Canada
1982	Jahangir Khan (Pakistan)	Dean Williams (Australia)	Birmingham, UK
1983	Jahangir Khan (Pakistan)	Chris Dittmar (Australia)	West Germany
1984	Jahangir Khan (Pakistan)	Qamar Zaman (Pakistan)	Karachi, Pakistan
1985	Jahangir Khan (Pakistan)	Ross Norman (New Zealand)	Cairo, Egypt
1986	Ross Norman (New Zealand)	Jahangir Khan (Pakistan)	Toulouse, France
1987	Jansher Khan (Pakistan)	Chris Dittmar (Australia)	Birmingham, UK
1988	Jahangir Khan (Pakistan)	Jansher Khan (Pakistan)	Amsterdam, The Netherlands
1989	Jansher Khan (Pakistan)	Chris Dittmar (Australia)	Kuala Lumpur, Malaysia
1990	Jansher Khan (Pakistan)	Chris Dittmar (Australia)	Toulouse, France
1991	Rodney Martin (Australia)	Jahangir Khan (Pakistan)	Adelaide, Australia
1992	Jansher Khan (Pakistan)	Chris Dittmar (Australia)	Johannesburg, South Africa
1993	Jansher Khan (Pakistan)	Jahangir Khan (Pakistan)	Karachi, Pakistan
1994	Jansher Khan (Pakistan)	Peter Marshall (England)	Barcelona, Spain
1995	Jansher Khan (Pakistan)	Del Harris (England)	Nicosia, Cyprus
1996	Jansher Khan (Pakistan)	Rodney Eyles (Australia)	Karachi, Pakistan
1997	Rodney Eyles (Australia)	Peter Nicol (Scotland)	Petaling Jaya, Malaysia
1998	Jonathon Power (Canada)	Peter Nicol (Scotland)	Doha, Qatar
1999	Peter Nicol (Scotland)	Ahmed Barada (Egypt)	Cairo, Egypt
2000–1	*Not held*		
2002	David Palmer (Australia)	John White (Scotland)	Antwerp, Belgium
2003	Amr Shabana (Egypt)	Thierry Lincou (France)	Lahore, Pakistan
2004	Thierry Lincou (France)	Lee Beachill (England)	Doha, Qatar

Women

	Winner	Runner-up	Venue
1979	Heather McKay (Australia)	Sue Cogswell (England)	Sheffield, UK
1981	Rhonda Thorne (Australia)	Vicki Hoffman (Australia)	Toronto, Canada
1983	Vicki Cardwell (née Hoffman) (Australia)	Rhonda Thorne (Australia)	Perth, Australia
1985	Susan Devoy (New Zealand)	Lisa Opie (England)	Dublin, Ireland
1987	Susan Devoy (New Zealand)	Lisa Opie (England)	Auckland, New Zealand
1989	Martine Le Moignan (England)	Susan Devoy (New Zealand)	Warmond, The Netherlands
1990	Susan Devoy (New Zealand)	Martine Le Moignan (England)	Sydney, Australia
1991	*Not held*		
1992	Susan Devoy (New Zealand)	Michelle Martin (Australia)	Vancouver, Canada
1993	Michelle Martin (Australia)	Liz Erving (New Zealand)	Johannesburg, South Africa
1994	Michelle Martin (Australia)	Cassie Campion (née Jackman) (England)	St Peter Port, Guernsey
1995	Michelle Martin (Australia)	Sarah Fitz-Gerald (Australia)	Hong Kong
1996	Sarah Fitz-Gerald (Australia)	Cassie Campion (née Jackman) (England)	Petaling Jaya, Malaysia
1997	Sarah Fitz-Gerald (Australia)	Michelle Martin (Australia)	Sydney, Australia
1998	Sarah Fitz-Gerald (Australia)	Michelle Martin (Australia)	Stuttgart, Germany
1999	Cassie Campion (née Jackman) (England)	Michelle Martin (Australia)	Seattle, USA
2000	Carol Owens (Australia)	Leilani Joyce (New Zealand)	Edinburgh, UK
2001	Sarah Fitz-Gerald (Australia)	Leilani Joyce (New Zealand)	Melbourne, Australia
2002	Sarah Fitz-Gerald (Australia)	Natalie Pohrer (England)	Doha, Qatar
2003	Carol Owens (Australia)	Cassie Jackman (England)	Hong Kong
2004	Vanessa Atkinson (The Netherlands)	Natalie Grinham (Australia)	Kuala Lumpur, Malaysia

British Open Champions

The British Open Championship was inaugurated in 1930 when C R Read was awarded the title. His reign as champion lasted only until the following year when Don Butcher defeated him.

Men

1931–2	Don Butcher (England)
1933–8	Abdel Fattah Amr Bey (Egypt)
1939	Jim Dear (England)
1940–6	*Not held*
1947–50	Mahmoud el Karim (Egypt)
1951–6	Hashim Khan (Pakistan)
1957	Roshan Khan (Pakistan)
1958	Hashim Khan (Pakistan)
1959–62	Azam Khan (Pakistan)
1963	Mohibullah Khan (Pakistan)
1964–6	Abou Taleb (Egypt)
1967–8	Jonah Barrington (Ireland)
1969	Geoff Hunt (Australia)
1970–3	Jonah Barrington (Ireland)
1974	Geoff Hunt (Australia)
1975	Qamar Zaman (Pakistan)
1976–81	Geoff Hunt (Australia)
1982–91	Jahangir Khan (Pakistan)
1992–7	Jansher Khan (Pakistan)
1998	Peter Nicol (Scotland)
1999	Jonathon Power (Canada)
2000	David Evans (Wales)
2001	David Palmer (Australia)
2002	Peter Nicol (England)
2003–4	David Palmer (Australia)

Women

1922	Joyce Cave (England)	**1961**	Fran Marshall (England)
1922	Silvia Huntsman (England)	**1962–77**	Heather McKay (Australia)*
1923	Nancy Cave (England)	**1978**	Sue Newman (Australia)
1924	Joyce Cave (England)	**1979**	Barbara Wall (Australia)
1925–6	Cecily Fenwick (England)	**1980–3**	Vicki Cardwell (Australia)**
1928	Joyce Cave (England)	**1984–90**	Susan Devoy (New Zealand)
1929–30	Nancy Cave (England)	**1991**	Lisa Opie (England)
1931	Cecily Fenwick (England)	**1992**	Susan Devoy (New Zealand)
1932–4	Susan Noel (England)	**1993–8**	Michelle Martin (Australia)
1934–9	Margot Lumb (England)	**1999–2000**	Leilani Joyce (New Zealand)
1940–6	*Not held*	**2001–2**	Sarah Fitz-Gerald (Australia)
1947–9	Joan Curry (England)	**2003–4**	Rachael Grinham (Australia)
1950–9	Janet Morgan (England)		
1960	Sheila Macintosh (England)		

* 1962–5 as Heather Blundell

** 1980–1 as Vicki Hoffman

The Khan dynasty

Roshan Khan from Pakistan won the British Open in 1957. He took the title from his cousin Hashim, who had first won it in 1951, and was to reclaim it from Roshan in 1958. However, no sooner had Hashim reclaimed lost ground than his brother Azam succeeded him as champion in 1959 and held on to the title until 1962. Then the title passed to Mohibullah Khan… Hashim's nephew. That might have been it but 20 years later Jahangir Khan, son of Roshan, won the first of his six world titles. It shouldn't come as any surprise to learn that Jahangir in Urdu means 'the conqueror'.

A-Z

ace — a service shot that the receiver cannot touch with his or her racket

alley — the area along the side walls of the court

angle — a shot that first hits the side wall and then the front wall without touching the floor

boast — any shot that hits three walls before bouncing

boast for nick — a **boast** that lands in the **nick** and dies

drop — a touch shot where the ball falls close to the front wall after hitting it

get — a difficult shot successfully reached and returned, eg *what an amazing get*

half-court line — a line marked on the floor of the court that divides the back of the court into two

let — a replayed point, at the referee's discretion, following unintentional obstruction

lob — a high soft shot to the back of the court played when one's opponent is at the front

nick — 1. the angle between two walls or between the wall and the floor 2. the name given to a shot that hits the angle between two walls and dies

not up — the call made when the ball is not successfully retrieved, ie bounces twice

quarter court	one half of the back part of the court. The **half-court line** splits the back part of the court into two quarter courts
rail	a shot hit close to or parallel to the side walls
rally	an exchange of shots, starting with the service
service box	a square area in each **quarter court** bounded by part of the **short line**, part of the side wall and by two other lines, and from within which the server serves
set	if you set a game, you decide to extend it by a specified number of points
short line	a line extending the full width of the court and lying 5.44m/18ft from the front wall
stroke	a point (or the right to serve, depending on the scoring system being used) awarded to a deliberately obstructed player
T	the T-shaped configuration formed by the juncture of the **half-court line** and the **short line**. Players aim to control possession of this area
telltale	same as **tin**
tight	a shot is tight if it is played such that the second bounce lands as close to a side wall as possible and is therefore unreturnable
tin	the strip that runs along the base of the front wall. Balls are judged out if they hit it. The referee can determine this because of the noise made by the ball hitting it. For that reason it is also sometimes known as a telltale
volley	a shot played before the ball bounces

Why yellow is slower than blue

Squash balls are generally black, but they are manufactured in a variety of different speeds: faster balls (which bounce more) for novice players and the slowest ones for world tournament play. The differences are indicated by a small coloured dot marked on the ball, as below.

double yellow	a super slow ball used at championship level
yellow	a super slow ball
white	a slow ball
green	a slow ball
red	a medium speed ball
blue	a fast ball

Some famous squash players

Susan Devoy, 1964–

Born in Rotorua, New Zealand, she moved to England in 1982 and won the British Open eight times (1984–90, 1992). Improving steadily, she won the world championship in 1985, 1987, 1990 and 1992, the only New Zealand woman to win the World Open. Devoy was awarded an MBE in 1988.

Sarah Fitz-Gerald, 1968–

Born in Melbourne, Australia, she is the most successful woman player of the modern age with five World Open titles (1996–8, 2001–2). She also won a gold medal at the 2002 Commonwealth Games. Fitz-Gerald was awarded the AM (Order of Australia) in 2004.

Geoff Hunt, 1947–

Born in Melbourne, Australia, he was the Australian amateur champion at the age of 17, the world amateur champion in 1967, 1969 and 1971, and the World Open champion in 1976–7 and 1979–80. Hunt also won eight British titles between 1969 and 1981. He was awarded an MBE and an AM (Order of Australia).

Jahangir Khan, 1963–

Born in Karachi, Pakistan, this youth prodigy won three world amateur titles (1979, 1983, 1985), six World Open titles (1981–5, 1988), and a phenomenal ten consecutive British Open titles (1982–91). He remained undefeated from April 1981 to November 1986, when he lost to Ross Norman of New Zealand in the World Open final. He is the son of Roshan Khan, winner of the 1957 British Open.

Jansher Khan, 1969–

Born in Peshawar, Pakistan, he won a record-breaking eight World Open titles (1987, 1989–90, 1992–6) as well as six British Open titles (1992–7). Seen as the heir to **Jahangir Khan** (though not closely related), he dominated the sport in the late 1990s.

Heather McKay, 1941–

Born in Queanbeyan, New South Wales, Australia, she won 14 Australian titles (1960–73), won the British Open for a record 16 successive years (1962–77), and was World Open champion in 1979. Such was her dominance of the sport that she was unbeaten between 1962 and 1980. In 1975 she moved to Canada, where she became a racketball champion.

SUMO WRESTLING

Origins

The Japanese form of wrestling known as sumo has its roots in the Shinto religion. The oldest written records date from the 8th century but sumo wrestling is believed to be more than 1,500 years old. During the Heian period (794–1185) sumo became a widespread spectator sport and in the 12th century the 'bushi' (warrior classes) developed it for battle combat.

Rules and description

A wrestling match is accompanied by much ceremony and ritual from the moment the wrestlers march in accompanied by their assistants – a 'tsuyu-harai' (personal attendant or herald) to the front and his 'tachi-mochi' (sword bearer) to the rear. The aim of the wrestlers is to push or throw their opponents out of the 'dohyo' (a ring about 3.6m²/3.9yd²) or to throw them to the floor. Traditionally there have been no weight categories and the most notable feature of the wrestlers is their size, starting at around 130kg/286.5lb and reaching as much as 200kg/441lb or more. Weight categories exist for the world championships, however. Techniques of wrestling involve pulling opponents' legs, grabbing belts and trying to throw or carry the opponent out of the ring. The bout is refereed by an official called a 'gyoji', who wears an elaborate silk kimono and a special black court hat. He traditionally bears a fan as a symbol of authority, and a dagger. Legend recounts that it was originally supplied so that the referee might disembowel himself if he gave a bad judgement.

The wrestlers are barefoot and naked except for a thick silk belt and loin covering known as a 'mawashi'. Their hair is styled into a top-knot 'chon-mage'. Other ceremonial traditions include the scattering of salt, a Shinto purification ritual. There are around 70 winning movements in sumo wrestling, including throws, twists and lifts. Women sumo wrestlers wear a leotard beneath the mawashi.

World Championships

World championships are held at four weight divisions: lightweight (men under 85kg/women under 65kg); middleweight (men under 115kg/women under 80kg); heavyweight (men over 115kg/women over 80kg); and the open division.

Men

	Team	**Open division**
1992	Japan	Kazunori Saito (Japan)
1993	Japan	Sunao Yasu (Japan)
1994	Japan	Badmaanyambuu Bat-Erdene (Mongolia)
1995	Japan	Emanuel Yarbrough (USA)
1996	Japan	Mark Robinson (South Africa)
1997	Japan	Naohito Saito (Japan)
1998	Japan	Keiji Tamiya (Japan)
1999	Japan	Levan Ebanoidze (Georgia)
2000	Germany	Tóru Kakizoe (Japan)
2001	Japan	Torsten Scheibler (Germany)
2002	Japan	Alan Karayev (Russia)
2003	*Not held*	
2004	Japan	Keisyo Shimoda (Japan)

Women

	Team	**Open division**
2001	Germany	Sandra Köppen (Germany)
2002	Japan	Rie Tsuihiji (Japan)
2003	*Not held*	
2004	Germany	Sandra Köppen (Germany)

A-Z

ashi-tori a move that involves grabbing an opponent's leg to bring him or her down

banzuke the official tournament ranking list

basho a sumo tournament

chanko nabe a protein-rich stew fed to **rikishi** to bulk them up ready for competition

chon-mage a sumo hairstyle that has hair slicked with camomile oil and a top-knot

dohyo the wrestling ring

dohyo-iri the rituals performed at the beginning of each match

gyoji the referee

haragei a form of abdominal exercises designed to strengthen the stomach

hataki-komi a quick sidestep and push

kachikoshi a wrestler's record; it indicates that he or she has more wins than losses; compare **makekoshi**

kesho mawashi a ceremonial apron worn by wrestlers during the their entrance ceremonies

ketaguri a move that pulls the opponent's legs away as he or she rushes in

kimarite a general term given to each of the 70 winning techniques that win a sumo bout

makekoshi a wrestler's record; it indicates that he or she has more losses than wins; compare **kachikoshi**

mawashi the thick silk belt of the wrestler. It is worn to protect the groin and offers a handhold for combatants to make grappling easier. Lower grades of **rikishi** wear black cotton mawashi. Juryo level (the top professional levels of rikishi) wear silks of various colours

morozashi an inside belt grip where both a wrestler's hands and arms are positioned under his or her opponent's arms

noda-wa thrusts to the throat

oicho-mage the gingko leaf-style top-knot worn by wrestlers. It resembles a little fan at the end of the top-knot

rikishi sumo wrestlers. Literally, it means 'strong man'

shiko a move that involves stamping down with each leg; it is used as a warm-up before bouts and in practice

sumotori same as **rikishi**

tachi-mochi the sword-bearer in the **dohyo-iri**

tsuppari slapping attacks; a series of hard slaps designed to drive the opponent out of the ring

tsuyu-harai the name given to the herald in the entrance ceremony, literally 'the dew sweeper'

yokozuna the highest rank (a grand champion). In 1993 the Hawaiian-born Chad Rowan (as Akebono) became the first foreign-born **rikishi** to become a yokozuna

yorikiri a move that involves grabbing the opponent's belt in an attempt to unbalance him or her

SURFING

Origins

Surfing originated in the Pacific Islands and was described by the seafaring explorer Captain James Cook when he reached the Hawaiian Islands in 1778. The birth of modern surfing is credited to the Hawaiian swimmer Duke Paoa Kahinu Makoe Hulikohoa Kahanamoku (1890–1968), who won three Olympic Games gold medals in the 1920s. He had been a surfer at home, and with surfboard designer Tom Blake, who created a hollow, lightweight board, he gave surfing demonstrations around the world. Surfing became truly popular in the USA and Australia in the 1960s.

Rules and description

Surfing is described as the sport of riding breaking waves on a surfboard. Surfers paddle their surfboards out to sea, and turn and 'ride' waves as they come back towards the shore. They start by pushing their boards and then mount them to end in a standing position. Offshore wind conditions provide the best sport. The best waves are to be found in Hawaii, where they can measure 9m or so. In competition, surfers not only 'ride' the waves but also perform various manoeuvres that are graded and judged according to a difficulty standard. Surfboards vary in size but are generally taller than the surfer. They are tapered hollow boards that float and are attached to the surfer's leg. Surfers 'steer' by adjusting their bodyweight on the board.

There are different surfing disciplines, including a men's and women's open. Bodyboarding, where surfers do not get to their feet, and kneeboarding are more modern developments.

Ruling body: In 1964, during the first World Surfing Championships, the ISF (International Surfing Federation) was created. This association organized world championships every year but in 1976, in Hawaii, the ISF was superseded by the ISA (International Surfing Association). It is the governing body for surfing and bodyboarding. The Association of Surfing Professionals (ASP) organizes the Professional World Championships and Championships Tour.

ASP World Professional Champions

Men

1976	Peter Townend (Australia)	**1987**	Damien Hardman (Australia)
1977	Shaun Tomson (South Africa)	**1988**	Barton Lynch (Australia)
1978	Wayne Bartholomew (Australia)	**1989**	Martin Potter (Great Britain)
1979–82	Mark Richards (Australia)	**1990**	Tom Curren (USA)
1983–4	Tom Carroll (Australia)	**1991**	Damien Hardman (Australia)
1985–6	Tom Curren (USA)	**1992**	Kelly Slater (USA)

1993	Derek Ho (Hawaii)*	**2000**	Sunny Garcia (Hawaii)*
1994–8	Kelly Slater (USA)	**2001**	C J Hobgood (USA)
1999	Mark Occhilupo (Australia)	**2002–4**	Andy Irons (Hawaii)*

*Surfing distinguishes between competitors from Hawaii and mainland USA.

Women

1977	Margo Oberg (USA)	**1989**	Wendy Botha (South Africa)
1978–9	Lynn Boyer (USA)	**1990**	Pam Burridge (Australia)
1980–1	Margo Oberg (USA)	**1991–2**	Wendy Botha (Australia)**
1982	Debbie Beacham (USA)	**1993**	Pauline Menczer (Australia)
1983	Kim Mearig (USA)	**1994–7**	Lisa Andersen (USA)
1984–6	Frieda Zamba (USA)	**1998–2003**	Layne Beachley (Australia)
1987	Wendy Botha (South Africa)	**2004**	Sofia Mulanovich (Peru)
1988	Frieda Zamba (USA)		

**Previously a South African citizen.

ASP World Longboard Champions

A separate world championship for longboards was instituted in 1986.

1986–7	Nat Young (Australia)	**1997**	Dino Miranda (Hawaii)*
1987–8	Stuart Entwistle (Australia)	**1998**	Joel Tudor (USA)
1988–90	Nat Young (Australia)	**1999**	Colin McPhillips (USA)
1991	Marty McMillan (Australia)	**2000**	Beau Young (Australia)
1992	Joey Hawkins (USA)	**2001–2**	Colin McPhillips (USA)
1993–5	Rusty Keaulana (Hawaii)*	**2003**	Beau Young (Australia)
1996	Greg Perkins (Hawaii)*	**2004**	Joel Tudor (USA)

*Surfing distinguishes between competitors from Hawaii and mainland USA.

A-Z

air	any move in which the surfer is in the air
barrel	the shape of the hollow wave when it is breaking
bodyboard	a board around 1.6m long on which the surfer lies
boogie board	same as **bodyboard**
carving	making large smooth turns on a wave
curl	a part of a hollow or semi-hollow wave that loops over as it breaks
cutback	a manoeuvre used to change direction and head back towards the breaking part of the wave
deck	the top surface of the surfboard
duck dive	the method of diving the board under an oncoming wave on the way out
dumper	a wave that crashes suddenly downwards with great force, causing surfers to fall
fall line	the line of fastest descent to the base of a wave

fins	small vertical projections on the rear of the bottom of the surfboard that are used for stability
floater	a move in which the surfer rides the very top of the wave
goofy foot	if a surfer rides goofy foot, he or she surfs with his/her right foot in front of the left
grommet	a derogatory term for a young surfer
hot-dog	a person who performs showy manoeuvres, such as spins and turns, while surfing
kneeboard	a shorter surfboard, measuring a maximum of 1.8m, ridden on the knees
layback	an extreme surfing manoeuvre where the surfer lays backwards on a wave
leash, leg rope	a rubber cord used to attach the surfboard to the surfer's ankle
longboard	a long, light surfing board
natural foot	a surfer who rides with his/her left foot in front of the right
nose	the front of the surfboard
nose riding	a surfing manoeuvre where the surfer stands on the very front of the surfboard
rails	the sides of the surfboard that run from **nose** to tail
skeg	same as **fin**
snap	a sharp turn back into the face of the wave, made at its top
tube	same as **barrel**
wipe-out	a fall from a surfboard after losing control or being knocked off by a wave

Some famous surfers

Layne Beachley, 1972–

Born in Sydney, Australia, she holds the record for the most world titles with six (1998–2003), an achievement which made her Australia's most successful surfer of all time and earned her the accolade of Australian Female Athlete of the Year in 2004. Once nicknamed 'Gidget' (after the character in the 1956 surfing film of that name and subsequent TV series), she is now more commonly referred to as 'Beach'. She became a professional surfer at 16 years old. In winning her first world title she set the biggest points margin in the history of the sport.

Bernard Farrelly, 1943–

Born in Paddington, Australia, he was the first from his country to win a major surfing title when he won the world championships in 1964. Nicknamed 'Midget', he also came second in 1968 and 1970. In 1963 he had won the Makaha title in Hawaii, which at that time was recognized as the unofficial world championship.

Duke Paoa Kahinu Makoe Hulikohoa Kahanamoku, 1890–1968

Born in Honolulu in Hawaii, the name Duke was given to him to commemorate a visit made to the islands by Queen Victoria's eldest son. Kahanamoku was a triple Olympic Games gold medallist as well as being an expert surfer. In 1917, during a great swell, he famously rode his board for over a mile.

Kelly Slater, 1972–

Born in Cocoa Beach, Florida, USA, he is popularly celebrated as the greatest surfer of all time. He won the World Professional Championships on six occasions (1992, 1994–8). His first title, aged 20, made him the youngest ever world champion. He is the first professional surfer to have made over $1 million in career earnings.

SWIMMING & DIVING

Origins

Although swimming dates from ancient times, and there is evidence it took place in Greek, Roman and Japanese societies, modern competitive swimming was first organized in England only in the late 18th century. The first national organization was the National Swimming Society, founded in London in 1837. Swimming was popularized by a number of Englishmen in the period that followed: Captain Matthew Webb, the first person to swim the English Channel in 1875; John Trudgen, who around 1873 devised a swimming stroke in which each arm was alternately raised out of the water and then thrown forward pulling water behind him (what we know today as the front crawl); and Frederick Cavill, who, after seeing South Sea islanders swimming a crawl-type stroke, invented the flutter kick and the overarm stroke, a further variant on the fastest swimming stroke and what became known as the Australian crawl. The first national British champion was Tom Morris, who won a mile race on the River Thames in 1869. Swimming was part of the programme of the first modern Olympic Games in 1896.

Rules and description

Swimming is the action of propelling oneself through water without mechanical aids. Four major strokes are now used in competitive swimming. The fastest is the front crawl. In competition, the event is known as the 'freestyle' because competitors freely choose to use the fastest stroke. It is a stroke where the swimmer lies face down and uses alternate overarm strokes to propel himself or herself forwards. The next fastest stroke is the 'butterfly' – the most tiring stroke – in which the arms move together through the water, and the feet pump together in a 'dolphin kick'. The butterfly was developed in the 1930s by Henry Myers and other American swimmers and recognized in the 1950s. The 'backstroke', the only event where the swimmer lies on his or her back, was also developed by an American swimmer (Harry Hebner who, at the 1912 Olympic Games, was the first to swim an alternating arm backstroke). The 'breaststroke' is the oldest known style and sees the swimmer push out water to the front and the sides using a circular arcing motion of the arms.

Swimming competitions are held in indoor or outdoor pools either 50m/54.7yd long (long course) or 25m/27.3yd long (short course) and distances range from 50m to 1,500m (800m for women). Each lane is marked off to ensure swimmers swim straight. In addition to individual events for all four strokes, there are relay races in the freestyle and 'individual medley' races. A 200m individual medley requires each swimmer to swim a length each of butterfly, backstroke, breaststroke and front crawl (in that sequence). In the 4x100m 'medley relay' a different swimmer takes each of the different strokes.

In **diving** events competitors jump from either an elevated rigid board or platform (at 10m height) or a sprung board (at 3m height) into a swimming pool, performing a variety of twists, somersaults and turns. Style gains marks, as does successfully completing the dive, based on the degree of difficulty of each attempt (which is used as a multiplying factor). Synchronized diving events engage divers in performing side by side. As well as the previous criteria they are also marked according to how closely they perform as mirror images of each other.

Synchronized swimming (or 'artistic swimming') is a relatively modern sport but traces its popularity to the Hollywood 'aqua musicals' of Esther Williams of the 1940s and 1950s. It is popular in Japan, Russia, Canada and the USA. Swimmers are given marks for the technical and artistic merits of their routines.

Ruling body: International Swimming Federation (FINA; Fédération Internationale de Natation)

World Championships

	Venues
1973	Belgrade, Yugoslavia
1975	Cali, Colombia
1978	Berlin, Germany
1982	Guayaquil, Ecuador
1986	Madrid, Spain
1991	Perth, Australia
1994	Rome, Italy
1998	Perth, Australia
2001	Fukuoka, Japan
2003	Barcelona, Spain
2005	Montreal, Canada

Men

	50m freestyle	**100m freestyle**	**200m freestyle**
1973	Jim Montgomery (USA)	Jim Montgomery (USA)	
1975	Andrew Coan (USA)	Tim Shaw (USA)	
1978	David McCagg (USA)	William Forrester (USA)	
1982	Jorg Woithe (East Germany)	Michael Gross (West Germany)	
1986	Tom Jager (USA)	Matt Biondi (USA)	Michael Gross (West Germany)
1991	Tom Jager (USA)	Matt Biondi (USA)	Giorgio Lamberti (Italy)
1994	Aleksandr Popov (Russia)	Aleksandr Popov (Russia)	Antti Kasvio (Finland)
1998	Bill Pilczuk (USA)	Aleksandr Popov (Russia)	Michael Klim (Australia)
2001	Anthony Ervin (USA)	Anthony Ervin (USA)	Ian Thorpe (Australia)
2003	Aleksandr Popov (Russia)	Aleksandr Popov (Russia)	Ian Thorpe (Australia)

	400m freestyle	800m freestyle	1,500m freestyle
1973	Rick DeMont (USA)	Steve Holland (Australia)	
1975	Tim Shaw (USA)	Tim Shaw (USA)	
1978	Vladimir Salnikov (USSR)	Vladimir Salnikov (USSR)	
1982	Vladimir Salnikov (USSR)	Vladimir Salnikov (USSR)	
1986	Rainer Henkel (West Germany)	Rainer Henkel (West Germany)	
1991	Jörg Hoffmann (Germany)	Jörg Hoffmann (Germany)	
1994	Kieren Perkins (Australia)	Kieren Perkins (Australia)	
1998	Ian Thorpe (Australia)	Grant Hackett (Australia)	
2001	Ian Thorpe (Australia)	Ian Thorpe (Australia)	Grant Hackett (Australia)
2003	Ian Thorpe (Australia)	Grant Hackett (Australia)	Grant Hackett (Australia)

	50m backstroke	100m backstroke	200m backstroke
1973	Roland Matthes (East Germany)	Roland Matthes (East Germany)	
1975	Roland Matthes (East Germany)	Zoltan Verraszto (Hungary)	
1978	Robert Jackson (USA)	Jesse Vassallo (USA)	
1982	Dirk Richter (East Germany)	Rick Carey (USA)	
1986	Igor Polyanski (USSR)	Igor Polyanski (USSR)	
1991	Jeff Rouse (USA)	Martin López-Zubero (Spain)	
1994	Martin López-Zubero (Spain)	Vladimir Selkov (Russia)	
1998	Lenny Krayzelburg (USA)	Lenny Krayzelburg (USA)	
2001	Randall Bal (USA)	Matt Welsh (Australia)	Aaron Peirsol (USA)
2003	Thomas Rupprath (Germany)	Aaron Peirsol (USA)	Aaron Peirsol (USA)

	50m breaststroke	100m breaststroke	200m breaststroke
1973	John Hencken (USA)	David Wilkie (Great Britain)	
1975	David Wilkie (Great Britain)	David Wilkie (Great Britain)	
1978	Walter Kusch (East Germany)	Nick Nevid (USA)	
1982	Steve Lundquist (USA)	Victor Davis (Canada)	
1986	Victor Davis (Canada)	Josef Szabó (Hungary)	
1991	Norbert Rósza (Hungary)	Mike Barrowman (USA)	
1994	Norbert Rósza (Hungary)	Norbert Rosza (Hungary)	
1998	Frédéric Deburghgraeve (Belgium)	Kurt Grote (USA)	
2001	Geoff Huegill (Australia)	Roman Sloudnov (Russia)	Brendan Hansen (USA)
2003	James Gibson (Great Britain)	Kosuke Kitajima (Japan)	Kosuke Kitajima (Japan)

	50m butterfly	100m butterfly	200m butterfly
1973	Bruce Robertson (Canada)	Robin Backhaus (USA)	
1975	Greg Jagenburg (USA)	Billy Forrester (USA)	
1978	Joe Bottom (USA)	Mike Bruner (USA)	
1982	Matt Gribble (USA)	Michael Gross (West Germany)	
1986	Pablo Morales (USA)	Michael Gross (West Germany)	
1991	Anthony Nesty (Suriname)	Melvin Stewart (USA)	
1994	Rafal Szukala (Poland)	Denis Pankratov (Russia)	
1998	Michael Klim (Australia)	Denis Silantiev (Russia)	
2001	Geoff Huegill (Australia)	Lars Frölander (Sweden)	Michael Phelps (USA)
2003	Matt Welsh (Australia)	Ian Crocker (USA)	Michael Phelps (USA)

	200m individual medley	400m individual medley	4x100m freestyle relay
1973	Gunnar Larsson (Sweden)	András Hargitay (Hungary)	USA
1975	András Hargitay (Hungary)	András Hargitay (Hungary)	USA
1978	Graham Smith (Canada)	Jesse Vassallo (USA)	USA
1982	Alexei Sidorenko (USSR)	Ricardo Prado (Brazil)	USA
1986	Tamás Darnyi (Hungary)	Tamás Darnyi (Hungary)	USA
1991	Tamás Darnyi (Hungary)	Tamás Darnyi (Hungary)	USA
1994	Jani Sievinen (Finland)	Tom Dolan (USA)	USA
1998	Marcel Wouda (The Netherlands)	Tom Dolan (USA)	USA
2001	Massi Rosolino (Italy)	Alessio Boggiatto (Italy)	Australia
2003	Michael Phelps (USA)	Michael Phelps (USA)	Russia

	4x200m freestyle relay	4x100m medley relay
1973	USA	USA
1975	West Germany	USA
1978	USA	USA
1982	USA	USA
1986	East Germany	USA
1991	Germany	USA
1994	Sweden	USA
1998	Australia	Australia
2001	Australia	Australia
2003	Australia	USA

Women

	50m freestyle	100m freestyle	200m freestyle
1973	Kornelia Ender (East Germany)	Keena Rothhammer (USA)	
1975	Kornelia Ender (East Germany)	Shirley Babashoff (USA)	
1978	Barbara Krause (East Germany)	Cynthia Woodhead (USA)	
1982	Birgit Meineke (East Germany)	Annemarie Verstappen (The Netherlands)	
1986	Tamara Costache (Romania)	Kristin Otto (East Germany)	Heike Friedrich (East Germany)
1991	Zhuang Yong (China)	Nicole Haislett (USA)	Hayley Lewis (Australia)
1994	Le Jingyi (China)	Le Jingyi (China)	Franziska Van Almsick (The Netherlands)
1998	Amy Van Dyken (USA)	Jenny Thompson (USA)	Claudia Poll (Costa Rica)
2001	Inge de Bruijn (The Netherlands)	Inge de Bruijn (The Netherlands)	Giaan Rooney (Australia)
2003	Inge de Bruijn (The Netherlands)	Hanna-Maria Seppala (Finland)	Alena Popchanka (Belarus)

	400m freestyle	800m freestyle	1,500m freestyle
1973	Heather Greenwood (USA)	Novella Calligaris (Italy)	
1975	Shirley Babashoff (USA)	Jenny Tunrall (Australia)	
1978	Tracey Wickham (Australia)	Tracey Wickham (Australia)	
1982	Carmela Schmidt (East Germany)	Kim Linehan (USA)	

	400m freestyle	800m freestyle	1,500m freestyle
1986	Heike Friedrich (East Germany)	Astrid Strauss (East Germany)	
1991	Janet Evans (USA)	Janet Evans (USA)	
1994	Yang Alhua (China)	Janet Evans (USA)	
1998	Chen Yan (China)	Brooke Bennett (USA)	
2001	Yana Klochkova (Ukraine)	Hannah Stockbauer (Germany)	Hannah Stockbauer (Germany)
2003	Hannah Stockbauer (Germany)	Hannah Stockbauer (Germany)	Hannah Stockbauer (Germany)

	50m backstroke	100m backstroke	200m backstroke
1973	Ulrike Richter (East Germany)	Melissa Belote (USA)	
1975	Ulrike Richter (East Germany)	Birgit Treiber (East Germany)	
1978	Linda Jezek (USA)	Linda Jezek (USA)	
1982	Cornelia Sirch (East Germany)	Cornelia Sirch (East Germany)	
1986	Cornelia Sirch (East Germany)	Cornelia Sirch (East Germany)	
1991	Krisztina Egerszegi (Hungary)	Krisztina Egerszegi (Hungary)	
1994	He Cihong (China)	He Cihong (China)	
1998	Lea Maurer (USA)	Roxanna Maracineanu (France)	
2001	Haley Cope (USA)	Natalie Coughlin (USA)	Diana Mocanu (Romania)
2003	Nina Zhivanevskaya (Spain)	Antje Buschschulte (Germany)	Katy Sexton (Great Britain)

	50m breaststroke	100m breaststroke	200m breaststroke
1973	Renate Vogel (East Germany)	Renate Vogel (East Germany)	
1975	Hannelore Anke (East Germany)	Hannelore Anke (East Germany)	
1978	Yulia Bogdanova (USSR)	Lina Kachushite (USSR)	
1982	Ute Geweniger (East Germany)	Svetlana Varganova (USSR)	
1986	Sylvia Gerasch (East Germany)	Silke Horner (East Germany)	
1991	Linley Frame (Australia)	Yelena Volkova (Russia)	
1994	Samantha Riley (Australia)	Samantha Riley (Australia)	
1998	Kristy Kowal (USA)	Agnes Kovacs (Hungary)	
2001	Luo Xuejuan (China)	Luo Xuejuan (China)	Agnes Kovacs (Hungary)
2003	Luo Xuejuan (China)	Luo Xuejuan (China)	Amanda Beard (USA)

	50m butterfly	100m butterfly	200m butterfly
1973	Kornelia Ender (East Germany)	Rosemarie Kother (East Germany)	
1975	Kornelia Ender (East Germany)	Rosemarie Kother (East Germany)	
1978	Mary Pennington (USA)	Tracy Caulkins (Australia)	
1982	Mary T Meagher (USA)	Ines Geissler (East Germany)	
1986	Silke Horner (East Germany)	Mary T Meagher (USA)	
1991	Qian Hong (China)	Summer Sanders (USA)	
1994	Liu Limin (China)	Liu Limin (China)	
1998	Jenny Thompson (USA)	Susie O'Neill (Australia)	
2001	Inge de Bruijn (The Netherlands)	Petria Thomas (Australia)	Petria Thomas (Australia)
2003	Inge de Bruijn (The Netherlands)	Jenny Thompson (USA)	Otylia Jedrzejczak (Poland)

	200m individual medley	400m individual medley	4x100m freestyle relay
1973	Angela Hubner (East Germany)	Gudrun Wegner (East Germany)	East Germany
1975	Kathy Heddy (USA)	Ulrike Tauber (East Germany)	East Germany
1978	Tracy Caulkins (Australia)	Tracy Caulkins (Australia)	USA
1982	Petra Schneider (East Germany)	Petra Schneider (East Germany)	East Germany
1986	Kathleen Nord (East Germany)	Kathleen Nord (East Germany)	East Germany
1991	Lin Li (China)	Lin Li (China)	USA
1994	Lu Bin (China)	Dai Guohong (China)	China
1998	Wu Yanyan (China)	Chen Yan (China)	USA
2001	Martha Bowen (USA)	Yana Klochkova (Ukraine)	Germany
2003	Yana Klochkova (Ukraine)	Yana Klochkova (Ukraine)	USA

	4x200m freestyle relay	4x100 medley relay
1973	East Germany	
1975	East Germany	
1978	USA	
1982	East Germany	
1986	East Germany	East Germany
1991	Germany	USA
1994	China	China
1998	Germany	USA
2001	Great Britain	Australia
2003	USA	China

Olympic Games

Men

In 1904 the first 50m freestyle event was held (won by Zoltán Halmaj of Hungary), but was then discontinued until 1988. Since that time the title of the world's fastest swimmer has been held by American Matt Biondi (1988); Aleksander Popov (1992, 1996); Americans Anthony Ervin and Gary Hall, Jr (2000), who could not be separated in a dead heat; and Gary Hall, Jr (2004).

	100m freestyle	200m freestyle	400m freestyle
1896	Alfréd Hajós (Hungary)	Paul Neumann (Austria)	
1900	Frederick Lane (Australia)		
1904	Zoltán Halmaj (Hungary)	Charles Daniels (USA)	Charles Daniels (USA)
1908	Charles Daniels (USA)	Henry Taylor (Great Britain)	
1912	Duke Kahanamoku (USA)	George Hodgson (Canada)	
1920	Duke Kahanamoku (USA)	Norman Ross (USA)	
1924	Johnny Weissmuller (USA)	Johnny Weissmuller (USA)	
1928	Johnny Weissmuller (USA)	Alberto Zorrill (Argentina)	
1932	Yasuji Miyazaki (Japan)	Buster Crabbe (USA)	
1936	Ferenc Csík (Hungary)	Jack Medica (USA)	
1948	Walter Ris (USA)	William Smith (USA)	
1952	Clarke Scholes (USA)	Jean Boiteux (France)	
1956	Jon Henricks (Australia)	Murray Rose (Australia)	
1960	John Devitt (Australia)	Murray Rose (Australia)	

	100m freestyle	200m freestyle	400m freestyle
1964	Donald Schollander (USA)	Donald Schollander (USA)	
1968	Michael Wenden (Australia)	Michael Wenden (Australia)	Michael Burton (USA)
1972	Mark Spitz (USA)	Mark Spitz (USA)	Bradford Cooper (Australia)
1976	James Montgomery (USA)	Bruce Furniss (USA)	Brian Goodell (USA)
1980	Jörg Woithe (East Germany)	Sergei Kopliakov (USSR)	Vladimir Salnikov (USSR)
1984	Rowdy Gaines (USA)	Michael Gross (Germany)	George DiCarlo (USA)
1988	Matt Biondi (USA)	Duncan Armstrong (Australia)	Uwe Dassier (East Germany)
1992	Aleksandr Popov (Russia)	Yevgeny Sadovyi (Russia)	Yevgeny Sadovyi (Russia)
1996	Aleksandr Popov (Russia)	Danyon Loader (New Zealand)	Danyon Loader (New Zealand)
2000	Pieter van den Hoogenband (The Netherlands)	Pieter van den Hoogenband (The Netherlands)	Ian Thorpe (Australia)
2004	Pieter van den Hoogenband (The Netherlands)	Ian Thorpe (Australia)	Ian Thorpe (Australia)

	1,500m freestyle	100m backstroke	200m backstroke
1896	Alfréd Hajós (Hungary)		
1900	John Jarvis (Great Britain)	Ernst Hoppenberg (Germany)	
1904	Emil Rausch (Germany)	Walter Brack (Germany)	
1908	Henry Taylor (Great Britain)	Arno Bieberstein (Germany)	
1912	George Hodgson (Canada)	Harry Hebner (USA)	
1920	Norman Ross (USA)	Warren Paoa Kealoha (USA)	
1924	Andrew Charlton (Australia)	Warren Paoa Kealoha (USA)	
1928	Arne Borg (Sweden)	George Kojac (USA)	
1932	Kusuo Kitamura (Japan)	Masaji Kiyokawa (Japan)	
1936	Noboru Terada (Japan)	Adolf Kiefer (USA)	
1948	James McLane (USA)	Allen Stack (USA)	
1952	Ford Konno (USA)	Yoshinobu Oyakawa (USA)	
1956	Murray Rose (Australia)	David Theile (Australia)	
1960	John Konrads (Australia)	David Theile (Australia)	
1964	Robert Windle (Australia)	Jed Graef (USA)	
1968	Michael Burton (USA)	Roland Matthes (East Germany)	Roland Matthes (East Germany)
1972	Michael Burton (USA)	Roland Matthes (East Germany)	Roland Matthes (East Germany)
1976	Brian Goodell (USA)	John Naber (USA)	John Naber (USA)
1980	Vladimir Salnikov (USSR)	Bengt Baron (Sweden)	Sándor Wladár (Hungary)
1984	Michael O'Brien (USA)	Richard Carey (USA)	Richard Carey (USA)
1988	Vladimir Salnikov (USSR)	Daichi Suzuki (Japan)	Igor Polyanski (USSR)
1992	Kieren Perkins (Australia)	Mark Tewksbury (Canada)	Martín López-Zubero (Spain)
1996	Kieren Perkins (Australia)	Jeffrey Rouse (USA)	Brad Bridgewater (USA)
2000	Grant Hackett (Australia)	Lenny Krayzelburg (USA)	Lenny Krayzelburg (USA)
2004	Grant Hackett (Australia)	Aaron Peirsol (USA)	Aaron Peirsol (USA)

	100m breaststroke	200m breaststroke	100m butterfly
1908	Frederick Holman (Great Britain)		
1912	Walter Bathe (Germany)		
1920	Håkan Malmroth (Sweden)		
1924	Robert Skelton (USA)		

	100m breaststroke	200m breaststroke	100m butterfly
1928	Yoshiyuki Tsuruta (Japan)		
1932	Yoshiyuki Tsuruta (Japan)		
1936	Tetsuo Hamuro (Japan)		
1948	Joseph Verdeur (USA)		
1952	John Davies (Australia)		
1956	Masaru Furukawa (Japan)		
1960	William Mulliken (USA)		
1964	Ian O'Brien (Australia)		
1968	Donald McKenzie (USA)	Felipe Munoz Kapamas (Mexico)	Douglas Russell (USA)
1972	Nobutaka Taguchi (Japan)	John Hencken (USA)	Mark Spitz (USA)
1976	John Hencken (USA)	David Wilkie (Great Britain)	Matt Vogel (USA)
1980	Duncan Goodhew (Great Britain)	Robertas Žulpa (USSR)	Pär Arvidsson (Sweden)
1984	Steve Lundquist (USA)	Victor Davis (Canada)	Michael Gross (West Germany)
1988	Adrian Moorhouse (Great Britain)	József Szabó (Hungary)	Anthony Nesty (Suriname)
1992	Nelson Diebel (USA)	Michael Barrowman (USA)	Pablo Morales (USA)
1996	Frédéric Deburghgraeve (Belgium)	Norbert Rózsa (Hungary)	Denis Pankratov (Russia)
2000	Domenico Fioravanti (Italy)	Domenico Fioravanti (Italy)	Lars Frölander (Sweden)
2004	Kosuke Kitajima (Japan)	Kosuke Kitajima (Japan)	Michael Phelps (USA)

	200m butterfly	200m individual medley	400m individual medley
1956	William Yorzyk (USA)		
1960	Michael Troy (USA)		
1964	Kevin Berry (Australia)	Richard Roth (USA)	
1968	Carl Robie (USA)	Charles Hickcox (USA)	Charles Hickcox (USA)
1972	Mark Spitz (USA)	Gunnar Larsson (Sweden)	Gunnar Larsson (Sweden)
1976	Mike Bruner (USA)	Rod Strachan (USA)	
1980	Sergei Fesenko (USSR)	Aleksandr Sidorenko (USSR)	
1984	Jonathon Sieben (Australia)	Alex Baumann (Canada)	Alex Baumann (Canada)
1988	Michael Gross (West Germany)	Tamás Darnyi (Hungary)	Tamás Darnyi (Hungary)
1992	Melvin Stewart (USA)	Tamás Darnyi (Hungary)	Tamás Darnyi (Hungary)
1996	Denis Pankratov (Russia)	Attila Czene (Hungary)	Tom Dolan (USA)
2000	Tom Malchow (USA)	Massimiliano Rosolino (Italy)	Tom Dolan (USA)
2004	Michael Phelps (USA)	Michael Phelps (USA)	Michael Phelps (USA)

	4x100m freestyle relay	4x200m freestyle relay	4x100m medley relay
1908	Great Britain		
1912	Australia and New Zealand		
1920	USA		
1924	USA		
1928	USA		
1932	Japan		
1936	Japan		
1948	USA		
1952	USA		
1956	Australia		

	4x100m freestyle relay	4x200m freestyle relay	4x100m medley relay
1960	USA	USA	
1964	USA	USA	USA
1968	USA	USA	USA
1972	USA	USA	USA
1976	USA	USA	
1980	USSR	Australia	
1984	USA	USA	USA
1988	USA	USA	USA
1992	USA	Russia	USA
1996	USA	USA	USA
2000	Australia	Australia	USA
2004	South Africa	USA	USA

Women

The women's 50m was introduced at the Seoul Games of 1988. Since that time the title of the world's fastest woman swimmer has been held by German swimmer Kristin Otto (1988); Chinese freestyler Yang Wenyi (1992); American Amy Van Dyken (1996); and Dutchwoman Inge de Bruijn (2000, 2004).

	100m freestyle	200m freestyle	400m freestyle
1912	Sarah Durack (Australia)		
1920	Ethelda Bleibtrey (USA)	Ethelda Bleibtrey (USA)	
1924	Ethel Lackie (USA)	Martha Norelius (USA)	
1928	Albina Osipowich (USA)	Martha Norelius (USA)	
1932	Helene Madison (USA)	Helene Madison (USA)	
1936	Rie Mastenbroek (The Netherlands)	Rie Mastenbroek (The Netherlands)	
1948	Greta Andersen (Denmark)	Ann Curtis (USA)	
1952	Katalin Szöke (Hungary)	Valéria Gyenge (Hungary)	
1956	Dawn Fraser (Australia)	Lorraine Crapp (Australia)	
1960	Dawn Fraser (Australia)	Christine Von Saltza (USA)	
1964	Dawn Fraser (Australia)	Virginia Duenkei (USA)	
1968	Jan Henne (USA)	Deborah Meyer (USA)	Debbie Meyer (USA)
1972	Sandra Neilson (USA)	Shane Gould (Australia)	Shane Gould (USA)
1976	Kornelia Ender (East Germany)	Kornelia Ender (East Germany)	Petra Thümer (East Germany)
1980	Barbara Krause (East Germany)	Barbara Krause (East Germany)	Ines Diers (East Germany)
1984	Nancy Hogshead (USA)	Mary Wayte (USA)	Tiffany Cohen (USA)
1988	Kristin Otto (East Germany)	Heike Friedrich (East Germany)	Janet Evans (USA)
1992	Zhuang Yong (China)	Nicole Haislett (USA)	Dagmar Hase (Germany)
1996	Le Jingyi (China)	Claudia Poll (Costa Rica)	Michelle Smith (Ireland)
2000	Inge de Bruijn (The Netherlands)	Susie O'Neill (Australia)	Brooke Bennett (USA)
2004	Jodie Henry (Australia)	Camelia Potec (Romania)	Laure Manaudou (France)

	800m freestyle	100m backstroke	200m backstroke
1924	Sybil Bauer (USA)		
1928	Maria Braun (The Netherlands)		

	800m freestyle	100m backstroke	200m backstroke
1932	Eleanor Holm (USA)		
1936	Dina Senff (The Netherlands)		
1948	Karen-Margrete Harup (Denmark)		
1952	Joan Harrison (South Africa)		
1956	Judith Grinham (Great Britain)		
1960	Lynn Burke (USA)		
1964	Cathy Ferguson (USA)		
1968	Deborah Meyer (USA)	Kaye Hall (USA)	Lillian Watson (USA)
1972	Keena Rothhammer (USA)	Melissa Belote (USA)	Melissa Belote (USA)
1976	Petra Thümer (East Germany)	Ulrike Richter (East Germany)	Ulrike Richter (East Germany)
1980	Michelle Ford (Australia)	Rica Reinisch (East Germany)	Rica Reinisch (East Germany)
1984	Tiffany Cohen (USA)	Theresa Andrews (USA)	Jolanda de Rover (The Netherlands)
1988	Janet Evans (USA)	Kristin Otto (East Germany)	Krisztina Egerszegi (Hungary)
1992	Janet Evans (USA)	Krisztina Egerszegi (Hungary)	Krisztina Egerszegi (Hungary)
1996	Brooke Bennett (USA)	Beth Botsford (USA)	Krisztina Egerszegi (Hungary)
2000	Brooke Bennett (USA)	Diana Mocanu (Romania)	Diana Mocanu (Romania)
2004	Ai Shibata (Japan)	Natalie Coughlin (USA)	Kirsty Coventry (Zimbabwe)

	100m breaststroke	200m breaststroke	100m butterfly
1924	Lucy Morton (Great Britain)		
1928	Hilde Schrader (Germany)		
1932	Clare Dennis (Australia)		
1936	Hideko Maehata (Japan)		
1948	Petronella van Vliet (The Netherlands)		
1952	Éva Székely (Hungary)		
1956	Ursula Happe (Germany)	Shelly Mann (USA)	
1960	Anita Lonsbrough (Great Britain)	Carolyn Schuler (USA)	
1964	Halyna Prozumenshchykova (USSR)	Sharon Stouder (USA)	
1968	Djurdjica Bjedov (Yugoslavia)	Sharon Wichman (USA)	Lynette McClements (Australia)
1972	Catherine Carr (USA)	Beverley Whitfield (Australia)	Mayumi Aoki (Japan)
1976	Hannelore Anke (East Germany)	Marina Koshevaia (USSR)	Kornelia Ender (East Germany)
1980	Ute Geweniger (East Germany)	Lina Kačiušytė (USSR)	Caren Metschuk (East Germany)
1984	Petra van Staveren (The Netherlands)	Anne Ottenbrite (Canada)	Mary Meagher (USA)
1988	Tania Dangalakova (Bulgaria)	Silke Hömer (East Germany)	Kristin Otto (East Germany)
1992	Yelena Rudkovskaya (Belarus)	Kyoko Iwasaki (Japan)	Qian Hong (China)
1996	Megan Quann (USA)	Penelope Heyns (South Africa)	Amy Van Dyken (USA)
2000	Megan Quann (USA)	Agnes Kovacs (Hungary)	Inge de Bruijn (The Netherlands)
2004	Luo Xuejuan (China)	Amanda Beard (USA)	Petria Thomas (Australia)

	200m butterfly	200m individual medley	400m individual medley
1964	Donna De Varona (USA)		
1968	Ada Kok (The Netherlands)	Claudia Kolb (USA)	Claudia Kolb (USA)

	200m butterfly	200m individual medley	400m individual medley
1972	Karen Moe (USA)	Shane Gould (Australia)	Gail Neall (Australia)
1976	Andrea Pollack (East Germany)	Ulrike Tauber (East Germany)	
1980	Ines Geissler (East Germany)	Petra Schneider (East Germany)	
1984	Mary Meagher (USA)	Tracy Caulkins (USA)	Tracy Caulkins (USA)
1988	Kathleen Nord (East Germany)	Daniela Hunger (East Germany)	Janet Evans (USA)
1992	Summer Sanders (USA)	Lin Li (China)	Krisztina Egerszegi (Hungary)
1996	Susie O'Neill (Australia)	Michelle Smith (Ireland)	Michelle Smith (Ireland)
2000	Misty Hyman (USA)	Yana Klochkova (Ukraine)	Yana Klochkova (Ukraine)
2004	Otylia Jedrzejczak (Poland)	Yana Klochkova (Ukraine)	Yana Klochkova (Ukraine)

	4x100m freestyle relay	4x200m freestyle relay	4x100m medley relay
1912	Great Britain		
1920	USA		
1924	USA		
1928	USA		
1932	USA		
1936	The Netherlands		
1948	USA		
1952	Hungary		
1956	Australia		
1960	USA	USA	
1964	USA	USA	
1968	USA	USA	
1972	USA	USA	
1976	USA	East Germany	
1980	East Germany	East Germany	
1984	USA	USA	
1988	East Germany	East Germany	
1992	USA	USA	
1996	USA	USA	USA
2000	USA	USA	USA
2004	Australia	USA	Australia

Synchronized Swimming

World Championships

	Venues
1973	Belgrade, Yugoslavia
1975	Cali, Colombia
1978	Berlin, West Germany
1982	Guayaquil, Ecuador
1986	Madrid, Spain
1991	Perth, Australia
1994	Rome, Italy
1998	Perth, Australia
2001	Fukuoka, Japan
2003	Barcelona, Spain
2005	Montreal, Canada

Women

	Duet	Team	Solo
1973	Teresa Andersen & Gail Johnson (USA)	USA	Teresa Andersen (USA)
1975	Robin Curren & Amanda Norrish (USA)	USA	Gail Johnson-Buzonas (USA)
1978	Michelle Calkins & Helen Vanderburg (Canada)	USA	Helen Vanderburg (Canada)
1982	Sharon Hambrook & Kelly Kryczka (Canada)	Canada	Tracie Ruiz (USA)
1986	Carolyn Waldo & Michelle Cameron (Canada)	Canada	Carolyn Waldo (Canada)
1991	Karen Josephson & Sarah Josephson (USA)	USA	Sylvie Fréchette (Canada)
1994	Becky Dyroen-Lancer & Jill Sudduth (USA)	USA	Becky Dyroen-Lancer (USA)
1998	Olga Sedakova & Olga Brusnikina (Russia)	Russia	Olga Sedakova (Russia)
2001	Miya Tachibana & Miho Takeda (Japan)	Russia	Olga Brusnikina (Russia)
2003	Anastasia Davydova & Anastasia Ermakova (Russia)	Russia	Virginie Dedieu (France)

Olympic Games

Women

	Duet	Team	Solo
1984	Candy Costie & Tracie Ruiz (USA)		Tracie Ruiz (USA)
1988	Michelle Cameron & Carolyn Waldo (Canada)		Carolyn Waldo (Canada)
1992	Karen Josephson & Sarah Josephson (USA)		Kristen Babb-Sprague (USA)
1996		USA	
2000	Olga Brusnikina & Maria Kisseleva (Russia)	Russia	
2004	Anastasia Davydova & Anastasia Ermakova (Russia)	Russia	

Diving

World Championships

	Venues
1973	Belgrade, Yugoslavia
1975	Cali, Colombia
1978	Berlin, West Germany
1982	Guayaquil, Ecuador
1986	Madrid, Spain
1991	Perth, Australia
1994	Rome, Italy
1998	Perth, Australia
2001	Fukuoka, Japan
2003	Barcelona, Spain
2005	Montreal, Canada

Swimming & Diving

Men

	3m springboard	10m platform	1m springboard
1973	Phil Boggs (USA)	Klaus Dibiasi (Italy)	
1975	Phil Boggs (USA)	Klaus Dibiasi (Italy)	
1978	Phil Boggs (USA)	Greg Louganis (USA)	
1982	Greg Louganis (USA)	Greg Louganis (USA)	
1986	Greg Louganis (USA)	Greg Louganis (USA)	
1991	Kent Ferguson (USA)	Sun Shuwei (China)	Edwin Jongejans (The Netherlands)
1994	Yu Zhuocheng (China)	Dmitri Sautin (Russia)	Evan Stewart (Zimbabwe)
1998	Dmitri Sautin (Russia)	Dmitri Sautin (Russia)	Yu Zhuocheng (China)
2001	Dmitri Sautin (Russia)	Tian Liang (China)	Wang Feng (China)
2003	Aleksandr Dobroskok (Russia)	Alexander Despatie (Canada)	Xu Xiang (China)

	Synchronized springboard	Synchronized platform
1998	Xu Hao & Yu Zhoucheng (China)	Sun Shuwei & Tian Liang (China)
2001	Peng Bo & Wang Kenan (China)	Tian Liang & Hu Jia (China)
2003	Aleksandr Dobroskok & Dmitri Sautin (Russia)	Mathew Helm & Robert Newbery (Australia)

Women

	3m springboard	10m platform	1m springboard
1973	Christa Koehler (East Germany)	Ulrika Knape (Sweden)	
1975	Irina Kalinina (USSR)	Janet Ely (USA)	
1978	Irina Kalinina (USSR)	Irina Kalinina (USSR)	
1982	Megan Neyer (USA)	Wendy Wyland (USA)	
1986	Gao Min (China)	Chen Lin (China)	
1991	Gao Min (China)	Fu Mingxia (China)	Gao Min (China)
1994	Tan Shuping (China)	Fu Mingxia (China)	Chen Lixia (China)
1998	Yulia Pakhalina (Russia)	Olena Zhupyna (Ukraine)	Irina Lashko (Russia)
2001	Guo Jingjing (China)	Xu Mian (China)	Blythe Hartley (Canada)
2003	Guo Jingjing (China)	Emilie Heymans (Canada)	Irina Lashko (Australia)

	Synchronized springboard	Synchronized platform
1998	Irina Lashko & Yulia Pakhalina (Russia)	Olena Zhupyna & Svetlana Serbina (Ukraine)
2001	Wu Minxia & Guo Jingjing (China)	Duan Qing & Sang Xue (China)
2003	Wu Minxia & Guo Jingjing (China)	Lao Lishi & Li Ting (China)

Olympic Games

Men

	3m springboard	10m platform
1904	George Sheldon (USA)	
1908	Albert Zürner (Germany)	Hjalmar Johansson (Sweden)
1912	Paul Günther (Germany)	Erik Adlerz (Sweden)
1920	Louis Kuehn (USA)	Clarence Pinkston (USA)
1924	Albert White (USA)	Albert White (USA)
1928	Peter Desjardins (USA)	Peter Desjardins (USA)

	3m springboard	10m platform
1932	Michael Galitzen (USA)	Harold Smith (USA)
1936	Richard Degener (USA)	Marshall Wayne (USA)
1948	Bruce Harlan (USA)	Sammy Lee (USA)
1952	David Browning (USA)	Sammy Lee (USA)
1956	Robert Clotworthy (USA)	Joaquín Capilla Pérez (Mexico)
1960	Gary Tobian (USA)	Robert Webster (USA)
1964	Ken Sitzberger (USA)	Robert Webster (USA)
1968	Bernard Wrightson (USA)	Klaus Dibiasi (Italy)
1972	Vladimir Vasin (USSR)	Klaus Dibiasi (Italy)
1976	Phil Boggs (USA)	Klaus Dibiasi (Italy)
1980	Aleksandr Portnov (USSR)	Falk Hoffmann (East Germany)
1984	Greg Louganis (USA)	Greg Louganis (USA)
1988	Greg Louganis (USA)	Greg Louganis (USA)
1992	Mark Lenzi (USA)	Sun Shuwei (China)
1996	Xiong Ni (China)	Dmitri Sautin (USSR)
2000	Xiong Ni (China)	Tian Liang (China)
2004	Peng Bo (China)	Hu Jia (China)

	Synchronized springboard	Synchronized platform
2000	Xiao Hailiang & Xiong Ni (China)	Igor Loukachine & Dmitri Sautin (Russia)
2004	Nikolaos Sirandis & Thomas Bimis (Greece)	Tian Liang & Yang Jinghui (China)

Women

	3m springboard	10m platform
1912	Margareta Johanson (Sweden)	
1920	Aileen Riggin (USA)	Stefanie Clausen (Denmark)
1924	Elizabeth Becker (USA)	Caroline Smith (USA)
1928	Helen Meany (USA)	Elizabeth Becker-Pinkston (USA)
1932	Georgia Coleman (USA)	Dorothy Poynton (USA)
1936	Marjorie Gestring (USA)	Dorothy Poynton Hill (USA)
1948	Vicki Draves (USA)	Vicki Draves (USA)
1952	Pat McCormick (USA)	Pat McCormick (USA)
1956	Pat McCormick (USA)	Pat McCormick (USA)
1960	Ingrid Krämer (Germany)	Ingrid Krämer (Germany)
1964	Ingrid Engel-Krämer (Germany)	Lesley Bush (USA)
1968	Sue Gossick (USA)	Milena Duchková (Czechoslovakia)
1972	Micki King (USA)	Ulrika Knape (Sweden)
1976	Jennifer Chandler (USA)	Elena Vaytsekhovskaya (USSR)
1980	Irina Kalinina (USSR)	Martina Jäschke (East Germany)
1984	Sylvie Bernier (Canada)	Zhou Jihong (China)
1988	Gao Min (China)	Xu Yanmei (China)
1992	Gao Min (China)	Fu Mingxia (China)
1996	Fu Mingxia (China)	Fu Mingxia (China)
2000	Fu Mingxia (China)	Laura Wilkinson (USA)
2004	Guo Jingjing (China)	Chantelle Newbery (Australia)

	Synchronized springboard	Synchronized platform
2000	Vera Ilina & Yulia Pakhalina (Russia)	Li Na & Sang Xue (China)
2004	Wu Minxia & Guo Jingjing (China)	Lao Lishi & Li Ting (China)

A-Z

armstand	a dive in a platform diving competition where the diver begins from a handstand position
backstroke flags	flags suspended above and across the pool, 5m from each end, to assist backstrokers in making turns
backward	any dive where the diver starts with his or her back towards the water and rotates away from the board
ballet leg	a position in synchronized swimming where one leg is extended perpendicular to the surface of the water, with the body in a back layout position
ballet leg double	a position in synchronized swimming where the swimmer has her legs together and extended perpendicular to the water surface, with the face at the surface
block	the platform from which a swimmer starts a race
boost	a rapid, headfirst rise out of the water in synchronized swimming where the swimmer aims to raise as much of her body as possible above the water surface
combined spin	a descending spin in synchronized swimming that travels through at least 360 degrees followed, without a pause, by an equal ascending spin in the same direction
continuous spin	a descending spin in synchronized swimming that travels through at least 720 degrees
degree of difficulty	a rating that measures the difficulty of a particular dive. It is based on a mathematical formula
dolphin kick	a kick performed in the butterfly stroke where the legs are held together and moved up and down by bending and straightening them at the knee twice in quick succession
eggbeater	a rotary action of the legs used to support and propel the upper body in an upright position in synchronized swimming
entry	the end of the dive when the diver hits the water. A perfect entry is judged on vertical body shape and little or no splash
flamingo	a position in synchronized swimming where one leg is extended perpendicular to the surface while the other leg is drawn to the chest, with the face at the surface
flutter kick	a kick, usually performed as part of the front crawl, where the legs are held straight and moved up and down alternately
fly	short for butterfly, eg *the 100m fly*
IM	short for individual **medley**
inward	a dive where the diver starts from a position with his or her back to the water and rotates towards the board
layout	a diving position where a diver's body and legs are straight, the feet are together, and the toes are pointed
medley	an individual or team race in which the four main strokes (backstroke, breaststroke, butterfly and freestyle) are used
negative split	a race strategy in which a swimmer completes the second half of a race faster than the first
pike	a diving position where the body is bent at the waist with the legs straight and toes pointed

reverse	any dive where the diver starts facing forwards and rotates back towards the board
rip	the ideal **entry** that creates little splash; it is named after the ripping sound as the diver enters the water
scull	a movement of the hands against the water in synchronized swimming, designed to provide balance and support
split	a swimmer's intermediate time in a race
tuck	a position in diving where the body is bent at the knees and the hips, with the knees held together close to the chest
tumble turn	an underwater roll at the end of a length that allows the swimmer to push off from the end of the pool with the feet

Some famous swimmers and divers

Matt Biondi, 1965–

Born in Moraga, California, USA, he won a record seven medals at the 1986 world championships, including three golds, and at the 1988 Olympics won seven medals, including five golds. He set the 100m freestyle world record of 48.74s in Orlando, Florida, in 1986. He won silver in the 50m freestyle at the 1992 Olympics, and announced his retirement in 1993.

Inge de Bruijn, 1973–

Born in Barendrecht, the Netherlands, she first swam competitively at the age of twelve and joined the top ranks in 1991, when she won four medals at the European championships. At the 2000 Olympics she created a sensation by winning gold medals in the 100m butterfly, 100m freestyle and the 50m freestyle events, setting new world records in each. She also won a silver medal in the 4×100m freestyle relay. Four years later she retained her 50m freestyle title. In between she won five individual sprint titles at the 2001 and 2003 world championships.

Gertrude Ederle, 1906–2003

Born in New York, USA, she won a gold medal at the 1924 Olympic Games as a member of the US 400m relay team, as well as two bronze medals. On 6 August 1926 she swam the English Channel from Cap Gris Nez to Kingsdown, the first woman to do so, in 14hrs 39mins, nearly two hours faster than the existing men's record.

Kornelia Ender, 1958–

Born in Bitterfeld, Germany, she won three Olympic silver medals in 1972, aged 13, and between 1973 and 1976 broke 23 world records (the most by a woman under modern conditions). At the 1973 and 1975 world championships she won ten medals, including a record eight golds. In 1976 she became the first woman to win four gold medals at one Olympic Games.

Janet Evans, 1971–

Born in Fullerton, California, USA, she won three gold medals at the 1988 Olympics (400m freestyle, 800m freestyle and 400m medley) and one at the 1992 Olympics (800m freestyle). She also set world records in the 400m freestyle, the 800m freestyle and the 1,500m freestyle.

Dawn Fraser, 1937–

Born in Balmain, Sydney, Australia, she broke 27 world records and won 29 Australian championships in her career. Her outstanding achievement was in winning gold medals at three successive Olympic Games – Melbourne (1956), Rome (1960) and Tokyo (1964), in each case setting a new Olympic record. At the Rome Olympic Games she broke three world records within one hour. In 1964 she became the first woman to break the 'magic minute' for the 100m with a time of 58.9s, a record that was to stand for 20 years.

Shane Gould, 1956–

Born in Brisbane, Australia, she set world records at every freestyle distance from 100m to 1,500m between 1971 and 1972. At the 1972 Olympics she also became the first woman to win three individual swimming golds in world record times. As well as breaking or equalling eleven world records throughout her short career, she won numerous Australian individual championships, all before retiring at the age of just 17.

Michael Gross, 1964–

Born in Frankfurt, Germany, he was a butterfly and freestyle swimmer who won 13 gold medals between 1981 and 1987 for West Germany at the European championships. He has won three Olympic gold medals: the 100m butterfly and 200m freestyle in 1984, and the 200m butterfly in 1988. He was nicknamed 'the Albatross' for his extraordinary armspan.

Greg Louganis, 1960–

Born in El Cajon, California, USA, of Samoan and Swedish ancestry, he won the gold medal in both the springboard and platform diving competitions at the 1984 Los Angeles Olympics, and won the world championship at both events in 1986. At the Seoul Olympics in 1988 he won gold medals in the same two categories despite injuring himself when he banged his head against the edge of the board during competition.

Michael Phelps, 1985–

Born in Baltimore, USA, he competed at the 2000 Olympic Games as a 15-year-old but first made an impact at the 2003 world championships with three gold medals (200m individual medley, 400m individual medley and 200m butterfly) as well as two world records. At the 2004 Athens Olympics he attempted to break the record of seven gold medals at a single games held by Mark Spitz; however, he had to settle for just six. Those and two further bronzes meant he became the most bemedalled swimmer ever at a single Games.

Mark Spitz, 1950–

Born in Modesto, California, USA, he earned worldwide fame at the 1972 Olympics by winning seven gold medals, achieving a world record time in each event. He also won two golds at the 1968 Games, and set a total of 26 world records between 1967 and 1972. He turned professional in 1972.

Ian Thorpe, 1982-

Born in Sydney, Australia, he marked his potential as a swimmer with selection for the Australian swimming team in 1997, aged just 14. Nicknamed 'the Thorpedo', he broke the world records for the 400m and 200m in 1999 and dominated the pool at the 2000 Olympic Games in Sydney, winning gold in the 400m freestyle (breaking his own record), silver in the 200m freestyle, and record-breaking golds in the 4×100m and 4×200m freestyle relays. Four years later in Athens he took two more individual golds. Thorpe took his tally of world titles to eleven in 2003 by winning six gold medals at the 2001 world championships in Fukuoka, Japan, and three at the 2003 world championships in Barcelona.

Johnny Weissmuller, 1903–84

Born in Freidorf, Romania, he emigrated with his family to the USA in 1908. He was the first man to swim 100m in under a minute, and 440yd/402m in less than five minutes. Undefeated from 1921 to 1928, he won a total of five Olympic gold medals. After turning professional in 1932 he modelled swimwear. His physique, swimming prowess and popularity won him the film role of Tarzan in 19 films (1932–48).

TABLE TENNIS

Origins

Table tennis, called indoor tennis in its earliest days, was played by British Army officers in India and South Africa who improvised an after-dinner game that could be played on dining tables. Corks were used as balls and cigar-box lids as rudimentary bats, with books laid across the table serving as a net. The game became popular and was marketed under various guises at the end of the 19th century: 'whiff-whaff', 'flim-flam', 'gossima', and 'Ping-Pong' (patented by Parker Bros). The early rules of the game were codified by Ivor Montagu in 1922 and the International Table Tennis Federation (ITTF) was formed in 1926.

Rules and description

Table tennis is a game like lawn tennis that is played on a table. There are singles (men and women), doubles and mixed doubles tournaments. Players use a small wooden, rubber-coated bat (also known as a paddle) to propel a small hollow ball of celluloid or a similar light material over a net strung across the table. The table is 9ft/2.74m by 5ft/1.52m with its upper surface 76cm/2.5ft above the floor. Its surface is dark green with white line markings. The net, 6in/15.25cm high, divides the playing surface in two. The aim of the game, as in tennis, is to score points by making winning shots or causing the opponent to make losing shots (hitting the ball off the table, hitting the ball into the net, or failing to retrieve the ball). The server must ensure the ball bounces on his or her side of the table before bouncing on the opponent's side. Until recently, serve changed every five points and the winner was the first to 21 points (a two-point advantage being required). In the modern scoring system, however, serve changes hands after every two points. A game is won by the first to 11 points; at 10-all the service changes after every point until a two-point advantage is gained.

Ruling body: International Table Tennis Federation (ITTF)

World Championships

	Men's singles	Men's doubles
1926	Roland Jacobi (Hungary)	Roland Jacobi & Daniel Pécsi (Hungary)
1927	*Not held*	
1928	Zoltán Mechlovits (Hungary)	Alfred Liebster & Robert Thum (Austria)
1929	Fred Perry (England)	Viktor Barna & Miklós Szabados (Hungary)
1930	Viktor Barna (Hungary)	Viktor Barna & Miklós Szabados (Hungary)
1931	Miklós Szabados (Hungary)	Viktor Barna & Miklós Szabados (Hungary)
1932	Viktor Barna (Hungary)	Viktor Barna & Miklós Szabados (Hungary)
1933	Viktor Barna (Hungary)	Viktor Barna & Sándor Glancz (Hungary)
1934	Viktor Barna (Hungary)	Viktor Barna & Miklós Szabados (Hungary)
1935	Viktor Barna (Hungary)	Viktor Barna & Miklós Szabados (Hungary)
1936	Stanislav Kolár (Hungary)	Robert Blattner & James McClure (US)
1937	Richard Bergmann (Austria)	Robert Blattner & James McClure (US)
1938	Bohumil Vána (Czechoslovakia)	James McClure & Sol Schiff (US)
1939	Richard Bergmann (England)	Viktor Barna & Richard Bergmann (England)
1940–6	*Not held*	
1947	Bohumil Vána (Czechoslovakia)	Adolf Slár & Bohumil Vána (Czechoslovakia)
1948	Richard Bergmann (England)	Ladislav Stipek & Bohumil Vána (Czechoslovakia)
1949	Johnny Leach (England)	Ivan Andreadis & Frantisekk Tokár (Czechoslovakia)
1950	Richard Bergmann (England)	Ferenc Sidó & Ferenc Soós (Hungary)
1951	Johnny Leach (England)	Ivan Andreadis & Bohumil Vána (Czechoslovakia)
1952	Hiroji Satoh (Japan)	Norikazu Fujii & Tadaski Hayashi (Japan)
1953	Ferenc Sidó (Hungary)	József Koczian & Ferenc Sidó (Hungary)
1954	Ichiro Ogimura (Japan)	Zarko Dolinar & Vilim Harangozo (Yugoslavia)
1955	Toshio Tanaka (Japan)	Ivan Andreadis & Ladislav Stipek (Czechoslovakia)
1956	Ichiro Ogimura (Japan)	Ichiro Ogimura & Yoshio Tomita (Japan)
1957	Toshio Tanaka (Japan)	Ivan Andreadis & Ladislav Stipek (Czechoslovakia)
1959	Rong Guotuan (China)	Teruo Murakami & Ichiro Ogimura (Japan)
1961	Zhuang Zedong (China)	Nobuyo Hoshino & Koji Kimura (Japan)
1963	Zhuang Zedong (China)	Zang Xielin & Wang Zhiliang (China)
1965	Zhuang Zedong (China)	Zang Xielin & Xu Yinsheng (China)
1967	Nobuhiko Hasegawa (Japan)	Hans Alser & Kjell Johansson (Sweden)
1969	Shigeo Itoh (Japan)	Hans Alser & Kjell Johansson (Sweden)
1971	Stellan Bengtsson (Sweden)	István Jónyer & Tibor Klampar (Hungary)
1973	Xi Enting (China)	Stellan Bengtsson & Kjell Johansson (Sweden)
1975	István Jónyer (Hungary)	Gabor Gergeley & István Jónyer (Hungary)
1977	Mitsuru Kohno (Japan)	Li Zhenshi & Liang Geliang (China)
1979	Seiji Ono (Japan)	Dragutin Surbek & Anton Stipancic (Yugoslavia)
1981	Guo Yuehua (China)	Li Zhenshi & Cai Zhenhua (China)
1983	Guo Yuehua (China)	Dragutin Surbek & Zoran Kalinic (Yugoslavia)
1985	Jiang Jialiang (China)	Mikael Appelgren & Ulf Carlsson (Sweden)

	Men's singles	Men's doubles
1987	Jiang Jialiang (China)	Chen Longcan & Wei Qingguang (China)
1989	Jan Ove Waldner (Sweden)	Jorg Rosskopf & Steffen Fetzner (West Germany)
1991	Jörgen Persson (Sweden)	Peter Karlsson & Thomas von Scheele (Sweden)
1993	Jean-Philippe Gatien (France)	Wang Tao & Lu Lin (China)
1995	Kong Linghui (China)	Wang Tao & Lu Lin (China)
1997	Jan-Ove Waldner (Sweden)	Kong Linghui & Liu Guoliang (China)
1999	Liu Guoliang (China)	Kong Linghui & Liu Guoliang (China)
2001	Wang Liqin (China)	Wang Liqin & Yan Sen (China)
2003	Werner Schlager (Austria)	Wang Liqin & Yan Sen (China)

	Women's singles	Women's doubles
1926	Mária Mednyánszky (Hungary)	
1927	*Not held*	
1928	Mária Mednyánszky (Hungary)	Erika Flamm (Austria) & Mária Mednyánszky (Hungary)
1929	Mária Mednyánszky (Hungary)	Erika Metzger & Mona Rüster (Germany)
1930	Mária Mednyánszky (Hungary)	Mária Mednyánszky & Anna Sipos (Hungary)
1931	Mária Mednyánszky (Hungary)	Mária Mednyánszky & Anna Sipos (Hungary)
1932	Anna Sipos (Hungary)	Mária Mednyánszky & Anna Sipos (Hungary)
1933	Anna Sipos (Hungary)	Mária Mednyánszky & Anna Sipos (Hungary)
1934	Marie Kettnerová (Czechoslovakia)	Mária Mednyánszky & Anna Sipos (Hungary)
1935	Marie Kettnerová (Czechoslovakia)	Mária Mednyánszky & Anna Sipos (Hungary)
1936	Ruth Aarons-Hughes (US)	Marie Kettnerová & Marie Smídová (Czechoslovakia)
1937	*Vacant*	Vlasta Depetrisová & Vera Votrubcová (Czechoslovakia)
1938	Gertrude Pritzi (Austria)	Vlasta Depetrisová & Vera Votrubcová (Czechoslovakia)
1939	Vlasta Depetrisová (Czechoslovakia)	Hilde Bussmann & Gertrude Pritzi (Germany)
1940–6	*Not held*	
1947	Gizella Lantos-Gervai-Farkas (Hungary)	Gizella Lantos-Gervai-Farkas (Hungary) & Gertrude Pritzi (Austria)
1948	Gizella Lantos-Gervai-Farkas (Hungary)	Margaret Franks & Vera Thomas (England)
1949	Gizella Lantos-Gervai-Farkas (Hungary)	Helen Elliot (Scotland) & Gizella Lantos-Gervai-Farkas (Hungary)
1950	Angelica Rozeanu (Romania)	Dora Beregi (England) & Helen Elliot (Scotland)
1951	Angelica Rozeanu (Romania)	Diane Rowe & Rosalind Rowe (England)
1952	Angelica Rozeanu (Romania)	Shizuki Narahara & Tomi Nishimura (Japan)
1953	Angelica Rozeanu (Romania)	Gizella Lantos-Gervai-Farkas (Hungary) & Angelica Rozeanu (Romania)
1954	Angelica Rozeanu (Romania)	Diane Rowe & Rosalind Rowe (England)
1955	Angelica Rozeanu (Romania)	Angelica Rozeanu & Ella Zeller (Romania)
1956	Tomie Okawa (Japan)	Angelica Rozeanu & Ella Zeller (Romania)
1957	Fujie Eguchi (Japan)	Livia Mosoczy & Agnes Simon (Hungary)
1959	Kimiyo Matsuzaki (Japan)	Taeko Namba & Kazuko Yamaizumi (Japan)
1961	Gui Zonghui (China)	Maria Alexandru & Geta Pitica (Romania)
1963	Kimiyo Matsuzaki (Japan)	Kimiyo Matsuzaki & Masako Seki (Japan)
1965	Naoko Fukazu (Japan)	Zheng Minzhi & Lin Huiqing (China)
1967	Sachiko Morisawa (Japan)	Saeko Hirota & Sachiko Morisawa (Japan)
1969	Toshiko Kowada (Japan)	Svetlana Grinberg & Zoya Rudnova (USSR)
1971	Lin Huiqing (China)	Zheng Minzhi & Lin Huiqing (China)
1973	Hu Yulan (China)	Maria Alexandru (Romania) & Miho Hamada (Japan)
1975	Pak Yung-sun (North Korea)	Maria Alexandru (Romania) & Shoko Takashima (Japan)

	Women's singles	Women's doubles
1977	Pak Yung-sun (North Korea)	Yang Ying (China) & Pak Yong-ok (North Korea)
1979	Ge Xinai (China)	Zhang Li & Zhang Deying (China)
1981	Tong Ling (China)	Zhang Deying & Cao Yanhua (China)
1983	Cao Yanhua (China)	Shen Jianping & Dai Lili (China)
1985	Cao Yanhua (China)	Dai Lili & Geng Lijuan (China)
1987	He Zhili (China)	Yang Young-ja & Hyun Jung-hwa (South Korea)
1989	Qiao Hong (China)	Deng Yaping & Qiao Hong (China)
1991	Deng Yaping (China)	Chen Zihe & Gao Jun (China)
1993	Hyun Jung-hwa (South Korea)	Liu Wei & Qiao Yunping (China)
1995	Deng Yaping (China)	Deng Yaping & Qiao Hong (China)
1997	Deng Yaping (China)	Deng Yaping & Yang Ying (China)
1999	Wang Nan (China)	Wang Nan & Li Ju (China)
2001	Wang Nan (China)	Wang Nan & Li Ju (China)
2003	Wang Nan (China)	Wang Nan & Zhang Yining (China)

The ultimate women's doubles team

To play well as a pairing it is essential that you are on the same wavelength as your partner. The world doubles champions of 1951 and 1954 had that little bit more insight into each other – English players Diane and Rosalind Rowe were identical twins, and they had the table covered with one being left-handed and the other right-handed.

Olympic Games

	Men's singles	Men's doubles
1988	Yoo Nam-kyu (South Korea)	Chen Longcan & Wei Qingguang (China)
1992	Jan-Ove Waldner (Sweden)	Lu Lin & Wang Tao (China)
1996	Liu Guoliang (China)	Kong Linghui & Liu Guoliang (China)
2000	Kong Linghui (China)	Wang Liqin & Yan Sen (China)
2004	Ryu Seung-min (South Korea)	Chen Qi & Ma Lin (China)

	Women's singles	Women's doubles
1988	Chen Jing (China)	Hyun Jung-hwa & Yang Young-ja (South Korea)
1992	Deng Yaping (China)	Deng Yaping & Qiao Hong (China)
1996	Deng Yaping (China)	Deng Yaping & Qiao Hong (China)
2000	Wang Nan (China)	Li Ju & Wang Nan (China)
2004	Zhang Yining (China)	Wang Nan & Zhang Yining (China)

Swaythling and Corbillon Cups

The Swaythling Cup is awarded to the world's men's team champions. It was donated by Lady Swaythling, mother of the ITTF's first president, Ivor Montagu. It has been won on most occasions by China with 14 titles. The women's equivalent event is the Marcel Corbillon Cup (Corbillon was the President of the French Table Tennis Association). It has been won on no fewer than 15 occasions by China.

A-Z

backhand a stroke with the hand turned backward, and to the left of the elbow for a right-hander and right of the elbow for a left-hander

backspin reverse spin imparted by striking the ball with a downward movement or **chop** of the bat

blade the wooden bat excluding its rubber covering

block a return shot, where the ball is played shortly after the bounce with little bat movement at the point of contact

chop a defensive downward stroke that produces **backspin**

cross-court a cross-court shot is one that is hit diagonally from corner to corner of the table

dead a dead shot is one with no spin

drop shot a touch shot that falls just over the opponent's side of the net; it is generally played when the opponent is far away from the table

forehand a stroke with the hand facing forward

high toss serve a serve where the ball is thrown high into the air. It increases the spin and deception the player can impart to the serve

let a point that is replayed at the umpire's discretion

lob a high defensive return of a **smash**

loop a shot played with a closed-face bat that places heavy **topspin** on the ball

penholder a popular grip in Asia where the bat is held as if holding a pen, with the tip of the bat pointing downward; compare **shake-hands**

pips the small raised bits of rubber that cover the surface area of the bat

push a defensive or containing shot played with **backspin**

rally the series of exchanged shots that decide a point

shakehands a grip that resembles 'shaking hands' with the bat; compare **penholder**

side line a white line along each side of the playing surface

sidespin spin imparted by striking the ball with a sideways movement of the bat

smash a hard, flat attacking stroke

third-ball attack a strategy that attempts to win the point on the third shot of the rally, with the server attempting to **loop** or **smash** the return of serve

topspin forward spin imparted by striking the ball with an upward movement of the bat

western grip same as **shakehands**

Some famous table tennis players

Viktor Barna, 1911–72

Born in Budapest, Hungary, Barna is considered the world's greatest player. Between 1930 and 1939 he was men's singles world champion five times, doubles champion eight times, and mixed doubles champion on two occasions. He broke his playing arm in a car accident in 1935 but still returned to win his final doubles world title.

Richard Bergmann, 1920–70

Born in Vienna he was part of the winning Austrian Swaythling Cup team in 1936 and won his first world singles title a year later. Shortly before World War II he fled to Britain and took British citizenship and won his world singles and doubles titles for Great Britain. In the mid-1950s, Bergmann became the world's first professional table tennis player.

Liu Guoliang, 1976–

Born in Xinxiang, Henan province, China, he started playing at the age of six and was a member of the national team at 17. He took the singles title at the world championships (1996, 1999), Olympics (1996) and World Cup (1996), and had many doubles and team successes. After retiring in 2002, he was appointed national coach.

Mária Mednyánszky, 1901–78

Born in Budapest, Hungary, she based her game on heavy attacking spin and was successful in winning a record total of 18 world titles. She competed in doubles with her great rival **Anna Sipos**.

Angelica Rozeanu, 1921–

Born in Bucharest, Romania, as Angelica Adelstein, she is considered the greatest women's player, winning 17 world titles, including an unbeaten series of women's singles titles (1950–5). Rozeanu won the Romanian singles title for the first time in 1936 as a 15-year-old and held it until she retired. She emigrated to Israel in 1960.

Anna Sipos, 1908–72

Born in Szeged, Hungary, she won eleven gold medals in world championship table tennis competition. She won doubles titles with **Mária Mednyánszky**, Istvan Kelen and **Viktor Barna**. Sipos was the first woman player to use the penholder grip but changed it to win her singles world titles.

Wang Nan, 1978–

Born in Fushun, Liaoning province, China, she took up table tennis at the age of seven and joined the national team at just 15. In 2003 she took all four titles (singles, doubles, mixed and team) at the world championships, the first time that this had been achieved since **Angelica Rozeanu** did it in 1953. It was the third consecutive championships in which she had taken singles and doubles titles. Her dominance of the women's game also yielded Olympic gold in the singles in 2000 and doubles in 2000 and 2004.

TAEKWONDO

Origins

Taekwondo (Korean, 'tae', 'foot'; 'kwon', 'fist'; 'do', 'way') is a Korean form of karate developed in the 1950s. Its roots go back much further in time, although its precise origins are unknown.

Rules and description

Like all modern martial arts, taekwondo aims for a synthesis of mind, body and spirit. In its physical form taekwondo players (or 'taekwondoka') use flying kicks and punches against their opponents to score points and knockdowns. The white uniform is similar to a karate uniform and is known as a 'dobok'. A protective piece of body armour (the 'hogu') is worn over the top, and further protection is provided by a helmet and shin and arm guards. As in other martial arts, the grade of taekwondoka is shown by a coloured belt: 'kup' or 'keup' pupil grades wear belts graduating from white to yellow, to green, blue and red. The 'dan' grades wear a black belt. The contest area is a 12m² mat and each contest lasts for three rounds of three minutes each, or two minutes each for women. During the contest one player wears red ('hong') and the other blue ('chung'). The aim is to punch or kick the opponent on specific parts of the body above the waist, including kicks to the head and face. Two of the three judges need to recognize an effective blow before it is scored as a point ('deuk-jeom'). Taekwondoka gain extra points for knock-downs. Grabbing, pushing, holding, feigning injury and turning the back on an opponent are forbidden. There are eight weight categories for men and women. For men they range from fin (under 54kg) to heavyweight (84kg and over); for women, from fin (47kg) to heavy (over 72kg). In Olympic Games competition there are four weight categories for men and women.

Ruling body: World Taekwondo Federation (WTF)

World Championships

The first World Championships were staged in 1973, and thereafter biennially. Women's events were first held unofficially in 1983 and became part of the official competition in 1987.

Men

	Under 54kg (Fin)	Under 58kg (Fly)
1991	Gergely Salim (Denmark)	Kim Cheol-ho (South Korea)
1993	Chin Seung-tae (South Korea)	Javier Argudo (Spain)
1995	Chin Seung-tae (South Korea)	Cihat Kutluca (Turkey)
1997	Juan Antonio Ramos (Spain)	Chin Seung-tae (South Korea)
1999	Min Byeong-seok (South Korea)	Yoon Jong-il (South Korea)
2001	Choi Yeon-ho (South Korea)	Behzad Khodada Kanjobeh (Iran)
2003	Choi Yeon-ho (South Korea)	Chu Muyen (Taiwan)

	Under 62kg (Bantam)	Under 67kg (Feather)*
1991	Ángel Alonso (Spain)	Jang Hyuk (South Korea)
1993	Kim In-kyung (South Korea)	Kim Byong-cheol (South Korea)
1995	Chang Dae-soon (South Korea)	Kim Byong-uk (South Korea)
1997	Huang Chihhsiung (Taiwan)	Kim Dong-in (South Korea)
1999	Ko Dae-hyu (South Korea)	No Hyun-ku (South Korea)
2001	Kang Nam-won (South Korea)	Niyameddin Pashayev (Azerbaijan)
2003	Huang Chihhsiung (Taiwan)	Kang Nam-won (South Korea)

*Until 1999 under 64kg

	Under 72kg (Light)*	Under 78kg (Welter)**
1991	Yang Dae-seung (South Korea)	Park Yong-woon (South Korea)
1993	Park Se-jin (South Korea)	Lim Young-ho (South Korea)
1995	Aziz Acharki (Germany)	José Jesús Marquez (Spain)
1997	Tamer Abdel Monem (Egypt)	José Jesús Marquez (Spain)
1999	Hadi Saei Boneh Kohal (Iran)	Jang Jong-oh (South Korea)
2001	Steven Lopez (USA)	Mamedy Doucara (France)
2003	Kim Kyo-sik (South Korea)	Steven Lopez (USA)
	*Until 1999 under 70kg	**Until 1999 under 76kg

	Under 84kg (Middle)*	Over 84kg (Heavy)**
1991	Yoon Soon-cheul (South Korea)	Tonny Sørensen (Denmark)
1993	Mikael Meloul (France)	Kim Je-kyoung (South Korea)
1995	Lee Dong-wan (South Korea)	Kim Je-kyoung (South Korea)
1997	Lee Dong-wan (South Korea)	Kim Je-kyoung (South Korea)
1999	Majid Aflaki Khamseh (Iran)	Moon Dae-sung (South Korea)
2001	Bahri Tanrikulu (Turkey)	Ferry Greevink (The Netherlands)
2003	Yossef Karami (Iran)	Morteza Rostami (Iran)
	*Until 1999 under 83kg	**Until 1999 over 83kg

Women

	Under 47kg (Fin)	Under 51kg (Fly)	Under 55kg (Bantam)
1991	Elizabeth Delgado (Spain)	Arzu Tan (Turkey)	Park Dong-seon (South Korea)
1993	Isabel Cruzado (Spain)	You Su-mi (South Korea)	Tang Huiwen (Taiwan)
1995	Huang Chinchin (Taiwan)	Hamide Bikcin Tosun (Turkey)	Won Sun-jin (South Korea)
1997	Yang So-hee (South Korea)	Chi Shuju (Taiwan)	Hwang Eun-suk (South Korea)
1999	Belén Asensio (Spain)	Chi Shuju (Taiwan)	Wang Su (China)
2001	Kadriye Selimoglu (Turkey)	Lee Hye-young (South Korea)	Jung Jae-eun (South Korea)
2003	Brigida Yague (Spain)	Lee Ji-hye (South Korea)	Ha Jeoung-yeon (South Korea)

	Under 59kg (Feather)	Under 63kg (Light)*	Under 67kg (Welter)**
1991	Tung Yaling (Taiwan)	Jeong Eun-ok (South Korea)	Arlene Limas (USA)
1993	Lee Seung-min (South Korea)	Kang Hae-eun (South Korea)	Kim Mi-young (South Korea)
1995	Lee Seung-min (South Korea)	Park Kyung-suk (South Korea)	Cho Hyang-mi (South Korea)
1997	Jung Jae-eun (South Korea)	María Jesús Santolaria (Spain)	Cho Hyang-mi (South Korea)
1999	Kang Hae-eun (South Korea)	Cho Hyang-mi (South Korea)	Elena Benítez (Spain)
2001	Jang Ji-won (South Korea)	Kim Yeon-ji (South Korea)	Kim Hye-mi (South Korea)
2003	Areti Athanasopoulou (Greece)	Kim Yeon-ji (South Korea)	Lee Sun-hee (South Korea)
		*Until 1999 under 60kg	**Until 1999 under 65kg

	Under 72kg (Middle)*	Over 72kg (Heavy)**
1991	Yang In-deok (South Korea)	Lynette Love (USA)
1993	Park Eun-sun (South Korea)	Jung Myoung-sook (South Korea)
1995	Irene Ruíz (Spain)	Jung Myoung-sook (South Korea)
1997	Woo Eun-joung (South Korea)	Jung Myoung-sook (South Korea)
1999	Kim Yoon-kyung (South Korea)	Kao Chingyi (Taiwan)
2001	Sarah Stevenson (Great Britain)	Sin Kyung-hyen (South Korea)
2003	Wei Luo (China)	Youn Hyun-jung (South Korea)
	*Until 1999 under 70kg	**Until 1999 over 70kg

TENNIS

Origins

The modern game of tennis can be traced back to the courtyards of medieval France, where a racketless version known as *jeu de paume* ('palm game') was popular. 'Field tennis' was played in the 18th century, but the first true incarnation of the modern game, christened 'sphairistike' by its creator, Walter Wingfield, was invented in Wales in 1873. Wingfield patented the game and it became widely known for a time by this name, which comes from the Greek *sphairistike techne* 'the art of playing ball', from *sphaira* 'ball'. It later became known as lawn tennis, tennis coming from the French word *tenez*, the imperative of *tenir* meaning 'to take or receive'.

Rules and description

Racket-and-ball game for two or four players, played on a rectangular court, 78 x 27ft/23.77 x 8.3m wide (36ft/10.97m wide for doubles). Players on opposite sides of the court hit a ball over a 3ft/91.4cm-high net dividing the court at the centre, until a point is won by a player hitting a shot that lands in the court and cannot be returned, or by the opponent's shot landing out of the court or failing to clear the net. Each point begins with a serve, where the ball is thrown up into the air and hit diagonally across the net to the opponent. The server continues to serve until four points and hence a game have been won. These four points are called 'fifteen', 'thirty', 'forty' and 'game'. There must be at least a two-point margin for a game to

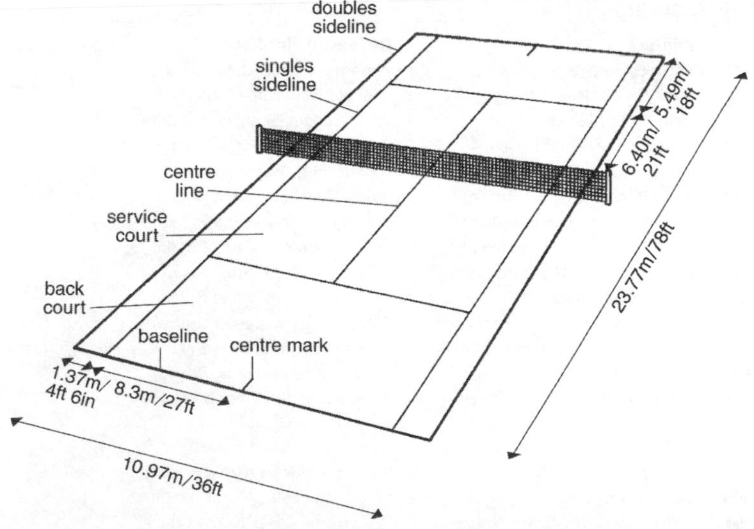

be won. If the score reaches forty apiece, 'deuce' is called; the first player to secure a two-point margin after this wins the game. Games are grouped into 'sets', with a player awarded a set when they win six games, provided a two-game margin is secured. If the set reaches six games apiece, a tie-break is played. The first player to win seven points in the 'tie-break', with at least a two-point margin, wins the set. Matches are decided on a best of three-set basis, or best of five in major men's championships.

Ruling bodies: Association of Tennis Professionals (ATP), Women's Tennis Association (WTA)

Scoring

The scoring system in tennis may be inspired by the presence of a clock face at the head of early courts. As players won points, the appropriate hand was moved to reflect this. Therefore the first point was fifteen (minutes), the second thirty, the third forty-five and finally, when the hour was reached, game. Forty-five was later shortened to forty as it took less time to call out.

Wimbledon

The third Grand Slam event of the year and the oldest tennis tournament in the world, Wimbledon is held in June on the grass courts of the All England Lawn Tennis and Croquet Club in London, England (SW19 is the famous postcode). Between 1878 and 1921 the holder of the men's singles title would not compete until the Challenge Round, when he met the winner of the singles to decide The Championship. This also applied to the women's singles and men's doubles from 1886 to 1921.

Men's Singles

	Winner	Defeated finalist
1877	Spencer Gore (Great Britain)	William Marshall (Great Britain)
1878	Frank Hadow (Great Britain)	Spencer Gore (Great Britain)
1879	John Hartley (Great Britain)	Vere St Leger Goold (Great Britain)
1880	John Hartley (Great Britain)	Herbert Lawford (Great Britain)
1881	Willie Renshaw (Great Britain)	John Hartley (Great Britain)
1882	Willie Renshaw (Great Britain)	Ernest Renshaw (Great Britain)
1883	Willie Renshaw (Great Britain)	Ernest Renshaw (Great Britain)
1884	Willie Renshaw (Great Britain)	Herbert Lawford (Great Britain)
1885	Willie Renshaw (Great Britain)	Herbert Lawford (Great Britain)
1886	Willie Renshaw (Great Britain)	Herbert Lawford (Great Britain)
1887	Herbert Lawford (Great Britain)	Ernest Renshaw (Great Britain)
1888	Ernest Renshaw (Great Britain)	Herbert Lawford (Great Britain)
1889	Willie Renshaw (Great Britain)	Ernest Renshaw (Great Britain)
1890	William Hamilton (Great Britain)	Willie Renshaw (Great Britain)
1891	Wilfred Baddeley (Great Britain)	Joshua Pim (Great Britain)
1892	Wilfred Baddeley (Great Britain)	Joshua Pim (Great Britain)
1893	Joshua Pim (Great Britain)	Wilfred Baddeley (Great Britain)
1894	Joshua Pim (Great Britain)	Wilfred Baddeley (Great Britain)
1895	Wilfred Baddeley (Great Britain)	Wilberforce Eaves (Great Britain)

	Winner	Defeated finalist
1896	Harold Mahoney (Great Britain)	Wilfred Baddeley (Great Britain)
1897	Reggie Doherty (Great Britain)	Harold Mahoney (Great Britain)
1898	Reggie Doherty (Great Britain)	Laurie Doherty (Great Britain)
1899	Reggie Doherty (Great Britain)	Arthur Gore (Great Britain)
1900	Reggie Doherty (Great Britain)	Sidney Smith (Great Britain)
1901	Arthur Gore (Great Britain)	Reggie Doherty (Great Britain)
1902	Laurie Doherty (Great Britain)	Arthur Gore (Great Britain)
1903	Laurie Doherty (Great Britain)	Frank Riseley (Great Britain)
1904	Laurie Doherty (Great Britain)	Frank Riseley (Great Britain)
1905	Laurie Doherty (Great Britain)	Norman Brookes (Australia)
1906	Laurie Doherty (Great Britain)	Frank Riseley (Great Britain)
1907	Norman Brookes (Australia)	Arthur Gore (Great Britain)
1908	Arthur Gore (Great Britain)	H Roper Barrett (Great Britain)
1909	Arthur Gore (Great Britain)	M J G Ritchie (Great Britain)
1910	Tony Wilding (New Zealand)	Arthur Gore (Great Britain)
1911	Tony Wilding (New Zealand)	H Roper Barrett (Great Britain)
1912	Tony Wilding (New Zealand)	Arthur Gore (Great Britain)
1913	Tony Wilding (New Zealand)	Maurice McLoughlin (USA)
1914	Norman Brookes (Australia)	Tony Wilding (New Zealand)
1915–18	*Not held*	
1919	Gerald Patterson (Australia)	Norman Brookes (Australia)
1920	Bill Tilden (USA)	Gerald Patterson (Australia)
1921	Bill Tilden (USA)	Brian Norton (South Africa)
1922	Gerald Patterson (Australia)	Randolph Lycett (Great Britain)
1923	Bill Johnston (USA)	Frank Hunter (USA)
1924	Jean Borotra (France)	René Lacoste (France)
1925	René Lacoste (France)	Jean Borotra (France)
1926	Jean Borotra (France)	Howard Kinsey (USA)
1927	Henri Cochet (France)	Jean Borotra (France)
1928	René Lacoste (France)	Henri Cochet (France)
1929	Henri Cochet (France)	Jean Borotra (France)
1930	Bill Tilden (USA)	Wilmer Allison (USA)
1931	Sidney Wood (USA)	Francis Shields (USA)
1932	Ellsworth.Vines (USA)	Henry 'Bunny' Austin (Great Britain)
1933	Jack Crawford (Australia)	Ellsworth Vines (USA)
1934	Fred Perry (Great Britain)	Jack Crawford (Australia)
1935	Fred Perry (Great Britain)	Gottfried von Cramm (Germany)
1936	Fred Perry (Great Britain)	Gottfried von Cramm (Germany)
1937	Don Budge (USA)	Gottfried von Cramm (Germany)
1938	Don Budge (USA)	Henry 'Bunny' Austin (Great Britain)
1939	Bobby Riggs (USA)	Elwood Cooke (USA)
1940–5	*Not held*	
1946	Yvon Petra (France)	Geoff Brown (Australia)
1947	Jack Kramer (USA)	Tom Brown (USA)
1948	Bob Falkenburg (USA)	John Bromwich (Australia)
1949	Ted Schroeder (USA)	Jaroslav Drobny (Czechoslovakia)
1950	Budge Patty (USA)	Frank Sedgman (Australia)
1951	Richard Savitt (USA)	Ken McGregor (Australia)
1952	Frank Sedgman (Australia)	Jaroslav Drobny (Egypt)

	Winner	Defeated finalist
1953	Vic Seixas (USA)	Ken Nielsen (Denmark)
1954	Jaroslav Drobny (Egypt)	Ken Rosewall (Australia)
1955	Tony Trabert (USA)	Ken Nielsen (Denmark)
1956	Lew Hoad (Australia)	Ken Rosewall (Australia)
1957	Lew Hoad (Australia)	Ashley Cooper (Australia)
1958	Ashley Cooper (Australia)	Neale Fraser (Australia)
1959	Alex Olmedo (USA)	Rod Laver (Australia)
1960	Neale Fraser (Australia)	Rod Laver (Australia)
1961	Rod Laver (Australia)	Chuck McKinley (USA)
1962	Rod Laver (Australia)	Marty Mulligan (Australia)
1963	Chuck McKinley (USA)	Fred Stolle (Australia)
1964	Roy Emerson (Australia)	Fred Stolle (Australia)
1965	Roy Emerson (Australia)	Fred Stolle (Australia)
1966	Manuel Santana (Spain)	Dennis Ralston (USA)
1967	John Newcombe (Australia)	Wilhelm Bungert (West Germany)
1968	Rod Laver (Australia)	Tony Roche (Australia)
1969	Rod Laver (Australia)	John Newcombe (Australia)
1970	John Newcombe (Australia)	Ken Rosewall (Australia)
1971	John Newcombe (Australia)	Stan Smith (USA)
1972	Stan Smith (USA)	Ilie Nastase (Romania)
1973	Jan Kodes (Czechoslovakia)	Alex Metreveli (USSR)
1974	Jimmy Connors (USA)	Ken Rosewall (Australia)
1975	Arthur Ashe (USA)	Jimmy Connors (USA)
1976	Björn Borg (Sweden)	Ilie Nastase (Romania)
1977	Björn Borg (Sweden)	Jimmy Connors (USA)
1978	Björn Borg (Sweden)	Jimmy Connors (USA)
1979	Björn Borg (Sweden)	Roscoe Tanner (USA)
1980	Björn Borg (Sweden)	John McEnroe (USA)
1981	John McEnroe (USA)	Björn Borg (Sweden)
1982	Jimmy Connors (USA)	John McEnroe (USA)
1983	John McEnroe (USA)	Chris Lewis (New Zealand)
1984	John McEnroe (USA)	Jimmy Connors (USA)
1985	Boris Becker (West Germany)	Kevin Curren (USA)
1986	Boris Becker (West Germany)	Ivan Lendl (Czechoslovakia)
1987	Pat Cash (Australia)	Ivan Lendl (Czechoslovakia)
1988	Stefan Edberg (Sweden)	Boris Becker (West Germany)
1989	Boris Becker (West Germany)	Stefan Edberg (Sweden)
1990	Stefan Edberg (Sweden)	Boris Becker (West Germany)
1991	Michael Stich (Germany)	Boris Becker (Germany)
1992	Andre Agassi (USA)	Goran Ivanisevic (Croatia)
1993	Pete Sampras (USA)	Jim Courier (USA)
1994	Pete Sampras (USA)	Goran Ivanisevic (Croatia)
1995	Pete Sampras (USA)	Boris Becker (Germany)
1996	Richard Krajicek (The Netherlands)	MaliVai Washington (USA)
1997	Pete Sampras (USA)	Cédric Pioline (France)
1998	Pete Sampras (USA)	Goran Ivanisevic (Croatia)
1999	Pete Sampras (USA)	Andre Agassi (USA)
2000	Pete Sampras (USA)	Pat Rafter (Australia)
2001	Goran Ivanisevic (Croatia)	Pat Rafter (Australia)

	Winner	Defeated finalist
2002	Lleyton Hewitt (Australia)	David Nalbandian (Argentina)
2003	Roger Federer (Switzerland)	Mark Phillippoussis (Australia)
2004	Roger Federer (Switzerland)	Andy Roddick (USA)

Three sides to every (fairy) story

Big-serving Croat Goran Ivanisevic became the first wild-card entry to win Wimbledon, when he beat Pat Rafter in a marathon five-setter in 2001. His career had suffered as he struggled to control multiple personalities, which he referred to as 'good Goran', 'bad Goran', and 'emergency Goran' – he was once forced to withdraw from a match in Brighton after smashing all his available rackets. However, he seemed to have them under control in 2001, with 'emergency Goran' finally coming through when he needed him.

Women's Singles

	Winner	Defeated finalist
1884	Maud Watson (Great Britain)	Louise Watson (Great Britain)
1885	Maud Watson (Great Britain)	Blanche Bingley (Great Britain)
1886	Blanche Bingley (Great Britain)	Maud Watson (Great Britain)
1887	Lottie Dod (Great Britain)	Blanche Bingley (Great Britain)
1888	Lottie Dod (Great Britain)	Blanche Bingley Hillyard (Great Britain)
1889	Blanche Bingley Hillyard (Great Britain)	Lena Rice (Great Britain)
1890	Lena Rice (Great Britain)	M Jacks (Great Britain)
1891	Lottie Dod (Great Britain)	Blanche Bingley Hillyard (Great Britain)
1892	Lottie Dod (Great Britain)	Blanche Bingley Hillyard (Great Britain)
1893	Lottie Dod (Great Britain)	Blanche Bingley Hillyard (Great Britain)
1894	Blanche Bingley Hillyard (Great Britain)	Edith Austin (Great Britain)
1895	Charlotte Cooper (Great Britain)	Helen Jackson (Great Britain)
1896	Charlotte Cooper (Great Britain)	Alice Simpson Pickering (Great Britain)
1897	Blanche Bingley Hillyard (Great Britain)	Charlotte Cooper (Great Britain)
1898	Charlotte Cooper (Great Britain)	Louise Martin (Great Britain)
1899	Blanche Bingley Hillyard (Great Britain)	Charlotte Cooper (Great Britain)
1900	Blanche Bingley Hillyard (Great Britain)	Charlotte Cooper (Great Britain)
1901	Charlotte Cooper Sterry (Great Britain)	Blanche Bingley Hillyard (Great Britain)
1902	Muriel Robb (Great Britain)	Charlotte Cooper Sterry (Great Britain)
1903	Dorothea Douglass (Great Britain)	Ethel Thomson (Great Britain)
1904	Dorothea Douglass (Great Britain)	Charlotte Cooper Sterry (Great Britain)
1905	May Sutton (USA)	Dorothea Douglass (Great Britain)
1906	Dorothea Douglass (Great Britain)	May Sutton (USA)
1907	May Sutton (USA)	Dorothea Douglass Chambers (Great Britain)
1908	Charlotte Cooper Sterry (Great Britain)	Agatha Morton (Great Britain)
1909	Dora Boothby (Great Britain)	Agatha Morton (Great Britain)
1910	Dorothea Douglass Chambers (Great Britain)	Dora Boothby (Great Britain)
1911	Dorothea Douglass Chambers (Great Britain)	Dora Boothby (Great Britain)
1912	Ethel Larcombe (Great Britain)	Charlotte Cooper Sterry (Great Britain)
1913	Dorothea Douglass Chambers (Great Britain)	Winifred McNair (Great Britain)
1914	Dorothea Douglass Chambers (Great Britain)	Ethel Larcombe (Great Britain)
1915–18	*Not held*	

	Winner	Defeated finalist
1919	Suzanne Lenglen (France)	Dorothea Douglass Chambers (Great Britain)
1920	Suzanne Lenglen (France)	Dorothea Douglass Chambers (Great Britain)
1921	Suzanne Lenglen (France)	Elizabeth Ryan (USA)
1922	Suzanne Lenglen (France)	Frances Mallory (USA)
1923	Suzanne Lenglen (France)	Kitty McKane (Great Britain)
1924	Kitty McKane (Great Britain)	Helen Wills (USA)
1925	Suzanne Lenglen (France)	Joan Fry (Great Britain)
1926	Kitty McKane Godfree (Great Britain)	Lili de Alvarez (Spain)
1927	Helen Wills (USA)	Lili de Alvarez (Spain)
1928	Helen Wills (USA)	Lili de Alvarez (Spain)
1929	Helen Wills (USA)	Helen Jacobs (USA)
1930	Helen Wills Moody (USA)	Elizabeth Ryan (USA)
1931	Cilly Aussem (Germany)	Hilde Krahwinkel (Germany)
1932	Helen Wills Moody (USA)	Helen Jacobs (USA)
1933	Helen Wills Moody (USA)	Dorothy Round (Great Britain)
1934	Dorothy Round (Great Britain)	Helen Jacobs (USA)
1935	Helen Wills Moody (USA)	Helen Jacobs (USA)
1936	Helen Jacobs (USA)	Hilde Krahwinkel Sperling (Germany)
1937	Dorothy Round (Great Britain)	Jadwiga Jedrzejowska (Poland)
1938	Helen Wills Moody (USA)	Helen Jacobs (USA)
1939	Alice Marble (USA)	Kim Stammers (Great Britain)
1940–5	*Not held*	
1946	Pauline Betz (USA)	Louise Brough (USA)
1947	Margaret Osborne (USA)	Doris Hart (USA)
1948	Louise Brough (USA)	Doris Hart (USA)
1949	Louise Brough (USA)	Margaret Osborne du Pont (USA)
1950	Louise Brough (USA)	Margaret Osborne du Pont (USA)
1951	Doris Hart (USA)	Shirley Fry (USA)
1952	Maureen Connolly (USA)	Louise Brough (USA)
1953	Maureen Connolly (USA)	Doris Hart (USA)
1954	Maureen Connolly (USA)	Louise Brough (USA)
1955	Louise Brough (USA)	Beverly Fleitz (USA)
1956	Shirley Fry (USA)	Angela Buxton (Great Britain)
1957	Althea Gibson (USA)	Darlene Hard (USA)
1958	Althea Gibson (USA)	Angela Mortimer (Great Britain)
1959	Maria Bueno (Brazil)	Darlene Hard (USA)
1960	Maria Bueno (Brazil)	Sandra Reynolds (South Africa)
1961	Angela Mortimer (Great Britain)	Christine Truman (Great Britain)
1962	Karen Susman (USA)	Vera Sukova (Czechoslovakia)
1963	Margaret Smith (Australia)	Billie Jean Moffitt (USA)
1964	Maria Bueno (Brazil)	Margaret Smith (Australia)
1965	Margaret Smith (Australia)	Maria Bueno (Brazil)
1966	Billie Jean King (USA)	Maria Bueno (Brazil)
1967	Billie Jean King (USA)	Ann Jones (Great Britain)
1968	Billie Jean King (USA)	Judy Dalton Tegart (Australia)
1969	Ann Jones (Great Britain)	Billie Jean King (USA)
1970	Margaret Smith Court (Australia)	Billie Jean King (USA)
1971	Evonne Goolagong (Australia)	Margaret Smith Court (Australia)
1972	Billie Jean King (USA)	Evonne Goolagong (Australia)

	Winner	Defeated finalist
1973	Billie Jean King (USA)	Chris Evert (USA)
1974	Chris Evert (USA)	Olga Morozova (USSR)
1975	Billie Jean King (USA)	Evonne Cawley (Australia)
1976	Chris Evert (USA)	Evonne Cawley (Australia)
1977	Virginia Wade (Great Britain)	Betty Stove (The Netherlands)
1978	Martina Navratilova (USA)	Chris Evert (USA)
1979	Martina Navratilova (USA)	Chris Evert Lloyd (USA)
1980	Evonne Cawley (Australia)	Chris Evert Lloyd (USA)
1981	Chris Evert Lloyd (USA)	Hana Mandlikova (Czechoslovakia)
1982	Martina Navratilova (USA)	Chris Evert Lloyd (USA)
1983	Martina Navratilova (USA)	Andrea Jaeger (USA)
1984	Martina Navratilova (USA)	Chris Evert Lloyd (USA)
1985	Martina Navratilova (USA)	Chris Evert Lloyd (USA)
1986	Martina Navratilova (USA)	Hana Mandlikova (Czechoslovakia)
1987	Martina Navratilova (USA)	Steffi Graf (West Germany)
1988	Steffi Graf (West Germany)	Martina Navratilova (USA)
1989	Steffi Graf (West Germany)	Martina Navratilova (USA)
1990	Martina Navratilova (USA)	Zina Garrison (USA)
1991	Steffi Graf (Germany)	Gabriela Sabatini (Argentina)
1992	Steffi Graf (Germany)	Monica Seles (USA)
1993	Steffi Graf (Germany)	Jana Novotna (Czech Republic)
1994	Conchita Martinez (Spain)	Martina Navratilova (USA)
1995	Steffi Graf (Germany)	Arantxa Sanchez-Vicario (Spain)
1996	Steffi Graf (Germany)	Arantxa Sanchez-Vicario (Spain)
1997	Martina Hingis (Switzerland)	Jana Novotna (Czech Republic)
1998	Jana Novotna (Czech Republic)	Nathalie Tauziat (France)
1999	Lindsay Davenport (USA)	Steffi Graf (Germany)
2000	Venus Williams (USA)	Lindsay Davenport (USA)
2001	Venus Williams (USA)	Justine Henin (Belgium)
2002	Serena Williams (USA)	Venus Williams (USA)
2003	Serena Williams (USA)	Venus Williams (USA)
2004	Maria Sharapova (Russia)	Serena Williams (USA)

Martina Mk II

Coached by her mother, who named her after Martina Navratilova, Swiss teenager Martina Hingis burst onto the scene in the mid-nineties. Reaching world number one at the tender age of 16 years, 6 months, Martina appeared aptly named as she went on to win the Australian Open, Wimbledon and the US Open in 1997. She retained the Australian title for the next two years but, while her namesake continued playing well into her forties, Hingis retired from tennis in 2002, aged just 22.

Men's Doubles

	Winners	Defeated finalists
1980	Peter McNamara & Paul McNamee (Australia)	Bob Lutz & Stan Smith (USA)
1981	Peter Fleming & John McEnroe (USA)	Bob Lutz & Stan Smith (USA)
1982	Peter McNamara & Paul McNamee (Australia)	Peter Fleming & John McEnroe (USA)
1983	Peter Fleming & John McEnroe (USA)	Tom Gullikson & Tim Gullikson (USA)

	Winners	Defeated finalists
1984	Peter Fleming & John McEnroe (USA)	Pat Cash & Paul McNamee (Australia)
1985	Heinz Gunthardt (Switzerland) & Balazs Taroczy (Hungary)	Pat Cash & John Fitzgerald (Australia)
1986	Joakim Nystrom & Mats Wilander (Sweden)	Gary Donnelly & Peter Fleming (USA)
1987	Ken Flach & Robert Seguso (USA)	Sergio Casal & Emilio Sanchez (Spain)
1988	Ken Flach & Robert Seguso (USA)	John Fitzgerald (Australia) & Anders Jarryd (Sweden)
1989	John Fitzgerald (Australia) & Anders Jarryd (Sweden)	Rick Leach & Jim Pugh (USA)
1990	Rick Leach & Jim Pugh (USA)	Pieter Aldrich & Danie Visser (South Africa)
1991	John Fitzgerald (Australia) & Anders Jarryd (Sweden)	Javier Frana (Argentina) & Leonardo Lavalle (Mexico)
1992	John McEnroe (USA) & Michael Stich (Germany)	Jim Grabb & Richey Reneberg (USA)
1993	Todd Woodbridge & Mark Woodforde (Australia)	Grant Connell (Canada) & Patrick Galbraith (USA)
1994	Todd Woodbridge & Mark Woodforde (Australia)	Grant Connell (Canada) & Patrick Galbraith (USA)
1995	Todd Woodbridge & Mark Woodforde (Australia)	Rick Leach & Scott Melville (USA)
1996	Todd Woodbridge & Mark Woodforde (Australia)	Byron Black (Zimbabwe) & Grant Connell (Canada)
1997	Todd Woodbridge & Mark Woodforde (Australia)	Jacco Eltingh & Paul Haarhuis (The Netherlands)
1998	Jacco Eltingh & Paul Haarhuis (The Netherlands)	Todd Woodbridge & Mark Woodforde (Australia)
1999	Mahesh Bhupathi & Leander Paes (India)	Paul Haarhuis (The Netherlands) & Jared Palmer (USA)
2000	Todd Woodbridge & Mark Woodforde (Australia)	Paul Haarhuis (The Netherlands) & Sandon Stolle (Australia)
2001	Donald Johnson & Jared Palmer (USA)	Jiri Novak & David Rikl (Czech Republic)
2002	Jonas Bjorkman (Sweden) & Todd Woodbridge (Australia)	Mark Knowles (Bahamas) & Daniel Nestor (Canada)
2003	Jonas Bjorkman (Sweden) & Todd Woodbridge (Australia)	Mahesh Bhupathi (India) & Max Mirnyi (Belarus)
2004	Jonas Bjorkman (Sweden) & Todd Woodbridge (Australia)	Julian Knowle (Austria) & Nenad Zimonjic (Serbia)

Women's Doubles

	Winners	Defeated finalists
1980	Kathy Jordan & Anne Smith (USA)	Rosie Casals (USA) & Wendy Turnbull (Australia)
1981	Martina Navratilova & Pam Shriver (USA)	Kathy Jordan & Anne Smith (USA)
1982	Martina Navratilova & Pam Shriver (USA)	Kathy Jordan & Anne Smith (USA)
1983	Martina Navratilova & Pam Shriver (USA)	Rosie Casals (USA) & Wendy Turnbull (Australia)
1984	Martina Navratilova & Pam Shriver (USA)	Kathy Jordan & Anne Smith (USA)
1985	Kathy Jordan (USA) & Elizabeth Smylie (Australia)	Martina Navratilova & Pam Shriver (USA)
1986	Martina Navratilova & Pam Shriver (USA)	Hana Mandlikova (Czechoslovakia) & Wendy Turnbull (Australia)

	Winners	Defeated finalists
1987	Claudia Kohde-Kilsh (West Germany) & Helena Sukova (Czechoslovakia)	Betsy Nagelsen & Elizabeth Smylie (Australia)
1988	Steffi Graf (West Germany) & Gabriela Sabatini (Argentina)	Larisa Savchenko & Natasha Zvereva (USSR)
1989	Jana Novotna & Helena Sukova (Czechoslovakia)	Larisa Savchenko & Natasha Zvereva (USSR)
1990	Jana Novotna & Helena Sukova (Czechoslovakia)	Kathy Jordan (USA) & Elizabeth Smylie (Australia)
1991	Larisa Savchenko & Natasha Zvereva (USSR)	Gigi Fernandez (Paraguay) & Jana Novotna (Czechoslovakia)
1992	Gigi Fernandez (USA) & Natasha Zvereva (CIS)	Larisa Neiland* (Latvia) & Jana Novotna (Czechoslovakia)
1993	Gigi Fernandez (USA) & Natasha Zvereva (Belarus)	Larisa Neiland* (Latvia) & Jana Novotna (Czech Republic)
1994	Gigi Fernandez (USA) & Natasha Zvereva (Belarus)	Jana Novotna (Czech Republic) & Arantxa Sanchez-Vicario (Spain)
1995	Jana Novotna (Czech Republic) & Arantxa Sanchez-Vicario (Spain)	Gigi Fernandez (USA) & Natasha Zvereva (Belarus)
1996	Martina Hingis (Switzerland) & Helena Sukova (Czech Republic)	Meredith McGrath (USA) & Larisa Neiland* (Latvia)
1997	Gigi Fernandez (USA) & Natasha Zvereva (Belarus)	Nicole Arendt (USA) & Manon Bollegraf (Netherlands)
1998	Martina Hingis (Switzerland) & Jana Novotna (Czech Republic)	Lindsay Davenport (USA) & Natasha Zvereva (Belarus)
1999	Lindsay Davenport & Corina Morariu (USA)	Mariaan de Swardt (South Africa) & Elena Tararkova (Ukraine)
2000	Venus Williams & Serena Williams (USA)	Julie Decugis (France) & Ai Sugiyama (Japan)
2001	Lisa Raymond (USA) & Rennae Stubbs (Australia)	Kim Clijsters (Belgium) & Ai Sugiyama (Japan)
2002	Venus Williams & Serena Williams (USA)	Virginia Ruano Pascual (Spain) & Paola Suarez (Argentina)
2003	Kim Clijsters (Belgium) & Ai Sugiyama (Japan)	Virginia Ruano Pascual (Spain) & Paola Suarez (Argentina)
2004	Cara Black (Zimbabwe) & Rennae Stubbs (Australia)	Liezel Huber (South Africa) & Ai Sugiyama (Japan)

* née Savchenko

Mixed Doubles

	Winners	Defeated finalists
1980	John Austin & Tracy Austin (USA)	Mark Edmondson & Dianne Fromholtz (Australia)
1981	Frew McMillan (South Africa) & Betty Stove (The Netherlands)	John Austin & Tracy Austin (USA)
1982	Kevin Curren (South Africa) & Anne Smith (USA)	John Lloyd (Great Britain) & Wendy Turnbull (Australia)
1983	John Lloyd (Great Britain) & Wendy Turnbull (Australia)	Steve Denton & Billie Jean King (USA)
1984	John Lloyd (Great Britain) & Wendy Turnbull (Australia)	Steve Denton & Kathy Jordan (USA)
1985	Paul McNamee (Australia) & Martina Navratilova (USA)	John Fitzgerald & Elizabeth Smylie (Australia)

	Winners	Defeated finalists
1986	Ken Flach & Kathy Jordan (USA)	Heinz Gunthardt (Switzerland) & Martina Navratilova (USA)
1987	Jeremy Bates & Jo Durie (Great Britain)	Darren Cahill & Nicole Provis (Australia)
1988	Sherwood Stewart & Zina Garrison (USA)	Kelly Jones & Gretchen Magers (USA)
1989	Jim Pugh (USA) & Jana Novotna (Czechoslovakia)	Mark Kratzmann & Jenny Byrne (Australia)
1990	Rick Leach & Zina Garrison (USA)	John Fitzgerald & Elizabeth Smylie (Australia)
1991	John Fitzgerald & Elizabeth Smylie (Australia)	Jim Pugh (USA) & Natalia Zvereva (USSR)
1992	Cyril Suk (Czechoslovakia) & Larisa Neiland* (Latvia)	Jacco Eltingh & Miriam Oremans (The Netherlands)
1993	Mark Woodforde (Australia) & Martina Navratilova (USA)	Tom Nijssen & Manon Bollegraf (The Netherlands)
1994	Todd Woodbridge (Australia) & Helena Sukova (Czech Republic)	T J Middleton & Lori McNeil (USA)
1995	Jonathan Stark & Martina Navratilova (USA)	Cyril Suk (Czech Republic) & Gigi Fernandez (USA)
1996	Cyril Suk & Helena Sukova (Czech Republic)	Mark Woodforde (Australia) & Larisa Neiland* (Latvia)
1997	Cyril Suk & Helena Sukova (Czech Republic)	Andrei Olhovskiy (Russia) & Larisa Neiland* (Latvia)
1998	Max Mirnyi (Belarus) & Serena Williams (USA)	Mahesh Bhupathi (India) & Mirjana Lucic (Croatia)
1999	Leander Paes (India) & Lisa Raymond (USA)	Jonas Bjorkman (Sweden) & Anna Kournikova (Russia)
2000	Donald Johnson & Kimberley Po (USA)	Lleyton Hewitt (Australia) & Kim Clijsters (Belgium)
2001	Leos Friedl (Czech Republic) & Daniela Hantuchova (Slovakia)	Mike Bryan (USA) & Liezel Huber (South Africa)
2002	Mahesh Bhupathi (India) & Elena Likhovteva (Russia)	Kevin Ullyett (Zimbabwe) & Daniela Hantuchova (Slovakia)
2003	Leander Paes (India) & Martina Navratilova (USA)	Andy Ram (Israel) & Anastasia Rodionova (Russia)
2004	Wayne Black & Cara Black (Zimbabwe)	Todd Woodbridge & Alicia Molik (Australia)

* née Savchenko

Fastest serves

In their quarter-final at Queen's Club, London, on 11 June 2004, American Andy Roddick sent down a monster 153mph serve (244.8 kph) to his Thai opponent Paradorn Srichaphan. The fastest women's serve was recorded by Venus Williams on 16 October 1998 against Mary Pierce of France. Her serve, at the European Indoor Championships in Zurich, Switzerland, was clocked at 127.4mph (205kph).

French Open

The second Grand Slam event of the year, the French Open is held on the clay of Roland Garros, Paris, in late May. Starting in 1891 as a domestic event, the championships were opened up to an international field in 1925.

Men's Singles

	Winner	Defeated finalist
1980	Björn Borg (Sweden)	Vitas Gerulaitis (USA)
1981	Björn Borg (Sweden)	Ivan Lendl (Czechoslovakia)
1982	Mats Wilander (Sweden)	Guillermo Vilas (Argentina)
1983	Yannick Noah (France)	Mats Wilander (Sweden)
1984	Ivan Lendl (Czechoslovakia)	John McEnroe (USA)
1985	Mats Wilander (Sweden)	Ivan Lendl (Czechoslovakia)
1986	Ivan Lendl (Czechoslovakia)	Mikael Pernfors (Sweden)
1987	Ivan Lendl (Czechoslovakia)	Mats Wilander (Sweden)
1988	Mats Wilander (Sweden)	Henri Leconte (France)
1989	Michael Chang (USA)	Stefan Edberg (Sweden)
1990	Andres Gomez (Ecuador)	Andre Agassi (USA)
1991	Jim Courier (USA)	Andre Agassi (USA)
1992	Jim Courier (USA)	Petr Korda (Czechoslovakia)
1993	Sergi Bruguera (Spain)	Jim Courier (USA)
1994	Sergi Bruguera (Spain)	Alberto Berasategui (Spain)
1995	Thomas Muster (Austria)	Michael Chang (USA)
1996	Yevgeny Kafelnikov (Russia)	Michael Stich (Germany)
1997	Gustavo Kuerten (Brazil)	Sergi Bruguera (Spain)
1998	Carlos Moyá (Spain)	Alex Corretja (Spain)
1999	Andre Agassi (USA)	Andrei Medvedev (Ukraine)
2000	Gustavo Kuerten (Brazil)	Magnus Norman (Sweden)
2001	Gustavo Kuerten (Brazil)	Alex Corretja (Spain)
2002	Albert Costa (Spain)	Juan Carlos Ferrero (Spain)
2003	Juan Carlos Ferrero (Spain)	Martin Verkerk (The Netherlands)
2004	Gaston Gaudio (Argentina)	Guillermo Coria (Argentina)

Women's Singles

	Winner	Defeated finalist
1980	Chris Evert Lloyd (USA)	Virginia Ruzici (Romania)
1981	Hana Mandlikova (Czechoslovakia)	Sylvia Hanika (West Germany)
1982	Martina Navratilova (USA)	Andrea Jaeger (USA)
1983	Chris Evert Lloyd (USA)	Mima Jausovec (Yugoslavia)
1984	Martina Navratilova (USA)	Chris Evert Lloyd (USA)
1985	Chris Evert Lloyd (USA)	Martina Navratilova (USA)
1986	Chris Evert Lloyd (USA)	Martina Navratilova (USA)
1987	Steffi Graf (West Germany)	Martina Navratilova (USA)
1988	Steffi Graf (West Germany)	Natasha Zvereva (USSR)
1989	Arantxa Sanchez-Vicario (Spain)	Steffi Graf (West Germany)
1990	Monica Seles (Yugoslavia)	Steffi Graf (West Germany)
1991	Monica Seles (Yugoslavia)	Arantxa Sanchez-Vicario (Spain)
1992	Monica Seles (Yugoslavia)	Steffi Graf (Germany)
1993	Steffi Graf (Germany)	Mary-Joe Fernandez (USA)
1994	Arantxa Sanchez-Vicario (Spain)	Mary Pierce (France)
1995	Steffi Graf (Germany)	Arantxa Sanchez-Vicario (Spain)
1996	Steffi Graf (Germany)	Aranxta Sanchez-Vicario (Spain)
1997	Iva Majoli (Croatia)	Martina Hingis (Switzerland)

	Winner	Defeated finalist
1998	Arantxa Sanchez-Vicario (Spain)	Monica Seles (USA)
1999	Steffi Graf (Germany)	Martina Hingis (Switzerland)
2000	Mary Pierce (France)	Conchita Martinez (Spain)
2001	Jennifer Capriati (USA)	Kim Clijsters (Belgium)
2002	Serena Williams (USA)	Venus Williams (USA)
2003	Justine Henin-Hardenne (Belgium)	Kim Clijsters (Belgium)
2004	Anastasia Myskina (Russia)	Elena Dementieva (Russia)

US Open

The final Grand Slam event of the year, the US Open takes place in late August. Originating in 1881 as a men's singles grass court championship, it was held in Newport until 1918. The equivalent women's singles began in Philadelphia in 1887 and from 1919 the two were staged simultaneously at Forest Hill, New York. In 1978 the US Open moved to Flushing Meadows in Queens, New York, and is now held on Decoturf hard courts.

Men's Singles

	Winner	Defeated finalist
1980	John McEnroe (USA)	Björn Borg (Sweden)
1981	John McEnroe (USA)	Björn Borg (Sweden)
1982	Jimmy Connors (USA)	Ivan Lendl (Czechoslovakia)
1983	Jimmy Connors (USA)	Ivan Lendl (Czechoslovakia)
1984	John McEnroe (USA)	Ivan Lendl (Czechoslovakia)
1985	Ivan Lendl (Czechoslovakia)	John McEnroe (USA)
1986	Ivan Lendl (Czechoslovakia)	Miloslav Mecir (Czechoslovakia)
1987	Ivan Lendl (Czechoslovakia)	Mats Wilander (Sweden)
1988	Mats Wilander (Sweden)	Ivan Lendl (Czechoslovakia)
1989	Boris Becker (West Germany)	Ivan Lendl (Czechoslovakia)
1990	Pete Sampras (USA)	Andre Agassi (USA)
1991	Stefan Edberg (Sweden)	Jim Courier (USA)
1992	Stefan Edberg (Sweden)	Pete Sampras (USA)
1993	Pete Sampras (USA)	Cédric Pioline (France)
1994	Andre Agassi (USA)	Michael Stich (Germany)
1995	Pete Sampras (USA)	Andre Agassi (USA)
1996	Pete Sampras (USA)	Michael Chang (USA)
1997	Pat Rafter (Australia)	Greg Rusedski (Great Britain)
1998	Pat Rafter (Australia)	Mark Philippoussis (Australia)
1999	Andre Agassi (USA)	Todd Martin (USA)
2000	Marat Safin (Russia)	Pete Sampras (USA)
2001	Lleyton Hewitt (Australia)	Pete Sampras (USA)
2002	Pete Sampras (USA)	Andre Agassi (USA)
2003	Andy Roddick (USA)	Juan Carlos Ferrero (Spain)
2004	Roger Federer (Switzerland)	Lleyton Hewitt (Australia)

Women's Singles

	Winner	Defeated finalist
1980	Chris Evert Lloyd (USA)	Hana Mandlikova (Czechoslovakia)
1981	Tracy Austin (USA)	Martina Navratilova (USA)
1982	Chris Evert Lloyd (USA)	Hana Mandlikova (Czechoslovakia)
1983	Martina Navratilova (USA)	Chris Evert Lloyd (USA)
1984	Martina Navratilova (USA)	Chris Evert Lloyd (USA)
1985	Hana Mandlikova (Czechoslovakia)	Martina Navratilova (USA)
1986	Martina Navratilova (USA)	Helena Sukova (Czechoslovakia)
1987	Martina Navratilova (USA)	Steffi Graf (West Germany)
1988	Steffi Graf (West Germany)	Gabriela Sabatini (Argentina)
1989	Steffi Graf (West Germany)	Martina Navratilova (USA)
1990	Gabriela Sabatini (Argentina)	Steffi Graf (West Germany)
1991	Monica Seles (Yugoslavia)	Martina Navratilova (USA)
1992	Monica Seles (Yugoslavia)	Arantxa Sanchez-Vicario (Spain)
1993	Steffi Graf (Germany)	Helena Sukova (Czech Republic)
1994	Arantxa Sanchez-Vicario (Spain)	Steffi Graf (Germany)
1995	Steffi Graf (Germany)	Monica Seles (USA)
1996	Steffi Graf (Germany)	Monica Seles (USA)
1997	Martina Hingis (Switzerland)	Venus Williams (USA)
1998	Lindsay Davenport (USA)	Martina Hingis (Switzerland)
1999	Serena Williams (USA)	Martina Hingis (Switzerland)
2000	Venus Williams (USA)	Lindsay Davenport (USA)
2001	Venus Williams (USA)	Serena Williams (USA)
2002	Serena Williams (USA)	Venus Williams (USA)
2003	Justine Henin-Hardenne (Belgium)	Kim Clijsters (Belgium)
2004	Svetlana Kuznetsova (Russia)	Elena Dementieva (Russia)

19 years later...

Ken Rosewall of Australia is both the oldest and youngest Australian Open champion, winning in 1953 at the age of 18 and again in 1972, aged 37.

Australian Open

The first Grand Slam event of the year, the Australian Open is played in January on a hard surface known as Rebound Ace. Starting in 1905 as the Australasian Championships, it became the Australian Championships in 1927 and the Australian Open in 1969. The championships moved to their current Melbourne home in 1972.

Men's Singles

	Winner	Defeated finalist
1980	Brian Teacher (USA)	Kim Warwick (Australia)
1981	Johan Kriek (South Africa)	Steve Denton (USA)
1982	Johan Kriek (South Africa)	Steve Denton (USA)
1983	Mats Wilander (Sweden)	Ivan Lendl (Czechoslovakia)
1984	Mats Wilander (Sweden)	Kevin Curren (South Africa)
1985	Stefan Edberg (Sweden)	Mats Wilander (Sweden)

	Winner	Defeated finalist
1986	*Not held*	
1987	Stefan Edberg (Sweden)	Pat Cash (Australia)
1988	Mats Wilander (Sweden)	Pat Cash (Australia)
1989	Ivan Lendl (Czechoslovakia)	Miloslav Mecir (Czechoslovakia)
1990	Ivan Lendl (Czechoslovakia)	Stefan Edberg (Sweden)
1991	Boris Becker (Germany)	Ivan Lendl (Czechoslovakia)
1992	Jim Courier (USA)	Stefan Edberg (Sweden)
1993	Jim Courier (USA)	Stefan Edberg (Sweden)
1994	Pete Sampras (USA)	Todd Martin (USA)
1995	Andre Agassi (USA)	Pete Sampras (USA)
1996	Boris Becker (Germany)	Michael Chang (USA)
1997	Pete Sampras (USA)	Carlos Moyá (Spain)
1998	Petr Korda (Czech Republic)	Marcelo Rios (Chile)
1999	Yevgeny Kafelnikov (Russia)	Thomas Enqvist (Sweden)
2000	Andre Agassi (USA)	Yevgeny Kafelnikov (Russia)
2001	Andre Agassi (USA)	Arnaud Clément (France)
2002	Thomas Johansson (Sweden)	Marat Safin (Russia)
2003	Andre Agassi (USA)	Rainer Schüttler (Germany)
2004	Roger Federer (Switzerland)	Marat Safin (Russia)

Women's Singles

	Winner	Defeated finalist
1980	Hana Mandlikova (Czechoslovakia)	Wendy Turnbull (Australia)
1981	Martina Navratilova (USA)	Chris Evert Lloyd (USA)
1982	Chris Evert Lloyd (USA)	Martina Navratilova (USA)
1983	Martina Navratilova (USA)	Kathy Jordan (USA)
1984	Chris Evert Lloyd (USA)	Helena Sukova (Czechoslovakia)
1985	Martina Navratilova (USA)	Chris Evert Lloyd (USA)
1986	*Not held*	
1987	Hana Mandlikova (Czechoslovakia)	Martina Navratilova (USA)
1988	Steffi Graf (West Germany)	Chris Evert Lloyd (USA)
1989	Steffi Graf (West Germany)	Helena Sukova (Czechoslovakia)
1990	Steffi Graf (West Germany)	Mary Jo Fernandez (USA)
1991	Monica Seles (Yugoslavia)	Jana Novotna (Czechoslovakia)
1992	Monica Seles (Yugoslavia)	Mary Jo Fernandez (USA)
1993	Monica Seles (Yugoslavia)	Steffi Graf (Germany)
1994	Steffi Graf (Germany)	Arantxa Sanchez-Vicario (Spain)
1995	Mary Pierce (France)	Arantxa Sanchez-Vicario (Spain)
1996	Monica Seles (USA)	Anke Huber (Germany)
1997	Martina Hingis (Switzerland)	Mary Pierce (France)
1998	Martina Hingis (Switzerland)	Conchita Martinez (Spain)
1999	Martina Hingis (Switzerland)	Amélie Mauresmo (France)
2000	Lindsay Davenport (USA)	Martina Hingis (Switzerland)
2001	Jennifer Capriati (USA)	Martina Hingis (Switzerland)
2002	Jennifer Capriati (USA)	Martina Hingis (Switzerland)
2003	Serena Williams (USA)	Venus Williams (USA)
2004	Justine Henin-Hardenne (Belgium)	Kim Clijsters (Belgium)

Royal tennis

King George VI competed (briefly) in the men's doubles at Wimbledon in 1926. Playing with Wing Commander Louis Greig, he lost in straight sets to 58-year-old Arthur Gore and 52-year-old Roper Barrett.

Masters Cup

The end of season showcase for men's tennis, the Masters Cup features the top eight players in the world that year, split into two groups of four, playing each other on a round robin basis. The top two players in each group qualify for the semi-finals. Previous incarnations include the ATP Tour World Championships (1990–9) and the Masters (1970–89).

	Winner	Defeated finalist	Venue
2000	Gustavo Kuerten (Brazil)	Andre Agassi (USA)	Lisbon, Portugal
2001	Lleyton Hewitt (Australia)	Sebastian Grosjean (France)	Sydney, Australia
2002	Lleyton Hewitt (Australia)	Juan Carlos Ferrero (Spain)	Shanghai, China
2003	Roger Federer (Switzerland)	Andre Agassi (USA)	Houston, USA
2004	Roger Federer (Switzerland)	Lleyton Hewitt (Australia)	Houston, USA

Davis Cup

The Davis Cup, the men's international team competition, began in 1900 as a challenge match between Great Britain and the USA. The two founder nations were joined by Austria, Belgium and France in 1904 and Australasia a year later. By 1970, there were 50 nations competing, and in 2001, 142. Ties are played over three days of competition and decided on a best-of-five basis – two singles matches on the first day, doubles on the second day, and the return singles on the third day. The 16 highest-ranked nations compete on a knockout basis in the World Group, with the other nations separated into three geographic zones, with promotion and relegation between ranked groups within each zone. The leading nations from the zones play off against the losing nations from the first round of the World Group for the right to compete in the World Group next year. USA leads the way with 31 wins, closely followed by Australia (28). Sweden is the most successful nation in recent years, with seven victories since 1975.

	Winner	Defeated finalist	Score	Venue
1980	Czechoslovakia	Italy	4–1	Prague, Czechoslovakia
1981	USA	Argentina	3–1	Cincinnati, USA
1982	USA	France	4–1	Grenoble, France
1983	Australia	Sweden	3–2	Melbourne, Australia
1984	Sweden	USA	4–1	Gothenburg, Sweden
1985	Sweden	West Germany	3–2	Munich, West Germany
1986	Australia	Sweden	3–2	Melbourne, Australia
1987	Sweden	India	5–0	Gothenburg, Sweden
1988	West Germany	Sweden	4–1	Gothenburg, Sweden
1989	West Germany	Sweden	3–2	Stuttgart, West Germany
1990	USA	Australia	3–2	St Petersburg, USA
1991	France	USA	3–1	Lyon, France

	Winner	Defeated finalist	Score	Venue
1992	USA	Switzerland	3–1	Fort Worth, USA
1993	Germany	Australia	4–1	Düsseldorf, Germany
1994	Sweden	Russia	4–1	Moscow, Russia
1995	USA	Russia	3–2	Moscow, Russia
1996	France	Sweden	3–2	Malmo, Sweden
1997	Sweden	USA	5–0	Gothenburg, Sweden
1998	Sweden	Italy	4–1	Milan, Italy
1999	Australia	France	3–2	Nice, France
2000	Spain	Australia	3–1	Barcelona, Spain
2001	France	Australia	3–2	Melbourne, Australia
2002	Russia	France	3–2	Paris, France
2003	Australia	Spain	3–1	Melbourne, Australia
2004	Spain	USA	3–1	Seville, Spain

Fed Cup

The Fed Cup, the international women's team tennis championships, began as the Federation Cup in 1963. Originally a week-long 16-team knockout tournament, played in a different venue each year, it shortened its name in 1995 and changed its format to reflect that of the Davis Cup. Matches are contested on a best-of-five basis (singles on the first day, return singles on the second day and doubles on the final day). World Group teams are drawn into first round ties, with the eight winners advancing to the quarter-finals, and the losers playing off against the eight regional qualifiers for the right to compete in next year's World Group. The USA has traditionally dominated, with 17 victories, although Spain won five times in the 1990s.

	Winner	Defeated finalist	Score	Venue
1980	USA	Australia	3–0	Berlin, West Germany
1981	USA	Great Britain	3–0	Tokyo, Japan
1982	USA	West Germany	3–0	Santa Clara, USA
1983	Czechoslovakia	West Germany	2–1	Zurich, Switzerland
1984	Czechoslovakia	Australia	2–1	Sao Paulo, Brazil
1985	Czechoslovakia	USA	2–1	Nagoya, Japan
1986	USA	Czechoslovakia	3–0	Prague, Czechoslovakia
1987	West Germany	USA	2–1	Vancouver, Canada
1988	Czechoslovakia	USSR	2–1	Melbourne, Australia
1989	USA	Spain	3–0	Tokyo, Japan
1990	USA	USSR	2–1	Atlanta, USA
1991	Spain	USA	2–1	Nottingham, England
1992	Germany	Spain	2–1	Frankfurt, Germany
1993	Spain	Australia	3–0	Frankfurt, Germany
1994	Spain	USA	3–0	Frankfurt, Germany
1995	Spain	USA	3–2	Valencia, Spain
1996	USA	Spain	5–0	Atlantic City, USA
1997	France	The Netherlands	4–1	Den Bosch, The Netherlands
1998	Spain	Switzerland	3–2	Geneva, Switzerland
1999	USA	Russia	4–1	Stanford, USA
2000	USA	Spain	5–0	Las Vegas, USA

	Winner	Defeated finalist	Score	Venue
2001	Belgium	Russia	2–1	Madrid, Spain
2002	Slovakia	Spain	3–1	Gran Canaria, Spain
2003	France	USA	4–1	Moscow, Russia
2004	Russia	France	3–2	Moscow, Russia

Olympic Games

Tennis was included in the Olympics until 1924, but then did not feature again until the Seoul Games in 1988.

Men's Singles

	Winner	Defeated finalist
1988	Miloslav Mecir (Czechoslovakia)	Tim Mayotte (USA)
1992	Marc Rosset (Switzerland)	Jordi Arrese (Spain)
1996	Andre Agassi (USA)	Sergi Brugera (Spain)
2000	Yevgeny Kafelnikov (Russia)	Tommy Haas (Germany)
2004	Nicolas Massu (Chile)	Mardy Fish (USA)

Women's Singles

	Winner	Defeated finalist
1988	Steffi Graf (West Germany)	Gabriela Sabatini (Argentina)
1992	Jennifer Capriati (USA	Steffi Graf (Germany)
1996	Lindsay Davenport (USA)	Arantxa Sanchez-Vicario (Spain)
2000	Venus Williams (USA)	Elena Dementieva (Russia)
2004	Justine Henin-Hardenne (Belgium)	Amélie Mauresmo (France)

Grand Slam winners

Only five players share the honour of having won all four Grand Slam tournaments in a calendar year: Don Budge (USA) in 1938, Rod Laver (Australia) in 1962 and 1969, Margaret Connolly (USA) in 1953, Margaret Court (Australia) in 1970, and Steffi Graf (West Germany) in 1988. Steffi Graf also won tennis gold at the 1988 Seoul Olympics, thus completing a unique 'golden slam'.

A-Z

ace — a point-winning **serve** that the opponent fails to hit

advantage — the first point after **deuce**

advantage court — the left side of the court, from which the **serve** is made and received at odd-numbered points

alley — the space between the **tramlines** at the side of the court

approach shot — a shot hit deep, enabling a player to move into the net

backcourt — the area of the court lying between the **service line** and **baseline**

backhand — a stroke with the back of the hand turned towards one's opponent

ballboy, ballgirl — a boy or girl who collects out of play balls and returns them to the server

Tennis

baseline	the boundary line at the back of the court
baseliner	a player who plays mainly from the **baseline** and rarely approaches the net
block volley	a **volley** played with a stationary racket
break	to win a game in which one's opponent was serving
break back	to win one's opponent's **service game** immediately after losing one's own service game
break point	an opportunity to win one's opponent's service game if the next point is won, eg *he has two break points for a 4-2 lead*
centre service line	the line parallel to the **tramlines**, dividing the right and left **service courts**
cross-court	if a player plays cross-court, he or she hits a shot diagonally across the court
deuce	the score of forty-forty, where a player must win two successive points to win the game (from the French *à deux de jeu* meaning 'at two to play')
deuce court	the right side of the court, from which the **serve** is made and received at even-numbered points
double fault	two **faults** in succession on service, giving a point to one's opponent
drive	a fast and straight shot
drop shot	a gently hit stroke that lands close behind the net after just clearing it
fault	when a **serve** fails to land the ball within the **service box**
foot fault	to step over the **baseline** when serving
forecourt	the area between the net and the **service line**
forehand	a stroke with the front of the hand turned towards one's opponent
ground stroke	any stroke played after the ball has bounced, usually used to refer to shots from the **baseline**
hold serve	to win one's own **service game**
let	1. a **serve** that hits the **net cord** before landing in and is therefore replayed 2. a point replayed at the umpire's discretion
line call	a decision on the status of a shot, articulated by an **umpire** or a **line judge**
line judge	an official who watches a line to adjudicate whether shots are in or out
lob	if a player lobs the ball, he or she sends it arcing upwards over the opponent, either to drop sharply and win a point (offensive) or to allow him/her to regain position (defensive)
love	no score (either from the French *l'oeuf* meaning 'egg', from the resemblance of zero to an egg, or from the phrases 'neither for love nor money' and 'a labour of love' where 'love' means 'nothing')
love game	a game in which a player fails to score a point
match point	an opportunity to win the match by winning the next point
midcourt	the area at the centre of the court
mixed doubles	a match with male and female players as partners on each side
net cord	a string or tape supporting the net
net judge	an official who used to sit with their hand on the **net cord** in order to feel whether a service should be called **let**; this position has now largely been superseded by an electronic aid
overhead	a shot played from above the head

overrule a call by the **umpire** to overturn the call of a **line judge**

pass if a player passes their opponent, he or she hits a passing shot beyond the opponent's reach

passing shot a shot played beyond the reach of one's opponent

rally the series of exchanged strokes that decide a point

return if a player returns the ball, he or she reaches the opponent's shot and plays it back

runback the area behind the **baseline** at either end of the court

second service the second of a player's two permitted **serves**, often struck with less pace and more accuracy to avoid a **double fault**

serve the opening shot of a point that puts the ball into play

serve and volley a style of play characterized by a charge to the net after serving in order to gain position to **volley** the opponent's **return**

service court the box on the other side of the net into which a server must place the ball when serving

service game when it is a player's service game, it is his or her turn to serve

service line the boundary of the **service court**, 6.4m/21ft from the net

set a series of games, the winner being the first to win at least six games and at least two games more than the opponent

set point an opportunity to win the set by winning the next point

shotmaker a player who has a full repertoire of skilful strokes

slice a shot played with a slicing motion to give the ball a lot of back-spin

smash a powerful strike of the ball downwards from above the head

sweet spot the optimum hitting spot on the face of the racket

tie-break the thirteenth game of a set, only played when a set reaches six games all, where a player must win seven points and at least two more than his or her opponent to win the set

tramlines lines marking the sides of the court and those lines inside the court running parallel to them

two-handed a stroke played with both hands holding the racket

umpire the official in charge of the match, who sits in a raised chair at the side of the court

volley a stroke played before the ball bounces

winner the stroke that ends a **rally**, winning a point, eg *she played a forehand winner down the line to take the set*

wood shot a shot inadvertently played off the frame of the racket (once wooden)

Some tennis slang

bagel, bagel job a set won in six straight games, from the resemblance of the loser's zero score to a bagel. Popularized by US player Eddie Dibbs in the 1970s

get a difficult shot successfully reached and returned, eg *what a great get*

good if a shot is good, it bounces within the court

hacker a poor player

kill if a player kills the ball, he or she smashes it downwards so hard that its upward bounce renders it impossible to return

long if a shot is long, it bounces outside the court

mini-break a point against the serve in a **tie-break**

slam dunk smash a style of **smash** made famous by US player Pete Sampras, where a player jumps above the ball to smash it downwards with as much power as possible (from its likeness to the basketball move)

Some famous tennis players

Andre Agassi, 1970–

Born in Las Vegas, Nevada, USA, he was known initially for his flamboyant on-court clothing, before proving himself as a serious player, winning Wimbledon in 1992. He won the US Open in 1994 and 1999, the French Open in 1999, and the Australian Open in 1995, 2000 and 2001. Sidelined by injury, he slipped to 141st in the world in 1997, before climbing to the top of the rankings in 1999. In 2001 he married **Steffi Graf**.

Arthur Ashe, 1943–93

Born in Richmond, Virginia, USA, he won the US national singles championship in 1968 and the first US Open championship later the same year. He was a professional tennis player from 1969 to 1979 and won the men's singles at the Australian Open (1970) and at Wimbledon (1975) when he defeated **Jimmy Connors**. He was the first black male tennis player to achieve world ranking. He retired in 1980 and became an AIDS Awareness campaigner, having contracted the virus himself, allegedly after a blood transfusion during his second heart bypass operation in 1983.

Boris Becker, 1967–

Born in Leimen, West Germany, he first came to prominence in 1984 when he finished runner-up in the US Open. In 1985, at the age of 17, he became the youngest-ever winner of the men's singles at Wimbledon, as well as the first unseeded winner. He successfully defended his title in 1986, won it for a third time in 1989, and was a beaten finalist in 1988, 1990, 1991 and 1995. He also won the US Open in 1989, the Australian Open in 1991 and 1996 and led West Germany to Davis Cup successes in 1988 and 1989.

Björn Borg, 1956–

Born in Soldertaljie, Sweden, he left school aged 14 to concentrate on tennis, and at 15 was selected for the Swedish Davis Cup team. He was Wimbledon junior champion at 16, and became the dominant player in world tennis in the 1970s, his athletic ability helping him to a record five consecutive Wimbledon singles titles (1976–80). He also won the French Open six times between 1974 and 1981. His Wimbledon reign ended in 1981 when he lost in the final to **John McEnroe**. Borg refused to follow the entire men's tour, preferring a long vacation; the ensuing row, where he was told he would have to qualify for Grand Slam events unless he committed himself to entering the required number of tournaments, led to his early retirement in 1983.

Jean Borotra, 1898–1994

Born near Biarritz, France, he was the most famous of the so-called Four Musketeers (with Lacoste, Cochet and Brugnon) who emerged in France in the 1920s. Nicknamed 'the Bounding Basque', he won the Wimbledon men's singles title in 1924, and his extraordinary fitness enabled him to compete in veterans' events at that same venue when he was almost 80. He also won the French and Australian championships, as well as several Davis Cup medals between 1927 and 1932. He was secretary of Physical Education in the Vichy government (1940–2), but was imprisoned by the Nazis from 1943 to 1945.

Evonne Cawley, 1951–

Born in Barellan, New South Wales, Australia, she left for Sydney at the age of ten to be coached in tennis. As a teenager she won 37 junior titles and in 1971 beat **Margaret Court** at Wimbledon, becoming the second-youngest woman to win, and the first Aboriginal to do so. During the 1970s, she won 92 major tennis tournaments, including the Australian Open four times, and was ranked second in the world. In 1980 she won her second Wimbledon title against **Chris Evert**, becoming the first mother to take the title.

Maureen Connolly, 1934–69

Born in San Diego, California, USA, she made tennis history by becoming the first woman to win the Grand Slam of the four major titles (British, US, French and Australian) in the same year (1953). Known as 'Little Mo', she won the US title in three consecutive years (1951–3) and the Wimbledon singles in three consecutive years (1952–4). She also won the French Open again in 1954. Her career ended before she turned 20, when she was forced to retire following a serious injury sustained while horse riding. She died of cancer in 1969.

Jimmy Connors, 1952–

He was born in East St Louis, Illinois, USA. He was Wimbledon men's singles champion in 1974 and 1982, won the Australian Open in 1974, and the US Open in 1974, 1976, 1978, 1982 and 1983. Tenacious, passionate and outspoken, crowds either saw him as a great entertainer or an embarrassment to tennis. A left-handed player, he was one of the first to use the double-fisted backhand and in 1991 reached the US Open semi-finals at the age of 39.

Margaret Court, 1942–

Born in Albury, New South Wales, Australia, she was the winner of more Grand Slam events (64) than any other player, including eleven Australian Open singles (1960–6, 1969–71, 1973), five French Open singles (1962, 1964, 1969–70, 1973), three Wimbledon singles (1963, 1965, 1970) and five US Open singles (1962, 1965, 1969–70, 1973). A tall, strong player, nicknamed 'The Arm' by **Billie Jean King**, she is the only player to achieve a Grand Slam in doubles and singles, winning all four mixed doubles titles with Ken Fletcher in 1963.

Roy Emerson, 1936–

Born in Queensland, Australia, he holds the record for the most Grand Slam titles – 28 (12 singles and 16 doubles) – and his record twelve Grand Slam singles titles was only surpassed by **Pete Sampras** in 2000. These victories, however, were at a time when the majority of his rivals had turned professional and were therefore ineligible for those championships. A classic all-court player, he is celebrated as the first man to play a serve-volley game for five sets.

Chris Evert, 1954–

She was born in Fort Lauderdale, Florida, USA. Renowned for her two-handed backhand, her success helped popularize women's tennis in the USA and Europe. She won 157 professional titles including 18 Grand Slam singles titles. She was married for a time to the English tennis player, John Lloyd. She retired in 1989 after reaching the quarter-finals of the US Open to become a mother and a television commentator.

Steffi Graf, 1969–

Born in Brühl, West Germany, she first came to prominence in 1984 when she reached the last 16 at Wimbledon. In 1988 she won the Grand Slam of singles titles as well as the gold medal at the Seoul Olympics. Other singles wins include the French Open (1987, 1993, 1995–6, 1999), the Australian Open (1989–90, 1994), the US Open (1989, 1993, 1995–6), and the Wimbledon championship (1989, 1991–3, 1995–6). In 2001 she married **Andre Agassi**.

Billie Jean King, 1943–

She was born in Long Beach, California, USA. She won the ladies doubles title at Wimbledon in 1961 (with Karen Hantze) at her first attempt, and between 1961 and 1979 won a record 20 Wimbledon titles, including the singles in 1966–8, 1972–3 and 1975, and four mixed doubles. She also won 13 US titles, four French titles and two Australian titles. Towards the end of her playing career she became involved in the administration of tennis, and as president of the Women's Tennis Association (1980–1) she played a prominent role in working for the improvement of remuneration and playing conditions for women in professional tennis. In 1973 she challenged the male player Bobby Riggs in the Houston Astrodome, watched by a crowd of 30,472, the biggest for a tennis match; a further 50 million television viewers witnessed her 6–4, 6–3, 6–3 victory.

Rod Laver, 1938–

He was born in Rockhampton, Queensland, Australia, and first won the Wimbledon title in 1961, winning it again in 1962 in the course of a Grand Slam. Nicknamed 'Rocket', he turned professional in 1962 and won the professional world singles title five times between 1964 and 1970, becoming the first player to earn $1 million in prize money. When Wimbledon first allowed professionals to participate in 1968, he won it in that year, and again in the following year, as part of his second Grand Slam.

Ivan Lendl, 1960–

He was born in Ostrava, Czechoslovakia. A solid baseline player, he won the singles title at the US Open (1985–7), French Open (1984, 1986–7) and Australian Open (1989). He was runner-up at Wimbledon in 1986–7 and was the Masters champion (1986–7) and the World Championship Tennis champion (1982, 1985). He became a US citizen in 1992 and retired from tennis two years later.

Suzanne Lenglen, 1899–1938

Born in Compiègne, France, she was trained by her father, and became famous in 1914 by winning the women's world hard-court singles championship at Paris at the age of 15. She won the French Open singles six times (1920–3, 1925–6), and also won six singles titles at Wimbledon (1919–23, 1925), and the mixed doubles (1920, 1922, 1925). She won gold medals in singles and mixed doubles at the 1920 Olympic Games in Antwerp. She retired in 1926 after a lucrative exhibition tour of the USA.

John McEnroe, 1959–

Born in Wiesbaden, West Germany, to US parents, he reached the semi-final at Wimbledon as a pre-qualifier in 1977, turned professional in 1978, and was runner-up to **Björn Borg** in the 1980 Wimbledon final. He won the Wimbledon title three times (1981, 1983–4), the US Open singles four times (1979–81, 1984), as well as eight Grand Slam doubles events. Throughout his professional career, his on-court outbursts resulted in much adverse publicity; he was nicknamed 'Superbrat' and was renowned for his tendency to greet umpires' decisions with cries of 'You cannot be serious!' More recently he has become a popular commentator and television presenter, working for the BBC and American networks.

Martina Navratilova, 1956–

Born in Prague, Czechoslovakia, she defected to the USA in 1975 and became a tennis professional, gaining citizenship in 1981. Her rivalry with **Chris Evert** was one of the great features of the game from 1975. She won a record nine singles titles at Wimbledon (1978–9, 1982–7, 1990) and the US Open four times (1983–4, 1986–7). Her record of 58 career Grand Slam titles is second only to Margaret Court. In 2003, at the age of 46, she won the mixed doubles at the Australian Open and Wimbledon with Indian partner Leander Paes.

Fred Perry, 1909–95

He was born in Stockport, Cheshire, England. His first sport was table tennis, at which he was world singles champion in 1929. He only took up lawn tennis when he was 19, and between 1933 and the end of 1936, when he turned professional, he won every major amateur title, including the Wimbledon singles three times, the US singles three times, and the Australian and French championships, and helped to keep the Davis Cup in Great Britain for four years. He was the first man to win all four major titles. He later took US citizenship (1938), and pursued a career in coaching, writing and broadcasting.

Pete Sampras, 1971–

Born in Washington DC, USA, he dominated men's tennis in the 1990s, winning Wimbledon seven times (1993–5, 1997–2000). With 14 Grand Slam championships overall, including five US Open titles (1990, 1993, 1995–6, 2002), he is the game's most successful player and was ranked number one in the world between 1993 and 1998. Nicknamed 'Pistol Pete', he was especially known for his powerful serves and his trademark 'slam dunk' smash and in 1993 became the first player to serve over 1,000 aces in a season.

Bill Tilden, 1893–1953

Born in Philadelphia, USA, he became the first American to win Wimbledon (1920). Known as 'Big Bill', he won Wimbledon twice more (1921, 1930) and the US Open seven times (1920–5, 1929). His ten Grand Slam victories remained a record until surpassed by **Roy Emerson** in the sixties. He was later ostracized from the tennis world because of his homosexuality and served a prison sentence in 1947 after making sexual advances to a minor. He died in poverty in 1953.

Serena Williams, 1981–

Born in Saginaw, Michigan, USA, she and her older sister **Venus** were acknowledged as the dominant forces in women's tennis at the beginning of the 21st century. Coached by her father from a young age, she won the US Open singles in 1999. She went on to win numerous doubles titles in partnership with Venus, including Olympic gold in 2000 and Wimbledon in 2002. She lost to her sister in the singles semi-finals at Wimbledon in 2000 but defeated her in the final in 2002. Rising to number one in the world, Serena also beat

Venus in finals at the US Open and French Open (2002) and the Australian Open and Wimbledon (2003).

Venus Williams, 1980–

Born in Lynwood, California, USA, she and her younger sister **Serena** emerged as the leading forces on the women's circuit at the beginning of the 21st century. Coached by her father from the age of four, she reached the final of the US Open in 1997. Her first Grand Slam singles victory came in 2000 when she won the Wimbledon title. She added the US Open and the Olympic singles titles that same year and won Wimbledon and the US Open for the second time in 2001. She lost to Serena in three Grand Slam finals in 2002 and two in 2003. Her many doubles titles with her sister have included an Olympic gold medal in 2000.

Helen Wills Moody, 1905–98

Born in Centreville, California, USA, she dominated women's tennis from the retirement of **Suzanne Lenglen** in 1926 until the outbreak of World War II, winning eight singles finals at Wimbledon, seven US championships and four French Opens. Of the 22 Grand Slams she entered in her career, she won 19, reaching the final in the other three. She also won gold medals in the women's singles and doubles at the 1924 Olympics.

TENPIN BOWLING

Origins

Evidence from ancient Egypt (around 5200 BC) indicates that bowling at pins or skittles has long existed as a pastime. The Greeks and Romans also had forms of bowling. In the Middle Ages it was particularly popular in Germany, the Netherlands and England. Dutch or German emigrants took the game of ninepins to the United States where, in the early 19th century, it became extremely popular. The sport was accompanied by much gambling and as a result the game was banned. The law was easily circumvented, however, with the addition of a tenth pin and the popularity of the sport was reignited.

Rules and description

Tenpin bowling is an indoor sport for individuals and teams where the aim is to knock down as many targets as possible by rolling a ball down a 20yd/18.3m long, polished wooden pathway called the 'lane'. The targets, wooden upright skittles 15in/38cm tall, are known as 'pins' and are arranged at the end of the lane in a triangular fashion with the apex pointing towards the bowlers. Running along either side of the 3.41 to 3.51ft/104 to 107cm wide lane are 'gutters'; if the ball falls into either gutter the turn is void. The game is divided into ten 'frames' with each player having two shots in each frame. Scoring is progressive. If the bowler knocks over all ten in a single shot (a 'strike') ten points are gained plus the score of the next two balls bowled. If the player knocks down some of the pins with one ball and the remaining pins with the second ball, a 'spare' is scored, and to the ten points thus scored the player adds the points gained on the first ball rolled during the next frame. When a spare is scored in the tenth frame, a third ball is bowled. The highest possible score is 300. Modern tenpin bowling has automated systems that add up the scores so mathematical prowess is not necessary.

The ball must not exceed 26.77in/68cm in circumference and 15.43lb/7kg in weight; it has either two or three holes, for the thumb and the middle and ring fingers. To make a throw, bowlers start their approach near the scoring area, then release the ball at the foul line.

Ruling body: Fédération Internationale des Quilleurs (FIQ)

FIQ World Championships

The world championships were inaugurated by the FIQ in 1954 and since 1963 have been held every four years.

Prior to 1952 the sport's governing body was the International Bowling Association (IBA); it organized four world championships between 1923 and 1936. Team competitions are for five players a side.

Men

	Singles	Pairs	Team
1963	Les Zikes (USA)	USA	USA
1967	David Pond (Great Britain)	Great Britain	Finland
1971	Ed Luther (USA)	Puerto Rico	USA
1975	Bud Staudt (USA)	Great Britain	Finland
1979	Ollie Ongtawco (Philippines)	Australia	Australia
1983	Armando Marino (Colombia)	Great Britain/Australia	Finland
1987	Patrick Rolland (France)	Sweden	Sweden
1991	Ma Ying-cheih (Taiwan)	USA	Taiwan
1995	Marc Doi (Canada)	Sweden	The Netherlands
1999	Gery Verbruggen (Belgium)	Sweden	Sweden
2003	Mika Luoto (Finland)	Sweden	Sweden

Women

	Singles	Pairs	Team
1963	Helen Shablis (USA)	USA	Mexico
1967	Helen Weston (USA)	Mexico	Finland
1971	Ashie Gonzales (Puerto Rico)	Japan	USA
1975	Anne-Dore Häfker (West Germany)	Sweden	Japan
1979	Lita de la Rosa (Philippines)	Philippines	USA
1983	Lena Sulkanen (Sweden)	Denmark	Sweden
1987	Edda Piccini (Mexico)	USA	USA
1991	Martina Beckel (Germany)	Japan	South Korea
1995	Debby Ship (Canada)	Thailand	Finland

	Singles	Pairs	Team
1999	Kelly Kulick (USA)	Australia	South Korea
2003	Zara Glover (England)	England	Malaysia

A-Z

anchor the last bowler to bowl for a team; generally the team's best bowler

arrows target lines marked on the **lane**, used to help guide the ball to the pins

barmaid a pin that is hidden behind another pin

foul line the line at the end of the lane behind which the player must release the ball

frame a pair of attempts by each player to score points

gutters the gulleys that run the length of the **lane** and to either side of it. A shot is void if the ball falls into the gutter

half-strike same as **spare**

head pin, kingpin the frontmost pin of the triangular arrangement

lane the smooth wooden runway along which the balls are delivered at the pins

leave the pins that remain standing after the first ball

perfect game a score of 300 points resulting from twelve successive **strikes**

pin spotter the device that replaces the pins in position after each player's turn

spare knocking down all ten pins in two attempts

split a **leave** situation where the remaining pins are widely spaced, making them difficult to hit with a single ball

strike knocking down all ten pins in one attempt

turkey three successive **strikes**

THAI BOXING

Origins

Thai boxing, otherwise known as 'muay thai', is believed to date from more than 2,000 years ago. One of the earliest recorded mentions of Thai boxing comes from an era after the Thai kingdom of Ayutthaya was ended following the sack by the Burmese in 1767. Legend has it that an expert boxer named Nai Khanom Tom, captured by the Burmese, so impressed their ruler with his ability to fend off his attackers that he was rewarded with his freedom. The rules of the modern sport were codified in the 1930s.

Rules and description

Thai boxing differs from Western boxing in that a combination of blows is thrown by the hands and the feet, as well as the elbows and knees. For this reason it is also known as 'the Science of Eight Limbs'. Points are scored for aggression and style as well as blows scored. A knockout is scored if a fallen fighter remains down for a count of ten. If both fighters are standing at the end of five three-minute rounds, then the judges decide the winner based on the points scored.

The fight is traditionally accompanied by ritual music and dance. The music, called 'sarama', is played by a three-piece ensemble comprising a 'pee java', or Java pipe; a pair of tom-tom drums called the 'klong khaek'; and small cymbals called 'ching'. The fight is preceded by a 'wai kru' dance, performed by the fighters in honour of their teachers. During this ritual the boxers wear a sacred cord around their heads – known as the 'mongkol', it is removed before fighting. Armbands are worn throughout the bout as they are believed to offer protection; called 'kruang rang', they consist of a piece of cloth inscribed with Sanskrit text.

Boxing gloves are worn, weighing a minimum of 172g/6oz. Footwear is not allowed.

Ruling body: World Muay Thai Council

Muay Thai World Championships 2003

Up to 51kg
Andrei Klokov (Ukraine)

Up to 54kg
Laafissi Issam (Morocco)

Up to 57kg
Andrei Kulebin (Belarus)

Up to 60kg
Bogdan Lukin (Ukraine)

Up to 63.5kg
Aleksandr Khimoroda (Belarus)

Up to 67kg
Edgar Arutiunian (Ukraine)

Up to 71kg
Dulkun Mamentov (Kazakhstan)

Up to 75kg
Habib Gadjiev (Russia)

Up to 81kg
Magamed Magamedov (Russia)

Up to 86kg
Andrei Molchanov (Belarus)

Up to 91kg
Aleksandr Pantukov (Belarus)

Over 91kg
Sergei Archipov (Ukraine)

TRAMPOLINING

Origins

Trampolining acts were popular at circuses in the 19th and 20th centuries but as a competitive sport it can be dated from 1936 when the first modern trampoline was produced by a US diving and tumbling champion named George Nissen, allegedly in his father's garage. Nissen was also fond of acrobatics and, familiar with bouncing on a safety net, dreamt up a smaller version. The first official competition was held in the United States of America in 1947.

Rules and description

Trampolining is an acrobatic sport performed by men and women on a piece of apparatus known as a trampoline.

The trampoline consists of a nylon canvas stretched taut within a metal frame and attached to it by springs or an elastic suspension. Trampolining, also originally known as 'rebound' or 'rebound tumbling', sees gymnasts performing acrobatic tumbles, twists, bounces and somersaults off the 'bed' (the bouncing area) of the trampoline. Men and women perform in individual events and there are also synchronized events where competitors perform simultaneously and attempt to mirror each other's movements. Competitors perform set and voluntary routines.

Ruling bodies: Fédération Internationale de Trampoline (FIT); Fédération Internationale de Gymnastique (FIG)

From diving board to bouncing bed

The name trampoline comes from the Spanish 'trampolin' (meaning diving board) and was chosen by inventor George Nissen after he heard the term during a tour of Mexico. He registered the term as a trademark and, in 1942, set up with his partner Larry Griswold the Griswold-Nissen Trampoline & Tumbling Company in Cedar Rapids, Iowa, the first trampoline manufacturing company in the world.

World Trampolining Championships

	Men's individual	Women's individual	Venue
1964	Danny Millman (USA)	Judy Wills (USA)	London, UK
1965	Gary Irwin (USA)	Judy Wills (USA)	London, UK
1966	Wayne Miller (USA)	Judy Wills (USA)	Lafayette, USA
1967	David Jacobs (USA)	Judy Wills (USA)	London, UK
1968	David Jacobs (USA)	Judy Wills (USA)	Amersfoort, The Netherlands
1970	Wayne Miller (USA)	Renée Ransom (USA)	Bern, Switzerland
1972	Paul Luxon (Great Britain)	Alexandra Nicholson (USA)	Stuttgart, West Germany
1974	Richard Tisson (France)	Alexandra Nicholson (USA)	Johannesburg, South Africa
1976	Richard Tisson (France)/ Yevgeny Yanes (USSR)	Svetlana Levina (USSR)	Tulsa, USA
1978	Yevgeny Yanes (USSR)	Tatyana Anisimova (USSR)	Newcastle, Australia
1980	Stewart Matthews (Great Britain)	Ruth Keller (Switzerland)	Brig, Switzerland
1982	Carl Furrer (Great Britain)	Ruth Keller (Switzerland)	Bozeman, USA
1984	Lionel Pioline (France)	Sue Shotton (Great Britain)	Osaka, Japan
1986	Lionel Pioline (France)	Tatyana Lushina (USSR)	Paris, France
1988	Vadim Krasnochapka (USSR)	Rusudan Khoperia (USSR)	Birmingham, UK
1990	Aleksandr Moskalenko (USSR)	Yelena Merkulova (USSR)	Essen, Germany
1992	Aleksandr Moskalenko (Russia)	Yelena Merkulova (Russia)	Auckland, New Zealand
1994	Aleksandr Moskalenko (Russia)	Irina Karaveyeva (Russia)	Porto, Portugal

	Men's individual	Women's individual	Venue
1996	Dmitri Polyarush (Belarus)	Tatyana Kovaleva (Russia)	Vancouver, Canada
1998	German Knytshev (Russia)	Irina Karaveyeva (Russia)	Sydney, Australia
1999	Aleksandr Moskalenko (Russia)	Irina Karaveyeva (Russia)	Sun City, South Africa
2001	Aleksandr Moskalenko (Russia)	Anna Dogonadze (Germany)	Odense, Denmark
2003	Henrik Stehlik (Germany)	Karen Cockburn (Canada)	Hanover, Germany

TRIATHLON

Origins

The first triathlon was held in San Diego, California, USA, in September 1974. In 1977 American John Collins invented the 'ironman race' on the Hawaiian island of Oahu. He proposed a swim of 2.4mi, a round-the-island cycle race of 112mi and the Honolulu marathon. Fifteen people entered in February 1978 and the first winner was Gordon Haller in a time of 11hrs and 46mins.

Rules and description

Triathlon is a single-race event where athletes need to excel at three separate disciplines: swimming, cycling and running. There are no rests between each discipline, though the triathletes enter a 'transition period' after getting out of the water to don shoes and helmet before the bike ride and then another period after riding the bike and preparing to run. In the swimming phase, triathletes wear swimming caps, and a wetsuit if the water temperature is below 20 degrees Celsius. The winner is the first to cross the finishing line at the end of the run.

There are four types of triathlon: classic, sprint, half, and ironman. The classic triathlon (the type competed for at the Olympic Games) consists of a 1.5km swim, a 40km bike ride and a 10km run. The sprint is 750m, 20km and 5km respectively. The ironman is 3.8km, 180km and 42.2km (with the 'half' describing a 1.9km swim, a 90km cycle ride and a 21km run).

Ruling body: International Triathlon Union

World Championships

	Men	Women	Venue
1989	Mark Allen (USA)	Erin Baker (New Zealand)	Avignon, France
1990	Greg Welch (Australia)	Karen Smyers (USA)	Orlando, USA
1991	Miles Stewart (Australia)	Jo-Anne Ritchie (Canada)	Gold Coast, Australia
1992	Simon Lessing (Great Britain)	Michellie Jones (Australia)	Muskoka, Canada
1993	Spencer Smith (Great Britain)	Michellie Jones (Australia)	Manchester, UK
1994	Spencer Smith (Great Britain)	Emma Carney (Australia)	Wellington, New Zealand

Triathlon

	Men	Women	Venue
1995	Simon Lessing (Great Britain)	Karen Smyers (USA)	Cancun, Mexico
1996	Simon Lessing (Great Britain)	Jackie Gallagher (Australia)	Cleveland, USA
1997	Chris McCormack (Australia)	Emma Carney (Australia)	Perth, Australia
1998	Simon Lessing (Great Britain)	Joanne King (Australia)	Lausanne, Switzerland
1999	Dimitri Gaag (Kazakhstan)	Loretta Harrop (Australia)	Montreal, Canada
2000	Olivier Marceau (France)	Nicole Hackett (Australia)	Perth, Australia
2001	Peter Robertson (Australia)	Siri Lindley (USA)	Edmonton, Canada
2002	Ivan Rana (Spain)	Leanda Cave (Great Britain)	Cancun, Mexico
2003	Peter Robertson (Australia)	Emma Snowsill (Australia)	Queenstown, New Zealand
2004	Bevan Docherty (New Zealand)	Sheila Taormina (USA)	Funchal, Portugal

Olympic Games

First held in 2000.

	Men	Women
2000	Simon Whitfield (Canada)	Brigitte McMahon (Switzerland)
2004	Hamish Carter (New Zealand)	Kate Allen (Austria)

Ironman Triathlon World Championship

	Men	Women
1978	Gordon Haller (USA)	No finishers
1979	Tom Warren (USA)	Lyn Lemaire (USA)
1980	Dave Scott (USA)	Robin Beck (USA)
1981	John Howard (USA)	Linda Sweeney (USA)
1982	Scott Tinley (USA)	Kathleen McCartney (USA)
1982	Dave Scott (USA)	Julie Leach (USA)
1983	Dave Scott (USA)	Sylviane Puntous (Canada)
1984	Dave Scott (USA)	Sylviane Puntous (Canada)
1985	Scott Tinley (USA)	Joanne Ernst (USA)
1986	Dave Scott (USA)	Paula Newby-Fraser (Zimbabwe)
1987	Dave Scott (USA)	Erin Baker (New Zealand)
1988	Scott Molina (USA)	Paula Newby-Fraser (Zimbabwe)
1989	Mark Allen (USA)	Paula Newby-Fraser (Zimbabwe)
1990	Mark Allen (USA)	Erin Baker (New Zealand)
1991	Mark Allen (USA)	Paula Newby-Fraser (Zimbabwe)
1992	Mark Allen (USA)	Paula Newby-Fraser (Zimbabwe)
1993	Mark Allen (USA)	Paula Newby-Fraser (Zimbabwe)
1994	Greg Welch (Australia)	Paula Newby-Fraser (Zimbabwe)
1995	Mark Allen (USA)	Karen Smyers (USA)
1996	Luc Van Lierde (Belgium)	Paula Newby-Fraser (Zimbabwe)
1997	Thomas Hellriegel (Germany)	Heather Fuhr (Canada)
1998	Peter Reid (Canada)	Natascha Badmann (Switzerland)
1999	Luc Van Lierde (Belgium)	Lori Bowden (Canada)
2000	Peter Reid (Canada)	Natascha Badmann (Switzerland)
2001	Timothy DeBoom (USA)	Natascha Badmann (Switzerland)

	Men	Women
2002	Timothy DeBoom (USA)	Natascha Badmann (Switzerland)
2003	Peter Reid (Canada)	Lori Bowden (Canada)
2004	Normann Stadler (Germany)	Nina Kraft (Germany)

TUG OF WAR

Origins

The term 'tug of war' is believed to have originated in Britain in the 19th century but the sport of displaying great team strength by pulling against an opposing side on a rope with bare hands certainly predates this by many centuries. Various origins have been proposed, none of them verified. The first rules for tug of war were drawn up in 1879 by the New York Athletics Club.

Rules and description

Tug of war is a sport where two teams of eight members pull against one another at opposite ends of a thick rope. The rope must be at least 33.5m/36.6yd long with a tape marking the mid-way point and further markings denoting 4m and 5m from the centre. The person at each end of the rope is known as the 'anchor'. Pullers can use resin on their hands to get a better grip of the rope but cannot use artificial aids to hold it. Spiked shoes are forbidden. A match is won when a team moves the rope the required distance, or when one of the rope markers passes beyond a centre line marked on the ground. Matches are generally the best of three pulls.

Ruling body: Tug of War International Federation (TWIF)

Olympic Games

	Winner	Runner-up	Venue
1900	Sweden/Denmark	France	Paris, France
1904	USA (Milwaukee AC)	USA (St Louis SouthWest Turnverein)	St Louis, USA
1908	Great Britain (City of London Police)	Great Britain (Liverpool Police)	London, UK
1912	Sweden	Great Britain	Stockholm, Sweden
1920	Great Britain	The Netherlands	Antwerp, Belgium

World Championships

World championships were first held for men in 1975 and for women in 1986. Indoor championships were inaugurated in 1991. Individual clubs compete as well as national teams.

Men 720kg (heavyweight)

England	1975–8, 1980, 1982
Ireland	1984, 1986, 1988, 1990
Switzerland	1985, 1992, 2000
The Netherlands	1994, 1998, 2002, 2004

Men 680kg (cruiserweight)

Switzerland	1990, 1994, 2000
Sweden	1998
The Netherlands	2004

Men 640kg (middleweight)

England	1975–6, 1978, 1980, 1986, 1988, 1998
Ireland	1982, 1984, 1990
Switzerland	1985, 1992, 1994, 2000, 2002
Germany	2004

Men 560kg (lightweight)

Switzerland	1982, 1985, 1990, 2000, 2002
England	1984, 1988, 1993, 2004
Ireland	1986
Spain	1992, 1994, 1998

Men's catchweight (no weight specification)

England	1984

Women 560kg

Sweden	1986, 1988, 1990, 1992, 1994 2000
The Netherlands	1998, 2002
Switzerland	2004

Women 520kg

Sweden	1986, 1988, 1994, 2004
Switzerland	1990, 2000
The Netherlands	1992, 1998, 2002

VOLLEYBALL

Origins

Volleyball was invented by William G Morgan at Springfield College, Holyoke, Massachusetts, in 1895. He named the game 'mintonette', and it was intended as a less strenuous version of basketball, invented just a few years previously at the same college. It was spread via the YMCA movement and the US armed forces. The game was introduced to the Olympic Games in 1964. It has developed into two forms: the original volleyball is now frequently called indoor volleyball to differentiate it from beach volleyball, which originated in California, USA, in the 1920s.

Rules and description

Volleyball is a six-a-side court game for both men and women in which a large ball is volleyed by hand over a high net. The court measures 18 x 9m/19.68 x 9.84yd; the 1m-high net is suspended across the centre of the court. The top of it stands 2.43m/2.65yd high for men and 2.24m/2.45yd for women. Parallel lines are marked on the court and divide each half into front (attacking) zones and back (defending) zones. Each set commences with three attacking players (the left, right and centre forwards) in the attacking zone, and two players in the defending zone. The server serves from behind the backline with an underarm or overarm strike of the ball. The object of the game is to score points by returning the ball over the net so that the opposition cannot retrieve it. Except for the serve (which must go straight into the opposing team's court), each side can hit the ball up to three times before it has to go over the net, with no single player allowed to hit the ball twice in sequence. Players rotate their positions after every serve. Matches are the best of five sets; the best of 25 points wins a set (15 points if the match reaches a final fifth set).

Beach volleyball is very similar but is played barefoot on an outdoor sandy court measuring 16 x 8m/17.49 x 8.74yd and each team comprises only two players. As in the indoor game, no player may make consecutive hits. The first two sets are played to 21 points, with the final tie-breaker set being played to 15 points. A team must win a set by two points.

Ruling body: International Volleyball Federation (FIVB; Fédération Internationale de Volleyball)

Indoor volleyball

World Championships

The world championships were inaugurated in 1949, with a women's event being introduced in 1952. The competition is held every four years. From 1980 the Olympic champions have been deemed that year's world champions.

	Men's winner	Venue	Women's winner	Venue
1949	USSR	Prague, Czechoslovakia		
1952	USSR	Moscow, USSR	USSR	Moscow, USSR
1956	Czechoslovakia	Paris, France	USSR	Paris, France
1960	USSR	Rio de Janeiro, Brazil	USSR	Rio de Janeiro, Brazil
1962	USSR	Moscow, USSR	Japan	Moscow, USSR
1966	Czechoslovakia	Prague, Czechoslovakia	Japan*	Tokyo, Japan
1970	East Germany	Sofia, Bulgaria	USSR	Varna, Bulgaria
1974	Poland	Mexico City, Mexico	Japan	Guadalajara, Mexico
1978	USSR	Rome, Italy	Cuba	Leningrad, USSR
1982	USSR	Buenos Aires, Argentina	China	Lima, Peru
1986	USA	Paris, France	China	Prague, Czechoslovakia
1990	Italy	Rio de Janeiro, Brazil	USSR	Beijing, China
1994	Italy	Athens, Greece	Cuba	Sao Paulo, Brazil
1998	Italy	Tokyo, Japan	Cuba	Tokyo, Japan
2002	Brazil	Buenos Aires, Argentina	Italy	Berlin, Germany

* Held in 1967

Olympic Champions

	Men	Women
1964	USSR	Japan
1968	USSR	USSR
1972	Japan	USSR
1976	Poland	Japan
1980	USSR	USSR

Volleyball

	Men	Women
1984	USA	China
1988	USA	USSR
1992	Brazil	Cuba
1996	The Netherlands	Cuba
2000	Yugoslavia	Cuba
2004	Brazil	China

World Cup

The World Cup has generally been held every four years since 1965 for men (and from 1973 for women).

	Men	Women
1965	USSR	
1969	East Germany	
1973	*Not held*	USSR
1977	USSR	Japan
1981	USSR	China
1985	USA	China
1989	Cuba	Cuba
1991	USSR	Cuba
1995	Italy	Cuba
1999	Cuba	Russia
2003	Brazil	China

Beach volleyball

World Championships

	Men	Venue
1997	Para Ferreira & Guilherme Marques (Brazil)	Los Angeles, USA
1999	Emanuel Scheffer & Jose Loiola (Brazil)	Marseilles, France
2001	Mariano Baracetti & Martin Conde (Argentina)	Klagenfurt, Austria
2003	Mariano Baracetti & Martin Conde (Argentina)	Rio de Janeiro, Brazil

	Women	Venue
1997	Jackie Silva & Sandra Pires (Brazil)	Los Angeles, USA
1999	Adriana Behar & Shelde Bede (Brazil)	Marseilles, France
2001	Adriana Behar & Shelde Bede (Brazil)	Klagenfurt, Austria
2003	Kerri Walsh & Misty May (USA)	Rio de Janeiro, Brazil

It's the sand that brings out the best in the Brazilians

If Brazilian footballers are so skilful because they learn to play their sport on Rio de Janeiro's Copacabana Beach, then it seems only natural that some of the world's best beach volleyball teams should also be Brazilian. The first Olympic medals (gold and silver) in women's beach volleyball went to two Brazilian teams – the first ever medals won by women for that country in the history of the Olympic Games.

Olympic Champions

	Men	Women
1996	Karch Kiraly & Kent Steffes (USA)	Jackie Silva & Sandra Pires (Brazil)
2000	Eric Fonoimoana & Dain Blanton (USA)	Kerri Pottharst & Natalie Cook (Australia)
2004	Ricardo Santos & Emanuel Rego (Brazil)	Kerri Walsh & Misty May (USA)

A-Z

ace	a serve that lands in the opposing team's court without being touched
attack line	a line marked 3m from the net that delineates the furthest advance of defending players
block	a wall of hands at the top of the net created to prevent a **spike** from getting through. Players' hands can reach over the net but they are not permitted to touch it
dig	a defensive shot made with the forearms together that keeps the ball up in the air
double-touch	a description indicating that the ball was not played cleanly
dump	a dummied **spike** that tips the ball just over the net or the **block**
kill	same as **spike**
libero	a designated, specialized defensive player who can be brought on at any time in a defensive role only; he or she wears a contrasting coloured shirt to the rest of the team
rotation	the clockwise movement of players when the service changes
screen	to shield the opponent's view of the ball during the serve
setter	a player who **volleys** the ball upwards for a team-mate to **spike**
shoot set	a fast volleyed pass that has a low trajectory over the net
spike	to smash a volleyball overarm so that it flies forcefully downwards into the opposing team's court and cannot be retrieved
volley	to play the ball with the fingertips of both hands in an overhead shot

WALKING

Origins

The origins of competitive race walking can be traced to the Victorian pastime of pedestrianism. Wagers were often taken on the walkers and extreme walking over long distances became a popular activity. Famous pedestrians, or 'peds' as they were known, included Captain Barclay Allardice, who walked 1,000 miles in 1,000 hours at Newmarket in 1809, and won himself 1,000 guineas.

Rules and description

Competitive race walking has few rules but the single most important one is the definition and judging of what exactly the difference between walking and running is. To walk legally, unbroken contact with the ground must be maintained. The front foot must make contact with the ground before the rear foot leaves it. If the contact is broken the walker is adjudged to be 'lifting'; in competition two warnings are given before the walker is disqualified on the third offence. The issue of whether contact is broken is made by eye. The leg that is in contact with the ground also needs to be straightened at some point.

Ruling body: International Association of Athletics Associations (IAAF)

Olympic Games

From 1912 to 1924, and again once the event was restored in 1948 and 1952, the Olympic walk event was a 10km track event. In 1956 the length was increased to 20km. Meanwhile a 50km event was inaugurated at the 1932 Olympic Games. The first Olympic walking race for women was the 10km in 1992. It was superseded in 2000 by a 20km event.

Men

	20km	**50km**
1912	George Goulding (Canada)*	
1920	Ugo Frigerio (Italy)*	
1924	Ugo Frigerio (Italy)*	
1928	*Not held*	
1932	*Not held*	Thomas Green (Great Britain)
1936	*Not held*	Harold Whitlock (Great Britain)
1948	John Mikaelsson (Sweden)*	John Ljunggren (Sweden)
1952	John Mikaelsson (Sweden)*	Giuseppe Dordoni (Italy)
1956	Leonid Spirin (USSR)	Norman Read (New Zealand)
1960	Vladimir Golubnichy (USSR)	Don Thompson (Great Britain)
1964	Ken Matthews (Great Britain)	Abdon Pamich (Italy)
1968	Vladimir Golubnichy (USSR)	Christoph Höhne (East Germany)
1972	Peter Frenkel (East Germany)	Bernd Kannenberg (West Germany)
1976	Daniel Bautista (Mexico)	*Not held*
1980	Maurizio Damilano (Italy)	Hartwig Gauder (East Germany)
1984	Ernesto Canto (Mexico)	Raúl González (Mexico)
1988	Jozef Pribilinec (Czechoslovakia)	Vyacheslav Ivanenko (USSR)
1992	Daniel Plaza (Spain)	Andrei Perlov (Russia)
1996	Jefferson Pérez (Ecuador)	Robert Korzeniowski (Poland)
2000	Robert Korzeniowski (Poland)	Robert Korzeniowski (Poland)
2004	Ivano Brugnetti (Italy)	Robert Korzeniowski (Poland)

*10km

Women

1992	Chen Yueling (China)
1996	Yelena Nikolayeva (Russia)
2000	Wang Liping (China)
2004	Athanasia Tsoumeleka (Greece)

WATER POLO

Origins

Water polo was pioneered in Britain in the 1870s and in 1877 a Scotsman called William Wilson drew up a set of rules. Originally known as 'football in the water', it quickly became popular and was introduced to the Olympic Games in 1900.

Rules and description

Water polo is a team game played by teams of seven, one of whom is nominated as goalkeeper. During the match four reserves may be brought on as substitutes. Water polo takes place in a swimming pool; the playing area measures a maximum of 20 x 30m/21.8 x 31.2yd (17 x 25m/18.6 x 27.34yd for women) and is a minimum of 1.8m/1.97yd deep. Coloured flags (white, red, yellow and green) mark the goal line and half-distance line, and 2m, 4m and 7m from the goal line respectively. Each game lasts for four periods of seven minutes; the official clock stops when play halts. Goalkeepers wear red caps; the other players wear caps of a contrasting colour.

The object of the game is to throw the ball into the opposing team's netted goal. A goal may be scored by any part of the body except the clenched fist but the players (except the goalkeeper) may use only one hand. Fouls are given for holding, pulling back and impeding progress, and are penalized by a free throw or a penalty throw.

Ruling body: Fédération Internationale de Natation (FINA)

World Champions

	Men	**Women**	**Venue**
1973	Hungary		Belgrade, Yugoslavia
1975	USSR		Cali, Colombia
1978	Italy		Berlin, Germany
1982	USSR		Guayaquil, Ecuador
1986	Yugoslavia	Australia	Madrid, Spain
1991	Yugoslavia	The Netherlands	Perth, Australia
1994	Italy	Hungary	Rome, Italy
1998	Spain	Italy	Perth, Australia
2001	Spain	Italy	Fukuoka, Japan
2003	Hungary	USA	Barcelona, Spain
2005			Montreal, Canada

Water Polo

Olympic Champions

Men

1900	Great Britain	**1936**	Hungary	**1976**	Hungary
1904	*Not held*	**1948**	Italy	**1980**	USSR
1908	Great Britain	**1952**	Hungary	**1984**	Yugoslavia
1912	Great Britain	**1956**	Hungary	**1988**	Yugoslavia
1920	Great Britain	**1960**	Italy	**1992**	Italy
1924	France	**1964**	Hungary	**1996**	Spain
1928	Germany	**1968**	Yugoslavia	**2000**	Hungary
1932	Hungary	**1972**	USSR	**2004**	Hungary

Women

2000	Australia
2004	Italy

World Cup

The World Cup was instituted by FINA in 1979.

Men

	Winner	**Venue**
1979	Hungary	Rijeka, Yugoslavia
1981	USSR	Long Beach, USA
1983	USSR	Malibu, USA
1985	West Germany	Duisburg, West Germany
1987	Yugoslavia	Thessaloniki, Greece
1989	Yugoslavia	Berlin, Germany
1991	USA	Barcelona, Spain
1993	Italy	Athens, Greece
1995	Hungary	Atlanta, USA
1997	USA	Athens, Greece
1999	Hungary	Sydney, Australia
2002	Russia	Belgrade, Yugoslavia

Women

	Winner	**Venue**
1979	USA	Merced, USA
1980	The Netherlands	Breda, The Netherlands
1981	Canada	Brisbane, Australia
1983	The Netherlands	Sainte-Foy, Canada
1984	Australia	Irvine, USA
1988	The Netherlands	Christchurch, New Zealand

	Winner	Venue
1989	The Netherlands	Eindhoven, The Netherlands
1991	The Netherlands	Long Beach, USA
1993	The Netherlands	Catania, Italy
1995	Australia	Sydney, Australia
1997	The Netherlands	Nancy, France
1999	The Netherlands	Winnipeg, Canada
2002	Hungary	Perth, Australia

WATER-SKIING

Origins

Water-skiing became possible as a competitive and recreational sport after the invention of the motorboat, as it provided the driving force for pulling skiers across water. The first water-skier was Ralph Samuelson, who in 1922 practised with boat and skis on Lake Pepin, Minnesota, USA. Water-skiing developed in the 1950s with more sophisticated equipment and diversified into different events.

Rules and description

Water-skiing is the skill of travelling across water ('planing') on one or two skis, or even barefoot, while being towed by a motorboat. The skier holds a bar handle attached to a rope that is secured to the boat and performs tricks ('figures'), slalom or distance jumping. The tow-rope is approximately 20m/21.8yd long and motorboats travel at speeds from 24 to more than 56kph. Barefoot skiers compete at speeds of around 68kph, and speed skiers can achieve speeds surpassing 150kph. Water-skis are generally made of fibreglass and vary in length from 1.7 to 1.8m/5.57 to 5.9ft according to the discipline. There are fins located on the underside to promote stability and to help the skier make sharp turns. The events in traditional water-skiing tournaments are slalom, jumping and tricks.

In slalom the skier zigzags across the wake of the boat, negotiating a series of buoys. Competitors are marked on the number of buoys achieved. Over a series of rounds the rope is shortened, making the runs progressively more difficult. In the jumping events the skier is towed up and off a waxed, fibreglass surfaced ramp, with the longest flights determining the winner. Championship jumps measure around 60m. In tricks, each skier has a timed run and executes as many tricks as possible, each being graded according to difficulty.

'Wakeboarding' uses a board similar to a snowboard and shares many terms with that sport. In 'kneeboarding' the rider sits on his or her heels. Wakeboarding and kneeboarding competitions include slalom and tricks.

The first Barefoot World Championships were held in 1978 and have been dominated by American and Australian skiers. Events include the wake slalom, tricks, start methods and jump as well as an overall competition. The World Ski-Racing

Water-skiing

Championships were inaugurated in 1979. Latterly (since 1998), there have been World Cableski Championships in which a cable, rather than a boat, tows the skier.

Ruling body: The International Water Ski Federation (IWSF)

World Championships

The world championships were first held at Juan les Pins, France, in 1949 and are now held biennially. Individual competitions include (for both men and women) slalom, tricks and jumping. The points scored from each go to make an overall champion.

Overall

	Men's winner	Women's winner
1949	Guy de Clercq (Belgium)/ Christian Jourdan (France)	Willa Worthington (USA)
1950	Dick Pope, Jr (USA)	Willa McGuire* (USA)
1953	Alfredo Mendoza (USA)	Leah Marie Rawls (USA)
1955	Alfredo Mendoza (USA)	Willa McGuire* (USA)
1957	Joe Cash (USA)	Marina Doria (Switzerland)
1959	Chuck Stearns (USA)	Vickie Van Hook (USA)
1961	Bruno Zaccardi (Italy)	Sylvie Hulsemann (Luxembourg)
1963	Billy Spencer (USA)	Jeanette Brown (USA)
1965	Roland Hillier (USA)	Liz Allan (USA)
1967	Mike Suyderhoud (USA)	Jeanette Stewart-Wood (Great Britain)
1969	Mike Suyderhoud (USA)	Liz Allan (USA)
1971	George Athans (Canada)	Christy Weir (USA)
1973	George Athans (Canada)	Lisa St John (USA)
1975	Carlos Suarez (Venezuela)	Liz Allan-Shetter (USA)
1977	Mike Hazelwood (Great Britain)	Cindy Todd (USA)
1979	Joel McClintock (Canada)	Cindy Todd (USA)
1981	Sammy Duvall (USA)	Karin Roberge (USA)
1983	Sammy Duvall (USA)	Ana Maria Carrasco (Venezuela)
1985	Sammy Duvall (USA)	Karen Neville (Australia)
1987	Sammy Duvall (USA)	Deena Brush (USA)
1989	Patrice Martin (France)	Deena Mapple** (USA)
1991	Patrice Martin (France)	Karen Neville (Australia)
1993	Patrice Martin (France)	Natalia Rumyantseva (Russia)
1995	Patrice Martin (France)	Judy Messer (Canada)
1997	Patrice Martin (France)	Elena Milakova (Russia)
1999	Patrice Martin (France)	Elena Milakova (Russia)
2001	Jaret Llewellyn (Canada)	Elena Milakova (Russia)
2003	Jimmy Siemers (USA)	Regina Jaques (USA)

* née Worthington

** née Brush

A-Z

bindings	the fastenings that secure the shoe-like fittings to the skis
bridle	the Y-shaped portion of the tow-rope that attaches to the tow handle
deepwater start	a start executed when the boat pulls the water-skier, wakeboarder or barefooter up out of the water while the skier is holding on to the tow-rope
dock start	a start executed when the water-skier, wakeboarder or barefooter begins his or her run by being pulled into the water by the boat while standing or sitting on a dock or pier
double-wake cut	an approach in jumping where the skier crosses the wake of the motorboat twice to build up speed. It is also known as a 'crack-the-whip' manoeuvre and enables jumpers to attain speeds in excess of 96 kph as they reach the ramp
fakie	the skill of riding backwards on a wakeboard
mono skiing	the skill of performing tricks on one ski
step-over turns	turns performed on one or two skis where the skier lifts a ski over the tow-rope while performing a 180-degree turn
trick release	a device that disconnects a trick skier from the boat in the event that the skier falls with his or her foot caught in the tow handle
wake	the V-shaped water behind the boat that is created by its forward motion

WEIGHTLIFTING

Origins

The impulse for an athlete to pit his or her strength against a rival is as old as mankind and there are records showing that it was a popular activity in ancient Greek and Roman societies, with the ancient Greeks lifting huge boulders. The lifting of barbells, a metal bar with weights at either end, became a recognized sport at the end of the 19th century and strongman exhibitions were popular attractions at circuses and fairs. The first organized weightlifting world championships were held in 1891 in London and the first Olympic events five years later in 1896.

Rules and description

Weightlifting is a sport in which competitors attempt to lift and hold above their heads a barbell made increasingly heavy as the competition progresses. The sport recognizes two lifts: the 'snatch' and the 'clean and jerk'. In the snatch the competitor has to lift the bar from the floor to above the head in one movement, and then hold the position for two seconds. The three referees determine whether it is a 'clean' lift; a white light indicates a clean lift and only a majority decision of the judges is needed. Each competitor is allowed three attempts at each weight. The 'clean and jerk', sometimes shortened to just 'jerk', is a lift with two parts. The first movement is to bring the weight up to shoulder level, with the bar momentarily resting on the chest before being pumped overhead. Again, the weightlifter needs to hold the position to ensure the weight is under his/her control and the referees judge as before. The best weights for the snatch and the clean and jerk are added together to give a final winning total. Where there is a tie, the weightlifter with the lower or lowest bodyweight wins.

The steel bar weighs 20kg/44lb (15kg/33lb in women's competition) and the weights are rubber-coated metal discs that are secured on each end of the barbell using collars.

Ruling body: International Weightlifting Federation (IWF)

World Championships

The world championships were first held in 1891, with women's world championships being instituted in 1987. There are frequent changes to weight divisions, and from time to time divisions are dropped or merged. Currently there are eight weight divisions in the men's competition (over 105kg; under 105kg; under 94kg; under 85kg; under 77kg; under 69kg; under 62kg; and under 56kg) and seven in women's (over 75kg; under 75kg; under 69kg; under 63kg; under 58kg; under 53kg; under 48kg). Since 1984 (for men) and 2000 (for women), not held in Olympic years.

Men

	Over 105kg*
1980	Sultan Rakhmanov (USSR)
1981–3	Anatoli Pisarenko (USSR)
1984	Dean Lukin (Australia)
1985–6	Antonio Krastev (Bulgaria)
1987, 1989	Aleksandr Kurlovich (USSR)
1990	Leonid Taranenko (USSR)
1991	Aleksandr Kurlovich (USSR)
1993	Ronnie Weller (Germany)
1994	Aleksandr Kurlovich (Belarus)
1995, 1997–9	Andrei Chemerkin (Russia)
2001	Saeed Salem Jaber (Qatar)
2002–3	Hossein Reza Zadeh (Iran)

* Until 1993 over 110kg/ until 1999 over 108kg

	Under 105kg**
1980	Leonid Taranenko (USSR)
1981	Valeri Kravchuk (USSR)
1982	Sergei Arakelov (USSR)
1983	Vyacheslav Klokov (USSR)
1984	Norberto Oberburger (Italy)
1985–7	Yuri Zakharevich (USSR)
1989–90	Stefan Botev (Bulgaria)
1991	Artur Akoev (USSR)
1993–4	Timur Tamaizov (Ukraine)
1995	Igor Razorenov (Ukraine)
1997	Cui Wenhua (China)
1998	Igor Razorenov (Ukraine)
1999	Denis Gotfried (Ukraine)
2001	Vladimir Smorchkov (Russia)
2002	Denis Gotfried (Ukraine)
2003	Assad Saif Assad (Qatar)

** Until 1993 under 110kg/ until 1999 under 108kg

	Under 94kg*
1980	Peter Baczako (Hungary)
1981–3	Blagoi Blagoyev (Bulgaria)
1984	Nico Vlad (Romania)
1985	Anatoli Khrapaty/ Viktor Solodov (USSR)

	Under 85kg**
1980–1	Yurik Vardanyan (USSR)
1982	Asen Zlatev (Bulgaria)
1983	Yurik Vardanyan (USSR)
1984	Petre Becheru (Romania)
1985	Yurik Vardanyan (USSR)

Under 94kg*

1986–7 Anatoli Khrapaty (USSR)
1989–90
1991 Sergei Sirtsov (USSR)
1993 Ivan Tchakarov (Bulgaria)
1994 Alexei Petrov (Russia)
1997 Maxim Agapitov (Russia)
1998–9 Akakios Kakiasvilis (Greece)
2001 Koroush Bagheri (Iran)
2002 Nizami Pashaev (Azerbaijan)
2003 Milen Dobrev (Bulgaria)

* Until 1993 under 90kg/
until 1998 under 91kg

Under 85kg**

1986 Asen Zlatev (Bulgaria)
1987 László Barsi (Hungary)
1989 Kiril Kunev (Bulgaria)
1990 Alty Orazdouriev (USSR)
1991 Ibrahim Samadov (USSR)
1993 Pyrros Dimas (Greece)
1994 Marc Huster (Germany)
1995 Pyrros Dimas (Greece)
1997 Andrzej Cofalik (Poland)
1998 Pyrros Dimas (Greece)
1999 Shahin Nassirinia (Iran)
2001 George Asanidze (Georgia)
2002 Zlaten Vanev (Bulgaria)
2003 Valeriu Calancea (Romania)

** Until 1993 under 82.5kg/
until 1998 under 83kg

Under 77kg*

1980 Yanko Rusev (Bulgaria)
1981 Joachim Kunz (East Germany)
1982 Pjotr Mandra (Poland)
1983 Joachim Kunz (East Germany)
1984 Yao Jingyuan (China)
1985–7 Mikhail Petrov (Bulgaria)
1989 Israel Milotosyan (USSR)
1990 Kim Myong-nam (North Korea)
1991, 1993 Yoto Yotov (Bulgaria)
1994 Fedail Guler (Turkey)
1995 Zhang Xugang (China)
1997–8 Zlaten Vanev (Bulgaria)
1999 Saleem Nayef Badr (Qatar)
2001 Nader Abbas (Qatar)
2002 Georgy Markov (Bulgaria)
2003 Mohammad Falahati-Nejad (Iran)

* Until 1993 under 67.5kg/
until 1998 under 70kg

Under 69kg**

1980 Viktor Masin (USSR)
1981 Beloslav Manolov (Bulgaria)
1982–3 Yurik Sarkisyan (USSR)
1984 Chen Weiqiang (China)
1985–6 Naim Suleymanoglu (Bulgaria) †
1987 Stefan Topurov (Bulgaria)
1989 Naim Suleymanoglu (Turkey)
1990 Nikolai Peschalov (Bulgaria)
1991, 1993–5 Naim Suleymanoglu (Turkey)
1998 Plamen Yeliazkov (Bulgaria)
1999, 2001 Galabin Boevski (Bulgaria)
2002–3 Zhang Guozheng (China)

† as Neum Shalamanov
** Until 1993 under 60kg/
until 1998 under 64kg

Under 62kg*

1980 Daniel Nunez (Cuba)
1981–2 Anton Kodiabashov (Bulgaria)
1983 Oksen Mirzoyan (USSR)
1984 Wu Shude (China)
1985 Neno Terziski (Bulgaria)
1986 Mitko Grablev (Bulgaria)
1987 Neno Terziski (Bulgaria)
1989 Hafiz Suleimanov (USSR)
1990 Liu Shoubin (China)
1991 Chun Byung-kwan (South Korea)

Under 56kg**

1980–1 Kanybek Osmonalyev (USSR)
1982 Stefan Leletko (Poland)
1983 Neno Terziyski (Bulgaria)
1985–6 Sevdalin Marinov (Bulgaria)
1987 Shamil Marinov (Bulgaria)
1989–91, 1993 Ivan Ivanov (Bulgaria)
1994 Halil Mutlu (Turkey)
1995 Zhang Xiangsen (China)
1997 Lan Shizhang (China)
1998–9, 2001 Halil Mutlu (Turkey)

Under 62kg*

1993–4	Nikolai Pechalov (Bulgaria)
1995	Leonidas Sabanis (Greece)
1997	Stefan Georgeyev (Bulgaria)
1998	Leonidas Sabanis (Greece)
1999	Le Maosheng (China)
2001	Henadzi Aliaschuk (Belarus)
2002	Yong Su-im (North Korea)
2003	Halil Mutlu (Turkey)

* Until 1993 under 56kg/ until 1998 under 59kg

Under 56kg**

2002–3	Wu Meijin (China)

** Until 1993 under 52kg/ until 1998 under 54kg

Women

Over 75kg*

1987–9	Han Changmei (China)
1990–3	Li Yajuan (China)
1994	Karolina Lundahl (Finland)
1995	Erika Takacs (Hungary)
1996	Wan Ni (China)
1997	Ma Runmei (China)
1998	Tang Gonghong (China)
1999	Ding Meiyuan (China)
2001	Albina Khomich (Russia)
2002	Agata Wrobel (Poland)
2003	Ding Meiyuan (China)

* Until 1993 over 82.5kg/ until 1998 over 83kg

Under 75kg**

1987–8	Li Hongling (China)
1989–90	Milena Trendafilova (Bulgaria)
1991	Zhang Xiaoli (China)
1992–3	Ju Hua (China)
1994	Panagiota Antonopolou (Greece)
1995–6	Li Yan (China)
1997	Ju Hua (China)
1998	Karolina Lundahl (Finland)
1999	Jiao Xu (China)
2001	Gyöngyi Likerecz (Hungary)
2002	Svetlana Chabirova (Russia)
2003	Nahla Ramadan (Egypt)

**From 1993 to 1997 under 76kg

Under 69kg*

1987	Gao Lijuan (China)
1988–9	Guo Qiuxiang (China)
1990	Wang Genying (China)
1991	Lei Li (China)
1992	Gao Lijuan (China)
1993	Milena Trendafilova (Bulgaria)
1994	Zhou Meihong (China)
1995–6	Tang Weifang (China)
1997	Xiang Fenglan (China)
1998	Tang Weifang (China)
1999	Sun Tianni (China)
2001	Valentina Popova (Russia)
2002	Pawina Thongsuk (Thailand)
2003	Liu Chunhong (China)

* Until 1993 under 67.5kg/ until 1998 under 70kg

Under 63kg**

1987	Zeng Xinling (China)
1988	Yang Jing (China)
1989	Ma Na (China)
1990	Maria Christoforidou (Greece)
1991	Han Lixia (China)
1992–4	Li Hongyun (China)
1995	Chen Yui-lien (Taiwan)
1996	Li Hongyun (China)
1997	Chen Yanqing (China)
1998–9	Chen Yui-lien (Taiwan)
2001	Xiao Ying (China)
2002	Xia Liu (China)
2003	Natalia Skakun (Ukraine)

** Until 1993 under 60kg/ until 1998 under 64kg

Under 58kg*

1987	Cui Aihong (China)
1988	Ma Na (China)

Under 53kg**

1987	Yan Zhangqun (China)
1988–9	Peng Liping (China)

Under 58kg*

1989	Xing Liwei (China)
1990	Wu Haiqing (China)
1991–3	Sun Caiyan (China)
1994	Zhou Fei'e (China)
1995–6	Chen Xiaomin (China)
1997	Patmawati Patmawati (Indonesia)
1998	Kuo Pin-chun (Taiwan)
1999	Chen Yanqing (China)
2001	Alexandra Klejnovska (Poland)
2002	Song Zhujuan (China)
2003	Sun Caiyan (China)

* Until 1993 under 56kg/
until 1998 under 59kg

Under 48kg*

1987–9	Huang Xiaoyu (China)
1990	Cai Jun (China)
1991	Izabela Rifatova (Bulgaria)
1992–3	Liu Xiuhua (China)
1994	Robin Byrd (USA)
1995–6	Liu Xiuhua (China)
1997	Winarni Binti Slamet (Indonesia)
1998	Li Yunli (China)
1999	Donka Mincheva (Bulgaria)
2001	Wei Gao (China)
2002–3	Wang Mingjuan (China)

* Until 1993 under 48kg/
until 1998 under 50kg

Under 53kg**

1990	Liao Shuping (China)
1991–2	Peng Liping (China)
1993	Chen Xiaomin (China)
1994–5	Karnam Malleswary (Indonesia)
1996	Zhang Xixiang (China)
1997	Meng Xianjuan (China)
1998	Wang Xiufen (China)
1999, 2001	Li Feng-Ying (Taiwan)
2002	Ri Song-hui (North Korea)
2003	Polsak Udomporn (Thailand)

** Until 1993 under 52kg/
until 1998 under 54kg

Sheer brute strength!

Powerlifting is a weightlifting competition that emphasizes pure strength and has the lifter competing against others in performing a bench press (lying on his or her back, the lifter attempts to raise the barbell to an arm's-length position); a squat (where the lifter squats with the barbell across the shoulders and then attempts to stand up again); and a two-handed dead lift (the lifter raises a barbell from the floor until he or she is standing upright).

A-Z

barbell, bar the weightlifting bar with attached **disc weights** and **collars**

bench press a weightlifting exercise in which a lifter lies on a bench with feet on the floor and raises a weight from chest level to arm's length

chalk the substance used by weightlifters on their hands to help them grip the bar. The chalk is magnesium carbonate powder

clean the first phase of the clean and jerk movement that has the weightlifter lifting the bar to shoulder height in preparation for the second phase, the **jerk**

collar the device that secures the **disc weights** to the **bar**

disc weights the differing weights of disc that are attached to the bar to make

	it heavier. The discs are colour coded as follows: red (25kg); blue (20kg); yellow (15kg); green (10kg); white (5kg); black (2.5kg); chrome (1.25kg, 0.5kg, 0.25kg)
good lift	a lift that has the approval of the majority of the three judges. In competition it is indicated by two or three white lights on a scoreboard
jerk	the second phase of the clean and jerk movement that follows the **clean** and has the weightlifter lifting the bar from the shoulder to above the head with straightened arms
no lift	an unsuccessful lift as judged by the majority of the three judges. In competition it is indicated by two or three red lights on a scoreboard
press-out	an illegal move where the arms are not straight and the lifter attempts to straighten them once the lift has been completed
simple grip	a grip for holding the bar that has four fingers on one side of the bar balanced by the thumb on the other side
snatch	a type of lift in which the barbell is raised from the floor to an overhead position with straightened arms in one continuous movement

Some famous weightlifters

Vasili Alexeyev, 1942–

Born in Pokrov, USSR (now Russia), he was a super-heavyweight who was probably the most famous weightlifter of all time. He won gold medals at both the 1972 and 1976 Olympic Games. He remained undefeated in super-heavyweight competition from 1970 until 1978 but suffered an injury during the 1978 world championships, and two years later he failed to win a medal at the 1980 Olympics. He broke more than 80 world records in his career.

John Davis, 1921–84

Born in Smithtown, New York, USA, he was the dominant weightlifter of the 1940s and won two Olympic Games gold medals (1948 and 1952) and six world titles (1938, 1946–7, 1949–51). Davis set 18 world records, and was the first lifter to clean and jerk over 400lb. He remained unbeaten from 1938 to 1953.

Naim Suleymanoglu, 1967–

Born in Ptichar, Bulgaria, of Turkish parentage, he set his first world record at 15 years old. In 1986 he defected to Turkey and won a gold medal in the featherweight division at the 1988 Olympic Games. His combined total was higher than that for the winner of the (heavier) lightweight title. At the 1992 Olympic Games he again won a gold and retained his title at the 1996 Olympics four years later, the first lifter to win golds at three different Games. Suleymanoglu also won seven world titles.

Yuri Zakharevich, 1963–

Born in the USSR (modern-day Ukraine), he was a world junior champion in 1981 and followed this victory up with senior world titles in 1985–7 and an Olympic Games gold medal in 1988, despite dislocating his elbow when 20 attempting to break the world record for the snatch. In his career he set more than 40 world records.

WINDSURFING

Origins

It is claimed that windsurfing was invented in 1958 on Hayling Island, Hampshire, UK, by Peter Chilvers, who created the first board with an attached sail. Around ten years later a commercial design (called a Windsurfer) was produced by Hoyle Schweitzer of California. In 1984 the windsurfer class was introduced to the Olympic Games sailing programme.

Rules and description

Windsurfing, also known as boardsailing, is a sailing sport where the surfer is propelled across lakes and the sea by waves and wind. Speeds of 80kph can be achieved. The windsurfer consists of a board and a 'rig'. The rig is the technical term that covers the sail, the mast and the boom (the horizontal bar gripped by the surfer that is used to help steer the craft). Located beneath the board is a 'centreboard', a pivoting device that can be deployed to increase stability. The surfer stands sideways on the board, facing the way in which he or she intends to travel, with the feet strapped into position.

Sailing events in which many windsurfers take part are called 'fleet races'; they take place on waterways delineated by marker buoys and the winner is the first to cross the finishing line. In regattas where there is more than one race, the combined totals are added together. Generally, one point is awarded to the winner, two points to the person in second place, and so on. In that way the winner of a competition is the person with the lowest mark. As well as racing there is 'freestyle sailing' or 'wave sailing' in which sailors attempt to become airborne and perform tricks and loops on the wave edges (as in surfing).

Ruling bodies: International Sailing Federation (ISAF); International Windsurfing Association

Olympic Games

In the inaugural 1984 competition the sailboard brand was a Windglider; it was superseded by a Lechner Division II for the 1988 and 1992 Games before the Mistral Class was introduced in 1996. The Mistral is 3.72m long and 0.6m wide and weighs 17kg.

	Men	Women
1984	Stephan van den Berg (The Netherlands)	
1988	Bruce Kendall (New Zealand)	
1992	Franck David (France)	Barbara Kendall (New Zealand)*
1996	Nikolaos Kaklamanakis (Greece)	Lee Lai-Shan (Hong Kong)
2000	Christoph Sieber (Austria)	Alessandra Sensini (Italy)
2004	Gal Fridman (Israel)	Faustine Merret (France)

* Barbara Kendall is the younger sister of Bruce Kendall

WRESTLING

Origins

Wrestling is probably the world's oldest sport. Depictions of men wrestling appear on Egyptian wall paintings that date back more than 5000 years. When the first Olympic Games took place in Greece in 776 BC, wrestling was regarded even then as an ancient sport and the wrestling competition was the main event. The sport featured prominently in Greek myth and literature, and was later adopted by the Romans who developed the sport into a less brutal form of combat. In the Middle Ages wrestling was very popular in Europe with all classes. It enjoyed royal patronage, including that of Henry VIII of England who was a keen wrestler in his youth.

After a long absence, the Olympics were resurrected in 1896 and the organizers attempted to capture a flavour of the ancient Olympiads by adopting the Graeco-Roman form of wrestling. This variety of the sport involves just the arms and upper body. 'Catch-as-catch-can' wrestling, which allows moves involving the legs and holds below the waist, was more popular in Europe and North America than Graeco-Roman at the time of the first modern Olympic Games. It was decided, therefore, to add it to the list of events at the 1904 Olympiad, whereupon it became known as freestyle wrestling.

Rules and descriptions

A combat sport in which two contestants attempt to achieve 'falls' by forcing each other's shoulders to the floor of a mat on which contests or 'bouts' take place. Points are also awarded for various moves such as 'escapes' and 'reversals' during the bout and, if a fall is not achieved during the permitted time period, the competitor with the most points wins. The most popular forms of wrestling are freestyle and Graeco-Roman. Freestyle permits the use of the legs and allows holds below the waist. Graeco-Roman permits only holds above the waist and does not permit the use of the legs as a means of holding and tripping. Both Graeco-Roman and freestyle types of wrestling are competed for at the Olympic Games at various weight categories, of which there are now seven. Women competed in wrestling at the Olympic Games for the first time in the Athens games of 2004, in the freestyle discipline only and in weight categories from 48kg to 72kg.

Ruling body: FILA (Fédération Internationale de Lutte Amateur)

Olympic Freestyle Champions

Heavyweight competition first held in 1904, superheavyweight in 1972.

	Heavyweight	**Superheavyweight**
1904	Bernhuff Hansen (USA)	
1906	*Not held*	
1908	George O'Kelly (Great Britain)	

	Heavyweight	Superheavyweight
1912	*Not held*	
1920	Robert Roth (Switzerland)	
1924	Harry Steele (USA)	
1928	Johan Richthoff (Sweden)	
1932	Johan Richthoff (Sweden)	
1936	Kristjan Palusalu (Estonia)	
1948	Gyula Bóbis (Hungary)	
1952	Arsen Mekokishvili (USSR)	
1956	Hamit Kaplan (Turkey)	
1960	Wilfried Dietrich (West Germany)	
1964	Aleksandr Ivanitsky (USSR)	
1968	Aleksandr Medved (USSR)	
1972	Ivan Yarygin (USSR)	Aleksandr Medved (USSR)
1976	Ivan Yarygin (USSR)	Soslan Andiyev (USSR)
1980	Ilia Mate (USSR)	Soslan Andiyev (USSR)
1984	Louis Banach (USA)	Bruce Baumgartner (USA)
1988	Vasile Puscasu (Romania)	David Gobezhishvili (USSR)
1992	Leri Khabelov (UT)	Bruce Baumgartner (USA)
1996	Kurt Angle (USA)	Mahmut Demir (Turkey)
2000	Saghid Mourtasaliyov (Russia)	David Moussoulbes (Russia)
2004	Khadjimourat Gatsalov (Russia)	Artur Taymazov (Uzbekistan)

Olympic Graeco-Roman champions

	Heavyweight	Superheavyweight
1896	Carl Schumann (Germany)	
1900	*Not held*	
1904	*Not held*	
1906	Søren Marius Jensen (Denmark)	
1908	Richárd Weisz (Hungary)	
1912	Yrjö Saarela (Finland)	
1920	Adolf Lindfors (Finland)	
1924	Henri Deglane (France)	
1928	Rudolf Svensson (Sweden)	
1932	Carl Westergren (Sweden)	
1936	Kristjan Palusalu (Estonia)	
1948	Mersinli Ahmet Kireççi (Turkey)	
1952	Johannes Kotkas (USSR)	
1956	Anatoli Parfenov (USSR)	
1960	Ivan Bogdan (USSR)	
1964	István Kozma (Hungary)	
1968	István Kozma (Hungary)	
1972	Nicolae Martinescu (Romania)	Anatoli Roshin (USSR)
1976	Nikolai Balboshin (USSR)	Aleksandr Kolchinski (USSR)
1980	Georgi Raikov (Bulgaria)	Aleksandr Kolchinski (USSR)
1984	Vasile Andrei (Romania)	Jeff Blatnick (USA)
1988	Andrzej Wronski (Poland)	Aleksandr Karelin (USSR)
1992	Héctor Milián (Cuba)	Aleksandr Karelin (UT)

	Heavyweight	Superheavyweight
1996	Andrzej Wronski (Poland)	Aleksandr Karelin (Russia)
2000	Mikael Ljungberg (Sweden)	Rulon Gardner (USA)
2004	Karam Ibrahim (Egypt)	Khasan Baroev (Russia)

Graeco-Roman World Championship

During an Olympic year the winner of the Olympic gold is considered world champion. Winners below are at the heaviest weight division.

	Winner
1904	Rudolf Arnold (Austria)
1905	Søren Marius Jensen (Denmark)
1907	Hans Heinrich Egeberg (Denmark)
1908	Hans Heinrich Egeberg (Denmark)
1909	Anton Schmitz (Austria)
1910	Gustav Sperling (Germany)
1911	Yrjö Saarela (Finland)
1913	Anders Ahlgren (Sweden)
1920	Heinrich Bock (Germany)
1921	Johan Salila (Finland)
1922	Ernst Nilsson (Sweden)
1950	Bertil Antonsson (Sweden)
1953	Bertil Antonsson (Sweden)
1955	Aleksandr Masur (USSR)
1958	Ivan Bogdan (USSR)
1961	Ivan Bogdan (USSR)
1962	Istvan Kozma (Hungary)
1963	Anatoli Roschtschin (USSR)
1965	Nikolai Schmakow (USSR)
1966	Istvan Kozma (Hungary)
1967	Istvan Kozma (Hungary)
1969	Anatoli Roschtschin (USSR)
1970	Anatoli Roschtschin (USSR)
1971	Aleksandr Tomow (Bulgaria)
1973	Aleksandr Tomow (Bulgaria)
1974	Aleksandr Tomow (Bulgaria)
1975	Aleksandr Tomow (Bulgaria)
1977	Nikola Dinev (Bulgaria)
1978	Aleksandr Kolchinski (USSR)
1979	Aleksandr Tomov (Bulgaria)
1981	Refik Memisevic (Yugoslavia)
1982	Nikola Dinev (Bulgaria)
1983	Jewgeni Artjuchin (USSR)
1985	Igor Rostorotzki (USSR)
1986	Tomas Johansson (Sweden)
1987	Igor Rostorotzki (USSR)
1989	Aleksandr Karelin (USSR)
1990	Aleksandr Karelin (USSR)
1991	Aleksandr Karelin (USSR)
1993	Aleksandr Karelin (Russia)
1994	Aleksandr Karelin (Russia)
1995	Aleksandr Karelin (Russia)
1997	Aleksandr Karelin (Russia)
1998	Aleksandr Karelin (Russia)
1999	Aleksandr Karelin (Russia)
2001	Rulon Gardner (USA)
2003	Khasan Baroev (Russia)

Freestyle World Championship

During an Olympic year the winner of the Olympic gold is considered world champion. Winners below are at the heaviest weight division.

	Winner
1951	Bertil Antonsson (Sweden)
1954	Arsen Mekokishvili (USSR)
1957	Hamit Kaplan (Turkey)
1959	Ljutwi Dshiber Achmedov (Bulgaria)
1961	Wilfried Dietrich (West Germany)
1962	Aleksandr Ivanitsky (USSR)
1963	Aleksandr Ivanitsky (USSR)
1965	Aleksandr Ivanitsky (USSR)
1966	Aleksandr Ivanitsky (USSR)
1967	Aleksandr Medved (USSR)
1969	Aleksandr Medved (USSR)
1970	Aleksandr Medved (USSR)
1971	Aleksandr Medved (USSR)
1973	Soslan Andiyev (USSR)

1974	Ladislau Simon (Romania)
1975	Soslan Andiyev (USSR)
1977	Soslan Andiyev (USSR)
1978	Soslan Andiyev (USSR)
1979	Salman Khasimikov (USSR)
1981	Salman Khasimikov (USSR)
1982	Salman Khasimikov (USSR)
1983	Salman Khasimikov (USSR)
1985	David Gobedzhishvili (USSR)
1986	Bruce Baumgartner (USA)
1987	Aslan Chadarzew (USSR)
1989	Ali Reza Soleimani (Iran)
1990	David Gobedzhishvili (USSR)
1992	Andreas Schroeder (Germany)
1993	Bruce Baumgartner (USA)
1994	Mahmut Demir (Turkey)
1995	Bruce Baumgartner (USA)
1997	Zekeriya Gücü (Turkey)
1998	Alexis Rodriguez Valera (Cuba)
1999	Stephen Neal (USA)
2001	David Moussoulbes (Russia)
2002	David Moussoulbes (Russia)
2003	Artur Taymazov (Uzbekistan)

Worth the attendance money?

There must have been a few yawns among spectators during the wrestling competition of the 1912 Olympic Games. When Martin Klein of Estonia (representing Russia) took on Alfred Asikáinen of Finland, the bout took an amazing 11 hours and 40 minutes, the longest recorded wrestling match in history.

A-Z

action the referee's command to the competitors to start wrestling

ankle lace a hold in which a wrestler uses his arms to trap his opponent by the ankles, exposing his back to the mat

arm throw a move in which a wrestler throws his opponent over his shoulder while holding his opponent's arm

body lock a hold in which a wrestler locks arms around his opponent's body before taking him down to the mat

bout a wrestling contest

bridge an arched position adopted by a wrestler, with his back facing the mat, in order to avoid a fall

bridge out if a wrestler bridges out from an opponent's move, he escapes by rolling from a **bridge** onto his stomach

central circle the inner circle of a wrestling mat

central wrestling area the circle on the wrestling mat between the **passivity zone** and the **central circle**

chairman see **referee**

cross-body ride same as **grapevine**

danger position a position in which a wrestler has his opponent's back at less than right angles to the mat

double-leg tackle a move in freestyle wrestling in which a wrestler takes down his opponent by means of an arm tackle on his opponent's legs

exposing a scoring technique in which points are earned for exposing an opponent's back to the mat at an angle of 90 degrees or more

fall the forcing of an opponent's shoulders on to the mat

freestyle type of wrestling in which competitors may use their arms and legs as well as their bodies, and may hold opponents above and below the waist

Graeco-Roman	a type of wrestling in which only the upper body and arms may be used for moves and holds. Moves and holds on and using the legs are not permitted
grand amplitude	a throw in which the wrestler's centre of gravity is lower than the wrestler whom he is trying to throw
grapevine	a move in freestyle wrestling in which a wrestler uses his legs to turn his opponent
gut wrench	a move in which a wrestler rolls his opponent on his back while in a **bridge** position
judge	see **referee**
mat	the circular mat on which wrestling bouts take place
open	a referee's command for a wrestler to alter his position and use more open tactics
passivity	the adoption of negative, stalling tactics in which moves are avoided
passivity zone	the outer circle of the wrestling mat
pin	same as **fall**
protection area	the border of the wrestling mat beyond the **passivity zone**
referee	one of the three officials in charge of a bout. The referee adjudicates from the mat while the judge and chairman are positioned beyond the mat
reversal	a move in which a wrestler escapes from his opponent's hold and executes a move which gives him a controlling position
single leg tackle	a move in which a wrestler takes down his opponent using an arm tackle to one of his opponent's legs
souple	a hold in which a wrestler holds his opponent from behind and throws him in a wide arc of movement
takedown	a move in which a wrestler throws his opponent to the ground from a standing position
technical points	points scored during the match from successful moves other than falls
technical superiority	a ten-point lead of one wrestler over his opponent, resulting in a win

INDEX

Index

This index contains the names of sports, terms given in the A–Z section and the names of sportspeople who have biography entries.

A

B

D

E

F

H

I

J

K

L

M

N

O

P

Q

R

S

T

U

V

W

X

Y

Z